Northern Italy
Emilia-Romagna
including Bologna

the Bradt Travel Guide

Dana Facaros & Michael Pauls

edition
1

www.bradtgui

Bradt Trave
The Globe F

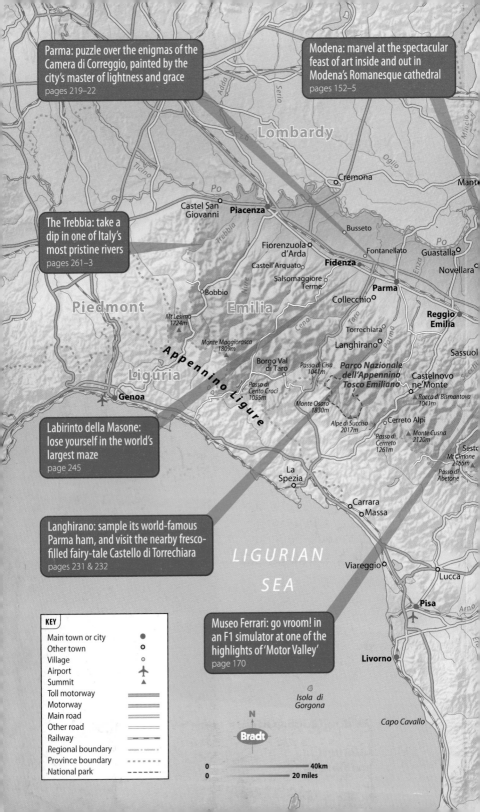

Parma: puzzle over the enigmas of the Camera di Correggio, painted by the city's master of lightness and grace
pages 219–22

Modena: marvel at the spectacular feast of art inside and out in Modena's Romanesque cathedral
pages 152–5

The Trebbia: take a dip in one of Italy's most pristine rivers
pages 261–3

Labirinto della Masone: lose yourself in the world's largest maze
page 245

Langhirano: sample its world-famous Parma ham, and visit the nearby fresco-filled fairy-tale Castello di Torrechiara
pages 231 & 232

Museo Ferrari: go vroom! in an F1 simulator at one of the highlights of 'Motor Valley'
page 170

Lombardy

Po

Cremona

Mant

Castel San Giovanni

Piacenza

Busseto

Fontanellato

Guastalla

Fiorenzuola d'Arda

Fidenza

Novellara

Castell'Arquato

Salsomaggiore Terme

Parma

Bobbio

Collecchio

Reggio Emilia

Piedmont

Emilia

Torrechiara

Sassuol

Mt Lesima 1724m

Langhirano

Monte Maggiorasca 1809m

Parco Nazionale dell'Appennino Tosco Emiliano

Castelnovo ne'Monte

Liguria

Borgo Val di Taro

Passo di Cisa 1041m

Rocca di Bismantova 1041m

Genoa

Passo di Cento Croci 1055m

Monte Osaro 1830m

Alpe di Succiso 2017m

Cerreto Alpi

Monte Cusna 2120m

Sesto

Passo di Cerrreto 1261m

Mt Cimone 2165m

Passo di Abetone

La Spezia

Carrara

Massa

LIGURIAN

SEA

Viareggio

Lucca

Pisa

Isola di Gorgona

Livorno

Arno

N

Bradt

Capo Cavallo

0   40km
0   20 miles

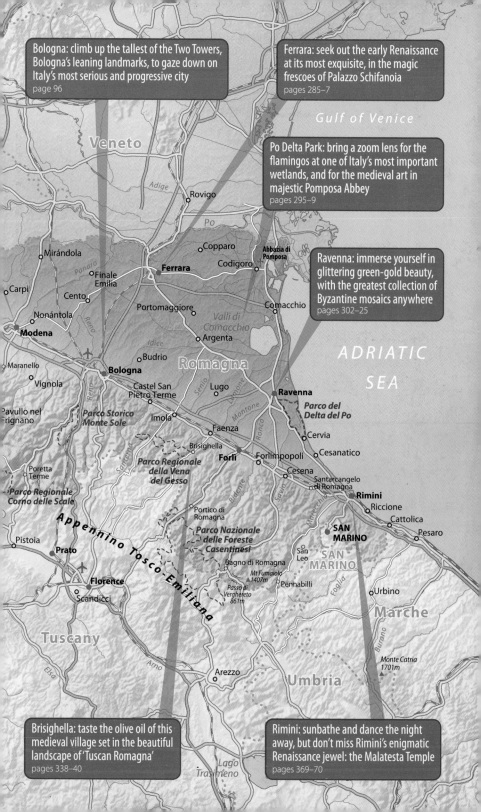

Bologna: climb up the tallest of the Two Towers, Bologna's leaning landmarks, to gaze down on Italy's most serious and progressive city
page 96

Ferrara: seek out the early Renaissance at its most exquisite, in the magic frescoes of Palazzo Schifanoia
pages 285–7

Po Delta Park: bring a zoom lens for the flamingos at one of Italy's most important wetlands, and for the medieval art in majestic Pomposa Abbey
pages 295–9

Ravenna: immerse yourself in glittering green-gold beauty, with the greatest collection of Byzantine mosaics anywhere
pages 302–25

Brisighella: taste the olive oil of this medieval village set in the beautiful landscape of 'Tuscan Romagna'
pages 338–40

Rimini: sunbathe and dance the night away, but don't miss Rimini's enigmatic Renaissance jewel: the Malatesta Temple
pages 369–70

Gulf of Venice

Veneto

Adige

Rovigo

Po

ADRIATIC SEA

Mirándola

Copparo

Codigoro

Abbazia di Pomposa

Finale Emilia

Panaro

Ferrara

Carpi

Cento

Portomaggiore

Comacchio

Nonántola

Reno

Valli di Comacchio

Modena

Idice

Argenta

Maranello

Budrio

Romagna

Vignola

Bologna

Pavullo nel Frignano

Castel San Pietro Terme

Lugo

Ravenna

Parco del Delta del Po

Parco Storico Monte Sole

Imola

Senio

Montone

Cervia

Faenza

Poretta Terme

Brisighella

Parco Regionale della Vena del Gesso

Forlì

Forlimpopoli

Cesenatico

Parco Regionale Corno delle Scale

Santerno

Cesena

Santarcangelo di Romagna

Ronco

Savio

Pistoia

Portico di Romagna

Bidente

Rimini

Appennino Tosco-Emiliana

Parco Nazionale delle Foreste Casentinesi

Prato

Riccione

Cattolica

Florence

San Leo

SAN MARINO

SAN MARINO

Pesaro

Scandicci

Bagno di Romagna

Mt Fumaiolo 1407m

Pennabilli

Arno

Passo di Viamaggio 861m

Foglia

Urbino

Marche

Tuscany

Elsa

Burano

Monte Catria 1701m

Arezzo

Umbria

Lago Trasimeno

Emilia-Romagna Don't miss...

Bologna
Under two leaning towers, a city of art, learning and fine cuisine
(VM/S) pages 59–129

Music
The home of Verdi and Rossini fills its historic theatres with opera and other spectacles throughout the year
(FD/S) pages 27 & 55

Cities of Art

Byzantine mosaics in Ravenna, medieval marvels in Modena and Parma, and Renaissance Ferrara, artistic rival to Florence

(PZ/S) pages 23–7

Nature on the Edges

Close to the cities are haunting lagoons on the Adriatic Sea, hiking and skiing in the Apennines and charming hill towns. Pictured here: flamingos in the Parco del Delta del Po

(RuS/S) page 295

Food

Emilia-Romagna is home to Italy's most refined cuisine, including its favourite ham, cured meats, cheese and balsamic vinegar

(ja/S) pages 40–4

Emilia-Romagna in colour

above left   Lighter-than-air saints float on the ceilings of Bologna's Baroque churches, like these in the Basilica di San Petronio (ZA/S) pages 88–90

above right   Gothic Palazzo della Mercanzia is one of the oldest of the grand *palazzi* that fill the city centre (V/S) page 99

below   The Quadrilatero: the city's medieval heart is devoted to food, with market stalls filling the streets by day, and restaurant tables after dark (LL/S) page 93

left   The world's oldest and smallest
republic, San Marino lives on a
high peak with its head in the
clouds (OP/S) pages 393–5

below   Pennabilli, one of the many
unspoiled hill towns in Emilia-
Romagna's Apennines
(CGC/S) pages 391–3

bottom   The region is a land of castles,
and many, like Torrechiara,
are filled with fascinating
Renaissance art
(d/S) page 231

AUTHORS

Travel writers **Dana Facaros** and **Michael Pauls** are old Italy hands, having lived in Umbria for three years with their young children while travelling and researching the country from Trieste to Lampedusa. Since then they have written more than 20 guidebooks to the country for the Cadogan Guides series, including their first guide to Emilia-Romagna. Among their recent works are also two apps (page 417). Dana is a regular contributor to the *Sunday Times Travel Magazine*. The couple are settled, at least for the time being, in southwest France.

FEEDBACK REQUEST AND UPDATES WEBSITE

At Bradt Travel Guides we're aware that guidebooks start to go out of date on the day they're published – and that you, our readers, are out there in the field doing research of your own. You'll find out before us when a fine new family-run hotel opens or a favourite restaurant changes hands and goes downhill. So why not write and tell us about your experiences? Contact us on ✆ 01753 893444 or e info@bradtguides.com. We will forward emails to the authors, who may post updates on the Bradt website at w bradtupdates. com/emilia. Alternatively you can add a review of the book to w bradtguides. com or Amazon.

PUBLISHER'S FOREWORD
Adrian Phillips, Managing Director

This guide further bolsters Bradt's growing reputation for in-depth coverage of some of Western Europe's most interesting corners. And Emilia-Romagna is certainly a colourful – even quirky – spot, with its settlements strung along a 200-mile road, its radical history, and its proud tradition in the arts. Furthermore, its food ranks among the very best you'll taste! Dana and Michael are longstanding Italy experts who arguably know the country better than any other guidebook writers out there. This is the perfect pair to show you around the region.

Published June 2018
Bradt Travel Guides Ltd
IDC House, The Vale, Chalfont St Peter, Bucks SL9 9RZ, England
www.bradtguides.com
Print edition published in the USA by The Globe Pequot Press Inc,
PO Box 480, Guilford, Connecticut 06437-0480

Text copyright © 2018 Dana Facaros and Michael Pauls
Maps copyright © 2018 Bradt Travel Guides Ltd. Includes map data © OpenStreetMap contributors
Photographs copyright © 2018 Individual photographers (see below)
Project Manager: Susannah Lord
Cover research: Pepi Bluck, Perfect Picture

ISBN: 978 1 78477 085 3 (print)
e-ISBN: 978 1 78477 550 6 (e-pub)
e-ISBN: 978 1 78477 451 6 (mobi)

British Library Cataloguing in Publication Data
A catalogue record for this book is available from the British Library

Photographs AWL Images: Francesco Ricardo Iacomino (FRI/AWL); Comune di Cervia (CdC); Comune di Rimini (CdR); Emilia-Romagna Tourist Board (ERTB); Shutterstock.com: Alexander Corne (AC/S), Agata Dorobek (AD/S), Alessia Pierdomenico (AP/S), Alessandro Zappalorto (AZ/S), Borisb17 (B/S), CervelliInFuga (CF/S), Claudio Giovanni Colombo (CGC/S), claudio zaccherini (CZ/S), dlaurro (d/S), ermess (e/S), Francesco Dazzi (FD/S), francesco de marco (fdm/S), Gimas (G/S), Giorgio Morara (GM/S), GoneWithTheWind (GWTW/S), iryna1 (i/S), javarman (ja/S), jorisvo (jo/S), Kevin George (KG/S), Luca Lorenzelli (LL/S), mountainpix (m/S), Mi.Ti. (MT/S), Natali22206 (N/S), Nickolay Vinokurov (NV/S), Oleg Proskurin (OP/S), peizais (p/S), Peter Zamorowski (PZ/S), Riccardofe (R/S), robertonencini (r/S), Roman Sigaev (RoS/S), Ruth Swan (RuS/S), Tupungato (T/S), vvoe (v/S), ValerioMei (VM/S), Zvonimir Atletic (ZA/S); SuperStock (SS); Ufficio Fiere (UF).

Front cover Bologna (FRI/AWL)
Back cover Mosaic detail, Neonian Baptistry, Ravenna (m/S), San Leo (NV/S)
Title page Bust, Palazzo Bolognini, Bologna (jo/S), Colourful houses, Modena (T/S), Abbey of San Colombano, Bobbio (MT/S)

Maps David McCutcheon FBCart.S; relief map bases by Nick Rowland FRGS

Typeset by Dataworks, and Ian Spick, Bradt Travel Guides Ltd
Production managed by Jellyfish Print Solutions; printed in India
Digital conversion by www.dataworks.co.in

Acknowledgements

We would like to thank our dear friend Rachel Fielding, who masterminded the creation of this book, and our editor, Susannah Lord, who waded through all the prose and tidied it up so neatly. Also thanks to the long-ago curator in Piacenza who back in 1986, while the museum was undergoing restoration, let Dana hold the famous Etruscan liver in the palm of her hand and feel its uncanny weirdness.

AUTHORS' STORY

We invaded Italy in 1981 by train from Victoria Station, with bags checked through to Catania. We didn't get our bags back, but instead we got a massive helping of Italy. Our affair with that gorgeous, delightful, sometimes maddening but deeply *simpatico* country has gone on for a long time since then. We started out pushing a baby stroller over the cobbles of every Italian island, destroying several strollers in the process. Our children learned reading, writing and dialect songs in an Umbrian village school, while we took turns roaming every corner of the country, coming home on Friday nights with lots of little presents and stories to tell.

That was 20 books ago. We've done guides to every region and major city, and we only had to stop because we ran out of Italy. We wish there were more of it. There's one part of it readers always ask about: Emilia-Romagna. That made us think too – with recollections of great works of art, walks in the spring fog and some memorable plates of tortellini. It's a fashionable place, suddenly, and we have been spending more time there, writing an app guide to Bologna and Modena, along with a second one, an Italian Food Decoder, and now this comprehensive guide to the region.

Contents

LIST OF MAPS

Introduction

The layout seems to have been designed by a government committee. Start with a road that runs almost perfectly straight for 320km (200 miles). String all the cities along it, at regular intervals. Put all the hills on one side of the road, and all the flatlands on the other. Sprinkle the whole thing liberally with red bricks, (former) Communists and tortellini, and you couldn't get anything else but Emilia-Romagna.

The joke is, it probably *was* designed by a committee. Sometime near the close of the Second Punic War, some Roman senators, engineers and military men sat down together and came up with the plan for developing this newly acquired territory. The biggest expanse of flat land in Italy gave them a chance to put the Roman passion for rationalism into practice on a massive scale, and their hard-nosed pragmatism has marked everything in the region's life for the last 2,200 years: its politics, its ways of thinking, and even at times its art. That straight-as-an-arrow Roman high road that ties everything together, the Via Emilia, gave the land its character along with its name.

After their orderly and efficient start as Roman colonies, the towns along the Via Emilia went their separate ways in the Middle Ages. Each one picked itself up from the rubble of the Dark Ages and built itself into a prosperous free city, and each had a busy career battling popes, emperors and each other. Eventually each one fell under the rule of city bosses, and as these *signori* turned into aristocratic dynasties, they added mightily to an already impressive hoard of castles and cathedrals, palaces, churches and frescoes.

Since then, the region's accomplishments have been many. Emilia-Romagna is the cradle of many of Italy's most innovative film directors: Fellini, Bertolucci and Antonioni. Before cinema, almost every town, large and small, built an ornate theatre-concert hall as a proud civic centrepiece, and a testimony to its devotion to the arts. So it shouldn't be surprising that the region is also the home of many of the nation's musical greats, from Verdi and Respighi to Toscanini and Pavarotti.

'Emilia-Romagna' is a slightly artificial region, given official status only in 1970 when Italy began decentralising power to local governments. Another committee decided to lump together Emilia, the stretch from Piacenza to Bologna, with the Romagna to the east, a territory with a history shaped by centuries of rule by the pope. But it does hang together. One feature that all its towns have in common is their radical politics, born over a century ago, and surviving two wars and Mussolini to blossom after 1945 as 'Red' Emilia-Romagna, where Communism with a human face gave the region Italy's most efficient and enlightened government, and at times even made the businessmen happy.

Along with radicalism, this region's other claim to fame is a well-established reputation as the home of Italy's finest cooking. When you begin to see how these two contradictory passions fit together, you'll understand the odd brand of earthy pragmatism that sets Emilia-Romagna apart. It helps to notice how simple this famous cuisine really is – all you need are the right ingredients, which the patient farmers of the region have had centuries to perfect. Here, even a *piadina* sandwich from a street-corner stand can be a strangely transcendent experience.

Yet, whether the food comes from the street or the serious, highly rated temples of tortellini that turn up in the most out-of-the-way villages, dukes and revolutionaries agree that living well is the best revenge. It all seems paradoxical at first. Emilia-Romagna is the place where plain brick churches conceal preposterously quadratura ceiling frescoes, where everybody knows the lyrics to at least one Verdi aria and one old socialist anthem, and where platoons of women in mink pedal bicycles through the town centres on their way to the grocer or the theatre. Stay around for a while, and it will all start to make sense…

HOW TO USE THIS GUIDE

MAPS
Keys and symbols Maps include alphabetical keys covering the locations of those places to stay, eat or drink that are featured in the book. Note that regional maps may not show all hotels and restaurants in the area: other establishments may be located in towns shown on the map.

Grids and grid references Several maps use grid lines to allow easy location of sites. Map grid references are listed in square brackets after the name of the place or site of interest in the text, with page number followed by grid number, eg: [103 C3].

FOLLOW BRADT

For the latest news, special offers and competitions, subscribe to the Bradt newsletter via the website **w** bradtguides.com and follow Bradt on:

- ⬛ BradtTravelGuides
- 🐦 @BradtGuides
- 📷 @bradtguides
- Ⓟ bradtguides
- ▶ bradtguides

Part One

GENERAL INFORMATION

EMILIA-ROMAGNA AT A GLANCE

Location In north central Italy, the great triangular wedge between the River Po, the Apennines and the Adriatic Sea, bordered to the north by Lombardy and the Veneto, to the south by Liguria, Tuscany, the Republic of San Marino and the Marche

Size 22,446km^2

Status One of Italy's 20 regions

GDP per capita €32,531 (2016), fourth among Italy's regions

Population 4,448,841 (2017)

Life expectancy Men 81 years, women 85 years

Climate Humid subtropical on the Po plain; warm continental climate in the mountains

Regional capital Bologna (population 386,200; 1 million in greater Bologna)

Other main towns Parma (population 187,195), Modena (population 185,228), Reggio Emilia (population 170,355), Ravenna (population 149,084), Rimini (population 138,060), Ferrara (population 131,907)

Main airport Bologna (Guglielmo Marconi Airport)

Language Italian. Main dialects: Emilian and Romagnol

Religion Roman Catholic

Currency Euro (€)

Exchange rate €1 = US$1.23, €1 = £0.88 (April 2018)

International telephone code +39 (but keep the first 0 in the number)

Time GMT +1

Electrical voltage 220V/50Hz, two-pin plugs

Public holidays 1 January, 6 January, 25 April, 1 May, 2 June, 15 August, 1 November, 8 December, 25 December, 26 December. See page 48

1

Background Information

GEOGRAPHY

Emilia-Romagna's nine provinces (Piacenza, Parma, Reggio Emilia, Modena, Bologna and Ferrara in Emilia, and Forlì-Cesena, Ravenna and Rimini in Romagna) have Italy's longest river, the Po, as a northern border, the Ligurian and Tusco-Emilian Apennines to the west and south, and the Adriatic Sea to the east. The Via Emilia (the SS9) neatly divides the flat fertile Po Valley, where three-quarters of the people live, from the hills and mountains.

The highest peaks are south of Modena, culminating in three over 2,000m: Monte Cimone at 2,165m, Monte Cusna at 2,121m and Alpe di Succiso at 2,017m. Thermal and saline springs bubble up in the region's 26 spas; rivers wind through scenic valleys – most importantly, the Trebbia, Taro, Secchia and Panaro, tributaries of the Po, and the Reno, Ronco, Montone and Savio flow directly into the Adriatic. The wetlands of the Po Delta are the biggest in Italy; south of these, long sandy beaches line the coast.

CLIMATE

The Po plain can be hot and muggy in summer, with daytime temperatures often above 30°C, but relieved by the occasional thunderstorm. Spring and autumn are mild, while winters are cool, wet and foggy. It occasionally snows, while up in the mountains there is enough white stuff in winter to maintain some modest ski resorts. The coast is reliably sunny and hot from June until August, but can get surprisingly rainy in September and surprisingly chilly in winter; in Rimini the average January high is 7°C, and in Parma 4°C.

NATURAL HISTORY AND CONSERVATION

Nearly 12% of Emilia-Romagna's territory is protected in 32 natural parks and reserves, including the two national parks that the region shares with Tuscany. The Parco Nazionale Foreste Casentinesi is one of the largest woodlands in Western Europe, covering some 368 square kilometres along the Romagna–Tuscany watershed. It encompasses the sources of the Tiber (on the Romagna side) and the Arno (on the Tuscan side), a thousand species of flora, Apennine wolves, badgers, fallow deer, boar, eagles, buzzards and tawny owls. In the heart of the forest are the towering silver firs of Campigna, planted by the Florentines for masts, and the primeval beech wood, the Riserva Naturale Integrale di Sasso Fratino, now a World Heritage Site and off limits to all but researchers since 1959.

The Parco Nazionale Tosco-Emiliano, created in 2001, encompasses the highest northern Apennines, dotted with crater lakes and rushing streams.

Below the alpine prairies are fir, beech and yew forests, home to boar, roe deer, wolves and golden eagles. The Emilian side has a striking landmark in the 1,047m-tall Rocca di Bismantova, a lofty isolated cylindrical plateau at Castelnovo ne' Monti.

One of the more unusual regional parks, the Vena del Gesso near Brisighella, surrounds Italy's largest gypsum ridge, a silver 25km outcrop pocked with dolines, ravines, swallow holes and 200 caves. An extremely rare fern, *Cheilanthes persica*, grows in the gypsum crevices, and in spring the forests bloom with wood anemone, dogtooth violet, lungwort, larkspur and primrose. The caves are home to mouse-eared, horseshoe and long-fingered bats and rare cave salamanders. Elsewhere, you might see crested porcupine, yellow-bellied toad, Sardinian warbler, Peregrine falcon or Eurasian eagle-owl.

The 54,000ha Parco Regionale Delta del Po, Emilia-Romagna's largest park, is scattered along the coast south of the Po to the salt pans of Cervia. Its wetlands, famous for their pink flamingos (notably at the marshes of Comacchio and Bertuzzi), lie along one of Europe's main migration routes and attract more than 250 species. Parasol pine woods dot the coast from Ravenna to Cervia; at Bosco della Mesola you can visit a patch of the forest that once covered the entire Po plain, and close to Ravenna, the Oasi di Punte Alberete is the last surviving example of the flooded forests that once covered the delta.

HISTORICAL OUTLINE

The 'region' of Emilia-Romagna is a political newborn, created only in the 1970s when all of Italy was divided into regions in a long-overdue move towards decentralisation. Some of Italy's regions have an obvious historical or geographical identity – Tuscany, the Veneto or Sicily for example. This one doesn't. Until relatively recently, the 'Emilian' part was considered part of Lombardy, while the Romagna followed a different destiny, first as part of the Byzantine Exarchate of Ravenna after the break-up of the Roman Empire, and then in the Papal State. The 'border' between Emilia and Romagna is generally considered to be the River Santerno, which flows by Imola.

Finds of tools and statuettes of fertility goddesses testify to the occupation of the Po plain in Palaeolithic times, and small farming settlements existed all through the Neolithic, but the first accomplished culture in the area was that of the remarkable Terramare people, who made the soggy plain habitable by digging the first drainage canals.

16th century BC	Arrival of the Terramare people in the Po Valley
12th century BC	Disappearance of the Terramare
c1000BC	Villanova people settle the area around Bologna, and the Apennine foothills around Rimini
9th century BC	Coming of the Etruscans

The Etruscans, arriving most likely from Asia Minor, imposed themselves as rulers on the existing Villanovan peoples, and the new hybrid culture, organised in confederations of city-states, became the most powerful and advanced nation in Italy. From their first centres in Tuscany and northern Lazio, the Etruscans expanded over the Apennines. From their new towns of Bologna and Spina, near Comacchio, the Etruscans gradually took over the entire Po plain by the 6th century BC. Already, though, they were facing a new enemy: the Celts.

c510BC	Etruscans found Velzna (Bologna)
5th century BC	Expansion of the Celts over the Alps
475BC	Defeats by the Greeks in southern Italy and by the Celts in the Po plain signal the decline of the Etruscans
390BC	Celts sack Rome
c350BC	Celts take Bologna

Even in Caesar's time, the part of Italy north of the Apennines was not 'Italy' at all, but called by the Romans Cisalpine Gaul, an area dominated by two main tribes, the Insubri in the west and the Boii around Bologna. Roman historians described a Celtic world in northern Italy that sounds a good deal like medieval Ireland. From 343 to 290 Rome fought its climactic battle for the rule of Italy – the Samnite Wars, in which that powerful southern Italic people was allied with the Celts and some Etruscans. Roman victories on all fronts opened the Po plain to Roman conquest and colonisation.

295BC	Victory of the Romans over the Celts at the Battle of Sentinum
268BC	Founding of Ariminium (Rimini), the first Roman colony north of the Apennines
223BC	Romans achieve final conquest of Cisalpine Gaul

The historian Polybius called the fight between Romans and Celts 'unsurpassed by any other war in history' in terms of the size and courage of the armies involved. The Romans built their great roads and established Latin colonies on the Po plain, but even after their defeat the Celts weren't done and the struggle in Gaul became part of an even bigger conflict, the Second Punic War, in which the Celts allied themselves with Carthage and served in great numbers in Hannibal's army.

220BC	Opening of the Via Flaminia, from Rome to Rimini
218BC	Opening of the Via Aemilia, founding of Placentia (Piacenza) Hannibal crosses the Alps, defeats the Romans at Trebbia, near Piacenza, winters at Bologna
202BC	Defeat of Carthage, end of the Second Punic War
189BC	Founding of Latin colony at Bononia (Bologna), conquered from the Celts
187BC	Opening of the Via Postumia, connecting Genoa with Heracleia via Piacenza
183BC	Founding of Parma
175BC	Founding of Reggio Emilia
132BC	Opening of the Via Popilia, the Adriatic coastal road through Rimini
115–102BC	Last Celtic raids into Italy

Roman surveyors, as relentless and methodical as the soldiers, carved the entire Po plain into a grid of straight roads, rectilinear towns and rectilinear land parcels called *centuriae*. Most of the land was expropriated from Celtic farmers and built into large estates (*latifundiae*) to enrich the Roman elite, though considerable areas around the new towns were granted as smallholdings to the colonists: Latins and army veterans.

49BC	Caesar crosses the Rubicon, ceases Rome expansion of Roman citizenship to all inhabitants of Cisalpine Gaul

AD98–180	The height of the Roman Empire, in which an unbroken line of good emperors (Trajan, Hadrian, Antoninus Pius and Marcus Aurelius) preside over a period of peace and prosperity

The decline began directly afterwards. In an empire increasingly oppressive and costly, run by and for the army, commerce and cities decayed greatly. After an unsettled period in the 3rd century that saw Germanic raids into the peninsula, Italian towns began building walls.

AD310	Legendary founding of San Marino by Christians fleeing Diocletian's persecutions
AD330	Constantine orders the closing of the pagan temples
AD364	Final division of the Empire into eastern and western halves
AD402	Ravenna becomes capital of the Western Empire

Vandal general Stilicho defended Italy (with a mostly German army) against German invasions. After his treacherous murder by Emperor Honorius, the army had no chance of holding the Western Empire together. For its last two decades, western emperors were puppets while German generals held the real power; after AD476 Italy was a German-run kingdom, with its capital at Ravenna. It enjoyed a period of recovery under the strong and enlightened rule of King Theodoric.

AD408	Murder of Stilicho
AD409	Invasion of the Visigoths, followed by their sack of Rome
AD450	Death of Galla Placidia
AD452	Attila the Hun invades Italy
AD476	End of the Western Roman Empire
AD476–93	Reign of Odoacer, King of Italy
AD488	Ostrogoths cross the Alps into Italy
AD493–526	Reign of King Theodoric
AD525	San Vitale (Ravenna) begun by Theodoric; execution of the philosopher Boethius
AD529–53	Greek–Gothic Wars

The greatest disaster in the history of Italy, the result of the ambition of Emperor Justinian to reconquer the lost lands of the west, led to a long, terrible war in which the flourishing Gothic Kingdom of Italy was destroyed, the Eastern Empire gravely weakened, and Italian civilisation dealt a near death blow. As Italy lay in ruins, a Germanic tribe heretofore quiet and backward, the Lombards, migrated over the Alps to fill the vacuum.

AD539	Widespread famine
AD540	Ravenna falls to the Byzantines under the great General Belisarius
AD567–68	The Lombards under King Alboin overrun most of Italy
circa AD590	Creation of the Exarchate of Ravenna

This period initiated the political divide between the two parts of our region, as the western half under Lombard control began to be considered part of 'Lombardia', while the east, still under the rule of the Empire, was known as 'Romania'. Here some important centres got their start: the Abbey of Pomposa, and the cities of

Ferrara (originally a Byzantine fort) and Comacchio, protected like Ravenna and Venice by its lagoons. Elsewhere, the devastation of the wars and invasions and the decrease of population had created a wasteland. In the 6th and 7th centuries most rural areas on the plain of the Po, which had depended on the upkeep of their drainage canals, once again became largely deserted, though none of the old cities except Velleia south of Parma died completely.

AD612	St Columbanus founds the Abbey of Bobbio
AD727	Lombards capture Bologna; Ravenna revolts against Byzantine rule
AD751	Lombards capture Ravenna
AD752	Lombards found abbey of Nonántola
AD754–56	Frankish invasion of northern Italy

As the Lombard Kingdom finally consolidated its power, and threatened papal rule in Rome, the papacy was alarmed enough to invite in King Pepin and the Franks, whose military superiority made short work of the Lombards. The origins of the Papal State came about with the 'Donation of Pepin' – the Franks, upholding their end of the deal with Rome, ceded the Romagna (and much of central Italy) to the temporal rule of the popes. Though they held on to this dubious claim tenaciously, they were in fact rarely able to wield much authority over these regions until the 1500s.

AD800	Charlemagne crowned Emperor
AD952	Otto the Great occupies northern Italy, is crowned Emperor the same year; creation of the Marquisate of Canossa

In this complex, feudal north Italy, the new house of da Canossa was not the only great power in the region. Another was the Obertenghi, a family of Lombard origins. They ran much of northwest Italy in the 10th century and held substantial lands in Germany, too. Branches of the Obertenghi eventually grew into the houses of Este, Malaspina and Pallavicini, three of the most powerful families of medieval Emilia-Romagna. Meanwhile, the rule of Otto and his successors, in the new Holy Roman Empire centred in Germany, restored order after the decay of the Carolingian Empire, and cities and culture throughout Italy started to revive.

After AD1000 the revival gained speed, inaugurating three centuries of nearly constant economic expansion. The booming cities organised themselves into free *comuni*; their efforts to increase their freedom from imperial or papal control provide most of the plot of Italian medieval history.

1055	Birth of Irnerius, first of Bologna University's *glossatori*
1071–1115	Reign of Matilda, Countess of Tuscany
1073–80	Reign of Pope Gregory VII
1077	Penance of Henry IV at Canossa, settling the investiture conflict between popes and emperors
1088	Founding of the University of Bologna
1095	First Crusade proclaimed at Piacenza
1099	Modena Cathedral begun, consecrated 1184
1115	Ferrara gains its independence from Canossa
1119	Building of the Two Towers of Bologna
1122	Piacenza Cathedral begun

By God, why shouldn't I rule this city?

Uberto Pallavicini, addressing the Capitano del Popolo
Ghiberto da Gente and the people of Parma

Italian medieval history may be a brilliant pageant of great men and great women, of stirring tales that would put any novelist to shame, but its study does require just a modicum of masochism. In its endless infernal complexity, it resembles one of those fractal pictures generated from the Mandelbrot set, where you can focus on any tiny corner of the image and see the whole pattern reproduced in all its twists and turns. While Guelphs and Ghibellines battled in an unending struggle for mastery of Italy, every city and every town was going through a similar drama of its own, with its own cast of characters, its own memorable events and moral fables – not so much a novel as a soap opera, full of intertwined plots, sudden reverses of fortune and surprises.

To see what sort of actor thrived in these potboilers, consider Uberto Pallavicini of Busseto, the great Marchese who built the family's little empire between Piacenza and Parma. A baron of the old school, regarded by his contemporaries as generous, frank and wise, Uberto had only one eye; the story went that a crow had pecked out the other one while he was a baby. He signed on early with the Ghibellines and never changed sides, serving Frederick II as *podestà* in several Italian cities. In the 1240s he was 'Imperial Vicar' in three regions of northern Tuscany, and by 1251 he was 'Captain General and Vicar of the Empire', the main military man looking out for the emperor's interests. With Frederick's death, things got hot for his partisans, and especially for Uberto, top Ghibelline in an area where the Guelphs were victorious almost everywhere. Think of it as a game of Monopoly, where the players circle around a board in which the stops are walled merchant towns – some cheap properties, and some quite choice ones. In 1254, Uberto held the titles to four *comuni*: Piacenza, Pavia, Cremona and Vercelli. On that turn he landed on 'Chance' and picked up a card that said 'You have been excommunicated by the pope; other players may jump you and help themselves to your money and properties'. (This was the worst card in the pack; Frederick himself got it twice.)

Uberto had always been a staunch anticleric, and a protector of the area's numerous Cathars. The pope found this a convenient excuse not only to excommunicate him, but to preach a crusade against him. This was largely a matter of politics, lining up a string of Uberto's enemies and promising them whatever of his lands they could capture. Uberto lost his four prize properties, but the 'crusaders' soon fell out in quarrels among themselves, and by 1259 Uberto came out stronger than before. He got Brescia for a while, before his ally Ezzelino da Romano tricked him out of it, and he won a share in the rulership of Milan and its dependent towns. Cremona fell in his lap, and finally Piacenza came back, when the *comune* granted him a four-year term of rule in 1261. He also picked up three cities in Piedmont: Asti, Tortona and Alessandria. Fortune then turned on him again, as the Guelphs came once more to the ascendant, and he lost nearly all his cities before his death in the late 1260s.

If you didn't follow all that, it doesn't matter, no more than the plot of any soap opera or game of Monopoly. Thirteenth-century Italy produced a score of men whose careers were just as colourful and complex. The times were fluid, and all the commotion and seemingly constant war did little damage to the sophisticated and wealthy life of the cities. It was in fact the presence of the cities that made the medieval chronicles so interesting. Emilia-Romagna's were surrounded by three powerful states, each a power on a European scale: Florence, Milan and Venice. There was also an emperor, who claimed authority over them all but was rarely able to enforce it, a pope, whose pretensions were even greater, and whose power might vary from the overwhelming to the laughable and back again overnight, and plenty of old-fashioned feudal barons up in castles, especially in the Apennines, where the economic revolution of medieval Italy hadn't quite arrived.

The cities themselves, however, were the important part. After AD1000 they had formed republican *comuni*, electing their own officials and running their own affairs. They stood up for their rights, forming the Lombard League against Emperor Frederick I, and they won. The *comuni* had all of the money, and most of the brains, and in their heyday in the 1100s they carved the territory of northern and central Italy into a patchwork quilt of city-states, each a compact and well-ordered economic unit of *città* and *contado*. They had wrested control away from the rural nobles, and often they forced them to live in town where they thought they wouldn't get up to any mischief.

What the cities could not do was evolve a fair and orderly way of governing themselves. The nobles still had plenty of money and influence. They usually monopolised the *comune*'s offices, and their vassals, clients and retainers made up private armies that often put them beyond the reach of the *comune*'s justice. They remained addicted to factionalism and vendettas, and by the 1200s the old feudal quarrels of the past had turned into civil wars within the *comune*'s walls. Most cities saw their middle classes organise as the *popolo* to make a stand against noble power and violence, but this usually only added another complexity to the game: nearly always they would choose a noble to lead them as Capitano del Popolo. Uberto himself held that office in several towns.

The titanic battle between Frederick II and the popes was the time when the weaknesses of the *comuni* started to unravel them. Local factional fights, between city and city or baron and baron, folded neatly into the greater struggle of Guelphs and Ghibellines, and the pope and emperor were always ready to give a prod and a push whenever any pair of local opponents looked like settling their differences peacefully. Every noble with an armed force became, quite simply, a politician. He had a party to answer to, clients to support, allies to plot with (or against), and divided cities to overawe or seduce. The stakes were high: as the conflict got hotter, any leader or faction that gained control of a city might exile the opponents and burn down their houses; that is how Dante Alighieri ended up in Ravenna.

The cities couldn't take the strain. The strongest, Florence, Siena and Venice, held on to their republican institutions for centuries more, but most of them, including every *comune* in Emilia-Romagna, sooner or later succumbed to the lure of boss rule. Uberto Pallavicini was one of the prototypes for the *signori* who would soon be ruling everywhere; only, unlike Uberto's, their rule would be permanent, often hereditary, and the interests of the city and its ruling family would become one – the Este in Ferrara and Modena, the da Polenta in Ravenna, the Malatesta in Rimini, and less enduring families in the other towns. Sometimes the old offices and laws of the *comuni* were maintained for a while, but eventually even that pretence was dropped.

The precocious republican experiment of the Middle Ages had failed, and dictatorship had taken its place. As a chronicler of Ferrara put it on the assumption of power of Obizzo II d'Este: 'The new ruler has more power than God eternal, who is not able to do unjust things.'

1135	Ferrara Cathedral begun
1152–90	Emperor Frederick I Barbarossa
1167	Founding of the Lombard League, an alliance of the *comuni* to uphold their rights against Frederick
1178	Parma Cathedral completed; baptistry begun in 1196
1198	Peace of Constance between the Emperor and the Lombard League
1212–46	Reign of Emperor Frederick II
1221	Death of St Dominic in Bologna
1226	Death of St Francis of Assisi
1236	Founding of the Second Lombard League
1240	Guelphs under Azzo d'Este control Ferrara, beginning three centuries of Este rule
1248	Siege of Parma, defeat of Imperial forces; Guelphs under Malatesta da Verucchio take control of Rimini
1249	Guelph victory of Fossalta (Modena), and capture of the emperor's son, King Enzo

The cities had won the first round, against Barbarossa; against his grandson Frederick II they had another hard fight, full of dramatic reverses of fortune. By now, all Italy was divided into two factions, the pro-imperial Ghibellines and the Guelphs, supporters of the free cities and their ally, the pope. Of course, one of the rights most important to the *comuni* was the right to battle each other, and in the shifting course of events 'Guelph' and 'Ghibelline' were often merely labels of convenience in purely local struggles.

After 1248, the Guelphs were victorious almost everywhere in north Italy, and the cities were generally free from imperial interference. But the factional fights within them continued, and nearly every city found the only solution was rule by a single boss, a *signore*, whose family often continued in power as a dynasty.

1255	Destruction of the castle of Canossa by the *comune* of Reggio
1256	Bologna abolishes feudalism in the communal territory
1275	Guido da Polenta establishes his family's rule in Ravenna
1278	Rudolph of Habsburg cedes sovereignty over Bologna and the Romagna to papacy
1295	Malatesta da Verucchio becomes *signore* of Rimini; San Marino adopts its Statutes and becomes an independent Republic
1307	Este rule in Modena
1314	Dante completes the *Commedia*; the poet dies in exile in Ravenna in 1321
1325	The 'Rape of the Bucket' by the Modenesi from Bologna
1331	Beginning of the rule of the Pio family in Carpi; they last until 1525
1346	The Visconti seize Parma, beginning a century of Milanese rule there
1348–49	The Black Death wipes out one-third of the Italian population

The plague returned throughout the region in 1361, in Bologna, Ferrara and Forlì in 1362, in Bologna and the Romagna in 1374 and again in 1382 and 1383. Much of Italy had a similar fate, and the plagues marked the first interruption of the medieval economic expansion. The cities recovered, and in the 15th century, Ferrara, and to a lesser extent Rimini and Bologna, became important centres of Renaissance art.

1360s	Campaigns of Cardinal Albornoz to establish papal control in the Romagna; Cesena taken in 1357, Bologna in 1360
1376	Bolognese throw out papal legate, establish oligarchic rule of the 'Sixteen Reformers of the State of Liberty'
1377	Bloody repression of revolt against papal rule in Cesena
1385	Building of the Castello Estense at Ferrara
1390	Basilica di San Petronio begun in Bologna
1401	The Bentivoglio gain control of Bologna
1441	Venice establishes rule over Ravenna
1446	Malatesta Temple begun at Rimini
1462	Excommunication of Sigismondo Malatesta, who loses most of his lands in the Romagna and Marche to the popes the following year
1470s	First printing presses in Ferrara and Bologna
c1475	Frescoes of the Palazzo Schifanoia at Ferrara
1482–83	War of Ferrara, prelude to the Wars of Italy
1494	Wars of Italy begin with the invasion of Charles VIII of France

After 1494, the delicate equilibrium of the small and wealthy Italian states was wrecked once and for all by the intervention of ambitious nation states France and Spain. The popes did as much as the foreign powers to keep the pot boiling in the decades of confusing and bitter war that followed. There was a string of calamitous popes – Alexander VI, Julius II, Leo X, Clement VII and Paul III – all intelligent men and patrons of learning and the arts, but their egomania, devotion to their families' interests and constant intrigues with foreign powers resulted in the end of Italian liberty and the subjection of nearly all of the nation to the eventual victor Charles V, who was both King of Spain and Holy Roman Emperor. For its part, the papacy won undisputed direct control of the lands of the Papal State, including the Romagna and Bologna, for the first time.

1495	Battle of Fornovo, demonstrating the ineffectuality of the Italians against the foreigners
1499	Campaigns in the Romagna of Cesare Borgia, son of Pope Alexander VI; captures Imola, Forlì and Rimini
1501	Marriage of Lucrezia Borgia and Alfonso I of Ferrara; Cesare Borgia's conquests dissolve on the death of his father and the transfer of the papacy to his enemies
1506	The Bentivoglio deposed in Bologna; papal rule established
1509	Pope Julius II raises a powerful coalition against Venice (League of Cambrai), which loses all its possessions in the Romagna
1519	Correggio paints the Camera di San Paolo in Parma
1527	Sack of Rome by Imperial troops
1530	Coronation of Charles V in Bologna
1532	Publication of Ariosto's *Orlando Furioso*
1534	Alessandro Farnese becomes Pope Paul III
1539	Famine and plague in the Romagna

| 1545 | Paul III creates the Duchy of Parma and Piacenza for his son Pier Luigi |
| 1547–63 | Council of Trent |

While Italy was subject to the unholy alliance of pope and Spaniard, the Reformation in northern Europe and the reform of the Church at Trent brought the liberal, humanistic culture of the Renaissance to an end in Italy. The new totalitarian Church that emerged from the council wiped out free thought and put severe strictures on art and the conduct of everyday life. Even the independent small states of Parma and Modena were seldom able to resist the pressure.

1553	Inquisition installed at Bologna
1559	Treaty of Câteau-Cambrésis confirms Spanish control over most of Italy
1564	Duke Cosimo of Florence builds Terra del Sole in the Tuscan Romagna
1593	Jews expelled from Bologna and Romagna
1598	Pope Clement VIII ousts the Este from Ferrara

As if Italy did not have enough troubles, after 1600 the economy began a rapid decay, caused partly by the shift of the richest trade routes from the Mediterranean to the Atlantic, and partly by papal and Spanish misrule and the loss of initiative in the merchant cities. Some agricultural prosperity remained, especially from silk and hemp cultivation around Bologna, but in this period the region was best known as a source of soldiers for the wars of northern Europe; opportunities at home were scarce. In the Baroque era Italy became a backwater, and no part of it suffered more than the Papal State, in which by 1650 the only thriving trades were church-building and banditry.

1618	Farnese Theatre begun in Parma
1630–31	Great plague in Emilia and most of Italy
1672	Earthquake at Rimini
1713	The close of the War of the Spanish Succession leaves Austria as the guarantor of the existing order in northern Italy
c1720	Introduction of maize as a food crop; Emilians discover polenta
1731	Extinction of the House of Farnese in Parma; rule passes to Charles of Bourbon
1735	Founding of the Gazzetta di Parma, Italy's oldest newspaper
1759	Enlightenment reformer Guillaume du Tillot transforms Duchy of Parma
1796	Napoleon enters Italy; creation of the 'Cispadane Republic' at Modena
1797	Cispadane Republic merged into a new 'Cisalpine Republic'
1813	Giuseppe Verdi born
1814	End of French rule
1815	Austrian garrison installed at Ferrara to protect the Papal State from revolts

The Congress of Vienna re-established the Papal State, gave the Duchy of Parma to Napoleon's estranged wife, Marie-Louise, and restored the Este to Modena, in the person of reactionary Francesco IV. In reality, all Italy was to be managed by Austria, but after the Napoleonic shake-up things would never be the same. In the decades of the 'Risorgimento', liberal thought and Italian nationalism were reborn. The secret societies called the Carbonari and revolutionaries such as Mazzini and Garibaldi led the fight for a united, democratic Italy, while conservative patriots hoped for unification under the Kingdom of Sardinia (Piedmont); Bolognese poet Giosuè Carducci and composer Giuseppe Verdi also played important roles.

1830–31	Revolution in Bologna, followed by Modena, Parma, and the Romagna. Government of the 'United Italian Provinces' set up; the revolt is soon crushed by Austrian troops
1843	Beginnings of Rimini as Italy's first beach resort
1845	Short-lived revolt in Rimini against papal rule
1847	Death of Marie-Louise
1848	Revolutions across Europe, and Italy; Carlo Alberto of Piedmont wars against Austria, and loses
1849	Collapse of revolutionary regimes; Garibaldi flees across the Romagna to Venice
1858	Railway reaches Bologna
1859	Revolt in Modena throws out the Este after 553 years; revolt in the Romagna. Both join Piedmont by plebiscite
1860	Parma incorporated into Piedmont, whose King Vittorio Emanuele II becomes king of a united Italy in 1861
1867	Arturo Toscanini born in Parma

Italian unity proved a disappointment to many under the oppressive and corrupt governments of the following decades; their liberal economic policies, while building modern industry, caused considerable hardship and dislocation in rural areas. Emilia-Romagna, where a large class of landless agricultural labour existed, became the most radicalised section of the nation, the birthplace of the Italian Socialist and co-operative movements.

1869	Severe riots in Parma and elsewhere against the Grist Tax, designed to build up the new Italy's army
1872	Large land-clearance and drainage programmes in the Romagna
1874	Socialist-anarchist revolt in Bologna
1881	Andrea Costa founds the Revolutionary Socialist Party of Romagna, and a year later becomes the first Socialist deputy in Parliament
1889	Imola elects Italy's first Socialist administration
1895	Guglielmo Marconi of Bologna sends the first radio signal
1896	First consumers' co-operative founded at Molinella, near Bologna

After World War I and Italy's disappointment at Versailles, the nation became polarised between the revolutionary movements and unions of the left, and the frightened propertied classes, who turned to the new Fascist party, led by the Romagnolo and former Socialist Mussolini, for salvation. In the years before Mussolini's assumption of power, Emilia-Romagna was the key battleground.

Mezzanotte in fondo   (In the deepest midnight,
Si sente un gran rumor'   What noise is this?
Ecco gli scariolanti   Here they are, the wheelbarrow men,
Chi vengano da lavor'   coming home from work)

Folk song from Ferrara province

The *scariolanti* pushed their wheelbarrows home so late because their villages were often many miles away from the unhealthy marshes of the Po where they worked. In the decades after Italian unification in 1860, times when men were glad to get any kind of work at all, they worked hard and long for pennies, raising levees and digging hundreds of miles of ditches and drainage canals, all by hand. Slightly luckier ones became farm hands on new estates created by the vast land reclamation projects, or on older farmlands that were being transformed by the economic changes of the 19th century.

For both, life was as nasty, brutish and short as in any part of Italy; to their horrific working conditions were added chronic malaria from the marshes, and pellagra from a diet over-dependent on corn polenta. These men and their families were a new phenomenon, a desperate rural proletariat with no roots in the soil, no heritage of village life and traditions and deference to the local lords – no old habits at all, in fact, to keep them from becoming the most thoroughly radicalised rural population of Europe.

The new Italian state was proving a disappointment, especially for working people. The landless and illiterate were excluded from voting. The politicians promised land reform, which they did try to follow through, but while this created a new class of peasant proprietors in Lombardy and other northern regions, in Emilia-Romagna it had little effect. In parts of the region feudal conditions still prevailed; Ferrara province, for example, had 20 families owning 60% of the land. Only eight years after unification, a widespread revolt against high taxes on grain had to be put down by the army.

Already, the rural workers were starting to organise themselves, and a region that had distinguished itself in the revolts against Austrian and papal rule before 1861 proved fertile ground for the new ideas of anarchism and socialism. The year 1872 saw the first meeting of the Italian branch of the First International at Rimini, where workers sat in on the arguments between the followers of Marx and those of Bakunin. The anarchist theorist himself, after his escape from Siberia, turned up in 1874, just in time to participate in the anarchist revolt of that year in Bologna.

The revolt was not a serious threat, and Bologna was hardly the place to try it. While other parts of Europe opposed radicalised industrial cities with a conservative hinterland, here the bourgeois cities felt besieged by a countryside full of Reds. In those days the metropolis of Emilia was called 'Bologna *rossa*' only for the colour of its bricks. Before 1900, despite its large working-class population, the city was still a centre of reaction. Along with the new proletariat came a new class of antagonists. Some of the old noble families had managed to hold on to parts of their estates, but the rest, along with the lands that had once belonged to the Church, fell into the hands of investors from the towns, or foreign corporations.

For the rest of the century the Reds built their movement pragmatically and carefully, step by step, with the police looking over their shoulders all the way. Italy's first Socialist party, the Socialist Party of the Romagna, appeared in

1881; its leader Andrea Costa of Imola became the first Socialist parliamentary deputy in the next elections. It became a national party in 1884, the same year its newspaper *Avanti!* was founded in Imola. The rest of the decade witnessed the first big agricultural strikes, in Emilia-Romagna and across the Po in Mantua province, and the split between the revolutionary anarchists and the Socialists. The latter worked on more practical concerns such as universal suffrage, labour rights and welfare issues. They also founded their first co-operatives, and made the region the strongest co-op centre south of Scandinavia. Urban industrial trade unions were growing too; the first appeared in Piacenza in 1891.

In the years up to World War I, the movement had its ups and downs. The strikes and fierce repression of 1898, especially rough around Ferrara, were followed by more than a decade of sympathetic government under the moderate Giovanni Giolitti, in which labour rights were extended and the co-operatives even got a share of government contracts. Agricultural strikes such as the huge one around Parma in 1908 usually ended in failure, but the co-ops, the unions and the Socialist Party grew a little stronger every year. A sharp recession caused the fall of Giolitti, and not long after came a spontaneous uprising called 'Red Week', when 100,000 troops had to be sent to the Romagna. This put such a scare into the powers that be that it helped convince them to drag Italy into World War I.

As soon as the war was done, the Socialists rose up again, and with a little leadership they might easily have accomplished the revolution. Instead, this time the powers raised up Mussolini and his blackshirts to beat them into the ground once and for all. Or so they thought. All through the dictatorship, the leftist organisations, increasingly led by the Communist Party, continued to organise underground, and some even got their newspapers out on a fairly regular basis.

The movement was reborn in the resistance of World War II, and here too the Communists took the lead; two-thirds of the *partigiani* were Party members. Resistance here was as strong as any part of Italy. At first the *partigiani* tried to make a stand in the mountains, establishing the free zone of the 'Republic of Montefiorino' in 1943. That strategy was a failure, and they soon learned that, paradoxically enough, their guerrilla war worked better in the flat Po Valley and in the cities, where they proved such a bother that the Germans responded with horrific massacres of civilians, at Ferrara in 1943 and Marzabotto in 1944.

New explosions on the level of 1914–22 were avoided after the war by an increasing maturity on both sides. In 1947, one in five adults in Emilia-Romagna was a Party member. Together, the Communists and Socialists could command more than 60% of the vote at any election. The rightists in Rome finally realised that Emilia-Romagna radicalism was utterly unkillable; they were content to run Italy and leave the region to the Reds. The Communists, for their part, had learned the hard way what happened when they tried revolution, and instead of trying to bring the system down they learned to work with it, while evolving the most humane and constructive brand of Communism the world has ever seen – ironically, with Stalin's blessing.

The old streak of Emilia-Romagna pragmatism led to a remarkable political cohabitation. The Communist-run local governments, of which Bologna was the showcase, were by far the best-run, most honest and most efficient in all Italy.

continued overleaf

Public transport, housing development and social services became models for Europe. In the 1960s, the Reds even won support from many of the region's employers. Emilia-Romagna was spawning large numbers of successful small manufacturing businesses, and the Communists demonstrated how such businesses were as much disadvantaged by monopoly capital as the workers. Whenever a businessman needed something done, he found a sympathetic Communist mayor ready to lend a hand.

Nowadays the Reds of Emilia-Romagna are to a certain extent victims of their own success. Their region has climbed to the top in average income for Italy, and some of the co-operatives have grown so posh they are quoted on the stock market. When Italians think of Emilia-Romagna, visions of tortelli and truffles, Ferraris and Maseratis are likely to dance in their heads, not agitators and picket lines. In 2,000 years, the region has metamorphosed from Cisalpine Gaul to Cisalpine Scandinavia: well-organised, intelligent and conspicuously caring, pink and plump, and (as some Italians might tell you) perhaps a little bit dull.

The great social experiment survives, however, and builds on its successes, and whatever the future has in store for Emilia-Romagna it seems that the region will be able to adapt and evolve and stay true to its principles. The question remains though, why should this region, out of all the world, be the one where socialism really makes sense? Perhaps the answer goes back to the *scariolanti*, and the land reclamation programmes dating back to the Middle Ages. Like the Dutch, the people of this region have a quiet sense of solidarity and a proprietary feeling about their land. After all, they built it.

1918–20	The 'Red years', waves of strikes throughout industrialised northern Italy
1921–22	Wave of violence by Fascist gangs against leftist institutions, co-operatives and municipal governments (see box, pages 14–16)
1922	Mussolini's March on Rome; he becomes head of the government
1925	Planning of the Città del Duce at Forlì
1926	Murder of defiant Socialist leader Giacomo Matteotti (from Fratta Polesine)
1937	Hundreds of Emilia-Romagna men escape Italy to fight with the International Brigades in Spain
1940	First Ferrari built in Modena
1943	The Allies invade Italy

The Allies' concentration on opening a new front in France led to stagnation on the Italian front. A failed offensive in August 1944 against the German Gothic Line, which extended across Emilia-Romagna, let the Germans and Fascist militias mop up Resistance groups, while allowing more time for Allied bombers to wreak havoc on the region's cities. Rimini was perhaps the most heavily bombed city in Italy. Bologna and Ravenna were also hard-hit, and artistic monuments such as the Teatro Farnese in Parma were partially destroyed.

1943	The partisans set up a short-lived free zone in the Apennines, the 'Republic of Montefiorino', and then conduct pitched battles with the Germans in Bologna

1944	The 'march of death'; SS massacres in several villages, notably Marzabotto, in reprisal for partisan activities
1946–48	The first post-war elections give Italy a Christian Democrat government, while Emilia-Romagna votes solidly Communist in local elections
1947	Massive, successful strikes by tenant farmers in the Po plain

After liberation, the Americans saw to it (quite understandably, in the context of the Cold War) that the new Italian Republic was a limited democracy at best. But while Italy was manipulated to ensure permanent control by the centre-right Christian Democrats, Emilia-Romagna bucked the trend by becoming a bastion of enlightened Communism. Their government did business no harm at all, and the region paradoxically also became a bastion of the 'third Italy' of small, successful, often family-run manufacturing firms.

Recovery was rapid, especially in agriculture (while the percentage of workers in that sector fell from more than 50% of the workforce to 10%), so much so that the Po plain saw extensive deforestation. A quarter of Italy's pigs called Emilia-Romagna home. A big chemical industry grew up in Ravenna and Ferrara and metals and machinery thrived in Bologna and Modena, along with ceramic products and textiles in several centres, and beach tourism in Rimini.

1956	Khrushchev's revelations about Stalin and the Hungarian revolt cause a split and soul-searching among the Communists
1964	Death of painter Giorgio Morandi
1970	Region of Emilia-Romagna created, with elections for a regional assembly
1970s	The Anni di Piombo, a decade of political crime and right-wing terrorism climaxing in the Bologna rail station bombing, killing 85 people
1974	Federico Fellini's Amarcord released
1998	Election of conservative Mayor Giorgio Guazzaloca in Bologna
2004	Bologna elects leftist academic Flavio Delbono
2007	Death of singer Luciano Pavarotti in Modena
2009	After a referendum, seven comuni in the Marche join the province of Rimini
2010	'Cinzia-gate': Flavio Delbono's girlfriend and secretary spills the beans of fraud and corruption, forcing Delbono from office; replaced by centre-left Virginio Merola
2012	Earthquakes on 20 and 29 May leave 27 dead, 200 injured and 14,000 homeless across the region
2016	Merola re-elected mayor of Bologna

GOVERNMENT AND POLITICS

Italy's 1948 Constitution divided the country into administrative regions. The borders weren't always tidy. Here, two regions that never thought much of each other landed in the same box. So far they have got on quite well, though occasionally some Romagnolo malcontent will call for secession. The regional government has a parliament (the Consiglio Regionale) and a President, along with ministers (called assessori). It lives in a gargantuan, horrific Brutalist compound on Viale Aldo Moro in Bologna.

> Our programme is simple. We wish to govern Italy. They ask us for programmes, but there are already too many.
>
> Benito Mussolini, in an article he wrote on Fascism for the *Enciclopedia Italiana*

Mussolini was born in Verano di Costa, a hamlet near Predappio. His father Alessandro, a blacksmith by trade, was an ardent and somewhat thuggish Socialist activist, his mother a pious Catholic schoolteacher. Their house, like many others in Italy, had two pictures on the wall, one of Garibaldi and the other of the Madonna. Alessandro named his first-born son Benito Amilcare Andrea, for three of his revolutionary heroes: Benito Juárez of Mexico, Amilcare Cipriani, a Romagnolo who had fought with Garibaldi and in the Paris Commune, and the Romagnolo Socialist leader Andrea Costa.

Little Benito was a prize student in the Catholic boarding school where his mother sent him, a boy with a passion for books. He also had a reputation as a bully, one who especially picked on girls (it was to be a lifelong habit). At the age of 11, he got expelled for stabbing a schoolmate in the hand with a knife. At 15, in another school, he stuck another classmate in the backside, but this time he got off with a short suspension. At 17, he was already well known in the bordellos of Forlimpopoli, and he was chosen by his school to give an oration to the town for a ceremony on the death of Giuseppe Verdi.

Reality, as it will do, was breaking in on this charmed life. Benito was 18, and a graduate, faced with the unpleasant prospect of earning a living. The best he could do was a job as schoolteacher in the woebegone village of Gualtieri on the Po, teaching seven-year-olds to conjugate verbs. The girlfriends he picked up and the company of fellow radicals – for Benito was as much a revolutionary as his dad – held few thrills, and reality had another dirty trick to play, the prospect of two years in the army.

To avoid conscription, he fled to Switzerland in 1902. At the time, his father was on trial back home for trying to steal an election by intimidating non-Socialist voters at the polls. Among the Swiss, Mussolini carried loads of bricks to the bricklayers, bummed his way from town to town, learned French and occasionally slept under bridges. Switzerland provided a refuge, if a precarious one, for radicals from all over Europe in those days, and Mussolini spent most of his time with them, attending political meetings and writing poems and articles for socialist papers. He started to make a name for himself, and the Swiss police started to make half-hearted attempts to deport him back to Italy; their failure, an odd lapse in Swiss efficiency, might be explained by later allegations that he had been in their pay, spying on his friends.

There was only one way he could ever return to Italy. It was either life in Switzerland or the army, and in 1904 Mussolini made the only intelligent choice. Amazingly, they sent this nearly useless revolutionary tramp to the elite corps, the Bersaglieri, and he seems to have thoroughly enjoyed it. With typical Mussolinian bombast, he later wrote of his 21 months as a soldier that 'a man must learn to obey before he can learn to command'. After the army came three more wasted years, but in 1909 Mussolini finally found his calling, as the editor of a socialist newspaper in Trento, then under Austrian rule. He also found his style, blunt and rough, typically Romagnolo, and seldom did he ever again write or speak a paragraph that did not impugn someone's virtue or intelligence, or scream for their blood.

The year 1909 was the height of Italietta, the 'little Italy' of a booming economy, ice cream, motorcars and modest bourgeois happiness, presided over by the liberal Prime Minister Giovanni Giolitti. Never before had Italy been so contented and prosperous; even the working classes were making impressive gains. All the intellectuals hated it. An odd change came over Benito Mussolini, as if he were emerging from a cocoon. Now wearing a decent suit, he began to write a bit dismissively about the common man; the word *gerarchia*, the hierarchy, started to figure prominently in his articles on the elite that would be necessary to create a 'new Italy'. He began to acquire odd habits. Like Hitler, the new Mussolini was a vegetarian, a non-smoker and a teetotaller. Even worse than Hitler, he became a fitness nut and an amateur violinist. Since he was going bald anyhow, he started shaving his head.

Mussolini was still enough of an internationalist in 1911 to oppose the imperialist war against Turkey, which was designed to steal Libya and take people's minds off an economic recession. He wrote fierce editorials, and organised demonstrations against the departing soldiers. Some Socialists had supported the war, including the editor of the national party newspaper *Avanti!*. Mussolini got him kicked out of the party, and took his job. His talents for demagoguery soon made him the most successful editor the paper ever had; its circulation tripled within a year.

Mussolini was now somebody. His next metamorphosis came, like so many other unexpected and unpleasant things, with the outbreak of World War I. Leftists were divided over whether Italy should join in. Mussolini threw away his old principles to call for war: this time it was his turn to get thrown out of the party and lose his job. He started a new paper in Milan, *Il Popolo d'Italia*, with a little help from some new friends – the French and Belgian governments, who financed the paper and Mussolini's campaign to bring Italy into the war.

The perfection of the former Socialist's sell-out came right after the armistice. When the Allies at Versailles broke all their promises to Italy, it wasn't only the Socialists who were pointing out that 600,000 Italians had just died for nothing. Accounts that had been put off for four years were now being settled. The Socialists convulsed Italy in a wave of strikes and factory occupations; they swept the local elections, and the propertied classes were terrified that Italy was going the way of Russia. How Mussolini felt is only too easy to imagine. He had guessed wrong about the war. He was politically dead, and the revolution was happening without him.

His rapid conversion into a gangster boss at the service of the rich was one of the cleverest political comebacks in history. Already during the war, Mussolini had been making contacts with the Milan industrialists and the big landowners of his home region. Tellingly, the first meeting of the Fasci di Combattamento in 1919 was held at the Milan Chamber of Commerce.

The next four years, when the Fascist *squadristi* terrorised the nation and forced their will on it while the police turned a blind eye, can look very much like an Emilia-Romagna civil war. Socialist and democratic opposition to the Fascists

continued overleaf

1

was strongest here, but paradoxically the region also gave Mussolini some of his strongest supporters, from the middle classes and especially among the class of landlords, who finally saw a chance to get back at the socialist and anarchist farmers with their agitation, their strikes and their co-operatives. Many of the top Fascist leaders came from the region: not only Mussolini, but Count Dino Grandi, from Mordaro near Bologna, and Italo Balbo, from Ferrara. Balbo, who was Jewish, and would die early in the war before he got a chance to regret what he had helped create, was the roughest and smartest of the *squadra* chiefs.

While the Fascists began their terror campaign bashing Slavs in Trieste, it was clear that the Red heartland, Emilia-Romagna, would have to be their prime objective. Their weapons were clubs and pistols, torches and petrol, and bottles of castor oil to pour down the throats of opponents – small-time stuff, compared with what Europe would be seeing in the 1930s and 40s, but in Italy it had just the desired effect. Mussolini sent Balbo to begin the campaign in 1920 with a raid on Bologna. He spent most of 1921 destroying the co-operatives in the region by violence and intimidation, and the next year led many of the attacks on Emilia-Romagna's cities, including his home town, where he assembled some 60,000 Fascists to seize control of the city government. Two weeks later they did the same in Bologna, though they were nearly stopped by a brave prefect named Cesare Mori, who barricaded himself inside his office until the government in Rome ordered him to let the Fascists have their way. Ironically, the same Mori would later become a Fascist and work for Mussolini as prefect in Sicily, where he did his job so well he nearly drove the Mafia out of business.

In one day, 29 July 1922, Balbo's *squadri* torched the buildings of every Socialist and Communist organisation in Ravenna and Forlì provinces. Only Parma held out against the Fascists, thanks on one occasion to the working men of the Oltratorrente, who built and defended barricades across the city, and on another to a democratic army commander who refused just to stand by, the only time such a thing happened.

All through their subjugation of Emilia-Romagna, the small numbers of *squadristi* had the near-total support of the army, the police, the king and the Church. Still, they never would have succeeded if the Socialists and democrats had not proved so totally bereft of courage and leadership. Despite Parma, the war in Emilia-Romagna was over, and the *squadri* moved on to bully the rest of the country; the King made Mussolini Prime Minister in October.

The rest of the story is familiar enough. Cynical opportunism is such a feature of Italian politics that there's even a name for it – *trasformismo*. Even so, the blacksmith's boy from Predappio is a truly special case: the Socialist who wrecked the unions and outlawed the Socialist Party, the atheist who signed the Concordat with the Church, the man who had briefly gone to jail for opposing one Italian imperialist war in Africa, and later started one himself, the implacable foe of the Germans and Austrians who became Hitler's best pal. His story would make a marvellously squalid historical novel or film, though it might not sell in Italy; the average Italian of today would never be convinced that such things actually happened.

Post-war Italian governments allowed the new regions little power – primarily because of worries over Emilia-Romagna, which was run by the Communists. That began to change with the reforms of 1980. Now regions have some measure of control over education, planning and health care. Many of their new powers came at the expense of the provinces. Emilia-Romagna has eight of these; limited to strictly local matters, they are roughly equivalent to counties. Bologna's is a special case, reformed under a new statute as a metro urban government, the Città Metropolitana di Bologna.

Ever since the war, government at all levels in the region has been dominated by the left, first under the Communists, who collapsed in 1991 and re-emerged as the Partito Democratico della Sinistra, which collapsed seven years later and turned into the Democratici della Sinistra and splinter parties. Amid endless factional and ideological quarrels, this morphed into the Ulivi (Olive Tree Movement) and then the Partito Democratico. It's always complicated here.

But as the showcase for Italy's left, the permanent majority has generally seen to it that the region's affairs are clean and well managed. There are always hiccups along the way. Emilia-Romagna's idea of a scandal is the 2013 Chioscopoli, in which the president of the region Stefano Bonaccini was dragged into court for abuse of office in an affair involving rights to a snack kiosk (*chiosco*) in a Modena park. Bonaccini won his case.

We can't leave without mentioning the Most Serene Republic of San Marino, the world's oldest. Its constitution, written in Latin, dates from the 16th century. San Marino has a 60-member parliament and two heads of state, the Capitani Reggenti. Traditionally they are selected one each from the opposing parties. Italy handles most of San Marino's foreign policy matters. San Marino uses the euro, though it doesn't even belong to the EU. Still, the little republic has a seat of its own at the Council of Europe.

ECONOMY

Emilia-Romagna is one of Italy's wealthiest and most dynamic regions, with a well-balanced economy and a GDP per capita of €32,531. Its unemployment rate of 7.6% is well below the national rate of 12%. The exceptionally strong manufacturing sector boasts some 50,000 companies producing cars, chemicals, farm machinery, ceramic tiles, pharmaceuticals, clothing, food and appliances. With its broad plains and abundant water, it's also Italy's most important agricultural region (although this sector only employs some 3% of the population), supplying a large percentage of the country's wheat (Barilla, the world's largest pasta producer, is based in Parma), corn, sugar beets, wine, vegetables, fruit and fodder for its important dairy and livestock industries. Tourism is less intense than elsewhere in Italy, and mainly concentrated along the Adriatic Riviera.

Yet along with all its wealth, Emilia-Romagna is the world capital of social co-operatives. Rather than maximise their profits, social co-operatives are dedicated to harmonising the interests of all stakeholders. Two of the biggest are the Coop supermarkets and Unipol insurance companies, both headquartered in Bologna. Social co-operatives also help smaller businesses, such as the Parmigiano Reggiano cheese makers, to thrive in a globalised economy.

EDUCATION

The importance of education is deeply instilled here. Bologna boasts the world's oldest university (see box, page 106) and consistently rates among the top two or three in the nation. Those in Reggio-Modena, Parma and Ferrara also date from the Middle Ages.

Reggio Emilia is world famous for the innovative 'Reggio approach' to early childhood and primary school education, developed by child psychologist Loris Malaguzzi in the immediate aftermath of World War II. The approach is based on the belief that children are the collective responsibility of the community, and on the need to nurture each child's own personality and interests. The Reggio approach places an emphasis on children's expression 'in a hundred languages', with an emphasis on art and beauty. Reggio-style nurseries are spread across the region.

PEOPLE

Although to the outsider the differences might seem subtle, the peoples of Emilia (where the barbarian Lombards settled) and Romagna (where the Western Roman Empire had its last hurrah) have distinct identities, notably in their dialects (page 23) and in their cuisine (pages 40–6). They like to argue about exactly where the 'border' lies between the two around Imola.

Emilia-Romagna's population of 4,448,841 (2017) includes a half-million foreign born, the second-highest percentage of any Italian region, who help to keep the population ticking over in spite of a low native birth rate. Romanians and Poles have large communities; the region's 180,800 non-EU residents include large Argentine, Albanian, Swiss, Brazilian and Russian populations and, increasingly, new arrivals from Africa and China. These last two are busy in small-scale international trading; whenever it starts raining you'll find a 'Chinese bazaar' nearby to sell you an umbrella. After the UK, Italy has the largest Sikh population in Europe, many of whom tend the cows in Emilia-Romagna's dairies.

RELIGION

The majority of residents are Catholic, and sometimes radical leftists at the same time, in the spirit of Giovannino Guareschi's characters in his *Don Camillo* stories: the village priest and Communist mayor who always bickered but shared a keen interest in the well-being of their town (and personified the spirit behind Emilia-Romagna's social co-operatives). Today both Communism and Catholicism are on the decline – as everywhere else – and many churches are open for only one mass a week. You'll also find Protestant (Italians call them 'Evangelical') churches in the cities, and a smattering of Greek Orthodox, Seventh Day Adventists and Jehovah's Witnesses.

Bologna had an important Jewish population, with 11 synagogues, a rabbinical school and Jewish printing press, although the vibrant cultural life was much diminished after the papal persecutions and forced ghettoisation in the 1550s. However, thanks to the protection of the Este dukes, communities thrived in Modena and especially Ferrara, which has the best-preserved Jewish quarter in Italy after Venice. Many Jews have remained, even after the intolerance of papal rule and the deportations and horrors of World War II; there are still active synagogues in Bologna Ferrara, Modena, Parma and Soragna (where Jews expelled from Parma and Piacenza by the Farnese took refuge in the 1500s).

Even though Islam isn't officially recognised by the Italian state, a third of Italy's foreign-born population is Muslim, mainly of Albanian, Turkish and Pakistani origin. They are served by 23 small mosques and cultural centres, mostly around Bologna and Modena.

LANGUAGE

Everyone speaks Italian, but many also speak various dialects of Emiliân-rumagnōl, a branch of the Gallo-Italic languages of northern Italy, spoken not only in Emilia-Romagna but also in neighbouring parts of Lombardy, Umbria, Tuscany, Liguria, the Marche and San Marino. Characterised by many diacritical marks (it has a lot more vowel and consonant sounds than Italian) and nouns that don't end in vowels, it is the main spoken language in 10.5% of households, and understood, alongside Italian, in 28%.

Emilian, which has never been standardised, has numerous recognised dialects, while Romagnol has had a dictionary since 1840 and an important literary tradition throughout the 20th century. Regional theatre groups and radio and television stations are doing their best to keep the language alive, and you may see it on menus.

ART

In art, Emilia-Romagna defies generalisations: look at it not as a matching pearl necklace but rather as a charm bracelet, with charms that evolved in various cities at various times in history. Influences came from every direction and, when the patronage was there, the efforts often merged into a coherent school. The region's talent for making pretty things goes back to the Villanovans and at various times in history it set the standard of excellence in Italy – in late Roman–Byzantine mosaics, in medieval illumination, in Baroque theatre and stage sets, and in painting during the late 16th and 17th centuries, when paintings by the Bologna school were in demand throughout Europe.

As much art as Emilia-Romagna has to offer today, an extraordinary amount of it was destroyed in various wars or is now in museums outside the region: for instance, nothing remains in the region by the major Renaissance painter Melozzo da Forlì. On the other hand, the region has a whole cast of lesser-known artists, local obsessions and talents. Faenza gave the world faience, but the whole region, like anywhere Etruscans once lived, has a knack with terracotta, and used it to produce mournful statue groups of the *Deposition of Christ*, as well as the characteristic decorative friezes of its simple brick churches and palaces. The Renaissance brought a mania for intarsia (wood inlay), employed most often in choir stalls – every church had to have a set, and most depict townscapes and simple everyday objects, both meant to show the artists' skill in perspective. Emilia-Romagna's castles, especially around Parma and the Romagna, are among the most striking in Italy, and often have lavish interiors added in or after the Renaissance, when they were converted into stately residences.

Except for the castles, architecture is a subject that Emilia-Romagna people do not often choose to bring up. In fact, the region has always been strangely allergic to architectural achievement of any kind. On the rare occasions when they cared to build ambitiously, they were usually content to find their inspiration, or their builders, from somewhere else. Parma, Ferrara and Piacenza, to an extent, are exceptions, but Bologna, for all its attractive porticoes, is unquestionably the most architecturally deprived great city of Italy.

For information on individual artists, see pages 408–14.

ANCIENT AND MEDIEVAL The finds from Villanovan and Etruscan cemeteries are scattered in the archaeology museums of the region, with the biggest concentrations in Bologna and Ferrara. Special mention must go to Verucchio near Rimini, where

1

a Villanovan cemetery yielded unusually well-preserved artefacts, including textiles and wood from the 7th century BC. Like their compatriots to the south, the Etruscans of the Po Valley made beautiful bronzes, ceramics and jewellery, and had a taste for ancient Greek pots (Ferrara has an extraordinary collection of red figure vases), besides making copies of their own. Unlike the Etruscans of Tuscany, however, they did not bury their dead in tumuli or painted tombs, but often under remarkable large circular tombstones carved with reliefs. The region was neither particularly wealthy nor accomplished in Roman times; the best collections of art and artefacts from that period are in Parma, Bologna and Rimini, and at the lost city of Velleia.

In the so-called Dark Ages, the Greek heirs of the Roman Empire in Constantinople gave the region one of the most dazzling charms on its bracelet in Ravenna. Although its 6th-century churches and splendid mosaics exerted more immediate influence on Byzantium's protégé Venice (which could afford such fancies), you'll find echoes of Ravenna throughout the region, in the belltowers of its churches and mosaic pavements, and Byzantine miniatures.

Outside Ravenna, you'll find early medieval traces in Bologna's Santo Stefano complex, the Abbey of Nonántola near Modena, and Bobbio, a great centre of learning in the Dark Ages. Among the Romanesque churches, the brightest jewels are Modena Cathedral, decorated by the sculptor Wiligelmo, his followers and the Campionese Masters of Lombardy, and Parma Cathedral and Baptistry, with fine sculptures by Antelami. A favourite was the *Allegories of the Months*, at Modena (Duomo), Parma (Duomo and Baptistry), Ferrara (Duomo and the Palazzo Schifanoia), Argenta (San Giorgio), Bobbio (San Colombo) and Piacenza (San Savino).

Other notable Romanesque churches include Castell'Arquato's Collegiata, Fidenza's Duomo and the Abbey of Pomposa, the region's greatest shrine of trecento art, with beautiful frescoes by Emilia-Romagna's two medieval schools of painting, Bologna and Rimini.

The Bolognese school grew up alongside the university. The city's artists excelled in illuminated manuscripts, Bibles and religious texts, but also legal codices and books of guild statutes or poetry (Biblioteca Estense in Modena, Biblioteca Comunale in Bologna). Although Byzantine influences were initially strong, by the late 13th century Giotto's more naturalistic, volumetric style led to a wealth of invention, foreshortening, movement and the individualisation of characters. Although most works are anonymous, Jacopino da Reggio, Bernardino da Modena and Franco Bolognese (highly praised by Dante) are among the names that have come down to us. The only important Bolognese artist of the trecento to work on a larger scale was Vitale da Bologna.

The often charming Rimini School blossomed in the early 14th century, initially inspired by Byzantine miniatures from Ravenna, and later by the frescoes in Assisi by Giotto and the finest Roman and Umbrian artists of the day. Little is known of its artists beyond their names (if that): the 'Pseudo Jacopino', Pietro da Rimini, Giuliano da Rimini and Giovanni Baronzio are among those identified, each with their individual quirks, joy in decoration, genre details and tendency to exuberant narrative.

RENAISSANCE AND MANNERISM In the quattrocento, the Ferrara school was the first in Emilia-Romagna to shine, thanks to the unflagging enthusiasm and deep pockets of the Este. They founded a university to attract leading scholars to their city, commissioned works from the greatest painters, and did all they could to encourage local talent. Cosmè Tura, their court artist, had a style unto himself – a very nervous and elegant line, creating highly energised dreamlike scenes, reflected

There is very little stone, much less marble, in Emilia-Romagna, but no end of quality clay. The Etruscans were the first ones here to sculpt and bake clay figures for their temple decoration and for funeral sculpture, especially banqueting couples lounging nonchalantly on their own urns.

The 16th century was the great age of life-size terracotta statues and altarpieces, and Bologna and Modena produced masters of the art who were admired by Michelangelo, even if most art historians since have tended to ignore them as being less 'noble' than marble. The best of them were Guido Mazzoni, Antonio Begarelli, Niccolò dell'Arca and Vincenzo Onofri.

Their life-size terracotta groups, which still adorn churches in the region, were incredibly tricky to make. Various kinds of clay were excavated, dried, cleaned of impurities, combined, kneaded together and then reconstituted. An internal armature was made to support the weight of the wet clay during the modelling. Here the work was distinctly easier than stone; instead of a chisel, fingers were the main tool.

Once modelled, the sculpture was left to dry completely, before being cut into sections to remove the armature. Each piece was then hollowed out for even baking in an open flame kiln for up to 24 hours and cooked until stone hard. Then the statues would be reassembled, using stucco for the glue, then finished. At any point along the way something could go horribly wrong, and there would be nothing to do but start over.

to varying degrees in the work of the other great quattrocento Ferraresi: Francesco del Cossa, Dosso Dossi, Lorenzo Costa and especially Ercole de' Roberti.

By the early 1500s the Duchy of Parma joined Ferrara among the leading artistic centres of northern Italy, where sophisticated patrons had an insatiable appetite for the luxurious and for precious art, especially if it came with scholarly allusions, visual puns and illusionistic effects. Art no longer imitated life, but life imitated art, in the costumes and spectacles and the striving for a refined, artificial air. In Parma, Correggio and Parmigianino were the men of the hour: Correggio's Camera di San Paolo has as many mysterious allusions as the region's other great Renaissance shrine, Rimini's Tempio Malatestiano; his proto-Baroque domes are full of illusionistic effect, and his mythological paintings among the most sensuous. He inspired Parma's two great painters, the exquisite Mannerist Parmigianino, with his elongated hyperelegant and sensuous forms, and the early Baroque master, Lanfranco.

HIGH RENAISSANCE AND BAROQUE In the late 16th century, Bologna became a cradle of reaction against the exaggerations and distortions of Mannerism, a fight led by the Carracci, brothers Annibale and Agostino and cousin Ludovico, who started off together painting palaces, and in the 1580s founded a school of painting with the startlingly inaccurate name of the Accademia degli Incamminati ('the progressives'). Their success was not necessarily due to any change in Italian tastes. The Council of Trent, which concluded its reform of the Church in 1563, decreed that religious art was to fall under the close supervision of the clergy, and clear rules were set down for it. Painting and sculpture must be simple and intelligible, realistic, and filled with emotional appeal to encourage piety. The Carracci's genius was to hit on a formula that the Counter-Reformation Church could approve. They emphasised draughtsmanship, life drawing, perfect polish and the restoration of classicism; their approach discouraged thinking, vision and imagination, which made their followers in the Bolognese school exceedingly popular and gave the region's museums and churches their acres of virtuoso wallpaper.

There were notable exceptions. The most gifted of the Carracci, Annibale, revived interest in the then-neglected art of Correggio before moving off to Rome to paint the ceiling of the Galleria Farnese, his masterpiece and a fundamental point of departure for Baroque painting. He is also credited with the invention of the 'ideal landscape', an art perfected by Poussin, and was the first to draw caricatures. Many graduates of the Accademia followed Annibale to Rome. The most talented, Guido Reni, soon returned to Bologna, where his huge studio sent religious paintings to patrons around Europe. Domenichino and Giovanni Lanfranco of Parma became rivals in Rome; Lanfranco surpassed Domenichino with his more dynamic, illusionistic work, full of the dramatic foreshortening he had learned while growing up and looking at Correggio's domes. The much younger Guercino, a great draughtsman, flirted with a more exuberant and natural Baroque style before returning to Bologna in 1624 to take over Reni's studio, and spent the next 30 years churning out classical Reni-style sleeping pills.

But Bologna had more up its sleeve: from the time of the Carracci it was the European centre of quadratura painting, illusionist decoration that makes a room appear to extend into imaginary space – a technique invented by the ancient Romans and revived by Andrea Mantegna in nearby Mantua. Specialist quadraturistas were used by other artists around Italy to paint backgrounds: the first leaders in the field were Girolamo Curti, 'Il Dentone', followed by Michele Colonna and Agostino Mitelli, who invented quadratura with multiple vanishing points. Even when demand for Bologna's hackneyed Grand Manner petered out in the 18th century (in 1847 Ruskin damned it as having 'no single virtue, no colour, no drawing, no character, no history, no thought'), the imaginative quadraturistas were still in demand such as Gerolamo Mengozzi Colonna of Ferrara who worked with Giambattista Tiepolo. This reflected the region's importance in theatre building – the reconstructed Baroque Teatro Farnese in Parma is considered the first modern theatre, and the Bibiena family of Bologna were in demand around Europe for their theatre designs.

18TH–21ST CENTURIES Ducal Parma is well endowed with 18th- and 19th-century Neoclassical architecture and art. The Glauco Lombardi Museum, the Teatro Regio and Biblioteca Palatina, the ducal palace at Colorno and the Teatro Municipale in Reggio Emilia are highlights; another centre of the Neoclassical was Faenza. Painting in Bologna and elsewhere in the region had run out of ideas, and almost nothing of value was produced. The low ebb of art in the 1700s did not prevent churches and cathedrals from being demolished (Ravenna and Rimini) or redecorated in the worst possible taste, no doubt destroying much earlier work in the process (Ferrara, Imola, San Mercuriale at Forlì).

Almost all of the region's museums end with a section of 19th-century painting and, though the names are obscure and the styles and subject matter not especially original, these are always worth a look. Liberty style (the Italian Art Nouveau, named after the London department store) found its greatest expression in the region's spas (especially Salsomaggiore) and in the grand hotels and villas built in the newly fashionable seaside resorts along the Adriatic. If you see anything in Emilia-Romagna's cities that looks too medieval to be true, with Gothic mullioned windows and carved coats of arms, it probably dates from the period 1890–1930, which saw a fad for romantic and imaginative restorations of genuine medieval buildings (Alfonso Rubbiani's transformation of the palaces of Bologna's

Piazza Maggiore is a good example). In Forlì, there's a fair amount of Fascist (or 'Rationalist') architecture provided by Il Duce.

In 1917–19, Ferrara witnessed a brief revival of its Renaissance affinity for dreamlike, atmospheric art when Futurist Carlo Carrà and poet Filippo de Pisis (both natives of Ferrara) met up with Giorgio de Chirico, who was in the city for his military service, and in contact with Giorgio Morandi of Bologna. Rebelling against the Futurist doctrines of machines, motion and modernity, the Metaphysical School was based on the 'eternal, passionless and unalterable' ideal, which the painters tried to depict while evoking its magical, mysterious quality. At first all experimented like de Chirico with dressmakers' dummies and other hermetical subjects, and by 1919 all had moved on in other directions, although Morandi didn't move too far.

The province of Reggio has a special affinity for naïve art: the well-known naïve painter Antonio Ligabue was born at Gualtieri; nearby at Luzzara, there's a charming Museo Comunale dei Pittori Naïf. Contemporary Bologna has a reputation for street art, with the anonymous but internationally known figures Blu and Ericailcane.

MUSIC

Italian music took a big step forward in the quattrocento, with great wealth, generous courts and new ideas in the air. The increasing professionalisation of music in this time was perfect for a city like Bologna, with its big student population and Church patronage. Music became a course of study at Bologna's University in 1450, by request of Pope Nicholas IV. The same era saw the founding of new church *scolae* and choirs, of which the most renowned were in Bologna's San Petronio. Bologna also became one of the first centres for the printing of musical scores.

Though the new advances and the best music usually came from Florence and Venice, Emilia had its share of successes. The late Renaissance fashion for *intermezzi*, the precursor of opera, is usually associated with Florentine composers, but the very first one was performed at Ferrara for the marriage of Lucrezia Borgia and Duke Alfonso I in 1502.

Bologna remained an important centre in the Baroque era, although very much under the control of the Counter-Reformation Church, and its music was as conventional as its art. Still, its Accademia Filarmonica was the most prestigious in Italy.

In the 19th century, opera became the people's art par excellence, often with political overtones. Emilia was at the centre of it, and every city in the region built grand concert halls, still in use today. Its first great composer, Giuseppe Verdi (1813–1901) was the son of an innkeeper in Busseto and spent his last years there. Gioacchino Rossini (1792–1868) lived most of his life in Bologna, and composed many of his famous operas there.

In the 20th century the region gave the world composer Ottorino Respighi (1879–1936), also of Bologna, conductor Arturo Toscanini (1867–1957) from Parma, and the great tenor Luciano Pavarotti (1935–2007) of Modena. Bologna keeps its traditions up today as one of the most important places for music in Europe, recently ranked as a UNESCO Creative City of Music, and the home of the International Museum and Library of Music. In the city and around the region, audiences are as knowledgeable and enthusiastic as anywhere in the world.

LITERATURE

The story here begins with none other than Dante Alighieri (1265–1321), exiled in Ravenna from political quarrels at home in Florence. He finished his

Paradiso here, and is buried in a modest tomb that has become a national shrine (page 315).

Following Dante, most of the achievement of Italian poetry came from over the mountains in Tuscany, but in the Renaissance, the poets of Emilia invented a new form for the classical epic, creating some of the most celebrated works in the Italian language under the patronage of the Este dukes of Ferrara. The new epics were episodic, packed with great stories, colour and drama, with casts worthy of grand opera. The new printing presses quickly spread them around Europe. In England, they became the inspiration and model for Spenser's *Faerie Queene*, and more than a few of the tales they related found their way into Shakespeare. The three great poets are:

GIOSUÈ CARDUCCI

Born in Valdicastello di Pietrasanta, Tuscany, poet Giosuè Carducci (1835–1907) was the eldest son of a physician, a well-educated liberal and fervent supporter of Garibaldi and Italian unification. A precocious child, he was reading in Latin and Greek at an early age, and especially appreciated the classic, restrained economy in the poetry of Horace, Ovid and Virgil. After winning a scholarship to the Scuola Normale Superiore di Pisa he began teaching, and in 1857 published his first book of poetry, *Rime*. He moved to Bologna in 1860 when he was appointed Chair of Italian Eloquence at the university, and remained in the city for the rest of his life.

In 1863, Carducci, a lifelong atheist and Masonic freethinker (Masonic lodges in Italy were major hotbeds of revolutionary activity), composed his most notorious verse: a drinking toast to the devil which he recited to friends, and then published two years later as the *Inno a Satana* (Hymn to Satan). For Carducci, Satan symbolised resistance to the 19th-century earthly power of the papacy and personified all the things the Church condemned: freedom of thought and speech, human reason, sensuous pleasure in love, art and beauty, and political progress and justice.

In 1869, when republicans across Italy were agitating for a death blow to the last of the Papal States, Carducci published the poem again in Bologna's radical newspaper *Il Popolo*, to coincide with the 20th Vatican Ecumenical Council. Even some sympathisers thought it was too provocative; the Church condemned him for blasphemy, but Carducci never backed down. And the republicans won the day.

His greatest works would come later, including the *Rime Nuove* (New Rhymes) and *Odi Barbare* (Barbarian Odes). In the latter, he adapted the meter and style of the ancient Latin poets to modern Italian. He left 20 volumes of writing, criticism, biographies, essays and translations of Homer, Heine and Goethe. He was an inspiring teacher and fierce critic of his fellow poets for their romantic sentimentality.

In 1906, Carducci became the first Italian to win the Nobel Prize for Literature, 'not only in consideration of his deep learning and critical research, but above all as a tribute to the creative energy, freshness of style, and lyrical force which characterise his poetic masterpieces'. Too ill to attend the ceremony in Stockholm, he died the next year.

His former home in Bologna is now a library and museum dedicated to the poet's life and letters (page 127).

Matteo Boiardo (1440–94) Count of Scandiano, his birthplace, and a favourite of the courts of dukes Ercole and Borso d'Este. Boiardo initiated the genre with his *Orlando Innamorato*, combining classical forms and medieval legends – the hero 'Orlando' is Charlemagne's knight Roland.

Ludovico Ariosto (1474–1533) Born in Reggio, he served the Este and continued Boiardo's work with *Orlando Furioso*, considered the greatest of the Italian epics, while also writing satires and comedies. Ariosto coined the word 'humanism'.

Torquato Tasso (1544–95), a southerner, spent much of his most productive period at Ferrara, where he completed his epic poem on the Crusades, *Gerusalemme Liberata*. 'Tasso', fittingly for this poet, means badger in Italian, but Duke Alfonso II had to suffer his ill-temper for years, in fear that the poet would run off to Florence and dedicate his epic to the Medici instead of him. In 1586, Alfonso locked him up in a madhouse.

So many epics, it's not surprising that a satire would appear. Alessandro Tassoni of Modena supplied it with his mock-epic *La Secchia Rapita* (1622), the tale of the famous bucket the Modenesi stole from the town well of Bologna.

Once the Este were banished from Ferrara, patronage and poetry ceased. The next major figure to come from the region was Giosuè Carducci (1835–1907; see box, opposite), notorious for his anticlerical *Inno a Satana* (Hymn to Satan) and revered as the great poet of Italy's national awakening.

CINEMA

The post-war decades were the golden age of Italian cinema, and Emilia-Romagna contributed some of its greatest names. Top of the list is Federico Fellini, with a 50-year career and too many classics to name. Caught between the twin nightmares of Duce and Church, Fellini drew a mocking, sometimes tragic, yet affectionate caricature of Italy, and especially his native Rimini, captured with its pants down for all time in *Amarcord* (1973; see box, pages 374–5).

At the same time, a number of other directors from the region were redefining Italian cinema, each with an individual style but all heavy on ambiguity, sometimes with a touch of fantasy and almost always with striking visual effects.

Michelangelo Antonioni of Ferrara made a series of notable films at Cinecittà before hitting the international scene in the 1960s (*Blow Up, Zabriskie Point*). Pier Paolo Pasolini, writer, painter and director, made his name with *Accatone* (1961), based on Pasolini's own novel and perhaps the last of the post-war era's stark *cinema verità* films (1961). Bernardo Bertolucci, from Parma, was Pasolini's friend and frequent collaborator. He became a worldwide success with such films as *Last Tango in Paris* (banned in Italy) and *The Last Emperor*.

Besides the great directors, other famous names made lasting contributions to Italian cinema. Screenwriter and Romangolo-language poet Tonino Guerra wrote some of his best for Fellini (*Amarcord*) and Antonioni, among many others. Cesare Zavattini directed a few pictures, though he is better known for his brilliant screenplays in such post-war classics as *Bicycle Thieves* and *Miracle in Milan*. Among the actors from the region are Giulietta Masina (wife of Fellini and star in several of his films), Lino Ventura, Rossano Brazzi, Serena Grandi and Franco Nero.

2

Practical Information

WHEN TO VISIT

Emilia-Romagna is a year-round destination. In summer millions come from around the world to bake on the beaches along the Adriatic Riviera. In August, hotel prices are at their highest on the coasts, but lowest in the cities as the locals abandon them for the beach (although many of the best restaurants close then).

As elsewhere in Italy, spring and autumn are the loveliest times for touring. The sights are rarely crowded and temperatures are mild. In many ways the cities are at their best in winter: opera season runs from December to March, hotels are cheaper (though beware of major trade fairs), you can have many sights to yourself and the rich, hearty food of the region tastes best.

HIGHLIGHTS

Art, cities, food, beaches, music, castles and super-cars are Emilia-Romagna's main draws. Each of its great cities has an immaculately maintained historic centre and its own distinct character, formed over the past 2,000 years. Away from the cities, there's more art: in the great medieval abbeys of Pomposa and Bobbio, in smaller towns such as Carpi and Faenza, in the palaces at Colorno and Sassuolo and in the striking castles, notably in the former Duchy of Parma and southern Romagna, which behind their stern walls have truly delightful frescoed interiors, and usually a ghost.

Most Italians will agree that you eat better here than anywhere else outside of their mamma's; the locals certainly believe it. The intensely farmed Po Valley is 'Food Valley', a land of pasta, cheese, ham, a hundred cured meats, balsamic vinegar, and some surprisingly good wines – it's no accident that Eataly built their new theme park of food in Bologna. Another nickname is 'Motor Valley': around Modena and Bologna you can visit the Ferrari, Lamborghini, Ducati and Pagani factories and three collections of classic cars. Then there's music: Busseto and Parma are Verdi country, and Bologna is a UNESCO Creative City of Music, and major festivals throughout the year fill the region with music. The beaches are long, and their resorts, especially Rimini and Riccione, are packed with summer fun by day and all through the night at Italy's top clubs.

Other Italian regions may have more spectacular nature, but never far from the cities of the flatlands you can escape south into Emilia-Romagna's best-kept secret: vine-clad hills and valleys, often reminiscent of Tuscany (but without all the tourists) under the Apennines, where wolves and eagles dwell.

SUGGESTED ITINERARIES

A WEEK'S ART TOUR Start in Bologna. The 'Big Tortellino' needs three days minimum – it's a subtle city behind its endless porticoes, one that takes some effort to know. Visit the Two Towers, the University and art churches (SS Petronio, Francesco, Domenico, Stefano and Maria dei Servi), the museums, markets and lively *osterie*. Next up, Modena: one day to see the Duomo and Galleria Estense; and then another day in Parma for its masterpieces by Antelami and Correggio. Arrive day six in Ferrara, where the springtime brilliance of the early Renaissance shines through the Po mists, before a grand finale on day seven at Ravenna, for the mosaics in San Vitale, Sant'Apollinare Nuovo and the Mausoleum of Galla Placida.

It's a hectic schedule, but great rail connections and short distances make it easy to do if you're in a hurry; from Ravenna it's just over an hour by train back to Bologna.

TWO WEEKS BY RAIL Emilia-Romagna's great art towns are strung out like pearls along the Via Emilia and the main rail line. Ideally, fly into Milan (close to Piacenza) and out of Venice (a short hop from Ferrara). After a day in Piacenza, spend two in Parma, with a day trip perhaps to Colorno or Busseto. Spend a morning in Reggio Emilia before heading to Modena for two nights, including a day trip to Sassuolo, the summer home of the Este family. Give Bologna three days, then carry on to Rimini for a look at the magical Tempio Malatestiana and the Museo della Città before hitting the beach. Next afternoon, head to Ravenna for two days, then end with two days in Ferrara.

THREE WEEKS BY CAR After three days in Bologna, head south into the hills to Marzabotto, Riola and Lizzano in Belvedere for a trek under the Corno alle Scale. Wind around Monte Cimone and foothills to the landscapes around Rocca di Bismantova to arrive south of Parma, by the beautiful castle of Torrechiara. Give Parma two days, then stop for Fidenza's cathedral before heading south to the lovely Castell'Arquato and Roman Velleia, ending up near Rivergaro.

Start week two in the Trebbia Valley with its castles, beaches and Dark Age Bobbio. Give Piacenza a day; then take in Busseto and the castles at Soragna and at Fontanellato before taking the A1 to Reggio Emilia. Give it a morning before heading to Sassuolo, Maranello and Modena. Next up, the art towns of Carpi and Cento before ending up at Ferrara. Then head north for the Po Delta park, the medieval frescoes in the Abbey of Pomposa and Romagna's 'Little Venice', Comacchio.

Begin the third week with Ravenna, followed by a day exploring Cervia, Cesena and Santarcangelo before heading to Rimini. Then, take in the tiny Republic of San Marino, and the beautiful Romagna hills, castles and hill towns. Tootle along the back roads to Bagno di Romagna and the Casentinesi National Forest, before winding back towards Bologna via Terra del Sole and Forlì, Faenza for its faience, pretty Brisighella, Imola and Dozza, with the regional enoteca.

WINE AND FOOD ITINERARIES Emilia-Romagna has set up 15 'Strade dei Vini e dei Sapori', or Routes of Wines and Flavours. For maps and more details, check the provincial tourist offices' websites.

TOURIST INFORMATION

Along with the regional and provincial offices listed below, every town and nearly every village has a local office.

Bologna Via Benedetto XIV 3; 051 659 8761; w www.cittametropolitana.bo.it/turismo

Emilia-Romagna Region Via Aldo Moro, 38 Torre, 40127 Bologna; 051 527 3353;

w emiliaromagnaturismo.com; also see
w emiliaromagnawelcome.com
i Ferrara Largo Castello 1; ☎0532 299274;
w www.ferraraterraeacqua.it
i Forlì-Cesena Piazza Morgagni 9, Forlì;
☎0543 714312; w www.provincia.fc.it
i Modena Piazza Grande 14; ☎059 203 3660;
w visitmodena.it
i Parma Piazza Garibaldi; ☎0521 218 889;
w turismo.comune.parma.it

i Piacenza Corso Garibaldi 50; ☎0523 795370;
w turismo.provincia.pc.it
i Ravenna Piazza San Francesco 8; ☎0544
35755; w turismo.ra.it
i Reggio Emilia Via Toschi 1/B; ☎0522 451152;
w turismo.comune.re.it
i Rimini Via Dario Campana 64; ☎0541
716377; w en.riviera.rimini.it

TOUR OPERATORS

While you'll find numerous day or half-day tours offered by local tourist offices and private firms (often dedicated to food!), several tour operators from abroad (mostly in the UK) also organise visits.

ACE Culture Tours ☎+44 (0) 1223 841055 (UK);
w aceculturaltours.co.uk. Offers tours of Piacenza & Val Trebbia, & arranges visits to the Verdi Festival in Parma.
Andante Travels ☎+44 (0) 1722 713800 (UK); w andantetravels.co.uk. Arranges tours of Ravenna, & visits to Festive Food in Bologna & the Verdi Festival in Parma.
Bluone Food & Wine Tours m 348 262 9794;
w bluone.com; see ad, page 58. Bologna-based company offering culinary & New Year's tours of Bologna; & seasonal tours & day trips around Emilia-Romagna.
Cyclomundo ☎+33 450 872109 (France), +1 646 233 1354 (USA & Canada); w cyclomundo. com. Organises 8-day 'Gastronomic Cycling from Parma to Bologna'.
Footprint Holidays ☎+44 (0) 1932 837633;
w footprint-holidays.com. Romagna food-&-wine tour based in Santarcangelo.

Genuine Italian Food Tours ☎+44 (0) 1892 652838 (UK); w genuineitalianfoodtours.co.uk. Offers a 5-day 'Discovering Bologna – culture, history & gastronomy' tour.
Hooked on Cycling and Walking ☎+44 (0) 1506 635399; w hookedoncycling.co.uk. Guided road bike tours in Romagna.
Kirker ☎+44 (0) 20 7593 1899 (UK);
w kirkerholidays.com. Verdi Festival tours to Parma.
Martin Randall ☎+44 (0) 20 8742 3355;
w martinrandall.com. Christmas in Emilia-Romagna, Verdi Festival, Courts of Northern Italy, Ravenna, Art in the Po Valley, Courts of Northern Italy, etc.
Railbookers ☎+44 (0) 20 3780 2222;
w railbookers.co.uk. Arranges rail holidays in Emilia-Romagna.
Sapori e Saperi m +44 (0) 7768 474610;
w sapori-e-saperi.com. Offers small-group visits to culinary artisans & in-depth courses in *salumi* & cheese-making.

RED TAPE

VISAS According to the Schengen Agreement, citizens of EU member states and holders of passports from some 50 nations do not need a visa for stays of 90 days or less. These include Australia, Canada, Hong Kong, Israel, Japan, Malaysia, Mexico, New Zealand, South Korea, Singapore, Switzerland, the USA and, very likely, the post-Brexit UK.

Theoretically, all foreigners are required to register their presence with the police within eight days of their arrival in the country, but in practice few people bother; in any case, your hotel will take your passport and residence details for this exact purpose. Be aware, however, that if you are a non-EU citizen and get in a jam with the police, they can take your failure to report your arrival as evidence that you have already overstayed the legal period.

EU citizens can stay beyond 90 days if they have employment, sufficient resources, or an approved course of study. Even so, it will require filling out a form at the local police station or *anagrafe* (registry office). Non-EU family members will need to apply for a residence permit, a *permesso di soggiorno*. After five years, EU citizens and family members have the right to a permanent residence card.

For citizens of non-EU countries, extending your stay in Italy beyond 90 days can be rather difficult; you'll need to come with an entry visa, before applying for a *permesso di soggiorno* through the provincial Questura (state police office). An entry visa is based on study, work and elective residence, few of which are entirely clear in their regulations or what's required in order to secure one. Whichever you need, expect the rules to be infernally complex, onerous and confusing. See the websites of the Polizia di Stato (**w** *poliziadistato.it*) and the Foreign Ministry (**w** *vistoperitalia.esteri.it*), although their information is often contradictory.

EMBASSIES

There are a number of consulates (mostly honorary) in Bologna; for a complete list, see **w** bolognawelcome.com/en/embassies-and-consulates. For most countries (including the UK, Ireland, Canada, the USA, Australia and New Zealand) the closest consular services will be in Milan or Rome. For a complete list of embassies and consulates in Italy (with complete contact information), as well as Italian embassies and consulates overseas, see **w** embassypages.com/italy.

GETTING THERE AND AWAY

BY AIR Bologna is the main gateway to the region, with flights from 92 destinations around Europe and North Africa (all listed on the airport's website). There are no direct flights from North America (the nearest airports with direct connections are Milan and Venice) or from Australia or New Zealand, although the daily direct flights on Air Emirates via Dubai make it the most direct route to the region.

To Bologna Aeroporto Guglielmo Marconi (BLQ) (*Via Triumvirato 84;* \051 647 9615; **w** *bologna-airport.it*) is 6km to the northwest of Bologna city centre.

From the UK and Ireland

✈ **Aer Lingus** **w** aerlingus.com. Flights from Dublin.

✈ **British Airways** **w** britishairways.com. Flights from London Heathrow.

✈ **EasyJet** **w** easyjet.com. Flights from London Gatwick.

✈ **Ryanair** **w** ryanair.com. Flights from London Stansted, Bristol, Edinburgh, Manchester & Dublin.

To Rimini Rimini (*Via Flaminia 409;* \0541 379800; **w** *riminiairport.com*) is served mainly by regular and charter flights from Eastern Europe.

To Parma Parma's airport (*Via Licinio Ferretti 50A;* \0521 951511; **w** *parma-airport.it*) has links to Sardinia, Trapani and Moldova only.

BY RAIL From the UK, take the Eurostar (**w** *eurostar.com*) across the Channel and connect with a fast train; if you're lucky, a journey from London St Pancras to Bologna can take as little as 12 hours, changing in Paris (Gare du Nord to Gare de Lyon) and Turin. **Trenitalia** (\892021; **w** *trenitalia.it*) operates much of

BOLOGNA Buses (w *aerobus.bo.it*) link the airport to Bologna Stazione Centrale every 11 minutes between 07.00 and 21.00 (less frequently between 05.30 and 07.00, and between 21.00 and 00.15). Tickets cost €6 each way.

FERRARA Ferrara Bus and Fly (m *333 200 5157*; w *ferrarabusandfly.it*) offers direct connections in an hour from Bologna airport and Stazione Centrale to Ferrara eight times a day. A one-way fare is €15.

MODENA SACA (↖ *059 236530*; w *sacaonline.it*) links the airport to Modena's train and bus stations eight times a day, taking 40 minutes and costing €15 one way.

RIMINI AND RICCIONE Shuttle Rimini–Bologna (↖ *0541 600100*; w *shutteriminibologna.it*) connects the airport to Rimini station (*10/day Apr– Oct, 7 rest of the year*), and carries on to Riccione from April to October. It also stops at Cesena if you book at least 2 hours in advance. The one-way fare is €25, or €20 if booked online. There's also a less frequent connection from the airport to Cesenatico.

Italy's domestic rail network. Note that all the high-speed Freccia ('arrow') trains (Frecciarossa, Frecciargento, etc) require a reservation, though these come with the ticket. Some city-centre agencies sell Trenitalia tickets, and you can also buy e-tickets online or from the machines at the stations. Trenitalia's competition, **Italo** (↖ *892020*; w *italotreno.it*), operates state-of-the-art high-speed trains, with stations in Bologna, Reggio Emilia and Ferrara; trains zip from Milan to Bologna in 53 minutes.

BY COACH A number of coach companies operate services from various European countries to Emilia-Romagna. Check out Bus Web (w *busweb.it*) for information on services including times, prices and booking options.

BY CAR It's 1,340km from Calais to Bologna by way of Grenoble, the Mont Blanc Tunnel and Milan, and costs €152 in tolls. It's much cheaper (*tolls €20*), if slightly longer, to travel instead via the A61 and A2 (Brussels, Cologne, Basel, Lugano and Milan). Italy has an excellent network of toll motorways (*autostrade*). For a useful journey planner, visit their website (w *autostrade.it*).

HEALTH AND SAFETY

You can insure yourself for almost any possible mishap – cancelled flights, stolen or lost baggage and ill health. Check any current policies you hold to see if they cover all the activities you plan to do in Emilia-Romagna and under what circumstances, and judge whether you need a special travel insurance policy for the journey.

HEALTH Aside from the risks posed by exposure to the sun (both in summer and winter), and the nuisance of mosquitoes, health issues in Emilia-Romagna are no different from those in other westernised countries. In most cases,

EU citizens with an EHIC (European Health Insurance Card) are entitled to free care in Italy from the national health system, the SSN (Servizio Sanitario Nazionale). For more information, call Emilia-Romagna's health hotline (✆ *800 033 033*).

There will be a hospital, clinic or local health unit (Azienda Sanitaria Locale, ASL) with a Pronto Soccorso (casualty/first aid department) in every town of any size. Pharmacy staff are trained to assist with most minor problems. If a pharmacy is closed when you need it, look for the card in the window with the schedule of the *farmacia di turno* (the closest one open) or call ✆ 1100 for the details of the three nearest pharmacies.

Most Italian doctors speak at least rudimentary English; otherwise the US Consulate in Florence (✆ *055 266 951*; w *it.usembassy.gov/embassy-consulates/florence*), which serves Emilia-Romagna, has a list of English-speaking doctors and dentists.

Travel clinics and health information A full list of current travel clinic websites worldwide is available on w istm.org. For other journey preparation information, consult w travelhealthpro.org.uk (UK) or w wwwnc.cdc.gov/travel (USA). Information about various medications may be found on w netdoctor. co.uk/travel. All advice found online should be used in conjunction with expert advice received prior to or during travel.

SAFETY While Emilia-Romagna's cities (especially Rimini and Bologna) get their share of petty crime – purse-snatchings, pickpocketing, minor thievery of the white-collar kind (always check your change), car break-ins and theft – violent crime is very rare. Nearly all mishaps can be avoided with adequate precautions. Scooter-borne purse-snatchers can be foiled if you stay on the inside of the pavement and keep a firm hold on your property (sling your bag-strap across your body, not dangling from one shoulder).

Remember that pickpockets strike in crowded buses or trams and gatherings; don't carry too much cash, and split it so you won't lose the lot at once. In cities

INFORMATION FOR TRAVELLERS WITH A DISABILITY

Emilia-Romagna is one of the best-equipped Italian regions for visitors with disabilities, although wheelchair users may well have difficulties in steep Apennine villages. Most hotels have at least one room designed for wheelchair travellers; public toilets and most restaurant toilets are accessible.

Trenitalia provides free assistance to wheelchair users if you let them know your plans 24 hours in advance. Big city stations have a Sala Blu for travellers with disabilities where journeys can be arranged. Ring the helpline (✆ *199 303060;* ⊕ *07.00–21.00 daily*) for more information.

Useful resources include: **Accessible Italy** (m *378 941 111;* w *accessibleitaly. com*); **Gov.uk** (w *gov.uk/guidance/foreign-travel-for-disabled-people*), which provides general advice and practical information for travellers with disabilities preparing for overseas travel; **Disability Travel** (w *disabilitytravel. com*), a comprehensive US site written by wheelchair users; and **Global Access News** (w *globalaccessnews.com/index.htm*), which provides general travel information, reviews, tips and links. **Disabled Holidays** (w *disabledholidays. com*) offers accessible holidays to Emilia-Romagna; **Camping Freedom** (w *campingfreedom.com*) lists 27 accessible campgrounds.

and popular tourist sites, beware groups of scruffy-looking women with babies or children with pieces of cardboard, apparently begging. They use distraction techniques to perfection. The smallest and most innocent-looking child is generally the most skilful pickpocket. If you are targeted, grab hold of any vulnerable possessions or pockets and shout furiously; Italian passers-by or plain-clothes police will often come to your assistance if they realise what is happening. Be extra careful in train stations, don't leave valuables in hotel rooms, and park your car in garages, guarded lots or on well-lit streets, with portable temptations well out of sight. For Italian emergency numbers, see inside front cover.

WOMEN TRAVELLERS

Women travelling alone or in small groups should not encounter any particular problems in Emilia-Romagna. If possible, try to avoid arriving or leaving big city stations late at night. There have been complaints in the past of harassment etc, though no more or less than in any other European city.

LGBTQ+ TRAVELLERS

Emilia-Romagna is the most tolerant region in Italy, so much so that Pope John Paul II called it a 'Sodom and Gomorrah'. Politically left-wing Bologna is the home to the national headquarters of Arcigay, Italy's first and largest LGBTQ+ organisation (see box, page 83). In country towns, a certain amount of discretion may be called for as you may encounter confusion and animosity, especially among teenagers and the elderly. However, hotel workers are unlikely to question a gay or lesbian couple requesting a double room.

TRAVELLING WITH CHILDREN

Italians adore children, and you shouldn't encounter any problems travelling with yours. However, if you are travelling with minor children with different surnames, you may need proof of guardianship. Contact your Italian consulate before you leave.

Many hotels now offer family rooms; staying in an *agriturismo* on a farm can be a great experience for kids. Children usually get half-price admission in museums. Children aged 4–11 years inclusive pay the child fare on Trenitalia; on long-distance trains those under 15 qualify for the child fare. Children under four travel for free, although you'll still have to pay a small fee for a reservation. On Italo trains, children under two travel for free, while those aged 2–16 are eligible for a child rate.

WHAT TO TAKE

Pack any medications you need to take regularly, plus sunblock, a torch and even binoculars for those lofty frescoes in churches and *palazzi*. Layers of warm clothing are a good idea for winter and at least a light jacket for summer evenings or trips into the mountains. You'll be doing a lot of walking: comfortable, broken-in shoes are essential.

As in the rest of mainland Europe, Italy uses **electricity** at a current of 220 volts at 50 cycles per second (50Hz). If you don't have the necessary plug adaptors and power converters, they are easy to find at the airport or your local electronics shop before you leave, but much harder to find once you arrive.

MONEY

Italy's currency is the euro (€). Credit cards are accepted at most major points of sale, though rarely at B&Bs, *agriturismi* and small family-run restaurants. Be sure to ask if there's any doubt. **ATMs** (Bancomats) are widely available and will spout cash with your bank card and PIN number, albeit for the price of a significant commission. Ask your bank if it has an agreement with any banks in Italy which will allow you to withdraw cash without paying international ATM access fees.

BUDGETING

On a shoestring, excluding accommodation, you could get by on around €30 a day for food, drink and the occasional bus or admission fee: a €2 breakfast (a cappuccino and cornetto), €5 lunch (a *piadina* and a drink), a €20 dinner at an inexpensive restaurant. If your budget is mid-priced, then you can expect to do well on around €40–50, again not including accommodation. This will allow for better meals at a good restaurant. Around €70–80 a day will get you excellent meals and even a taxi here and there. For accommodation budgeting, see pages 38–9.

GETTING AROUND

Emilia-Romagna has excellent public transport, and you really can see its great art cities and towns by riding its frequent and affordable trains or buses without the expensive headache of finding a place to park and/or dealing with the limited traffic regulations in most historic centres. Before setting off, check Google Transit or the Go Euro website (**w** *goeuro.com*) to find the quickest or most economical ways of getting around, including rides on the car-pooling BlablaCar (**w** *blablacar.com*).

BY RAIL Trenitalia (*national call centre* ✆ *06 6847 5475;* **w** *trenitalia.it*) still often called by its old name, the Ferrovie dello Stato (FS), operates much of the country's rail network. Tickets can be purchased up to three months in advance – your best chance to bag a discount (for more on where to buy tickets, see page 70). Economy fares and family fares are available if you purchase the ticket at least two days in advance. If you change your mind about the date, you have up until 23.59 on the day before travel to change it one time only. Tickets must be validated (*convalidato*) in the green or yellow machines located in the ticket hall or on the platform before boarding.

Italo (✆ *892020;* **w** *italotreno.it*) is Trenitalia's state-of-the-art high-speed competitor. At present, it serves Bologna, Reggio Emilia and Ferrara. There is a variety of tickets available at the stations or online: low-cost, purchased up to three days in advance; economy, which allows you to change times and dates up to 3 minutes before departure, and offers 60% refund if you cancel; and Flex, similar to economy with an 80% refund if you cancel.

Left luggage Left luggage (*deposito bagagli*) is expensive and not available at all rail stations, but if you need to drop off your bags, try **w** bagbnb.com (inexpensive, but it must be booked in advance).

BY BUS Italian bus services are excellent: modern, clean, frequent, punctual and inexpensive, generally cheaper to travel on than trains. Four firms serve the region: **SETA** (✆ *840 000216;* **w** *setaweb.it*) for the provinces of Piacenza, Reggio Emilia and

Modena); **Tep** (✎ *0521 2141;* **w** *tep.pr.it*) for Parma; **TPER** (✎ *051 290290;* **w** *tper.it*) for Bologna and Ferrara; and **StartRomagna** (✎ *199 115577;* **w** *startromagna.it*) for Ravenna, Forlì–Cesena and Rimini.

A new service, **Mi Muovo Multibus** (✎ *800 388988;* **w** *mobilita.regione.emilia-romagna.it/mi-muovo*) allows you to travel all through Emilia-Romagna with a single €15 bus pass on all the region's bus lines; good for twelve 75-minute journeys, in any combination (three people, for instance, can make four journeys). Pick up tickets at any of the local offices.

Buses reach even the smaller villages, and they'll be indispensable if you're travelling without a car. Note that the lines are based in the provincial capitals; so, for example if you want to go from Bologna to a nearby village in Modena province, you'll probably have to go through Modena.

Also check schedules with **Baltour** (✎ *0861 199 1900;* **w** *en.baltour.it*), a low-cost bus line that serves parts of Emilia-Romagna.

BY CAR Driving can be fun and fast on the *autostrade* but slow and frustrating elsewhere. Every city and town centre is enclosed in a pedestrian zone, or ZTL (*zona traffico limitata*); trying to tour them with a car will only make you miserable. The only place where you'll really wish you had one is in the Apennines, where connections between villages aren't always convenient. Petrol stations are generally open 07.00–12.30 and 15.30–19.00 Monday to Saturday. There are 24-hour stations along the *autostrade*.

Car hire Car-hire companies are the same you would expect to find anywhere else in Italy: Hertz (**w** *hertz.co.uk*), Avis (**w** *avis.co.uk*), Europcar (**w** *europcar.co.uk*), Sixt (**w** *sixt.co.uk*) and Maggiore (**w** *maggiore.it/en*). Most have branches in the major cities, at Bologna and Rimini airports and at the main train stations; most domestic one-way rentals carry no surcharge. You must be at least 18 (age may vary by car category) and have held your licence for at least a year. Some companies will only rent to drivers aged 21 and over; drivers under 25 may incur a surcharge. There is no maximum age.

ACCOMMODATION

At the top end of the market, Emilia-Romagna has a number of sybaritic resorts and smart hotels, often in historic buildings, furnished and decorated with real panache. Good-value, interesting accommodation in cities can be difficult to find; in the listings, we've put in the ones we know. In Bologna, Parma and Ravenna, guests over the age of 14 will be charged a tourist tax from €5 (luxury hotels) to €0.50 (hostels and campsites) per person per night.

HOTELS Italian *alberghi* are rated from one to five stars, depending on the facilities they offer. The ratings are some indication of price, but for tax reasons not all hotels choose to advertise themselves at the rating to which they are entitled, so you may find a modestly rated hotel just as comfortable as a higher rated one. Tourist offices can help find one, and if they're not open ask a police officer (a local officer, not a *carabiniere*; the national force is recruited from all over Italy, and *carabinieri* tend to know little of local affairs).

Price lists, by law, must be posted on the door of every room, along with meal prices and any extra charges. Most display two or more rates, depending on the season; with most people booking online these days, prices often change by the day of the week. If you have paid a deposit, your booking is valid under Italian law, but don't

ACCOMMODATION PRICE CODES

Prices for a double room; expect to pay about two-thirds the rate for single occupancy.

€€€€€	Luxury	€150+
€€€€	Upmarket	€100–150
€€€	Mid-range	€70–100
€€	Budget	€50–70
€	Shoestring	less than €50

expect it to be refunded if you have to cancel. You will be asked for your passport for registration; they should give it back as soon as they fill out the form for the police.

Extra beds are usually charged at a third more of the room rate, although most offer discounts for children sharing their parents' rooms. For a double bed, specify a *camera matrimoniale*. If breakfast is not included, you can usually get better value by eating breakfast in a bar. In high season you might be expected to take half-board in resorts, and one-night stays may be refused.

AGRITURISMI Emilia-Romagna has nearly 1,200 *agriturismi*, offering rooms or apartments. Italy pioneered this concept in the 1970s. Originally it meant simply accommodation and/or meals on a working farm; today the definition is a lot broader – the only thing you can be sure of with an *agriturismo* is that it will be in the countryside. They can be basic or luxurious. Some offer home cooking, often with their own produce; others offer riding, swimming pools, cookery courses, tours and more. Complete listings by province are at w agriturismo.emilia-romagna.it.

APARTMENTS/SELF-CATERING Besides w airbnb.com, there are more than a thousand self-catering holiday homes and apartments in the region listed with Rentalia (w *rentalia.com*). Increasingly, hotels offer apartments as well as rooms.

BED AND BREAKFAST These can be anything from glam and romantic to very basic. Besides the Airbnb and *agriturismi* websites, check out dedicated sites such as BB Italia (w *bbitalia.it, bedandbreakfast.com*).

CAMPING The majority of Emilia-Romagna's campsites are on the coast (often as part of family-oriented holiday villages), but you can also find them scattered around the rest of the region, in the Apennines and near major towns. Most offer bungalows, mobile homes or other accommodation, as well as pitches. Check the listings at Eurocampings (w *eurocampings.co.uk*).

HOSTELS The region's six youth hostels (two in Bologna, and one each in Parma, Modena, Reggio Emilia and Ferrara) welcome all ages. Some offer small discounts if you have a youth hostel card.

RIFUGI Emilia-Romagna has 30 *rifugi* (singular: *rifugio*) in the Apennines. These vary from simple mountain huts, offering dormitory accommodation and basic meals, to purpose-built places with mod cons – and higher-than-expected prices that reflect the high costs of access. For a complete list with contact details, see w rifugiappennino.it.

Life is a combination of magic and pasta
Federico Fellini

Emilia-Romagna is Italy's 'Food Valley', the queen of culinary delights, home of the nation's favourite ham, cured meats, cheese and balsamic vinegar, not to mention a cornucopia of fruit and vegetables, seafood, wild mushrooms and truffles. Every province, every village even, has its own specialities, which often appear on menus in Emilio-Romagnolo dialect to complete the bewilderment of the innocent diner. In general, dishes tend to be meaty but vegetarians need not despair; there will nearly always be options or that old standby, pizza. Vegans, however, may find it tough going.

SALUMI *Salumi* means cured pork products – cold cuts, if you will – and no place in Italy does them as well and as abundantly as Emilia-Romagna, where the most typical antipasto is a selection of *salumi*, called an *affettati* or *tagliere* (literally, 'cutting board'). This may include **prosciutto di Parma** (see box, page 232) and **culatello di Zibello** (page 242). *Culatello* has a little brother, *fiocco* or *fiocchetto*, the smaller, less fatty muscle from the back of the hog's leg. The off-cuts of *culatello* and other prized hams are made into a gourmet *salame* called **strolghino**.

But that's only the tip of the *salumi*-berg. Essentials include **mortadella** (see box, below), *lardo stagionato* (not 'lard', but the layer of fat found on the back and flanks), which is cured, spiced and good enough to eat by itself, and *ciccioli* ('little fatties'), golden fried pork crackling, which can even turn up on pizza. There's *salame di Felino*, a slender, delicate cured sausage, *spalla cotta di San Secondo* (pork shoulder, salted for a month then cooked in bouillon and Marsala wine, first recorded in 1170 and a favourite of Verdi), *coppa di Piacentina* and *coppa di Carpaneto* (cured meat from the neck with a lot of spice) and the dark, red, coarse-grained *salame di Piacenza*.

PIADINE AND OTHER OBSESSIONS What goes with your plate of *salumi*? A foaming glass of dry Lambrusco (see box, page 44) and a something else, depending where you are. In Romagna it's sure to be a hot and savoury *piadina*, a soft round flatbread traditionally made with flour and lard. The main source of carbohydrates for the poor for at least a thousand years, and the essential ingredient of any *festa*, *piadine*

MORTADELLA: IT'S NO BALONEY

Mortadella, 'the most noble of all pork parts', was so prized in the 14th and 15th centuries that it was used for currency in the contracts of the Cathedral Chapter of Bologna. The word comes from the mortar used to grind the pork into a smooth paste, before kneading it with peppercorns and stuffing it into a casing: the recipe was registered with the Corporazione dei Salaroli (the sausage-makers' guild) in 1367. The biggest ones, as thick as tree trunks, can weigh 200kg. The Americans, who loved it, are responsible for the confusion over the name: after 1899 they started calling any kind of sausage 'mortadella' or 'Bologna sausage', or just plain 'baloney'. A lot of sausage made elsewhere that's labelled 'mortadella' might as well be baloney. A good mortadella must be sliced as thinly as possible; in the days before machines, there were contests to see who could slice it thinnest and fastest.

are served in the traditional *osterie*, where someone will be flipping them out fresh and hot. They (and their cousins *guscioni*, *cassoni* or *crescioni*) have also enjoyed a renaissance as street food, filled with whatever you fancy – ham, salami, mozzarella, aubergines, tomatoes, cheese, anchovies, wild herbs, etc. A *piadina* with sausage and onions can be transcendent. Always remember this bit of Romagnolo folk wisdom: '*Con la piadina è meglio*' ('It's better with a *piadina*').

Each province on the Emilia side also has its own flatbread or focaccia or **paste fritte** or **gnocco fritto** – deep-fried little golden pillows. Otherwise sane folks will drive an hour just to eat them (many places prepare them only at weekends or in the evenings). In Reggio, you might get a flaky **chizza**, served with butter and cheese; in Piacenza, the **burtléina**; in Parma, the triangular **torta fritta**; in Ferrara **pinzini** and the striking **coppia ferrarese**, a twisted sourdough X-shaped bread knotted together like a couple in love. In Modena and Bologna, look for **crescentine**, traditionally cooked between chestnut leaves and two stone discs in the hot ashes of the hearth. Stuff a similar dough with potatoes (or pumpkin), pancetta and grated pecorino, then cook it on a griddle and you have a **bartolaccio**.

Throughout Emilia you'll find **tigelle**, made with yeast and lard baked in a round waffle-iron, and **borlenghi,** enormous crêpes usually cooked out of doors and traditionally topped with **cunza** – a mix of chopped rosemary, garlic and *lardo* – folded and served, although some heretics replace the *lardo* with Parmesan.

In Reggio and elsewhere, look for **erbazzone**, a very thin rustic pie filled with spinach or chard, onions and sometimes pancetta or cheese.

PRIMI
Pasta, pasta, pasta Pasta is the classic *primo*, or first course. Many of Italy's favourite forms originated here, and taste better here than anywhere else. Several come from the word *torta*, or twist, which describes how they're made: the pasta is rolled and cut, the filling is spooned on, and sealed in a ring with a twist. The classic **tortellini** are part of the region's mythology (see box, page 77), and ideally served in capon broth. In Bologna they are filled with pork, ham, mortadella and Parmesan. Bigger ones are **tortelloni**. **Tortelli**, usually stuffed with herbs and ricotta, or pumpkin or other fillings, can be twisted but are usually square or shaped like half-moons and served with melted butter and Parmesan, or a sauce.

Another classic, **tagliatelle** (see, box page 42) should be ideally served with a *ragù* – the mother of 'spag bol', a dish as bastardised in the UK as mortadella has been baloneyed in America. The original *ragù* is a smooth sauce of very finely minced pork and veal, prosciutto, onions, carrots, celery, butter and tomato; in general, when a dish is labelled *alla Bolognese* it means with *ragù* (one exception is **maccheroni alla bolognese**: macaroni baked with truffles and chicken livers and doused in fresh cream). But these days you are more likely to see **gramigna**, squiggly hollow noodles served with a simple sauce of sausage, onions and tomatoes.

Bologna also claims its own lasagne. In most places you'll find it as **lasagne al forno,** layered with *ragù* and cheese and topped with béchamel (which incidentally was served in Cesena in the 14th century – long before it was supposedly invented by Louis XIV's maître d'hôtel, the Marquis de Béchameil). Bologna, however, is the mother of green lasagne, made with spinach; a proper **lasagne verde alla bolognese** has prosciutto, chicken livers, bacon and béchamel. In autumn, look for lasagne with truffles or wild mushrooms.

In Parma and Piacenza, the favourite *primo* is **anolini** (or **anvein**), stuffed pasta made into delicate circles filled with stewed beef, Parmesan, eggs, breadcrumbs and nutmeg, served in a clear beef broth. Also look for **garganelli** (intricate ridged

Feminine pulchritude, the inspiration for tortellini (see box, page 77), was also the secret behind tagliatelle, invented in Bologna in 1487 to celebrate Lucrezia Borgia's wedding to the Duke of Ferrara. The pope's daughter had long golden hair, and a chef named Zafirano from the village of Bentivoglio, called upon to help prepare the wedding feast, created the long fair strips of pale golden egg pasta in her honour. According to one old authority, the pasta must be rolled out until a person holding it up can be seen through the dough.

The Academy of Italian Cuisine, based in Bologna, has solemnly decreed that for pasta to be called tagliatelle, the width of the ribbons must be precisely 1/1,270th of the height of the Torre Asinelli, ie: 9mm, no more, no less. It takes only 15 years of practice to get it exactly right.

pasta tubes rolled and cut with a device resembling a loom card, and often served with duck sauce), fat *strozzapreti* ('priest-chokers') and *passatelli in brodo*, little dumplings made of spinach or beef marrow, breadcrumbs, eggs and Parmesan. In Romagna, you'll see *tagliatelle al ragù di Mora Romagnola* made with the local breed of black pig.

As a reaction to all the pasta fussiness, you'll also find *maltagliati* ('badly cuts'), made by chopping a sheet of pasta any which way. When cooked with beans, it's nicknamed 'chin sprinkler'.

Other first courses *Risotti* have long been popular (the rice paddies of Lombardy are just across the Po). *Risotto al sugo* incorporates minced chicken and cheese. Comacchio serves a risotto cooked in eel broth. Then there are the specialities from the Duchy of Parma: *bomba di riso*, cheese-flavoured rice, with a rich mushroom sauce with pieces of boned pigeon topped with butter and baked in the oven; and *savarin di riso*, a Parmesan risotto in a mould, wrapped in cooked ham and topped with veal meatballs and porcini *ragù*.

In Piacenza and Parma, a favourite dish is *pisaréi e fasò* (borlotti bean stew with bread dumplings); you may also find a *frità cui bavaron* (leek omelette), or truffle omelette, or *melanzane alla parmigiana* (fried aubergine slices, baked with mozzarella and tomato sauce).

SECONDI Main courses (*secondi*) tend to be on the hearty side as well. One heraldic dish is *stracotto*, topside of beef, cooked for hours (or days, by some extremists) in wine with herbs and vegetables until it becomes incredibly tender; sometimes it has sausage and a garnish of mushrooms. You may also find *rosa di Parma*: a fillet of beef tenderloin, stuffed with Parmesan and prosciutto, rolled up, roasted and sliced. Another classic, *bollito misto*, is several boiled meats served with sauces, which often comes on a cart (*carrello dei bolliti*), allowing diners to pick and choose. *Coppa arrosto,* a speciality of Piacenza, is pork cooked in butter, oil, garlic and rosemary, then doused with wine and roasted in the oven. Rabbit is popular: *coniglio alla cacciatora*, sweet and sour, or *coniglio saporito*, rabbit stew with chicken livers, anchovies and capers, or even the elaborate *coniglio in porchetta*, a speciality around Cesena, made with deboned rabbit, flavoured with fennel, garlic and rosemary, bacon and rabbit liver then stuffed with minced beef and pork, rolled up and baked.

You'll find lamb dishes such as *agnello con piselli alla romagnola* (lamb and pancetta cooked with peas), and poultry dishes – stewed or roast duck and goose, or *anatra* or *faraona alla creta* (duck or guinea fowl cooked in a terracotta dish), or *duchessa di Parma*, fried rolls of turkey breast, prosciutto and Parmesan in a Marsala and cream sauce. Tripe (*trippa* or *buzeca*) is often cooked *alla parmigiana*, and various veal dishes, among them *punta di vitello* (or *cima) ripiena* or *picaja* (stuffed breast of veal). Horse and even donkey meat have their aficionados, especially in Piacenza; the former is often served raw and minced, or cooked with diced vegetables (*picula ad cavàll*). Game dishes are increasingly popular, not just in the Apennines where they've always been a staple. They usually appear as roasts with polenta (either maize or made of chestnuts) and wild mushrooms in season.

Ferrara is famous for its haggis-like *salama da sugo*: minced pork, tongue and liver mixed with Vino di Bosco and spices, stuffed in a pig's bladder and hung for a year or so before it's boiled for up to 8 hours. When it comes out of the bladder, it's an intense, gooey love-it-or-hate-it hash, served traditionally with mashed potatoes. Modena is renowned for *zampone*: a hollowed out and deboned trotter filled with pork and spices crushed into a smooth paste then cooked for hours until it has the consistency of butter. The similar *cotechino*, another Modena speciality, is a slightly gelatinous cooked sausage served with lentils or in a *bollito misto*. Both are popular around Christmas.

Like all Italians, the locals love seafood. The Po Delta is famous for eels, and the marinated ones, *anguilla marinata tradizionale delle Valli di Comacchio* are especially prized – there are roadside restaurants that serve almost nothing else. As elsewhere along the Adriatic, you'll find *brodetto* or *zuppa di pesce* (seafood soup) and seafood fry-ups, along with dishes such as *triglie vestite al prosciutto di Parma* (red mullets baked with ham and courgettes) and *seppie alla romagnola* (cuttlefish with tomatoes and peas).

CHEESE Besides Parmesan (see box, page 243) and its Grana Padano cousins, Emilia's cheeses include *stracchino* (delicious soft cow's cheese, often eaten on an antipasti plate with *salumi*, in a *piadina* or even mixed in mashed potatoes) and fresh semi-soft *ribiòla* made in Piacenza. In the Apennines, try soft white *raviggiolo*, one of the country's oldest cheeses; unlike most, the curd isn't cut, but is simply left to drain on fern or fig leaves. It's usually eaten fresh with olive oil and pepper, or stuffed in pasta. In Romagna, look for *formaggio di fossa*, or 'pit cheese' (see box, page 391).

SWEET STUFF Unlike some regions in Italy, desserts are serious business in Emilia-Romagna, and often there are special dessert menus. Among the most traditional are *sbrisolona*, a crumbly, cookie-like cake, often flavoured with lemon zest or almonds; *torta di riso*, a delicate cake of rice, sugar, almonds and milk; *zuppa inglese*, the Italian version of trifle (the name seems to derive from the trifle that members of the Este family enjoyed while visiting the court at London); *buslàn*, hard ring-shaped biscuits flavoured with lemon zest, for dunking in dessert wine at the end of a meal; *spongata*, a dense cake filled with honey, nuts and candied fruit; and a dense chocolate-and-coffee cake from Modena. For sheer decadence, it's hard to beat a *torta di Duchessa di Parma*, a hazelnut cake laden with pastry cream, zabaglione, and chocolate ganache.

The biggest sugar rushes come with the holidays. For carnival, there are *sfrappole* (or *crespelli*), twisted ribbons of deep-fried dough dusted with vanilla sugar. The dense Christmas cake, *pampapato*, invented by Ferrara's nuns of Corpus Domini in the 17th century, is made with almonds, cocoa, orange peel, lemons, cinnamon,

2

cloves and candied fruit and topped with chocolate; *panspeziale* in Bologna is similar. The Bolognesi also make *certosino*, a fruitcake dating from the Middle Ages baked by monks in the Certosa. Prepared weeks before Christmas, the recipe includes honey, candied lemon and orange, almonds, pine nuts, *mostarda* (candied fruit in a mustard syrup), red wine and chocolate. The weirdest Christmas cake is the viper-shaped *biscione* of Reggio Emilia, topped with a meringue and sweets to make a snake face.

WINE AND LIQUEURS Stretching from north of Genoa to the Adriatic, Emilia-Romagna is Italy's fourth biggest wine producer. Much of the wine ends up as cardboard boxes of supermarket plonk, but the region also produces some gems among its 77 DOC (Denominazione di Origine Controllata) wines. Two of the region's finest, Pignoletto from the Colli Bolognesi and Romagna Albana, get Italy's strictest rating: DOCG (Denominazione di Origine Controllata e Garantita). Best known of the DOC wines are **Lambrusco** (see box, below) in Emilia and the ruby-red, fuller-bodied **Sangiovese** (the 'blood of Jove') of Romagna, made from one of the main grapes of Tuscany's Chianti, although the results are usually lighter and fresher; the finest bottles, however, can hold their own with the noble Tuscans. The third by volume is straw-coloured **Trebbiano**, a refreshing single-grape wine, best drunk young.

Piacenza and Parma The traditional white wines from the Colli Piacentini are Monterosso Val D'Arda and Trebbiano Val Trebbia – the grape, as Pliny the Elder acknowledged in his praise of *trebulanus*, is indigenous to Piacenza's River Trebbia, where Hannibal first defeated the Romans, although nowadays most of the Trebbiano is grown in Romagna. Sauvignon and Pinot Grigio are also popular. Or try the Colli Piacenza's Malvasia di Candia, a varietal of Cretan origin. Reds include Barbera and Bonardo, which here are best blended into DOC Gutturnio,

LAMBRUSCO: EMILIANS AT THEIR MOST EFFERVESCENT

The name Lambrusco will sender shivers down the spine of anyone who remembers the 1970s and 80s, when the sweet fizzy soda-pop stuff was Italy's top wine export. But here in its native land, Lambrusco is a different creature altogether: a young, light-bodied (11%) wine that foams like purple champagne out of the bottle, slightly bubbly (*frizzante*), acidic, dry and full of berry notes, a perfect match for platters of fatty *salumi* and rich pasta dishes.

Native to Emilia and cultivated by the Etruscans, the Lambrusco grape in its 60 variations is one of Italy's rare indigenous varietals. Cato the Elder was the first to mention it (he was impressed by its yield), but the Romans never much cared for it – unlike the Celts and Lombards who settled the western half of this region, and found that bubbles helped them digest their rich meat and dairy diet.

The three finest Lambruschi, all from Modena province, are hard to find outside Emilia. Look for deep dark purple Lambrusco Grasparossa di Castelvetro, the most tannic of the bunch; Lambrusco Salamino di Santa Croce, lighter in colour and named after the grape bunches that resemble hanging salamis; and Lambrusco di Sorbara grown around Sorbara, the rarest and most fragrant. Give them a try: you may even end up doing as the hipsters do, sloshing a bit of Lambrusco in the dregs of your *tortellini in brodo*.

famous since the time when Julius Caesar's father-in-law was a leading producer. For something different, try Ortrugo, made from an ancient varietal that until the 1970s was used only as a table grape. The hills of Parma (Colli di Parma) produce two white wines, a Sauvignon and Malvasia, nearly always *frizzante*, and a red from Barbera and Bonarda.

Reggio Emilia and Modena Besides the frothing fresh Lambruschi from the hills around Modena, there's the much-exported DOC Lambrusco Reggiano, from Reggio. The Colli di Scandiano e di Canossa produce a *frizzante* white Lambrusco, Bianco di Scandiano, as well as Cabernet, Chardonnay and Pinot.

Modena is also Emilia's top distiller, best known for *nocino*, made from green walnuts picked on St John's Day, 24 June: a chocolate-brown liqueur, smooth and sweet but with an underlying bitterness. Other liqueurs are Sassolino (made from star anise, at Sassuolo), *alchermes* (made with spices), *laurino* (made of bay leaves), raspberry *lamponcino*, lemon *limoncino*, and grappa.

Bologna and Imola The big news coming out of the Colli Bolognesi south of Bologna is the 'next Prosecco': energetic Pignoletto, once believed to be a native of Bologna province (although it was recently found to be the same (or very similar to) northern Umbria's Grechetto, leading to arguments about the grape's true roots). Top DOCG Pignolettos come from Monteveglio, west of Bologna. The Colli Bolognesi also grow Sangiovese, Barbera and Merlot, and whites Cabernet Sauvignon, Chardonnay and a fine Riesling Italico. The Reno Valley north of Bologna is known for its Montuni del Reno. To the east, the DOC Colli di Imola grow similar varieties to the Colli Bolognesi and a white DOCG Albana.

Ferrara and Ravenna The coastal areas of Ferrara and Ravenna are the home of DOC Vino di Bosco Eliceo or the Vini delle Sàbbia, or 'wines of the sands' that (precisely because of the sand) survived the phylloxera that killed nearly all of Europe's vines in the 19th century. In 1528, Renée of France brought the first vine cuttings from Burgundy's Côte d'Or with her when she wed Ercole II d'Este. Still known as the *uva d'oro* ('golden grape' – a bit confusing as it's black and produces a very black wine) or Fortana, it produces a wine that is slightly tart and acidic when young. Try it with those eels.

Forlì-Cesena and Rimini Much of this area is part of DOC Vini di Romagna, producing Sangiovese di Romagna, Trebbiano and Albana di Romagna Secco, the first Italian white wine raised to DOCG status; the same grapes go into a *passito* dessert wine. Others are white Pagadebit ('pay the bill') and Cagnina, a fragrant purple-red dessert wine, recommended with roast chestnuts or a *ciambella*.

BEER With its huge student population and thirsty summer tourists, beer has always been a serious tipple, though not a distinguished one. Now, however, Emilia-Romagna is playing a big role in Italy's momentous beer revolution, with more than a hundred craft breweries (*microbirrifici*) and brew pubs, nearly all founded in the last decade or so. The best known, so far, is the Birrificio del Ducato, which since its foundation in 2007 has won awards and exports all over the world.

RESTAURANTS AND BARS The terms for restaurants – *ristorante*, *trattoria*, *osteria*, and even *enoteca* – have been blurred, although as a general rule a *ristorante* is more formal. In a traditional osteria, drinking is as important as eating, especially in the

Based on the average price of a main course.

€€€€€	Expensive	€25+
€€€€	Above average	€20–24
€€€	Moderate	€15–19
€€	Cheap & cheerful	€10–14
€	Rock bottom	less than €10

university towns; an enoteca is a wine shop or bar, often serving wine by the *calice* ('chalice' aka a glass), but many serve food and even full meals. As a general rule, the fancier the fittings, the fancier the bill.

In Emilia-Romagna, the best restaurants are often hidden away in alleys or on the edge of town, where you normally wouldn't come across them (this book should help); the Italian mania for motoring means that many are out of town altogether, where it's easy to park.

Breakfast Although some hotels now serve morning buffets, breakfast (*prima colazione*) is traditionally a wake-up shot to the brain, with few pretensions to nutrition: a cappuccino or a caffè latte, accompanied by a croissant-like *cornetto*, or a brioche or fancy pastry. The place to sample these delights is a bar, with newspapers to peruse while standing at the counter. Beware the factory-made cardboardy pastries with great lumps of sugar on top; stand up for civilisation and find another bar. At larger ones, the barista will expect you to pick up a receipt (*scontrino*) from the cashier (*cassa*) before making your order.

Lunch *Pranzo*, served around 13.00, is traditionally the most important meal of the day, the full whack including an antipasto (it could be anything), a *primo piatto* (pasta, broth or soup, or risotto), a *secondo piatto* (meat or seafood) accompanied by a *contorno* or side dish (potatoes, or the fashionable grilled or roasted vegetables), followed by fruit or dessert, all accompanied by wine and mineral water (*acqua minerale*) and ending with an espresso, maybe *corretto* ('corrected' with a squirt of brandy or grappa), or else a *digestivo* (Fernet Branca among many others), which invariably tastes like medicine but can be weirdly addictive. Then, in an ideal world, one has a nice long nap.

Although people in rural areas maintain the classic big lunches, modern urban life has made them a strictly Sunday affair for many. Many restaurants serve special express lunches, or offer fixed menus at affordable prices; bars often double as sandwich bars (*paninoteca*); *piadina* kiosks are common in city centres.

Dinner *Cena* is usually eaten around 20.00. This is much the same as *pranzo*, though lighter and (if you're Italian) without the pasta; that's for lunch. Pizza is popular in the evening and rare in the afternoon, so if you want one for lunch look for places that advertise *pizza anche a pranzo*.

Prices and tipping The bill (*conto*) will very often include a bread and cover charge (*pane e coperto*; usually €1–3 – it's an old Italian tradition), and maybe a 15% service charge (*servizio compreso*); if not, the bill will say *servizio non compreso* (or just *snc*) and you'll have to do your own arithmetic. Leaving a tip (*mancia*) is discretionary.

When you leave, you will be given a receipt (*scontrino* or *ricevuto fiscale*), which by law you must take out of the door and carry for at least 60m. There is a slim chance the tax police (Guardia di Finanza) may have their eye on you or the restaurant, and if you don't have a receipt they could slap you with a heavy fine.

FESTIVALS AND ANNUAL EVENTS

Emilia-Romagna puts on hundreds of annual festivals and events. Music festivals and swanning around in medieval costumes are mainstays, but most of all you'll find celebrations of local food and wine in the infinite number of *sagre* (singular: *sagra*). Dates are fluid and in general change every year. Check listings, organised region by region, on the Eventi e Sagre website (w *eventiesagre.it, sagreinromagna.it*).

JANUARY

Bologna	**Bologna Festival** (w *bolognafestival.it*): a classical music festival with international star performers; runs until May.
Modena	**Corrida di San Geminiano** (w *corridadisangeminiano.it*): a 13.35km footrace through the streets of Modena, on the 31st.

FEBRUARY

Bologna	**Harp Festival** (w *millearpeggi.com*): first half of February.
Cento	**Carnival** (w *carnevalecento.com*): one of the best in the region; dates vary.
Imola	**Sfilata dei Fantaveicoli** (w *carnevalefantaveicoli.it*): carnival and competition featuring homemade fantastical vehicles.
Ponticelli	**Sagra dei Maccheroni** (w *visitareimola.it*): celebrating macaroni for over a century; first Sunday of the month.
San Giovanni in Persiceto	**Carnival** (w *comunepersiceto.it*) with a parade of satirical floats, revealing their true meaning on Sunday at the *spillo* or 'transformation', when they open up.

MARCH

Bologna	**Salsa Festival** (w *bolognasalsafestival.com*): held mid-month.
Forlimpopoli	**Segavecchia** (w *segavecchia.it*): week-long festival with folklore, music, food and parades, culminating in the burning of the effigy of the Old Woman of Winter; third week.
Ravenna	**Ravenna Jazz** (w *ravennajazz.org*): seminars and concerts with an impressive line-up of performers; first two weeks of the month.
Rocca San Casciano	**Festa del Falò** (w *festadelfalo.it*): bonfire festival; second weekend.

APRIL

Bologna	**Live Arts Week** (w *liveartsweek.it*): featuring the latest in live media, sponsored by MAMbo (page 117); at the end of the month.

1 January	New Year's Day (Capodanno)
6 January	Epiphany (Epifania)
March/April	Easter Monday (Pasquetta; variable)
25 April	Liberation Day (Festa della Liberazione)
1 May	Labour Day (Festa dei Lavoratori)
2 June	Anniversary of the Republic (Festa della Repubblica)
15 August	Assumption (Ferragosto)
1 November	All Saints' Day (Tutti i Santi)
8 December	The Immaculate Conception (Immacolata Concezione)
25 December	Christmas Day (Natale)
26 December	St Stephen's Day (Santo Stefano)

Ferrara	**Vulandra** (**w** *vulandra.it*): kite and kite-makers' festival; third week.
Gambettola	**Float races** (**w** *comune.cesena.fc.it*): a humorous procession, on Easter Monday and the following Sunday.
Tredozio	**Sagra e Palio dell'Uovo** (**w** *comune.tredozio.fc.it*): egg-cracking contests and the Italian hard-boiled egg-eating championship, on Easter Sunday and Monday.
Vignola	**Festa dei Ciliegi in Fiore** (**w** *centrostudivignola.it*): cherry blossom festival; held in the second week.

MAY

Busseto	**Verdi Voice** (**w** *vociverdiane.com*): competitions in May/June.
Cervia	**Lo Sposalizio del Mare** (**w** *cerviasposaliziodelmare.it*): Ascension Day 'Marriage to the Sea', dating back to 1445.
Ferrara	More than two weeks of events in mid-May, the lead-up to the **Palio di San Giorgio** (**w** *paliodiferrara.it*).
Imola	**Imola in Musica** (**w** *imolainmusica.it*): late May to early June.
Modena	**Voliamo Festival** (**w** *voliamofestival.it*): with hot air balloons, hang gliders, horses and shows; late May to early June.
Quattro Castella	**Corteo Matildico** (**w** *corteomatildico.it*): three days of re-enactment of the Investiture of Matilda of Canossa as Vicereine of Italy by Henry V; late May.
Ravenna	**Ravenna Festival** (**w** *ravennafestival.org*): opera, classical music and ballet in the churches; mid-May to mid-July.
	Ravenna Jazz Festival (**w** *ravennajazz.org*): second week.

JUNE

Bologna	**Il Cinema Ritrovato** (**w** *festival.ilcinemaritrovato.it*): festival of silent films; late June.
	Sotto le Stelle del Cinema (**w** *cinetecadibologna.it*): free outdoor films, often in Piazza Maggiore.

Brisighella	Medieval Festival (w *festemedioevali.org*): with music, sports, feasts, games and more; in early June.
Castelvetro di Modena	Mercurdo – Mercato dell'Assurdo (w *mercurdo.it*): 'Market of the Absurd', a wild contemporary arts festival; first weekend.
Cervia	Festival Danza (w *festivaldanzacervia.it*): ballroom dancing competition; third week.
Codigoro	Musica Pomposa (w *comune.codigoro.fe.it*): free concerts at the abbey until the end of August.
Faenza	Palio del Niballo (w *paliodifaenza.it*): first weekend.
Ferrara	Ferrara Sotto le Stelle (w *ferrarasottolestelle.it*): rock festival; mid-June to mid-July.
Modena	Modena Cento Ore (w *modenacentooreclassic.it*): four-day historic car race.
Spilamberto	Fiera di San Giovanni (w *fierasangiovanni.it*): with a balsamic vinegar competition; around the 21st.

JULY
Bobbio	Irlanda in Musica (w *irlandainmusica.com*): Irish music festival; mid-month.
Castel del Rio	Feste Rinascimentali (w *festerinascimentali.it*): Renaissance festival; mid-month.
Fiorenzuola d'Arda	Dal Mississippi al Po (w *festivaldalmississippialpo.com*): focusing on the blues; mid-month.
Gatteo Mare	Settimana della Micizia (w *gatteomareturismo.it*: cat festival; mid-month.
Porretta Terme	Porretta Soul Festival (w *porrettasoulfestival.it*): soul music festival; third week.
Rimini	Cartoon Club (w *cartoonclubrimini.com*): festival of animation from around the world; mid-month.
Santarcangelo	Santarcangelo Festival (w *santarcangelofestival.com*): street theatre festival; second week.
Savignano sul Rubicone	Piadiniamo (f *piadiniamo.comeunavolta*): *piadina* love fest; mid-month.
Stellata di Bondeno	Bundan Celtic Festival (w *bundan.com*): at the Rocca di Stellata; late July.

AUGUST
Ravenna	Festival Internazionale di Musica d'Organo (w *turismo.ra.it*): organ concerts every Monday in San Vitale; throughout August.
Cesenatico	Festa di Garibaldi (w *cesenaticoholidays.com*): with big fireworks; first weekend.
Casina	Fiera del Parmigiano Reggiano (f *fieradelparmigianoreggianocasina*): Parmesan cheese fair; first week.
Ferrara	Ferrara Buskers Festival (w *ferrarabuskers.com*): the largest festival of its kind in Europe; ten days in mid-August.
Mondaino	Palio de lo Daino (w *mondainoeventi.it*): mid-month.
Pontenure	Concorto Film Festival (w *concortofilmfestival.com*): short film festival with first prize, the Golden Donkey; mid-month.

SEPTEMBER

Argenta

Fiera d'Argenta (w *comune.argenta.fe.it*): big fair with music, food and events; second weekend.

Bologna

Danza Urbana (w *danzaurbana.eu*): contemporary dance in locations around the city; first week.

Castelvetro di Modena

Dama Vivente/Festa in Castello (w *visitcastelvetro.it*): in even-numbered years, a live game of draughts in which the pieces are ladies in Renaissance gowns; or, in odd-numbered years, a parade and a Renaissance banquet for everyone who books ahead, and comes in Renaissance costume; 2nd weekend in September.

Cervia

Sapore di Sale (w *cerviasaporedisale.it*): 'Taste of Salt', in all its forms, including snacks and tours; second week.

Langhirano/Parma

Festival del Prosciutto di Parma (w *festivaldelprosciuttodiparma.com*): taste more than a thousand kinds of ham at this Parma ham festival; three days in early September.

Parma/Busseto

Festival Verdi (w *parmaincomingtravel.com*): opera performances; running from the end of September to the end of October.

San Marino

Palio delle Balestre (w *federazionebalestrieri.sm*): crossbow competitions; early September.

Terra del Sole

Palio di Santa Reparata (w *terradelsole.org*): medieval palio; third week.

Val Tidone

Valtidone Wine Fest (w *valtidonewinefest.it*): in four villages, on four weekends.

OCTOBER

Bologna

Bologna Jazz Festival (w *bolognajazzfestival.com*): one of the most important jazz festivals in Italy; October to November.

Mortadella Bò (w *mortadellabologna.com*): celebrating mortadella; third weekend.

Casola Valsenio

Festa dei Frutti Dimenticati (w *www.comune. casolavalsenio.ra.it*): celebrating heirloom fruit; second and third weekends.

Cesenatico

Il Pesce fa Festa (w *www.cesenatico.it*): the town turns into a giant outdoor seafood restaurant; end of the month.

Comacchio

Sagra dell'Anguilla (Eel Festival) (w *ferrarainfo.com/it/ comacchio*): over the first three weekends.

Fragno

Fiera Nazionale del Tartufo Nero di Fragno (w *tartufonerofragno.it*): black truffle fair; every Sunday from mid-October to mid-November.

Sant'Agata Féltria

Fiera del Tartufo Bianco (w *santagatainfiera.com*): the national white truffle fair; every Sunday in October.

Spilamberto

Mast Còt (Cooked Must) (w *mastcot.it*): streets are filled with pots of boiling grape juice to be made into balsamic vinegar; first weekend.

NOVEMBER

Bologna	**BilBOlbul** (w *bilbolbul.net*): a three-day international comic-book and cartoon festival; third week.
Brisighella	Every Sunday a different *sagra* (w *brisighella.org*): pork, Volpina pears and cheese, truffles and olive oil.
Ravenna	**Ravenna Festival** (w *ravennafestival.org*): opera, classical music and ballet in the churches; mid-month.
Sogliano al Rubicone	**Fiera del Formaggio di Fossa** (w *www.comune.sogliano. fc.it*): third and fourth Sundays, and the first Sunday of December.
Talamello	**Fiera del Formaggio di Fossa** (w *comune.talamello. rn.it*): celebration of the town's 'pit cheese'; mid-month.

DECEMBER

Campagnola Emilia	**Cicciolo d'Oro** (w *ilcicciolodoro.com*): 'Golden Crackling Festival'; second weekend.
Imola	**Corto Imola** (w *cortoimolafestival.it*): international short-film festival; second week.
Porretta Terme	**Festival del Cinema di Porretta Terme** (w *porrettacinema.com*): film festival; second week.
Savignano sul Rubicone	**Fiera di Santa Lucia** (f *Fiera-Santa-Lucia-Savignano*): Christmas market, music and many events; lasting three days, ending the 13th.

OPENING TIMES

In general, Sunday afternoons and Mondays are dead periods for the sightseer – you may want to make them your travelling days.

CHURCHES Italy's churches are a prime target for art thieves and as a consequence small or remote ones are usually locked, with limited opening hours (often at weekends); you may also have to hunt down the keyholder. The most important churches are open all day, while others keep shop hours, closing for lunch. Don't come to see paintings and statues in churches the week preceding Easter – you may find them covered with mourning shrouds.

MUSEUMS AND MONUMENTS Public ones tend to close on Sunday afternoons and all day Monday, although it varies according to season. Opening hours on public holidays are nearly always the same as those on Sundays, except at Christmas, New Year and on Easter Day, when everything is shut.

EATING AND DRINKING For **restaurants,** usual lunchtime hours are anywhere between 12.30 and 14.30, whereas dinner can range from 19.30 to 23.00. You would be hard pressed to find a restaurant serving dinner before 19.30, unless it's in a hotel. **Cafés and bars** usually open from very early in the morning (around 06.00–07.00) and close late at night, particularly during summer.

OTHER PRACTICALITIES Banks open at 08.30 Monday to Friday and close for lunch around 13.00–13.30. Afternoon hours are 14.45–16.00. **Pharmacies** are generally open Monday to Friday 09.00–13.00 and 15.30–19.30 (16.00–20.00 in summer). In reality, they work on a rota basis, where the times change frequently

Twice a year, in spring and autumn, Parma holds the week-long **Mercanteinfiera** [210 B1] (*Fiere di Parma, Viale delle Esposizioni 393A;* w *mercanteinfiera.it*), said to be the world's biggest antiques and vintage market, with more than a thousand exhibitors from Italy and abroad. Other important ones are:

Bologna Piazza Santo Stefano; ⊕ 2nd w/end of every month exc Jul, Aug & Jan
Ferrara Piazza Municipale; ⊕ 1st w/end of every month exc Aug
Fontanellato ⊕ every 3rd Sun. Huge antiques fair in the centre.
Modena Parco Novi; ⊕ 4th w/end of every month
Piacenza Porta Galera; ⊕ 4th Sun of month
Ravenna Piazza Einaudi & Piazza Garibaldi; ⊕ 3rd w/end of month

but are displayed at the entrance, with information on the nearest open *farmacia*. Normal **post office** opening hours are Monday to Friday 08.30–13.30 and Saturday 08.30–12.30.

Shops are usually open Monday to Saturday 09.00–13.00 and 16.00–20.00. In winter, this often (and without notice, depending on the shop) changes to 10.00–13.00 and 15.30–19.30.

SHOPPING

Emilia-Romagna is packed with things to take home: perhaps a Ferrari, Maserati or Lamborghini, ceramics from Faenza, Ferrara or Sassuolo, or hand-printed linens from Santarcangelo. But nothing sums up this area so well as food: cheese, cured meats, olive oil, pasta and wine. Just be sure that anything that could be deemed a 'substance' (including cheese) is packed in a checked-in bag. Bargain-hunting fashionistas after Italian clothes and accessories should come during the sales periods (January–February and July–August) or hit the factory outlets. The two biggest are the outlet malls **Fidenza Village** (page 235) and **Castel Guelfo** (page 334). For complete listings in English, see w factoryoutletsitaly.com.

Non-EU citizens should save all receipts for customs. If you spend at least €154.45 in a single shop that posts a sign that it belongs to either Global Blue (w *globalblue.com*), Premier Tax Free (w *premiertaxfree.com*), Tax Refund for Tourists (w *taxrefund.it*) or Tax Free VAT Refund Service (w *www.taxfreeservice. com*), ask for a tax-free invoice to be eligible for a VAT rebate at the airport.

ACTIVITIES

BEACHES AND WATERSPORTS Eighty per cent of all tourists to Emilia-Romagna come to sprawl on the beach, and if you join them you'll find plenty to do, including all the usual watersports – sailing, windsurfing, waterskiing and scuba-diving. Six beaches (Bellaria Igea Marina, Cervia, Cesenatico, Comacchio, Lidi Ravennati and Misano Adriatico) fly the eco-friendly Blue Flag for their cleanliness.

Stabilimenti Because Italians tend to like each others' company and their creature comforts, the resorts are plagued (or blessed, according to your point of view) by that peculiarly Italian phenomenon, the *stabilimento balneare*: beach clubs with raked sand

and ranks of sunbeds (*lettini*), deckchairs (*sdraie*) or chairs (*sedie*), fake palms and brollies, which charge all comers for the privilege of clean sand and watching your neighbours. They also offer changing rooms, a bar and food; some have full fancy restaurants, jacuzzis, massages, playgrounds, sports facilities, etc. Although places are leased by the season, they will let day visitors in according to availability (although most beach hotels have reserved places). By law they cannot deny the public access to the sea and must leave the first 5m of sand by the water free of obstacles. Resorts all have free beaches, too, but they may be strewn with litter and cigarette butts.

CANOEING AND KAYAKING The River Enza, between the provinces of Parma and Reggio Emilia, is one of Europe's top kayaking rivers, the setting for the International Kayak Enza races every April since 1965. Other key spots are the rivers Taro, Trebbia and Ceno in Parma province, lakes Suviana and Brasimone, and the white-water River Limentra south of Bologna.

CYCLING In Emilia-Romagna, everyone has a bike. Many hotels lend bicycles to guests, or at least can tell you where you can hire one. Although the traffic would make general touring between the cities a dismal proposition, three transnational **Eurovelo Routes** (w *eurovelo.com*) crisscross the region: Ciclovia Destra Po (Eurovelo 8), follows the south bank of the Po; the Ciclopista del Sole (EuroVelo7) goes from Mantua via Bologna towards Pistoia; and the Ciclovia Francigena (Eurovelo 5) follows the Via Francigena (see box, page 235) from Piacenza and Fidenza to Pontrémoli in Tuscany. **Albergabici** (w *albergabici.it*) is a national network of places to stay from hotels to campsites with bicycle-friendly facilities.

Terrabici (w *terrabici.com*) lists ten of the best areas for less ambitious rides. The Ferrara tourist office's 'Bike Book and Bike Maps', available on their website (w *ferraraterraeacqua.it*), is also useful. In the nearby Po Delta, you can easily combine boat and bike rides (*see* w *visitcomacchio.it*). If you want to tackle hills, **Riccione** (pages 380–2) with its many bike hotels is the queen bee of Italian cycling resorts, with day rides into the Apennines. Also see **Bicitalia**, the national cycling organisation (w *bicitalia.org*). **Bikemap** (w *bikemap.net*) and its mobile app have itineraries and advice on hundreds of routes in Emilia-Romagna.

Besides all the good cycling routes, there is one dangerous lorry-filled road to avoid: the SS309 north of Ravenna to Mestre.

Bikes on trains If your bike can be disassembled to fit in a case no larger than 80cm x 110cm x 40cm, it is treated as any other piece of luggage and free to transport. If it can't be disassembled, look for the bike icon on the timetable and purchase a €3.50 bike ticket.

Mountain bikes Mountain bikes (same word in Italian) are extremely popular in the Apennines. One of the most exciting routes is the five-day **Via degli Dei**, or the Way of the Gods (w *viadeglidei.it*) from Bologna to Florence, a route used from the 7th century BC by the Etruscans into the Middle Ages, and restored in the 1990s. The name comes from the various mountains along the way named after gods: Adonis, Venus, Monzuno (Mount Jove) and Lunario (after Lua, the Roman goddess of atonement).

Other favourites include **Cimone Bike Park** on Mount Cimone south of Modena, rated one of the best in the world (page 183), and the Salti dei Diavolo 'Devil's Leaps' – three off-road trails in the Parmense Apennines, part of the province's **Grande Giro MTB** (w *ilgrandegiromtb.it*) with 900km of trails.

FISHING You don't need a permit for sea-fishing, but Italy's coastal waters may disappoint. Many freshwater lakes and streams are stocked. To fish here you need to buy a year's membership card from the Federazione Italiana della Pesca Sportiva (w *fipsas.it*), which has an office in every province; they will inform you about local restrictions. Bait and equipment are readily available.

FOOTBALL Soccer (*calcio*) is a national obsession. For many, *calcio* far outweighs tedious issues such as the state of the nation – not least because of the weekly chance (slim but real) of becoming an instant millionaire in the Lotteria Sportiva. All major cities, and most minor ones, have at least one team. Rivalries are intense; scandals, especially involving bribery and cheating, are rife, although crowd violence is minimal. Five-a-side football is so popular that nearly every town has a pitch dedicated to it: there are five in Rimini alone.

Bologna FC Founded in 1909 (w *bolognafc.it*), Emilia-Romagna's only club in Serie A usually sits somewhere in the middle of the pack and has a massive fan base. The lively home matches take place on Sunday afternoons from September to May in the Stadio Renato dall'Ara west of the centre (*Via A Costa 174; for tickets* \051 611 1177; w *bolognafc.vivaticket.it*), a 25-minute walk from Piazza Maggiore or a short bus ride away (route 14, 20 or 21).

GOLF Italians have been slow to appreciate the delights of biffing a small white ball into a hole, but they're catching on fast. Emilia-Romagna has 25 championship courses; for information on all the courses and golf packages, see w emiliaromagnagolf.com.

HIKING The Apennines have a good system of way-marked trails and mountain refuges run by the Italian Alpine Club, CAI (*Via Stalingrado 105, Bologna;* \051 234856; w *caiemiliaromagna.org*). Some of the most breathtaking treks are in the Parco Nazionale Appennino Tosco-Emiliano (w *www.parcoappennino.it*), which straddles the highest mountains between Tuscany and Emilia.

Walking at high altitudes is generally practicable between May and October, after most of the snow has melted, although come prepared at any time of the year: even summer in the high Apennines can be fickle and stormy. Hiking boots, backpack, wind jacket or waterproof cape, and water bottle are essential.

Long-distance treks The longest trail through the mountains is the **Grande Escursione Appenninica** (GEA), a 375km, 28-stage trek from the Due Santi Pass in the Marche to Bocca Trabaria in Tuscany, much of it through dense forests. Shorter, less strenuous walks include the **Grande Circuito della Romagna** (13 stages, possible all year) or the **Sentiero dei Ducati**, a nine-stage walk from Canossa to Luni. Local tourist offices sell maps and provide details for refuges and lodging along the way.

HORSERIDING The region has more than 250 riding stables, particularly in the Apennines and Po Delta (where white Camargue horses have been introduced). Many are connected to *agriturismi*. The region has set up a riding trail stretching over 1,000km called La Grande Ippovia across the entire region (*see* w *trekappennino.it*).

SKIING AND WINTER SPORTS Although Emilia-Romagna's mountains aren't about to challenge the Alps in height, prestige (or prices), there are 15 winter resort areas in the Apennines, most of them with snow machines that deal with the erratic snow cover. There are ice rinks (including an Olympic-size one at Fanano, and another at Cereto Laghi), 5,000km of cross-country and snowshoe routes, indoor pools, snowboarding parks and lessons in kite skiing or ice-climbing. Equipment hire is generally not too expensive, but lift passes and accommodation can push up the cost. Prices on the pistes are highest during the Christmas and New Year holidays. For a complete list, see w appenninoeverde.it.

SPAS Emilia-Romagna has a great underground current of hot mineral water that has given rise to a large spa industry, with some 19 spa towns and hundreds of hotels and beauty and wellness centres, all of which are listed at w emiliaromagnaterme. com.

TENNIS If football is Italy's most popular spectator sport, tennis is probably the game most people actually play. Every *comune* has public courts, especially in the resorts. Hotel courts can often be used by non-residents for a fee.

ARTS AND ENTERTAINMENT

CINEMA No Italian city loves film more than Bologna, which sells more cinema tickets per capita than any other, and is home to the Cineteca and the country's most important film archives (page 80); it's also your best chance to see a film in VO (*versione originale*), the original language, as Italians nearly always dub films.

MUSEUMS With two or three works of art per inhabitant, the Italians have a hard time financing the preservation of their national heritage. Even so, entrance charges are not exorbitant; few will be over €5, and others may be completely free. EU citizens under 18 and over 65 years of age get free admission to state museums, with identification.

MUSIC Music is everywhere in the homeland of Giuseppe Verdi, Arturo Toscanini, Niccolò Paganini, Ottorino Respighi, Luciano Pavarotti, Carlo Bergonzi and Mirella Freni. Bologna, a UNESCO Creative City of Music, has a permanent orchestra, as do Ferrara and Parma. Historic theatres (the oldest, Parma's Teatro Farnese, dates from 1628), churches and oratories host concert, chamber music and opera seasons; music festivals (pages 47–51) range from the Verdi festival to Ferrara's festival of buskers.

PHOTOGRAPHY Museums and churches often prohibit the use of flash photography because it damages the artwork. Some museums may ban photos altogether. The Apennines and the wetlands of the Po Delta offer the most evocative landscapes, especially early in the morning or in the 'golden hour' before sunset.

MEDIA AND COMMUNICATIONS

PRINT AND ONLINE MEDIA The main dailies in Bologna are *Il Resto del Carlino* (no, it doesn't mean the 'Remains of Little Charles' but the change from an old coin called the Carlino – you bought a cigar, and instead of change you could have a newspaper) and the *Corriere di Bologna* (the local edition of the national paper of Milan, the *Corriere della Sera*). Nearly every province has a local paper or two, which offer interesting insights and listings if you read Italian. The main ones –

La Gazzetta di Modena, *Modena Today* and *Il Nuovo Giornale di Modena*, Ferrara's *Estense*, Parma's *Zerosette* and *La Gazzetta di Parma*, Piacenza's *Libertà* and Rimini's *Corriere di Romagna* – have online editions, as does the English-language *Bologna Press* and *Bologna Magazine*.

TELEVISION AND RADIO Free-to-air television stations are those shared by the rest of the nation. The main ones are Rai 1, Rai 2, Rai 3, Rete 4, Canale 5 and Italia 1. Rai airs TGR (Telegiornale Regione), with regional news and weather at 14.00 and 19.28 every day. There are also dozens of small regional stations, most of which seem to be devoted to adverts for fortune tellers.

POST Dealing with the Poste Italiane (w *poste.it*) has always been a frustrating, time-consuming affair. It is one of the least competent and slowest postal services in Europe, and although it has improved in recent years, it's easy to understand the Italians' love affair with email. Stamps (*francobolli*) may be purchased in post offices or at tobacconists (*tabacchi*; identified by their blue or black signs with a white T). Stamps to the UK (for normal letters and postcards) are about €1; to America, around €2.20; and to Australia about €2.90. Red post boxes can be found outside post offices and scattered throughout towns. For opening times, see page 52.

INTERNET Nearly every hotel and B&B in the region offers free Wi-Fi, although you might have to go into the public areas to get a connection. Italo trains offer free excellent internet; Trenitalia's Frecciarossa or Frecciargento high-speed trains do as well, though, unlike the Italo network, to get online you have to obtain a username and password and pay €0.01/24 hours – and it doesn't work in tunnels.

The Italian government has recently launched an English and Italian-language Wi-Fi Italia app designed to allow travellers to connect instantly to hot spots in railway stations, public institutions, hotels and elsewhere. For even more coverage, several companies offer 4G and 4G+ mobile Wi-Fi hot spot rentals for €3–6 a day: see Expressowifi (w *expressowifi.com*), Witourist (w *witourist.com*) and My Webspot (w *my-webspot.com*).

TELEPHONES Confusingly, Italian numbers can have anything from eight to twelve digits. If you're calling from abroad or from your non-Italian mobile phone, dial '00 39' and then the whole number, *including* the first '0'. Numbers beginning with a '3' are mobile numbers; numbers starting with a 1 are for emergency services; toll-free numbers (*numeri verdi*) start with '80'. Other numbers starting with an '8' may have an extra charge.

CULTURAL ETIQUETTE

Dress respectfully when visiting churches, and don't visit during a service. Avoid eating and drinking on church steps or in a historic monument; not only does this really annoy the locals, but you may even be fined. If you're invited to someone's house for dinner, bring flowers or chocolates (but never chrysanthemums, which are associated with death). Even if you don't speak Italian, the basics such as *buongiorno* (good day), *per favore* (please) and *grazie* (thank you) go a long way.

Part Two

THE GUIDE

3

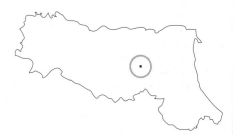

Bologna

'You must write all the beautiful things of Italy,' said the Venetian on the train, but the man from Bologna vehemently shook his finger. 'No, no,' he insisted. 'You must write the truth!'

And it is precisely that, a fervent insistence on the plain truth as opposed to the typical Italian delight in appearance and *bella figura*, that sets Bologna apart. A homespun realism and attention to the detail of the visible, material world are the main characteristics of the Bolognese school of art (recall Petrarch's comment that, while only an educated man is amazed by a Giotto, anyone can understand a Bolognese picture). The city's handsome, harmonic and well-preserved centre disdains imported marble or ornate stucco, preferring honest red brick. Bologna's municipal government, which was long in the hands of the Italian Communist Party (now the PDS), is considered the most efficient of any large city in Italy.

In the 11th century it was the desire for truth and law that led to the founding of the University of Bologna, whose first scholars interpreted the law codes of Justinian in settling disputes over investitures between pope and emperor. And it is Bolognese sincerity and honest ingredients in the kitchen that has made *la cucina bolognese* by common consent the best in all Italy, a fact recently confirmed by the opening of FICO Eataly World (page 129), the world's first theme park dedicated to food.

The city's historic centre is considered one of the best preserved and maintained in Italy, to the credit of its policy of 'active preservation', developed in the 1970s – old houses were gutted and renovated for municipal public housing, maintaining the character of the old quarters. Nor is this the first time Bologna has found a creative solution to its housing needs.

One of the first things you notice is how every street is lined with arcades, or *portici*. The originals date from the 12th century, when the *comune*, faced with a housing shortage compounded by the presence of 2,000 university students, allowed rooms to be built on to existing buildings over the streets. Over time the Bolognesi became attached to them and the shelter they provided from the weather. Along with the absurdly tilting Two Towers, they are the city's soul, its identity; to the Bolognesi, their special world is the *pianeta porticata*, the 'porticoed planet'. The city claims 70km (including the single 4km portico that climbs up to San Luca), more than any other city in the world.

La Dotta, La Grassa and La Rossa (the Learned, the Fat and the Red) are Bologna's sobriquets. It may be full of socialist virtue, but the city is also very wealthy and cosy, with a quality of life often compared to Sweden's. The casual observer could well come away with the impression that the reddest things about Bologna are its bricks and its suburban street names such as Via Stalingrado, Via Yuri Gagarin and Viale Lenin. But Bologna is hardly a stolid place – its bars, cafés and squares are brimming with youth and life, and there's a full calendar of concerts from rap to jazz to Renaissance madrigals, as well as avant-garde ballet, theatre and art exhibitions.

The area around Bologna was first settled as early as 1000BC by the people of the Villanovan culture, who occupied much of northcentral Italy; Villanova di Castelnaso itself, with the site that gives these people a name, is just outside the city.

The Villanovans, once believed to be an Italic people who were conquered by the Etruscans, are now generally accepted as an earlier phase of Etruscan culture, before its great economic expansion of the 8th and 7th centuries BC brought it into the Mediterranean main stream and opened it to influences from the Greek world. The Etruscans expanded over the Apennines sometime in the 6th century, and founded the town of Velzna in c510BC

Finds in Bologna's archaeology museum are sufficient testament to the wealth and sophistication of Etruscan Velzna in the century that followed, even though the city and other settlements in the Po Valley were only frontier outposts of the great Etruscan civilisation centred in Tuscany and northern Lazio. The Etruscan world was a collection of city-states, organised in religiously based confederations, and Velzna may have been the chief town of a *dodecapolis*, or league of 12 cities, similar to that of Tuscany.

Velzna grew quickly and grew fat from trade with the other towns of Italy and Greece, but its good fortune was not to last. In the 4th century BC everything seemed to go wrong for the Etruscans. While the cities south of the Apennines were getting battered in trade wars against the Greeks, and beginning to feel the threat from the new power of Rome, the Po Valley cities found themselves overwhelmed by invaders from the north, the Celts.

The Celtic Boii tribe conquered the region around Velzna in c350BC, and gave the city its new name, Bononia. (The Boii also gave their name to Bohemia, whence they had originally come.)

The Celts cared more for poetry, hospitality and other people's cattle than for cities and commerce, and Bononia languished under their control. In the Punic Wars, the Boii and the rest of the Celts sided with Carthage against Rome. Hannibal's army wintered at Bononia in 217BC, but after his defeat the Celts of Cisalpine Gaul were doomed. Bononia succumbed to Rome's legions in 189BC, and was soon after refounded as a Latin colony.

For the next six centuries this town had almost nothing to say for itself. With its prime location, at the intersection of the Via Emilia and the Via Cassia, the main road to Venetia and central Europe, Bononia grew into a prosperous though undistinguished *municipium*, and variously enjoyed the benefits or suffered the vicissitudes of the Roman state.

If little is known about the city in this era, it is only because the centre has been continuously occupied through all the centuries since, and opportunities for archaeological excavations are few. A bit of the old Via Aemilia, complete with wagon ruts in the stone paving, is visible on the pedestrian underpass beneath Via Rizzoli, and the Roman theatre has been located on Via Carbonesi, almost entirely covered with buildings.

On any map, you can see clearly the extent of Roman Bononia in the grid of rectilinear streets between the Two Towers and Via Nazario Sauro, Via Riva di Reno and Via Farini. In the troubles that accompanied the fall of the Empire, the area west of Via Galliera seems to have been abandoned, and sometime after AD300 a defensive wall was built around the shrunken town. The town's top patron saint, St Petronius, was a 5th-century bishop who assumed control of the city and did good work keeping things together in hard times.

Like Romagna, but unlike Emilia to the west, Bononia was never conquered by the Lombards when they overran Italy in the AD570s, and the city remained under the rule of the Byzantine Exarchate of Ravenna until the Lombard King Liutprand finally seized it in AD727. They in turn lost it to Charlemagne in AD774. There is evidence that the city was thriving even in the Dark Ages – it was one of the few cities to expand its walls, if slightly. In the curving streets between the Torre Asinella and Piazza Rossini you can trace on the map the course of an unusual semicircular addition, most likely made in the 8th century.

A MEDIEVAL BOOM TOWN All Europe started to revive around AD1000, and in few places was the sudden upsurge of medieval civilisation more pronounced than in Bologna. This previously sleepy and unremarkable community started off the new millennium with a bang, founding one of Italy's first free *comuni* and starting what would become Europe's first university. Bologna had benefited from the new trade fostered in the Po Valley by the first great commercial metropolis of Western Europe, Venice, and now the city was starting to generate wealth of its own, from wool, linen and hemp (for ropes), as well as luxury goods, especially silk. The presence of 2,000 students provided another boost to the economy, and led to a new industry – Bologna was the first city in Italy where books were copied for sale.

In the 1100s Bologna was a boom town on an American scale, with tower-fortresses of the urban nobility zooming up like modern skyscrapers – some 180 of them, more perhaps than any city outside Florence. By 1200 Bologna, with its 50,000 inhabitants, had become one of the great cities of Europe, surpassed only by Venice, Constantinople, Paris and Milan (Genoa and Palermo were probably about the same size). Thanks to its university it had become the intellectual centre of Italy, and the money was flowing – there were 242 goldsmiths in the town, compared with only 60 in Rome.

Like Modena and Ferrara, medieval Bologna was a city of canals. The most important, now under Via Riva di Reno, powered mills for the manufacturies and provided a shipping outlet to the Po. The extent to which the city was thriving can be seen in its walls. From the original rectangle of Roman times, the city expanded to fill a new circuit in the 1100s that was nearly six times the original size (following Piazza Malpighi, Via Marconi, Via Riva di Reno, Via Righi, Piazza Aldrovandi and Via Guerazzi, then down to the Palazzo di Giustizia).

Only a century later, the city had quadrupled in size again, and had to build its final wall, now traced by the 6.5km ring of boulevards (the Circla) around the *centro storico*.

Bologna played its part in the political battles of the time as one of the principal cities of the Lombard League. In the 1200s it was occupied with the typical factional strife, in which the local Guelphs (the Geremei) usually had the better of it over the Ghibellines (the Lambertazzi). The Guelph merchants and nobles helped secure the abolition of serfdom in Bologna's territory by the Paradisius law of 1256, and warred continuously with Ghibelline Modena. Bologna defeated that city decisively at the Battle of Fossalta in 1249, capturing the talented Enzo, King of Sardinia and natural son of Emperor Frederick II. Defying custom, Bologna refused to ransom him and kept him locked up until he died in 1272.

Soon after, Bologna formally became part of the Papal States through a legal sleight-of-hand – Pope Gregory X got his supporter Rudolph of Habsburg crowned as Emperor and King of Italy, and in return Rudolph donated Bologna and the Romagna to the papacy.

The popes (now in Avignon) attempted to assert their control in 1327, sending Cardinal Bertrand du Pouget to rule the city. He did his best to destroy the *comune*, abolishing most of its offices and functions, while building a fortress at the Porta Galliera to intimidate the citizens. After only six years he had so infuriated the Bolognesi that they ran him out of town. But, as in so many other cities, the inability of the factions ever to behave themselves made the city ready to hand power to a single boss, a *signore*. The first was a banker, Taddeo Pepoli (1337–47), and when he died his sons shocked the Bolognesi by selling the office to the Visconti of Milan.

The city had bigger things to worry about. The Black Death of 1348 carried off a third of the population, as elsewhere in Italy. Trade was severely disrupted, and the huge spaces enclosed by the newly completed city wall would remain empty for a century or more.

Still, Bologna was worth fighting over. The Visconti ruled through their man Giovanni da Oleggio until 1360, when he was forced to relinquish it to the formidable Gil Albornoz, a veteran of the wars against the Moors in Spain who spent a decade leading armies through Italy trying, with considerable success, to re-establish papal control.

The Bolognesi found their second spell of papal rule no more palatable than the first, and they regained their independence in a revolt of 1376, setting up a council called the 'Sixteen Reformers of the State of Liberty' to govern them. For a while, it worked just fine. As the economy recovered, the Reformers began an ambitious building programme, including many of the public buildings around Piazza Maggiore and San Petronio, a municipal (not a Church) effort that was intended to be the biggest basilica in the world.

Eventually, however, the council and the city came to be dominated by a single family, the Bentivoglio, whose name – which might be translated as either 'Wish-you-well' or 'I-love-you' – contains a good dose of irony either way. Their rule continued the flowering of local culture, despite a sensational family saga of violence, assassination and questionable legitimacy – the paternity of Annibale Bentivoglio was decided by a throw of the dice.

The first Bentivoglio *signore*, Giovanni I, lasted little more than a year before being murdered by a mob (1401–02). His son Anton Galeazzo seized power in 1420, but Pope Martin V eventually forced him out and he too was killed. Another interim of papal predominance and factional strife was resolved in 1445 by bringing Annibale back from exile. He got the knife within a year, but this time the family held on a bit longer. Annibale was followed by another Bentivoglio bastard, Sante (1446–63), and then by the energetic, cultivated and thoroughly tyrannical Giovanni II, who lorded it over the city for 43 years.

Despite the patronage of Giovanni, Bologna had little to contribute to the arts of the Renaissance. In painting, sculpture and architecture, the city took its cues from Florence, and the greatest works are all by outsiders: plenty of Tuscans, notably Jacopo della Quercia, Niccolò dell'Arca from Puglia, the dalle Masegne from Venice and Giovanni da Modena.

THE POPES TAKE OVER In 1506, that most warlike and irascible of popes, Julius II, took time off from browbeating Michelangelo and Raphael to bring a big army over the Apennines to vindicate his claims on the Romagna and Bologna. The Bolognesi, who had had their fill of Bentivoglios, were delighted to see him, and in their enthusiasm they sacked and demolished the Bentivoglio Palace and chased Giovanni out of town. It did not occur to them at the time that they had exchanged a weak local despot for a distant and powerful one. By the time it sunk in, Julius had put an end to Bologna's independence once and for all, and a revolt against him in 1511 was crushed. From then on, the city was ruled by papal legates, with a consultative senate of nobles, and the popes themselves made several lengthy stays.

During one of these, in 1530, Bologna witnessed a turning point in Italian history. The Emperor, Charles V, insisted on being crowned Holy Roman Emperor in its basilica of San Petronio instead of in Rome, which his troops had mercilessly sacked three years previously. Charles (who had been emperor for 11 years but was always too busy for a formal coronation) felt that going to Rome would seem like an act of contrition, and such was the low standing of papal authority that, when he told Pope Clement VII that he 'did not need to seek crowns, but that crowns ran after him', the pope could only agree.

Charles's double coronation, as Emperor (in San Petronio) and King of Italy (in the Palazzo Comunale), was celebrated with tremendous pomp, but it marked the beginning of three centuries of foreign domination in Italy, and the first symptoms of death for the Renaissance. Luigi Barzini notes that from then on the Italians put away their bright clothes and began to wear black in the Spanish style, as if they were in mourning – just as the Fascisti donned black shirts under Mussolini.

In Bologna it was a great age for palace building, as out of the shadow of the Bentivoglio the other families could once more express themselves. But in many ways the century was a disaster for Bologna. The new totalitarian Church that emerged from the Council of Trent (which briefly held its sessions in Bologna) was determined to control every aspect of Italy's intellectual and artistic life, and the cities under its direct control suffered the most. Carlo Borromeo, the grim Svengali of the Counter-Reformation himself, was briefly legate, and he set the tone for the years to come. The university, already something of a backwater (like that of Paris, and many other once-great institutions), was now doomed to increasing senility in an atmosphere of book-burnings, intimidation and the exile, incarceration or killing of humanist scholars. The Inquisition arrived in Bologna in 1553. Two years later the authorities locked up Bologna's Jews in the Ghetto and, after they had squeezed every last penny out of them, they expelled the lot in 1593.

Ironically, this age was also marked by Bologna's only period of prominence in art, as local talent such as the Carracci family and Guido Reni defined a new classicising style in art, one entirely in tune with the dictates of the Counter-Reformation Church. Bologna remained a major art centre for a century, while new churches and monasteries went up all over town. By 1650 there were 96 monastic complexes in Bologna; foreign visitors reported that the city seemed entirely populated by monks and beggars. Times were bad, though never quite as bad as in the papal provinces further south, such as Lazio and Umbria, reduced by the misrule of the clerics to utter penury. Bologna still made a sort of living from textiles and hemp, but carrying the weight of the Church and a decadent nobility, and closed off from the new trade routes and technological advances of northern Europe, the city's economic prospects were nil.

For the next 200 years Bologna had practically no history at all. It slumbered peacefully through the 18th century, and through the big shake-up provided by Napoleon. The Bolognesi surprised even themselves when they started Italy's wave of rebellions in 1831, booting out the papal legate who was, however, soon restored by Austrian troops. They revolted again in 1848. In the last year of papal rule – 1858 – Bologna finally got a railway; that, and the new climate of united Italy, helped get the old town going again. The population doubled before the century was out, in a city that was turning into one of Italy's major industrial centres.

MODERN BOLOGNA In the 19th century Bologna was the birthplace of Guglielmo Marconi, who carried out his first experiments with radio at the Villa Griffone, and of composer Ottorino Respighi (1879–1936), whose music was popularised abroad by fellow Emilian Arturo Toscanini.

It was also at this time that Bologna took the lead in the Italian socialist movement, building strong industrial unions in town and prosperous rural co-operatives on the plains – as well as in enduring the brunt of the Fascist reaction in the 20th century. In 1944, Bologna participated fully in the big wave of courageous strikes meant to slow down the Fascist war effort, and partisan activity in the hinterlands led to brutal Nazi reprisals such as the massacre at Marzabotto. Although it was on the 'Gothic Line', where the Germans held the Allies at bay in 1944–45, and the scene of fervid partisan activity, including pitched battles between the Nazis and partisan brigades, Bologna emerged from the war relatively unscathed.

After the war, Bologna's Communists got their chance to run the city, and they made the most of it. An excellent mayor, Giuseppe Dozza, made the city the showcase of Italy's brand of Communism, providing the most honest, efficient and innovative municipal government in the country. Dozza improved public transport and health care, while leading the nation in building new schools, housing and other facilities – even municipal launderettes.

The new housing projects may have been 'vomit-coloured cement barracks', as conservative historian Indro Montanelli put it, but that after all was the style of the time, and in the middle of a huge housing crisis the most important thing, as everywhere else in Europe, was getting something built. Nevertheless, the shabby planning that gave the city its distinctly unpleasant band of sprawl is something that Bologna, like most prosperous Italian cities, is going to have to live with for a long time.

Like the rest of Italy, Bologna in the late 1960s and 70s had more than its share of troubles. Italy was making a sharp left turn. While the Communist vote increased greatly in local and national elections, a younger generation was forsaking the PCI for more radical alternatives. The climax of a wave of student agitation in Bologna came in March 1977, when the shooting of a demonstrator by the police led to riots.

In these Anni di Piombo, the 'Years of Lead', shadowy rightist groups in the armed forces and security police infiltrated and manipulated the so-called Red Brigade and other operations, along with radical rightist groups they controlled directly, into fomenting terrorism, with the hope of destabilising democracy and perhaps even staging a coup.

Now that it's over, most Italians would like to forget all about the Anni di Piombo. Others, however, are still trying to get to the bottom of this murky business. There's even a word, *dietrologia* (the study of who was *dietro*, or 'behind', the attacks), to describe the conspiracy theories and speculation about which national figures and institutions were directly involved. Investigations have established the existence of Operation Gladio, in which the infamous P2 'masonic lodge' led by Licio Gelli (a wartime fascist and an officer in the SS at the war's end, who pulled a lot of strings in Italy for decades afterwards thanks to his co-operation with the CIA) co-ordinated the terrorist effort, along with the leaders of the Italian secret service, the SID (almost all of whom were P2 members, along with many army chiefs, business leaders and Christian Democrat politicians) and elements in the CIA.

Bologna's Communists, labour leaders and the city itself were prime targets. In 1974 the terrorists blew up a Bologna–Florence train, killing 12 and wounding 105. In 1978 they assassinated Prime Minister Aldo Moro, who favoured bringing the Communists into the government coalition, and two years later made their bloodiest strike ever – the bomb in Bologna's Stazione Centrale which killed 85 people and wounded more than 200 on 2 August 1980.

Things gradually calmed down after that – the ghouls had made their point. Bologna's earnest Reds soldiered on, despite a national 'reform' that severely limited local government powers in the 1970s. Even the most useful regimes, however, grow old and tired, and in the 1990s many Bolognesi became increasingly discontented with the way their city was moving; a sharp increase in crime and drug addiction, and a general decline in the quality of life were the main concerns (spray-paint graffiti is always an indicator of urban disarray, and Bologna had more of it than almost any Italian city). Many also found the city government becoming too rigid, bureaucratic and out of touch with the citizens. The 'catastrophe', as local leftists call it, came in the mayoral election of 1998, when a conservative businessman and head of the Chamber of Commerce named Giorgio Guazzaloca squeaked in with 50.69% of the vote.

The right crowed and cackled across Italy. The great Red bastion had capitulated, and in their enthusiasm some even spoke of the election as the 'fall of the Berlin Wall'. Guazzaloca, who was often compared to New York's Rudy Giuliani, was not quite the bogey that leftists feared. He didn't have much of a detailed programme during the campaign, and his most controversial move was to cut back on the limitations on cars in the *centro storico*, the reversal of a policy that had been expanded since 1972, when Bologna became one of the first cities in Europe to create pedestrian zones and limit traffic in the centre.

Bologna soon tired of its flirtation with conservatism, and the left climbed back into power in 2004, where they have remained ever since. Many came to regret it, when Mayor Flavio Delbono, a much-touted academic who also held the Chair of Economics at Bologna's University, got nabbed in one of Italy's more colourful recent scandals. 'Cinziagate', so called after Delbono's girlfriend and secretary Cinzia Cracchi, who spilled the beans, told a sordid tale of corruption, fraud and abuse of office that left the proud Bolognesi wondering if their virtuous city had somehow overnight turned into Naples. Delbono was forced out of office in 2010, and Italy's forgiving justice system let him off with only 40 days in jail. His replacement, centre-left mayor Virginio Merola, won a second five-year term in 2016.

Bologna, in its quiet way, takes very good care of itself. One of the wealthiest cities in Europe, and one where the quality of life is constantly rated among the very highest, Bologna bases its prosperity not so much on the university and research spin-offs as a good old-fashioned industrial base. The metro population of just over half a million produces Lamborghini cars and Ducati motorcycles. It's big in high-tech machinery, foodstuffs, clothing, printing and publishing, not to mention insurance and banking. Firms headquartered here range from big fashion names (Bruno Magli, La Perla and Mandarina Duck) to Italy's biggest supermarket chain which, fittingly for Bologna Rossa, is the Coop. And now it has the world's first theme park anywhere dedicated to its great passion: food.

GREATER BOLOGNA

For listings, see pages 72–3 & 75–6

Where to stay

1	4 Viale Masini Design Hotel.................F4
2	Boutique Hotel Calzavecchio............A7
3	Centro Turistico Città di Bologna.....H2
4	Hotel Villa Azzura............................H6
5	Palazzo Trevi
	Charming House..........................E5
6	Santo Stefano...................................F6
7	Touring...E6
8	We_Bologna Hostel...........................E3

Off map

	Casa Fluò Relais................................E7
	Relais Bellaria Hotel & Congressi......H7

Where to eat and drink

9	All'Osteria Bottega...........................E5
10	Antica Trattoria del Cacciatore..........A4
11	Cremeria Santo Stefano......................F6
12	Danilo e Patrizia...............................H3
13	Drogheria della Rosa...........................F5
14	Il Gelatauro.....................................F5
15	Osteria al 15....................................E6
16	Ranzani 13..G4
17	Ristorante Pizzeria Caruso.................H5
18	Trattoria Meloncello..........................C6

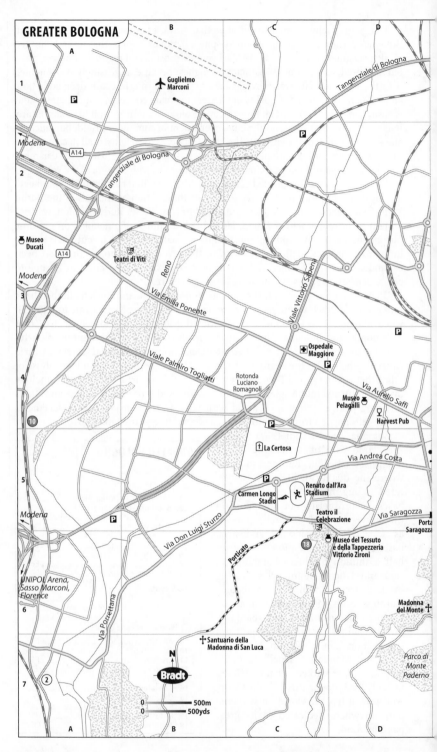

GREATER BOLOGNA

Guglielmo Marconi

Tangenziale di Bologna

Modena

A14

Trangenziale di Bologna

Museo Ducati

A14

Modena

Teatri di Viti

Reno

Via Emilia Ponente

Viale Vittorio Sabena

Ospedale Maggiore

Via Aurelio Saffi

Viale Palmiro Togliatti

Rotonda Luciano Romagnoli

Museo Pelagalli

Harvest Pub

La Certosa

Via Andrea Costa

Carmen Longo Stadio

Renato dall'Ara Stadium

Via Saragozza

Porta Saragozza

Teatro il Celebrazione

Modena

Museo del Tessuto e della Tappezzeria Vittorio Zironi

Via Don Luigi Sturzo

UNIPOL Arena, Sasso Marconi, Florence

Porticato

Madonna del Monte

Via Porrettana

Santuario della Madonna di San Luca

Parco di Monte Paderno

N

Bradt

0 — 500m
0 — 500yds

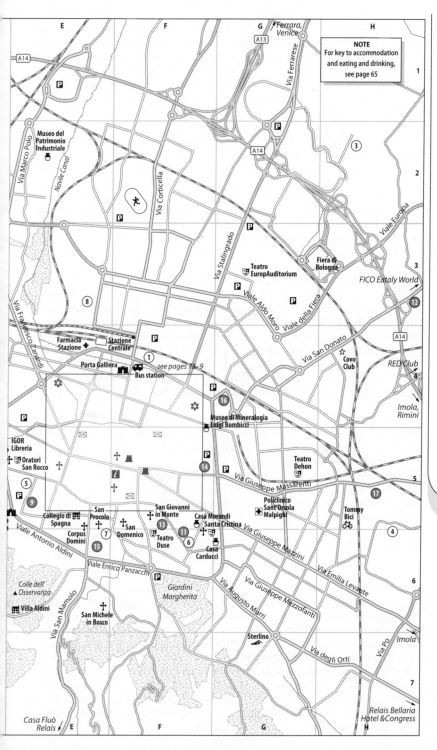

NOTE
For key to accommodation
and eating and drinking,
see page 65

Ferrara,
Venice
A13
Via Ferrarese

A14

Via Marco Polo

Museo del
Patrimonio
Industriale

Navile Canal

Via Corticella

Viale Europa

Via Stalingrado

Teatro
EuropAuditorium

Fiera di
Bologna

FICO Eataly World

Viale Aldo Moro

Viale della Fiera

Via Francesco Zanardi

Farmacia
Stazione

Stazione
Centrale

Via San Donato

A14

Covo
Club

RED Club

Porta Galliera

Bus station

see pages 78–9

Imola,
Rimini

Museo di Mineralogia
Luigi Bombicci

Teatro
Dehon

IGOR
Libreria

Oratori
San Rocco

Via Giuseppe Massarenti

Policlinico
Sant'Orsola
Malpighi

Collegio di
Spagna

San
Procolo

San Giovanni
in Monte

Casa Morandi

Tommy
Bici

San
Domenico

Santa Cristina

Via Giuseppe Mazzini

Corpus
Domini

Teatro
Duse

Casa
Carducci

Via Emilia Levante

Viale Antonio Aldini

Viale Enrico Panzacchi

Colle dell'
Osservanza

Villa Aldini

Via San Mamolo

San Michele
in Bosco

Giardini
Margherita

Via Augusto Murri

Via Giuseppe Mezzofanti

Imola

Sterlino

Via degli Orti

Via Po

Casa Fluò
Relais

Relais Bellaria
Hotel &Congress

In short, a little bit of everything, where no one corporation or industry dominates; with more than 16,000 businesses Bologna ranks third in Italy, behind only the much bigger cities Milan and Rome. Despite the current economic hard times, the virtuous old post-war model hangs on: economic diversity, medium and small enterprises, enlightened labour relations and strong social policy. Opportunity and quality of life have made the city a very attractive destination. Over 15% of Bolognesi are immigrants, and they come from all over the world, with no more than a few thousand from any one country.

Many people, in Italy and beyond, think of Bologna as a stolid, fusty, highbrow sort of town, its endless arcades reminiscent of a university cloister. Serious culture is certainly well served here. Few cities in the world have as many imposing theatres, galleries and concert halls, or such a full schedule of events. But behind the Baroque stage curtain there's a city that does its honest best to stay up to date and relevant. Bologna is known in Italy as a centre for everything trendy and new, from comics to street art to alternative music. The Bolognesi will never let modernity change their city, but they're not too proud to assimilate whatever catches their fancy.

GETTING THERE AND AWAY

BY AIR Bologna's Aeroporto Guglielmo Marconi [66 B1] (w *bologna-airport.it*) is 6km from the city centre. Regular **shuttle buses** (w *aerobus.bo.it*) make a loop, linking the airport to Bologna's Stazione Centrale, with stops at Pontelungo, Ospedale Maggiore and Mille in the city centre. Buses run every 11 minutes between 07.00 and 21.00 (with less frequent services 05.30–07.00 and 21.00–00.15). Allow 20 minutes, but during peak traffic it can take an hour. Tickets cost €6 each way and can be purchased online or at the automatic machines at the airport or train station. **Taxis** (page 70) are available outside the arrivals hall and cost about €15 to central Bologna.

BY RAIL All trains arrive at the Stazione Centrale [67 E4], although high-speed (Alta Velocità) services arrive in the new section, Bologna Centrale AV, located under the old station and linked by walkways and escalators. For details of getting to Bologna by train, see pages 33–4.

Trains from Bologna to other towns in Emilia-Romagna: Reggio Emilia (*54/ day; 19mins*); Modena (*54/day; 17mins*); Parma (*50/day; 46mins*); Ferrara (*26/day; 20mins*); Rimini (*29/day; 1hr 30mins*); Ravenna (*15/day; 1hr 19mins*); Forlì (*33/ day; 31mins*).

BY CAR OR BUS For details, see pages 34 and 38.

ORIENTATION

The *autostrade* approaching Bologna skirt the city to the north in a ring road, the *tangenziale*, which links to most major routes. At Bologna, the A1 from Milan leaves the Via Emilia and turns south to Florence, but the A14 continues on to Ravenna and Rimini. The A13 runs north from Bologna to Ferrara and Padua.

Within the *tangenziale*, the state roads to Bologna join an inner ring road, although the SS9/Via Emilia still runs through the city centre. The SS64 (or Via Stalingrado, inside the *tangenziale*) branches off north for Ferrara, while the SS253 runs east for Ravenna and the SS64 goes south to Pistoia and the SS65 to Florence. Since the centre is closed to traffic (page 70), you'll be routed around it on the ring of boulevards that follow the course of the demolished city walls, the *circla* or *corona semicentrale*.

The award-winning non-profit Associazione Succede Sola a Bologna, or the 'It Only Happens in Bologna Association' (w *succedesoloabologna.it*) was founded in 2010 to spread the members' love of their city and promote its art, architecture, culture and dialect. They run a range of guided tours in several languages designed for both the hearing and deaf, and recently raised more than €200,000 for repairs to San Petronio.

At the very centre is Bologna's heart, Piazza Maggiore, in a grid of streets dating from its Roman foundations. Via dell'Indipendenza links Piazza Maggiore to the train and bus stations and just north of the big square forms the **T-Zone** with Bologna's other main shopping streets, Via Rizzo (east) and Via Ugo Bassi (west), where from 08.00 on Saturdays until 22.00 on Sundays and holidays, it's pedestrians and bicycles only.

GETTING AROUND

Much of Bologna is easily explored on foot, with the main sights a short distance from the Piazza Maggiore; other advantages are the city's flatness and its famous porticoes that shelter pedestrians from the rain and sun.

BY BUS Bologna's very efficient bus system, TPER, is an excellent way to get around the city. All the routes and their hours may be found on its website (w *tper.it*). Single tickets cost €1.30, or €1.50 if purchased on the bus (no change given) for 75 minutes of travel; day tickets are €5, and a city pass good for ten trips costs €12. You can buy tickets from the red machines near the major stops (*€1.50, exact change only*), or pick up tickets and passes at the TPER kiosks around town. Board the bus through the front or back doors (the middle door is for descending, although it can be used if the bus is really crowded) and validate your ticket in the machines.

The **City Red Bus** (w *cityredbus.com; adults €14, ages 6–10 €7, under 6s €3*) offers hop-on, hop-off tours to 13 stops around the main city sights of Bologna, running every 30–45 minutes, with main stops at Piazza Maggiore and Stazione Centrale. The same company runs the **San Luca Express Bus** (*adult return €10, ages 6–10 €5, under 5s €3*) up to the Madonna di San Luca church between Piazza Maggiore and San Luca at weekends in January and February, and daily in March–December. A combined City Red Bus–San Luca Express ticket is also available (*adult €21, ages 6–10 €10, under 6s €3*).

BY BICYCLE Flat, with limited traffic in the centre, and with miles of bike paths, Bologna was made for cycling. There's no city rental scheme, but you can hire wheels at several locations.

Dynamo Velostation [79 E1] Via Indipendenza 71/Z; ☏ 051 1990 0462; w dynamo. bo.it; ⊕ 06.30–22.30 Mon–Thu, 06.30–00.30 Fri, 07.30–00.30 Sat, 08.30–22.30 Sun. Every city should have a Dynamo, a combo bike centre, music bar (with frequent DJ sets) & cultural centre. 5mins' walk from Stazione Centrale, it occupies a former garage & air-raid shelter under the Parco della Montagnola. It rents out city & mountain bikes (*€5/2hrs, €8/half-day, €15/24hrs, €24/48hrs, €30/72hrs*), as well as cargo bikes, e-bikes & wheelchair transporting bikes. Child seats are free, & you can book 2hr guided tours (*€25*) or self-guided tours (*€10*) online. Dynamo is also a bike parking garage & repair shop, & daytime left-luggage facility (€5).

Bike in Bo [79 E1] Via Indipendenza 69/a; m 347 001 7996; w bikeinbo.it; ⏰ 08.30–20.30 daily. Offers bike rentals in the shop or will deliver your bike to your accommodation for a small fee. Prices, including helmet, raincoat & bike path map, are €5/2hrs (*child's bike €4*), €15/day (*€20 if delivered, child's bike €11*) & €58/week (*€65 if delivered, child's bike €50*). Child seats on an adult bike are €2. It also offers 2hr guided tours of Bologna with a guide & radio guide for €35, including bike rental (book online).

Tommy Bici [67 H5] Via Azzurra 36/B; ☎ 051 341218; w tommybici.com; ⏰ 09.00–19.00 Mon–Fri, 09.00–noon Sat. Specialist that rents city, mountain, racing or e-bikes. Prices for a city bike are €10/half-day & €20/whole day; half price for a child's bike.

BY TAXI Taxis cannot be hailed on the street but there are stands at Piazza Maggiore [66 D6], the Stazione Centrale [79 E4] and in a few other key locations. The city has two 24-hour radio taxi companies, both of which have taxis equipped for users of wheelchairs: **COTABO** (☎ *051 372727*) and **Taxi CAT** (☎ *051 4590*).

BY CAR Much of the city centre is a Zona Traffico Limitato (ZTL), where traffic is restricted from 07.00 to 20.00 and controlled by cameras posted at all access roads. If you're driving and staying in a hotel or bed and breakfast within the ZTL, the management will assist you with the registration of your car licence plate number. A day pass costs €9 and is valid 24 hours for parking in all pay parking areas (marked by blue lines) in the city.

Otherwise, the best thing is to leave your car in one of the many car parks on the periphery, all of which are connected by bus to the centre; you'll find a complete list on the tourist office's website (w *bolognawelcome.com*). The easiest way to find a car park, prices and to pay for parking in the blue lines is with the MyCicero app (w *mycicero.eu*).

TOURIST INFORMATION

Bologna Welcome [78 D6] Piazza Maggiore 1; ☎ 051 658 3111/3190; w bolognawelcome.com; ⏰ 09.00–19.00 Mon–Sat, 10.00–17.00 Sun & holidays. The city's main tourist office is extremely helpful, & can book hotels, make restaurant or city tour reservations, arrange airline tickets, & make train or ferry reservations. Also sells advance tickets to cultural & sporting events.

Bologna Welcome (airport) [66 B1] Ground floor; ☎ 051 647 2113; ⏰ 09.00–19.30 Mon–Sat, 09.00–17.00 Sun & holidays. Besides offering information & maps, this office sells tickets to trains, cultural & sporting events & can make hotel, restaurant & city tour reservations.

 WHERE TO STAY

Accommodation in Bologna ranges from boutique hotels in the centre and large modern hotels on the outskirts, with a mainly business clientele bound to the city's many trade fairs; during major ones (Cosmoprof/Cosmopack in mid-March, Children's Book Fair in early April, Cersaie in late September, and the Motorshow in early December), room rates often soar – that is if you can find one. You'll probably want to stay in the historic centre, in walking distance of the sights (though beware Bologna can be noisy at night, so you may want to request a courtyard rather than a front room). If you're driving, you might consider avoiding the complications of the ZTL and expense of parking garages by staying on the fringes and taking the bus into town.

Prices are usually at their lowest at weekends, and in February and August; if you arrive without a reservation, the Bologna Welcome Tourist office (page 70) has a free room-finding service. If you want to stay more than a few days, check its online list of apartments, holiday homes and studios.

CENTRE: AROUND PIAZZA MAGGIORE & THE TWO TOWERS

🏠 **Art Hotel Orologio** [78 D6] (40 rooms) Via IV Novembre 10; 📞051 745 7411; bolognarthotels.it/en/hotel-orologio. Charming 3-star boutique hotel located just behind the clocktower of the Palazzo d'Accursio in a pedestrian zone, although it does have a private garage nearby where you can arrange to leave a car. Friendly staff, free bikes & buffet b/fast are all part of the deal. €€€€€

🏠 **Corona d'Oro** [79 E5] (40 rooms) Via Oberdan 12; 📞051 745 7611; w hco.it. This swish & popular hotel occupies a palazzo from 1300 on a narrow cobbled street. Some rooms have coffered ceilings & frescoes, & the newly restored *fin de siècle* reception hall under a glass cupola makes a delightful setting for the generous b/fast buffet & *aperitivi* in the evening. B/fast inc. €€€€€

🏠 **Torre Prendiparte** [79 E5] (1 suite) Via Sant'Alò 7; m 335 561 6858; w prendiparte.it. This is your chance to sleep in a medieval skyscraper, the 60m Torre Prendiparte (only the Torre Asinelli is taller). The first 2 floors, linked by a 16th-century spiral stair built in the 2m-thick walls, form a romantic antique-furnished suite. Stays include a tour to the top of the tower with its spectacular views, & a welcome drink with owner, Matteo Giovanardi. For a special occasion, Matteo can arrange a private tête-à-tête candlelit gourmet dinner, complete with live music. €500, b/fast inc €€€€€

🏠 **Al Cappello Rosso** [78 C6] (33 rooms) Via Fusari 9; 📞051 261891; w alcappellorosso.it. Another luxurious central hotel, named for the red hat of Cardinal Albornoz who first requisitioned the building to lodge the builders of Bologna's cathedral in 1375. In the 1800s it became an inn proper, & is now one of the city's smartest hotels. Pay a bit more for a room designed in conjunction with the Biografilm Festival: rooms dedicated to composer John Cage, fashion designer Elsa Schiaparelli, the Typewriter, comic strips, etc. It also has a garage & several apts & studios to let in the vicinity. €€€€–€€€€€

🏠 **Commercianti** [78 D6] (44 rooms) Via de' Pignattari 11; 📞051 745 7511; w en.art-hotel-commercianti.com. In the shadow of San Petronio, this atmospheric, award-winning hotel in an 11th–13th-century palazzo couldn't be more central. Some of the pricier rooms & romantic suites on the top floors have fascinating histories, as well as frescoes & views. Staff & the buffet b/fast (inc) are exceptional. Guests can pedal away on free bikes, & parking is available by reservation (from €28/day). It also has 3 luxury apts nearby sleeping 4. €€€€–€€€€€

🏠 **Albergo delle Drapperie** [79 E6] (20 rooms) Via Drapperie 5; 📞051 223995; w albergodrapperie.com. On a pedestrian lane near the Mercato di Mezzo, only 3mins from Piazza Maggiore, this little boutique hotel has richly coloured rooms, some with decorated ceilings, in a 19th-century building. The staff couldn't be nicer, & it serves up a good Italian continental b/fast (inc). €€€€

🏠 **B&B Piazza Grande** [78 D6] (3 rooms) Via Massimo D'Azeglio 5; m 389 318 3509. Tidy en-suite dbls & trpls a stone's throw from Piazza Maggiore, run by a friendly couple. Good Wi-Fi, plus self-serve b/fast from a well-stocked kitchen. €€€

🏠 **Centrale** [78 C5] (25 rooms) Via della Zecca 2; 📞051 006 3937; w albergocentralebologna.it. A friendly 2-star hotel in an old palazzo in the centre of the action. Rooms on the 3rd & 4th floors have views over the roofs of Bologna, all have free Wi-Fi & AC, & some sleep up to 5, though not all are en suite. It also rents rooms out for day use (🕐 10.00–17.00). B/fast inc. €€€

🏠 **Roma** [78 D6] (85 rooms) Via Massimo D'Azeglio 9; 📞051 226322; w hotelroma.biz. An old-fashioned 3-star hotel in the medieval *centro storico*, 1min from Piazza Maggiore. Large sound-proofed rooms with floral wallpaper & fabrics, & a convenient laundry service & parking. B/fast inc. €€€

NORTH/NORTHWEST: TOWARDS STAZIONE CENTRALE

🏠 **Grand Hotel Majestic già Baglioni** [78 D5] (109 rooms) Via dell'Indipendenza 8; 📞051 225445;

3

w grandhotelmajestic.duetorrihotels.com. A few steps from Piazza Maggiore, the opulent 16th-century Palazzo Ghisleri-Fava was converted into a hotel in 1912 & is deeply embedded in Bologna's history (Morandi's paintings were first exhibited here, in 1914; the Futurists hung out in the retro Café Marinetti, & the guest list includes the likes of Clark Gable, Frank Sinatra, Ava Gardner, the Dalai Lama, Princess Diana & Paul McCartney, the latter 2 checking into the truly majestic Royal Giuseppe Verdi Suite). Antiques line the rooms, each different & there's an underground garage, & a beautiful restaurant frescoed by the Carracci which specialises in Bolognese cuisine. €€€€€

🏠 I Portici [79 E1] (89 rooms) Via Indipendenza 69; ☎ 051 42185; w iporticihotel.com. Located in between the station & Piazza Maggiore, this swanky 4-star hotel occupies part of the Palazzo Maccaferri, with a pretty winter garden & Michelin-star restaurant (page 74). Choose between luminous minimalist contemporary or Liberty-style rooms with frescoes & ceiling decorations, all with superb beds & showers. Excellent b/fast €15. €€€€€

🏠 Royal Hotel Carlton [78 D1] (236 rooms) Via Montebello 8; ☎ 051 249361; w royalhotelcarltonbologna.com. Comfortable, contemporary hotel 5mins from the station, with one of the best spas in the city, good restaurant & a garden with a cocktail pagoda, plus shuttles to major events at the Fiera. B/fast inc. €€€€€

🏠 Hotel Internazionale [78 D2] (126 rooms) Via Indipendenza 60; ☎ 051 245544; w hotelinternazionalebologna.com. An 8min walk from the Stazione Centrale, this reliable mid-range choice is popular with both pleasure & business travellers (there are handy shuttles to the Fiera di Bologna [67 G3] during major events). The restaurant will cater for gluten-free & vegan diets, & packages using the spa in the Internazionale's sister establishment, the Royal Hotel Carlton, are available, as well as special w/end, last-minute & advance rates. B/fast inc. €€€–€€€€€

🏠 4 Viale Masini Design Hotel [67 F4] (82 rooms) 4 Viale Masini; ☎ 051 255035; w 4vialemasini.com. Chic contemporary-styled hotel with a lounge bar 200m from the Stazione Centrale on the busy boulevard that circles the *centro storico*; an underground garage makes it a good bet for motorists. Piazza Maggiore is a 15min walk. B/fast inc. €€€–€€€€

🏠 Bologna Center Town [78 B3] (3 rooms) Via Guglielmo Marconi 28; m 331 273 1318; w bolognacentertown.com. A 10min walk from Piazza Maggiore, this B&B has large rooms & big beds & shared but immaculate bathrooms. Mario, the charming owner, knows Bologna well. B/fast inc. €€€

🏠 Hotel Atlantic [78 D2] (24 rooms) Via Galliera 46; ☎ 051 248488; w hotelatlanticbologna.it. Cosy little bargain midway between the station & Piazza Maggiore, with simple but tidy rooms & caring, helpful staff. B/fast inc. €€–€€€

🏠 Hotel Paradise [79 E3] (18 rooms) Vicolo Cattani 7; ☎ 051 231792; w hotelparadisebologna.it. Perhaps not quite everyone's vision of paradise, but a cheap & cheerful choice on a quiet side street, only minutes from Piazza Maggiore, with some trpl rooms & apts in the annex. Friendly staff, & good ample b/fast inc. €€–€€€

🏠 We_Bologna Hostel [67 E3] (62 rooms) Via de' Carracci 69/14; ☎ 051 039 7900; w we-gastameco.com. Located north of the train station, in the former railway workers' dormitory, AC en-suite twins & quads. Kids welcome. €

NORTHEAST: AROUND THE UNIVERSITY

🏠 Casa Bertagni [79 H3] (3 rooms) Via G B De Rolandis 7; m 346 323 9893; w casabertagni.it. Local architect Guido Carlo Vincenzi has lovingly converted his family home into a boutique guesthouse combining antiques & contemporary styling, with en-suite dbls, all equipped with smart TVs & herbal tea pantries (the pick of the 3 is Temperance, with private whirlpool bath & door into the garden). Exceptional b/fasts (*inc*) are served around the communal table in the designer kitchen. €€€€–€€€€€

🏠 Albergo Rossini 1936 [79 G5] (20 rooms) Via dei Bibiena 11; ☎ 051 232412; w mchotels.it/albergorossini. This friendly 2-star hotel, 2mins from the university, offers modern en-suite rooms, complete with minibars & basic kitchen facilities, making it a good bet for families. €€€

🏠 Casa Ilaria [79 G4] (3 rooms) Largo Respighi 8; ☎ 051 412 4760; w casailaria.com. Very welcoming B&B run by chef Tiziana, not far from the Two Towers, with airy dbl rooms (1 sleeping up to 4 for families) & a professional kitchen that guests can use; cookery lessons & cooking parties also available. Minimum stay 3 nights; b/fast inc. €€€

🏠 **Ostello Dopa** [79 G3] (7 rooms) Via Irnerio 41; 📞051 095 2461; w dopahostel.com. New hip hostel located in a 19th-century building, with everything from private en-suite dbls to 8-bed shared dorms & 6-bed dorms for women only. Bike rentals, book swaps, AC, free Wi-Fi, fully equipped kitchen all included. Dbls inc b/fast €€; dorm beds inc b/fast. €

SOUTH/SOUTHEAST: AROUND SAN DOMENICO & SANTO STEFANO

🏠 **Antica Casa Zucchini** [79 G7] (3 rooms) Via Santo Stefano 36; m 347 911 0731; w anticacasazucchini.it. Near the church of Santo Stefano, this well-preserved Renaissance-era house has a beautiful 18th-century stair & stunning portal & door, said to have originally graced the demolished Bentivoglio palace. Rooms combine high frescoed ceilings & antiques with the mod cons, & there's a charming library guests are welcome to use. B/fast inc. €€€€–€€€€€

🏠 **B&B Farini 26** [79 F7] (4 rooms) Via Farini 26; m 335 636 5930; w bnbfarini26.com. Spacious B&B rooms in a historic building not far from Piazza Maggiore, surrounded by some of the city's best boutiques. Some rooms en suite & some not, but there's a super-friendly & helpful staff, who serve a delicious continental b/fast on elegant porcelain. €€€€

🏠 **Santo Stefano** [67 F6] (13 rooms) Via Santo Stefano 84; 📞051 308458; w bedandbreakfastsantostefano.com. Cool, contemporary-styled AC rooms & suites a short walk from the Giardini Margherita; big buffet b/fast. €€€–€€€€

🏠 **Touring** [67 E6] (39 rooms) Via Mattuiani 1/2; 📞051 584305; w hoteltouring.it. On the corner of Piazza de' Tribunale, this is 1 of the city's nicest 3-star hotels with comfortable rooms & a parking garage. The Terrazza Mattuiani lounge bar & summer jacuzzi on the roof offer fine views over the city centre, & guests can pedal away on a hotel bike. €€€

WEST OF PIAZZA MAGGIORE TOWARDS SAN FRANCESCO

🏠 **Hotel Novecento** [78 C6] (28 rooms) Piazza Galileo 4/3; 📞051 745 7311; w bolognarthotels.it/en/hotel-novecento.

Glamorous 4-star hotel designed in the 1930s Viennese Secessionist style, only 2mins from Piazza Maggiore. The lavish b/fast (*inc*) is part of the charm. €€€€–€€€€€

🏠 **Palazzo Trevi Charming House** [67 E5] (6 rooms) Via Frassinago 31; 📞051 580230; w palazzotrevi.it. Designer rooms in pale woods & cream tones, with a wonderful staff, buffet b/fast & a terrace for eating it alfresco on fine days. Very near San Francesco. 2 nights min stay; b/fast inc. €€€€

🏠 **Casa della Zia** [78 A6] (3 rooms) Via Nosadella 19; 📞051 716 2926; w 3bnb.it/bed-and-breakfast-bologna-centro-casa-della-zia. If you don't have your own relatives to visit in Bologna, the 'Aunt's house' B&B just south of San Francesco, a 10min walk to Piazza Maggiore, is the next best thing. 2 of the en-suite rooms have colourful Murano light fixtures; another has a private terrace. B/fast inc. €€

OUTSIDE THE CENTRE

🏠 **Casa Fluò Relais** [67 E7] (4 rooms) Via di Paderno 9; 📞051 589484; w casafluo.it. In the quiet of the Bolognese hills, this B&B of unusual name (derived from the discovery here in the 17th century of a phosphorescent stone) is only 10mins from the centre by bus 52 from Piazza Cavour. Each room comes with its own scent, colour & unique pieces & docking stations. The attic room can sleep 2 children & 2 adults. Actor, director & owner Angelica Zanardi also runs the nearby Fienile Fluò, with a small theatre & workshops (notably morning Qigong) in a former hay loft, which also hosts concerts, dance & other performances; the restaurant features farm-fresh ingredients & produces its own La Rovere Colli di Paderno wine. B/fast inc. €€€€

🏠 **Relais Bellaria Hotel & Congressi** [67 H7] (108 rooms) Via Altura 11/bis, San Lazzaro di Savena; 📞051 453103; w hotelrelaisbellaria. com. A 20min drive from Bologna centre, this comfortable, modern hotel set in a park has well-equipped rooms & an outdoor pool, fitness room, free parking, & a good restaurant that will prepare vegan, vegetarian & gluten-free menus. On Fri nights it hosts excellent live blues sessions with a buffet dinner that attracts punters from the city. B/fast inc. €€€

🏠 **Boutique Hotel Calzavecchio** [66 A7] (80 rooms) Via Calzavecchio 1, Casalecchio di Reno;

\051 376 1616; w hotelcalzavecchio.eu. Recently renovated, this is a comfortable, convenient choice for motorists (it's near a major *autostrada* junction) with free parking, but only 2km from the Sanctuary of the Madonna di San Luca & a few mins' walk from a train station (on the Bologna–Porretta Terme line) or bus stop into city centre. Good restaurant, too, with roots that go back 400 years; try its speciality, Angus beef *tagliata* in a pistachio crust seasoned with balsamic vinegar. Prices (*b/fast inc*) depend very much on events, but generally plunge at w/ends. **€€–€€€€€**

🏠 **Hotel Villa Azzurra** [67 H6] (9 rooms) Viale Felsina 49; \051 535460; w hotelvillaazzurra. com. Simple, tidy rooms 3km east of the centre (linked by frequent bus 37 from Stazione Centrale) in a 19th-century villa with a shady garden, free parking & friendly owners, who offer 24hr check-in. B/fast inc. **€€**

🏠 **Centro Turistico Città di Bologna** [67 H2] (50 bungalows) Via Romita 12/4a; \051 325016; w hotelcamping.com. Northeast of centre (15mins by bus 68 from the coach station), this basic complex combines a campsite, chalet mobile homes sleeping 2 & bungalows sleeping 4. There's a pool open Jun–mid-Sep, bar, restaurant & pizzeria. **€**

✖ WHERE TO EAT AND DRINK

In Italy's gastronomic capital, eating out is a pleasure whether you plump for a meal in a fancy shrine to *cucina petroniana*, as they call it, or head to one of the city's traditional late-night inns or *osterie*, which grew up over Bologna's millennium of hosting students. It's always best to book to avoid disappointment – the smarter restaurants allow you to do so online. Many close for all or part of August.

CENTRE: AROUND PIAZZA MAGGIORE

✖ **Battibecco** [78 C6] Via Battibecco 4; \051 263579; w battibecco.com; ⏲ closed Sat, Sun lunch. For more than 30 years 1 of the city's gastro-temples located a stone's throw from San Petronio. Battibecco offers Bolognese classics with an elegant twist & delicious fresh seafood in a chic contemporary setting, complete with a wooden ceiling & trompe l'œil backlit wall. Excellent wine list, too. **€€€€€**

✖ **Pappagallo** [79 E6] Piazza delle Mercanzia 3; \051 232807; w alpappagallo.it; ⏲ daily from 11.00. You can join the celebrities or just study the photos of past diners at the most famous restaurant in Bologna, housed in a quattrocento palace & in business since 1919. **€€€€€**

✖ **La Baita Vecchia Malga** [78 D6] Via Pescherie Vecchie 3/A; \051 223940; w vecchiamalganegozi.it; ⏲ 09.00–23.00 Mon–Fri, 09.00–01.00 Sat–Sun. Gorgeous food shop in the heart of the Quadrilatero, but also a lively & atmospheric wine bar offering superb platters of meat & cheese to go with the wine. **€€**

✖ **Pigro Mortadelleria** [78 D6] Via De' Pignattari 1; m 366 508 9699; ⏲ closed Mon, Tue. Friendly & right off Piazza Maggiore, & perfect for the classic Bolognese snack or lunch: genuine mortadella, a choice of breads & glasses of fizzy Franciacorte. **€**

✖ **Zanarini** [78 D7] Piazza Galvani 1; \051 275 0041; ⏲ 06.00–21.00 daily. Located in the Archiginnasio building, this elegant *caffè-pasticceria* with a large terrace in front is where the Bolognese love to meet over b/fast, an exquisite pastry, lunch or cocktail while nibbling the beautiful *aperitivi* buffet (€8). **€**

NORTH/NORTHWEST: TOWARDS STAZIONE CENTRALE

✖ **I Portici** [79 E1] Via Indipendenza 69; \051 42185; w iporticihotel.com; ⏲ eves only, closed Sun & Mon. Chef Agostino Iacobucci from Naples is in charge of this hotel restaurant located in a beautiful setting in a former theatre, with a tinkling piano, superb staff & magnificent *degustazione* menus (land, sea or *Espressione di Agostino Iacobucci*) that have earned it Bologna's only Michelin star, starting at €85. There's also a more affordable bistro on the 2nd floor with a terrace. **€€€€€**

✖ **Caminetto d'Oro** [78 D3] Via de' Falegnami 4; \051 263494; w caminettodoro.it; ⏲ closed Sun & Aug. The 'Golden Chimney' started as a bakery that in 1980 evolved under self-taught chef Maria Di Giandomenico into one of Bologna's best-loved restaurants, a favourite of artists whose works decorate the walls. Still run by her family & talented apprentice, they still make their own bread, pasta & desserts in the old oven. Their *tagliatelle al ragù* is among the best in Bologna & they do delicious things with beef – from raw beef pounded with different dressings to a grilled *bistecca Fiorentina* – but they also have vegetarian choices & a great wine list. €€€€

✖ Diana [78 D3] Via Indipendenza 24; ☎051 231302; w ristorante-diana.it; ⏱ closed Mon. Since the 1920s, this classy restaurant with crisp white tablecloths, mirrors & ornate stucco ceiling has been an institution for properly prepared classics (its tortellini in broth is renowned) but there's always a list of specials, updated daily on its website. The wine list has more than 200 choices. €€€€

✖ Da Bertino [78 A3] Via della Lame 55; ☎051 522230; w ristorantedabertino.it; ⏱ closed Sun. Another family-run institution with an early 1970s décor, Da Bertino is renowned for its *bollito misto al carrello* – a trolley of various meats, potatoes & greens. Even the website looks like it's from the 1970s. €€€

✖ Franco Rossi [78 D4] Via Goito 3; ☎051 238818; w ristorantefrancorossi.it; ⏱ closed Sun. Good enough to get a mention in John Grisham's novel *The Broker*, a pleasant, friendly ambience that makes every customer feel like a VIP. There are 2 menus: traditional Bolognese & seafood. Great wines, some available by the glass. €€€

✖ E' Cucina Leopardi [78 C2] Via G Leopardi 4; ☎051 275 0069; w cesaremarretti.com/e-cucina-leopardi; ⏱ closed mid-Jun–Aug. Near the Cineteca (page 80), this cool restaurant with bicycles hanging from the ceiling is run by Jamie Oliver disciple Cesare Marretti, who offers lovely gourmet market cuisine at fast-food prices. No menu – just choose meat, fish or vegetarian & let the friendly staff bring as many courses as you're up for. Be sure to book. 4-course lunch €20, inc water, glass of wine & coffee; full dinner €30. €€

✖ Trattoria Serghei [79 E3] Via Piella 12; ☎051 233533; ⏱ closed all day Sat, & Sun eve. There are only 35 covers at this welcoming family-run restaurant celebrated for its wonderful pasta dishes, made with grandmotherly care: *tortellini in brodo*, *gramigna con salsiccia* & *tagliatelle al ragù*. €€

✖ Twinside [78 D3] Via de' Falegnami 6; ☎051 991 1797; w caminettodoro.it; ⏱ 12.30–23.30

Mon–Sat. The less-pricey bistro of the Caminetto d'Oro (page 74) has similar lovely food until late for the after-theatre crowd. €€

♟ Galliera 49 [78 D2] Via Galliera 49/B; ☎051 246736; w galliera49.it; ⏱ noon–midnight daily. A must for ice cream lovers – renowned for gorgeous, award-winning fruity granitas. €

NORTHEAST: AROUND THE UNIVERSITY

✖ Alcenero Berberè [79 G5] Via Giuseppe Petroni 9; ☎051 275 9196; w berberepizza.it; ⏱ closed Mon eve. Delicious organic handcrafted pizzas, made from a variety of special flours & changing seasonal ingredients, many in the Slow Food Ark of taste; also delicious set lunches, small plates, organic wines & artisanal beers. €–€€

✖ Ranzani 13 [67 G4] Via Camillo Ranzani 5/12; ☎051 849 3743; w ranzani13.it; ⏱ until 01.00 Tue–Sun, closed Mon, & Sat–Sun lunch. Just outside of the old walls, shabby chic & popular for its pizzas & burgers, & craft beers from around the world. €–€€

✖ Enoteca Storica Faccioli [79 E5] Via Altabella 15/b; m 349 300 2939; w enotecastoricafaccioli.it; ⏱ closed Mon–Wed lunch, Sun exc Oct–Mar. Specialists in organic & biodynamic wines & bubblies from around the world, the refined wine bar was established in 1924 & serves a wide choice of delicious nibbles (*stuzzichi*), *salumi* & cheese platters, & hot & cold dishes & desserts, all carefully sourced from artisanal suppliers. €

✖ Osteria dell'Orsa [79 F4] Via Mentana 1; ☎051 231 576; w osteriadellorsa.com; ⏱ 12.30–midnight. A favourite student beer cellar with OK food, including *piadini* pasta & frites. Get here early, or queue; it doesn't take reservations. €

✖ Tamburini [79 E6] Via Caprarie 1; ☎051 234726; w tamburini.com; ⏱ noon–18.00 daily. A deli filled with meats, cheeses, fresh pasta & prepared dishes, but also a self-service *tavola calda* for lunch, with tables in & out, & wine bar (⏱ *noon–23.30 Mon–Thu, noon–00.30 Fri & Sat, noon–22.30 Sun*). Inexpensive & very popular with the locals. €

♟ Il Gelatauro [67 F5] Via San Vitale 98/b; ☎051 230 049; w ilgelatauro.wordpress.com; ⏱ closed Aug. The 3 Figliomeni brothers, owners of this charming ice cream & pastry shop, hail from Calabria, & their superb *gelato*, granitas and pastries are all packed with the freshness of the south, without any artificial ingredients or colours. Their hot chocolate in winter is famous; in summer they sell *gelato* from the window from midnight until 01.00. €

SOUTH/SOUTHEAST: AROUND SAN DOMENICO & SANTO STEFANO

✖ **Drogheria della Rosa** [67 F5] Via Cartoleria 10; ☎ 051 222 529; w drogheriadellarosa.it. Sit under the portico or amid apothecary jars, books & bottles of fine Emilian wine in an atmospheric old pharmacy. Emanuele Addone, a native of southern Italy, & his staff offer a warm welcome, great atmosphere & great food & wine. No written menu or prices, but expect around €35 pp for a full meal. €€€

✖ **Osteria al 15** [67 E6] Via Mirasole 15; ☎ 051 331 806; ⊕ eves only. Intimate, warm & welcoming, with casual wooden tables under its ceiling collage, super-simpatico waiters, & famous *tortelloni ai carciofi* (artichoke cream pasta). €€€

✖ **Trattoria Meloncello** [66 C6] Via Saragozza 240/a; ☎ 051 614 3947; w trattoriameloncello.it. It might not look like much, but stop off here if you need fortifying before making the trek up the hill to San Luca. Founded in 1918 & renowned throughout the city for its pasta, which comes as close to melting in the mouth as is possible. Lots of locals know how good it is, but vegetarians should stay away. €€€

✖ **La Tua Piadina** [79 G7] Via Borgonuovo 17; ☎ 051 270 959; w latuapiadina.it; ⊕ closed all day Sat, & Sun lunch. Delicious homemade *piadine* & *crescioni* with both fresh meat & vegetarian fillings, with artisanal beers from the White Dog Brewery in Modena. Eat in or take away; perfect for a quick lunch. €

♥ **Cremeria Santo Stefano** [67 F6] Via Santo Stefano 70; ☎ 051 227 045; ⊕ 11.00–23.30 Tue– Sun. Charming, intimate pastry/chocolate shop with only a few tables, but luscious homemade *gelato* & sorbets in unique flavours; try the sublime Brontë pistachio. €

WEST OF PIAZZA MAGGIORE TOWARDS SAN FRANCESCO

✖ **All'Osteria Bottega** [67 E5] Via Santa Caterina 51; ☎ 051 585 111; osteriabottega@ alice.it; ⊕ closed Mon. One of Bologna's best-kept secrets, the little restaurant hidden behind a nondescript store front serves some of

the best food in Emilia-Romagna. Expect top-quality, locally sourced ingredients, & a mania for authenticity few can match. Everything is delicious. €€€€€

✖ **Banco 32** [78 B4] Mercato delle Erbe; ☎ 051 269 522; w banco32.it; ⊕ closed Mon. When you need a change from tortellini, try Bologna's freshest seafood tapas in an informal market atmosphere next to a fish stand. Nibble them with a glass of white wine or concoct a full meal out of the menu of raw or cooked choices on a menu that changes daily: try raw *bonito* with a dried tomato pesto, a perfectly cooked mini tuna steak with asparagus & a sweet wine reduction, or a classic *fritto misto* of prawns, squid & anchovies. Delicious homemade desserts, too, but no reservations; get here early. €€

♥ **Cremeria San Francesco** [78 A5] Piazza San Francesco 1/b; ☎ 051 233 230; ⊕ closed Mon. The place for delicious homemade vegan *gelato* made from almond milk & seasonal ingredients sourced from local farmers. €

OUTSIDE THE CENTRE

✖ **Antica Trattoria del Cacciatore** [66 A4] Via Caduti di Casteldebole 25; ☎ 051 564 203; w ristoranteilcacciatore.com; ⊕ closed Sun eve. Vast rustic establishment north of the centre, near the banks of the River Reno, & founded in the early 1800s for hunters, who would wade here through the shallow river. Well known for its heaving carts of delicious antipasti, side dishes & desserts but also excellent pasta dishes, mushrooms & plenty of game. More than 300 wines. Dine out on the garden veranda in summer (book online). €€€€

✖ **Danilo e Patrizia** [67 H3] Via Pilastro 1; ☎ 051 633 2534; w ristorantedaniloepatrizia.com; ⊕ closed all day Mon, & Sun eve. Northwest of the centre, this restaurant in the Savoia Hotel is run by Danilo & Patrizia, who are passionate for mushrooms & truffles. Expect delicious updated Bolognese cuisine, gorgeous pasta & extensive wine list. Choice of tasting menus including drinks from €35–40. €€€

✖ **Ristorante Pizzeria Caruso** [67 H5] Via del Parco 13 (extension of Via San Vitale, east of centre); ☎ 051 531 341; w ristorantepizzeriacaruso. com; ⊕ closed Mon. Superb Neapolitan-style pizza, as well as pizzas made with kamut & spelt dough for easy digestion, & other dishes from the south, including seafood. Book at w/ends. €€–€€€

TORTELLINI, THE NAVEL OF VENUS

If the first father of the human race was lost for an apple, what would he not have done for a plate of tortellini?

An old saying in Bologna

The Bolognese are not an excitable race, but they go as gaga as Neapolitans on the subject of tortellini. For many, even the university pales before the plump rings of pasta as Bologna's culminating cultural achievement. Men have fought for the honour of tortellini; in the 1920s, when a visiting Venetian dared to insult them, a postman beat him up so badly that one ended up in the hospital and the other in jail (sentenced to six months without tortellini).

They may even be as old as the university; the first reference to 'turtlein', as they are known in Bolognese dialect, goes back to the 12th century when they were given to priests at Christmastide, and to this day no Christmas table in Emilia is complete without a bowl of tortellini in capon broth. A recipe discovered in a 14th-century manuscript prescribes a stuffing similar to the one used today, though with the addition of medicinal herbs.

It has also been revealed that a certain Adelaide, wife of a Bolognese notary, produced in the year 1821 the first canonical tortellini filled with minced ham, veal, mortadella, Parmesan cheese and nutmeg. In 1963, the Accademia del Tortellino was founded to pursue perfection in Adelaide's recipe. Although tortellini machines have simplified the lives of countless Bolognese chefs, connoisseurs disdain them; a handmade *tortellino* contains 20–30% more filling, which is why they cost more.

In Bologna, tortellini have passed beyond the realm of culinary science into myth. Their shape in particular makes the Bolognese go all dewy-eyed, for they are supposedly modelled on a woman's navel, a navel so beautiful that it could belong only to Venus herself. In the 17th century, a Tuscan poet named Ceri wrote a satirical poem telling how the goddess of love stopped at an inn, disguised as a mortal; the cook there had a glimpse of her naked, and was moved to model his pasta on the shape of her navel. In 1925, a play in Bolognese dialect called *The Man Who Invented Tortellini* follows the same theme, only the navel in this case belonged to the wife of the cook's employer. The cook had been found in the wife's bedroom, and he invented tortellini as a love letter.

The official recipe for tortellini, along with Bologna's other most cherished treasures (such as the measure for the canonical width of tagliatelle) is kept closely guarded by the city's Chamber of Commerce in the Palazzo della Mercanzia.

Bologna ENTERTAINMENT AND NIGHTLIFE

3

ENTERTAINMENT AND NIGHTLIFE

Not surprisingly, a thousand-year-old university city like Bologna stays up later than most other Italian cities. People here eat late – often around 22.00 – and there are plenty of bars and cafés open until 03.00. During term time you have only to take a look at posters in the bars around the university to find out about concerts, films, exhibitions, performances and clubs. But even outside term time and the cultural season (September–June) the city goes out of its way to entertain residents and visitors with a range of festivals. The tourist office in Piazza Maggiore sells tickets to most events. For LGBTQ+ Bologna, see the box on page 83.

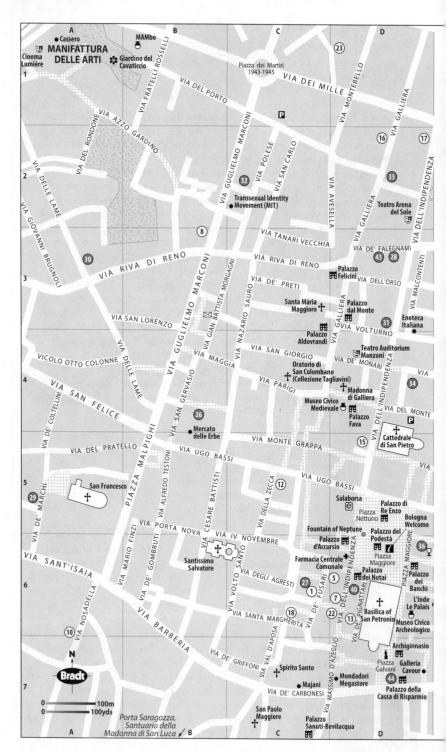

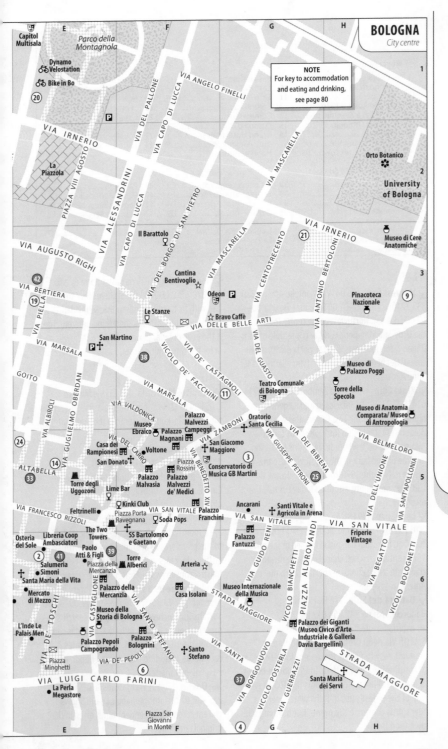

BOLOGNA City centre
For listings, see pages 70–6

⊖ Where to stay

1	Al Cappello Rosso............C6	9	Casa Bertagni......................H3
2	Albergo delle	10	Casa della Zia.....................A6
	Drapperie.........................E6	11	Casa Ilaria...........................G4
3	Albergo Rossini 1936.....G5	12	Centrale................................C5
4	Antica Casa Zucchini....G7	13	Commercianti....................D6
5	Art Hotel Orologio.........D6	14	Corona d'Oro.......................E5
6	B&B Farini 26.......................F7	15	Grand Hotel Majestic
7	B&B Piazza Grande.........D6		già Baglioni.......................D5
8	Bologna Center Town....B3	16	Hotel Atlantic....................D2

17	Hotel Internazionale...D2
18	Hotel Novecento..........C6
19	Hotel Paradise.................E3
20	I Portici...............................E1
21	Ostello Dopa....................G3
22	Roma...................................D6
23	Royal Hotel Carlton.....D1
24	Torre Prendiparte..........E5

⊗ Where to eat and drink

25	Alcenero Berberè...........G5	32	E' Cucina Leopardi.............C2	39	Pappagallo.......................E6
26	Banco 32...............................B4	33	Enoteca Storica Faccioli....E5	40	Pigro Mortadelleria....D6
27	Battibecco..........................C6	34	Franco Rossi......................D4	41	Tamburini..........................E6
28	Caminetto d'Oro.............D3	35	Galliera 49.........................D2	42	Trattoria Serghei.........E3
29	Cremeria San		I Portici.......................(see ip)	43	Twinside.............................D3
	Francesco.........................A5	36	La Baita Vecchia Malga.....D6	44	Zanarini.............................D7
30	Da Bertino..........................A3	37	La Tua Piadina.................G7		
31	Diana...................................D3	38	Osteria dell'Orsa................F4		

BARS

♀ **Harvest Pub** [66 D4] Via Montello 4/a; m 339 832 7210; ⏲ 18.00–01.00 Sun, Tue–Thu, 18.00–02.00 Fri & Sat. Northwest of the centre towards the Ospedale Maggiore, this bar is a temple of craft Italian & foreign beers, & often packed with a jolly crowd. Get here by buses 13, 19 (stop: Saffi) or 14 (stop: Crocetta).

♀ **Kinki Club** [79 F5] Via Zamboni 1; m 338 716 6141; ⏲ 23.20–04.00, closed Aug. Legendary nightspot next to the Two Towers, this was Bologna's first real club (in 1958 it was called 'Whisky a Go Go'), where Jimi Hendrix & Jackson Browne played back in the day; it was also the first in Italy in the 1970s to openly welcome the LGBTQ+ community, although today DJs rule the roost.

♀ **Le Stanze** [79 F3] Via del Borgo San Pietro 1; ☎ 051 228767; w lestanzecafe.it; ⏲ 11.00–01.00 Tue–Sat. Beautiful bar-bistro housed in the private 16th-century frescoed chapel of the Bentivoglio clan, with a vast choice of cocktails from the American-style bar.

♀ **Osteria del Sole** [78 D6] Vicolo Ranocchi 1/d; m 347 968 0171; w osteriadelsole.it; ⏲ 10.30–21.30 Mon–Sat. Off Via degli Orefici in the Quadrilatero (but not easy to find, & there's no sign), this atmospheric osteria with its long wooden tables & memorabilia opened its doors in 1465, & is one of the oldest pubs in Italy. Wine, beer & a few spirits comprise the menu, but bringing your own food is fine.

♀ **Soda Pops** [79 F5] Via Castel Tialto 6; ☎ 051 272 079; ⏲ 23.00–04.00. Students love this disco bar, with its tasty cocktails, music & tiny dance floor; every night there's something different. Tue is the ever-popular Erasmus Night; Sat crowds pack in for the thrumming DJ set.

CINEMAS

🎞 **Capitol Multisala** [67 E1] Via Milazzo 1; ☎ 051 241002; w capitolmultisala.com. Screening the latest blockbusters, some in their original language.

🎞 **Cinema Lumière** [78 A1] Via Azzo Gardino 65; ☎ 051 219 5311; w cinetecadibologna.it. Bologna's very active Cineteca screens films nightly here using old-fashioned projectors, nearly always in the original language with subtitles. There are 2 rooms: the Sala Scorsese is dedicated to the premieres of art films & events with visiting directors, while the Sala Offcinema/ Mastroianni shows historic, restored classic films. The **Cineteca's** Renzo Renzi library is here too (⏲ 13.30–19.30 Tue–Fri, 11.00–17.00 Sat). Its film archive, dedicated to research & preservation, is unique in Italy & includes some 13,000 international films, documentaries & recordings, including everything Chaplin or Pasolini ever made.

🎞 **Odeon** [79 F3] Via Mascarella 3; ☎ 051 227916; w circuitocinemabologna.it. Shows current & some independent films, often in the original language.

CONCERT HALLS

☺ **Conservatorio di Musica G B Martini**
[79 F5] Piazza Rossini 2; ☎051 221483; w consbo.
it. A key reason why UNESCO designated
Bologna a Creative City of Music in 2006 is this
conservatory, founded in 1804; 1 of its first pupils
was Gioacchino Rossini. It occupies the convent
of San Giacomo Maggiore, where free concerts
regularly take place.

☺ **Oratorio di San Rocco** [67 E5] Via Monaldo
Calari 4/2; ☎051 983 474; w circolodellamusica.
it/oratorio-di-san-rocco. This oratory of 1614 was
the headquarters of a pious confraternity that
practised self-flagellation & was wealthy enough
(many of the members were silk-makers) to hire
the top pupils of the Carracci to fresco the walls
with scenes from the life of San Rocco. Restored in
1954, it frequently hosts classical concerts & piano
recitals by the Circolo della Musica di Bologna.

☺ **Santa Cristina** [67 F6] Piazzetta Morandi;
☎051 275 4127; w genusbononiae.it/palazzi/
santa-cristina. Santa Cristina was built in 1602
with exceptional acoustics in its single nave to
highlight the singing of the Camaldolesi nuns.
An *Ascension* by Ludovico Carracci hangs over the
high altar, & there are also works by Guido Reni:
statues of SS Peter & Paul, his only known forays
into sculpture. Restored as a concert venue in
2007, it also hosts the headquarters of the Schola
Gregoriana Benedetto XVI, dedicated to promoting
Gregorian chant in a series of free concerts from
October to May.

☺ **Teatro Auditorium Manzoni** [78 D4] Via Dè
Monari 1; ☎051 261 303; w auditoriumanzoni.it;

ticket office ☺ 15.00–18.30 Tue–Sat, or buy tickets
online via its website. Built in the Liberty style in
1933 as a cinema & theatre, & renovated in 2003, this
is the home of the Orchestra Filarmonia del Teatro
Comunale di Bologna. It hosts a full programme of
classical music, dance, jazz, rock & pop including
everyone from the Kelemen Quartet to Patti Smith.

☺ **Teatro Comunale di Bologna** [79 G4]
Largo Respighi 1; ☎051 529 958; w tcbo.it;
ticket office ☎051 529019; ☺ 14.00–18.00
Tue–Fri, 11.00–15.00 Sat. One of Italy's great
opera temples, the Comunale dates back to 1745
& was the 1st ever theatre commissioned by a
municipality (previously all had been built by
private citizens). Designed by the Bologna-based
Bibiena family, a famous clan of Baroque theatre
builders, it preserves four tiers of Baroque boxes
that the Bibiena did much to popularise. After
a star-studded 19th century of Rossini, Bellini,
Verdi & Wagner productions (see box, below),
Arturo Toscanini served as conductor from 1894
until World War II. Today the theatre stages
8 opera productions a year, along with a full
programme of concerts & dance recitals. Tickets
sell out fast, so book online.

☺ **Teatro Duse** [67 F6] Via Cartolerie 42; ☎051
231836; w teatrodusebologna.it; ticket office
☺ 15.00–19.00 Tue–Sat. This 17th-century
theatre in the Palazzo del Giglio was renamed
after the famous actress Eleonora Duse. The prose
season runs from Oct to early May, but the theatre
is also used for the various dance, circus, musical &
other events, including the Bologna Jazz Festival
in Nov.

WAGNER VS VERDI

In the 19th century, the Bolognesi went gaga over Wagner, pouring into the
Teatro Comunale for the Italian premieres of *Tannhäuser*, *Der fliegende Holländer*,
Tristan und Isolde and *Parsifal* and making the composer an honorary citizen.

On 1 November 1871, during a production of *Lohengrin*, there was a
VIP in the front row: Giuseppe Verdi. Verdi had never heard Wagner before
(although they were both born in 1813) and sat with the vocal score on his
lap, taking notes. He wasn't terribly impressed with his arch-rival: 'Wagner
surpasses every composer in his rich variety of instrumental colour, but in
both form and style he went too far … so the monotony, which he avoided
with such success, now threatens to dominate him.'

Wagner, for his part, had nothing but mockery for the bel canto tradition of
Italian opera; his follower, conductor Hans von Bülow, summed up Wagnerian
opinion when he called Verdi 'the Attila of the throat'.

🎭 **Teatro EuropAuditorium** [67 G3] Piazza Costituzione 4; ☎051 372540; w teatroeuropa.it; ticket office ⏰ 15.00–19.00 Mon–Fri & 1hr before a show. The largest & newest theatre in Emilia-Romagna, seating 2,696, this multipurpose venue puts on musicals, Italian pop concerts, modern dance & more.

🎭 **Unipol Arena** [66 A6] Via Gino Cervi 2, Casalecchio di Reno; ☎051 758758; w unipolarena.it. When the likes of Justin Bieber & the Red Hot Chili Peppers tour central Italy, they play just outside Bologna at this 18,000-seat arena, also home to Bologna's beloved Virtus basketball team.

LIVE MUSIC

☆ **Arterìa** [79 F6] Vicolo Broglio 1E; m 346 614 9292; w arteria.bo.it; ⏰ 22.00–03.00 Wed & Thu, 22.00–05.00 Fri & Sat. This student favourite occupies a brick cellar near the Two Towers, featuring live rap, rock, indie & underground sounds & art exhibitions.

☆ **Bravo Caffè** [79 F3] Via Mascarella 1; ☎051 266 112; w bravocaffe.it; ⏰ 19.00–02.00 Mon–Sat. Intimate cool, high-design club & wine bar that features big-name events during the week (Suzanne Vega & Terence Trent d'Arby have performed here), soul & funk on Fri, easy listening on Sat & jazz on Sun. The food is great, too: excellent traditional & creative land & sea dishes, homemade desserts & a big fat wine list. Book via its website.

☆ **Cantina Bentivoglio** [79 F3] Via Mascarella 4/B; ☎051 265 416; w cantinabentivoglio.it; ⏰ 20.00–01.00. Since 1987, this smart, lively restaurant-enoteca in the wine cellar of the 16th-century Palazzo Bentivoglio has been *the* best place in Bologna to hear live acoustic jazz. Book a table for an excellent full meal at the restaurant, or have a snack, accompanied by drinks from a list of 400

wines from Italy & beyond, Caribbean rums & single malts. Download the programme from their website.

☆ **Covo Club** [67 H4] Viale Zagabria 1; ☎051 505081; w covoclub.it/bo; ⏰ 22.00–04.00 Fri & Sat. One of Italy's top indie meccas, the Covo Club is still going strong since it first opened in 1980, with big-name performers (Franz Ferdinand, Mumford & Sons, The Gossip, The XX, The Drums, The Wombats & Libertines have all played here) & DJs. Expect a lot of university students & good cocktails. Entrance costs around €10 depending on the act, & entrance is for members only (there's a form you can download online, or join at the entrance; free before midnight, afterwards €5).

THEATRES

🎭 **Teatri di Viti** [66 B3] Via Emilia Ponente 485; ☎051 566330; w teatridivita.it. 'The theatre that sees where others don't look' is the motto of this highly original award-winning complex in the Parco dei Pini northwest of the city, featuring contemporary theatre & dance troupes from around the world. 5mins' walk from Bologna Panigale Station (trains from Stazione Centrale) or take bus 13 from the centre.

🎭 **Teatro Arena del Sole** [78 D2] Via Indipendenza 44; ☎051 291 0910; w arenadelsole. it. Managed since 2015 by the Emilia-Romagna region, presents both classical & experimental theatre Oct–May.

🎭 **Teatro Dehon** [67 G5] Via Libia 59; ☎051 342934; w teatrodehon.it. A mix of new & classic theatre including Shakespeare, musicals, operettas & more.

🎭 **Teatro il Celebrazione** [66 C5] Via Saragozza 234; ☎051 439 9123; w teatrocelebrazioni.it. Stages special events, dance, theatre & musicals.

SHOPPING

Bologna has no lack of small boutiques: Via Rizzoli, Via Ugo Bassi and Via dell'Indipendenza are the main centres for fashion shops. Chic outlets line Via Farini, including an arcade of upscale designer shops in Via Clavature and Via d'Azeglio. Don't miss an excursion into the Quadrilatero, a kasbah of sublime food shops just east of Piazza Maggiore inside Via Rizzoli, Piazza della Mercanzia and Piazza Galvani. In food-obsessed Bologna, edible goodies are irresistible and make great gifts for the folks back home.

LGBTQ+ BOLOGNA

One reflection of Bologna's progressive open-mindedness is that it has long been the most LGBTQ+-tolerant city in Italy. Proud to have been the birthplace of openly gay director Pier Paolo Pasolini, the city was the chosen home of Marcella Di Folco (1943–2010), who played in several Fellini films before serving as president of the Transsexual Identity Movement (MIT) [78 C2] (*Via Polese 15;* w *mit-italia.it*), founded in Bologna in 1982 . In 1995, when she was elected to the Bologna Municipal Council, she became the world's first trans politician to achieve public office.

Bologna is the HQ of Italy's largest gay organisation, **Arcigay**, and is the only city in the country to have a municipally supported LGBTQ+ centre, the **Cassero** [78 A1] (*Via Don Giovanni Minzoni 18;* \ *051 095 7200;* w *cassero.it*), located in the 18th-century Salara, a fortified salt depot in the Manifattura delle Arti. It hosts a wide-ranging programme from theatre to dance, drag artists and disco nights (there are women-only nights one Saturday a month) and operates a gay-friendly info service, **Telefono Amico Gay** (\ *051 555 661;* ⊕ *20.00–23.00 Mon–Fri*). The city also has Italy's first, only and very active LGBTQ+ bookshop, **IGOR Libreria** [66 D5] (*Via Santa Croce 10;* m *328 693 3884;* ⊕ *10.00–13.00 & 16.00–19.30 Mon–Sat*) with books in English and information about the scene in Bologna. Also see the online Bologna-based *Gay News* (w *gaynews.it*) (in Italian only).

Across the board, the nightlife scene is more gay-friendly than exclusively gay. Try:

♀ **Il Barattolo** [79 F3] Via del Borgo di San Pietro 26; m 328 857 1529; f barattolo.bo; ⊕ 17.00–02.00 Mon–Thu, 17.00–03.00 Fri, 18.00–03.00 Sun. Chilled, fashionable & friendly, with a wide choice of beers.

♀ **Lime Bar** [79 E5] Via Zamboni 3; m 333 362 6548; f limebar.cocktail.bologna; ⊕ 08.00–01.30 Mon, 08.00–02.30 Tue–Fri, 10.00–03.30 Sat; 15.00–01.30 Sun. Affordable & tasty cocktails by the Two Towers.

☆ **RED Club** [67 H4] Via del Tipografo 2; \ 051 601 1241; w redbologna.it; ⊕ 23.30–06.30 Sat. LGBTQ+ dance club with a pool for over 18s only; sign up for a membership online.

BOOKS

Feltrinelli [79 E5] Piazza di Porta Ravegnana 1; \ 051 261392; ⊕ 09.00–20.00 Mon–Sat, 10.00–13.30 & 15.30–20.00 Sun. Located near the Two Towers, this is one of the biggest bookshop chains in Italy, with one of the largest selections in English & occasional events. There's another branch at Via dei Mille 12 (⊕ *same hrs*).

Libreria Coop Ambasciatori [79 E6] Via degli Orefici 19; \ 051 220131; ⊕ 09.00–midnight Mon–Sat, 10.00–23.15 Sun. Beautiful bookstore in a palazzo with a glass ceiling, big shelves of English-language books & an Eataly café.

Mondadori Megastore [78 D7] Via Massimo d'Azeglio 34; \ 051 275611; w mondadoristore. it; ⊕ 09.00–20.00 Mon–Sat, 10.00–20.00 Sun. Large shop owned by Italy's largest publisher, with an extensive English-language collection in all fields.

CLOTHES, SHOES & ACCESSORIES

Ancarani [79 G5] Via San Vitale 34D; \ 051 348882; w www.ancaranilescarpe.com; ⊕ 10.00–13.00 & 15.30–19.30 Tue–Sat. Beautiful, sophisticated women's street shoes 'with a soul' designed by Bologna-born Daniele Ancarani.

Friperie Vintage [79 H6] Via San Vitale 49/a; w friperie.it; ⊕ 10.30–13.30 & 15.30–19.30 Tue–Fri, 11.00–19.30 Sat. Cool women's fashions from the 1940s–90s.

L'Inde Le Palais [79 E6] Via dei Musei 6; \ 051 648 6587; w lindelepalais.com; ⊕ 15.30–19.30 Mon, 10.30–14.00 & 15.30–19.30 Tue–Fri,

10.30–19.30 Sat. 2 floors of seriously designer retail therapy featuring a wide range of luxury clothes, bags, shoes & accessories for women, from Aliaia, Givenchy & Haider Ackerman. Plus ancient Greek sandals.

L'Inde Le Palais Men [79 E7] Via de Foscherari 19/c; ☎051 030 1108; ☺ as for L'Inde Le Palais. The boutique for young & hip dudes, by designers such as Raf Simons, Alexander McQueen & Dries Van Noten, plus a café/cocktail bar.

La Perla Megastore [79 E7] Via Farini 11; ☎051 273363; w laperla.com; ☺ 10.00–13.30 & 15.30–19.30 Mon–Sat. New flagship store of a famous Bologna brand, featuring beachwear & menswear alongside silken lingerie.

FOOD & WINE

Enoteca Italiana [78 D3] Via Marsala 2; ☎051 235989; w enotecaitaliana.it; ☺ 07.30–21.30 daily. Extraordinary, affable & informal neighbourhood wine bar & shop run by 2 former sommeliers, Marco Nannetti & Claudio Cavallari, who have gathered 1 of Bologna's most remarkable selections of wines. Slices of cheese & *salumi* are available if you want to linger – as well you might.

Majani [78 C7] Via de' Carbonesi 5; ☎051 234302; w majani.it; ☺ 09.00–13.00 & 15.30–19.30 Mon–Wed & Fri, 09.00–13.00 Thu. In 1796 Teresa Majani founded this company, which in 1832 invented 'hard' chocolate (previously it was only a drink) with its Scorza ('bark', a bit like a Cadbury Flake). Its beautiful Liberty-style shop is worth a look just for itself.

Paolo Atti & Figli [79 E6] Via Caprarie 7; ☎051 220425; & Via Drapperie 6; ☎051 233 3349; w paoloatti.com; ☺ 07.30–19.15 Mon–Thu, 07.30–19.30 Fri & Sat, 10.30–13.30 Sun. In business since 1880, this shop sells excellent homemade pasta & some of the city's most mouthwatering pastries: take home a box of tortellini or the shop's classic *certosino* fruit, nut & chocolate cake.

Salumeria Simoni [79 E6] Via Drapperie 5/2a; ☎051 231880; w salumeriasimoni.it; ☺ 08.00–13.30 & 16.30–19.00 Mon–Thu, 08.00–19.30 Fri & Sat. Even if you aren't in the market for a Parma ham, a wheel of Parmesan or a dozen exquisite handmade tortellini, pop into this temple of gastronomic delights, featuring rows of top-quality cheeses & cured meats from Emilia-Romagna & beyond, preserves in oil & vinegars.

MARKETS Bologna's biggest market, **La Piazzola** [79 E2] (*Montagnola Park & Piazza VIII Agosto;* ☺ *06.30–20.00 Fri & Sat*) started out as a cattle market in 1251 and has been going strong ever since, with some 400 stalls selling everything from underpants and coats to plants and jewellery. Piazza VIII Agosto hosts the **Mercato del Collezionismo** (☺ *08.30–17.00 Thu*) selling books, postcards, old posters and such. If you like rummaging around for previously owned treasures, there's the **Mercato Antiquario Città di Bologna** (*Piazza Santo Stefano & surrounding streets;* ☺ *08.30–18.00 2nd w/end of each month exc Jul & Aug*) and the weekly **Mercato del Vintage** (*Piazza Puntoni;* ☺ *Mar–Jun & Sep–Dec 09.00–16.00 Tue*) for clothes, handbags, jewellery, etc.

Then of course there's food. The city's oldest and most visited covered market, the **Mercato di Mezzo** [79 E6] (*Via Clavature 12;* ☺ *08.30–midnight daily; see also page 93*) has also recently been restored, with three floors of food and market stalls for buying or eating in, the regional enoteca and craft beer bar, and outdoor seating in Via Clavature; one shop, the Antica Aguzzeria del Cavallo, has superb cheffy tools. The less touristy but spectacular glass-and-iron **Mercato delle Erbe** [78 B4] (*Via Ugo Bassi 25;* 🅵; ☺ *07.00–midnight Mon–Thu, 07.00–02.00 Fri & Sat*) was given a facelift in 2014 and is a shrine to food: besides all the heavenly delights of Emilia-Romagna in spades, there's even Maichan, a dim sum stand, with dumplings made by Bolognesi pasta specialists. There's also an informal food court with a dozen 'mini-restaurants' to choose from (including a take-away vegetarian) which can get very lively in the evening.

Slow Food's weekly **Mercato della Terra** [78 A1] (*Piazzetta Pier Paolo Pasolini in the Manifattura delle Arti;* w *mercatidellaterra.com;* ☺ *Sep–Jun 09.00–14.00 Sat; May–Aug 17.30–23.00 Mon*) is the best place to discover all the gorgeous local food from the immediate area around Bologna as well as Slow Food rarities, plus wines from indigenous grapes and local craft beers. On summer evenings there's often music and tables set out for feasting on your purchases then and there.

SPORTS AND ACTIVITIES

WALKING AND CYCLING From March to December, the Italian Alpine Club, CAI (*Via Stalingrado 105, Bologna;* \051 234856; **w** *caiemiliaromagna.org*) offers hiking and cycling excursions around Bologna with CAI guides for €5 per person, using public transport to get to the starting point and back (which you are responsible for). Many of the guides are English speaking. Download the programme at Trekking col Treno (**w** *trekkingcoltreno.it*).

SWIMMING POOLS Bologna has 15 public pools and lidos, all run by SO.GE.SE (**w** *sogese.com*). Tickets are around €7, and bathing caps are required. The two listed below are the most central (ring first because they're often fully booked by school groups).

Carmen Longo Stadio [66 C5] Via A Costa 174, in the Bologna FC complex (bus 14 or 21); \051 615 2520. Beautiful 25m pool with tiered seating.

Sterlino [67 G7] Via Murri 113 (bus 13 or 38); \051 623 7034. Has both a 25m indoor pool & a 50m outdoor pool.

FOOD TOURS AND COOKING CLASSES These are great fun and offer a chance to get under the delicious skin of Italy's gastro capital.

Italian Days **m** 338 421 6659; **w** italiandays.it. Bologna-based operator offering a wide range of visits, including a morning food walking & tasting tour in Bologna (*€79, ages 5–15 €39.50*); visits to producers of Parma ham, Parmigiano Reggiano cheese & balsamic vinegar (*full day inc lunch €150*); wine tours (*from €150 inc gourmet lunch*); & tours into Motor Valley (*full day inc lunch & test drive from €150*).

Taste Bologna **w** tastebologna.net. Run by locals who love their city & its food; the Classic Bologna small group tour starts with a visit to the best shops in the Quadrilatero & includes pasta demonstrations, tastings, gourmet coffee & *gelato* (*4hrs inc lunch €80, ages 6–12 €40*). They also do a 3hr pizza & *gelato* tour (*€60/30*) & cooking classes. Book online.

OTHER PRACTICALITIES

Bologna was one of the first cities in Italy to have free internet hot spots (Rete Civica Iperbole), all of which are mapped on **w** comune.bologna.it/wireless. In the city centre you're never far from a bank or an ATM (Bancomat) machine.

HOSPITALS
✚ **Ospedale Maggiore** [66 C4] Largo Nigrisoli 2; \051 647 8111
✚ **Policlinico Sant'Orsola Malpighi** [67 G5] Via Pietro Albertoni 15; \051 636 1111; **w** aosp.bo.it

INTERNET
ⓔ **Salaborsa** [66 D5] Piazza Nettuno 3; ⏲ 14.30–20.00 Mon, 10.00–20.00 Tue–Fri, 10.00–19.00 Sat; free with ID.

LEFT LUGGAGE (*DEPOSITO BAGAGLI*)
Airport terminal [66 B1] 1st floor; \051 647 9664; ⏲ 24hrs daily; €6/item/day or €12 for a large item.
Stazione Centrale [67 E4] \051 258 3033; ⏲ 07.00–21.00. €6/item for the 1st 5hrs; €0.90/hr for next 6hrs; then €0.40/hr.

✚ **Farmacia Centrale Comunale** [78 D6]
Piazza Maggiore 6; ☎051 239 690; ⏰ 24hrs daily
✚ **Farmacia Stazione** [67 E4] Viale Pietro
Pietramellara 22; ☎051 246 603; ⏰ 07.30–23.00
Mon–Sat, 08.00–22.00 Sun

POST OFFICES

✉ [79 E7] Piazza Minghetti 4; ⏰ 08.20–19.05
Mon–Fri, 08.20–12.35 Sat
✉ [79 F3] Via delle Belle Arti 9; ⏰ 08.20–13.35
Mon–Fri, 08.20–12.35 Sat
✉ [78 B3] Via Gian Battista Morgagni 6;
⏰ 08.20–13.35 Mon–Fri, 08.20–12.35 Sat

WHAT TO SEE AND DO

BOLOGNA'S HEART: AROUND PIAZZA MAGGIORE

Piazza Maggiore [78 D6] This is the centre stage of public life, where all Bologna seems to come together in the evening. Italy is famous for its central piazzas, usually combining a cathedral with the seat of civic government in a beautiful architectural ensemble. Almost every city north of Rome has a brilliant example – but not poor old Bologna. This is the homeliest square in Italy; it's like a cultured old woman in galoshes and a tatty brown coat from the charity shop, with hair that hasn't been brushed for centuries. But the Bolognese don't care. She's friendly, familiar and they love her to pieces.

Piazza Maggiore and its antechamber, Piazza Nettuno, grew into their present shape in fits and starts, replacing the narrow streets and tiny *piazze* of the medieval city's marketplace.

Fountain of Neptune [78 D5] Piazza Nettuno is graced with this virile and vaguely outrageous fountain, where a very out-of-place sea god has, as the Bolognese say, 'abandoned the fishes to make friends with the pigeons'.

Erected in 1564–46 at the exact centre of ancient Bologna (where the two main Roman streets, the *cardo* and *decumanus*, met), the fountain was commissioned by Pope Pius IV and designed by Tommaso Laureti of Palermo. The sculptures were provided by Giambologna (who, despite his name, wasn't a Bolognese at all, but Jean Boulogne from Flanders; he spent most of his life in Florence, but this is the work that made his reputation). Portraying the god calming the waves with a simple gesture was intended as an allegory of serene papal government. The serene governors knocked down a whole block to make room for it, and forced the adjacent property owners to pay for the job.

The fountain made headlines in early 2017, when Facebook banned a photo of Neptune as too sexually explicit (and felt a bit silly afterwards). But had Giambologna had his way, 'Il Gigante', as Neptune is known, would have been even better endowed. His patrons in the Curia said 'no'. So Giambologna adjusted the statue's pose so that if you look up at it from a certain angle (stand in front of the Sala Borsa with your back to Via Indipendenza), Neptune's thumb looks just like an erection.

BOLOGNA WELCOME CARD

Both tourist offices (page 70) sell the Bologna Welcome Card (*€20*), which is especially good value if you plan to spend the next two days in a lot of museums. Valid for 48 hours, it offers a map, admission to ten museums, discounts on special exhibitions and events and specialised guided tours, and a 2-hour guided walking tour of the city centre. They also have a €30 version good for 72 hours which includes the City Red Bus (page 69).

For company, Giambologna gave Neptune a riot of putti and mermaids, squirting water from their breasts; the vaguely outrageous teenagers that crowd over the fountain at all hours of the day and night came later. Any who are purposefully walking anticlockwise twice around the fountain are superstitious students about to take an exam.

Neptune's distinctive trident may seem familiar; in 1914, the Maserati brothers borrowed it as a logo for their automobile company.

Palazzo del Podestà and the Palazzo Re Enzo (*Both ⏲ only during special exhibitions*) In the corner between Piazza Nettuno and Piazza Maggiore, this peculiar two-headed 13th-century complex was the medieval centre of power.

Palazzo del Podestà [78 D6] The Palazzo del Podestà grew up around the Torre dell'Arrengo (1212), with its bell that was used to warn the city in case of danger. Like the Basilica di San Petronio, which faces it across Piazza Maggiore, this clumsy palace is a testament to old Bologna's odd incapacity for ever coherently completing a major project. Giovanni II Bentivoglio had the Palazzo del Podestà remodelled with a Renaissance façade in 1484 by hometown architect Aristotele Fioravanti, who later went on to design parts of the Kremlin.

Under the popes the Palazzo del Podestà languished; in the 16th–18th centuries, the *piano nobile* was used as a theatre, and in the 19th century for a game resembling court tennis. In the early 20th century, the fashionable Art Nouveau painter Adolfo De Carolis and his students decorated the palace with scenes of the history of Bologna.

Stroll through the ground floor's shopping arcades to see the Voltone: a large frescoed vault, decorated with terracotta statues of four of Bologna's patron saints,

---

BOLOGNA'S MOST FAMOUS PRISONER

The illegitimate son of Emperor Frederick II 'Stupor Mundi', Enzo (c1218–72) was his father's fair-haired boy, a fine soldier and a poet like his father. He married the widow of the King of Sardinia and inherited the title in 1238.

His father appointed Enzo imperial vicar general in Lombardy and General-Legate in Romagna, and he won several battles against his father's papal enemies before being captured at the Battle of Fossalta near Modena. 'With a handsome body and angelic face, and golden hair down to his belt', he was brought into the city behind Bologna's *carroccio*, the ox-drawn 'war cart' possessed by every Italian *comune*.

His entry into Bologna, on 24 August 1249, made such an impression that the anniversary was celebrated thereafter with the Festa de la Porchetta, which involved horse races, fireworks, theatre and *porchetta* (stuffed roast pork) hurled down from the Palazzo Re Enzo to the crowd waiting in Piazza Maggiore. Napoleon, ever the party pooper, put an end to it when he took Bologna in 1796.

Enzo seems to have been more of a well-guarded guest than a prisoner, receiving a constant stream of female visitors, at least during the day, when he was free to roam in the palazzo (at night he was kept in a cage suspended from the ceiling). Enzo mentioned three daughters in his will, and there's an old story that says the first Bentivoglio was his bastard son. Bologna's own Ottorino Respighi wrote a comic opera about him, *Re Enzo*.

by Alfonso Lombardi (most cities were content with one or two patrons; Bologna, hedging its bets, has eight). The Voltone covers what was once the intersection of two medieval lanes, where merchants and notaries once had their stalls, and where blasphemers were pilloried and criminals hanged. It's famous for an acoustical trick. Have someone whisper in one corner of the Voltone, and you can hear it loud and clear in the other.

Palazzo Re Enzo [78 D5] Facing Neptune's fountain, the Palazzo Re Enzo was built in 1244 and, formerly known as the 'New Palace', takes its name from Enzo, son of Emperor Frederick II, who was captured by the Bolognesi at the Battle of Fossalta in 1249 and locked up here until he died (see box, page 87). If you manage to get in, the most lavish room is the Sala dei Trecento, or Hall of the Three Hundred, built in 1369 by Antonio di Vincenzo.

Basilica di San Petronio [78 D6] (*Piazza Maggiore;* \ *051 231 415;* w *basilicadisanpetronio.it;* ⊕ *07.45–18.30 daily. For security reasons, avoid bringing along large bags or backpacks; unlikely as it seems, this basilica is a terrorist target: page 90*) Begun by Antonio di Vincenzo in 1390, Bologna's main church (but not its cathedral) is mastodonic and preposterous, with a never-to-be-finished façade. It's one of the largest in Christendom – yet, had the Bolognesi had their way, this temple to their most important patron saint would have been far, far grander, and even larger than St Peter's in Rome. An entire city neighbourhood, eight other churches and countless towers were cleared for the site, but that wasn't enough. The Bolognesi constantly remind us that Pope Pius IV himself, in 1565, ordered that the money be spent instead on the university's Archiginnasio, instead of on municipal prestige.

As it is, San Petronio (132m by 60m) is the fifth-largest church in Italy, and the Pope's decision may have been less about maintaining Rome's bragging rights than simple economy.

Façade On the other hand, if the models inside are any indication, the Pope might well have saved Bologna a large, marble-coated civic embarrassment. The white and red marble stripe cladding, recalling the city's heraldic colours, only made it up to the level of the portals. Imagine them covering the entire building, and you would have something as eccentric as Florence's Duomo, which has been memorably described as 'a cathedral wearing pyjamas'.

Bologna was so miffed by the pope's decree that in more than 400 years it has never even bothered finishing the Basilica's façade. Italian cities have any number of bare, brick-front churches, testaments to exhausted ambitions or civic disasters, but this is the most conspicuous, although even some of Italy's greatest architects, including Vignola and Palladio, submitted design proposals. Even staid old Florence felt sufficiently embarrassed finally to tack up a façade for its Duomo in 1888. But not Bologna. Somehow, San Petronio's grimy cliff face is very Bolognese, a disregard for appearances that says, 'Love me as I am'.

Like St Mark's in Venice, San Petronio was a civic project that had little to do with the powers that be in Rome. It was the venue for all the solemnities of Bologna's Senate, and was given to the diocese only in 1929, and consecrated only in 1954. In 2000, the relics of Petronius were finally transferred here from Santo Stefano.

The façade does have a remarkable **portal**, with a stately Madonna surrounded by reliefs of Old and New Testament scenes and prophets by the great Sienese sculptor Jacopo della Quercia, begun in 1425. Like Ghiberti's contemporaneous

Baptistry doors in Florence, they are landmarks in the visual evolution of the early Renaissance, and seem strangely modern – almost Art Deco in sensibility. Amico Aspertini sculpted the central arch; Alfonso Lombardi contributed the *Resurrection* (left door) and the *Deposition* (right door).

Missing from the front of San Petronio, however, is Michelangelo's colossal bronze statue of Pope Julius II, a work that had consumed two years of the sculptor's life, commissioned by that pope in 1506 after he regained the city for the Papal States. Julius also built a large castle in the city centre. Both were torn to bits by the population as soon as the pope's luck changed; and to rub salt into his wounded pride the bronze was sold as scrap to his arch-enemy, Alfonso I of Ferrara, who melted it down to cast an enormous cannon.

Interior The lofty, spacious interior was probably built much as architect Antonio di Vincenzo imagined it. It saw the crowning of Charles V as Holy Roman Emperor by Pope Clement VII in 1530. This would be the last papal coronation of an emperor, but perhaps it was one too many. According to local tradition, it occasioned the conversion of a visiting monk named Martin Luther, who became so nauseated by papal pomp and pageantry that he decided to go home and start the Reformation.

Around the nave you'll see four crosses, set atop antique columns. These once stood at the four gates leading into the city; according to legend they were placed there by Petronius, or St Ambrose, as part of a magic circle that protected the city (actually they are 8th-century, and typical of the crossroads monuments common throughout medieval Emilia).

Meridian In 1655, while teaching astronomy at Bologna University, Giovanni Cassini (future royal astronomer to Louis XIV in Paris, and namesake of NASA's space probe to Saturn) traced a meridian on the floor of the basilica and designed the huge astronomical clock, which marks noon and tells the hour of sunrise and sunset with the shaft of light admitted through a small aperture in the vaulting at noon (solar noon, not clock time).

Cassini's *meridiana* is the longest in the world in a closed space, exactly 1/600,000 of the earth's circumference, and the length of the shadow on it also tells the date. An optical illusion makes the image of the sun look heart-shaped if you see it at just the right time on certain days of the year; seeing the illusion has always been taken as good luck for newly-weds. The *meridiana* isn't just a toy, though; creating it was serious work that helped to determine precisely the movements of the earth, necessary for Pope Gregory's 17th-century calendar reform. It also helped to prove the earth wasn't the centre of the universe.

Chapels Many of the chapels hold fine works of art. The first on the left, **Chapel I**, was the site of Charles V's coronation in 1530 and has some exceedingly strange (and exceedingly bigoted) frescoes by Giovanni da Modena on the *Triumph of the Church over the Synagogue* and the *Redemption of the Original Sin*. **Chapel II** was designed to house St Petronius's head; in **Chapel III** you'll find the *Madonna of St Luke with SS Emidio and Ivo* by Gaetano Gandolfi and Alessandro Tiarini's *Apparition of the Virgin to St Francesca Romana*. The clocks hanging on the adjacent pillar date from 1758 and are said to be the first in Italy with adjustable pendulums.

The famous Chapel IV, the **Cappella Bolognini** or **Cappella dei Tre Magi** (⏲ *10.00–18.00 daily; €3*) is next to a giant figure of St Christopher. It was frescoed by Giovanni da Modena and his assistant, Jacopo di Paolo. In his will, Bartolomeo Bolognini provided the funds and requested a Paradise, which was interpreted by

Giovanni quite intentionally to resemble a Church Council, with rows of saints seated at benches, gazing raptly at the Coronation of the Virgin.

But Bolognini's will also stipulated an *Inferno* 'as horrible as possible'. Giovanni duly filled his craggy underworld place with one of the most dramatic, most populous *Last Judgement* scenes ever painted, full of interesting detail, much of it taken from Dante: there's a Heaven painted with allegorical figures of the Seven Deadly Sins, a Wood of the Suicides, and a Devil with two mouths (one in the nether regions), one devouring Judas, the other Brutus – sacred and secular treachery are damned equally.

He also placed (and labelled) Muhammad as an elderly man just to the right of Satan, bound to a rock and tortured by a demon. His presence in Hell wasn't unusual in medieval art (Dante placed him there among the 'Sowers of Discord' in his Inferno), but it has seen St Petronio receiving some unwanted notoriety. In 2002 and 2006, plots to blow up the basilica by Muslim terrorists who claimed the art was insulting to Islam were thwarted by the police. Islamists in Italy are still calling for the fresco to be destroyed, and the police keep a close watch on it – which explains the metal detectors installed at the doors.

Bolognini also specified scenes of the *Legend of the Magi*, but didn't say which, so Giovanni chose to depict the three kings sailing home after their visit to Bethlehem. Other scenes in the chapel are on the *Legend of St Petronius*, which show the Bologna of the early 15th century. One, depicting the installation of a bishop by the anti-pope John XXIII, allowed scholars to date it c1412–20. The stained glass was designed by Jacopo di Paolo.

Chapel V has an *Annunciation*, with the Virgin by Lorenzo Costa and the angel by Il Francia. Costa also painted the *Twelve Apostles*, and *Madonna Enthroned with Saints*, one of his finest works, in **Chapel VII**. The latter, formerly belonging to the Baciocchi family, contains the tomb of Elisa Bonaparte, the only one of Napoleon's sisters who had any actual political powers, as the Princess of Lucca and Piombino, and later Grand Duchess of Tuscany; she is buried with her husband, Prince Felice Baciocchi.

Chapel VIII has a *San Rocco* by Parmigianino, one of the few paintings by the most elegant of Mannerists in Bologna, while **Chapel IX** has an *Archangel Michael Defeating the Fallen Angels* (1582) by Donato Creti and a bust in terracotta of Andrea Barbazza by Vincenzo Onofri (1479). **Chapel X**, the chapel of the city of Bologna, has a *Martyrdom of St Barbara*, by Alessandro Tiarini.

Over the **high altar**, the Tribuna, supported by red marble columns, was designed by Vignola, with an enormous 15th-century *Crucifixion*. A large fresco of the *Virgin, Child and St Petronius* fills the apse, overlooking a set of 15th-century intarsia choir stalls by Agostino de' Marchi, featuring large figures of SS Petronius and Ambrose by Francesco del Cossa.

The altarpiece in **Chapel XIV** boasts a statue of *St Anthony of Padua*, attributed to the great Renaissance sculptor Jacopo Sansovino; on the altar of **Chapel XV** is a throne by Alessandro Algardi, sculpted from ancient Roman marbles. **Chapel XVII** has another work of Costa, *St Jerome*; **Chapel XVIII** houses Amico Aspertini's *Pietà*.

Museo Storico (*Entrance to the left of the high altar;* ⊕ *10.00–17.00 Tue–Sat, 15.00–17.00 Sun; admission free*) Here are some of the instruments Cassini used to lay out the Meridian, and drawings and original models of most of the grand, doomed, schemes for the church and its façade. It also has nine illuminated choir books used by the Cappella Musicale.

CAPPELLA MUSICALE DI SAN PETRONIO

For centuries San Petronio was renowned for music. The Cappella Musicale, founded by Pope Eugenius IV in 1436, initially had a singing master and 24 boy clerics singing plainchant, although within a few years paid performers were added. Gradually they moved towards polyphony, with two choirs accompanied by various instruments: a new organ in 1476, and another facing it in 1596 (both restored in 1974–82 and still in excellent working condition). Trombones, cornets, strings, bassoons, oboes, a *theorbo* (a long-necked lute) and serpents (a curling ancestor of the tuba) were added.

By the early 17th century, the Cappella regularly employed 42 musicians, with as many as 150 extra singers and musicians for the most important occasions. Large-scale, complex compositions featuring up to nine soloists were especially written for San Petronio (where the harmonic possibilities were somewhat limited in extremely long 12-second reverberations in the enormous church) by its great *maestri di cappella*, who formed the core of the Baroque Bolognese School of Music: Maurizio Cazzati (1657–71), Giovanni Paolo Colonna (1674–95) and Giacomo Antonio Perti (1696–1756).

In the 19th century, the Cappella Musicale slowly declined, only to be completely abolished in 1929. But in the 1980s it was revived, with the mission of studying and reviving works from San Petronio's Renaissance and Baroque glory days. It was the first orchestra in Italy to use original instruments, and performs in the original choir setting here and all over the world.

Palazzo dei Notai [78 D6] (*Via de' Pignattari 1, facing Piazza Maggiore;* ⊕ *only during special exhibitions*) To the right of San Petronio, this palace of 1287 was renovated by cathedral architect Antonio di Vicenzo. It housed the guild of the notaries, who established the legal basis of the *comune* in 1282 with the Sacred Ordinances by notary Rolandino Passageri. This put the guild in charge of the city's administration, replacing an elite coalition of bankers and merchants. The notary guild's coat of arms still emblazons the façade.

Palazzo d'Accursio (or Comunale) [78 D6] (*Piazza Maggiore 6;* ✆ *051 203040;* ⊕ *Ex Sala Borsa: 10.00–20.00 Tue–Fri, 10.00–19.00 Sat, Sala del Consiglio: 10.00–13.00 Tues–Sun, archaeological excavations: 10.00–13.30 & 15.30–18.00 Tue–Sat, other rooms by request; admission free, exc Collezioni Comunali d'Arte, page 92*) Filling the western side of the big square, Bologna's crenellated City Hall incorporates the Casa Accursio of 1287 (the arcaded section, once the home of the great medieval Jurist and law professor Accursio), and the 1425 annexe by Fioravante Fioravanti. It has been the centre of local politics ever since 1336, when the Casa Accursio became the seat of the Anziani (Elders), the magistrates in charge of the commune.

The Palazzo took on its current fortresslike appearance in a rebuilding of 1365, when Cardinal Albornoz had taken over the city and feared a revolt. Fioravanti also added the tower; other remodellings took place in the 16th century after the fall of the Bentivoglio clan.

The Palazzo has seen its share of violence. On 21 November 1920, it was scene of the infamous massacre that marked the beginnings of the Fascist party in Bologna. Newly elected Socialist mayor Enio Gnudi, who had served as president of the railway union, was presiding over his first session of the city council when a band of *squadristi* entered the piazza and started shooting at the Palazzo d'Accursio; the carabinieri inside shot back; some Communists threw bombs at both sides. Eleven were killed, including a member of the opposition, and 50 were wounded; the city government was dissolved by the prefect.

Ground floor Galeazzo Alessi designed the main **portal**, presided over by a bronze statue of Pope Gregory XIII (1580), the reformer of the calendar and a native of Bologna. Originally this spot held a gilded statue of another pope – bad old Julius II – but this was destroyed in 1511 during an attempted coup by the Bentivoglio. Under a canopy just to the left is a beautiful terracotta Madonna (1478) by Niccolò dell'Arca.

The **Ex Sala Borsa**, the old stock exchange on the ground floor which covers remains of what was probably the Roman forum (the archaeological excavations are visible through the glass floor), has been transformed into a 'Piazza Coperta', a kind of indoor extension of the square to hold exhibitions, office space and the city's new multimedia library, including the English-language collection from the British Council.

Near the entrance is Bologna's **Shrine to the Resistance**, with photos of all 2,000 of the *partigiani* who died in the war and during the massacre of Marzabotto (page 138). Also present are the names of all the 'victims of fascist terrorism' who died in the 1980 bombing at the Stazione Centrale.

Upstairs Bologna's city council meets in the **Sala del Consiglio Comunale** on the first floor, under quadratura frescoes painted in the 1670s by Angelo Michele Colonna and Gioacchino Pizzoli. The Sala d'Ercole is named for a statue of *Hercules Battling the Hydra* (1519) by Alfonso Lombardi; here, too, is a fresco of the *Madonna del Terremoto* (1505) by Il Francia, commissioned after an earthquake struck the city. The **Sala Farnese** on the second floor saw Charles V crowned king with the Iron Crown of Italy before he was crowned Emperor in San Petronio. Prospero Fontana frescoed the Cappella Palatina here, while the walls are covered with scenes of Bologna's history from the Middle Ages to the 1500s.

Collezioni Comunali d'Arte (*2nd floor;* ☏ *051 219 3998;* w *museibologna.it/ arteantica;* ⊕ *09.00–18.30 Tue–Fri, 10.00–18.30 Sat–Sun; adults €5, concessions €3, under 19s free*) Reached via Bramante's grand staircase, the **Collezioni Comunali d'Arte** occupies the Sala Urbana, originally winter quarters for Bologna's Cardinal legates. It includes paintings, sculptures, miniatures, furniture and more donated to the city over the centuries, notably by arch-collector Pelagio Palagi, as well as pieces from deconsecrated churches. Under ceilings lavishly frescoed by Girolamo Curti, Agostino Mitelli and Angelo Michele Colonna are works by artists ranging from Lippo di Dalmasio and Vitale da Bologna to Aspertini and Passerotti, to Ludovico Carracci and Giuseppe Maria Crespi.

Non-Emilians are here, too, including Luca Signorelli and Tintoretto and, perhaps best of all, the *Portrait of a Gonfaloniere* (1622) by Artemisia Gentileschi and *Ruth* by Francesco Hayez. The core of the collection occupies the frescoed Galleria Vidoniana: 18 larger-than-life *Mythologies* (1713–23) by Donato Creti, donated to the city senate in 1744. The *Education of Achilles by Chiron* is perhaps the only one ever painted showing the young hero riding bareback on his centaur teacher.

The Museo Morandi, originally here as well, was 'temporarily' moved to MAMbo (page 117) after the 2012 earthquake, and at the time of writing is still there.

Palazzo dei Banchi [78 D6] (*Via dell'Archiginnasio, facing Piazza Maggiore 6*) On the eastern side stands perhaps the only architecturally notable building on the square, a work of distinguished Renaissance architect Vignola (1568). The façade was all he needed to do: the project was simply to give a common front to a number of buildings that made up Renaissance Bologna's banking district. Walk through its archways and you'll be in the Quadrilatero, the heart of culinary Bologna, centred around the Mercato di Mezzo.

Il Quadrilatero When the city chased all the market stands off Piazza Maggiore and Via Rizzoli in the 1870s, much of the food trade took refuge in this 'quadrilateral' of ancient narrow streets east of the piazza. They've been there ever since, making this area the heart and soul of Bologna's culinary traditions and the best place to start your education in Emilian cooking. It's where you'll find some of the best meat, cheese and produce shops in Bologna, if not the entire galaxy. There's no shortage of places to eat and drink too, including real Bologna institutions such as Tamburini on Via Caprarie, a great *tavola calda*/delicatessen, or old-fashioned bars such as the Osteria del Sole (since 1465; page 80) on Vicolo Ranocchi.

Recently the Quadrilatero has become one of the city's biggest tourist attractions. Plenty of new restaurants and shops have appeared; on warm nights they put out tables with white napery and candles, blocking the streets with frantic waiters and happy diners.

Mercato di Mezzo [79 E6] (*Via Clavature 12;* ⏱ *08.00–midnight daily*) Built in the 1870s to rehouse the old stands on the piazza, this was the city's first covered market. Closed for years, it was lavishly refurbished in 2014 by the local Coop chain and Eataly into something a bit more than a range of stands selling fruit and veg. On the ground floor's Centrale del Gusto, you can try Bologna's best breakfast, or buy your Lambrusco or other Emilia-Romagna wines at the Enoteca Regionale dell'Emilia-Romagna, eat pizza at the Eataly Pizzeria upstairs, or try the beers from Teo Musso's micro-brewery, Baladin. So far it has been a spectacular success, with outdoor seating in Via Clavature near the church of Santa Maria della Vita. Best of all, it's open every day, and you can get a meal or a snack until midnight.

Museo Civico Archeologico [78 D6] (*Via dell'Archiginnasio 2;* ☎ *051 275 7211;* w *museibologna.it/archeologico;* ⏱ *09.00–15.00 Tue–Fri, 10.00–18.30 Sat–Sun; adults €5, concessions €3, under 19s free, free 1st Sun of month*) Next to the Palazzo dei Banchi, facing the great, gloomy wall of San Petronio, is Bologna's excellent archaeology museum, occupying the building of an old hospital with the reassuring name of Ospedale della Morte. It boasts one of Italy's best collections of antiquities – beautifully wrought items from the Iron Age Villanova culture, finely crafted urns and jewellery that clearly show these people as the precursors of the Etruscans.

These are followed by artefacts from Etruscan *Velzna* (the Etruscan name of Bologna, Latinised as *Felsina*). Velzna may have been a frontier town, compared with the wealthy and cultivated Etruscan metropolises of Tuscany and northern Lazio, but it is richly represented here with funerary art. It has a notable collection of spectacular circular tombstones, a form found nowhere else in the Etruscan world, carved with proud warriors or ships; some are more than 3m in diameter. There is a famous embossed bronze urn, the Situla di Certosa, similar to others found in Tuscany. Many of the best pieces are housed in Room X, which has kept its original 19th-century character, complete with its colourful Etruscan-style frescoes.

The Etruscans of Bologna traded through their Adriatic port of Spina with the Greeks, whose Attic vases are one of the highlights of the museum. There are a few items from Gallic Bononia, Roman artefacts (a lovely copy of Phidias's bust of Athena Lemnia), and an unexpected surprise – the third most important Egyptian collection in Italy.

Archiginnasio [78 D7] (*Piazza Galvani;* ✆ *051 276811;* ⏰ *10.00–18.00 Mon–Fri, 10.00–19.00 Sat, 10.00–14.00 Sun; adults €3, under 18s free*) The long, porticoed façade to the left of San Petronio is the former home of the university, the Archiginnasio, its walls covered with the escutcheons and memorials of famous scholars. Bologna's university, although the oldest in Europe, was not provided with a central building until 1563; before then classes were held in public buildings or cloisters. The monument in front, in **Piazza Galvani** [78 D7], commemorates Luigi Galvani of Bologna, the 18th-century discoverer of electrical impulses in the nerves who gave his life and name ('galvanise') to physics.

The Archiginnasio is the building Bologna got for its money instead of the expansion of San Petronio; the Counter-Reformation popes, always worried about heresy and political opposition, apparently wanted to keep all the intellectuals here in one place where they could keep a close eye on them. After the university expanded to its new quarters in 1803, the Archiginnasio became the municipal library, the **Biblioteca Comunale**, which always has a selection of old books, manuscripts, prints and sketches on display. The library's reading room occupies one of the two former *aule magne*, or lecture rooms. The other, the atmospheric **Aula dello Stabat Mater** was named after the premiere of Rossini's piece conducted here on 18 March 1842 by Donizetti. Albert Einstein held a famous series of conferences on relativity here in 1921.

Anatomical Theatre The visit includes the ornate 18th-century Anatomical Theatre, shattered by a bomb in World War II and painstakingly rebuilt in 1950. It's a sumptuous, spruce-panelled monument in the history of science, where statues of great surgeons, ancient and modern, peer down from niches to concentrate the attention of the real surgeon at the marble table, where dissections were carried out by candlelight. Hippocrates and Galen, the Greek and Roman fathers of medicine, dominate, but you might also notice Bologna's own Gaspare Tagliacozzi, holding a nose in his hand. In the 16th century, he was one of the pioneers of plastic surgery. Rebuilding noses was a well-studied issue in a day when duelling with rapiers was popular, and Tagliacozzi found the first practical way to do it.

Piazza Minghetti One of the most pleasant corners of Bologna's centre, this shady, intimate square behind the Archiginnasio provides a welcome oasis among all the bricks and porticoes. Laid out in the 1890s as a kind of urban renewal project, it boasts some good architecture: the impressive, eclectic **Palazzo della Cassa di Risparmio** [78 D7], designed by Giuseppe Mengoni, and the **Main Post Office** [79 E7] of 1911. In mid-April each year the piazza hosts a colourful flower fair.

The piazza's name and statue honour Marco Minghetti, a Risorgimento figure and ally of Cavour who became one of the first prime ministers of united Italy, in 1863 and again in 1873. Minghetti ran an honest administration, as one would expect from a Bolognese, and he was the first (and perhaps only) prime minister to balance the budget.

To the mink-coat brigades, though, Piazza Minghetti means only one thing: shopping. On the western edge are the entrances to the **Galleria Cavour** [78 D7] (w *galleriacavourbologna.com*), an austere modernist mall of 1959 tucked behind older façades, with some 30 shops including Italy's best-known fashion and jewellery chains.

Santa Maria della Vita [79 E6] (*Via Clavature 8;* ☎ *051 230260;* w *genusbononiae. it/palazzi/santa-maria-della-vita;* ⊕ *10.00–19.00 Tue–Sun*) In the midst of the Quadrilatero shops, this church houses one of Emilia-Romagna's masterpieces.

Back in the 11th century, Pier Damiani, a Doctor of the Church, wrote a treatise called *De laude flagellorum* ('In praise of flagellation'), establishing the concept that participating in Christ's sufferings promised a share of his glory in paradise. Both founders of the great 13th-century preaching orders, SS Francis and Dominic, were keen practitioners, Francis wanting to keep 'Brother Donkey' (the body) in line. Dominic went a step further: 'three times every night he would whip himself with an iron chain: once for himself, once for the sinners in the world, and one for the sinners who are suffering in purgatory'.

In Italy, in particular, a number of aesthetic-minded, penitential brotherhoods known as *battuti* sprang up. Santa Maria della Vita was built in 1260 by Riniero Barcobini Fasani of Perugia, the founder of the Confraternità dei Battuti Bianchi ('Brotherhood of the White-robed Whipped Ones'). Next to the church, the brotherhood set up a hospital, the Ospedale della Vita e della Morte ('of life and death') to treat the poor and shelter passing pilgrims.

After the church collapsed in 1686, the Sanctuary of Santa Maria della Vita was rebuilt from scratch with all the Baroque trimmings; in 1754, it was crowned with an impressive dome by Antonio Bibiena, frescoed by Gaetano Gandolfi.

Compianto (⊕ *10.30–18.30 Tue–Sun; adults €3, concessions €1*) The church houses the greatest of all the region's Renaissance terracotta groups, the *Compianto sul Cristo Morto* (Lament over the Dead Christ) by Niccolò dell'Arca. Commissioned by the Confraternity in 1463, with figures of the dead Christ, the Virgin, the Three Marys, St John the Evangelist and Joseph of Arimathea, the Compianto is harrowing in its grief and terror, a 15th-century version of Edvard Munch's *The Scream*, or '*l'urlo in pietra*' as Gabriele d'Annunzio called it.

A trecento fresco of the *Madonna Enthroned* by Simone de' Crocefissi was rescued from the collapsed church. And during the Christmas season, the Sanctuary displays Santa Maria's historic *presepe* (Christmas nativity scene).

Oratorio della Confraternità dei Battuti The adjacent Oratory, designed by Floriano Ambrosini in the early 1600s, is dedicated to the Virgin and the Blessed Riniero, whose life is depicted in the canvases around the altar (note how some of the gilded putti in the décor grip little whips). The Oratory houses another slightly larger-than-life-size terracotta tableau, with 15 figures (including an angel suspended from the ceiling) of the *Transito del Vergine* (Dormition of the Virgin; 1522) by Alfonso Lombardi.

Museo della Sanità (*Entrance from the Oratory;* ⊕ *same as the church*) The former hospital houses the Museum of Health, with pharmaceutical jars, silver chalices, furniture and other items relating to the history of the Confraternity.

EAST OF PIAZZA MAGGIORE: THE TWO TOWERS AND RADIAL STREETS The east end was the fashionable part of medieval Bologna, and remains so today. So different was this aristocratic corner from the more plebeian San Felice district (west of Via Marconi) that to Dante the people seemed to speak two different languages. From

Piazza Porta Ravegnana and the Two Towers, five streets fan out to gates in the eastern walls of the old city: Via Castiglione, Via Santo Stefano, Strada Maggiore, Via San Vitale and Via Zamboni. The first, Via Castiglione, heads due south from the Two Towers, a winding and aristocratic street that follows the course of a now-buried canal.

The Two Towers (I Due Torri) [79 E5] (*Piazza Porta Ravegnana; stairs up Torre Asinelli* ☉ *Nov–Feb 09.30–17.45 (last entrance 17.00), Mar–Oct 09.30–19.30 (last entrance 18.30); €5; book timed tickets online at* w *duetorribologna.com*) This beautiful piazza at the east end of Via Rizzoli (the ancient Via Aemilia) was the site of the main gate in Bologna's Roman walls. Today it holds the city's landmark, a pair of towers that might have wandered off the set of *The Cabinet of Dr Caligari*. After the initial shock wears off, however, fondness invariably sets in for this odd couple, the Laurel and Hardy of medieval architecture, built during the great 12th-century tower-building boom (see box, page 98).The taller of the two, the 97m **Torre degli Asinelli**, was originally at least 3m higher; and probably the champ among such towers. It stood at the heart of what was then Bologna's market area, the place where riots and insurrections were most likely to break out – it was a handy reminder to the people to behave themselves. The crenellated base was added in 1480 as a guardhouse. It tilts just over 2m out of true, making it Italy's tallest leaning tower (Pisa's at 57m is a pipsqueak in comparison); 64 different state-of-the-art measuring tools have been installed to monitor its strength every day. The 498 steps that lead to the top are more likely to make your head spin than the tilt, but the view over Bologna is worth the trouble.

Its sidekick, the **Torre della Garisenda**, sways tipsily to the south, 3m out of true; the Garisenda contingent failed to prepare a solid foundation and, when they saw their tower pitching precariously, gave up. In 1360 it became such a threat to public safety that 12m were lopped off its top, leaving only a squat 48m stump; inscribed on its base you can read what Dante wrote about it in the *Inferno* (see box, opposite). Like Pisa's leaning tower, it needs a lot of attention to keep it from tipping over and squashing a good bit of central Bologna.

Between the towers, the statue of San Petronio watched over the old marketplace for centuries – until it was hauled away in the 1870s as an obstacle to traffic. The city recently polished up the saint and put him back on his pedestal. In front of the towers, the **Palazzo dei Drappieri** (1486; now housing the Feltrinelli bookshop) is a fine example of the somewhat Florentine, Gothic-windowed style of palaces popular in the days of the Bentivoglio.

FAULTY TOWER TRICKS

Dante's mention of the Garisenda Tower comes in Canto XXXI of the *Inferno*, when he and Virgil encounter the giant Antaeus frozen in ice at the bottom of Hell:

Qual pare a riguardar la Garisenda
Tal parve Anteo a me, che stava a bada
Sotto 'l chinato, quando un nuvol vada
Di vederlo chinare, e fu tal ora
Sovr'essa si, che ella incontro penda
Ch'i' avrei voluto ir per altra strada.

('Like looking at the Garisenda, under the leaning side, when a cloud comes; so seemed Antaeus to me, about to fall – to see him leaning so, I wished I had taken another path.')

Dante is referring to an illusion that every child in Bologna knows. If you stand underneath the leaning side of the tower when clouds are passing over it against the direction of the tilt, it seems to be falling over on top of you. Try it and see.

Museo della Storia di Bologna [79 E6] (*Via Castiglione 8;* ✆ *051 1993 6370;* w *genusbononiae.it/palazzi/palazzo-pepoli;* ⊕ *10.00–19.00 Tue–Sun (last entry 18.00); admission inc audio guide in English: adults €10, ages 19–26 & over 70s €8, ages 6–18 €5, under 6s free*) Bologna's new history museum occupies the massive 14th-century Palazzo Pepoli Vecchio (or Antico) in the shadow of the Two Towers. Property of the Pepoli, Bologna's earliest bosses, it was continuously improved until 1723: a grand stair, stuccoes, paintings, frescoes and statues were added to the medieval fabric.

In 2003, the Fondazione Cassa di Risparmio purchased the palazzo and held a competition for its conversion into a museum, won by architects Mario Bellini and Italo Lupi. They restored the palace's original features and converted the courtyard into a striking steel and glass tower, described by Bellini as 'a tower-umbrella' or 'a magic lantern flooded with white sunlight which gradually descends and dematerialises into pure transparency. It is practically a moment of revelation which leads one to ponder on the passing of time.'

Exhibits in the museum vividly survey the city's history, starting in the entrance with its 1:1 scale reproduction of the great Map of Bologna of 1575 (the original is in the Apostolic Palace, Vatican City), said to be largest fresco map of a city ever executed. From there, displays follow the history of Bologna from its beginnings as Etruscan Felsina (complete with a 3D film) to its growth along the Via Aemilia, its medieval forest of towers, the advent of Napoleon, and a virtual-reality walk through the city's mostly hidden canals that helped to make it a medieval industrial powerhouse. Allow a couple of hours; at the end there's the de rigueur café and shop.

Palazzo Pepoli Campogrande [79 E6] (*Via Castiglione 7;* ✆ *051 420 9411;* w *pinacotecabologna.beniculturali.it;* ⊕ *Sep–Jun 08.30–19.30 Tue–Sun, Jul & Aug 08.30–14.00 Tue & Wed, 13.45–19.30 Thu–Sun; joint admission with the Pinacoteca Nazionale (pages 110–12): adults €6, ages 18–26 €3, under 18s free*) The Pepoli must

3

Imagine you're in the Middle Ages, on your way to Bologna over the Apennine foothills from Florence (that's walking, most likely, or on horseback if you're a nobleman or a military captain, or on a mule if you're a posh cleric). If it's a clear day, you will see the city ten miles before you reach it, and it's an astounding sight: a dense forest of slender towers glittering on the plain, the skyline of a proper modern city.

It's hard to imagine, but most northern Italian cities were like this. Before the 20th-century Americans, no people in history had such an insatiable lust for verticality as the medieval Italians. Between church campaniles, public buildings and private fortifications, towers of over 70m (and up to 100m) were extremely common. The Two Towers are among the few survivors. The remains or sites of 194 others have been located so far in Bologna, and no doubt quite a few have disappeared altogether.

Nearly all were simple, square defence towers. Along with Florence, Bologna probably had the most, monuments of the time when the city was dominated by contending nobles. As these, after the year 1000, found their economic interests ever more tied up with the booming cities, they started building fortified residences in town to complement their castles in the country. In an age when family vendettas were the main subject of the chronicles, they were a good thing to have. They also became status symbols, and families would strive to see who could build the highest. According to legend the Two Towers were built in just such a competition in c1109–19. The winner, the svelte 97m Torre degli Asinelli, is still the tallest building in Bologna.

The age of the towers came to a close with the advent of strong free cities, the *comuni*. Endless street battles, and occasional all-out sieges had become intolerable nuisances, and just as the new governments were figuratively cutting the nobles down to size, they often lopped down their towers. Quite a few fell down by themselves over the centuries, from earthquakes and lightning. In Bologna, some 20 towers survive; and while you're tramping the back streets, keep an eye out for the stumps of the rest, hiding among the old houses. Often the giveaway is an impressive, incongruous arched entrance, or a foundation of great stones that hasn't been stuccoed over. Once you start looking, you'll see them everywhere.

have been attached to the neighbourhood; the aforementioned Palazzo Pepoli Vecchio and the earlier, 13th-century, Casa Gadda Pepoli are right across the street. This one was called 'Campogrande' after the big field Taddeo Pepoli (boss of Bologna in 1337–47) had to clear to build it. Taddeo's heirs at one point sold Bologna to Milan for 200,000 florins – not a popular move, but they later kissed and made up with the Bentivoglio – so when Odoardo Pepoli was made a senator in 1653, there was still enough gold in the pot to rebuild the palace from scratch and commission lavish frescoes from Bologna's best Baroque painters.

Along the grand stairway, Domenico Canuti painted a history of the Pepoli family. In 1665, he also frescoed one of two extraordinary ceilings on a theme dear to the Pepoli heart, the *Triumph of Hercules*. Canuti's version is florid and busy, and Giuseppe Maria Crespi's *Triumph* is later (1691) and more restrained, with Allegories of the Seasons in the four corners. A third ceiling shows *Alexander Cutting the Gordian Knot* (1708) by Donato Creti.

Today the palazzo belongs to the Pinacoteca Nazionale (pages 110–12), and houses archives, photos and the **Collezione Zambeccari** donated by the Marchese Zambeccari in the 18th century, including paintings by Ludovico Carracci, Guercino, Albani and Crespi.

Palazzo della Mercanzia [79 E6] (*Piazza della Mercanzia, at the top of Via Santo Stefano*)

Just south of the Two Towers this handsome Gothic palace of 1384 was the merchants' exchange and customs house, headquarters of their guilds and the 12 consuls, who were charged with settling business disputes and keeping up the city's canals. It has an ornate Gothic loggia by the architect of San Petronio, Antonio di Vincenzo – though it owes much of its current appearance to the indefatigable 19th-century restorer Alfonso Rubbiani. From the little balcony above it, the news of the day and the decisions of the consuls would be announced. Beneath it, swindlers and other financial miscreants would be chained to the central pillar to receive the crowd's jeers.

The medieval system based here lasted, somewhat anachronistically, until the Napoleonic occupation. Today, fittingly enough, it is home to the Chamber of Commerce, and it is where Bologna solemnly guards its greatest treasures – the official measure for the width of tagliatelle, and the official recipes for tortellini, *ragù*, *certosino* (Christmas fruitcake) and *lasagne verde*.

Other houses on Piazza della Mercanzia are equally as old; around the corner on Via Santo Stefano is another surviving tower, the 13th-century **Torre Alberici** [79 F6]. Continuing down Via Santo Stefano, the **Palazzo Bolognini** (1517) [79 F6] on the right at number 11 is a *palazzo senatorio* – as the Bolognesi call their most impressive palaces – designed for the 'senatorial' class of the most powerful families. This one is known for its graceful portico, decorated with a series of busts in between the arches, some by Alfonso Lombardi. Everything above that level is a 19th-century restoration.

Santo Stefano [79 F7] (*Via Santo Stefano 24;* \ *051 648 0611;* ⊕ *08.00–19.00; donations*)

One of the city's most extraordinary churches, or rather seven churches, Santo Stefano is the Jerusalem Bononiensis, the 'Jerusalem of Bologna'. Dedicated to the first Christian martyr, it was founded according to legend in AD430 by St Petronius, who had visited the hermit-saints of the Holy Land as a youth. Petronius's intent was to reproduce the seven holy sites of Jerusalem over the much-venerated tombs of the first Bolognese martyrs SS Vitale and Agricola, enabling the faithful to make at least a symbolic pilgrimage.

Most of the work in this unique complex dates from the 8th–12th centuries. It was held in the highest esteem by the Lombards, but then considerably altered in modern restorations. These uncovered the interesting fact that Santo Stefano was built over the site of an ancient temple of the Egyptian goddess Isis (Egyptian religion was extremely popular in the Roman Empire and promoted by several emperors, especially Domitian).

Three of the churches of this unique and harmonious Romanesque ensemble face Piazza Santo Stefano. The entrance is through the **Chiesa del Crocifisso,** with a Renaissance pulpit in its façade, begun in the 11th century and containing an **ancient crypt** below its raised choir; here are the relics of SS Vitale and Agricola, discovered in AD393 by St Ambrose and Bologna's Bishop Eusebius in a Jewish cemetery and brought here.

To the left is the entrance to **San Sepolcro**, an irregular polygonal temple modelled after Jerusalem's Holy Sepulchre and containing the equally curious **Edicola di San Petronio**, a large pulpit adorned with reliefs; in a macabre touch, the saint's bones

3

are visible through a tiny hole at floor level. The circle of columns around it survives from Isis's temple, which was used as a baptistry in the 5th century and rebuilt in its present form in the 11th.

Outside the circle, a single lone column represents the pillar to which Christ was bound during his flagellation. A door behind this column leads directly into evocative **SS Vitale e Agricola**, Bologna's oldest church; built in the 5th century, it incorporates bits and pieces of old Roman buildings and alabaster windows.

Beyond it is the **Cortile di Pilato** in patterned brick with interlacing arches, replicating the courtyard where Pontius Pilate tried Jesus. Its centrepiece is an 8th-century basin, donated to the church by Lombard kings Luitprand and Ilprand, which somehow gained the sinister reputation of being the basin in which Pilate washed his hands.

From here you can enter the fourth church, the 13th-century **Trinità**, which may originally have been the east end of a 4th-century church, or a Lombard church of the AD800s – like most of the complex, it has been rebuilt and reconfigured so often that scholars have endless opportunity to debate what was what. The Trinità, also called the Martyrium, contains a striking if rather sombre wooden *Adoration of the Magi* from the 1370s, with the figures painted by Simone de' Crocefissi.

A passage from the Cortile di Pilato leads into the lovely double-decker 10th-century **cloister**, with some fascinating capitals, including a bare-bottom figure with its head on backwards, and a curious diving man pulling his beard. A room facing it contains the **museum**, with a collection of mostly 14th-century paintings, including works by Simone de' Crocifissi, Michele di Matteo (the *Lives of St Stephen and St Petronius*), and a fresco of the *Massacre of the Innocents* by Berlinghero di Lucca.

No Jerusalem would be complete without a Mount of Olives, and the small hill to the south of Santo Stefano was called Monte Oliveto in the Middle Ages. On top, in a picturesque piazza off Via Santo Stefano, **San Giovanni in Monte** [79 F7] was built in 1286 on the site of the original church founded by St Petronius. Largely remodelled in the late 1400s, it contains paintings by Guercino and Lorenzo Costa. The terracotta eagle over the portal is the work of Niccolò dell'Arca.

SS Bartolomeo e Gaetano [79 F5] (*Strada Maggiore 4;* ☎ *051 227692;* ⊕ *07.00–12.30 & 15.30–18.45 Mon–Sat, 08.30–13.00 & 15.30–19.00 Sun*) The third street radiating from Piazza Porta Ravegnana, palace-lined Strada Maggiore, traces the continuation of the Roman Via Aemilia, starting with this church in the shadow of the Two Towers. Built in the 5th century as a Benedictine monastery, it was rebuilt starting in 1516 around an unfinished palazzo with a portico, hence its unusual façade (or lack of one). It was given to the Order of the Theatines, who redid the interior and added a dome, and in 1617 added a new dedication to their newly canonised founder, St Gaetano (Cajetan) Thiene. It has its share of Baroque art: the nave ceiling is by Angelo Michele Colonna, while Ludovico Carracci painted *San Carlo Borromeo* on the second altar on the right. The left transept has a *Madonna* by Guido Reni, while the apse contains the *Martyrdom of San Bartolomeo* and *Two Miracles of the Saint* by Marcantonio Franceschini.

Casa Isolani [79 F6] (*Strada Maggiore 13*) This is one of the best-preserved 13th-century houses left in Bologna, with one of the city's oldest and highest porticoes, supported on wooden beams. The adjacent Corte Isolani, a charming covered street with a string of little courtyards, dates from the 1450s. The Isolani family, who trace their origins to the Lusignan rulers of Cyprus during the Crusades, still own both today, and they have restored the Corte as an arcade of shops and cafés.

Museo Internazionale della Musica [79 G6] (*Strada Maggiore 34;* \ 051 275 7711; w *museibologna.it/musica;* ⊕ *09.30–16.00 Tue–Fri, 10.00–18.30 Sat–Sun;* €5; *audioguides available – & worth getting to hear the music*) The 16th-century Palazzo Sanguinetti was remodelled in the early 19th century and, after 1832, owned by tenor Domenico Donzelli. In 1986 the last owner, Eleonora Sanguinetti, donated it to the city, suggesting that in honour of her music-loving father it become a museum of music.

Much of its contents come from the remarkable musician, composer, teacher, collector and historian Father Giambattista Martini (1706–84), in his day considered the world's leading authority on music. Among his many distinctions Martini taught counterpoint to the 14-year-old Mozart. The museum houses his massive hoard of early print music from the 16th–18th centuries, codices, 11,000 *opera libretti* and letters to and from composers and musicians, forming one of the top collections of its kind in Europe.

Among the exhibits are scores, posters, photos and memorabilia and the first printed music book (1501), as well as instruments: a clavichord made for Camillo Gonzaga in 1606, Rossini's Pleyel piano, a twisty 'serpentone' and a rare heckelphone. The theatre isn't neglected. There are old prints of fabulous stage sets, more posters and handbills, and even architect Bibiena's model for his Teatro Comunale (Bologna never throws *anything* away).

Padre Martini also commissioned and collected the hundreds of portraits of musicians, not all by great artists, that line the walls. Back in the day having a portrait in his collection was, according to James Reel, the 'equivalent to a modern Hollywood celebrity having "arrived" by getting a set of footprints on to the Walk of Fame'. The ones that stand out are of the original diva, Maria Malibran, the great lady of 1830s opera and Maria Callas of her day.

On the ground floor, the Laboratorio di Liuteria is the workshop of Otello Bignami, one of Bologna's top violin-makers, donated to the city by his children after his death in 1989.

Palazzo dei Giganti (Museo Civico d'Arte Industriale and the Galleria Davia-Bargellini) [79 G6] (*Strada Maggiore 44;* \ 051 236 708; w *museibologna. it;* ⊕ *09.00–14.00 Tue–Sat, 09.00–13.00 Sun*) Properly the Palazzo Davia-Bargellini, this palace of 1638 is better known by its nickname from the two huge Baroque *telamones* carved by Gabriele Brunelli around the main entrance. Inside, have a peek through the window at the stair to see the colossal stone Hercules, the centrepiece of the palace courtyard.

The two museums here have now merged. The **Museo Civico d'Arte Industriale** first confronts you with a room chock full of antique locks and keys, handles and drawer pulls (the one you need to restore that old armoire is probably here). It's a queer, dear sort of museum, devoted to the applied arts, and it has some interesting 'curiosities' going back to the 1400s, including a gilt carriage, a Venetian marionette theatre, a marvellous 18th-century French doll's house for some duke's daughter, and works in wrought iron and terracotta.

The rooms that follow make up the **Galleria Davia-Bargellini**, a small but excellent array of Bolognese painting, mostly from the Bargellini family collection, including a *Pietà* by Simone de' Crocefissi as well as Vitale da Bologna's famous smiling *Madonna dei Denti* (the 'Madonna of the Teeth'), perhaps the most characteristic work of the 14th-century Bolognese school. Later paintings commissioned by the family include portraits of themselves by Bartolomeo Passerotti; there are others by father and daughter Prospero and Lavinia Fontana, and Giuseppe Maria Crespi;

his *Giocattori dei Dadi* ('the Dice Players') illustrates his delight in the details of everyday life.

Santa Maria dei Servi [79 H7] (*Strada Maggiore 43;* ☎ *051 226807;* ☺ *winter 07.30–12.30 & 15.30–19.00 daily, summer 07.30–12.30 & 16.00–20.00 daily; Cimabue frescoes* ☺ *09.30–12.30 Sat only*) The city's Gothic jewel, Santa Maria dei Servi is preceded by a rare and lovely *quadroporticus* mingled amid the porticoes of the Strada Maggiore. This is in the Early Renaissance Tuscan style, with slender columns and iron braces; one side dates from the 1390s, while the rest had to wait until 1855. The church was a little slow too; begun in 1346, according to a design by Friar Andrea da Faenza, and assisted by Antonio di Vincenzo, it wasn't completed for another two centuries. Typical for Bologna, however, they never got around to the façade.

Also typical is the interior, where the brick ribs vaulting the three naves and the brick pillars handsomely contrast with the white walls. And on the walls there's a fine mix of medieval and Baroque art. The first chapel on the right contains the *Virgin with the Seven Founders of the Servites* by Marcantonio Franceschini and *God the Father* by Guido Reni.

In the ambulatory, the *Maestà di Santa Maria dei Servi* (1280s) holds pride of place: a rare enthroned *Madonna and Child* by Giotto's teacher, Cimabue (or his workshop – the attribution is hotly disputed); be sure to bring a €1 coin for the light. Nearby is a polyptych in an unusual painted terracotta frame by Lippo di Dalmasio, and the all-terracotta *Madonna with SS Lorenzo and Eustachio* by Vicenzo Onofri, not one of his best works, though his *Monument to Gian Giacomo e Andrea Grati* is. Also of note is Alessandro Tiarini's *Presentation of the Virgin at the Temple*.

Then there are the sadly damaged fragments of a late trecento fresco cycle by Vitale da Bologna. Among these is a rare scene of the *Madonna del Parto* – the pregnant Virgin, shown here seated, dozing, with a book on her lap, her long hair symbolising her youth and virginity. Next to her on the table, the potted bush with three branches symbolises the Tree of Jesse; the little dragon at her foot was the dragon of the Apocalypse.

The 16th-century Servite friar Giovanni Angelo Montorsoli, a pupil of Michelangelo, sculpted the marble high altarpiece of the *Resurrection*. Lastly on the left, have a look at a *Noli me tangere* (second chapel) and *St Andrew* (fifth chapel), both by Francesco Albani.

From the 14th century, but especially in the 17th, Santa Maria dei Servi was famous for music, boasting no fewer than four organs to belt out the sound. Today it has only one, but it's a humdinger: a mechanical-action Tamburini, built in 1967. The church's once-renowned Cappella Musicale dei Servi was revived in 1933, and regularly performs here; check its website (**w** *musicaiservi.it*) for schedules.

Casa Morandi [67 F5] (*Via Fondazza 36, a block off Strada Maggiore; book in advance via MAMbo:* ☎ *051 649 6611;* ☺ *Oct–May 14.00–16.00 Fri & Sat, 11.00–13.00 Sun, Jun–Sep 17.00–19.00 Fri & Sat, 11.00–13.00 Sun; admission free*) In 2009, the house where Morandi and his three sisters moved after their father's death, and lived together for the rest of their lives, was opened to the public. Along with family furnishings and art, the enigmatic painter's atelier has been restored to its original appearance, with the familiar – almost numinous – vases, bottles and shells that featured in most of his 1,350 paintings.

The house has the serenity and minimalist atmosphere you'd expect, while other rooms have been converted into a library and exhibition area with audiovisual installations and photos of the famous people Morandi knew.

Along Via San Vitale The radial street north of the Strada Maggiore, Via San Vitale, was the medieval Via Salaria, the 'salt road', along which that commodity was brought from the salt pans along the Adriatic. Its monuments are two fine palaces of the 16th century, the dilapidated **Palazzo Franchini** [79 F5] (*Via San Vitale 31*) and the **Palazzo Fantuzzi** [79 G6] (*Via San Vitale* 23), complete with carved elephants that play on the family name, *ele-fantuzzi*. The church of **Santi Vitale e Agricola in Arena** [79 G5] (*Via San Vitale 50;* ⊕ *08.15–noon & 15.40–19.30 Mon–Sat, 09.00–12.30 & 16.00–20.30 Sun*) commemorates the 4th-century martyrs of Bologna who died in AD304 under Emperor Diocletian, in a story first mentioned in AD394 by St Ambrose, the bishop of Milan, who did much to popularise their cult. Agricola was a Christian who converted his slave Vitalis. Vitalis was executed, and Agricola was tortured to make him recant his religion, then crucified in the Roman amphitheatre on this site, at that time outside the walls. The church was rebuilt in the 16th century by the Benedictines, but retains its original early Romanesque crypt and the Renaissance Cappella di Santa Maria degli Angeli.

Via Zamboni Northernmost of the radial streets, Via Zamboni connects the Two Towers to the university and the Porta San Donato. Originally called Strada San Donato, it was renamed to honour Luigi Zamboni, a law student at the university who distinguished himself as a spy and soldier against the pope in the tumults that accompanied the French Revolution. Before his death in a papal prison, Zamboni invented the red-white-and-green *tricolore* that would become the Italian flag.

In the Middle Ages, one of the noble family compounds in the area belonged to the Bentivogli, the family who would rise to become Bologna's tyrant bosses. They built their great Renaissance palace on this street, setting the scene for it to become the city's most fashionable address. The Bentivogli were expelled in 1507, but in the decades that followed, as Bologna enjoyed its last flush of Renaissance prosperity, this street filled up with more imposing palaces. The university was already here, and narrow Via Zamboni became the place where dons and dukes rubbed shoulders. It certainly is one of the narrower streets in Bologna, and made even narrower by the porticoes that lined it – but Bologna is a city where even the wealthy have to grow accustomed to living in the shadows.

Via Zamboni heads eastward from the Two Towers. The first sight along the way is the little deconsecrated church of **San Donato** [79 F5], with its curious painted Rococo façade. Adjacent to this, the **Palazzo Malvasia** (1535) [79 F5] was perhaps the first palace built on the street after the fall of the Bentivogli; now it's a hotel. Between the palace and church, note the archway underneath a leering grotesque mask. This is the **Voltone** [79 F5] of the Malvasia family, the only surviving entrance to what was once Bologna's Jewish Ghetto to the north (page 112). There was a system of pipes leading to the mask and, whenever one of the Malvasia was named to a public office, the family would throw a party for the neighbourhood and wine would pour out of the Voltone's mouth.

Next comes the **Palazzo Magnani** [79 F5], at number 20, designed by Domenico Tibaldi (son of Pellegrino). Today it's a branch of the Unicredit bank, but they'll let you in to see the palace's lively series of frescoes on the *Founding of Rome* painted in 1590 by all three Carracci (🕿 *051 640 8221;* ⊕ *by appointment only*).

Across the street is **Piazza Rossini**, a little square that should be an attractive neighbourhood gathering place, but is instead a miserable car park. Wherever you see this in a prominent place in an Italian historic centre, there are probably politicians about, and here they infest the **Palazzo Malvezzi de' Medici** (1560) [79 F5], now the home of the Provincial Government.

3

San Giacomo Maggiore [79 F5] (*Piazza Rossini–Via Zamboni;* \ *051 225970;* ⏲ *07.30–12.30 & 15.30–18.30 Mon–Fri, 08.30–12.30 & 15.30–18.30 Sat–Sun; Cappella Bentivoglia:* ⏲ *09.30–12.30 Sat only, when volunteers of the Touring Club Italiano offer tours)* Begun in 1267 by an order of Augustinian hermits and completed in 1344, Romanesque San Giacomo Maggiore is hugged by a graceful **portico**, arguably the most beautiful in Bologna, with Corinthian columns and a terracotta frieze. It was paid for by Bologna's godfather, Giovanni II Bentivoglio. In 1802, after the Augustinians were ejected by Napoleon, part of their monastery was given over to the Conservatorio Giovanni Battista Martini, where Rossini once presided as musical director.

San Giacomo was the parish church of the Bentivogli, who built their family chapel in the 1460s, then filled it with some of Bologna's finest Renaissance art. Giovanni II hired Lorenzo Costa to paint the frescoes – the *Triumph of Death,* the *Apocalypse* and a *Madonna Enthroned* – in the midst of *Giovanni II and His Family,* a fresco commissioned in thanksgiving for the big boss's escape from hired assassins. Even with the usual artistic flattery, Giovanni still comes off looking the cultured Renaissance thug.

The altarpiece in the chapel is by Francesco Francia while the high-mounted tomb of Anton Galeazzo Bentivoglio (1435), opposite the chapel, is by the great Sienese sculptor Jacopo della Quercia. In the other chapels of the ambulatory you can see a polyptych by Paolo Veneziano and an altarpiece of the *Crucifixion* by Simone de' Crocifissi.

San Giacomo continued to accumulate notable works after the Bentivoglio were gone. On the right side of the nave is the beautiful **Cappella Poggi**, built for the Bologna-born Cardinal Giovanni Poggi (d1556), who is buried here. Poggi had met his fellow Bolognese Pellegrino Tibaldi in Rome, and sent him home to build and fresco his palace (pages 106–7) and this chapel with *St John Preaching in the Wilderness* and the *Division of the Elect from the Damned,* and two portraits of the cardinal, one in his role as papal nuncio to Spain.

Appropriately enough for a church surrounded by music, **San Giacomo**'s 55m campanile has the most musical bells in Bologna.

Oratorio Santa Cecilia [79 G4] (*Via Zamboni 15;* \ *051 225970;* ⏲ *Jun–Sep 10.00–13.00 & 15.00–19.00 daily, Oct–May 10.00–13.00 & 14.00–18.00 daily)* St Cecilia, thanks to the song in her heart, is the patroness of musicians, so appropriately the oratorio is used for concerts, notably during the March–June San Giacomo Festival.

In 1504, Giovanni Bentivoglio commissioned the decoration of this oratory from the same masters who frescoed his chapel in San Giacomo Maggiore: Lorenzo Costa, Il Francia and Amico Aspertini, along with some of their students and helpers. They gave him his money's worth, with some of Bologna's finest frescoes, all of which have been recently restored, depicting the *Lives of SS Valerian and Cecilia.* The rather obscure story and artists are:

Panel 1	*Marriage of Cecilia and Valerian* by Il Francia. Cecilia was a noble Christian convert forced by her parents to marry the pagan Valerian. During her wedding, her story goes that she 'sang in her heart to the Lord' that Valerian would become a Christian and respect her vows of virginity.
Panel 2	*Valerian Converted by Pope Urban I* (Costa)
Panel 3	*Baptism of Valerian by Pope Urban* (attributed to the otherwise little-known Giovanni Maria Chiodarolo and Cesare Tamaroccio)

Panel 4   *SS Cecilia and Valerian Crowned by an Angel* (attributed to Costa and Il Francia's students, Bagnacavallo and Biagio Pupini). Celia had told Valerian on their wedding night that an angel was watching over her, who would punish him if he tried to consummate the marriage, but if he let her remain a virgin, the angel would love him. Valerian asked to see the angel, and Cecilia told him to go to the third milestone of the Via Appia, where the angel crowned them both and the pope baptised him.

Panel 5   *Decapitation of Valerian and His Brother Tiburzio* (Aspertini)

Panel 6   *Burial of the Martyrs* (Aspertini)

Panel 7   *Trial of St Cecilia* (Bagnacavallo and Biagio Pupini)

Panel 8   *Decapitation of St Cecilia* (Giovanni Maria Chiodarolo and Cesare Tamaroccio)

Panel 9   *St Cecilia Donates All Her Goods to the Poor* (Costa). The chronological order again may seem a bit bizarre but the story goes that, although she was struck three times by the sword, she survived for three days, enough time to distribute her goods.

Panel 10   *Burial of St Cecilia* (Il Francia)

Palazzo Malvezzi Campeggi [79 F5] (*Via Zamboni 22*) Across from San

Giacomo's portico, this elegant Renaissance palazzo (begun 1560) was the home of the Malvezzi, the bitter enemies of the Bentivogli who helped chase them out of town. It has a stunning courtyard, embellished with a statue of Hercules by Giuseppe Maria Mazza. For years it was the home of the university's famous law school, but the lawyers have recently moved out for more spacious quarters, and the Palazzo's fate is still undetermined.

Maybe the Malvezzi were just bad neighbours, for just one palazzo away, where Via Zamboni widens (slightly) into Piazza Giuseppe Verdi, stood the biggest palace ever built in Bologna, the fabulous lost Palazzo Bentivoglio, 40 years in the building, with a façade stretching 150m and a tower second in height only to the Torre degli Asinelli.

By 1507, only four years after the palace was completed, the Bolognesi had become thoroughly tired of the Bentivogli, their brawling offspring, their greed and their leaden rule. And Giovanni II, the last of the dynasty, made the fatal mistake of offending the ferocious Pope Julius II, who egged on the people to throw the bosses out, and rip down their proud new palace to help make sure they never came back.

But only a few years of papal rule were enough to make many think the Bentivogli maybe weren't so bad after all. In 1519, one of the family's many branches convinced the city to let him build a new Palazzo Bentivoglio near the site of the old one, just north at Via delle Belle Arti 8. The site of the original palace is now occupied by the **Teatro Comunale** (page 81). The street to the right of the theatre, Via del Guasto ('of the broken'), got its name from the ruins, which were too extensive to clear and remained here for decades.

THE UNIVERSITY OF BOLOGNA AND ITS MUSEUMS

Museo di Palazzo Poggi [79 H4] (*Via Zamboni 33;* \ *051 209 9610;* w *museopalazzopoggi.unibo.it;* ⊕ *10.00–16.00 Tue–Fri, 10.30–17.30 Sat–Sun; adults €5, ages 6–26 & over 65s €3, under 6s free*) The university puts on a dazzling display of art and science in its former home, Palazzo Poggi (1549–60, although some parts are a century older). One of the grandest palaces in Bologna, the work of Bartolomeo Triachini, it was completed just when family boss Giovanni Poggi

Bononia Culta was an epithet first given to the city by Roman poet Martial. Nobody has the faintest idea what the Roman-era city did to deserve it but, starting in the 11th century, Bologna did its best to live up to it.

The Bolognesi like to claim that their university is the oldest in the world and give it a founding date of 1088 – but the matter isn't so clear. All the medieval universities had very informal beginnings, as loose communities of teachers and students; some grew out of cathedral schools that date back to the AD800s, and their growth into institutions was gradual and poorly documented.

What is certain, though, is that – along with the school at Paris – Bologna's was the most important centre of learning in medieval Europe. Unlike Paris's, this one was at first run by the students, not the teachers, and they organised into guilds to maintain their rights.

Originally there were four of these, called 'universities' (the original use of the word), although soon these merged into two, the Cismontane for Italians and the Transmontane for all foreigners; later on, each nation had its own guild and building. From the earliest times the student guilds were able to get fixed prices set for their lodgings and books and, since they provided the professors' income directly through fees, they could dispose of incompetent or merely unpopular ones by the simple means of a boycott. The emperors were usually only too glad to give them a hand, and a decree of 1158 from Frederick Barbarossa even granted them exemption from the legal jurisdiction of the *comune*. Eventually the professors formed guilds of their own; membership of one was the origin of the university degree.

Almost from the beginning, Bologna was known best of all for its studies of the written law. This grew out of the subject of rhetoric, the basis of the education for lawyers and politicians in classical times. In the 1200s the university established faculties of Philosophy and Medicine. In the latter it was replacing Salerno, where the university was already in decline, and it soon became renowned for it as the first place in Europe to revive the practice of human dissection.

Paris may have had the greater reputation for the liberal arts and theology, but besides medicine Bologna also gradually achieved distinction in the sciences, particularly astronomy. By this time Bologna had also become a mother of other universities, as groups of students broke away to found new schools in Modena, Reggio, Vicenza and Padua. Bolognese masters were also instrumental in staffing the universities of Naples, Palencia, Salamanca and Montpellier, and one alumnus, Vacarius, founded the law school at Oxford in 1144. Today the university has campuses in Rimini, Ravenna, Forlì and Cesena, as well as in Argentina.

was made cardinal nuncio to Spain, the pope's ambassador to Emperor Charles V, a position that brought in the cash Poggi needed to make his new palace a showcase of Mannerist art at the hands of Pellegrino Tibaldi and Niccolò dell'Abate.

For a cardinal, Poggi's tastes tended more towards mythology and Renaissance humanism than religious themes. The main hall of the palazzo is adorned with Pellegrino Tibaldi's witty frescoes of the *Story of Ulysses* (1549), an early and influential example of Mannerist illusionistic quadratura ceiling painting that would later inspire Annibale Carracci's great fresco cycle in the Palazzo Farnese in Rome. Elegant scenes of banqueting and concerts by Niccolò dell'Abate and others on religious themes by Prospero Fontana adorn the *piano nobile*, or first floor.

In 1712, the Palazzo Poggi became home to the Istituto delle Scienze, founded by Count Luigi Ferdinando Marsili to bring the new empirical sciences of the day into Bologna and to breathe some life into a university that was growing mouldy under papal rule. In all fairness, the Church fully supported his efforts, especially after Prospero Lambertini of Bologna became Pope Benedict XIV. Laboratories and workshops were installed under the frescoed ceilings. A new library wing was built, and Marsili added the Torre della Specola, an observation tower for astronomers.

In 1803, the Palazzo Poggi became the seat of the University of Bologna under Napoleon's men, who worried that students could always cause trouble and that their former base, the Archiginnasio (page 94), was too central. Today many of the university's collections inherited from the Istituto delle Scienze are open to the public after a major revamp, designed to recreate the spirit of the collections in the time of Luigi Marsili.

The first room houses what remains of the fabled 'Microcosm of Nature' – the natural history collections that once filled the home of the Father of Modern Natural History, Ulisse Aldrovandi (see box, page 108). Next are the **Sala di Davide** and **Sala di Mosè** with Biblical frescoes by Prospero Fontana, the first housing minerals and other specimens that Marsili (who was a soldier and diplomat before he left the busy world behind for scholarship) collected during his travels around Europe. The second holds the institute's Museum Diluvianum, with fossils that for centuries were set up as proof of the Biblical flood. The **Sala di Susanna** frescoed by Pellegrino Tibaldi is used for special exhibitions.

Niccolò dell'Abate's charming frescoes adorn the next four rooms, now dedicated to the Anatomy and Obstetrics, and weirdly compelling rooms they are, too. This starts in the **Sala di Camilla** with scenes from Virgil's *Aeneid* (page 162), while below are models and equipment from the School of Obstetrics founded by surgery professor Giovanni Antonio Galli in the 18th century to instruct doctors and midwives.

Bologna was the first medical school to make use of wax anatomical models. The **Sala dei Paesaggi**, decorated with eight charming imaginary landscapes, houses wax 'flayed' figures (*ecorches*) by Ercole Lelli (1702–66), one of the leading anatomical artists of his day, who used human skeletons as the base (with papal permission, of course). Lelli taught his craft to Giovanni Manzolini (1700–55), who in turn taught his wife, Anna Morandi (1714–74), a remarkable wax artist and perhaps the world's first female professor of anatomy. Among their waxworks in the **Sala dei Concerti e delle Fatiche di Ercole**, adorned with delightful scenes of courtly life interspersed with the Labours of Hercules, is one of the most surprising things you'll see in Bologna: Anna Morandi's portrait of her husband and of herself, dressed up for a fancy ball while dissecting a brain.

The **Camerino dei putti vendemmiatori**, named after its pictures of grape-harvesting cherubs, houses 'La Venerina', the masterpiece of Clemente Susini (1754–1814). Susini is considered the greatest of all anatomical artists: the contrast of a beautiful, sensuous reclining, naked pregnant woman, surrendering to death, but split wide open with removable organs is a purposefully disturbing and fascinating example of early sensitivity training.

The **Sala dello Zodiaco e delle Stagioni** decorated by Prospero Fontana is dedicated to early optical and other equipment, including lenses and moulds. It has a model based on Giambattista Pittoni and Domenico and Giuseppe Valeriani's *Allegorical*

ULISSE ALDROVANDI: FATHER OF NATURAL HISTORY

Born to a noble family in Bologna, Ulisse Aldrovandi (1522–1605) is the founder of modern Natural History. During his university studies in 1549, he got in trouble with the Church for doubting the doctrine of the Trinity. He was taken to Rome and placed under house arrest in order to weed out any heretical thoughts.

Aldrovandi's time in Rome changed his life, but perhaps not as the Church intended. Before he was released in 1550 he met many fellow scholars, who introduced him to the delights of the natural world. Back in Bologna he became the Professor of Philosophy (1554) before becoming the university's first Professor of Natural Sciences (1561). He invented the word 'geology', and established botany, zoology and entomology as distinct scientific disciplines; and he made Bologna an important centre for their study.

In his own time, Aldrovandi was compared to Aristotle; known throughout Europe, he was called the 'second Pliny'. His remarkable collection of specimens, sent to him by contacts from all over the world and numbering more than 18,000, was the first and perhaps largest of all the 'cabinets of curiosities' that became popular in the 17th century. Modern science was still in its infancy, and Aldrovandi thought it perfectly natural to take the fables of the ancient writers at face value. One of the first to investigate fossils, he was certain that some local finds belonged to dragons, a subject in which he held a great interest. Among his voluminous works is the *Monstrorum Historia*, or 'History of Monstrosities'.

Aldrovandi conducted the first-ever botanical expedition, to Umbria's Monti Sibellini in 1557, and planted the university's Orto Botanico (see opposite), one of the first botanical gardens in the world. His collections were largely dispersed over the centuries; the Museo di Palazzo Poggi houses what has survived.

Monument to Sir Isaac Newton in Cambridge's Fitzwilliam Museum, which shows Newton performing his optical experiment with a prism. Bologna's physicists performed their own experiments on Newton's theories in this very room. The **Sala dei Telamoni**'s partly damaged frescoes of telemons and landscapes with ruins are also by Fontana. Exhibits here are dedicated to Electrical Physics, and in particular the work of Luigi Galvani (1737–98), whose experiments paved the way for the study of electromagnetism and neurophysiology.

The last rooms (without frescoes) are dedicated to military science, geography and navigation, subjects dear to the heart and career of Luigi Marsili. There are paintings of his proudest moments (between 1682 and 1704 he fought in the service of Emperor Leopold I of Habsburg), scale models of cannons and fortifications and other instruments dedicated to the study of geometry, mechanics and ballistics for advances in artillery. There are ships' models and maps, globes and navigational instruments that originally formed part of the Istituto delle Scienze, as well as the institute's library, which has been in operation since 1724.

And at the end, a change of pace: a room of **East Asian Art** with beautiful Japanese woodcuts, Chinese and Japanese paintings, and works in porcelain and ivory.

Torre della Specola [79 H4] (*Via Zamboni 33;* m *320 436 5356;* w *sma.unibo. it/il-sistema-museale;* ⊕ *guided tours only: 10.45, 12.15 & 15.00 Tue–Fri, 11.00 & 15.00 Sat–Sun; adults €5, ages 6–26 & over 65s €3, under 6s free*) After the Palazzo Poggi became the Istituto delle Scienze, its founder Count Marsili wanted to add an astronomical observatory. It was a period when the works of Isaac Newton were making inroads even in the Papal States, and the intellectually open Pope Clement XI sat on St Peter's throne – but even so Marsili needed the papal nod before proceeding.

He did it with a cultural bribe, commissioning Donato Creti to paint a charming series of landscapes lit by outsize astronomical bodies for the pope. Clement then gave his nod and, in 1725, Marsili added the Torre della Specola, where important astronomical work was done in the good old days before electric street lighting. Today it houses the **Museo della Specola**, which contains many of the instruments used in the 18th and 19th centuries, a fresco of the constellations and exhibits on the history of astronomy.

Museo di Mineralogia Luigi Bombicci [67 F5] (*Piazza di Porta San Donato;* \ *051 209 4926;* w *sma.unibo.it/il-sistema-museale;* ⊕ *09.00–13.00 Mon–Sun*) This collection of 40,000 rocks was begun in 1860, and anyone at all interested in geology and mineralogy might consider a visit. On display are some remarkable crystals (including sulphur and other minerals from Emilia's mines), amber, meteorites, and a collection of prehistoric tools made from flint, obsidian and jade.

Museo di Antropologia [79 H4] (*Via Selmi 3;* \ *051 209 4196;* w *sma.unibo.it/il-sistema-museale;* ⊕ *09.00–13.00 Mon, Wed & Fri, 09.00–15.00 Tue & Thu, 10.00–17.00 Sat–Sun*) This one is pretty didactic, dedicated to human evolution through skulls, casts and bones, the reconstructions of facial features, comparative skeletons, artefacts of prehistoric Italians, displays of bio-archaeology (including the oldest-known skeleton of a person afflicted with leprosy, from a 4th-century BC necropolis at Casalecchio di Reno), and a recent acquisition: a yurt from Kazakhstan.

Museo di Anatomia Comparata [79 H4] (*Via Selmi 3;* \ *051 209 4243;* w *sma.unibo.it/il-sistema-museale;* ⊕ *09.00–14.30 Mon–Fri; 10.00–17.00 Sat–Sun*) Even if you only have a passing interesting in anatomy, there is a strange beauty to the university's museum of animal skeletons, rather bizarrely chained to the walls, which does make you wonder what they get up to after dark. Detailed coloured wax models of nervous systems are the pride of the collection, begun in the early 19th century, along with the 16m skeleton of a sperm whale.

Museo di Cere Anatomiche [79 H3] (*Via Irnerio 48;* \ *051 209 1556;* w *sma.unibo.it/il-sistema-museale;* ⊕ *10.30–17.00 Mon–Thu, 10.00–14.00 Fri*) If the wax anatomical models in the Palazzo Poggi left you hankering for more, come here, two streets north of Via Zambeni. There's also a fine collection of 2,000 skulls, models of foetal deformities and other pathologies, the obsession of one of the anatomy professors, Cesare Taruffi (1821–1902).

Orto Botanico [79 H2] (*Via Irnerio 42;* \ *051 209 1325;* w *sma.unibo.it/il-sistema-museale;* ⊕ *08.30–15.30 Mon–Fri, 08.30–13.00 Sat*) The university's Botanical Garden, started by Ulisse Aldrovandi, is one of the oldest in the world. It's also the second-largest park in the city centre, with a collection of mostly Mediterranean flora, rock and herb gardens and ponds, along with such exotica as a fully grown sequoia, and greenhouses for cacti and insectivorous plants. There's also a Botanical Museum and Herbarium; the latter houses more than 100,000 dried plants, though this is open by appointment only to students and researchers with documents proving their studies.

Pinacoteca Nazionale [79 H3] (*Via Belle Arti 56;* ☎ *051 420 9411;* w *pinacotecabologna.beniculturali.it;* ⊕ *08.30–19.30 Tue–Sun; joint admission with the Palazzo Pepoli Campogrande (pages 97–9): adults €6, ages 18–26 €3, under 18s free)* Bologna's main art collection, stored among the university buildings, was begun by Cardinal Lambertini and expanded after 1740 when he became Pope Benedict XIV. Most of the works came from demolished city churches, especially after Napoleon suppressed so many of the city's monasteries. Napoleon, as was his wont, also took the best paintings to Paris, but unlike many places after 1815 Bologna was fortunate enough to get them back and moved to this old Jesuit monastery in 1816.

14th-century Bolognese artists The itinerary begins with Bolognese medieval masters, of which that singular painter Vitale da Bologna emerges as the star with his intense *St George and the Dragon* and *Life of St Anthony Abbot* (unlike most of his contemporaries, including Giotto, Vitale knew what a camel looked like). Brilliant colours, a hint of depth, and delight in nature are the rule with Vitale, excepting the grey and sombre *Cristo in Pietà* made in the plague year of 1348.

Some of Vitale's approach is reflected in his peers: the colourful *Morte della Vergine* by Pseudo Jacopino and a glowing *Madonna col Bambino* by Simone de' Crocefissi. Giovanni da Modena contributes a *Crocefissione adorato da San Francesco*, and another artist with a distinctive style and fine brush, Jacopo di Paolo, a *Crucifixion with Saints.*

The next room is devoted to 'foreign' painters, and pride of place is taken by the only Giotto in Bologna, a *Polyptych with the Madonna and Saints.* Other foreigners, many of whom had come to Bologna to work on San Petronio, include Lorenzo Monaco, Giovanni Martorelli of Brescia (known for intense, worried-looking saints, as in the *Life of St Anthony Abbot*), and the Sienese Andrea di Bartolo; from Spoleto, Rinaldo di Ranuccio contributes a wonderfully stylised Franciscan-style painted crucifix.

Next come three rooms of detached frescoes from Bologna churches. Again, Vitale da Bologna stands out with his *Madonna del Ricamo*, depicting an old legend where Mary sews the shirt that would be gambled for by the soldiers at the Crucifixion; he also painted many of the frescoes from Santa Maria (or Apollonia) di Mezzaratta, with help from Jacopo di Paolo. Pseudo Jacopino's cinematic *Battle of Clavijo* depicts the climactic fight that saved the last corner of Christian Spain after the 8th-century Arab conquest, when St James (Santiago) came down from heaven to help defeat the Moors. Other exceptional works are by Simone de' Crocefissi, Jacopo di Paolo and Francesco da Rimini, including a *Miracolo di San Francesco.*

The Renaissance This section contains more 'foreigners', with fine works of Antonio and Bartolomeo Vivarini and Cima da Conegliano of Venice; it shows the considerable influence of artists from Venice and Tuscany on the local artists present, notably in the big-canvas virtuosity of Ferrara's Lorenzo Costa and Bologna's Il Francia, the most popular painters in Bologna in the days of the Bentivoglio. There are two small fragments from elusive Ferrarese master Ercole de' Roberti, including a tearful *Magdalene*, del Cossa's *Pala dei Mercanti*, an early work of El Greco, the *Last Supper*, and a *Visitation* by Tintoretto.

The most famous painting in the museum is Raphael's *Ecstasy of St Cecilia*, a late work (1517) which the artist sent from Rome to hang in the church of San Giovanni in Monte. It shows the patron saint of music, holding a set of organ pipes and raptly listening to the angels sing, with a chamber orchestra's worth of instruments, unstrung and broken at her feet, symbolic of Cecilia's lack of interest in earthly things. Around her stand contemplative saints: Paul leaning on a sword, John the Evangelist with his eagle, Augustine and Mary Magdalene.

Mannerism From Emilia-Romagna's Mannerist decades come works by Parmigianino, Pellegrino Tibaldi, Niccolò dell'Abate (*Scenes from Orlando Furioso*), and some dependably tepid ones by Il Garofalo, sharing space with Perugino, Giulio Romano and Titian's *Jesus Crucified with the Good Thief.*

Baroque The Carracci, who initiated Bologna's move into the forefront of Italian art at the dawn of the Baroque, get a room all to themselves; among the many works present are Ludovico's *Caduta di San Paolo* and *Madonna dei Bargellini*, Annibale's *Madonna di San Ludovico*, and Agostino's *Comunione di San Gerolamo*, one of the most celebrated and influential works of its day.

From here it's a short and logical step to the strangely perfect little world of Guido Reni, Bologna's favourite son, who earns the most lavish chamber in the entire museum. Most of his best works are in Rome, but the selection here at least

SMALL FUN IN THE BIG MUSEUM

The Italian Baroque was indeed an exotic fruit, but like most exotic fruits it was sure to go off if not handled carefully. Bolognese art in the late 16th and 17th centuries does have a certain aroma to it. The Counter-Reformation and Italy's loss of political liberty created a quietly traumatised world, one in which a very sophisticated people was reduced to mouthing pious platitudes, with the police and the Inquisition looking over their shoulders. As long as they were careful, Italians could enjoy their last few decades of prosperity. They were impressed by the lavish, solemn spectacles provided by Church and state, and the new art, sanctioned by Rome and commissioned in vast quantities for churches and palaces, seemed an Olympian peak of beauty and elegance.

Something was missing. The Bolognese masters of the new official style, the Carracci and Guido Reni, may have dazzled with their technical perfection, but their innumerable imitators found them a hard act to follow. Bologna in this era has a lot to answer for, and the last rooms of the Pinacoteca Nazionale will amuse you with a flood of some of the most uninspired painting ever made. Lifeless virtuosity alternates with rare flashes of witless virtuosity, including perhaps the silliest high-fashion *Annunciation* ever painted, by Bologna's own Pietro Faccini.

The thought police of the popes can take most of the credit for this slow strangulation of art, but the Pinacoteca also provides a wonderful glimpse into the sort of people that inhabited this sad, twilight world. *La Famiglia Gozzadini* is a work by the popular portraitist Lavinia Fontana (1552–1602), capturing a prominent family on the cusp of the Renaissance and the Baroque. Fontana was a great artist, and it's hard to tell whether this strangely Victorian group is an intentional send-up, like Goya's brutally caricaturistic portraits of the Spanish royal family, or Rousseau's *Cart of Père Juniet*, or Grant Wood's *American Gothic*; perhaps there simply wasn't any other way to paint such creatures. The Gozzadini, jowly, smug and overdressed, are horrible enough, though the miserable little family dog steals the show, looking quite the Gozzadini herself in her bracelet and earrings.

gives a hint of why Reni was once considered one of the greatest painters of all time; even in his own day, his classical precision of line and total command of colour and composition were thought a refreshing advance on the fevered excesses of the Mannerists. Highlights include the hypnotic *Triumph of Samson*, the *Massacre of the Innocents*, *Madonna dei Mendicanti* and the *Madonna della Pietà*; and there is a portrait of the artist himself, by Simone Cantarini.

In the rooms that follow, true gems are mixed with a good helping of dross, a fair representation of the age itself. Among the artists to appear are Guercino (including his *Investiture of St William*, a painting so admired it was specially selected by Napoleon's men to take to France); Mastelletta (*Rest on the Flight into Egypt*), Domenichino, Francesco Albani, Alessandro Tiarini, Marcantonio Franceschini, Leonello Spada, Donato Creti (the precociously Neoclassical *Sigismonda*), Gaetano Gandolfi's masterpiece, the huge *Marriage of Cana* (1775–80), and Giuseppe Maria Crespi (*The Courtyard Scene*). Some of the larger paintings have been placed in the auditorium, the Aula Didattica at the end of the itinerary.

NORTH OF THE TWO TOWERS

Ghetto, and Museo Ebraico [79 F5] (*Via Valdonica 1/5;* \ *051 291 1280;* w *www. museoebraicobo.it/it;* ⊕ *10.00–18.00 Sun–Thu, 10.00–16.00 Fri; adults €4, under 25s & over 65s €3*) Strolling north of the Two Towers will take you into a claustrophobic nest of alleys off Via de' Giudei and Via dell'Inferno which before 1860 made up Bologna's Ghetto. Jews were segregated here, as in most Italian cities, at the instigation of the Church during the Counter-Reformation. This one was begun in 1555 under a truly loathsome pope, Paul IV, although having gone to all the trouble to wall it off Pope Clement VIII decided in 1593 it didn't go far enough, and forced all Jews to leave the Papal States. Later, they gradually trickled back, living in the old Ghetto 'unofficially' and subject to intermittent extortion and persecution by the papal authorities.

The museum tells their story, which for the moment consists mostly of historical displays; it also offers tours of Jewish sites in Bologna, Ferrara and other cities. The museum was an initiative not of Bologna's Jewish community, which currently numbers only about 200 people, but of the regional government.

The alleys of the Ghetto contain some medieval relics: the **Casa dei Rampionesi** [79 F5], a 12th-century house at Via del Carro 4, and the **Torre degli Uggozoni** [79 E5]. There's a plaque commemorating the Synagogue, which ironically was destroyed not by popes or Nazis, but by Allied bombings in 1943.

San Martino [79 E4] (*Via Oberdan 25;* \ *051 234662;* ⊕ *08.00–noon & 16.00– 19.00 Mon–Sat, 09.00–13.00 & 16.00–19.30 Sun*) Begun in 1227, this arty church was remodelled in the 15th century by the Carmelites, and given a Gothic-style façade in 1879. An 18th-century Virgin Mary high on a column overlooks a piazza filled with parked cars.

The interior, all white walls and red brick columns, is typically Bolognese. The first chapel on the right contains an *Adoration of the Magi* by Girolamo da Carpi. Further up there's a fresco of the Madonna by the 14th-century Lippo di Dalmasio, and Vitale da Bologna's *Crucifixion*, finished by another artist in the 16th century. Nearby is a column painted with a formidable *Sant'Onofrio* by Lippo di Dalmasio, and in the fifth chapel, a beautiful *Madonna* by Amico Aspertini. The 16th-century organ to the right of the presbytery is one of Bologna's oldest and most tuneful. Girolamo da Sermoneta's *Madonna Enthroned with Saints* (1548) holds pride of place on the high altar, set in a lavish golden frame.

The first chapel on the left holds the *Madonna della Carmine*, a rare statue in terracotta by Jacopo della Quercia, a *Madonna and Saints* by Il Francia and, below, a *Deposition* by Amico Aspertini. In the 15th century, Paolo Uccello painted a fresco of the *Nativity* by the sacristy, which was believed completely lost until 1981, when a fragment was discovered and moved to this chapel. Even from the bit that survived, it's easy to tell this was not your ordinary Nativity scene but a typically uncanny Uccello composition. A donkey and a cow hold centre stage over the Child; in the background, the Magi study a crescent moon.

Further up, the third chapel on the left has a *Crucifixion* by Bartolomeo Cesi, followed by a *San Girolamo* by Ludovico Carracci and an *Assumption* by Lorenzo Costa. Further up are fragments of frescoes by Vitale da Bologna and Simone de' Crocefissi that survived from the 15th-century remodelling.

NORTH AND WEST OF PIAZZA MAGGIORE

Cattedrale di San Pietro [78 D5] (*Via Indipendenza 7;* ✆ *051 222112;* ◷ *07.30–18.45; Campanile and Cathedral Treasure:* ◷ *14.00–16.30 Sat; €5; Crypt & Archaeological Area:* ◷ *14.00–18.00 Mon, Wed, Fri & Sat; admission free*) Founded in the 6th century, rebuilt in the 10th century and consecrated in 1184, and frescoed in the Renaissance by Francesco del Cossa and Ercole de' Roberto, Bologna's cathedral should be more interesting. But as it was being enlarged in the late 16th century, the vaults collapsed; only fragments of the frescoes that inspired Michelangelo survive in the Pinacoteca. Afterwards, it was rebuilt by Giovanni Ambrogio Mazenta in a showy Baroque style, with a façade added in 1747.

It was never a favourite of the locals. Like Venice's former cathedral (another St Peter's) this church represented Rome's authority in the city, as opposed to that of the municipality, embodied in the basilica of the city's patron saint, St Mark in Venice, and St Petronius in Bologna.

Inside are red marble lions from the portal of the original façade, and, in the first chapel on the right, a dramatic, terracotta *Lamentation of Christ* (1522) by Alfonso Lombardi. In the side chapels, look out for Donato Creti's *Pala of Saint Ignatius of Loyola* in the ornate third chapel on the left, and a *Sacred Family with SS Rocco and James the Greater* by Marcantonio Franceschini in the fourth chapel on the right.

The sanctuary houses a striking 12th-century polychrome *Crucifixion* in cedar wood, with a solemn crowned figure of Christ and two pillar-like figures of the Virgin and St John. Bartolomeo Cesi's paintings in the choir are among his last works; hovering over the ornate Cappella Maggiore is the *Eternal Father* (1579) by Prospero Fontana; also see the *Annunciation*, the last painting (1619) by Ludovico Carracci.

The slightly leaning Romanesque **campanile**, the second-tallest tower in Bologna, is a survivor of the original church. It houses a massive 3,330kg bell, nicknamed La Nonna (Grandma), which is hand rung in a circle 'Bolognese style' with three other massive bells (Bologna and Rome used to compete on their bells and ringing techniques).

Stroll past the campanile down **Via Altabella** and its adjacent lanes (especially Via Sant'Alò and Via Albiroli) for a look at medieval Bologna, with several medieval towers and houses dating from the 13th to the 16th centuries.

Museo Civico Medievale [78 D4] (*Via Manzoni 4;* ✆ *051 219 3930;* ☷ *museibologna.it/arteanticaen/luoghi/70083/offset/0/id/70109;* ◷ *09.00–15.00 Tue–Fri, 10.00–18.30 Sat–Sun; adults €5, ages 18–25 & over 65s €3, under 18s free*) Housed in the quattrocento Palazzo Fava-Ghisilardi, this is one of Bologna's top

3

sights. First, however, you'll have to wade through the delightfully screwy private collections accumulated by 18th-century museums, which are preserved here for no apparent reason beyond our entertainment. There's a mummified baby something, carved ostrich eggs and coconut shells, a smattering of pre-Columbian art, a carved narwhal tusk, and courtesans' slippers from Venice with 18-inch heels inspired by the harem of the Ottoman sultans.

Once through that, you'll see something that really brings old Bologna back to life – the tombs of the great doctors of the university. By convention, these would be carved with images of the professors in relief, expounding to a crowd of attentive students. Part of the convention was to make these scenes as lifelike as possible – so many students, with so many faces from over the centuries, earnest, daydreaming or perplexed. Some of the best, from the early Renaissance, are by Paolo di Bonaiuto (the *Sepolcro di Lorenzo Pini*), the Tuscan Andrea da Fiesole, and the dalle Masegne brothers (the *Arca di Carlo Roberto e Ricardo da Saliceti* of 1403). The dalle Masegne touch is also shown in the statues of Justice and four patron saints of Bologna (1391), which originally decorated the Loggia della Mercanzia.

Like any good medieval museum, this one has no end of surprising pretty things, such as the mosaic Byzantine *Madonna* from c1100 made from the tiniest of tesserae, and an exceptional collection of ivories, a field where medieval sculptors could display their skill in miniature. The best were made in Venice and France; here the Venetians of schools such as the 14th–15th-century Bottega degli Embriachi, with their trademark spiky foliage borders, compete with French artists who created little coffers for jewellery, and little portable altarpieces for personal devotion, carved with intricate scenes that capture medieval civilisation in full flower.

Along with the exquisite, there's a touch of the bizarre, such as the colossal *Statue of Pope Boniface VIII* in gilded copper plate, made by Manno Bandini da Siena (1301). This most grasping and arrogant pope, whose impostures wrecked the powerful medieval papacy, commissioned this statue and many like it across Italy, as an early sort of political propaganda; Boniface also invented the beehive triple tiara popes once wore, to show that they were three times mightier than mere kings and emperors. The massive cope nearby is a fine example of 13th-century English needlework, embroidered with the *Life of Christ*.

The collection of sculpture goes on to Jacopo della Quercia's group of the *Madonna and Saints*, with flowing draperies that proclaim the Renaissance has arrived (1410). Among the later works are a bronze bust of the Bolognese *Pope Gregory XV* by Bernini, and Giambologna's *Mercury* (a virtuoso work, one of the four versions he sculpted, showing the messenger of the gods poised on one foot) and a *St Michael the Archangel* by Bernini's great rival in Rome, Bologna native Alessandro Algardi.

Bologna had a fine school of miniaturists, and their work is displayed in music books and in the *Statutes of the Arte dei Merciai* (merchants' guild) of 1361. The collections of armour, ceramics, majolica plates, and glass include spectacular works from Murano.

In the courtyard of the museum is an additional exhibit: the 13th-century **Torre dei Conoscenti**, a typical example of the house-and-tower complexes of the Middle Ages. Near it you can see the only surviving bit of Bologna's original Roman–Dark Age city wall.

Palazzo Fava [78 D4] (*Via Manzoni 2;* \ *051 1993 6305;* w *genusbononiae.it/ palazzi/palazzo-fava;* ⊕ *10.00–19.00 Tue–Sun; adults €6, under 13s free – prices are at least double during exhibitions*) In 1583, Filippo Fava, scion of a prominent family, was visiting his tailor, who had heard that he was seeking artists to fresco his brand-new palace. The tailor recommended his sons, who had just returned from studying in other parts of Italy and had made great progress according to their slightly older cousin, and would work more for honour than a fee. Signor Fava decided to let them have a go painting a series of mythological scenes on the upper walls.

The brothers, of course, were the Carracci, Annibale and Agostino, and they worked together with their cousin Ludovico, sharing ideas and painting side by side on the *Story of Europa* (1583–84), the *Story of Jason* (1583–84), with a striking scene of Medea purifying herself by the light of the moon (which the critic Andrea Emiliani called the 'first truly modern female nude in Italian art'), and the *Story of Aeneas* (1586), which was partly frescoed by Bartolomeo Cesi.

Although the Carracci themselves always said they did it all together, scholars ever since have tried to pick out which Carracci did what: Agostino gets credit for the idea of adding the figures of the relevant gods in between the scenes, an idea more fully developed in the trio's later fresco series at the Palazzo Magnani (page 103). Annibale did much of the actual drawing and colouring, and Ludovico came up with the ideas and compositions.

Madonna di Galliera [78 D4] (*Via Manzoni 3;* ⊕ *07.30–noon, 13.15–14.00 & 16.00–19.00 Mon–Sat, 09.00–13.00 Sun*) This church across the street from the Palazzo Fava has a wonderful, richly sculpted Renaissance façade (1479). The interior, finally restored after wartime bomb damage, has works by Guercino, Marcantonio Franceschini and others.

Oratorio di San Colombano (Collezione Tagliavini) [78 C4] (*Via Parigi 5;* ☏ *051 1993 6366;* w *genusbononiae.it/palazzi/san-colombano;* ⊕ *11.00–19.00 Tue–Sun; adults €7, ages 19–26 & over 70s €5, ages 6–18 €4, under 6s free*) One of the city's oldest churches, San Colombano was founded in circa AD610 by Bishop Pietro of Bologna, a student of the scholarly Irish missionary monk Colombanus, around the same time that Columbanus founded the monastery and centre of learning at Bobbio (pages 263–6).

That church was built over a late Roman building, and in 1591 the Baroque Oratorio di Santa Maria di Colombano was built over that to house the church's treasures, especially the *Madonna dell'Orazione* by Lippo di Dalmasio. Upstairs, however, is one of Bologna's marvels: frescoes painted under the direction of Ludovico Carracci known as 'La Gloriosa Gara' of scenes of the *Passion and Resurrection of Christ* by some of the leading painters of the day: Guercino, Albani, Reni, Domenichino, Massari and Brizio.

In a thorough restoration financed by the Cassa di Risparmio, the medieval crypt and fragments of a 13th-century fresco of the *Crucifixion* by Giunta Pisano were uncovered. Today the Oratory is filled with beautiful musical instruments from the 16th to 19th centuries, many finely painted and all in working order, collected by the Bolognese musicologist, Luigi Ferdinando Tagliavini. From October to June, the instruments are used in the Musica in San Colombano series of concerts.

Via Galliera This was the main street leading north from Bologna's centre until broad, straight Via dell'Indipendenza was blasted through in 1890 to connect the centre with the railway station. Bombed in World War II, the area's mix of old and new was neglected for decades, but recently its low rents have attracted the young and creative.

3

The lower part of Via Galliera remains a street of impressive palaces, from the days of the Bentivoglio to the 1700s. The first of these palaces, at number 8, is the **Palazzo Aldrovandi** (1725) [78 C3], home of one of Bologna's great families, with a dash of Rococo style in its ornate window grilles; and across the street the cinquecento **Palazzo dal Monte** [78 D3]. Next to the Aldrovandi is the woebegone church of **Santa Maria Maggiore** [78 C3], sadly in need of restoration, and then the Renaissance **Palazzo Felicini** [78 D3] at number 14, from the 1490s. This stands at the corner of **Via Riva di Reno**, a street that followed the course of the Reno Canal. Once lined with mills, this was medieval Bologna's industrial zone.

At the top of the street, the **Porta Galliera** [67 F4] is the most ornate of Bologna's surviving gates, designed in 1661 by Bartolomeo Provaglia and still bearing its papal coat of arms. The originally medieval gate in the third ring of walls became part of a fortress, the Rocca di Galliera constructed in 1330 by the envoy of Pope John XXII, Cardinal Bertrand du Pouget, to bully the *comune*. It didn't work; the fort and gate were destroyed by the people.

Parco della Montagnola [79 E1] This is Bologna's oldest park (1662), the only sizeable one in the *centro storico*, and the only 'hill' north of Piazza Maggiore. The Bolognesi take it as a symbol of their love of liberty – it's really a mound of debris, from the Rocca di Galliera. In 1806, the pile was covered in earth and landscaped, ironically on the orders of the new tyrant Napoleon.

A fair, the Esposizione Emiliana, was held on the grounds in 1888, before the park took its current shape, complete with a charming turtle fountain. Get there by way of a grand stair from the 1890s that gave the park its nickname, the 'Pincio di

NORTHWEST BOLOGNA: THE VENICE OF EMILIA-ROMAGNA

You wouldn't know it today, but Bologna is criss-crossed by 60km of canals, dating from the 12th to the 16th century. Water from the Reno and Savena rivers was channelled through four main canals to power the flour mills and the massive wheels used to spin cloth, especially for the once-important hemp and silk industries. The extra humidity provided by the canals was ideal for raising silkworms. They were also useful for flood control; the water was used for watering animals and for laundry (preferably downstream). The network was linked to the 36km Navile Canal that connected Bologna to Ferrara and Venice. The main port, where 50 barges a day once transported passengers and tonnes of goods (they could make it to Venice in 40 hours) was closed in 1935; today the only surviving building is the Salara, or old salt depot (see box, page 83). Nearby is the Liberty-style Manifattura Tabacchi, the tobacco factory that once used the Reno Canal to power the tobacco-cutting mills; today the building houses the headquarters of the Cineteca (page 80).

In the boom years of the 1950s and 60s, the canals were paved over to become car parks and streets such as Via Riva Reno. Even so, here and there you can catch glimpses of the water: at the Grada where the Reno Canal entered Bologna (*Viale Giovanni Vicini 19*); at the former tannery, the Pellacaneria della Grada, now the headquarters of the Consortium of the Reno and Savena Canals (*Via della Grada 10*); from the bridge in Via Malcontenta; and at Via Capo di Lucca 10. The most Venetian view, however, is through the Finestrella (little window) cut into the wall at Via Piella 16. You may have to open the shutter for a peek.

Bologna'. On Fridays and Saturdays the park and nearby Piazza VIII Agosto host La Piazzola market from 06.30 to 20.00, with 400 stalls selling clothes, accessories, pots, pans, plants and more.

Manifattura delle Arti [78 A1] (*Via Azzo Gardino;* w *manifatturadellearti.org*)
Located at the meeting of the Reno and Cavaticcio canals, this part of Bologna was a hive of water-powered industry into the 19th century, filled with mills, factories and warehouses. But it was already on its way to abandonment when Allied bombs more or less finished the job.

The post-war decades saw the redevelopment of the area as a dismal modern neighbourhood. Then in 2003, the city and university combined forces to make the zone into the Manifattura delle Arti (Arts Factory), a centre of contemporary art and culture unique in Italy, a project designed by the late Pritzker Prize-winning architect Aldo Rossi.

Anchored by MAMbo and the **Cineteca** (page 80), the district hosts contemporary art galleries, public and student housing, the **Cassero LGBTQ+** centre in the Salara (see box, page 83), and the Slow Food-sponsored **Mercato della Terra** (pages 84–5). A walkway winds through the **Giardino del Cavaticcio** [78 A1], lined with sculptures by Giò Pomodoro. And summer sees a host of activities, concerts and festivals (Bio Park, Lady Stardust and the Cinema Ritrovato and Biografilm Festivals).

MAMbo [78 B1] (*Via Don Giovanni Minzoni 14;* \ *051 649 6611;* w *mambo-bologna.org;* ⊕ *10.00–18.00 Tue, Wed, Sun & holidays, 10.00–19.00 Thu, Fri & Sat; permanent collection: adults €6, over 64s & ages 18–25 €4, under 18s & students with ID free*)
In 2007, Bologna's former Gallery of Modern Art morphed into MAMbo and inaugurated its new home in the vast spaces of the Ex-Forno del Pane, a former industrial bakery in the Manifattura delle Arti.

It houses an exceptional collection of contemporary Italian art from the latter half of the 20th century to the present. The museum's permanent collection has thematically arranged works, starting with 'Arte e Ideologia', featuring Renato Guttuso's *I Funerali di Togliatti* (1972) on the death of Palmiro Togliatti, leader of the Italian Communist Party. The first floor hosts frequent special exhibitions, often solo shows by big-name Italian or foreign artists. The mezzanine has an extensive art book and newspaper library, and there's a cool shop and bar-bistro serving lunch, *aperitivi* and Sunday brunch.

Museo Morandi (*Admission inc in MAMbo ticket*)
After the earthquake of 2012 damaged its home in the Palazzo d'Accursio, the Museo Morandi was rehoused in the same building as MAMbo. It's a fascinating collection of works by Bologna's best-known modern artist donated to the city by his sister. These are some of the 20th century's most thoughtful paintings. His subject matter (bottles, boxes, a vase of flowers) is mundane, but Giorgio Morandi's fierce gaze transforms it with startling intensity; as Umberto Eco put it, he 'made the dust sing'. There are also landscapes of Grizzana where Morandi spent the summers (page 139), as well as portraits and drawings. MAMbo also offers tours of his house, the **Casa Morandi** (page 102).

BOLOGNA'S WEST END
Santissimo Salvatore [78 B6] (*Cnr Via IV Novembre & Via Cesare Battisti;* \ *051 648 0611;* ⊕ *09.00–19.30 daily*)
The parish for English students in Bologna for centuries, this dates back to 1136, but in 1623 it was completely rebuilt. The vanilla interior was inspired by the baths of ancient Rome, framed by Corinthian columns.

3

You cannot demonstrate your own greatness by remaining at one extreme, but by reaching out to both extremes at the same time, and filling the intermediate space.

Giorgio Morandi

Giorgio Morandi (1890–1964) is generally considered the greatest still-life painter of the 20th century, and one of the founders of Minimalism. An artist of geometry and tonal intimism, a few everyday objects formed his intensely contemplative and lyrical 'personal alphabet'. He belonged to no movement or school but his own, but was as timeless and contemplative as the painters who inspired him: Giotto, Masaccio, Piero della Francesca, Chardin and, probably most of all, Cézanne, who scrutinised the world just as closely.

Morandi's own life was a still life. For most of it he lived with his three sisters in the same house in his native Bologna. If they left, it was usually to spend the summer in the Apennine coolness of a modest cottage in Grizzana. Some have found echoes of Bologna itself in his art – in his austere colours, in his tower-like bottles.

One of Morandi's rare trips outside his home town took him to Florence in 1910, where he studied the great Tuscan masters at first hand. He attended Bologna's Accademia di Belle Arti and in 1914 had his first exhibition with fellow students in Bologna's Hotel Baglioni, while starting to teach drawing in elementary school. After joining the army in 1915, he suffered a serious breakdown and was discharged.

He briefly joined the Metaphysical art movement in 1918 along with Giorgio de Chirico and Carlo Carrà who were in nearby Ferrara at the time, but by 1922 had found the style he would paint in for the rest of his life. 'I am essentially a painter of the kind of still-life composition that communicates a sense of tranquillity and privacy, moods which I have always valued above all else.'

It preserves two exceptional works from its medieval predecessor: a gold-ground, venerated *Madonna della Vittoria* in a gem-studded frame painted by Simone de' Crocifissi, and a beautiful polyptych of the *Coronation of the Virgin* (1355) by Vitale da Bologna, with one of the artist's typically endearing Madonnas, commissioned for the chapel of the English students. On the left side, under a nativity scene, a panel shows St Petronius having a chat with St Scholastica. On the right side, under the figure of St Catherine (patron saint of philosophy), is St Thomas à Becket, who studied law in Bologna. The *Virgin in the Temple*, nearby, by Girolamo di Treviso, also came from the long-gone English Chapel.

The next chapel has a *Resurrection* by Mastelletta, with Christ wreathed in gold over a troubled blue-grey world. Also seek out the unusual *Story of the Crucifixion According to the Miracle of Beirut* by Mannerist Jacopo Coppi (1523–91), a mysterious figure who worked with Vasari and somehow earned the nickname 'Il Meglio' (The Best), the *Holy Family* by Alessandro Tiarini and a *St John the Baptist Blessed by His Father* by Il Garofalo. Painter Giovanni Francesco Barbieri, better known as Guercino, is buried in the centre of the nave.

There's electricity in the air in this corner of Bologna. At Via IV Novembre 7, a plaque marks the birthplace of Guglielmo Marconi, while nearby at Via Testoni 2,

Luigi Galvani conducted his famous experiments on electrical impulses in living things – making frogs' legs twitch with a jolt of current.

San Francesco [78 A5] (*Piazza Malpighi 9;* ☎ *051 221762;* ⏲ *06.30–noon & 15.00–19.00 daily*) Lovely Gothic San Francesco was begun when St Francis was still alive. Bologna had one of the first convents of his new order by 1211 and, when Francis himself visited Bologna in 1222, interest soared. In 1236, Pope Gregory IX himself gave his approval for a new more monumental complex for the growing order of Friars Minor.

Consecrated in 1251 by Pope Innocent IV, the church was partially inspired by the Gothic cathedrals of northern France. Its massive flying buttresses are a rarity in Italian churches. The façade, a lofty screen front typical of Emilia-Romagna's plains, was rebuilt four years after it was blown clean off the church by Allied bombers in 1944.

Inside, the striking, lofty interior is calm and elegant, all white contrasted with dark brick piers and vaulting, a style that would come to characterise Bologna's churches, culminating in San Petronio. In 1796, when Napoleon converted it into a barracks, much of its accumulated art was stolen or destroyed, before the church was returned to the Franciscans in 1886. Several Renaissance-era tombs have survived all the changes, including the Tomb of Pope Alexander IV (who died in Bologna in 1410), the work of Tuscan Niccolò Lamberti.

On the high altar the beautiful marble *Ancona* (1393) was sculpted by Jacobello and Pier Paolo dalle Masegne, with various saints (including eight busts bizarrely impaled on pinnacles) and superb naturalistic scenes from the life of St Francis. The Chiostro dei Morti is lined with the tombs of 14th-century university dons.

Around the back, take a look at the great apse with its flying buttresses, along with the elegant campanile added in the 1390s by Antonio di Vincenzo, and four unique monuments – little pavilions with pyramidal roofs raised off the ground on slender columns. These are the **Tombs of the Glossatori,** memorials to four notable professors of law of the 13th century: Accursio and his son Francesco Accursio, Odofredo Denario and Rolandino de' Romanzi.

They owe their current state to Alfonso Rubbiani, the arch-restorer Viollet-le-Duc of Bologna: finding the fragments of the tombs inside the basilica during his restoration, he decided to restore and erect them outside the church (similar to Verona's Scaliger Tombs), in the style of the Mausoleum of Halicarnassus, to make these founders of the University of Bologna into public theatre and a focal point of civic pride.

SOUTH OF PIAZZA MAGGIORE
Palazzo Sanuti-Bevilacqua [78 C7] (*Via d'Azeglio 31;* ☎ *051 234666;* ⏲ *by request*) One of the few Bolognese *palazzi* without any porticoes, the Palazzo Sanuti-Belivacqua (1482) seems out of place in this city, with heavily rusticated stonework and biforate windows that make it the very picture of a Florentine palace from that era.

The man who paid for it, Niccolò Sanuti, was well connected – his wife was the mistress of Sante Bentivoglio, tyrant of the city. After the fall of the Bentivogli it remained a top address. The Council of Trent, eternally debating the reforms of the Counter-Reformation Church, took refuge here from a plague in Trent in 1547–49.

The palace belongs to the Bevilacqua-degli Ariosti family today, but even if you haven't booked a visit you might be able to have a peek at the elegant courtyard, with its fountain, loggias and terracotta decoration.

Anyone who thinks our contemporary world is overrun with lawyers may be reassured (or depressed) to know that the Middle Ages had it just as bad. Blame it on Bologna, or specifically, on a man named Irnerius, the noble forebear of all the tribe, born in this city around 1055.

Irnerius was hardly the ivory tower sort of scholar. In his day no-one could afford such a luxury; there was serious work to be done. In fact, Irnerius was a protégé of Matilda of Canossa (page 197); it was she who first convinced him to take up the study of law and then made good use of his talents in diplomatic missions, although after her death Irnerius went over to the other side, serving Emperor Henry V.

But both sides had an interest in common: reviving Roman law to replace the many conflicting local codes, such as that of the Lombards in northern Italy, which were commonly based on archaic German tradition and feudal rights. In those days any man had the right to be judged according to the law of his birthplace, residence or station, which might be Lombard law, Byzantine law, or canon law if he was a cleric; the confusions are only too easy to imagine. The growing *comuni*, including Bologna itself, had an even greater interest in reform, since the Germanic codes were made for a rural population and had nothing useful to say about city rights or the regulation of commerce.

After Irnerius came the 'Four Doctors': Bulgarus, Martinus Gosia, Hugo da Porta Ravennate and Jacobus de Voragine. Legend says they were pupils of Irnerius, though that's probably not true. (It makes a good example of how everything in those times was cast into legend. Another set of legendary 'Four Doctors' was credited with founding the great medical university at Salerno in the same era.) All four were already acting as advisers to Emperor Frederick Barbarossa, following the eternal principle of civilisation: where there are clever lawyers, there's power and money too.

No profession was a surer road to riches – enough to pay for the most lavish tombs in Bologna. And in the Church, a legal education was the best guarantee of career

San Procolo [67 E5] (*Via d'Azeglio 54; \051 331223; ☉ 07.00–11.00 Mon–Fri, 09.00– 11.00 & 17.00–19.00 Sat, 09.30–noon Sun*) Begun in the 4th century and rebuilt over and over in the years since, this church commemorates a Roman legionary, St Proculus, a martyr under Diocletian who became one of Bologna's eight patron saints.

The pretty, peaceful Neoclassical interior is largely the work of Carlo Francesco Dotti, though after a big Napoleonic interruption work didn't get under way until 1826. Here, the highlight is the dome over the crossing, coffered and centred with an oculus to illuminate the main altar, like the Pantheon in Rome. Note the sarcophagus in front of the altar, with a little window that displays the saint's illuminated relics. Over this is a dramatic altarpiece of Proculus's beheading painted by Giuseppe Pedretti in the 18th century; the chapels include works by Leonello Spada, Bartolomeo Cesi and Alessandro Tiarini.

In the early days of the university, San Procolo and its monastery were connected with the School of Law. On the wall outside the church, the scholars left a small plaque with a tongue-twisting Latin riddle on it, dated 1393 – something about the campanile collapsing on a bell-ringer, or a student who died from overwork. It's so clever that no-one today can figure out what it really says.

The adjacent monastery later became a convent and hospice, the place for Bolognesi to leave anonymously *esposti e bastardini* – abandoned children and 'little bastards'.

advancement. In the heyday of the medieval papacy most of the popes started their careers as canon lawyers. Alexander III (1159–81), one of Bologna's four popes, had been a university *glossatore*; another alumnus, the great Pope Innocent III, may have been one of his students. Even Thomas Becket, future Archbishop of Canterbury, spent five years in the 1140s studying his glosses in Bologna.

Irnerius' major contribution was a gloss of the Code of Justinian; in other words, he wrote explanations of the difficult points in the margins, along with recommendations of how these 500-year-old laws would apply to modern cases.

His successors, who came to be known as *glossatori*, naturally carried this erudite pettifoggery to its logical extreme. By about 1250 ambitious doctors were writing not only glosses, but glosses on the glosses, each identified with the doctor's initial, and occasionally someone would add glosses on these. One scholar complained that the glosses were like a 'multitude of locusts' that literally covered up the text; in this age of expensive hand-copied books, only when all the space on the pages was filled would a new copy be commissioned. One of the doctors entombed at San Francesco, Francesco Accursio, helped put an end to the confusion with his *Glossa Magna* (1250), a commentary so comprehensive and trenchant that it made the earlier ones obsolete.

Whatever we think of lawyers, some respect is due for an effort that has been called 'the most brilliant achievement of the intellect of medieval Europe'. That intellect, with its passion for order, definition and classification, its reverence for the written word and its relentless chains of logic, eventually made philosophy and science into hidebound scholastic nightmares. But for the law, it was perfect. It sharpened arguments and minds, and turned reason loose on the practical things of this world; some have claimed that it was the greatest factor in setting Western civilisation on its dizzying trajectory over centuries to come. For better or worse, the processes and patterns of thought for that civilisation were made in Bologna.

San Domenico [67 F5] (*Piazza San Domenico;* \ *051 581718;* w *www. centrosandomenico.it;* ⊕ *09.00–noon & 15.30–18.00 Mon–Fri, 09.00–noon & 15.30– 17.00 Sat, 15.30–17.00 Sun*) This church was built in 1251 to house the relics of St Dominic, founder of the Order of Preaching Friars or Dominicans. Dominic had arrived in Bologna in 1218, and was so impressed by the scholarship of the university city that he built a convent by a small church on this site.

He died in Bologna in 1221 and was buried in a simple wooden coffin in the church floor (as was the custom: holy bodies had to be hidden to foil relic thieves). As the Dominicans' popularity soared, a bigger church was built to house the saint's tomb; Pope Innocent IV consecrated it in 1251, and although it's been frequently remodelled (the façade was added only in 1910), it is still one of the great treasure houses of art in Bologna.

Cappella di San Domenico Inside, the narrow Baroque nave only accentuates the effect of a church that is nearly as long as San Petronio. The main attraction is St Dominic's Chapel in the right aisle, originally Gothic but rebuilt and enlarged in the 17th century by Floriano Ambrosini to contain all the pilgrims who came to worship beside the saint's relics in the spectacular, and at the time revolutionary, **Arca di San Domenico**, mostly completed by 1261.

Many hands contributed to this sculptural ensemble, notably Niccolò Pisano, who had just completed the magnificent pulpit in Pisa's Baptistry and was deemed by the Dominicans to be the only man up to the task. Assisted by his followers (which included Arnolfo da Cambio, future architect of Florence's cathedral), he executed the sarcophagus and the beautiful reliefs of the saint's life.

Two centuries later, Niccolò dell'Arca (Niccolò da Bari, who gained his name and fame from this work) added the cover of the sarcophagus and the statues of Bologna's eight patron saints; Niccolò died before the group was finished, leaving the rest to the 20-year-old Michelangelo, who had to leave Florence during the political turbulence that followed the death of his patron Lorenzo de' Medici. During 1494, when Savonarola, a Dominican who had started his career in this very monastery, was gaining power in Florence, Michelangelo was here sculpting the figures of SS Petronius and Proculus.

Some of the biggest names of the Bolognese school decorated the walls with early Baroque extravaganzas, including Mastelletta, Alessandro Tiarini (*St Dominic Resuscitating a Child*) and Leonello Spada (a rather chilling *Burning of the Heretical Books*). Hovering above all in the ceiling is Guido Reni's *Apotheosis of St Dominic* (1615).

Cappella del Rosario Across the nave from the Arca, this large chapel was dedicated to the Virgin of the Rosary after she was credited with ending the plague in Bologna in 1630. Floriano Ambrosini designed the altar, under ceiling frescoes in quadratura by Angelo Michele Colonna and Agostino Mitelli. For the *Scenes of the Mystery of the Rosary* on the walls, the Dominicans again paid top dollar: Ludovico Carracci (*Annunciation*, *Visitation*, *Scourging* and *Christ Falling under the Cross*), Bartolomeo Cesi (*Nativity*, *Christ in the Garden*, *The Crowning with Thorns*, *The Crucifixion* and *Pentecost*), Denis Calvaert (*Presentation of Jesus in the Temple*), Lavinia Fontana (*Jesus among the Doctors* and *The Coronation of the Virgin*), Domenichino (*Assumption of the Blessed Virgin*) and Guido Reni (*Resurrection*); the chapel holds Reni's tomb. A young Mozart played the organ here in 1769.

Right transept This holds a *St Thomas Aquinas* by Guercino, but in the nearest chapel don't miss *The Mystic Marriage of St Catherine*, a late work by Florentine Filippino Lippi.

Left transept In one of the three chapels here, the grave of King Enzo of Sardinia, bastard son of Emperor Frederick II and the last of the House of Hohenstaufen (d1272) is marked by an 18th-century marble monument. The *Crucifixion* (1250) in the middle chapel of St Michael the Archangel is the masterpiece of Giunta Pisano, as well as being the first signed work by an Italian artist ('*Cuius docta manus me pixit Junta Pisanus*' – 'painted by the hand of Giunta Pisano'). One of the most notable paintings of trecento Italy, still powerfully stylised and influenced by Byzantine art, it was the first to make a move towards realism, showing Christ suffering on the cross (unlike the serene figure in Byzantine and Romanesque art, as in the 12th-century *Crucifixion* in San Pietro; page 113). Giunta's work would influence Cimabue's own more emotional, more realistic art, creating the first spark of the Italian Renaissance.

Here, too, is the 13th-century tomb of Taddeo Pepoli, Bologna's trecento boss (d1347), by an unknown Florentine artist, and a 14th-century fresco of *SS Thomas Aquinas and Benedict*.

Apse A triptych of the *Adoration of the Magi* by Bartolomeo Cesi is in the apse, along with one of the basilica's masterpieces: the 102 beautiful wooden intarsia **choir stalls** by the friar Damiano from Bergamo, with help from his brother Stefano (1528–51), with Old Testament scenes on the right, and New Testament scenes on the left. During the Renaissance they were known as the 'Eighth Wonder of the World' and were greatly admired by Emperor Charles V during his visit.

Museo di San Domenico (⊕ *By request, 09.00–noon & 15.30–18.00 Mon–Sat, 15.00–17.00 Sun; admission free*) To the right of altar is the entrance to this museum, with a good deal of church clutter in its two rooms. But there are also fine works relocated from the church and monastery, including a bust of *St Dominic* by Niccolò dell'Arca, more fine marquetry by Fra Damiano (*The Story of San Girolamo*); the *Madonna of the Velvet* by Lippo di Dalmasio and a *St Raymond* by Ludovico Carracci. There's also St Louis's finger in an elaborate gold Gothic reliquary, a gift to the church from French King Philip IV after the canonisation of his father.

Ghisilardi Chapel, and tombs (⊕ *Same as museum*) This chapel to the left of San Domenico's façade was designed by Sienese architect Baldassarre Peruzzi, who was in Bologna to plan a façade for San Petronio that was never built. While he was here, he built this chapel. Inspired by the writing of Vitruvius and his experience among the antiquities of Rome, Peruzzi created an elegant chapel with Corinthian columns in the form of a Latin cross, in a reworking of Classicism that wouldn't be seen again until the Venetian churches of Palladio. Alfonso Lombardi sculpted the figure of Christ.

Outside are two tombs of noted doctors of Law, Egidio Foscherari (1289) and Rolandino de' Passageri (1310), similar to the Tombs of the Glossatori (page 119).

San Paolo Maggiore [78 C7] (*Via Carbonesi 18;* ☏ *051 331 490;* ⊕ *08.00–11.30 & 16.00–18.30 Mon–Sat, 08.30–13.00 & 17.30–19.00 Sun*) Built in 1606–22 for the fashionable Counter-Reformation Order of the Barnabites, this church was designed by one of Bologna's leading Baroque architects, Giovanni Ambrogio Mazenta (himself a Barnabite priest), who also designed the cathedral and San Salvatore.

The interior has lavishly painted vaults (*Scenes of St Paul in the Aeropagus in Athens*) by brothers Antonio and Giuseppe Rolli, but what draws the eye is the high altar's sober and eloquent *Decapitation of St Paul*, a masterpiece by Bolognese sculptor Alessandro Algardi, commissioned by the Barnabites for this spot. Algardi has frozen the action in time, creating a breathless, tension-filled void between the two figures in a spiralling composition, contrasting the cruel muscular executioner preparing to strike and the kneeling, resigned saint, his eyes closed in a final prayer.

Algardi also sculpted the medallions on the altar; in the chapels are paintings by Ludovico Carracci (*Paradise*, one of his best), Giacomo Cavedoni, Guercino and Crespi.

Spirito Santo (Oratorio dei Celestini) [78 C7] (*Via Val d'Aposa 6*) Tucked away in the back streets behind San Petronio, this delightful little church stands pink and pretty with a façade made of nothing but brick and terracotta. The oratorio was built by the Celestines in 1481 to house an icon of the Virgin Mary. Later it served as the home of a confraternity called the Spirito Santo. Like so much else in Bologna, the façade was restored by Alfonso Rubbiani in the 1890s, which explains its pristine condition. The five *tondi* of saints and the other decoration may have been the work of Vincenzo Onofri.

Collegio di Spagna [67 E5] (*Via Collegio di Spagna 4;* ☏ *051 330408;* w *realecollegiospagna.it;* ⊕ *during exhibitions or by request*) This college was founded in 1365 for Spanish students by Cardinal Albornoz, the papacy's top man in Italy while the popes were hiding out in Avignon. It would later be the model for the colleges at the University of Salamanca and is claimed to be the oldest institution in the world, outside of Spain itself, with the word 'Spanish' in its title. In 1488, Ferdinand and Isabel placed the college under royal patronage, where it has remained ever since. Cervantes studied here, as did St Ignatius of Loyola.

Albornoz commissioned architect Matteo Gattapone of Umbria, who is best known for his striking engineering works in Spoleto. But it's a shame he didn't get a chance to design more buildings: the Collegio's combination of simplicity and sophistication has fascinated architects over the centuries. The courtyard is a delight, its loggia made up of two tiers of rounded arcades, the top arches half the height of the lower. The upper façade of Gattapone's church of San Clemente looming over the roof behind adds the perfect final touch.

In the late Middle Ages Bologna had many such colleges for various nationalities, but this one (still officially Spanish territory) is the only one to survive. After a meticulous 32-year restoration, which uncovered a number of long-lost frescoes in the royal chamber and antechamber, it won the Europa Nostra Prize in 2012 for conservation. It has several works inside, including the *Martyrdom of St Peter of Arbués*, appropriately by Giuseppe Crespi, the painter from Bologna nicknamed 'Lo Spagnuolo' (the Spaniard) for his natty dress sense.

Corpus Domini [67 E5] (*Via Tagliapietre 21;* ☏ *051 331277;* w *santuariocorpusdomini. it;* ⊕ *09.00–noon & 15.00–19.00 daily; Cappella della Santa* ⊕ *09.30–11.30 & 16.00– 17.45 daily; museum* ⊕ *same as Cappella Tue, Thu, Sat–Sun*) Born into a noble Bolognese family, Caterina de' Vigri (1413–63) was raised in the ducal court of Ferrara as a lady-in-waiting, where she was educated in literature, art and music. In 1426 she entered the Corpus Domini convent in Ferrara, but eventually Church superiors called her back to Bologna to serve as abbess here.

Caterina painted and wrote, and as a mystic became famous for her account of her visions of God and Satan in the *Treatise on the Seven Spiritual Weapons Necessary for Spiritual Warfare*, which she kept hidden until on her deathbed, but later went through 21 editions, and translations into most European languages. After she was buried, so many miracles occurred that 18 days later her body was exhumed and, found uncorrupted, was seated on a throne, where her mummy has remained ever since, now behind glass, in the **Cappella della Santa** (she was canonised as St Catherine of Bologna in 1712).

The convent is still partially cloistered, but the church and chapel are open to visitors; the church had to be repaired after bomb damage in World War II. It has a painting of baby Jesus, attributed to St Catherine herself (she is a patron saint of artists) and which was often taken to the homes of the ill.

Another painting by the saint, the *Madonna del Pomo*, is in a little **museum** off the second chapel to the left, in a room decorated with frescoes by Marcantonio Franceschini; it also has copies of her writings.

THE BOLOGNA HILLS Bologna may not be well endowed with parks and green space, but the city has the good fortune of being built next to a patch of wooded hills, the first foothills of the Apennines. Of course, these hills also made the city nearly indefensible after the invention of artillery – but good fortune kept anyone from ever besieging it.

Museo del Tessuto e della Tappezzeria Vittorio Zironi [66 D6] (*Via di Casaglia 3 (3km walk from the centre, or take bus 20);* \ *051 219 4528;* w *museibologna.it;* ☉ *09.00–14.00 Thu, 10.00–18.30 Sat–Sun; €5, free 1st Sun of month*) The 18th-century Neoclassical Villa Spada, surrounded by elegant box-hedged Italian gardens cascading down the slope, has seen its share of history. Once owned by tenor Antonio Poggi, it became the Austrian headquarters in Bologna in 1849 when its tower served as the prison of Garibaldi's fighting priest, Ugo Bassi, and his comrade Count Livraghi, who were shot by a firing squad near the villa wall. At the south end of the garden is the memorial (1975) to the 128 resistance fighters from Bologna province who were executed during World War II.

The garden's terracotta statues seem to be showing off their clothes, appropriately enough because the villa, purchased by the city in the 1960s, has housed a unique collection of textiles since the 1990s. Vittorio Zironi came up with the idea of a textile museum while being interned in a prisoner-of-war camp in Germany and hearing that a similar museum in Berlin had been bombed in the war. As soon as he returned to Bologna, he set off on his mission, accumulating a huge collection of 6,000 woven artefacts, embroideries, tapestries, upholstery textiles and clothing dating back to the 4th century AD from Europe, the Middle East and Asia, as well as looms and other machinery demonstrating how they have been woven since the Middle Ages, all displayed within the villa's pretty frescoed walls.

Above the second upper entrance to the gardens on Via di Casaglia is the *curvone*, the curve in the road with a magnificent 360-degree view over Bologna's *centro storico*.

The Porticato [66 C6] In the southwest corner of the *centro storico* is the Porta Saragozza [67 E5], the starting point of the portico to beat all porticoes – the Porticato, winding 4km up to the Sanctuary of the Madonna di San Luca, with 666 arches along the way, a kind of eccentric embellishment only possible in the Age of the Baroque (it was also quite a boost to the local pilgrimage trade).

It took them long enough to build it. Begun in 1674 and finished in 1793, each arch was financed by a different family, religious group, guild or corporation. Each set up a plaque by their contribution, although many have vanished or resemble ghosts of their former selves.

The Porticato was also intended as a meditation exercise, like the chapels representing the stations of the cross (Via Crucis) that were laid out on hillsides around Europe in this era. Beginning at the elaborate Baroque **Arco di Meloncello** (1732) designed by Carlo Francesco, there are 15 rest stops for prayer, corresponding to the 15 Mysteries of the Life of the Virgin Mary. Not even Bologna's numerous students of the occult can explain why there are exactly 666 arches. That at least is the traditional number; people often try to count them, and they never get the same answer twice.

Santuario della Madonna di San Luca [66 B7] (*Via di San Luca 36;* \ *051 614 2339;* ☉ *Apr–Oct 06.30–19.00, Nov–Mar 06.30–17.00 daily*) Bologna's chief religious patron saint (Petronio is the 'civic patron') is the Madonna of this icon attributed to St Luke, which according to local legend hung in the Hagia Sophia in Constantinople. A pious Greek named Theocles had a vision there, in which the Virgin commanded him to remove the icon to the 'sentinel mountain'. He wandered for years with it before coming to Rome, where he was taken in by a kindly Bolognese senator, who told him about the Colle della Guardia back home.

Nobody knows for sure when the icon turned up (studies have dated it to the 12th century), although the sanctuary seems to have begun as a pilgrim hostel, perhaps in the 11th century, before becoming a pilgrimage destination in its own right.

The sanctuary church was designed by Carlo Francesco Dotti in 1723, and completed by his son. It was a time when the impulse of Baroque architecture was running out of steam, and architects often tried to find inspiration by going back to the origins; this church, with its elliptical shape preceded by a curving portico, draws heavily on Bernini's revolutionary churches in Rome, built a century earlier.

Still, Dotti had a big problem – making a monument that would serve as a fitting end to the long pilgrimage walk, and at the same time be a conspicuous landmark visible from all over Bologna – and his retro creation does the job admirably. The interior is richly decorated; besides the miraculous icon it contains three paintings by Guido Reni and one by Guercino. From outside, there are fantastic views of the Apennines.

The Sanctuary can be reached either via the Porticato (page 125), or by bus 58 from the Arco di Meloncello, or the San Luca Express Bus from Piazza Maggiore (page 69).

Panoramic terrace (⊕ *09.00–12.30 & 14.30–19.00 Fri & Sat, 09.00–19.00 Sun; San Luca Sky Experience Card: adults €5, ages 10–18 €3, under 10s free*) As of April 2017, you can climb a hundred steps up a narrow spiral staircase to the church's attic for the unique 180-degree view of Bologna and the hills

Colle dell'Osservanza
Other famous viewpoints over Bologna are from the next hill east, the Colle dell'Osservanza (take bus 52 from Piazza Cavour or Via Farini). Near the top is the **Villa Aldini** [67 E6] and **Madonna del Monte** [66 D6] (*Via dell'Osservanza 35/a;* ✆ *051 219 3930;* w *museibologna.it; check website for guided tours*). Napoleon had admired the view from this prominent hill overlooking Bologna, and in 1811 his powerful minister Antonio Aldini, eager to please the emperor, commissioned Giuseppe Nadi to demolish the recently suppressed Benedictine monastery then on the site and build a Neoclassical summer villa in its place, complete with Olympian gods on the tympanum.

The monastery had a peculiar old round church, known as the **Madonna del Monte**. Legend has it that it was founded by a noblewoman, Picciola de' Galluzzi in 1116, who planned a shrine in memory of her husband. As she considered the site, a dove with a piece of straw in its mouth circled overhead, which Picciola took as a divine suggestion that she should build a perfectly round church oriented to the four cardinal points.

Made of brick and decorated with blind arcading (note the curious faces and symbols at the bottom of the arches, including a swastika) the church was visited by Dante and several saints, including Dominic, Anthony and Bernardino. Fortunately, rather than destroy the quirky little church, Aldini built around it and used it as a music and dining room.

In 1844 there was talk of reopening the church, but the cardinal refused because worshippers would have to enter a 'pagan' portal under the Olympian gods. In 1888 the property was donated to the *comune*, and in the 1930s architect Guido Zucchini was put in charge of its restoration. When he took down Aldini's wallpaper, he found a surprise: the original Byzantine-Romanesque frescoes of the 12 Apostles and Jesus, with big eyes and giant flipper hands (long fingers being a symbol of holiness), along with a striking modern-looking portrait of the Madonna that was detached and framed.

To the south, under the hill on Via San Mamolo, is the **Parco di Monte Paderno** [66 D7] (or Parco di Villa Ghigi), a large expanse of oak forests, meadows and trails, and a favourite picnic spot (buses 29 and 30 buses get within 1km of it). Monte Paderno made a big stir in 1603 when Vicenzo Cascariolo, a shoemaker-alchemist, discovered deposits of a luminescent mineral called barite ('Bologna stone'), and claimed he had found the Philosopher's Stone.

San Michele in Bosco [67 E6] (*Piazzale di San Michele in Bosco (bus 30 from Stazione Centrale or the Navetta A);* ☎ *051 636 6705; church* ⊕ *09.00–noon & 16.00–19.00 daily, library* ⊕ *10.00–17.30 Mon, 09.30–14.30 Tue–Thu, 10.00–13.30 Fri, 09.00–13.00 1st & 4th Sat, closed Aug*) The hilltop site of San Michele in Bosco (St Michael's in the Woods) was a favourite retreat for hermits in Lombard times. In the 14th century, Pope Urban V granted the land to the Olivetan Benedictine monks. They rebuilt and remodelled the church, lastly in 1523, giving it a marble portal by Baldassare Peruzzi of Siena.

Inside there's a tomb by another Sienese sculptor, Jacopo della Quercia. The walls are covered with frescoes by Girolamo da Carpi and *quadraturisti* Domenico Canuti and Angelo Michele Colonna. Next to the church is an unusual octagonal **cloister**, with remains of frescoes by Ludovico Carracci and Guido Reni.

The **monastery** became a barracks under Napoleon, then a prison, then a residence for the papal legate. The complex was purchased by surgeon Francesco Rizzoli, who made it into an orthopaedic hospital, the Istituto Rizzoli. Most of it is off limits, but take the door on the right side of the presbytery to the 150m gallery called the **Cannocchiale di Bologna**, cleverly designed to create an optical illusion; walk to the far end and look back towards the city, and you can see the Torre Asinelli zooming in as if through a telescope.

The peaceful **Library** at Via Putti 1 is worth a look as well: built in 1517, it is lined with old wooden bookshelves, cabinets and antique books, iced with colour-drenched frescoes by Amico Aspertini.

PERIPHERAL ATTRACTIONS

Casa Carducci [67 G6] (*Piazza Giosuè Carducci 5 (bus 32 from Stazione Centrale);* ☎ *051 347592;* w *casacarducci.it;* ⊕ *Sep–mid-Jul 09.00–13.00 Tue–Sat; adults €5, ages 18–25 €3, under 18s free, free 1st Sun of month*) With an irony he probably enjoyed, Italy's great atheist poet and Nobel Prize winner Giosuè Carducci (see box, page 28) lived in what was originally the church and oratory of the Confraternità di Santa Maria della Pietà, better known as Piombo or 'Lead' because it was built where a lead sheet engraved with a Pietà was discovered in 1502. The confraternity had been suppressed by Napoleon and, after Carducci's death, the building was made into this museum and library of his life and letters.

The ground floor also houses the **Museo Civico del Risorgimento**, dedicated to Bologna's role in the unification of Italy. Don't miss the adjacent **Giardino Memoriale**, with its very grand marble **Monument to Carducci** sculpted by Leonardo Bistolfi in 1928.

Giardini Margherita [67 F6] (*Piazza di Porta Santo Stefano, bus 32, 33, 38, 39, 17, 13, 90 or 96*) Bologna keeps its largest and most beautiful park southeast of the *centro storico* where few casual visitors ever see it. Named for the much-loved Queen of Italy who was on the throne when it was laid out in the 1870s (she also lent her name to a classic style of pizza), the park has artificial gypsum cliffs, tree-lined lanes and lawns, a splendid oak grove and a pretty lagoon with an island in the middle. On the south end, you can see a rare above-ground section of the Savena Canal, part of the network of artificial waterways that once powered the city. There's also a reproduction of a 2,800-year-old Villanova-culture round hut on display (perhaps fittingly, since an Etruscan necropolis was discovered in the park itself).

La Certosa [66 C5] (*Via della Certosa 18 (bus 19, 36, 38 or 39);* \051 615 0811; ⊕ *winter 08.00–17.00 daily, summer 07.00–18.00 daily*) Out in the western suburbs, the Certosa was a Carthusian monastery with a church dedicated to San Girolamo, decorated with scenes of the *Passion* by Bartolomeo Cesi and sporting two fine Renaissance cloisters. In 1800, it was chosen to become the city's main cemetery, and has acres of grandiose mausolea, as well as sections for non-Catholics and a separate Jewish cemetery.

The choice of La Certosa as a cemetery was curiously atavistic. In 1869, Etruscan tombs, dating back to the 4th century BC, were found here, making it one of the oldest cemeteries in any European city; the finds are now in the Museo Civico Archeologico (pages 93–4).

Museo Pelagalli [66 D4] (*Via Col di Lana 7;* \051 649 1008; w *museopelagalli. com;* ⊕ *2hr guided tours by appointment; €5*). In Marconi's home town, it's not surprising that this is one of Bologna's best-loved museums, with more than 2,000 historic working radios, televisions, mechanical musical instruments, cinema equipment, jukeboxes, telephones and computers accumulated over the decades by local enthusiast Giovanni Pelagalli, with rare and unique items dating from 1760 to the present. In 2007, the collection won a UNESCO prize; at the time of writing, however, it is seeking a new home.

Museo del Patrimonio Industriale [67 E2] (*Via della Beverara 123 (bus 30 from the centre or station towards Sostegno, stop: Beverara);* \051 635 6611; w *museibologna.it/patrimonioindustriale;* ⊕ *Sep–mid-Jun 09.00–13.00 Tue–Fri, 09.00–13.00 & 15.00–18.00 Sat, 15.00–18.00 Sun; mid-Jun–mid-Sep 09.00–13.00 Mon–Fri; adults €5, ages 18–25 & over 65s €3, under 18s free*) Bologna's canals converged at the Sostegno di Battiferro, a hydraulic lock that lowered the barges coming from Ferrara and points north along the Navile Canal to the level of Bologna's own canals. The original Sostegno was designed by Vignola in 1548, but was much rebuilt afterwards.

The easy access to water power attracted numerous industries, including Bologna's first hydro-electric plant, in 1901, and the Fornace Galotti, next to the Sostegno. Its massive Hoffmann furnace supplied Bologna with bricks from 1887 until it closed in 1966; in the 1990s it was restored and reopened as a museum.

Exhibits showcase Bologna's industrial and scientific prowess through the ages: its skills in bricks and terracotta, its canals and mills. The star attraction here is a half-scale working model of one of the hundred silk mills that helped to make Bologna one of Europe's top silk cities between the 15th and 18th centuries, thanks to technological innovations (the silk mills famously had no windows, to prevent any industrial espionage).

There's a handsome display of the machines that made Bologna 'the Capital of Packaging' after World War II, as well as a Zamboni tortellini-making machine, a Maserati, historic machines, tools and a large display of motorcycles from the 1920s to 40s made in Bologna, although of the manufacturers only Ducati survives.

FICO Eataly World [map, page 130] (*Via Paolo Canale 1 (bus 35 from Stazione Centrale);* w *eatalyworld.it;* ⊕ *10.00–midnight daily; admission free, though many activities (bookable online) carry a charge, inc hour-long guided tours €15*) FICO (Fabbricca Italiana Contadina, or 'Italian Farming Factory') is nothing less than the world's first theme park dedicated to food, a €100m+ creation of EATaly, all powered by 44,000 solar panels, the most on any single property in Europe. The 10ha grounds at the CAAB (Centro Agro Alimentare di Bologna) feature a demonstration organic farm with vegetables, orchards and various breeds of farm animals. Some 40 workshops and laboratories with 30 events and 50 courses (*most costing around €20*) take place every day, designed for all ages, where you can watch wheat become flour and then pasta, or watch a cow being milked and the milk turned into cheese ('field to fork' is the motto, although live slaughtering is off the cards). There are virtual-reality experiences and six educational 'rides' (*€10*) including a look at the future, 40 restaurants (often featuring Italy's top chefs) and snack bars, an organic market, a cinema, theatre and convention centre. And there are specially designed Bianchi tricycles equipped with shopping baskets to help you get around.

Museo Ducati [66 A3] (*Via Antonio Cavalieri Ducati 3, Borgo Panigale;* \ *051 641 3343;* w *ducati.com;* ⊕ *Oct–Mar 09.00–18.00 Mon, Tue, Thu–Sat, Apr–Sep 09.00–18.00 Thu–Tue; adults €15, Ducati owners with ownership card €10, under 11s free; guided factory tours (book online) plus museum:* ⊕ *Oct–Mar 09.15 & 13.45 Mon, Tue, Thu, Fri, Apr–Sep 09.15, 11.00, 13.45 & 15.30 Mon, Tue, Thu, Fri; adults €30, Ducati owners with ownership card & over 65s €20, under 11s free*) One of Bologna's best-known companies was founded in 1926 by Antonio Cavalieri Ducati and his three sons, Adriano, Marcello and Bruno. In their small laboratory they commercialised the inventions of Adriano, who was a pioneer in short-wave technology and the first to send a message from Italy to the USA. Originally known as the Società Scientifica Radio Brevetti Ducati, the company soon became known for its innovative radio parts, calculating machines and vacuum tubes. It expanded so quickly that a new factory was built here in 1935, employing 1,200 workers. They continued to work through the war, until the factory was bombed in October 1944.

By 1946 it was back in business, although by 1948 it was no longer managed by the Ducati family. That same year the company began to collaborate with the SIATA firm in Turin, which had invented the small, four-stroke Cucciolo (puppy) motor to attach to bicycles. In 1950, Ducati started to produce its own Cucciolo and Cruiser bikes; in 1954, the company split into an electronics firm (now Ducati Energia SpA) and a Ducati Meccanica SpA, devoted to motorcycles.

Designer Fabio Taglioni (1920–2001) was key to Ducati's success in the 1950s, building the first racing bikes (Ducati's motto would be 'win on Sunday, sell on Monday') and developing the three key features that set Ducati apart from its rivals: the desmodromic valve design (1956), the L-shaped twin-cylinder engine (1971), and the trellis frame (1979).

The company went through various owners: today it's owned by Lamborghini, which is owned by Audi, which is owned by Volkswagen. The newly refurbished museum in the Borgo Panigale factory tells the story with historic, unusual and famous race-winning motorcycles, along with the stories of their riders, while true aficionados can take the factory tour to see how they're made.

To get here, take the suburban train from central station platform Binario Ovest to the Borgo Panigale.

Around Bologna

THE NORTHERN PLAINS   *Map, below*

A considerable portion of Bologna's prosperity, medieval and modern, is due to La Bassa, the rich, well-watered plain north of the city, laced by rivers, streams and the canals, some of which go back as far as the 13th century. Even when you get beyond the sprawl and small industrial towns that surround the city, it's a monotonous bit of countryside, without any compelling attractions along the way. But if you're passing through…

GELATO MUSEUM CARPIGIANI (*Via Emilia 45, Anzola dell'Emilia;* \ *051 650 5306;* **w** *gelatomuseum.com;* ⏰ *guided visits 09.00–18.00 Tue–Sun; basic 1hr museum tour & tasting: adults €7, ages 3–13 €5; book online*) Opened in 2012 near the Carpigiani ice cream company headquarters, the Gelato Museum is a kids' favourite. Interactive displays tell the history of ice cream from ancient Mesopotamians fetching snow and ice from mountain tops to cool their drinks, to the Arabs in Sicily who invented

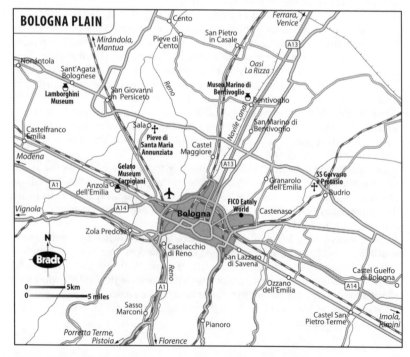

the essential sugar syrup and a multitude of flavours for their sorbets, to Florentine architect Bernardo Buontalenti, who gets credit for adding eggs and cream to the confection. In the 19th century, the invention of freezers and artificial ice led to a worldwide boom in ice cream and *gelato*, led by entrepreneurial Italians who always made it better than anyone else.

The museum has 20 of the firm's historic *gelato* machines, and fascinating photos, as well as displays showing how *gelato* is made today. Among the tours are various tastings, visits to the lab, and a masterclass on *gelato* making.

To get here, take bus 87 from Bologna Stazione Centrale to Via Magli in Anzola.

PIEVE DI SANTA MARIA ANNUNZIATA (*Via Gramsci 51, Sala Bolognese;* 📞 *051 828514;* 🕐 *closed at the time of writing for restoration*) This red-brick 11th-century church is a rare example of the Lombard Romanesque on the Emilian plain. Built over a 4th-century church, which itself stood on a pagan temple, the church is typical of the Lombard style: blind arcades and arches adorn the façade and central apse, while a Byzantine column divides a twin light window over the door. A Lombard-style campanile was added in the major 1926 restoration and given a fine nubbly, pigeon-proof roof, with a chapel honouring the locals who died in World Wars I and II.

The interior, laid out as a basilica, has three naves divided by simple selenite columns. Near the door is an ancient immersion font in red marble from Verona. Up the steps in the sanctuary is a relic from its pagan predecessor: an altar carved with a divinity sporting ram horns, identified as either Jupiter Ammon or the Celtic deity Kerunnos, recycled from a pagan temple and Christianised with a cross. There's a 15th-century fresco of the Annunciation and, on the parapet, a Swabian imperial eagle. The evocative crypt beneath the altar retains elements from the 4th-century church.

To get here, take the frequent S3 Suburban line from Bologna's Stazione Centrale [67 E4] northwest to Osteria Nuovo (*12mins*) and walk 3km to Sala Bolognese.

MUSEO LAMBORGHINI (*Via Modena 12, Sant'Agata Bolognese;* 📞 *051 681 7611;* w *lamborghini.com; museum* 🕐 *Nov–Mar 09.30–18.00 Mon–Sat, Apr–Oct 09.30–19.00 daily; adults €15, students, over 65s & caregivers with disabled visitor €12, ages 6–14 €5, under 6s & disabled visitors free. Museum & production line tours (book online)* 🕐 *10.00–16.00 Mon–Fri; adults €75, disabled visitors & ages 6–14 €50*) In 1963, after making a mint building tractors, Ferruccio Lamborghini decided it was time to realise his dream of founding a company to build luxury cars capable of competing with the likes of Ferrari. People scoffed, but he went ahead and purchased land in Sant'Agata, 25km northwest of Bologna, built a state-of-the-art factory, and produced the first 350 GTV in time to show it off at the Turin Auto Show.

In 1966, his two young engineers, Giampaolo Dallara and Giampaolo Stanzani, came up with a new concept for a high-powered touring car. Designer Marcello Gandini made his name by creating an eye-popping body for it, based on the racing cars of the era. Lamborghini named the new beast the Miura, after the Spanish fighting bulls of Seville (and Ferruccio Lamborghini's Taurus birth sign), and it became a sensation. From then on, nearly all the cars would have names associated with Spain and bulls.

When the world economy nose-dived in the late 1970s, the market for exclusive luxury sports cars dived with it. In 1987 the company was purchased by Chrysler, then in 1994 Chrysler sold it to a group of Indonesian investors, who in turn sold it to Audi in 1998. Audi has invested heavily in the company, and since 2014 business has boomed.

This museum opened in 2001 on two floors of Ferruccio Lamborghini's original factory building. It houses many a gleaming beast (look, but don't touch!), including one of the original 350 GTs, the Countach S, the Jalpa, the Espada, the Sesto Elemento, the Reventón, and the Murciélago (the 'Bat', also the name of a legendary bull of 1879, spared in the ring for his courage). Photos, motors and more tell the story, and you may even see the latest models being test driven on Via Modena, right in front of the museum.

To get here, take bus 576 from Bologna's bus station in Piazza XX Settembre [67 F4], to stop S Agata B Chiesa Frati (*approx 55mins*) and walk for 5 minutes.

CENTO On the road to Ferrara, in the gloomy northern fringes of the Metropolitan City of Bologna (as its province is now called), the River Reno divides the twin towns of Cento and Pieve di Cento. A role as a border town in the Middle Ages made this a double settlement; even today Cento is officially in Ferrara province, Pieve di Cento in Bologna's.

Cento is largely a creation of the medieval Bishops of Bologna, who oversaw the draining and settling of the land. To protect it, they built the 14th-century Rocca di Cento, a fort now used for exhibitions and concerts. In 1502 Pope Alexander VI included the town in the dowry of his daughter Lucrezia Borgia when she married Duke Alfonso of Ferrara.

Getting there and away For both Cento and Pieve di Cento (see below), take bus 97 from Bologna bus station in Piazza XX Settembre; the journey takes about 50 minutes.

Tourist information
🛈 **Piazza Guercino** 39; ☎ 051 684 3334;
w comune.cento.fe.it; ⏰ 09.00–12.30 Mon–Fri

What to see and do
Pinacoteca Civica Il Guercino (*Piazza A Costa 17; ⏰ closed for restoration*) Located in the 18th-century Palazzo del Monte di Pietà, this museum also contains paintings by other Bolognese artists, including one of the most acclaimed works by Ludovico Carracci, the *Holy Family with St Francis*. Unfortunately, much of Cento was damaged in the 2012 earthquake, including this museum, which is still closed for restoration. In the meantime, nine paintings by Guercino have been moved into the **Pinacoteca San Lorenzo**, in the church of San Lorenzo (*Corso Guercino 47/1;* ☎ *051 684 3334;* ⏰ *10.00–13.00 & 15.00–19.00 Fri, 10.00– 13.00 Sat, 15.00–19.00 Sun*).

More Guercino (he came back to spend 19 years in Cento, 1623–42) can be seen in the **Chiesa del Rosario** on Via Ugo Bassi; the artist himself is said to have helped with the design for the church.

PIEVE DI CENTO Cento's twin city, just over the River Reno, Pieve wears the nickname 'Little Bologna'. Little it certainly is, and with its old brick buildings and porticoes there is a definite resemblance. Some of these are wooden-beamed; they survive from the 1300s, along with the three gates, all that is left of Pieve's walls. Inside these, the **Collegiata di Santa Maria Maggiore** was damaged by the 2012 earthquake, which brought its cupola crashing to the ground. When reconstruction is completed, its paintings by Guercino, Lavinia Fontana and a very glossy *Assumption* by Guido Reni should be restored to their places.

Giovanni Francesco Barbieri (1591–1666), better known by his nickname Guercino or 'Squinter', because he was cross-eyed, was born into a poor family in Cento. Precocious, he was largely self-taught, but was encouraged by Ludovico Carracci and patronised by the Gonzaga Duke of Mantua and several influential clerics, notably the Bolognese Cardinal Alessandro Ludovisi. When he moved to Bologna in 1615, he became known for painting with dramatic chiaroscuro effects, echoing some of Ludovico's later works.

In 1616, he founded the 'Academy of the Nude' in Cento, similar to Carracci's school in Bologna, and produced a series of anatomical sketches for his students. An expert draughtsman whose lively drawings were in great demand among collectors, Guercino was famously fast with the brush, completing some 250 altarpieces and paintings in his career.

In 1618 he painted two of his most powerful, expressive works: *The Flaying of Marsyas* (in the Pitti Palace, in Florence) and the famous *Et in Arcadio Ego* (in the Galleria Nazionale d'Arte Antica in Rome), with its two shepherds contemplating a skull with a blowfly. Guercino was the first to use the phrase ('I too am in Arcadia'), seemingly a reminder that Death is present everywhere in this world; but the phrase and the painting have attracted no end of esoteric speculation about a special undercurrent of knowledge somehow linked to Rennes-le-Château in France, especially as Poussin painted two paintings of the same title and Goethe used it as the motto for his travel book, *Italian Journey*.

When Cardinal Ludovisi was elected Pope Gregory XV in 1621, he took Guercino to Rome, where he painted his greatest altarpiece, the moody *St Petronilla* for the Vatican, and the *Aurora* ceiling frescoes in the Villa Ludovisi for the Pope's nephew. After the death of the Pope, Guercino ran his studio from Cento, refusing requests to become official painter to the courts of England (1626) and France (1629 and 1639). Increasingly his palette lightened while his compositions became more classical, until his work began to be mistaken for paintings by Guido Reni. Reni hated him and accused him of copying but, after Reni's death in 1642, Guercino left Cento and took over as the most popular painter in Bologna.

✖ Where to eat and drink

✖ **Buriani** Via Provinciale Bologna 2/A; ☏051 975177; w ristoranteburiani.com; ⊕ closed Tue & Wed. This famous family-run restaurant founded in 1967 is still going strong, dedicated to the freshest & finest seasonal ingredients, marrying tradition with innovation on a frequently changing menu. More than 200 wines to choose from. €€€€

BENTIVOGLIO Northeast of Bologna is the town that gave the famous rulers of Bologna their name. They built their imposing **Castello** in 1475, now home to a medical institute. In San Marino di Bentivoglio, 3km south, the **Museo della Civiltà Contadina** (*Via Sammarina 35;* ☏ *051 891050;* w *www.museociviltacontadina. bo.it;* ⊕ *Mar–Nov 09.30–12.30 Mon, Wed & Fri, 09.30–12.30 & 14.30–17.30 Tue & Thu, Mar, Apr, Oct & Nov 15.00–19.00 Sun & holidays, May–Sep 16.00–20.00 Sun & holidays; adults €4, ages 14–18 & over 60s €2, under 14s free*) occupies the lovely Villa Smeraldi and its park on the Navile Canal, with extensive exhibits of traditional farm life and crafts.

Bentivoglio's former rice paddies, 2km north, are now a 21ha nature reserve, the **Oasi La Rizza**, a wetland home to a summer colony of white storks, managed by a local *agriturismo* (*Via Bassa degli Albanelli 13;* ✆ *051 664 0076*) of the same name, so you can combine birdwatching with lunch.

Getting there and away There are several buses (376, 95, 377, 378) from Bologna bus station.

BUDRIO Just east of Bologna, Budrio was once the centre of hemp production on the plains but is better known for its great contribution to music; here, in 1853, Giuseppe Donati took what had been a toy and invented the ocarina ('little goose' in the Bolognese dialect).

Getting there and away Budrio is 31 minutes by train from Bologna's Stazione Centrale on the Portomaggiore line.

What to see and do
Museo dell'Ocarina Franco Ferri (*Via Garibaldi 35;* ✆ *051 692 8306;* ⊕ *Oct–10 Jun 15.30–18.30 Sun, also 10.00–12.30 1st Sun of month, or by appointment*) People once took ocarinas more seriously; in the 19th century composers wrote sonatas for them. They are certainly still revered in Budrio, and if you ever wanted to buy a proper one in terracotta, this is the place.

Pinacoteca Civica (*Via Mentana 32;* ✆ *051 692 8306;* ⊕ *same as the Ocarina museum*) Located in the Palazzo della Partecipanza, the pinacoteca has a surprisingly good collection including works by Vitale da Bologna, Dosso Dossi and Lavinia Fontana, as well as a room of rare books and atlases, and local archaeological finds.

Around Budrio Budrio has more than its share of churches, but the one most worth seeing is just west of town, **SS Gervasio e Protasio** (w *pievedibudrio.it;* ⊕ *16.00–19.00 Sat, 09.30–11.30 Sun (for Mass); admission free*), where the Baroque façade conceals a Romanesque interior with a stunning Carolingian cross and other bits going back to the Lombards.

East of Budrio the empty spaces are empty indeed; near the village of Medicina, if you see something that looks like the head of a garden rake but 150m long, it's only Bologna University's radio telescope, the **Croce del Nord**.

On the road from Budrio to Bologna, the name of **Castenaso** has for more than 2,000 years kept alive the memory of the mighty Roman nose of Publius Scipio 'Nasica', a general otherwise famous for defeating the local Celts in the 2nd century BC.

SOUTH OF BOLOGNA: INTO THE APENNINES *Map, opposite*

Much of the interest here is along the River Reno, and the Bologna–Porretta–Pistoia railway and the SS64 which run alongside it as they climb into the Apennines. There's lovely scenery in the hills, although the lower valley is now more than a little compromised by the presence of the big A1 motorway for Florence. Because the sights are spread about, it's easiest to have your own wheels to explore, or be prepared to take taxis.

MONTEVEGLIO This medieval town 27km west of Bologna has a handsome church on a hill, surrounded by the wooded Parco Regionale Abbazia di Monteveglio and

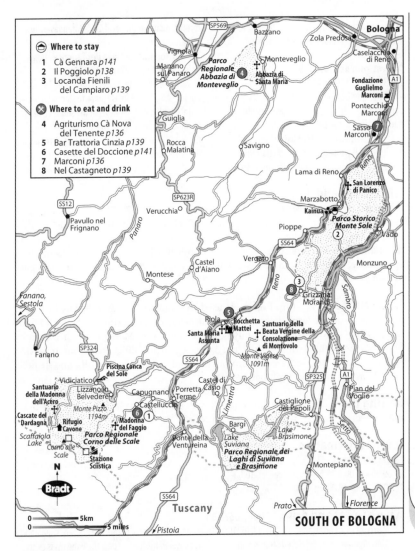

Where to stay
1 Cà Gennara *p141*
2 Il Poggiolo *p138*
3 Locanda Fienili del Campiaro *p139*

Where to eat and drink
4 Agriturismo Cà Nova del Tenente *p136*
5 Bar Trattoria Cinzia *p139*
6 Casette del Doccione *p141*
7 Marconi *p136*
8 Nel Castagneto *p139*

SOUTH OF BOLOGNA

Bologna's most prestigious Pignoletto vines. But the main reason most people make the journey is to eat in Monteveglio's exceptional clutch of restaurants.

Getting there and away Take bus 671 from Bologna bus station, then change at Bazzano Stazione for bus 657.

Where to eat and drink

Ponterosso Via dei Ponti 16; ☎051 670 2166; w ristoranteponterosso.com; ⊕ closed Tue & Aug. This is the fief of larger-than-life celebrity chef Massimo Ratti, a star on Italian TV, who prepares surprising variations on the region's classics; tortellini with strawberries really is better

than it might sound. Let Ratti be your guide. €€€€

Trattoria dai Mugnai Via Mulino 11; ☎051 670 2003; ✆; ⊕ 19.00–22.30 Tue & Fri, 11.30–14.00 & 19.00–22.30 Sat, 11.30–14.00 Sun. Historic restaurant in an old mill run by a lovely, welcoming family who have been at it for generations. Very traditional & very delicious. €€€

✖ Trattoria del Borgo Via San Rocco 12; ☎051 670 7982; w trattoriadelborgomonteveglio.it; ⏱ eves only exc Sun lunch, closed Tue. Cosy & stalwartly traditional up in the pedestrian-only area near the abbey, with a menu that features porcini mushrooms & truffles in season; a charming place for dining out on a summer's night on the

terrace, quaffing the local Colli Bolognesi wine. €€€

✖ Agriturismo Cà Nova del Tenente [map, page 135] Via Volta 27; m 348 228 3289; w canovadeltenente.it; ⏱ 19.30–22.00 Thu–Sat, noon–14.30 Sun. A lovely place to sit out on the terrace with gorgeous views in the summer, or inside by the open fire in winter. The fixed-price menu (€27) includes wines & liqueurs, & changes every week depending on what's available on the family farm; check it out on their website. €€

What to see and do
Abbazia di Santa Maria (*Via San Rocco 15;* ☎ *051 670 7931;* ⏱ *10.30–12.30 & 16.00–18.30 Sat, 11.00–noon & 16.00–18.30 Sun*) Built to celebrate Matilda of Canossa's victory here in 1092 over her arch-enemy emperor Henry IV, this handsome Romanesque abbey on the hill has been restored to its original appearance, complete with alabaster windows, a red Verona marble altar and a part of its original cloisters.

SASSO MARCONI Wealthy Bolognesi used to build their country villas here and quite a few survive, especially around Pontecchio in the *comune* of Sasso. One of these, Villa Griffone, was the family home of Guglielmo Marconi and it was from here that he sent off the world's first radio signal in 1895. There was only one receiver to pick it up – Marconi's brother manned a station in the hills, and he fired his rifle to tell the inventor it had worked.

Getting there and away Blue bus 92 leaves Bologna bus station every half-hour for Pontecchio-Marconi and the museum.

Tourist information
⑂ Via Porrettana 312; ☎051 675 8409; ⏱ 09.30–14.00 & 15.00–19.00 Tue–Fri, 10.00–12.30 & 14.30–19.00 Sat, 10.00–13.00 Sun

---

✖ Where to eat and drink *Map, page 135*
✖ Marconi Via Porrettana 291; ☎051 846216; w ristorantemarconi.it; ⏱ closed Mon, & Sun eve. Come here to this chic minimalist dining room for elegant, complex & bold Michelin-star cuisine prepared by Aurora Mazzucchelli with brother

Massimo in front of house; the gorgeous seafood is delivered fresh every day; the wine list is simply heavenly. 5 courses from €65, 8 from €85 or choose à la carte. €€€€

What to see and do
Museo Marconi (*Via Celestini 1, Pontecchio Marconi;* ☎ *051 846121;* e *info@fgm.it;* w *www.fgm.it; guided tours* ⏱ *10.00 Sun, w/days by reservation a few days in advance by phone or email; adults €5, students €2, under 6s free*) Today Villa Griffoni is home to a scientific institute, the Fondazione G Marconi, but you can visit the museum which retraces his first attempts at wireless telegraphy, with working replicas from the era, film clips and interactive exhibits for recreating some of Marconi's experiments. Admission includes access to Marconi's colossal **mausoleum** underneath the villa, built by Mussolini in the middle of the war (1941) in the style of the ancient Etruscans.

GUGLIELMO MARCONI

Have I done the world good, or have I created a menace?

Guglielmo Masconi

Guglielmo Marconi (1874–1937) was born in Bologna, the second son of aristocrat Giuseppe Marconi and his Irish wife, Annie Jameson, granddaughter of the founder of Jameson Whiskey. At Villa Griffone, young Marconi studied with his neighbour, physicist Augusto Righi, and became fascinated with electricity and especially Heinrich Hertz's research on electromagnetic 'Hertzian' or radio waves.

He carried out his first experiments at the age of 20 in the attic, and eventually succeeded in sending a transmission a mile and a half over a hill. Realising the potential of his discovery and needing more funding, he wrote to the Italian minister of Post and Telegraphs about the new wireless (the minister thought he was insane and never replied).

But Marconi was fortunate in having connections and knowing the right people. Through a family friend, he contacted the Italian ambassador in the UK, who advised him to come to England and to patent his discovery as soon as he arrived. Marconi duly did with the help of his cousin Henry Jameson Davis, filing the world's first patent for a system of telegraphy using Hertzian waves (2 June 1896). The following year he undertook a series of demonstrations for the UK government, each time transmitting messages further and further.

In 1899 he founded the London-based Wireless Telegraph & Signal Company (later the Marconi Telegraph Company, then Marconi PLC, now part of Ericsson), and two years later, on 12 December 1901, he sent and received the first wireless message across the Atlantic, from Cornwall to a military base in Newfoundland, using a 150m kite-supported antenna. Until then, it was widely believed the curvature of the earth would affect the transmission. Marconi proved them wrong.

The wireless revolutionised communications from ship to shore. In January 1909, 1,700 people were rescued off the east coast of the USA after the *RMS Republic* collided with Italian steamer the *Florida* in thick fog. Jack Binns, the Marconi radio operator aboard the *Republic*, sent out 200 messages to guide rescuing ships to his position.

That same year Marconi shared the Nobel Prize in Physics with Karl Ferdinand Braun 'in recognition of their contributions to the development of wireless telegraphy'. Three years later, the Marconi radio made headlines again when it was used by the crew of the *Titanic* to call for assistance. As Lord Samuel, UK Postmaster General, said at the time: 'Those who have been saved have been saved through one man, Mr Marconi.'

In charge of the Italian radio service in World War I, Marconi later worked on short-wave, beam transmissions and continuous wave transmission; on 15 June 1920, a Marconi 15kW telephone transmitter in Chelmsford hosted Britain's first public broadcast programme, a song recital by Dame Nellie Melba. Two years later, the BBC was born.

In later years, Marconi lived in Rome, and joined the Fascist party; in 1930 Mussolini made him the head of Italy's Royal Academy. He died in 1937 of a heart attack.

4

MARZABOTTO Italians know the town as the site of the worst Nazi massacre of civilians in Western Europe, the equivalent of Lidice in the Czech Republic or Oradour-sur-Glane in France. On a far happier note, it also has the ruins of Kainua, a rare example of an Etruscan town that never grew into a Roman city.

Getting there and away Marzabotto's train station is a stop along the Bologna–Pistoia line, 35 minutes from Bologna. Motorists should exit the Bologna–Florence *autostrada* at Sasso Marconi and follow the SS64 south.

 Where to stay, eat and drink *Map, page 135*
Il Poggiolo (10 rooms) Via San Martino 25; \051 678 7100. Combination visitors' centre (come here to pick up maps) with a basic hotel, including a dorm room sleeping 10, & a restaurant. €

What to see and do
Parco Storico di Monte Sole (*Via Porrettana Nord 4;* \ *051 932525;* ⊕ *always open*) Between 29 September and 5 October 1944, as the Nazis were being pushed back by the Allies, a Waffen SS column tore through Emilia-Romagna with the expressed purpose of brutalising the population, who were accused of supporting the Resistance. As they made their way up Monte Sole, they shot and killed 770 people, 155 under ten years old. The village priest, Don Fornasini, helped many escape the slaughter, but was shot when he returned to give his parishioners a dignified burial; he and two other priests of Marzabotto have since been beatified. Nobody forgot Marzabotto; prosecutions of the surviving German participants dragged on into 2007.

Marzabotto was awarded a gold medal for its heroism and Monte Sole, where many of the deaths took place, was made into Italy's only historic park: the **Parco Storico di Monte Sole**. The victims are buried in the church crypt (⊕ *Tue–Sun*), and are remembered in a harrowing memorial, the Sacrario dei Caduti. The rest of the park covers 6,300ha, much of it woods and meadows, with hiking trails, excellent views and more than 900 species of flowers.

Kainua Archaeological Site (*Via Porrettana Sud 13;* \ *051 932353;* w *www.archeobologna.beniculturali.it/marzabotto;* ⊕ *Apr–Oct 08.00–19.00, Nov–Mar 08.00–17.30; admission (inc museum): adults €3, ages 18–25 €1.50, under 18s free, free 1st Sun of month*) Once known as Misa (the name given it by the first archaeologists), Kainua was founded in the 6th century BC in the Reno Valley, along the main route between Etruscan Felsina (Bologna) and Tuscany.

The first Etruscans lived in simple thatched huts, but by the early 5th century BC Kainua was laid out as a proper city in a grid plan that looks ahead to the classic Roman colony, with 15m-wide main north–south and east–west streets and residential areas neatly laid out in the 'suburbs'. They abandoned Kainua in the mid 4th century BC, when the Gauls invaded the Po Valley. The invaders briefly moved in but soon abandoned the site, leaving behind the uniquely intact foundations of an Etruscan town (only the cemeteries survive of the famous Etruscan cities of Tuscany and Lazio).

Many of the tile-roofed houses had courtyards; the presence of kilns showed that many doubled as workshops. Fairly scant remains of Kainua's temples are on the acropolis hill to the northwest; another religious area, a fountain sanctuary, stood just northeast of the centre. On the far north and east edges, the Etruscans buried their dead in curious squarish rock tombs, made of travertine plates and marked by onion-shaped rocks or columns.

Museo Nazionale Etrusco Pompeo Aria (*within the archaeological site;* ⊕ *Apr–Oct 09.00–18.30 Tue–Sun, Nov–Mar 09.00–17.30 Tue–Sun*) The best finds are in Bologna's archaeology museum (pages 93–4), but this has some fine bits, including a bronze statue of the Etruscan goddess of love, Turan, Greek urns and Etruscan copies, and the reconstruction of part of the fountain sanctuary with its painted terracotta decoration.

San Lorenzo di Panico (*Via Lama di Reno 29, Panico, across the River Reno;* ☏*051 931230;* ⊕ *10.00–noon & 14.00–18.00 Fri–Wed*) One of Emilia's Romanesque gems, this handsome sandstone church was built in 1145 by the Comacini Masters for the Counts of Panico, in the Middle Ages the most powerful family in the Apennines and sworn Ghibelline enemies of the *comune* of Bologna, who only stopped causing trouble when the last one, Ugolino da Panico, was beheaded in Piazza Maggiore in 1389. Their church, however, is calm and evocative and decorated with roses, the symbol of the counts, notably on the apse.

GRIZZANA MORANDI AND RIOLA Giorgio Morandi (see box, page 118) often spent his summers in the cool altitudes of Grizzana, a village of attractive stone hamlets spread over the mountains, including part of the Monte Sole. According to Morandi, who admittedly never travelled far, these were the most beautiful landscapes in the world. It also has a striking folly, near the neighbouring village of Riola, which has its own marvel: a church by the great Finnish architect Alvar Aalto.

Getting there and away Some 25 trains a day leave Bologna Stazione Centrale for Grizzana (*35mins, on the Bologna–Florence line*), but Riola (*57mins from Bologna, on the Pistoia line*) is the closest station to the Rocchetta Mattei.

Where to stay, eat and drink *Map, page 135*

🏠 **Locanda Fienili del Campiaro** (4 rooms) Loc Campiaro 112/C; m 348 660 8847; w locandafienilidelcampiaro.it. In a lovely rural setting near Morandi's house, this old stone inn offers rustic en-suite rooms with beamed ceilings & wrought-iron beds, plus a big hay barn for special events. The restaurant serves Bolognese classics & tasty beef *secondi*, & some unusual dishes (pasta made from nettles, fried sage, chicken bites with turmeric). B/fast inc. €€

✕ **Nel Castagneto** Loc Stanco di Sopra 79; ☏051 913272; w nelcastagneto.it; ⊕ closed Mon, Fri & Sat lunch. Under a spreading chestnut tree, 1km from the centre of Grizzana, this is a charming little family-run spot for lunch. Start with sun-dried tomatoes with *focaccia*, seasonal dishes (in spring, with St George's mushrooms, or *prugnoli*; in winter, *tagliata* (slices of steak) with truffles). €€
✕ **Bar Trattoria Cinzia** Loc Riola Ponte 1; m 339 507 3192; ⊕ closed Mon. Cheap, laid-back spot for lunch run by an affable couple, specialising in *tigelle*, meats & cheeses. €

What to see and do

Casa Museo Morandi (*Loc Campiaro;* ☏ *051 673 0311; w casedellamemoria. it;* ⊕ *10.00–13.00 & 14.30–17.30 Sat–Sun; adults €2, ages 6–12 €1, under 6s free*) After Morandi died, Grizzana adopted his name and made his little house into a museum, not to be missed if you want to have a look at the master's little bed (even though he was quite tall), his Fiat 850 and his studio, with his easel and brushes, and some of his favourite subjects: jugs, bottles and vases.

Santuario della Beata Vergine della Consolazione di Montovolo

(*30mins south of Grizzana, on SP73 & Via Montovolo;* w *santuariomontovolo.
it;* ⊕ *May–Sep 10.00–17.00 Fri–Sun, also Jun–Aug 10.00–17.00 Thu*). Founded
in the 11th century, this isolated hilltop sanctuary houses a black statue of the
Virgin, an unusual 14th-century marble crucifixion and fragments of frescoes
and sculptural work by the Comacene Masters, who rebuilt the church in the
13th century.

There is something uncanny about the wooded, flat-topped, pyramid-shaped
Monte Vigese looming next to the church. It was sacred to the Etruscans,
possibly even the 'navel' of their world; the crypt of Montovolo, according to
at least one researcher, Professor Graziano Baccolini, may even be an intact
Etruscan shrine.

Rocchetta Mattei

(*SP62;* ☎ *051 916845;* w *rocchettamattei-riola.it;* ⊕ *Sat–Sun
only;* w *viviappennino.com (search: Appennino, Bolognese); adults €10, children €5,
free 1st Sun of month; book online with Vivi Appennino*) A folly crowned with turrets,
loggias, and bulbous and gilded neo-Moorish domes, the Rocchetta was built over
20 years (1850–70) on the foundations of a ruined castle by Count Cesare Mattei.
Born into a wealthy family in Bologna, Mattei (1809–96) was a founder of the Cassa
di Risparmio di Bologna bank whose hobbies were alchemy and travelling: he was
especially impressed with the Alhambra and the Kremlin, which he mishmashed
together to create his dream castle.

He is best known, however, as the inventor of 'electrohomeopathy', a non-surgical
cure for cancer, based on the 'natural electricity' in plant extracts. His claims of
remarkable cures attracted worldwide attention and numerous Russian aristocrats
to Riola, although most doctors condemned him as a quack. Some, however, credit
him with inventing placebos.

Santa Maria Assunta

(*Piazza Alvar Aalto, Riola;* ☎ *051 916355*) Built in 1978,
Riola's parish church is a Modernist masterpiece of pure white concrete and glass.
It was one of the last works of Alvar Aalto, built at the request of the local cardinal,
who wondered how a great architect would respond to the doctrines of Vatican II.
The exterior echoes the three surrounding peaks of Montovolo, Monte Vigese and
Monte Vigo; in the serene luminous interior, the soft northern light filters down
through a grid of asymmetrical ribs.

PORRETTA TERME

Sitting on the banks of the Reno up near the Tuscan border,
Porretta Terme traces its origins back to the spa-loving Etruscans. Now a charming
and busy little spa town, it loves soul music (there's a street named after Otis
Redding) and makes a great base for walking and taking in unchanged medieval
villages such as **Castel di Casio** and **Bargi**, where they used to make arquebuses, on
the mountain back roads to the east.

Getting there and away Porretta Terme (54km south of Bologna) is a station
along the Bologna–Pistoia line, 70 minutes from Bologna Stazione Centrale.

Tourist information

🛈 Piazza della Libertà; ☎ 0534 521103;
w discoveraltorenoterme.it; ⊕ summer 10.00–
13.00 & 16.00–19.00 Thu–Tue, winter 10.00–noon
Tue–Sat & 15.00–17.00 Sat

Where to stay, eat and drink

Helvetia Thermal Spa (48 rooms) Piazza Vittorio Veneto 11; 0534 22214; w helvetiabenessere.it. A 5min walk from the train station, this hotel's modern spa centre is in a large cave excavated as a bomb shelter during the war, with a large hammam, thermal pool with hot tub & water cascades, an indoor pool, Ayurvedic massages, technogym & beauty treatments available. The hotel's restaurant, Cipensoio (€€€), is one of the best in town & open to non-guests. B/fast inc. €€

Hotel Italia (32 rooms) Piazza della Libertà 2; 0534 22923; w hotelitaliaporretta.com. Friendly older hotel 220m from the train station. Functional, tidy rooms with a few trpls, & a restaurant (€€) serving dishes with a Caribbean/Venezuelan touch. €€

Cà Gennara B&B [map, page 135] (3 rooms) Via Cà Gennara 18, Fraz Capugnano; m 333 414 5415; w cagennara.com. On the edge of a chestnut forest, a 5min drive above Porretta, this rustic chic B&B in a big stone house makes a peaceful base for exploring the beautiful countryside. Two rooms are en suite; b/fast inc. €–€€

Casette del Doccione [map, page 135] Via Monte Cavallo, Fraz Castelluccio; 0534 29198; closed Tue & Sat, Sun eve. Worth the detour for delicious seasonal home cooking (porcini pasta, fresh fruit pies) in a gorgeous wooded setting. Great for families, with lots of space outside for scampering while the adults linger. €€

Il Poeta Via G Mazzini 6; 0534 21190; w shop.ilpoetawine.com; closed Mon. Cosy wine bar in a gourmet grocery, with delicious snacks & a good choice of bottles. €

What to see and do

Terme di Porretta (*Via Roma 5;* 0534 22062; w *www.termediporretta.it;* 08.30–13.00 & 14.30–18.00 Mon–Fri, 08.30–13.00 Sat) The spa-loving Etruscans were the first to appreciate Porretta's salso-bromo-iodine springs, and they were one of the many spots visited by Lorenzo the Magnificent of Florence in the hope that the waters would help his gout (they didn't). Porretta attracted the upper crust well into the 20th century, including many opera stars who believed the waters would soothe their overwrought vocal chords. Today the waters are touted for blood circulation, rheumatoid arthritis, vascular problems & relaxation, but wellness and beauty treatments are also on offer.

Museo delle Moto e dei Ciclomotori DEMM (*Via Mazzini 230/A;* m *335 721 4996;* 10.00–noon & 16.00–19.00 Sat, 16.00–19.00 Sun, or by ringing 0534 22021) For lovers of historic two wheelers: some 20 DEMM motorcycles and motorbikes collected by company vice president Giuliano Mazzini.

Castello Manservisi (*Fraz Castelluccio, 6km west;* w *castellomanservisi.it;* Jul & Aug 10.00–noon & 16.00–19.00 daily). One of the prettiest hamlets around Porretta, Castelluccio has gorgeous views and a big stone folly rebuilt from an older castle by a Bolognese textile magnate in the 1880s; it now houses the **Museo Laborantes**, a small museum of rural life, as well as special exhibitions in summer.

Madonna del Faggio (*6km from Castelluccio, on the road to Pennola;* summer 10.00–18.00 Sun, but ring the tourist office to check) One of the region's most picturesque pilgrimage churches, this sanctuary of 1772 is isolated in a gorgeous beech wood.

Parco Regionale dei Laghi di Suviana e Brasimone (*20min drive east of Porretta;* w *www.parks.it/parco.suviana.brasimone*) Near the highest peaks on the Tuscan border, these two artificial lakes immersed in woodlands, Suviana and the smaller Brasimon, are popular recreation areas and lovely spots for a picnic and swim. Suviana's Centro Velico USIP (*Località Piderla 74, Camugnano;* m *345 463*

2278; w *centrovelicosuviana.it*; ⏰ *09.00–19.00 Fri–Sun, Aug 09.00–19.00 daily*) rents sailboats, windsurfers, stand-up paddle boards, canoes and kayaks and offers lessons; the white-water rapids of the lake's outlet, the Limentra, make for the most exciting canoeing in the Apennines.

LIZZANO IN BELVEDERE The mountain resort of Lizzano and its constellation of hamlets are the base for visiting the regional park named after the 1,944m Corno alle Scale. Woods and meadows cover the mountain's southern and northwest slopes, but its northeast face is a dramatic vertical cliff corrugated with sandstone strata that gave it its name, the 'horn with steps'. Sport facilities are concentrated 1km up the road in Vidiciatico.

Getting there and away ATC bus 776 from Porretta train station goes to Lizzano (14km) and to the hamlet of Vidiciatico, and in winter up to the Corno alle Scale ski station. For information, ring ☎0534 31136.

Tourist information

🛈 Lizzano in Belvedere Piazza Marconi 6; ☎0534 51052; ⏰ 3rd Sun in Jun–1st Sun in Sep 09.00–noon & 14.00–19.00 Tue–Sun; rest

🛈 Vidiciatico Piazza XXVII Settembre 8; ☎0534 53159; ⏰ as for Lizzano in Belvedere of year 09.00–noon Tue, Thu, Fri, 09.00–noon & 15.00–18.00 Sat–Sun

Where to stay, eat and drink

🏠 **Hotel Montepizzo** (30 rooms) Piazza Montanari Don Alfonso 1, Lizzano; ☎0534 51055; w hotelmontepizzo.it. Cosy family-run hotel & restaurant with a small jacuzzi, hammam, massage & fitness area for relaxing after a day on the slopes. B/fast inc. €€€

🏠 **Hotel Montegrande** (14 rooms) Via Marconi 27, Vidiciatico; ☎0534 53210;

w hotelmontegrande.it. Comfortable, recently renovated 3-star lodge near the entrance to the park, a perfect refuge after long days on the mountain trails or ski slopes. Manager Bruno & his staff are experts on what to see & do in the area, & the restaurant is famous for its generous portions. HB terms are good value for money. B/fast inc. €€

What to see and do

Delubro (or Rotonda) (*behind Lizzano's modern church;* ⏰ *usually closed*) Built in the 7th or 8th century, perhaps under the rule of Charlemagne, this enigmatic, slightly tilted round church (Delubro means 'place of purification') with decorative arches and two doors, is the oldest building in Bologna province; originally it stood twice as high, with a conical roof.

Parco Regionale del Corno alle Scale (w *cornoallescale.net; for information in English* w *www.parks.it/parco.corno.scale*). This 4,974ha park covers the ridge of some of Emilia's wildest Apennines, in a cirque dominated by Corno alle Scale, amid pine, chestnut and beech forests. Wolves, deer, boar, mouflons and marmots, as well as birds of prey, especially royal eagles, are among the inhabitants; the orchids in spring and autumn leaves are a delight. The main road from Vidiciatico follows the valley of the River Dardagna and ends shortly after the **Rifugio di Lago Cavone** at c1,500m. From here you can make a 5-hour circular high mountain walk to the summit, taking in **Lake Scaffaiolo** (at 1,775m one of the highest lakes in the Apennines) and the **Balze dell'Ora** ravine; from here on a clear day views stretch to both the Adriatic and Tyrrhenian seas, the curve of the Alps and the top tip of Monte Cinto in Corsica. The park has a dozen other trails, most of moderate difficulty: one of the most popular is the easy 3½-hour walk from the Madonna dell'Acero (see below) to the five waterfalls of the **Cascate del Dardagna**, tumbling down in a beech forest.

Piscina Conca del Sole (*Vidiciatico;* ☎ *0534 53971;* w *cornoallescale.net;* ⏲ *early Jun–early Sep 08.30–19.00; full day/afternoon: adults €9/6, ages 5–11 €6/4, under 5s free*) After a morning's trekking, relax in this heated outdoor lido with a spectacular 50m slide.

Mountain biking Corno alle Scale and its surroundings boast ten superb mountain-bike routes of varying difficulty; pick up the *Il Corno alle Scale in Mountain Bike* map and guide (*€15*) at the tourist offices or visitor centre. The **Montagna SenzaFreni Association** (*Via Cà Gherardi 7A, Vidiciatico;* m *331 867 3013;* ⨍ *montagnasenzafreni*) rents out mountain bikes, helmets and protective gear, including for people with disabilities (*€60/day, €35/half-day*) and offers a shuttle to Monte Pizzo for exciting downhills on three free-ride paths.

Stazione Sciistica del Corno alle Scale (*Via Panoramica 21, Vidiciatico;* ☎ *0534 53735;* w *cornosci.it;* ⏲ *winter 09.00–16.30 Mon–Fri, 08.30–16.30 Sat–Sun*) Five chair lifts serve 36km of ski slopes, with guaranteed snow 150 days a year. This is where the Bolognesi, including the Bologna-born downhill champion Alberto Tomba, learn to ski; the two 3km uninterrupted Tomba pistes are the longest in the Apennines. Along with the slopes, there are cross-country trails and a modern snowboarding park.

Pianaccio Visitor Centre (*Via Roma 1, Fraz Pianaccio, 5km from Lizzano;* ☎ *0534 51761*) Four floors of exhibits on the forest and its traditions, with an emphasis on the once all-important chestnut, as well as maps and other info.

Monte Pizzo Hang-gliding (*8km from Lizzano; book with Gianluca:* m *347 255 4935;* ⨍ *vivereil.montepizzo; €80, inc shuttle back to Monte Pizzo*) At weekends in good weather, even novices can hang-glide (*parapendio*) in tandem from the summit of Monte Pizzo with a professional pilot.

Santuario della Madonna dell'Acero (*Via Madonna dell'Acero 189, 14km from Lizzano;* ☎ *0534 53029;* w *madonnadellacero.it;* ⏲ *Apr–Oct 09.00–19.00 daily*) The charming, stone-roofed 16th-century sanctuary of Our Lady of the Maple Tree marks yet another apparition of the Virgin in these mountains, in this instance to two young shepherds who had taken refuge under a maple. Her miracles are well attested to by a chapel crammed with votive offerings, including (displayed in summer only) the life-size wooden statues of the family of Brunetto Brunori, a Florentine commander who survived being pierced with a lance in a battle in 1530.

4

EMILIA-ROMAGNA ONLINE

For additional online content, articles, photos and more on Emilia-Romagna, why not visit w bradtguides.com/emilia?

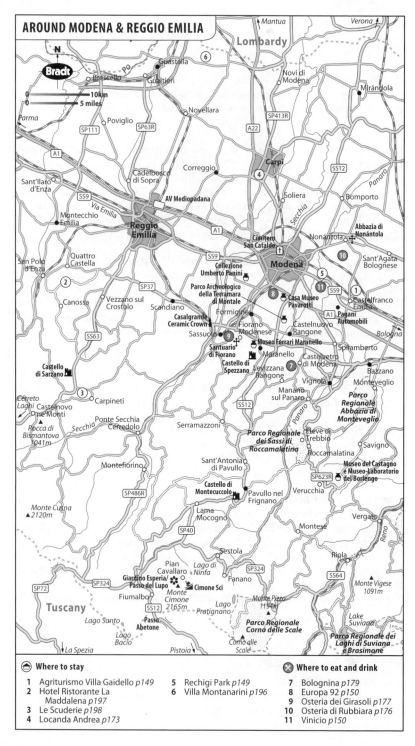

AROUND MODENA & REGGIO EMILIA

Lombardy

Tuscany

0 ____ 10km
0 ____ 5 miles

Where to stay

1 Agriturismo Villa Gaidello *p149*
2 Hotel Ristorante La
   Maddalena *p197*
3 Le Scuderie *p198*
4 Locanda Andrea *p173*
5 Rechigi Park *p149*
6 Villa Montanarini *p196*

Where to eat and drink

7 Bolognina *p179*
8 Europa 92 *p150*
9 Osteria dei Girasoli *p177*
10 Osteria di Rubbiara *p176*
11 Vinicio *p150*

5

Modena and Surrounds

Slow Food. Fast Cars
Modena's motto

Modena puts on a class act – 'Mink City' they call it, the city with Italy's highest per capita income, a city with 'a psychological need for racing cars' according to the late Enzo Ferrari, whose famous flame-red chariots compete with the shiny beasts churned out by cross-town rival Maserati. Sleek and speedy, Modena also has a lyrical side of larger-than-life proportions: Luciano Pavarotti was born here, and its scenographic streets take on an air of mystery and romance when enveloped in the winter mists rising from the Po.

Though it grew up as a feisty free *comune* in the Middle Ages, when it built one of Italy's finest cathedrals, Modena learned its graces and style in a more aristocratic age, under the House of Este. The city's formative years came between 1598 and 1859, when it stood among the capitals of Europe – if only as the capital of the Este's little duchy. In that period Modena was transformed into a model Baroque city, and its elegant streets filled up with churches, palaces and porticoes in the new style.

All this Baroque fussiness, however, is only a stage for a people as devoutly socialist as Bologna's. Italy's richest city is also one of its most progressive; Modena has the largest car-free centre in Emilia-Romagna, making it a delight to walk around. The serene old capital of the Este comes back to life, and the Baroque effect is made perfect by the cadets of the National Military Academy, who live in the old Ducal Palace and never go out without their hats and capes.

HISTORY

Known in ancient times as Mutina, the city began as a settlement of the Celtic Boii. The Romans took it in 183BC, and it made little account of itself until the end of the empire, when it had the honour of being sacked by both the Huns and the Lombards. Medieval Modena grew back to prominence as part of the 'Canossiana', the state founded by Atto Adalbert in the 10th century and made glorious by Countess Matilda, powerful ally of the pope; under her rule the city began its great cathedral (1099).

When it became an independent *comune*, however, Modena's Ghibelline party was to dominate in response to the Guelph allegiance of the city's chief rival, Bologna. Throughout the long campaigns of Frederick II in the north, Modena was to remain one of the emperor's most faithful allies. In 1288, after a long spell of fierce factional conflict, the city came under the control of Obizzo II d'Este, the powerful *signore* of Ferrara. A revolution of the *popolo* seized control of the city in 1306, but it lasted only a year. So frightened were the nobles by this outbreak that they put aside their differences and decided to put an end to the *comune* forever. With only a few brief interruptions, the Este would rule Modena for the next 553 years.

After the Este were thrown out of Ferrara by the pope (page 271), Cesare d'Este was allowed to keep Modena and Reggio Emilia. The Este Duchy of Modena endured, though it no longer played a prominent role in Italian history or culture. Not that the Este didn't try. Francesco I (1629–58) was a fervent patron of the arts (Velázquez and Bernini left memorable portraits of him), and he successfully kept his little state afloat despite his capital losing 70% of its population in the great plague of 1630–31. Francesco also had to navigate the treacherous currents of the Thirty Years War, finally dying on the battlefield against the Spanish. (Francesco's daughter Maria Beatrice, or 'Mary of Modena', married James II in 1673 and played a small role in British history simply by being Catholic and thereby increasing James's subjects' distrust of him. She fled the country with her husband after the Glorious Revolution of 1688.)

Francesco and his successors transformed the face of the city; with the building of the Ducal Palace, the Corso Canalgrande and other projects, Modena became a thoroughly up-to-date Baroque city, a capital fit for a duke. Despite their efforts, however, the resources necessary to support the pretensions of the House of Este just weren't available in Modena, and the charms of a long, pleasant slide into decadence proved too strong to resist.

Through the long reigns of Rinaldo I (1694–1737) and Francesco III (1737–80), the duchy remained a sleepy though reasonably well-run backwater. Rinaldo oversaw his duchy like a fond but grumpy paterfamilias, poking his nose in everyone's affairs and tossing adulterers into prison; he made his duchy the joke of Europe by forcing everyone in Modena to be in their houses by ten o'clock so that they wouldn't disturb his sleep. Francesco, except for building one of Italy's most impressive poorhouses (now the Palazzo dei Musei), generally left his subjects in peace and devoted his life to eating; he grew so fat he had to be carried upstairs.

When Napoleon's armies arrived at the gates, the good-natured Ercole III (1780–96) simply left town. Ercole left only a daughter for an heir, and she was forced into marriage with an Austrian archduke as part of the Habsburg schemes to solidify their control over northern Italy. Their son Francesco IV (1814–46) was propped back on his throne by Metternich after Napoleon's defeat. He proved as reactionary and useless as any Habsburg, distinguishing himself only by the bloody suppression of a revolt in 1831.

His subjects found comfort in food. 'The existence of Modena sausage makes up for the existence of the Duke', as their satirical poet Giuseppe Giusti put it. Francesco V was the last of the line; the Modenesi booted him out in 1859 in favour of Vittorio Emanuele II of Piedmont, soon to become the first King of Italy. The Este-Habsburgs, incidentally, are still around: if aristocracy ever makes a comeback, there is a pretender, Prince Lorenz of Belgium, Archduke of Austria-Este, who could claim the thrones of both Modena and Ferrara. He's a banker.

GETTING THERE AND AWAY

BY AIR SACA **Aerbus** operates a shuttle between Bologna's Guglielmo Marconi Airport and Modena's bus station [148 A1] (*about 50mins*). The price one way is €15, and tickets can be bought online (**w** *aerbus.it*). Coaches run about every 2 hours during the day; timetables are on the website.

BY RAIL Modena's **station** is on Piazzale Dante [148 D1], a 10-minute walk from the centre. The trip to Bologna averages 25 minutes, and trains can be as frequent as 20 minutes apart. The same is true for the opposite direction, towards Reggio and

Parma, and there are frequent trains all day for Milan and Turin, Rome (via Bologna) and eastward to Rimini and down the Adriatic coast. Regular suburban lines can take you to Carpi and Sassuolo, the latter run by a separate line, the **FER** (**w** *www.fer.it*).

For **Italo** high-speed trains, there is a shuttle bus provided by Italo to Modena station from the new AV Mediopadana station outside Reggio Emilia.

BY BUS Modena's **Autostazione** [148 A1] is on Via Fabriani, a 5-minute walk north of the Palazzo dei Musei. Provincial services are run by **SETA** (**℡** *840 000 216;* **w** *setaweb.it*). Modena is a **Flixbus** hub (**w** *flixbus.com*), with buses leaving from Via Glauco Gottardi, in the southeast suburbs near the SS12 ring road: there are services to Rome, Milan, Naples, Florence, Munich and many other destinations.

BY CAR The home of Ferrari is a major road junction. Just west of Modena, the A22 leaves the A1 from Verona, Trento and the Brenner Pass. The Via Emilia runs through the city but there is also a bypass to the north, linking with the SS12 (north, to Verona) and the SP3/SS12 south.

GETTING AROUND

Modena is a compact city and you won't need wheels to see the main sights. Most suburban attractions, such as the car museums (pages 169–71), are however far enough out that you'll need – a car.

All of the centre is a **ZTL** (*zona traffico limitato*); if you're staying in a central hotel, you can ask them for a pass to park, if available, or just to load and unload. Street parking around the periphery is difficult but not impossible, and there are garages on Viale Trento Trieste, east of the centre, in Piazza Roma and in Viale C Sigonio to the south.

BY BIKE There is municipal **bike rental** at the IAT tourist office (see below). Other locations are the Parco Novi Sad [148 B1] and the Policlinico [148 F4].

BY BUS The city's bus service is run by **SETA** (**℡** *840 000 216;* **w** *setaweb.it*); tickets cost €1.50 from the ticket machines or SETA sales outlets, or €2 from the driver.

BY TAXI For radio taxis 24/7, try **Area Taxi Modena** (**℡** *059 212 100;* **w** *areataxi.it*) – trips to Bologna airport from whatever location cost a flat €65, with no supplements.

TOURIST INFORMATION

❖ IAT tourist office [148 B3] Piazza Grande 14; **℡**059 203 2660; **w** visitmodena.it; ☼ 14.30– 18.00 Mon, 09.00–13.30 & 14.30–18.00 Tue–Sat, 09.30–13.30 & 14.30–18.00 Sun. A very helpful & well-organised tourist office in the town hall, across from the Duomo.

WHERE TO STAY

Surprisingly, Modena doesn't get a lot of tourists (it's more business oriented), and inexpensive places near the centre are very limited.

LUXURY

🏠 Best Western Milano Palace [148 D1] (55 rooms) Corso Vittorio Emanuele 68; **℡**059 223 011; **w** milanopalacehotel.it. Modern & functional, soundproofed, with posh bathrooms; lounge bar, spa with jacuzzi & steam room. **€€€€€**

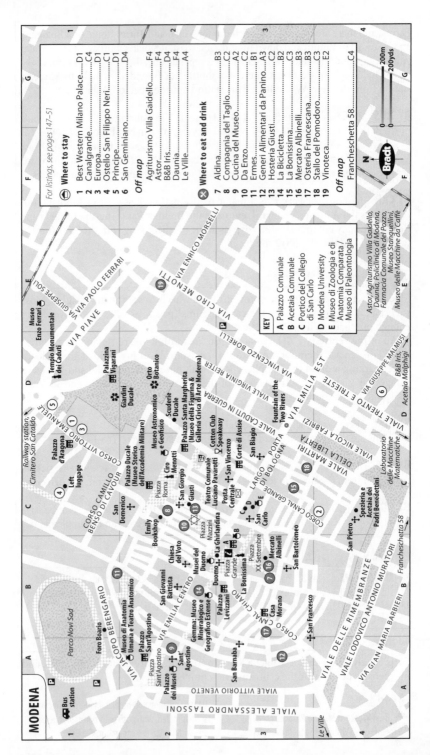

MODENA

Parco Novi Sad

Railway station;
Cimitero San Cataldo

For listings, see pages 147–51

Where to stay
1	Best Western Milano Palace	D1
2	Canalgrande	C4
3	Europa	D1
4	Ostello San Filippo Neri	C1
5	Principe	D1
6	San Geminiano	D4

Off map
Agriturismo Villa Gaidello	F4
Astor	F4
B&B Iris	D4
Daunia	F4
Le Ville	A4

Where to eat and drink
7	Aldina	B3
8	Compagnia del Taglio	C2
9	Cucina del Museo	A2
10	Da Enzo	C2
11	Ermes	B1
12	Generi Alimentari da Panino	A3
13	Hosteria Giusti	C2
14	La Bicicletta	B2
15	La Bonissima	C3
16	Mercato Albinelli	B3
17	Osteria Francescana	B3
18	Stallo del Pomodoro	C3
19	Vinoteca	E2

Off map
Franceschetta 58	C4

KEY
A Palazzo Comunale
B Acetaia Comunale
C Portico del Collegio di San Carlo
D Modena University
E Museo di Zoologia e di Anatomia Comparata / Museo di Paleontologia

Astor, Agriturismo Villa Gaidello,
Daunia, Policlinico di Modena,
Farmacia Comunale del Pozzo,
Museo Stanguellini,
Museo delle Macchine da Caffè

B&B Iris;
Acetaia Malphigi

Laboratorio
delle Macchine
Matematiche

Le Ville

Franceschetta 58

UPMARKET

🏠 **Le Ville** [148 A4] (72 rooms) Via Giardini 1,270, in Baggiovara, 7km south of town off the A1; 📞059 510051; w hotelleville.eu. Peaceful hotel with 3 buildings centred around an old villa in a large park with a pool & sauna. There's a restaurant (€€€) with some refined cooking & an outdoor terrace (📞 *059 512 240;* ⏰ *closed Sat lunch & Sun*); wide choice of grills & roasts, & five kinds of soup. €€€€

🏠 **Rechigi Park** [map, page 144] (72 rooms) 5km from the centre at Via Emilia Est 1,581; 📞059 283600; w rechigiparkhotel.it. Another converted noble villa, elegant, spacious & packed with mod cons. Some rooms have their own jacuzzis; there's a park & gym. €€€€

🏠 **Canalgrande** [148 C4] (44 rooms) Corso Canalgrande 6; 📞059 217160; w canalgrandehotel.it. In the centre, this palatial hotel is named after Modena's long-gone medieval canal. Once the Renaissance palazzo of the Marchesi Schedoni, it has richly decorated & stuccoed 18th-century public rooms, with crystal chandeliers, ceiling frescoes & plush rooms. Ancient trees grace the pretty inner garden. €€€–€€€€

🏠 **Principe** [148 D1] (50 rooms) Corso Vittorio Emanuele 94; 📞059 218670; w hotelprincipemodena.it. Modern & somewhat austere bedrooms; AC, garage (*extra charge*), bar, good b/fast. €€€–€€€€.

MID-RANGE

🏠 **Astor** [148 F4] (24 rooms) Via Minelli 61; 📞059 365037; w www.hotelastormodena.com. Near the university, a 20min walk east of the centre. Pleasant rooms with little balconies; free parking & a good b/fast buffet. €€€

🏠 **Daunia** [148 F4] (42 rooms) Via del Pozzo 158; 📞059 371182; w hoteldaunia.it. Another one near the university & hospital, this hotel

has a pleasant terrace, & old-fashioned but elegant & comfortable AC rooms; car park. €€€

🏠 **Europa** [148 D1] (67 rooms) Corso Vittorio Emanuele 52; 📞059 217721; w hoteleuropa.it. Occupying a 19th-century palazzo, all rooms come with AC, some smoking; bar & restaurant, private garage (*extra charge*). €€€

🏠 **San Geminiano** [148 D4] (22 rooms) Viale Moreali 41; 📞059 210303; w hotelsangeminiano. it. Just east of the centre off Via Trento e Trieste; basic, family-run. Parking. €€€

SHOESTRING

🏠 **B&B Iris** [148 D4] (3 rooms) Via Stuffler 22; m 348 713 2101; w bbiris.it. Quiet rooms near the university, 1.5km from the centre. AC & a small garden. €

🏠 **Ostello San Filippo Neri** [148 C1] Via Sant'Orsola 52; 📞059 234598; w ostellomodena. it. Sgl, dbl & trpl rooms, also dormitory accommodation at daily & weekly rates. Near the station. €

APARTMENTS

🏠 **EmiliaSuite** [not mapped] m 328 672 6128; w emiliasuite.it. Something new in Modena, a collection of apartments & suites at 9 different locations, all run as B&Bs & each with a personality of its own. All with AC, sharp modern design & services on offer that range from gastronomic tours to laundry to babysitting. €€€€–€€€€€

🏠 **Agriturismo Villa Gaidello** [map, page 144] (4 apts) Via Gaidello 18; 📞059 926806; w gaidello.com. Just north of Castelfranco Emilia, 10km east of Modena. An enchanting oasis of greenery, part of which is an organic farm. 4 apts, furnished with antiques, in a beautifully restored early 19th-century farmhouse. €€€€

✖ WHERE TO EAT AND DRINK

Modena's kitchen has a long and notable tradition. As well as the world-famous balsamic vinegar, Modena, in the heart of Emilia's pig country, prides itself on its variety of *salumeria* and prosciutto; minced pork fills its tortellini and its famous main course, *zampone* (pig's trotter), which is boiled and sliced. Modena is also the best place to taste true, natural Lambrusco (see box, page 44), which must be drunk young to be lively and sparkling; the test is to see if the foam vanishes instantly when poured into a glass.

EXPENSIVE

✖ Osteria Francescana [148 B3] Via Stella 22; ☎059 223912; w osteriafrancescana.it; ⊕ closed Sun–Mon. 3 Michelin stars, frequent acclaim as the 'best restaurant in the world' &, it must be said, an ocean of pretentiousness & puffery. There isn't much more for chef Massimo Bottura to achieve, but his legendary restaurant keeps going. It's fabulously expensive, & you'll need to book a month or more in advance. €€€€€

ABOVE AVERAGE

✖ Cucina del Museo [148 42] Via Sant'Agostino 7; ☎059 217429; w cucinadelmuseo.it; ⊕ closed Mon. An intimate restaurant & creative cooking, fond of seafood & dishes with *spugnole* (morels); a very interesting *menu degustazione* & an enormous wine list from around the world. €€€€–€€€€€

✖ Europa 92 [map, page 144] Stradello Nava 8, 5km south of Modena; ☎059 460067; w ristoranteuropa92.com; ⊕ closed Mon all day, Tue lunch. This was Pavarotti's favourite restaurant in all the world; just coincidentally he opened it himself on his farm, near what is now the Casa Museo Pavarotti (page 171). Excellent pastas & grills as you would expect, but it make its reputation on the elaborate antipasti & the incredible dessert trolley. €€€€

✖ Francheschetta 58 [148 C4] Via Vignolese 58; ☎059 309 1008; w franceschetta58.it; ⊕ closed Sun. This is the junior version of Massimo Bottura's Osteria Francescana, more informal & with more reasonable prices. The tasting menus & especially the €25 lunch menu are good bargains. €€€€

✖ Hosteria Giusti [148 C2] Vicolo Squallore 46; ☎059 222533; w www.hosteriagiusti.it; ⊕ lunch only, closed Sun & Mon. Hidden away behind the famous deli (page 152), a simple room with just 4 tables (book way ahead!). It's been around for decades & never changes, dedicated to serving all the Emilian classics with the best of ingredients. €€€€

✖ Vinicio [map, page 144] Via Emilia Est 1526; ☎059 280313; w ristorantevinicio.it; ⊕ closed Mon. A short drive out of the centre, an elegant room (plus tables outdoors in season) & a very rich menu, beginning with the spaghetti with lobster; excellent wine list. €€€€

MODERATE

✖ Stallo del Pomodoro [148 C3] Largo Hannover 63; ☎059 214664; w stallodelpomodoro.it. Takes its name from the former tomato market held here. Truly original cooking without affectation; very enticing, reasonably priced *menu degustazione* (€30, €40 with wine pairing); also a vegetarian menu & gluten-free dishes. Outdoor tables. €€–€€€

CHEAP & CHEERFUL

✖ Aldina [148 B3] Via Albinelli 40 (upstairs), opposite the Mercato Coperto; ☎059 236106; ⓕ trattoriaaldina; ⊕ closed Sun, Mon–Thu eves. A Modena institution, resolutely old-fashioned but good, which attracts a wide range of customers all happy to plonk down €20 for *tortellini in brodo*, a *secondo* & a bottle of Lambrusco. €€

✖ Da Enzo [148 C2] Via Coltellini 17; ☎059 225177; ⊕ closed Sun. Excellent trattoria, famous for homemade pasta, especially the pumpkin tortellini. €€

✖ La Bonissima [148 C3] Via Masone 16; m 335 542 5015. A very convivial neighbourhood trattoria, good for copious portions of pasta & *secondi*; good bargain too. €€

✖ Ermes [148 B1] Via Ganaceto 89; ☎059 238065; ⊕ lunch only, closed Sun. Another local favourite: simple, family-run place with great food on a fixed-price menu, which includes a dish of homemade pasta, a main course (*bollito misto* always on Sat), a side dish, Lambrusco & coffee. No reservations; come at noon sharp. €–€€

✖ Generi Alimentari da Panino [148 A3] Rua Freda 21; w dapanino.it; ⊕ closed Mon. 'Make love, not diets' is the motto of this hipster deli. It has a few tables & makes some bodacious panini & plates of pasta. €

✖ La Bicicletta [148 B2] Largo Sant'Eufemia 26; ☎059 875 4541; ⊕ until midnight Sun–Thu, till 01.30 Fri & Sat. In an area just west of the Duomo with lots of restaurants & cafés, this convivial place with outside tables has the usual *piadine* & *salumi*, as well as pastas, soups & salads. Good for b/fast too. €

✖ Mercato Albinelli [148 B3] Via Albinelli 17. Something brand new in Modena's famous market, an initiative of chef Massimo Bottura of the Osteria Francescana. The 'Food Hall' in the market, with common tables & take-away, so far consists of a few establishments offering pizza, chicken kebabs, vegetarian & vegan dishes, *gnocchi fritti* & *tigelle*, & lots of tortellini.

WINE BARS

♀ **Compagnia del Taglio** [148 C2] Via Taglio 12, upstairs; `059 210 377; ⊕ closed mid-Jul–mid-Sep. A classy wine bar in the *centro storico*;

big wine list, cocktails, delicious nibbles, pasta & salads; sometimes live music. €€

♀ **Vinoteca** [148 E2] Via Ciro Menotti 217; `059 241198; ◧ vinoteca.modena. Wine bar with a younger clientele; nice plates of cheese & *salumi*. Outside tables; jazz or rock on summer nights. €€

SHOPPING

Modena sponsors an antiques fair on the fourth Saturday and Sunday of every month in the Parco Novi Sad [148 B1] (except July and December). The big weekly food and clothes market is there too on Monday mornings, while the market in the city centre, in Piazza XX Settembre, is held Monday to Saturday. An organic foods market is held in Piazza Sant'Agostino on Tuesday mornings. There are *consorzi dei prodotti tipici* for balsamic vinegar, Lambrusco, cherries, chestnuts, cheeses and hams (quite as tasty as Parma's). It's often possible to visit the farms around the city where they're made; tours can be booked through the tourist office.

Acetaia Malpighi [148 D4] Via Barca 20; `059 467725; w acetaiamalpighi.it. In business since 1850, producing not only traditional balsamic vinegars but also caramels & chocolates filled

with the stuff (Vin Drop & Vin Royal respectively), designed for people who think they've tried everything – see the website about free tours & tastings. Near the Modena south *autostrada* exit.

THE ELIXIR OF MODENA

In 1944, when the frantically clanging bells of the Ghirlandina warned Modena that American bombers were approaching, thousands took to bicycles and pedaled desperately out of the city. Many of them had taken time to scoop up money, jewels and other easy-to-carry valuables; and on dozens of luggage carriers small kegs were securely strapped. They contained vinegar.

Waverly Root

The city's famous balsamic vinegar, now exported all over the world, is first documented in 1046, when Countess Matilda's dad gave a keg of it to the emperor; in those days it was prized as much for its supposed medicinal qualities – hence its name – as for dressing vegetables.

Now manufactured commercially, the vinegar is made according to strict rules from the cooked and fermented must of Trebbiana grapes, to which a squirt of aged 'mother vinegar' has been added. Then it is aged in a red oak barrel. Over the next ten years, the vinegar will be diligently poured from one barrel to another slightly smaller one (because of evaporation) in a specially prescribed sequence – each made of a certain wood, including mulberry and juniper, which gives the vinegar its perfume – until it achieves its distinctive glowing coffee colour, delicate aroma and a taste between sweet and tart. The most prized vinegars are more than 50 years old. Traditionally each family had its own set of six barrels, and would start a new one at the birth of a boy, so that by the time he married he would have his own stock.

Note that authentic, traditionally made balsamic vinegar always comes in an oval bottle, designed by Giorgetto Giugiaro (who also designed cars for Ferrari).

Emily Bookshop [148 C2] Via Fonte d'Abisso 9; m 349 536 9707. Books in English & other languages, tea & coffee, free Wi-Fi.
Giusti [148 C2] Via Farini 75 ⟍059 222533; w hosteriagiusti.it. An institution, this *salumeria* has been around more than 400 years, & it has the best of everything from the region: meats, cheeses, wines, fresh pasta & breads, & a fine little restaurant hidden away at the back (page 150).
Mercato Albinelli [148 B3] Via Albinelli 13; w mercatoalbinelli.it; ⏰ daily exc Sun 06.30–

14.30. One of the most beautiful market halls in Europe, with all the finest Emilia produce, & places to eat (pages 150–1). Coming here is a culinary education.
Spezieria e Acetaia dei Padri Benedettini [148 C4] Via San Pietro 7, in cloister of San Pietro; m 328 667 3338; ⏰ closed Mon morning & Sun. In business for more than 1,000 years, this monkish apothecary now sells food products & many other things made by Benedictines here & around the world.

ENTERTAINMENT AND NIGHTLIFE

♀ Cotton Club Speakeasy [148 C3] Corso Canalgrande 86; ⟍059 223023; w cottonclub-mo. it. Ring the bell – it's a speakeasy. Inside, 1920s atmosphere, serious cocktails & jazz. Best to book ahead, especially at w/ends.

🎭 Teatro Comunale Luciano Pavarotti [148 C2] Via del Teatro 8; ⟍059 203 3010 (box office); w teatrocomunalemodena.it. Modena's fabulous 18th-century theatre offers prestige concerts, opera & ballet in winter & spring, as well as more contemporary attractions.

OTHER PRACTICALITIES

HOSPITAL
✚ Policlinico di Modena [148 F4] Via del Pozzo, 1.5km southeast of the centre; ⟍059 422 2111

LEFT LUGGAGE
Ostello San Filippo Neri [148 C1] 51 Via Sant'Orsola; ⏰ 08.00–23.00. 15mins' walk south of the rail station, this hostel keeps bags for €6 each/day (free for hostel guests).

PHARMACY
✚ Farmacia Comunale del Pozzo [148 F4] Via Emilia Est 416; ⟍059 360 091; ⏰ 24hrs

POST OFFICE
✉ Posta Centrale [148 C3] Via Modenella 8, off the Via Emilia Est

WHAT TO SEE AND DO

THE DUOMO AND PIAZZA GRANDE
Duomo di San Geminiano [148 B3] (*Piazza Grande;* ⟍ *059 216078;* w *duomodimodena.it;* ⏰ *07.00–19.00 Tue–Sun, 07.00–12.30 & 15.30–19.00 Mon; €1.50. For the traditionalist faithful, the Duomo offers a Mass in Latin at 08.30 Sun, followed by one with Gregorian chant at 09.45*) The Via Emilia is Modena's main thoroughfare, and it is in the centre of this city where the old Roman highway picks up one of its loveliest gems, the UNESCO-listed Romanesque Duomo di San Geminiano. Begun with funds and support from Countess Matilda in 1099, Modena cathedral was designed by a master builder named Lanfranco and completed in the 13th century.

Complementing the Duomo's fine proportions are the magnificent carvings by 12th-century sculptor Wiligelmo (see box, opposite) above the three main entrances and elsewhere around the church. Wiligelmo's followers, and after them the anonymous Lombard sculptors and architects known as the Campionese Masters, carried on the work, making this cathedral a living museum of medieval sculpture.

There is some great work from the Renaissance, too – altogether, a church one can look at all day and not see everything.

Façade The façade is topped by the strange figure of the *Angel of Death Grasping a Lily*. Below this are figures of the *Four Evangelists* and *Samson and the Lion* by followers of Wiligelmo, and in the centre *The Redeemer*, by a Campionese sculptor, directly over the great 24-sided rose window, with four panes of 15th-century stained glass created after designs by Giovanni da Modena.

Below is a **loggia**, with capitals carved with imaginary beasts and monsters. Some of the more unusual subjects on this façade are carved on four small panels underneath this: an angel with a reversed torch and an ibis, symbolising Death and Sin; next, a hart with one head and two bodies, taking a drink and symbolising God knows what; a lion and lioness with lion-headed serpents coming out of their mouths; and on the right another Angel of Death.

Wiligelmo's four great **relief panels of Genesis** come next: over the left portal *Adam and Eve in Paradise* and the *Original Sin*; to the left of the main portal the *Flight from Paradise* and the *Labour of Adam and Eve*; to the right of the main portal the *Sacrifices of Cain and Abel* and the *Murder of Abel*; and over the right portal the *Murder of Cain* by Lamech and *Noah's Ark*. These reliefs are believed to illustrate scenes not so much from Genesis directly, but from the medieval mystery play on it, the *Jeu d'Adam*.

All the reliefs in the **Portale Maggiore** are Wiligelmo's too: 12 *Prophets of Israel*, and the familiar medieval subject of the *Labourers in the Vineyard*, where the grape harvest prefigures the harvest of souls in the last days. At the top, note the unusual intruder in this Christian scene: the two-headed Roman god Janus, still performing

WILIGELMO AND LANFRANCO

Perhaps of German origin, or perhaps from Como, Wiligelmo (active 1106–20) is considered as the first of the great Italian Romanesque sculptors. If so, his work seems less of a timid beginning than a fully formed and sophisticated art, intense and full of life, with a complex iconography that effortlessly combines scriptural interpretation and medieval fancy, along with a will to recapture the sculptural forms of antiquity. Some scholars see a French influence in his work, or even the collaboration of sculptors from Toulouse; others see the sometimes heavy, stocky figures as based on the illustrations in contemporary Ottonian manuscripts.

Wiligelmo's masterpiece is the sculptural work in Modena Cathedral. He was an architect too, and is often given credit for at least some of its design.

The main architect of the cathedral, though, was undoubtedly Lanfranco (active 1099–1110), one of the earliest medieval architects whose name is known. Lanfranco transformed the existing Lombard style of churches to create a major advance at the beginnings of Italian Romanesque architecture.

Nothing is known about his life, but medieval manuscripts suggest he was a big man in his day; one illustration pictures him with the powerful Countess Matilda of Canossa (page 197), a notable builder of churches who may have been his employer here. One account has it that Lanfranco helped discover the remains of San Geminiano, the event that occasioned the building of the cathedral. There is a 13th-century inscription honouring him in the cathedral's apse.

his ancient function as guardian of doors and gates. The lions supporting the portal's columns were recycled from a Roman building.

Wiligelmo also carved the inscription above and to the left of the portal recording the building of the cathedral, on a tablet supported by Enoch and Elijah: 'As Cancer overtook the Twins, five days before the Ides of June in the year of Our Lord eleven hundred minus one, this house was founded for the great Geminiano.' The presence of the two prophets here has caused much puzzlement – the two figures of the Old Testament who were translated to heaven without dying, they also play a role in the Apocalypse.

Later hands added another message at the bottom of the tablet: 'From your work here, O Wiligelmus, it is clear how worthy you are to be honoured among sculptors.'

South wall and apse With its conspicuous position facing Piazza Grande, this side has almost as much good sculpture as the façade. Of the two portals, the one on the left is the **Porta dei Principi**; its reliefs, by followers of Wiligelmo, were damaged by an Allied bomb in the war. On the lintel, the scenes from the *Life of San Geminiano* detail the legend of how the saint voyaged to Constantinople to exorcise a demon that was inhabiting the body of Emperor Jovian's daughter (the demon, who looks more like a winged tabby cat, appears in the third panel). Around the door, facing outwards are interlaced vines concealing charming figures of the professions: soldiers, peasants, smiths and musicians, even a sculptor. These share the vineyard with fantastical animals. On the inside facing the door are figures of the Apostles.

Above the door, to the right, is an inscription of 1184 detailing the consecration of the cathedral, and above that, on the roofline, the builders inserted two sculptures from Roman times, the heads of Jupiter and Matrona.

The right portal, the **Porta Regia**, was added after the completion of the cathedral by the Campionese Masters, who also designed the gabled false transept to the right. The graceful loggia above the door holds an odd 1376 copper statue of the saint himself, looking like he's about to give a sermon. To the right of this portal, on the transept, is another relief of the *Life of San Geminiano*, the earliest known work of a great Renaissance Florentine sculptor, Agostino di Duccio (1442), and a lovely balcony carved with rondels with symbols of the Evangelists by Jacopo da Ferrara (1500–11).

Around the back, the slightly listing **apse** was the first part of the cathedral to be completed. Around the lower, central window, where a figure of the Medusa hides amid the foliage, medieval Modena carved its standard measures – lengths and brick sizes – to keep the merchants and tradesmen honest.

Metopes and north wall Wiligelmo's unknown contemporary, known as the 'Master of the Metopes', executed these fascinating reliefs of mythological creatures and allegorical subjects on top of the buttresses – monsters relegated to the ends of the cathedral just as they are relegated to the ends of the earth (or perhaps, as some believe, mystic allegories, placed closest to heaven and farthest from profane eyes). Exactly what they represent is anyone's guess. Four face south, four north.

The **north wall** was originally built up with episcopal offices (Via Lanfranco, which runs along this side now, was cut through only in 1898), and consequently there is little decoration. The four metopes on the north roofline are hard to see. (But all the metopes are copies; the early 12th-century originals, which deserve a much closer look, are in the Musei del Duomo; pages 156–7).

Also on the north wall is the **Porta della Pescheria**, with carvings by Wiligelmo's followers of something else not quite canonical – **King Arthur**. Stories of Arthur and his knights were familiar in medieval Italy, especially in the south. The Normans and crusaders brought them down originally, and soon Italians were creating Arthurian stories of their own (in Sicily he sleeps eternally not in Avalon but under Mount Etna). This portal (1130s, or according to some much earlier), was meant to be seen only by the clergy as they entered the church; it pictures him with two of his knights coming to the aid of Guenevere, imprisoned in Modroc's castle surrounded by the sea.

This is the oldest sculptural representation of Arthurian stories anywhere, older in fact than the first appearance in literature of the tale of the *Abduction of Guenevere*. The versions of the names carved on the relief – 'Galvegin' for Gawain, 'Che' for Kay – are Breton; the Modenese must have heard the stories from knights from Brittany.

Beneath this are fine reliefs of the *Labours of the Months*, along with other fond medieval fancies, such as the fairy-tale scene of the *Funeral of the Fox* being born off by two giant chickens.

Inside the cathedral The Campionese Masters also added the final touches to Lanfranco's charming interior, with its rhythm of arches supported by slender columns and ponderous piers. If the cathedral seems rather austere inside, that was not the intent – most of it was originally covered in frescoes, fragments of which survive throughout.

The floor level is split in the Lombard style, the altar and choir raised above the rest of the church. To decorate the entrance to the crypt, the Campionese Masters created the great **pontile**, carved with lion pillars and polychromed reliefs of the life of Christ, and incorporating the *ambone*, a pulpit with pillars in the shape of telamones with excellent capitals. Behind the altar are intarsia **choir stalls** by Cristoforo and Lorenzo Canozi da Lendinara, and in the left aisle a polyptych by Serafino dei Serafini.

Underneath it all is a **crypt** of 32 columns with capitals carved by Wiligelmo and his followers, with more lions, Evangelists and strange devices from the Romanesque bag, including a chimaera and another fork-tailed mermaid, as well as two wonderful alabaster windows, left and right of the altar. San Geminiano is buried here in a Roman sarcophagus, and to the right is a terracotta *Adoration of the Shepherds* (Guido Mazzoni, 1480).

In the right aisle of the cathedral is a terracotta *presepe*, made by Antonio Begarelli (1527), and to the right of that an altar with frescoes by Cristoforo da Lendinara. Among the altars of the left aisle are one with fragments of frescoes by Tommaso da Modena, and another with an altarpiece by Dosso Dossi. Attached to one of the pillars on the left side of the nave, the pulpit is the work of Enrico da Campione (1322), with statues added a century later.

La Ghirlandina, and the Stolen Bucket [148 B3] (*Piazza della Torre, behind the Duomo;* ✆ *059 203 2660;* ⊕ *Apr–Sep 09.30–13.00 & 15.00–19.00 Tue–Fri, 09.30–17.30 Sat–Sun, Oct–Mar 09.30–13.00 & 14.30–17.30 Tue–Fri, 09.30–17.30 Sat–Sun; €3, or joint ticket with Palazzo Comunale, Acetaia Comunale & Musei del Duomo €6)* Modena's pride and symbol is the mighty, if slightly askew, campanile called the Ghirlandina. This too is a creation of the Campionese Masters. They got the lower part up in a single year (1169), and then left their grandsons the job of finishing the octagonal spire (completed 1319) that accounts for almost half the tower's 85m – the third-tallest campanile in Italy, after Cremona and Venice. The tower's name is often explained as referring to the 'garland' (*ghirlanda*) of arcading

around the base of the spire, though a more likely version says that the tower was originally La Ghiraldina, and that the Modenese were comparing their work to the most famous tower of the medieval world: La Giralda, the minaret of the Great Mosque of Seville.

The Campionese sculptors were able to follow their fancy in medallions at the corners, and in the capitals of the tower windows where few would ever see them: more fantastic beasts and mysterious figures, along with the story of a corrupt Modenese judge and scenes of King David with dancers and musicians. Of the four great bells, one goes back to the year 1350; they still ring it. At the base of the campanile is a photo memorial to Modena's martyred *partigiani*, as in Bologna.

The Ghirlandina houses a famous trophy – an ancient wooden **bucket** stolen from the town well of Bologna during a raid on that city in 1325, when the two cities were at war. It is the subject of Alessandro Tassoni's mock-heroic epic, *La Secchia Rapita* (1622), in which every episode starts out in total seriousness and gradually deteriorates into total absurdity, while the gods of Olympus take sides and interfere, as in Homer. Mozart's rival Salieri turned it into an opera in 1772.

The Bolognesi hatch periodic plots to steal back their bucket; according to rumour, they have it now, and the one you see is only a replica. Actually, it is a replica; the real one is in the Palazzo Comunale, where it is kept safe from the evil Bolognesi. There's a **statue of Tassoni** in the Piazza Torre, next to the tower.

Musei del Duomo [148 B2] (*Via Lanfranco 6;* \ *059 439 6969;* w *museidelduomodimodena.it;* ☉ *09.30–12.30 & 15.30–18.30 Tue–Sun; €4, or joint ticket with La Ghirlandina, Palazzo Comunale & Acetaia Comunale €6*) Next to the Ghirlandina, Modena's cathedral has two museums at the same address, both renovated for the Jubilee Year in 2000. The older **Museo Lapidario** houses one of Modena's treasures: the original eight **metopes** from the Duomo by the unknown 'Master of the Metopes', sculpted in the first decades of the 12th century but with an accuracy of proportions and brilliant stylisation that look startlingly modern. Originally they decorated the eight buttresses of the nave, projecting just above the cornice, where no-one could really see them. The Modenese thought them important enough to move out of the rain, and they have replaced them with copies. ('Metopes' is a misnomer; that term only applies to Greek and Roman art. There is really no word for these but just 'reliefs'.)

The metopes are masterpieces of elegance and mystery, dream-images in a medieval vocabulary utterly lost to us, but utterly fascinating. Are they just fantasy, or is there a hidden meaning? In order of their original placement we have, on the north side, from left to right: (1) a girl in an Eastern-style headdress and a long robe, dreaming, while behind her a disembodied masculine arm is menacingly raised, clutching a scroll; (2) a man with long, flowing hair, cornrows, handlebar moustache and full beard, who seems to be in a yoga position, flanked by unknown symbols; (3) a sleeping girl, holding what may be a flower, with an ibis, stork or pelican on her left and maybe a sphinx, with its head twisted upside down, on her right; and (4) a forked-tail mermaid, with a face and hair reminiscent of an ancient Greek Medusa. And on the south side: (1) a pair of sitting girls facing each other, one right-side up, with long braided hair and an eagle or falcon whispering in her ear, the other upside down (the Museum calls them the 'Antipodes'); (2) a hermaphrodite with proudly spread legs (like the mermaid); (3) a bird-headed man with one human foot and one bull's hoof, swallowing a fish, and behind him floating the head of a woman with closed eyes; (4) a naked girl affectionately holding a small dragon by the neck.

Scholars have not been much help in interpreting medieval mysteries such as these. The fork-tailed mermaid is extremely common in churches of the era. Italy has the most, notably at Otranto cathedral in Puglia, where the mermaid sits enthroned next to King Solomon. Bird-headed men are among the fantastical creatures mentioned in medieval books; often they are said to live in India (like the mount of Vishnu, Garuda). As for the rest – not a clue!

The **Museo del Duomo** contains a good deal of church clutter, much of it dedicated to patron saint San Geminiano, including a reliquary bust. There are tapestries made in Brussels on *Stories from Genesis* (1570) and others from the next century that were hung in the Duomo during Lent, along with a permanent display of medieval codices.

Palazzo Comunale [148 B3] (*Piazza Grande;* \ *059 206111;* ⏰ *09.00–19.00 Tue–Sat, 08.00–13.00 & 15.00–19.00 Sun; €2 Sun, free Mon–Sat, or joint ticket with La Ghirlandina, Musei del Duomo & Acetaia Comunale €6*)

The cathedral turns its side to the heart of Modena, Piazza Grande, a spacious and lovely square that is also home to the town hall. Though the façade is early 1600s, it conceals a complex of no fewer than ten buildings behind it, the oldest of which, the Palazzo Urbis Mutinae, goes back to 1046. The **Sale Storiche** (Historic Rooms) are the part open to visitors. Besides the sacred bucket, kept in the Camerino dei Confirmati, you can see a painting by Bartolomeo Schedoni, the *Sposalizio della Vergine*, in the same chamber, and in the Sala del Consiglio Vecchio a set of peculiar paintings by Schedoni and Ercole dell'Abate on patriotic themes, meant to inspire virtue in the town officials.

Modenese *campanilismo* finds its apotheosis in the Sala del Fuoco, with a series of frescoes by Niccolò dell'Abate on the *History of Modena* in Roman times.

Outside the Palazzo, the enormous slab of red Verona marble in the angle of the façade is the **Preda Ringadora**, a speakers' platform in use since the 1200s (an *arringadore* meant an orator; that's where we get our word 'harangue'). Another of Modena's civic icons stands on a pedestal high on the corner of the building, where the piazza meets Via Castellaro: **La Bonissima** [148 B3], a marble lady documented to have been on this spot at least since 1268. According to one story she is the image of a noblewoman famous for her charity in a time of famine; another one says she was the symbol of the Buona Stima, the municipal office that watched over dealings in the markets and among the moneylenders to make sure everything stayed on the level.

Acetaia Comunale [148 B3] (*Rear entrance on Via Scudari;* \ *059 203 2660;* ⏰ *guided tours 15.30 & 16.30 Fri, 10.30, 11.30, 15.30 & 16.30 Sat–Sun; €2, or joint ticket with La Ghirlandina, Palazzo Comunale & Musei del Duomo €6*)

Modena may be the only city on earth that makes vinegar in the attic of its town hall. The 'Municipal Vinegar Works' was opened in 2003 as a promotion for the city's most famous product. There isn't much to see but barrels, but you'll learn a lot about vinegar.

SOUTH OF PIAZZA GRANDE

The streets south of the Piazza Grande, around Corso Canal Chiaro and Via Canalino, are some of Modena's oldest. **Corso Canal Chiaro** in particular is a lovely, winding medieval street, lined with porticoed *palazzi*. These include the **Palazzo Levizzani** [148 B3], from the 1500s, and the next-door Palazzo Fogliani (1491); further down at Via dei Servi is the Renaissance **Casa Morano** [148 B3].

Few people notice it, but the cathedral and its surroundings also make up an exceptionally skilful ensemble of medieval urban design. Don't think for a minute there is anything accidental in the cathedral's seemingly random placement. People in the Middle Ages built cathedrals as the maximum expression of their faith and art. They were outrageously expensive, but their designers had the ability to combine aesthetics with practicality in ways that made the investment go as far as possible to embellish the town.

Like so many in medieval Europe, and particularly in Italy, this cathedral is sited to define and dominate three separate piazzas: the small one at the end of Corso Duomo in front of the façade, the Piazza Torre to the north, where the Ghirlandina is on display, and the Piazza Grande. To reduce the total cost, one or more sides of a cathedral would usually be set into a block of buildings, as in Parma or Modena, or else a side would run along a little alley, as in Ferrara. Either way, the town would save by cutting down the costly sculptural decoration required, and at the same time their cathedral would appear more an organic part of the city, woven into its fabric, instead of just a pretty objet d'art isolated in the middle of a square.

The two keys to medieval urban design are asymmetry and surprise. Any open space in a town was conceived as an aesthetic composition in three dimensions; a good piazza presents constantly changing aspects as one walks around it, any one of which could be the subject for a painting. The dramatic effect, however, comes when one first encounters the composition. Walking towards the centre down Via Castellaro, the Corso Canal Chiaro or the Via Emilia, there is no hint of what lies ahead.

Even in the Middle Ages, the aesthetics of town design were often defeated by practical considerations. Medieval new towns were customarily laid out in simple grids, a practice proven from ancient Greece to frontier America to be the

Like Venice, this was once a city full of canals. There's plenty of water about, spilling down from the Apennines into the marshy countryside around the city. To get rid of it, the medieval *comune* built no fewer than nine canals through its streets to channel the water towards the Po, of which the oldest was the 9th-century Canale Chiaro. All of them led to the moat around the original castle, and from there down the navigable Canale Naviglio, which connected the city to the Po down what is now Corso Vittorio Emanuele. Modena's dukes started bricking over the canals in the 1600s, and the last of them was gone by 1800.

Mercato Albinelli [148 B3] (*Via Albinelli 17;* w *mercatoalbinelli.it;* ⊕ *06.30–14.30 Mon–Sat*) Modena's marketplace was once Piazza Grande. Around the beginning of the 20th century, the city (under a mayor named Albinelli) decided to move the vendors indoors, to ease congestion in the piazza and to better keep an eye on the quality of what the stallholders were selling.

Plans were made but never followed up, though fortunately when they finally did build the market, in 1929, they used the original design, in the gracious, restrained version of Art Nouveau the Italians call Liberty style after the London department store.

A Londoner would not perhaps be reminded of Liberty's, but a miniature glass-roofed Covent Garden. It's a delight, a bright and airy place that makes the perfect produce and seafood – for this is a true big-league temple of food – look even fresher. The presiding angel of the market is the *Girl with a Fruit Basket*, a much-loved sculpture by Giuseppe Graziosi atop the market's fountain.

cheapest and easiest for surveyors (and for land speculators). In the Renaissance the subtleties of medieval design were forgotten, replaced by a mania for the straight line and the right angle perfected in Baroque Rome and Paris, with their broad vistas and strict symmetrical building ensembles. Medieval design reclaimed some popularity in the Romantic era, when painters and tourists learned to appreciate its 'picturesque' qualities without any understanding of the principles that governed them.

Those principles were rediscovered a century ago by a Viennese architect named Camillo Sitte. Sitte's method while travelling was to take a taxi from the station to the best bookstore in town, and there to ask three questions: the best map of the town, the hotel with the best dinners, and the tower with the best views. The result, after 30 years studying the cities of Italy and Europe, was a book published in 1889 called *Der Städtebau nach seinem künstlerischen Grundlage* (The Art of Building Cities).

Sitte's ideas were immensely popular in the decades that followed, influencing the design of new towns and suburbs throughout Europe. Then came World War I, and in its wake the grim cult of architectural Modernism. 'The street must be abolished!' declared Le Corbusier, and a triumphant new ideology proclaimed that modern people must live in tower blocks joined by motorways. The Modernists did not completely succeed in their goal of destroying the old convivial town centres, except in parts of Britain, and both Europe and America are gradually recovering from this brief attack of madness. Now that we're back at square one, with little notion of how to build correctly, it might be a good idea to look at Sitte's sophisticated medieval compositions once again. Take a walk around old Modena with your eyes open, and see if there's anything that strikes your fancy.

Needless to say, you can get everything you need here for a memorable picnic; or have a light lunch at the market's new Food Hall (pages 150–1).

San Barnabà [148 A3] (*Via Carteria 108;* 📞 *059 236327;* 🕐 *09.45–12.30 & 15.00–18.40 daily*) It's a sweet little surprise on the tiny back streets of Modena, just off the Corso Canal Chiaro. San Barnabà, built in 1660 to replace a medieval original, doesn't promise much from the outside, but the interior is one of the best in Modena. The architect may have been the Este's famous stage designer Gaspare Vigarani (see box, page 166), and though relatively small and intimate it certainly is theatrical.

The best part is the frescoed ceiling (begun 1699), with figures by Sigismondo Caula in a wonderful quadratura setting by Iacopo Antonio Mannini. These two carried on the tradition of Emilian quadratura spectaculars, teaming up just as their forebears Angelo Michele Colonna and Agostino Mitelli had done earlier. The theme is the life of St Francis di Paola, founder of the Friars Minim, to whom this church belonged.

San Bartolomeo [148 B3] (*Via dei Servi 8;* 🕐 *09.00–12.30 daily; Mass 10.30 daily*) Begun in 1607, the Jesuit church of San Bartolomeo's main feature is something without which no Jesuit church would be complete: a ceiling covered in trompe l'œil fresco; the works are by various hands, from the fake dome to the quadratura buildings that seem to rise above the roofline and offer parishioners a secret passage between them straight up to Heaven. Grandiose Jesuit piles like this one were the fashionable churches of their day and, as in the public squares and the palaces, theatricality was everything.

San Francesco [148 A3] (*Rua Frati Minori;* \ *059 236218;* ⊕ *06.45–19.00 daily*) Modena's first Franciscan church was founded in 1221, when St Francis was still alive, but the present one, begun in 1244, was still not competed by the mid 15th century, then was completely restructured along with its convent in 1535. After Napoleon, it served as a barracks and suffered other indignities before it was restored as a church in the mid 19th century.

It houses one exceptional work of art by Antonio Begarelli, relocated to San Francesco from the deconsecrated church of Santa Margherita: the life-size *Deposition of Christ from the Cross* with 13 terracotta figures (including *SS Francis and Anthony of Padua*) from around 1531, considered one of his masterpieces. There was another work of Begarelli's here, but Napoleon's troops smashed it up for fun. Over the last few years San Francesco has undergone a very thorough rebuilding, occasioned by structural issues and the need for earthquake proofing. The workmen found the pieces of Begarelli's statues under the floor, and the restorers are trying to see if they can put them together again.

Outside in the piazza, the charming **Fontana di San Francesco**, with a statue by G Graziosi of the saint preaching to the fish, was cast in 1938.

San Pietro [148 C4] (*Via San Pietro 1;* \ *059 214046;* ⊕ *06.15–noon & 15.00– 19.45 daily*) This church has a harmonious Renaissance façade (1530) with a strange terracotta frieze of winged satyrs and serpent-horses by the Bisogni brothers, perhaps inspired by some of the medieval carvings on the cathedral.

The interior is one of the most sumptuous in Modena, with ornate *pietra dura* altars, a painted organ case of 1524, stuccoed decoration and a wealth of painting by local artists of the 16th and 17th centuries, including works by Francesco Bianchi Ferrari and Scarsellino. Best of all are the terracotta sculptures by Antonio Begarelli: the *Dead Christ with the Virgin, St John and Joseph of Arimathea* and six large saints lined up along the nave.

There is a small Renaissance cloister, recently restored, and an 18th-century dispensary, the **Spezieria e Acetaia dei Padri Benedettini**, also restored and recently reopened; here the monks will sell you products from Benedictine abbeys around Europe.

Outside the church, note the little medieval column topped by a cross, the 10th-century **Croce di San Pietro**. In old Emilia, these were common monuments at crossroads or market squares; this one is Modena's only survivor.

ALONG THE VIA EMILIA

Piazza Mazzini [148 C2] The Via Emilia, Modena's elegant main street, runs just behind the Ghirlandina. Heading east, it passes Piazza Mazzini, the site of the Jewish ghetto, instituted by Francesco I in 1638 in a quarter where Jews had already lived since at least the 11th century. After Italian unification ghettos like this one were closed all over the nation. The oldest and most densely packed part was demolished for reasons of hygiene and made into this square, and a big new **synagogue** was built on one side in 1873.

Collegio di San Carlo Like Bologna, Modena is a city of porticoes. The longest, on the south side of Via Emilia, is the gracefully curving **Portico del Collegio di San Carlo** [148 C3], built in the late 17th century. Behind the portico, on Via Università, is the main building of **Modena University** [148 C3], one of Italy's oldest (1175). This complex of buildings, occupying the entire block, includes the portico and the university offices, as well as the **Collegio di San Carlo**, a school for young noblemen of the 17th century, and its church of **San Carlo** [148 C3] (1664–1766; ☏ *059 421204;* ⊕ *by appointment only*), with a painting inside by Marcantonio Franceschini commemorating the plague of 1576 in Milan.

San Biagio [148 C3] (*Via del Carmine 4;* ☏ *059 222 450;* ⊕ *07.30–11.45 & 15.30–19.15 daily*)

Farther down the Via Emilia, the medieval church of San Biagio was thoroughly baroqued in 1638, with paintings by a great southern Italian Baroque master, Mattia Preti. His nickname, the Cavaliere Calabrese, gives an idea of the picaresque life he led, and it shouldn't come as a surprise to see him a follower of Caravaggio, a lover of dark deeds illuminated against the darkness. Preti had psychological depth and a fanatical attention to detail, two qualities rare in his day; his best work comes with an electric spark the Emilian painters seldom manage. His greatest works are in Naples and on Malta, where he worked for the Grand Master of the Knights of St John; but before he went back down south, Preti left a sweet *Concerto di Angeli* in the choir here, where the angel musicians are kitted out with a full panoply of Baroque-era instruments, including a slide trombone. Preti also painted the spectacular dome, with a host of saints plus Evangelists, and Adam and Eve swirling around the heavenly vortex.

MODENA'S BOULEVARDS The old city ends at the **Porta di Bologna**. In place of the old gate is the **Fountain of Two Rivers** [148 C3], representing the Secchia and the little Panaro. It took Modena 30 years to demolish its walls, starting in 1882, and the city replaced them with a ring of tree-lined boulevards. The best part starts here, with Viale Martiri della Libertà and Viale delle Rimembranze, bordered by parks as they wind around the eastern and southern edges of the centre.

WEST OF THE DUOMO From the cathedral, the western stretch of Via Emilia will take you to Modena's other main attraction, the Palazzo dei Musei.

Chiesa del Voto [148 B2] (*Via Emilia;* ⊕ *closed for restorations*).

Though it gets only a passing mention in most histories, the great plague, or 'Plague of Milan' in 1630–31, was one of the most dramatic events of that troubled century, and it contributed greatly to Italy's economic and political decline. An outbreak of bubonic plague, it seems to have been spread by the movements of armies and dismissed soldiers. Modena, like all the cities of Emilia, was badly hit, and lost perhaps half its population.

A number of Italian cities built votive churches in thanksgiving for the end of the plague, most notably Santa Maria della Salute in Venice. The Chiesa del Voto is Modena's, with a stately, rather Venetian design by local architect Cristoforo Galaverna. The interior is restrained by Modenese standards, the only art of note being a quietly moving altarpiece by Lodovico Lana, an allegory depicting the plague.

San Giovanni Battista [148 B2] (*Piazza Matteotti;* ⊕ *before or after Mass, winter 18.00 Sat, 08.00 & 11.30 Sun, summer 18.30 Sat, 09.30 Sun*)

Originally dedicated to St Michael, this church was reconstructed in the 16th century. In 1774 it was rededicated to John the Baptist by the Confraternità di San Giovanni della Buona Morte, which remains in charge of it. The main reason to pop in if it's open is to see Guido Mazzoni's life-size painted terracotta *Lamentation over the Dead Christ*

5

(1477–80), commissioned by the confraternity and moved here in the 19th century. The rulers of Modena at the time are reflected in the figures' features: Ercole I d'Este is Nicodemus and his wife Eleonor represents Mary of Cleophas.

Palazzo Sant'Agostino [148 A2] At the old western entrance to the city, Via Emilia opens up into Largo Porta Sant'Agostino, part of a major building scheme of the 18th-century Este dukes.

The long, looming presence across from the Palazzo dei Musei is Modena's former hospital, now called the Palazzo Sant'Agostino. Duke Francesco III had it built in 1758, and then doubled its already impressive size to add a military hospital in the 1770s. When the hospital decamped for a more modern facility on the outskirts, Modena had to find a new use for the building. Inevitably, in the Europe of today, that meant some sort of 'cultural centre'. The city and the Cassa di Risparmio di Modena have been pushing the project, and Gae Aulenti, the Milanese architect famous for the conversion of the Gare d'Orsay in Paris, got the job.

Progress has been slow, complicated by the usual Italian bureaucratic tangles and the 2012 death of architect Aulenti, and it is hard to predict when work will finally get under way. When it is finished, the Polo Culturale, or Casa della Cultura, or whatever they finally decide to call it, will be a mixed-use project with a small auditorium, a school, an exhibition space for photography, shops, residences and a restaurant, as well as new homes for the Biblioteca Estense and the Biblioteca Poletti, both now in the Palazzo dei Musei.

Meanwhile, exhibitions are occasionally held inside, and if you should happen to find the palazzo open, have a peek inside for the beautiful 18th-century **pharmacy**, left completely intact and in its original state, with frescoes of the great physicians of antiquity.

Palazzo dei Musei [148 A2] (*Viale Vittorio Veneto 5*) This huge 'palace' was really built as the Albergo dei Poveri – the poorhouse. All over Europe in those days it was considered progressive to lock up the unemployed, disabled and orphans in buildings like this (and profitable too; usually they were subjected to forced labour); stately façades like the one here (1764) served to maintain the decorum of the city and to keep respectable folk from worrying too much about what went on inside.

In 1884 the complex was converted again into the Palazzo dei Musei to house the Este picture collections, the Galleria Estense. In later years, the Musei Civici were moved into the ground floor, including the **Museo Lapidario Estense**, which houses Duke Francesco IV's collection of Roman and medieval stone carvings, tombs and inscriptions.

Galleria Estense (*Largo Porta Sant'Agostino 337;* \ *059 439 5707;* w *gallerie-estensi.beniculturali.it;* ⊕ *08.30–19.00 Tue–Sat, 14.00–19.30 Sun & 08.30–19.30 1st Sun of month; €4, free 1st Sun of month*) On the upper floor of the Palazzo dei Musei, the Galleria Estense is a well-arranged collection founded by Francesco I d'Este. The dukes didn't bother much with anything before the 1400s (this is one of those museums that still calls them 'primitives'), but there is one work by medieval Modena's greatest painter, Tommaso da Modena, as well as some other good early Emilian paintings.

A room of quattrocento works shows that in the Renaissance Modena could play too. There's a scene from the *Aeneid* by Niccolò dell'Abate, the obscure Bartolomeo Bonascia's *Pietà with Symbols of the Passion*, and an animated *Crucifixion* by Francesco Bianchi Ferrari, a pupil of Cosmè Tura. Still, the Florentines steal the show, with works by Francesco Botticini and Andrea del Sarto, and especially Botticelli's ripe technicolour *Madonna and Child*.

Other highlights include the gentle *Madonna Campori* by Correggio; Lelio Orsi's dramatic *Martyrdom of St Catherine* (with sword-bearing angels descending through the gloom to find Catherine tied to a diabolical steampunk wheel), bronzes by Il Riccio of Padua, a good Flemish collection, an unusual portable altar painted on both sides, known as the *Modena Triptych* (1568) by El Greco, and several works by Venetian Renaissance artists (Palma Vecchio, Tintoretto, Cima da Conegliano and Veronese).

For all that, the painting you can't stop staring at will be the masterpiece and last-known work of the great quattrocento eccentric Cosmè Tura, the cadaverous, beautiful, horrific *St Anthony of Padua* (1484), a life-size vision of spiritual and anatomical deformity, captured in a garish pink sunset, that will send any good Catholic out in search of a stiff drink.

For another curiosity, there is the **Camera delle Meraviglie** of the later Este dukes. Like the later Medici in Florence, these Este cared less about serious art than exotic knick-knacks; most of them have been preserved here, including tiny working pistols, ostrich eggs and minuscule carved ships.

After the pope took over the city in 1598, the Este got to keep a Ferrara residence, the Palazzo dei Diamanti, and one of the palace's finest embellishments ended up here: a set of ceiling paintings (detachable panels, not frescoes) by Emilian artists including the Carracci and Niccolò dell'Abate; among these Ludovico Carracci's winsome *Flora* stands out. Another set of ceiling paintings called the *Ottagoni* has scenes from Ovid's *Metamorphoses* by Tintoretto, and was brought here from Venice in 1658.

The museum is especially rich in Emilian and other works of the 1600s: two notable canvases of Guercino (a *Martyrdom of St Peter*, and *Venus, Cupid and Mars*), Velázquez's *Portrait of Francesco I d'Este* and Salvator Rosa's *Veduta di una Baia* with a shipwreck, as well as works by Il Garofalo (his charming *Madonna Enthroned with Saints*, 1532), Lionello Spada, Guido Reni, Annibale Carracci, Carlo Bonone and Charles le Brun.

Musei Civici (*Largo Porta Sant'Agostino 337;* \ *059 203 3100;* w *museicivici. modena.it;* ⊕ *09.00–noon Mon–Fri, 10.00–13.00 & 16.00–19.00 Sat–Sun; admission free*) This museum is one of those charming old Italian institutions where nothing seems to have changed since the time of King Umberto. It comes in two parts. First is the **Museo Civico d'Arte**, with a collection of medieval paintings from the city's churches, including work by Tommaso da Modena and some by his followers, Antonio Begarelli's *Madonna della Piazza*, and a lovely room of **antique musical instruments** – psalteries, cembalos, on up to Neapolitan mandolins, all looking rather sad to be locked up in museum cases.

Next comes a room of scientific instruments and early machines, and a huge collection of old Modenese crafts and industrial products – a fascinating and peculiar atticful of everything under the sun, from lace to greeting cards; the display of bridle bits takes up an entire wall.

The **Museo Archeologico e Etnologico**, in the rear of the Palazzo dei Musei at Viale Vittorio Veneto 5, is low in excitement though rich in potsherds. The best parts are the exhibits on the fascinating Terramare people (see box, page 172) and the Etruscans, the 'Venus of Savignano', a fertility goddess some 20,000 years old, and the finds from a Lombard tomb. The ethnological section is a mixed bag from all over the world, from pre-Columbian figurines from Central America and Peru to samurai costumes from Japan.

5

Sant'Agostino [148 A2] (*Piazza Sant'Agostino;* ☎ *059 236327;* ⊕ *07.00–12.30 & 15.00–19.30 daily*) The Palazzo dei Musei had to be built around an existing church, the 14th-century Sant'Agostino. For a while, the Este considered making this their dynastic pantheon, and in 1660 they hired architect Giovanni Monti and theatre designer Gaspare Vigarani (see box, page 166) to remodel the interior into something more fitting for the grandiose ceremonials of a Baroque funeral.

The Este later dropped the idea, choosing San Vincenzo for their pantheon, but Sant'Agostino was left with a quite impressive interior, with rich stucco decorations and plenty of forgettable painting and sculpture. Look out for the slightly larger-than-life-size terracotta group, the *Lament over the Dead Christ* by Antonio Begarelli (1526). Another survivor from the original church is a rare work by medieval Modena's greatest painter, the *Madonna della Consolazione* of Tommaso da Modena.

Foro Boario [148 B1] (*Via Bono Da Nonántola 2, on the edge of Parco Novi Sad;* ☎ *059 20311;* w *fondazionefotografia.org;* ⊕ *generally Wed–Sun but hrs & admission prices change with the exhibitions – check the website*) Formerly a cattle market and military barracks, the enormous and imposing Foro Boario plays two roles today, as the University of Modena's faculty of economics and the exhibition hall of the Fondazione Fotografica.

NORTH OF PIAZZA GRANDE

Palazzo Ducale [148 C2] (*Piazza Roma 15; for info & booking* ☎ *059 220022 (Modenatur), 059 203 2660 (Tourist Office);* ⊕ *for guided tours most Sat–Sun, exc Aug, with advance booking; €8*) The huge Palazzo Ducale still dominates the historic centre of Modena, just as the Este who built it intended. Today though, the building houses the Italian National Military Academy, with its cape-wearing cadets who help give this city its picturesque character. After the Este were forced out of Ferrara, they took up residence in the original castle on this site, built by Obizzo II in 1288. Perhaps it was a little too medieval and draughty, or else it reminded Duke Francesco I too much of his lost home in Ferrara (which it resembled, in a smaller version); whatever, the castle was gone and work on a new up-to-date palace under way by 1635.

Despite the tiny confines of their state, the Este and their architect Bartolomeo Avanzini – with perhaps a little help from consulting architect Gianlorenzo Bernini – made a home that few princes of Europe could match. The façade, with its elegant window cornices and corner towers flanking an impressive entrance, makes a perfect picture of the 17th-century ideals of aristocratic gravity and refinement. Look closely, though, and you can see how hard-pressed the Este were to keep up their pretensions in their little capital on very limited resources: some of the window cornices and trim are just painted on, and half of the balustrade on the cornice is painted cement, not marble. The stone statues on the roofline were added only in the 1920s – in the originals the Este had to settle for wood.

The army takes good care of its landmark schoolhouse, which now includes a **Museo Storico dell'Accademia Militare**, with military memorabilia. If you're around for the weekend tours, they'll show you some of the restored rooms, including the **Salone d'Onore**, with frescoes by Marcantonio Franceschini (1696) and the gorgeous golden **Salottino d'Oro**, done in the 18th century in the style of Versailles. They might also take you downstairs to see the huge underground reservoir, the **Casa delle Acque**, which the dukes built to collect the water flowing from Modena's medieval canals.

And finally, to close the book on the Dukes of Modena, notice the **Monument to Ciro Menotti** [148 C2], which the Modenese erected right in front of the palace in 1879, after Italian unification. The romantically heroic figure up on the pedestal was a local patriot who organised a doomed rebellion against Austrian rule in 1831.

Behind the palace, **Corso Vittorio Emanuele**, once the Canale Naviglio, is a street of imposing palaces, notably the 1772 **Palazzo d'Aragona** [148 C1]. This street ends at Modena's northern gate, its main landmark the neo-Romanesque **Tempio Monumentale dei Caduti** [148 D1], built in the 1920s as a memorial to the dead of World War I.

Giardini Ducale
[148 D1] (*Corso Canalgrande;* ⊕ *Nov–mid-Apr 07.00–20.30 daily, rest of year 06.30–23.30; admission free*) Created in 1598 for the garden-mad Este dukes, the Giardini Ducale were once much more grand and extensive. As with the other great Este gardens, in Ferrara and Sassuolo, so much has been lost over the centuries that it's hard even to guess at the original design.

The gardens were given to the people of Modena in 1739 by Francesco III. Today, they include the **Orto Botanico** (see below), created in 1758 for the study of medicinal plants and still in use by the university, and the adjacent **Giardini Pubblici**, a public park. Centrepiece of the park is the charming **Palazzina Vigarani** [148 D1] (or Palazzina dei Giardini) built in 1634 as a 'casino' for summer balls and shows by the great stage designer Gaspare Vigarani. The Palazzina fell out of favour over the centuries; by the 1920s the *comune* was using it for a tool shed. Restoration came too late to save most of the interior decoration, but now the Palazzina is part of the Galleria Civica di Modena, which uses it for exhibitions of contemporary art; a prestigious annual photography show is held here.

Orto Botanico
[148 D2] (*Viale dei Caduti in Guerra;* ☏ *059 205 6011;* w *www. ortobot.unimore.it;* ⊕ *Apr–Jul & Sep 09.00–13.00 Mon–Fri; admission free; guided tours available by appointment*) This part of the park is a working research garden, owned by the university as part of its Department of Botany. Duke Francesco III founded it in 1758 on land that had been part of the palace gardens. Even if it's not really for show, this will be a treat for plant lovers and anyone else who needs some time in a green oasis in the heart of the city. There is an arboretum with more than 200 trees, special zones for mountain and lowland plants, and plenty of flowers, including more than a hundred species of iris. From the beginning the gardens have always concentrated on exotic species. Those from warmer climates are kept in the rather elegant greenhouse called the **Serre Ducali**. Some of these came from Eritrea and Ethiopia when they were Italian colonies. There's a separate greenhouse for succulents.

San Domenico
[148 C2] (*Piazza San Domenico;* ☏ *059 222958;* ⊕ *10.00–noon & 15.30–19.00 Mon–Fri, 09.00–noon Sat–Sun*) There was a medieval church here but it was in the way of the construction of the Palazzo Ducale, so it was demolished in 1707 and replaced with a new church of San Domenico designed by G A Torri, and opened in 1737. Huge semi-columns support the elliptical dome, the biggest in Modena; below, niches hold statues of the four Evangelists by Giuseppe Maria Mazza of Modena. The best art, from the original church, is just to the left of the entrance: a fine terracotta group of *Jesus in the House of Martha* (1544) by Antonio Begarelli.

San Giorgio
[148 C2] (*Largo San Giorgio;* ⊕ *07.30–11.30 & 17.00–19.30 daily*) Just outside the Palazzo Ducale, San Giorgio was rebuilt in 1647, in the time of

5

Gaspare Vigarani (1588–1663), from Reggio Emilia, was the 'Engineer and Chief Superintendent of the Workshops' for Duke Francesco I of Modena. Like every artist who worked for the Este, he had to do a little bit of everything, from building fortifications to reforming and embellishing the system of canals (the Canale del Naviglio). Mostly his time was divided between architecture and creating the sets and the stage mechanisms – the *macchine*, such as floating clouds, wave machines, fireworks, sea monsters and sea battles, floating gods and goddesses – for the legendary theatrical productions staged by the dukes. At these he was the master of his day, earning him the nickname Il Stregone, the 'great sorcerer'.

As an architect, Vigarani designed the Palazzina in the Giardini Ducale (1632; page 165) as a centrepiece for what was then the dukes' gardens, and a setting for the court's summer theatre. In his remarkable church of San Giorgio (pages 165–6), the interior itself becomes a kind of stage set. Other works include the richly decorated Sant'Agostino in Modena (page 164), and the ingenious SS Girolamo e Vitale in Reggio Emilia (pages 192–3), where three oratories on three different levels are squeezed into a tiny space.

As a great set designer, in an age passionately obsessed with operas and theatre, Vigarani was famous across Europe. In 1659, he and his son and assistant Carlo (1637–1713) were called to the greatest of all courts, that of Louis XIV, to oversee the celebrations for the King's marriage to Maria Teresa of Spain. The Vigaranis proved such a success that they were given permanent posts at Versailles as Intendants des Machines et Plaisirs du Roi. Here, with an almost unlimited budget, they staged the operas of Jean-Baptiste Lully and the plays of Molière and Racine.

The Vigaranis designed the famous stage machinery for the Théâtre des Tuileries (now lost), and they were able to translate many of their theatre tricks into landscape gardening, as assistants in the creation of the gardens at Versailles.

Francesco I d'Este, to house a miraculous image of the Virgin Mary, 'Our Lady of the Modenese People'. The church and its rare Greek-cross plan are the work of Gaspare Vigarani (see box, above), though the façade was added by other hands in the 1680s. Here though, the real interest is inside, where Vigarani translated his talent for stage design into religious architecture. The architectural constructions flanking the altar, with their Corinthian pilasters and balconies, may be unique in the history of church building. They make the east end of the church a proper stage set; the upper galleries were intended to accommodate the musicians accompanying the mass.

Corso Canal Grande Corso Canal Grande was the posh address of Baroque Modena. It's a rather narrow street, built along the path of the ancient Roman walls; you'll wonder how they found room for a canal in the middle of it. It starts at the Giardini Ducale, next to the Ducal Palace, and passes first the long, 18th-century **Scuderie Ducale** [148 D2], the arsenal and stables of the Este, and now a barracks of the Military Academy.

The palaces that follow as you continue southward are architecturally rather modest. One of the most impressive is the **Palazzo Santa Margherita** [148 C2], now the home of the Museo della Figurina and the Galleria Civica of modern art (see below). Like the dukes themselves, the great ones who buzzed around their court were often strapped for cash to keep up with the Baroque Joneses; in places you can see where the plaster 'stonework' has chipped away, revealing the bricks beneath.

Further down, on the left, the big, squat **Corte di Assise** [148 C3] – the provincial courthouse – occupies a 17th-century Theatine monastery built by the great Modena-born Guarino Guarini, who was a Theatine priest himself. Guarini went on to design wonderful arch-Rococo palaces and churches in Turin and Sicily; by comparison his only hometown work is very subdued.

Museo della Figurina [148 C2] (*Corso Canalgrande 103;* \ *059 203 2919;* w *comune.modena.it/museofigurina;* ⏲ *10.30–13.00 & 16.00–19.30 Wed–Fri, 10.30–19.30 Sat–Sun; admission free*) Giuseppe Panini, one of the founders of Modena's Edizione Panini publishing dynasty, accumulated the biggest museum collection in Modena. The Paninis printed books and comic books, but they made their real money from stickers and collectors' cards (*figurine* in Italian). Giuseppe's mad passion for these led to this museum, housed since 2006 in the Palazzo Santa Margherita. Here you'll find a choice selection of Panini's half a million cigarette cards and every other kind of collectors' cards going back to the 1860s, as well as matchboxes, menus, calendars, and no fewer than 43,000 19th-century letter seals.

Galleria Civica di Arte Moderna [148 C2] (*Corso Canalgrande 103;* \ *059 203 2940;* w *comune.modena.it/galleria;* ⏲ *during exhibitions only, check website for hours; admission free*) Housed in the Palazzo Santa Margherita, this museum has a permanent collection of drawings and photographs by 20th-century Italian artists, as well as regular temporary exhibitions by artists from around the world.

San Vincenzo [148 C3] (*Corso Canalgrande 75;* ⏲ *10.00–noon & 16.00–18.00 Sat–Sun*) Even in this city of overwrought churches, San Vincenzo stands out. It was a project of the Theatines, a powerful and aristocratic religious order that in the mid 16th century had the full backing of the popes. The Theatines built churches that were perfect exemplars of the Counter-Reformation ideals of beauty and spectacle for the masses: light and airy, opulently decorated with heavenly frescoed vaults and stucco laid on like thick cake frosting. Their great church of Sant'Andrea in Valle in Rome was the model, and it is recaptured on a smaller scale here.

Begun in 1617, the church is largely the design of Bartolomeo Avanzini, the court architect who also worked on the ducal palaces at Modena and Sassuolo (he isn't responsible for the restrained façade, a compromise solution that was added later). While still under construction, San Vincenzo got even fancier, as Duke Francesco IV decided to make it a kind of pantheon for the Este dynasty. Results from this include the odd, pyramidal tomb of Duke Ercole III, and the octagonal chapel of the 1830s where three dukes are buried, all named Francesco, as well as miscellaneous other Este family members, including Laura Martinozzi, mother of Francesco II and also of Maria Beatrice Anna Margherita Isabella d'Este (b1658) the 'Mary of Modena' who married James II and became Queen of England.

Some of the artworks inside were destroyed in a bombing raid in 1944, including the frescoes of the dome and apse. There was an altarpiece with a Madonna by Guercino (1630), but it was stolen in 2014. The theft of such a large and heavy painting mystified the Carabinieri until the following year, when this very unfortunate church almost blew itself up. A leak had filled the entire building with gas; it was discovered just in time, and the investigating firemen found a centuries-

5

old hidden entrance that led to a clothing shop next door. Mystery solved; painting, valued at €5 million, still missing.

Musei Universitari (w *musei.unimore.it*; ⊕ *all by appointment only*) Modena's university has been collecting things for centuries. The results are kept in six separate small museums, old-fashioned and a little dusty, seldom visited and relentlessly didactic – museums that are almost museum pieces in themselves. Two of the Musei Universitari are in the main building on Via Università; the others are scattered around town.

Museo di Zoologia e di Anatomia Comparata [148 C3] (*Via Università 4;* ✆ *059 205 6561*) A peculiar museum packed full of specimens, with thousands of skeletons, fossils and poor sad creatures in formaldehyde. It has resisted any and every urge to go interactive and high tech: it's a treat for anyone who loves old-fashioned wooden cases of specimens (3,300 vertebrates) with handwritten tags. They're proudest of their collections of parasites, poisonous animals and parrots.

Museo Astronomico e Geofisico [148 C2] (*Piazza Roma, in the east tower of the Palazzo Ducale;* ✆ *059 222239*) The university opened its astronomical observatory in 1826. It never threw anything away, leaving this interesting collection of old telescopes and instruments, maps and charts; right now it's working on the restoration of the observatory in the dukes' gardens as it was in 1896.

Laboratorio delle Macchine Matematiche [148 C4] (*Via Campi 213, off Via Vignolese, southeast of the centre;* ✆ *059 205 5039*) Somewhere in the world there must be a few geometers who will find this the most fascinating museum in Italy. It's a collection of geometrical instruments from the 16th to the 19th century, plus reconstructions of instruments from the ancient world, including everything from pantographs to perspective devices to a gadget that would supposedly let you legally trisect an angle.

Museo di Paleontologia [148 C3] (*Via Università 4;* ✆ *059 205 5832*) The highlight here is the Sala dei Dinosauri, with two recently reassembled skeletons found in Utah. The rest – the collection of otoliths (structures of the inner ear) from prehistoric fish, and microfossils – will be of interest only to specialists.

Museo di Anatomia Umana e Teatro Anatomico [148 A2] (*Via Berengario 14;* ✆ *059 205 7131*) A smaller version of the medical museums of Bologna's university, this one offers beautifully made terracotta and wax models of the human anatomy used by Baroque-era medical students, and an ornate wood-panelled operating theatre from the 18th century.

Gemma: Museo Mineralogico e Geografico Estense [148 B2] (*Largo Santa Eufemia 19, west of the Duomo;* ✆ *059 205 5873*) It's been around since 1786; the last dukes took a surprising interest in the subject. As you would expect, the collection includes lots of mineral specimens, but there is also a set of 'historic meteorites' they've been gathering since the 18th century.

SUBURBAN SIGHTS
Cimitero San Cataldo [map, page 144] (*Strada Cimitero San Cataldo;* ✆ *059 334013*; ⊕ *generally 08.00–noon & 14.00–16.00 daily, later in summer*) Though he

might try to deny it – 'I cannot be Postmodern, as I have never been Modern' – Aldo Rossi is a darling of the Postmodernists, the first Italian to win the Pritzker Prize. At first more an academic than a builder, Rossi made his name when he won a competition in the 1970s to build this cemetery expansion project in Modena's northern suburbs. The controversial project has not yet been finished, and may never be. What you can see now is a blank exterior wall, some long barracks-like buildings and the chillingly geometric 'ossuary cube'. The whole could be a haunted landscape from a Di Chirico painting, perhaps a fitting representation for a modern Europe where death has ceased to have much meaning.

Museo delle Macchine da Caffè [148 F4] (*Via Umberto Giordano 125, off Via Emilia Est just before the SS12 ring road;* ✆ *059 376811;* w *collezionecaffecagliari.it;* ⏲ *some w/ends, with guided tours & often special shows or cooking classes; admission free*) Caffè Cagliari is a century-old local roaster that makes a pretty good brew; you'll see it all over Emilia. The firm has assembled this collection of more than a hundred antique espresso machines, one of the largest in the world.

Coffee technology goes back at least to the 18th century. Back then, coffee was either just boiled or passed through a filter, and the earliest machines were intended only to keep the stuff warm. Real *espresso* (it means 'ready-made') arrived with the invention of the espresso machine, with its steam boiler, in the 1890s. The coffee-enslaved Italians soon made the new machine into a cult object, reigning as queen of the bar like some extra-planetary religious icon. More than anything, this museum is a parade of the best and flashiest Italian design. The machines from the Mussolini Deco years and the even spacier post-war decades are amazing. They deserve a museum.

See the website under 'News e Eventi' for full details including opening dates and times. Bookings can be made via the website or by phone.

Pagani Automobili [map, page 144] (*Via dell'Artigianato 5, San Cesario sul Panaro, between Modena & Bologna (actually closer to Castelfranco dell'Emilia, north of the A1);* ✆ *059 220 022 (Modenatur);* w *pagani.com/factory-tours;* ⏲ *factory tours Mon–Fri, by reservation only via Modenatur or the Pagani website; €35, under 12s free*) The burning desire to create the ultimate handcrafted luxury super-car in Italy's Motor Valley is far from dead. Horacio Pagani, born in Argentina in 1955, built and designed many things early in his career – bar furniture, camper vans, combine harvesters, orthopaedic beds and an F2 single-seater racing car – before he moved to Italy in 1983. After working with Lamborghini, designing parts of its F1 engine and the chassis of its Diabolo model, Pagani set up his own company in San Cesario sul Panaro and started production of the Zonda, which had its debut at the Geneva Motor Show in 1999. Pagani's second major model, the Huayra hyper-car, made its appearance in 2011, also at the Geneva Motor Show. If you don't have €1.3 million to buy the ultimate boy's toy, you can at least come and watch them being made.

Museo Stanguellini [148 F4] (*Via Emilia Est 756, Modena;* ✆ *059 361105;* w *stanguellini.it/museo;* ⏲ *by appointment only – closed for renovations, reopening date uncertain; admission free*) The oldest of Modena's car dynasties, the Stanguellini had mechanical aptitude in their blood. In 1879 Celso Stanguellini patented mechanically tuned kettle drums and founded a company in Modena to build them. In the early 1900s, his son Francesco became the first person in Modena to register a car, and later drove in some of the first car and motorcycle (on Modena-made Mignon motorcycles) races in Italy, founding the Stanguellini Racing Team while serving as the local Fiat agent.

After his death in 1932, his 19-year-old son Vittorio inherited the company and the passion for engines and cars, turning Fiat chassis into premier roadsters, often competing against his friend and rival Enzo Ferrari. Pre-war victories in the Mille Miglia race across Italy made Stanguellini famous.

FERRARI IN MODENA

There are *two* Ferrari museums. One is in Modena, the other by the factory in suburban Maranello. A dedicated shuttle connects the two, with a stop at the Modena train station (*051 612 0818; adult return €12, purchase online at* w *vivaraviaggi.it/happy_circle.php*), which also has the timetables.

MUSEO ENZO FERRARI [148 E1] (*Via Paolo Ferrari 85;* *059 439 7979;* w *musei. ferrari.com/en/Modena;* ⊕ *09.30–18.00 daily, Apr–Oct until 19.00; admission €16, combination ticket with Museo Ferrari Maranello €26*) Enzo Ferrari (1898–1998) loved his native Modena enough to put the city's yellow on his badge, behind the prancing pony, and Modena loves Ferrari right back. Open in 2012, this museum pays homage to his life and times. The house where Enzo was born, next to the workshop where his father worked on rail carriages, has been restored to house the Museo dei Motori, with various engines on display from a small two-cylinder model to F1, along with a collection of race cars and videos.

Next to it rises the curving glass façade of a slick, ultra-contemporary hall in the shape of a yellow Ferrari bonnet (big enough to get in the faces of workers in the nearby Maserati factory). Films cover Enzo's long, colourful life (he died at age 90, still working on the blueprints of his next car). There are changing exhibits, which not surprisingly focus on cars, set up on white plinths.

There are even three different sized Ferrari-shaped kennels where you can leave your pooch for free while you visit the museum.

MUSEO FERRARI MARANELLO [map, page 144] (*Via Dino Ferrari 43, Maranello;* *0536 949714;* w *musei.ferrari.com;* ⊕ *same hrs & prices as Museo Enzo Ferrari*) The older of the two museums was set up at the factory and testing track in Maranello: there are historic cars, F1 trophies and exhibits and films on the marque's history, which boasts no fewer than 5,000 race victories around the world since 1940. There's a 'pit stop' and tyre change to recreate just what goes on there during a race, and F1 simulators for young and old. Tours of the Ferrari factory and the Fiorano Test Track can be booked in advance via the website.

Enzo Ferrari, who had his start building tractors on his father's farm outside Modena, moved out to this village during war production in 1943, and promptly got bombed flat by the Allies. Since the rebuilding, Maranello has been Ferrari City, the place where people throughout the town hear the buzz of the cars on the testing track and, as the town's tourist bumph puts it, 'listen for a false sound in the engine, as if it were a wrong note at the opera'. In fact, one division in the factory is dedicated to perfecting the precise sound of the engine. Each model has its very own tune.

It's a strange little world: high tech, but at the same time an anachronistic stronghold of Renaissance-style Italian luxury craftsmanship. The town of Maranello also has an **Enzo Ferrari Park**, and a statue of the founder, 6m tall, unveiled for the centenary of his birth in 1998.

Right after the war, Vittorio continued where he left off. He became known as The Transformer; his workshop in Modena was nicknamed the Courtyard of Miracles as he made Stanguellini into one of the best of the 'Etceterini' (small Italian handmade racing cars, using Fiat running gear but building their own chassis, hand-hammered aluminium bodies, and engines). He concentrated on making the lightest cars and engines, and produced a stream of winners on the Formula Junior circuit. His streamlined Colibrì (Hummingbird) using a 250cc Moto Guzzi engine set six international speed records in 1962 at Monza.

With Vittorio's death in 1981, however, the company stopped making racing cars; the day of front-engine racers had passed, and today it specialises in vintage replicas. Francesco, son of Vittorio, set up this museum in 1996 next to the family's Fiat dealership. It contains not only historic Stanguellini cars, but also the family's personal collection of Ferraris, Maseratis, Porsches, Jaguars and a Lola T-160.

Casa Museo Pavarotti [map, page 144] (*Stradella Nava 6, 7km south of Modena off the SS12;* \ *059 460 778;* w *casamuseolucianopavarotti.it;* ⊕ *10.00–19.00 daily;* €8) Besides football and pasta, another of Luciano Pavarotti's passions was horses, and he designed this charming house with stables in 2005 on land he purchased in the 1980s for a show jumping competition. Although he died in the house after only two years, it has a comfortable lived-in feel, from the kitchen to the bathroom scales, packed throughout with memorabilia, photos, videos, costumes, awards, letters and more, all accompanied by an excellent audio commentary.

Collezione Umberto Panini [map, page 144] (*Azienda Agricola Hombre, Via Corletto 320, off Stradello Borrone, 10km southwest of Modena;* \ *059 220022;* w *paninimotormuseum.it;* ⊕ *Mar–Jul, Sep & Oct 09.00–12.30 & 14.30–18.00 Mon–Fri, 09.00–12.30 Sat, by appointment only; admission free*) Any child who grew up in Italy would instantly recognise the name Panini as the company that produces little collectable stickers of sports heroes and much, much more. The company was founded in Modena in 1961 by two Panini brothers, who worked in a print shop. Today the firm is worth hundreds of millions of euros, and the Paninis have created Modena's Museo della Figurina (page 167), as well as this museum of classic cars.

Umberto Panini (1930–2013) was the seventh of eight Panini siblings. As a young man he had worked as a welder in the workshops of Maserati and Stanguellini, and in 1957 went to Venezuela to seek his fortune (an experience that he said made him a real *hombre*). He returned to Modena in 1964 to join the family firm and in 1972 bought this farm, which he named 'Hombre', to raise cows organically to supply the perfect milk for Parmesan cheese. And in one of the barns, his descendants display 19 historic Maseratis, including a very rare A6GCS Berlinetta Pininfarina, three-time winner of the Mille Miglia race (along with a few BMWs, steam cars, vintage tractors, 1950s petrol pumps, and a little red Wolseley classic).

But the Maseratis are the stars. This unique collection was owned by the company itself. Founded in Bologna in 1914 by Alfieri Maserati and adopting, as its symbol, the trident of Neptune in Bologna's Piazza Maggiore, Maserati was purchased by the Orsi family in 1937 and relocated to Viale Ciro Menotti in Modena. The collection was in danger of being auctioned off in London by its owners after the rest of the company was purchased by Fiat in 1993. Faced with the prospect of losing such an important slice of Modena's history, everyone from the Minister of Culture down mounted a campaign to keep the collection in Modena ... when Umberto Panini and other members of the family stepped up and purchased the cars.

Parco Archeologico della Terramara di Montale [map, page 144] (*Via Vandelli, Montale, on the SS12 between Modena & Maranello;* \ *059 203 3101;* w *parcomontale.it;* ⊕ *Apr–Jun, Sep & Oct 9.30–13.30 & 14.30–18.30 Sun, Oct until 18.00, other times by appointment; €7*) Village sites from the Terramare culture are easy to find. Locals have been 'mining' them for centuries for their ultra-rich soil (caused by the huge amounts of rotted wood where the homes once stood). Here, on a site just south of Modena, archaeological excavations have been followed by the creation of an 'open-air museum' to give us an idea of what life for the Terramare people was like.

Two of the thatch-roofed *capanne* (cabins) have been reconstructed, along with a gate and part of the wooden-walled fortifications. The walls would have been surrounded by a moat, as in all Terramare villages; these served not only for protection, but as a water supply, connected to the system of canals that kept the

TERRAMARE MYSTERIES

In the 19th century farmers around the Po Valley knew of patches of land with an unusually rich peat-like soil. Called *terra marre*, it was dug up and sold as garden fertiliser. The farmers paid little attention to the potsherds and bits of metal that turned up in these sites, but eventually they attracted the attention of archaeologists, leading to the discovery of one of the most unusual and enigmatic cultures of ancient Italy. They're still putting together the pieces of this puzzle, but so far it is certain that the 'Terramare people' migrated down from the region of Lake Garda around the 16th century BC, and settled most of the Po Valley.

Another thing we know is that they were among the busiest beavers of antiquity. The Terramare people lived in carefully constructed wooden houses raised on piles, like the lake-dwellers of Switzerland (and the Italian lakes, and central Italy; they were probably all closely related). In this soggy valley such houses had to be rebuilt every 20 years or so; it was all this wood, piling up and rotting away over the generations, that made the soil under the villages so rich. A thousand years before the Romans turned Emilia-Romagna into an endless web of right angles, these people built villages that were neatly rectangular, with precise, straight streets. Around the villages they dug networks of canals for irrigation and drainage. It seems they had little time for art, though they did leave a wealth of little ceramic items that seem to be ex-voto offerings to their gods – miniature vases and wagons. Although they had the use of metal, their culture gives no evidence of any sort of social hierarchy. They probably held their fields in common, though not their livestock.

At first, Terramare life appears to have been peaceful. Weapons were few and the earliest villages had no fortifications. Later, however, they are surrounded by elaborate moats and defensive embankments. Were the villages fighting each other, or some foreign raiders? That isn't yet known, but something – war, invasion, climate change, disease or soil exhaustion and consequent migration – brought the Terramare world to an abrupt end in the 12th century BC – the same era that saw the fall of Troy, the collapse of Mycenaean Greece and so many other disasters around the Mediterranean. In one of history's great disappearing acts, the population of the Po Valley went from c120,000 to near zero in little over a generation; it would stay that way until the coming of the Etruscans three centuries later.

fields well drained. The houses, roofed with thatch and built up on piles to keep them off the damp ground, are furnished with household items copied after finds on the site.

The open-air museum includes a small farm with Terramare-era crops, and a kiln; demonstrations of pottery techniques and other ancient crafts are given on Sundays, or when school groups are around.

NORTH OF MODENA

CARPI North of Modena is Carpi, a wealthy, workaholic town with an illustrious past, one of the few smaller cities in the region worth going out of your way for. It is also one of the few towns not founded in Roman times or earlier. Carpi, named for the groves of hornbeam (*carpinus*) that once stood here, grew up as a fortified settlement under the Lombards in the 8th century. In the Middle Ages it became a prosperous city and established a *comune*, but its greatest days came between 1331 and 1525, when it was governed by the Pio family, clever fellows who could keep their little city independent while doing great service as patrons of the arts. Like so many other minor *signori* around Italy, the Pio lost control in the Wars of Italy. After a two-year Spanish occupation, Carpi and its *contado* ended up in the hands of the Este.

Getting there and away The Trenitalia Modena–Carpi service (on the Modena–Mantua line) is essentially a commuter run; there are usually about 20 a day, and the trip takes only 14 minutes.

Tourist information

i Piazza Martiri 59; \059 649255; w incarpi. info; ⊕ 10.00–18.00 Tue–Sun

⌂ Where to stay

⌂ **Duomo** (18 rooms) Via Battisti 25; \059 669592; w hotelduomocarpi.it; ⊕ closed Aug. Just behind the cathedral, this is the only hotel in the centre but it's comfortable, & stylish in a modest way, with parking; AC, b/fast inc; free bikes for guests. €€€€

⌂ **Touring** (65 rooms) Via Dallai 1; \059 681535; w hoteltouringcarpi.it; ⊕ closed Aug & Christmas. Modern & by the station, the most comfortable place to stay in Carpi; gym, parking & a restaurant (La Bottiglieria; see below). €€€–€€€€

⌂ **Locanda Andrea** [map, page 144] (7 rooms) SS per Correggio 43; m 388 794 2855; w locandaandrea.it. On the edge of town, good if you're driving; a small & basic, family-run place with some old-fashioned charms. Also has a very good & inexpensive restaurant (⊕ *closed Sun eve*; €€). €€

✕ Where to eat and drink

✕ **L'Incontro** Via delle Magliae 4; \059 693136; w www.lincontroristorante.it; ⊕ closed Sun in Jan–Feb & 2 weeks in Aug. Known for its pasta dishes – ravioli with duck, tortelli with beetroot & ricotta – also for seafood. Interesting tasting menus at €40 & €60, plus vegetarian & vegan menus. €€€

✕ **La Bottiglieria** Via Dallai 1; \059 863 7150; w hoteltouringcarpi.it/it/ristorante.html; ⊕ closed Sat lunch & Sun. Restaurant of the Hotel Touring; one of the best in the area, in an elegant setting with outside tables. There's a touch of south Italy in the cuisine: seafood pasta, orecchiette, *baccalà* fritters. €€€

✕ **Teresa Baldini** Via Livorno 30; \059 662691; ⊕ lunch, by reservation only, closed Thu & w/ends. 10km east of Carpi, at San Martino Secchia, is an old-fashioned & welcoming osteria; the *maccheroni al pettine* is perfect, the meats traditionally prepared, & the desserts homemade. €€

What to see and do

Piazza dei Martiri The city centre is dominated by the vast Piazza dei Martiri, formerly called the Borgogioioso. You will probably be reminded at least once in Carpi that this is the third-largest piazza in Italy; whether or not this is true would be hard to say, but it is about 300m long and it leaves an unforgettable impression. With a crowd receding into the distance, it seems like some perspectivist Renaissance painting of the 'ideal city'; without them it becomes positively oceanic, and crossing it on a still Sunday afternoon one feels tempted to stop the lone passer-by and ask for news from land. The piazza is bordered on one side by a long portico, and the view is closed on the short end by the **Cathedral of Santa Maria Assunta** (⊕ *07.30–noon & 15.30–19.30 Mon–Wed, Fri & Sun, 07.30–12.30 & 15.30–19.30 Thu & Sat*), with a sumptuous Baroque façade. Begun in 1515 by Alberto III, the last and greatest Pio, the city didn't get it completely finished and decorated until the 1800s. The cathedral was severely damaged in the earthquakes of May 2012. Parts of the dome and façade collapsed, but restoration work was completed in March 2017, and Pope Francis came to visit.

Castello dei Pio On the long side of Piazza Martiri stands the 16th-century Castello dei Pio. Everyone from the Lombards to the Spanish contributed something to this huge complex, but it was Alberto III who tied it all together with an elegant Renaissance façade. Inside, Carpi keeps its impressive collection of museums.

Musei Civici (☏ *059 649 955;* w *palazzodeipio.it/imusei;* ⊕ *10.00–13.00, 15.00–19.00 Thu, Sat–Sun, 10.00–13.00 Tue, Wed & Fri;* €8) The Musei Civici are three, with common hours and admission. First comes the **Museo del Palazzo**, in the rooms of Alberto III's residence, frescoed by Bernardino Loschi and others in the early 1500s. Besides the beautiful chapel, there are works in the Stanza dei Trionfi (a series of 'triumphs' like those in Ferrara's Palazzo Schifanoia), the Salone dei Mori, the Studiolo of Alberto II and other rooms. The museum also houses the former **Museo della Xilografica**, devoted to the work of Ugo da Carpi (1481–1532), who invented the chiaroscuro woodcut, using multiple blocks to create tinted shading and make the woodcut something closer to painting. Ugo was the father of a major revolution in art – not so much for his own talents, but because he made his living by copying the paintings of Raphael, Titian, Parmigianino and others as woodcuts for the artists to use as advertising, sending them around to the courts of Europe. For the first time, people could get an idea of what the great artists of the day were up to without travelling.

Next comes the **Museo della Città**, with exhibits on the history of Carpi, ceramics, fabrics and terracotta. In the passage to the palace courtyard, the **Museo Monumento al Deportato** remembers the prisoners and civilians deported to Germany during World War II from the **Campo di Concentramento di Fossoli**, 8km north of Carpi (ask the museum about visits). Originally built in 1942 for British Empire prisoners of war, this camp was later run by the SS, and it was the place where most of Italy's Jews and other Nazi victims were kept before their trip to Auschwitz.

Next to the Castello, the pretty **Teatro Comunale** (1860) replaced an original built by Gaspare Vigarani for the Este; in the opposite corner is the city's old grain market.

Pieve di Santa Maria in Castello (*Piazzale Re Astolfo;* ☏ *059 659255;* ⊕ *10.00– noon Thu–Sat, 15.00–17.00 Sun*) Carpi's real treasure is one-third of a church. The Pieve di Santa Maria, usually just called 'La Sagra', sits hidden away behind the Palazzo del Pio. The city's centre of gravity changed when the Palazzo del Pio was completed in the 1400s, and the Borgogioioso was laid out next to it. Before that, the Pieve and the little square in front of it made up the centre. 'Pieve' means a country church, and this one was the nucleus around which Carpi took shape some time in the 8th century.

Later on, the old walled medieval quarter became known as the 'Castello'; except for the church, almost all of it has disappeared. The first church on this site may have been part of a Roman villa. It was rebuilt in AD752 by Lombard King Aistulf, or Astolfo; the current incarnation was begun around 1120, one of the many churches financed by Countess Matilda of Canossa. After the city was re-centred, Signore Alberto III decided to tear the old church down. In the end, however, he left the rear third standing, building a new, plain façade (1514), and incorporating into it the portal from Matilda's church. Other survivors from the original church are the sculptural decoration of the apse by the followers of Wiligelmo, and the tall, tilted campanile, built in 1221.

The entrance is through the adjacent **Cappella di Santa Caterina**, with an excellent cycle of quattrocento frescoes on the *Life of St Catherine* by unknown artists, followers of Giovanni da Modena. Catherine of Alexandria was a favourite subject of medieval Emilian artists; her cult came back with the Crusaders. Her story is mostly fairy tale (she was one of the saints tossed out of the book by the Second Vatican Council), and you can follow all the episodes in the frescoes here: Catherine meets the Emperor Maxentius, converts the empress, argues with the pagan philosophers, and is finally martyred on her wheel, while the empress is decapitated; in the background note Mount Sinai, where the saint's supposed relics are still kept in an Orthodox monastery.

In the church proper is the **Cappella di San Martino**, with frescoes by the Ferrarese Antonio Alberti (1424) of the *Adoration of the Magi* and the *Doctors of the Church*. Fragments of medieval frescoes can be seen around the vaulting of the church, along with two fine sculptural works: a 12th-century *ambone*, the work of a follower of Wiligelmo named Niccolò, and the 1351 *Sarcophagus of Manfredo Pio*.

ABBAZIA DI NONÁNTOLA

[map, page 144] The Benedictine Abbey of Nonántola, 10km northeast of Modena, was one of the most prestigious and powerful in medieval Italy. Founded in AD752 by Lombard King Aistulf's brother-in-law, the abbot St Anselm, the richly endowed abbey soon became one of the greatest landowners in northern Italy. Emperors courted it and granted it favours. In the 9th century, two of its abbots served as imperial ambassadors to Constantinople.

In AD900 the invading Hungarians levelled the monastery and slew all the monks they could find. It was quickly rebuilt and became renowned for its scriptorium. In 1058, the abbot Gotescalco wrote a charter, donating 760ha of farm land surrounding the abbey to local families to be passed down in perpetuity from father to son in exchange for building walls and defending the monastery from attackers. The Partecipanza Agraria (Agricultural Attendance), as it's known, survives to this day (along with several others around Emilia), though much of the land once drained by canals has reverted to wetlands, now protected as the Oasi di Riequilibrio Ecologico di Torrazzuolo.

The monastery was rebuilt for the last time in the 12th century, when it became embroiled in the momentous Investiture Conflict over who had the power to appoint bishops, the popes or the emperors. Nonántola supported the emperors until Countess Matilda intervened and pressured the abbot to side with the pope. For good measure, one of the monks, Placidus, wrote the classic *De honore Ecclesiæ* defending the papal position in 1111.

5

In the 15th century Nonántola became a commendatory abbey, its rents going to an absentee cleric; two of the best known were Giuliano Della Rovere (later Pope Julius II) and St Charles Borromeo. It declined until Pope Clement XIII suppressed it in 1768; it became a monastery again in 1821 for a few decades and today belongs to the Italian state. Since 1986 the basilica has served as the co-cathedral of the Modena diocese. It was damaged in the 2012 earthquake.

Tourist information

i Palazzo Comunale, Via Marconi 11; ☎059 896555; w www.comune.nonantola.mo.it;

⊕ 08.30–12.30 Thu–Fri, 09.00–12.30 & 15.00–18.30 Sat–Sun

✖ Where to eat and drink

✖ Osteria di Rubbiara [map, page 144] Via Risaia 2, Rubbiara; ☎059 549019; w acetaiapedroni.it; ⊕ lunch only exc Fri & Sat eves (booking only); closed Tue. Near Nonántola at Rubbiara, this combination *acetaio* (vinegar distiller) & osteria has been in the Pedroni family since 1861. Mobile phones must be checked at the door (reason enough to come!); the good home cooking, in generous portions, is another. You'll get whatever's on offer, take it or leave it, but at least 1 dish will come with the family's balsamic vinegar. The shop offers all of their huge variety of vinegars & liqueurs. €€€

What to see and do

Basilica di San Silvestro *(Piazza Abbazia;* ☎ *059 549025. The abbey was badly damaged in the 2012 earthquake; parts of the Basilica are currently open, along with the Museo Diocesano & the Crypt* ⊕ *09.00–12.30 Mon–Thu, 09.00–12.30 & 14.00–18.00 Fri–Sun, closed Aug)* The large, red-brick Romanesque basilica is dedicated to and contains relics of the 4th-century St Sylvester, who served as pope under Constantine. The great **portal** retains its beautiful, vigorous reliefs by the workshop of Wiligelmo (see box, page 153): panels on the left tell the history of the monastery, while those on the right are on the story of Christ. Wiligelmo himself may well have sculpted the figures of Christ, two angels and symbols of the Evangelists in the lunette over the door.

Inside, the basilica is austere, the eye drawn to the presbytery raised high over the beautiful **crypt**, supported by a forest of 64 columns, half of them with carved capitals dating from the 9th to the 11th century. No fewer than seven saints are buried underneath the high altar: the founder St Anselm (died 3 March AD803), Pope St Adrian III, who died here in AD885; the virgin SS Fusca and Anseris; the martyrs SS Theopontus and Senesius, and possibly another great pope, St Sylvester, who died in AD335. The altar is decorated with 16th-century panels on the *Life of St Sylvester* by Giacomo Silla de' Longhi. More Lombard columns and capitals adorn the three majestic **apses**, along with blind arches and pilasters and a twin lancet window, echoing the façade.

Museo Diocesano *(⊕ Same as the Basilica; admission free)* Near the basilica is the Palazzo Abbaziale which, along with the Archives and Library, houses the Museo Diocesano, with a sumptuous collection of 11th- and 12th-century medieval reliquaries, including an 11th-century Byzantine reliquary of the Cross, depicting Constantine and his mother, Helen, along with a selection of manuscripts and rare books such as the *Graduale*, an 11th-century collection of Gregorian chant. The 4,500 parchments preserved in the library go back to AD751, and bear signatures by Charlemagne, Countess Matilda of Canossa and Frederick Barbarossa.

MIRÁNDOLA Mirándola is an ancient town that was ruled for four centuries (until 1711) by the Pico family. These names might ring a bell; one of the family was none other than Giovanni Pico della Mirándola, famous Renaissance philosopher, magician and friend of Lorenzo de' Medici.

In his day the Pico were turning Mirándola into an up-to-date Renaissance town, with one of Italy's first sets of modern fortifications; little of these walls has survived, but Mirándola still has its quattrocento Duomo and Palazzo Comunale.

The **Museo Civico**, with an archaeological collection and a pinacoteca with portraits of members of the Pico family, along with a section on biomedicine, was installed in 2010 in the Castello dei Pico on Piazza Guglielmo Marconi, but has been closed since the May 2012 earthquake, which hit Mirándola particularly hard, killing 17 people in the area and leaving 14,000 homeless.

SOUTH OF MODENA

SASSUOLO AND ITS PALACE Though now it's a rather gritty industrial town, the centre of Italy's ceramic tile industry, the Este favoured Sassuolo as a summer residence, especially so after the great plague of 1630 carried off 40% of Modena's population. Francesco I purchased an existing country estate here, and charged court architect Bartolomeo Avanzino in 1634 with transforming it into what he would call the Delizia, a fairy-tale palace that could compete with the great courts of Europe.

Tourist information
i Piazza Garibaldi 56; \ 0536 880801;
w sassuoloturismo.it; ⏲ 09.00–13.30 Mon–Wed
& Fri, 09.00–18.30 Thu, 09.00–12.30 Sat

✘ Where to eat and drink
✘ **Osteria dei Girasoli** [map, page 144] Via Circonvalazione Nord-Est 217; \ 0536 801223; w osteriadeigirasoli.com; ⏲ closed Mon eve & Sun. An unlikely setting, out in the industrial zone, for a very convivial restaurant. Ravioli with a touch of truffle, guinea fowl, horse tartare, rich desserts & a wide choice of wines from around Italy.

Land, sea & vegetarian tasting menus €40–50. €€–€€€
✘ **Enoteca Rivellino** Via Monzanbano 1, nr the Palace; \ 0536 580334; w rivellino.it; ⏲ closed Sun. Not just *gnocchi fritti* and *salumi*, but risottos & pasta, grills & desserts; big wine list (beers too). Jazz or blues every Thu. €€

What to see and do
Palazzo Ducale (*Piazzale della Rosa;* \ *0536 880801;* w *sassuoloturismo.it;* ⏲ *Apr–Oct 10.00–13.00 & 15.00–19.00 Tue–Sun, rest of year groups only, with advance booking; €4*) Duke Francesco's 'Delizia', the Palazzo Ducale, was just that, though its glory days were short. Later dukes spent little time here, and after Napoleon kicked out the Este the palace fell into disrepair. Eventually it became part of the Italian Military Academy. The soldiers did not treat it well; eventually they tired of the place, and now the slow work is under way of restoring one of the most stunning creations of the Emilian Baroque.

The palace entrance is on the enclosed, stately **Piazza della Rosa**, designed as part of Avanzino's plan for the palace ensemble. Just to the right of the palace façade is another original feature, the dukes' church of **San Francesco in Rocca**. Its austere façade hides a sumptuous interior decorated by some of the same artists that worked on the palace, including a great quadratura ceiling by Jean Boulanger, a Frenchman who studied under Guido Reni – apparently with help from the Bologna quadratura masters, Agostino Mitelli and Angelo Michele Colonna.

On the palace itself, the attraction is not so much the restrained architecture as the impressive statuary on it. Much has been lost, or was never completed, but there are allegories of *Civil and Military Architecture*, and flanking the portal, the spectacular statues of **Neptune** and **Galatea** by Antonio Raggi (1652). Raggi, a student of Bernini, was one of the most celebrated sculptors of his day; you can see his work all over Rome. Galatea, one of the Nereids, or sea nymphs, was a frequent subject for ancient and again Renaissance art. Her renewed popularity in this era may be due to Raphael, who painted a celebrated fresco of her in Rome; to him, she represented an ideal of perfect beauty.

The statues aren't marble, but stucco coated in marble dust – *marmorizzato*, as the Italians say. After the Este lost Ferrara, and were cooped up in their ruritanian Duchy of Modena, they never had the income to match their pretensions.

Passing these, the **courtyard** has another marine fantasy by Raggi, the Fountain of Neptune, possibly done from a design by Bernini. On the walls are traces of frescoes by Colonna and Mitelli, who also did the grand stair, the Scalone d'Onore; by the stair are two more sculptural allegories, representing *Happiness* and *Eternity*, by Roman sculptor Maschio Lattanzio.

Inside, the frescoed rooms of the *piano nobile* have been largely restored. Many artists, mostly obscure, contributed to these. There are several quadratura ceilings here, as in the lovely Camarino del Genio and the Camera della Fortuna; no doubt Mitelli and Colonna were busy here too. Much of the best is by Jean Boulanger, including the ducal apartments and what might be the highlight of the visit, the mind-blowing *Gallery of Bacchus*.

Now swallowed up by the town, the Palazzo retains only a sad remnant of its once-extensive **gardens**. These originally spread over 10km in length along the River Secchia, an expanse of garden walks, terraces, fountains and follies meant to recreate the fabulous gardens the Este once had at Ferrara, now also lost.

One bit that survives is the colossal, bizarre fountain called the **Peschiera** or 'Fontanazzo' (*Piazza Roverello, just south of the palace;* ⊕ *09.00–19.00 daily, winter 09.00–18.00 daily*). It was built along what was once part of the earlier palace's moat. A crumbling, purpose-built 'ruin', similar to the artificial rustic grottoes so popular among Renaissance princes, it continues the marine theme of the palace's decoration that began with Raggi's statues at the entrance. The fountain was once the centrepiece of an elaborate outdoor theatre, used for mock sea battles and other spectacles – and also to stock fish for the dukes' table.

Museo AMES (*Via San Giacomo;* m *348 781 0514;* ⊕ *15.00–18.00 Fri & Sat, closed Aug*) If you can stand another car museum, this one specialises in what Italians call *microvetture* – cute little underpowered models, mostly from the 1950s and 60s, including NSUs, Messerschmitts, Vespas and several Isettas (those crazy bugs with the doors in front).

Casalgrande Ceramic Crown (*SP467R Variante, at Dinazzano, 5km west of Sassuolo*) If you head from Sassuolo towards Reggio Emilia, you'll pass this striking 20m bauble, the work of fashionable architect Daniel Libeskind (World Trade Centre, New York). Casalgrande Padana, one of the world's biggest producers of advanced ceramics, commissioned it to decorate the entrance to their headquarters. The Crown is entirely covered in their architectural tiles; built in the architect's trademark jagged, prismatic forms, it assumes a different shape from every angle. The Crown is complementary to another Casalgrande commission, the **Casalgrande Ceramic Cloud** by Japanese architect Kengo Kuma, on the next roundabout up the road.

Santuario di Fiorano (*Fiorano Modenese, 18km south of Modena, between Sassuolo's Ducal Palace & the industrial zones of Maranello;* ☏ *0536 830042;* ⊕ *08.00–20.00 daily*) The Santuario della Beata Vergine del Castello di Fiorano stands on a commanding hilltop overlooking Sassuolo. Like Modena's Chiesa del Voto, this is a plague church, built not to thank the Virgin for finally ending the plague, as at Modena, but from keeping it away entirely. A powerful castle once occupied this spot, until the troops of that most troublemaking pope, Julius II, destroyed it during his campaigns to subdue Modena. An image of the Virgin was saved from the wreck and thereafter regarded as a miracle-worker. She had already saved Fiorano from a Spanish army bent on burning it down, and after she warded off the plague it was obvious to everyone she needed her own church.

The church was designed by Bartolomeo Avanzini, architect of the palace at Sassuolo; though begun in 1634, parts of the façade weren't finished until 1889. The two buildings went up at about the same time, and some of the same artists were employed in their decoration. Much of the interior painting, including the wild flying saints frescoed inside the cupola, was done by Sebastiano Caula, a student of Sassuolo's Jean Boulanger.

Castello di Spezzano (*Via del Castello in Fiorano Modenese;* ☏ *0522 532094;* ⊕ *Mar–Oct 15.00–19.00 Sat–Sun, Nov 15.00–18.00 Sat–Sun; €2*) Up in the hills south of Fiorano this castle began in the 11th century and later came into the hands of the Pio family of Carpi, who made it into a residence; eventually it was owned by the Este. The most interesting part is the **Sala delle Vedute** (Hall of the Views) with 57 frescoes of castles and towns owned by the Pio, painted in 1595–96 by Cesare Baglione. They make balsamic vinegar in the castle's old prisons, now the **Acetaia Comunale**, and another part of the complex now holds a small museum on the history of pottery, the **Museo della Ceramica**, from Neolithic to Roman times.

CASTELVETRO DI MODENA Set in the first foothills of the Apennines south of the city, Castelvetro is a village with a lovely skyline of towers, arranged around Piazza Roma. The piazza is paved in a chequer-board pattern, and the Castelvetrani use it each year in September for their **Dama Vivente**, a game of draughts where the pieces are ladies in Renaissance dress.

Tourist information
ℹ️ Piazza Roma 5; ☏ 059 758880;
w visitcastelvetro.it

Where to stay, eat and drink

🏠 **Locanda del Feudo** Via Trasversale 2; ☏ 059 708711; w locandadelfeudo.it; ⊕ closed Sun eve & Mon. In the lovely historic centre, 4 spacious luxury suites of 3 rooms each, individually & tastefully decorated, & a restaurant (€€€€) with very refined cooking & a lot of atmosphere. €€€€

✕ **Bolognina** [map, page 144] Via Medusia 59; ☏ 059 790265. Out in the country 2km west of Castelvetrano, a wonderful family trattoria with homemade pasta, *baccalà*, grilled meats & *cotechino*. Outside tables. Basic B&B accommodation is offered at 2 locations nearby (€€–€€€). €€

What to see and do In the Palazzo Rangoni, the **Museo del'Assurdo** (*Via Cavedoni 14;* ☏ *059 758818;* ⏰ *16.00–19.00 (Jun 16.30–19.30) Sun only, closed Jan, Jul & Aug; admission free*) has a collection of contemporary art dedicated to the 'absurd as a metaphor of existence' and designed to make you laugh, like the droll crocodile made of egg cartons. Every year the village celebrates **Mercurdo** (w *mercurdo.it*), the 'market of the absurd', in the first week of June, with a competition of wild performance art, installations and shows. In the same Palazzo, the **Mostra Fili d'Oro** (⏰ *Sun only, Apr–Sep 16.00–19.00, Oct–Mar 15.00–18.00; admission free*) is a small museum of the Renaissance costumes made for the Dama Vivente.

VIGNOLA In April the emerald-green foothills around Vignola are covered with the lacy, rosy-pink blossoms of Vignola's famous cherry trees. These are celebrated in a Cherry Blossom Festival in mid-April, with horse races, bicycle tours, medieval costumes, fair, exhibitions and other events (you can get here from Bologna by way of a special free 'Cherry Train', the Treno dei Ciliegi). Half of Italy's cherries come from Vignola, as did one of Italy's most talented 16th-century architects, Giacomo Barozzi – best known simply as 'Vignola'.

Tourist information
🛈 Via Belluci 1; ☏ 059 777 606

Where to stay, eat and drink
🏠 **Eden** Via C Battisti 49; ☏ 059 772847; w www.hoteledenvignola.it. There's 1 hotel in cherry town. Modern & well-kept; some rooms with balconies & a view. €€€

✗ **Trattoria Bolognese** Via Muratori 1; ☏ 059 771207; ⏰ closed Fri eve, Sat & Aug. In the centre of town, with a lovely interior courtyard next to the Rocca, where you can feast on excellent *tagliatelle alla Bolognese* & local Lambrusco. €€

What to see and do
Rocca di Vignola (*Piazza dei Contrari;* ☏ *059 775246;* w *roccadivignola.it;* ⏰ *winter 09.00–noon & 14.30–18.00 Tue–Sat, 10.30–12.30 & 14.30–18.00 Sun; summer 09.00–noon & 15.30–19.00 Tue–Sat, 10.30–13.00 & 15.30–19.00 Sun; admission free, with an audioguide in English*) Architect Vignola didn't leave anything in his home town, but it does have in its centre one of the best-preserved castles in Emilia-Romagna, the Rocca di Vignola. Founded in the 8th century by the abbots of Nonántola, and rebuilt with lofty towers in the 13th century, it was improved by the Contrari family in the 15th century, and since 1965 has been owned by a bank, which has financed its complete restoration. A number of rooms retain their frescoes; the chapel has frescoes by the so-called Maestro di Vignola. The castle often hosts important exhibitions and concerts.

Around the village The pretty hills around Vignola are great for hiking or biking, and they've laid out trails everywhere. Ask at the tourist office for details on the 48km **Percorso Belvedere** and the shorter **Percorso Sole**. In addition, there is a dedicated cycling route of 18km from Vignola to Modena, following a closed railway line.

PARCO REGIONALE DEI SASSI DI ROCCAMALATINA [map, page 144] The peculiar sandstone pinnacles of Roccamalatina, south of Vignola, rise over the chestnut woodlands and medieval hamlets of the 2,300ha Parco dei Sassi, a favourite Sunday getaway for the Modenesi (Malatina, the name of the local barons, seems to mean *malvagia tignola*, the 'evil moth'). In the Middle Ages, the natural grottoes in the sandstone were used for defence; here and there staircases and traces of scaffolding survive, as at the chestnut wood called the Bosco delle Tane, bounded by strange caverns and rock formations. Peregrine falcons and kestrels soar overhead; the spring brings plenty of wild orchids. Over 100km of trails criss-cross the park, including one up to the main rock above the hamlet of Borgo dei Sassi; pick up a map at the park information headquarters.

🛈 Centro Parco 'Il Fontanazzo' Loc Pieve di Trebbio, Roccamalatina; ☎ 059 795044; **w** parks. it/parco.sassi.roccamalatina; ⏱ Easter–Sep

08.30–13.00 Mon–Sat, also 15.00–17.00 Mon & Wed, 10.00–18.00 Sun. It has a small museum of the area's natural history.

Museo del Castagno e Museo-Laboratorio del Borlengo (⏱ *Easter–Nov only, 10.00–noon & 15.00–19.00 Sun, Aug 10.00–noon & 15.00–19.00 daily; admission free*) This museum celebrates the local cherries and chestnuts, as well as the traditional crêpes and flatbreads of the region: *tigelle, crescentine* and *borlenghi*.

Pieve di Trebbio The park's jewel is a charming country church near the information centre in Pieve di Trebbio. Built in the 10th or 11th century over a Carolingian church, which in turn replaced a pagan religious site, it's one of the most important churches in the region, packed with primitive Celto-Lombard details and artistic quirks. Interestingly, it seems to have once belonged to the Templars.

For starters, it sports a very unorthodox sarcophagus stuck right in the middle of the façade, probably from the 6th century and similar to ones in Ravenna, and decorated with peacocks (the peacock, which grows new tail feathers each year, was a symbol of resurrection and renewal). An ornamental architrave carved with Celtic knots from the 8th century spans the side door.

The church has two semicircular apses and a polygonal one, is decorated with intriguing Celto-Lombard reliefs, including a Lombard capital with a hand holding a bouquet, and a pulpit with a very rare winged figure of St John the Evangelist holding a codex taken straight from early Byzantine iconography. A dove decorates the ciborium over the altar. There's a tiny crypt, which once held a relic of St John.

The charming little octagonal baptistry, with its moss-covered roof, resembles a well inside, used for full immersion baptisms (although some say it was too small really to be used and was built as a symbol). Inside is a fresco with the Baptist, dressed in a short tunic and boots instead of the usual animal skin. The stout campanile was originally a defensive tower.

THE MODENESE APENNINES

South of Sassuolo, you can break away from the flatlands of the Po by heading south into the Apennines, which achieve majestic proportions near the border with Tuscany. The region has perfect updraughts for hang-gliding and sailplanes, especially around Pavullo and Montecreto.

At weekends, the Modenesi embark on gastronomic voyages into the Apennines: stop at any roadside restaurant (choose the one with the most cars parked outside), and you will find simple meals of smoked meats, cheeses, freshly baked breads and raw vegetables. Two other local treats, porcini mushrooms and black truffles, may also figure on the menu in season. The meal is called a *tigelle* or *crescente* after its distinctive breads – one like a flat, baked muffin, the other of thin dough fried in fat. During the week you won't have to wait for a table.

PAVULLO NEL FRIGNANO Pavullo is the largest village in the Modenese Apennines, the capital of a little region called the Frignano and the most popular base for visiting the region. The **tourist office** (*Via Giardini 3; \ 0536 29964; ⊕ 15.00–18.00 Tue & Thu, 10.00–13.00 Sat*) can give you maps and info on the various hiking and biking paths in the area, as well as opportunities for riding, nature walks and fishing. There's a load of information about everything in this area also at w appenninomodenese.net.

Pavullo is a lovely village though there isn't much to see besides the giant cedar of Lebanon in the gardens of the old **Palazzo Ducale**. Just south of Pavullo, the village of Montecuccolo lies in the shadow of a thoroughly charming and romantic little castle, the 11th–14th century **Castello di Montecuccolo**; recently restored, it has great views.

 Where to stay, eat and drink

 Corsini (36 rooms) Via Giardini Nord 127; \ 0536 20130; w albergocorsini.it. Welcoming & well-kept, with modern & colourful rooms & a very popular restaurant (€€€), known for homemade tortelli & other pasta, which often comes with fresh porcini mushrooms, abundant in this area. **€€€**

 Vandelli (40 rooms) Via Giardini Sud 7; \ 0536 20288; w hotelvandelli.it. Family-run since 1949, with great attention to detail. Lovely rooms:

clean, individually furnished & decorated with a homey touch, some with balconies. The restaurant offers summer dining in the garden pavilion (*booking necessary;* €€€). **€€€**

✗ **Parco Corsini** Viale Martiri 11; \ 0536 20129; ⊕ closed Tue. Excellent value, with a wide choice of pasta & meat dishes – lots of fresh seafood too, rare in these parts. Sometimes there's music & dancing on Sat nights. **€€**

MONTEFIORINO To the west of Pavullo, in one of the most inaccessible parts of the mountains, the *partigiani* set up the Repubblica di Montefiorino, a 'free zone' that held out for a few months against the Nazis in 1944. In the village of Montefiorino (*off the SP19 south of Sassuolo*), the **Museo della Repubblica di Montefiorino** (*Via Rocca 1; \ 0536 962815; w resistenzamontefiorino.it; ⊕ 10.00–13.00 & 15.00–18.00 (until 19.00 in summer) Sat–Sun, also Aug 10.00–13.00 & 15.00–18.00 Wed–Fri; €5*) tells the story with photos, documents and objects from the time.

SESTOLA The most striking mountain scenery is up at Sestola, a winter and summer resort near the highest peak of the northern Apennines, **Monte Cimone** (2,165m).

Tourist information

ℹ Via Passerini 18; \ 0536 62324

 Where to stay, eat and drink

 San Marco (38 rooms) Via delle Rose 2; \ 0536 62330; w hotelsanmarcosestola.it. With a pinewood for a backdrop, set in a large 19th-century villa with a panoramic terrace. It has comfortable rooms with AC, a gym & tennis courts in a lovely garden, a wellness centre & free transport to the ski lifts in season; in the summer it has a restaurant (€€€). Closed Oct & Nov. **€€€€**

 San Rocco (21 rooms) Corso Umberto I 47; \ 0536 62382; w hotelsanrocco.net/navbar.htm.

Gracious establishment with well-furnished rooms, but the real story here is the restaurant (€€€), one of the best in the area, with wild mushrooms & game dishes, quail, guinea fowl, & a great wine list. Closed Mon, May & Oct. **€€€**

 Tirolo (40 rooms) Via delle Rose 9; \ 0536 62523; w hoteltirolo.com. A very Tyrolean chalet indeed, with tennis courts & very comfortable rooms. Good, simple restaurant with homemade pasta; HB & FB offered, a bargain. Open mid-Jun– mid-Sep & mid-Dec–Mar. **€€€**

🏠 **Sport Hotel** Via delle Ville 116; 📞 0536 62502; **w** sporthotelsestola.it. A pleasant small hotel open all year; HB & FB available. **€€–€€€**

What to see and do Among other activities, there is a skating rink at nearby Fanano, the **Palaghiaccio di Fanano**; the **Baby Park**, with snow fun for children, at Locazione Cimoncino near the ski area (📞 0536 61133); and a **heated pool** in Sestola.

Musei del Castello (*Via Corso Umberto I;* 📞 *0536 62324;* ⊕ *Jul–Aug 10.00–noon & 14.00–19.00 daily, Sep–Jun 10.00–noon & 13.00–18.00 Sun only (winter 10.00– noon & 14.00–17.00), other days by appointment; €3*) Two separate museums here: the **Museo degli Strumenti Musicali Meccanici** with 120 calliopes and carillons, barrel organs, automated birds and singing dolls, most of them in working order. The **Museo della Civiltà Montanara** contains objects on local traditions and country life.

Mountain excursions From Sestola you can visit the pretty glacial **Lago della Ninfa**, just off the road to the Monte Cimone ski area. Another excursion from Sestola is to **Pian Cavallaro**, and from there to the summit of Monte Cimone for a unique view – on a clear day you can see the Tyrrhenian and Adriatic seas, and all the way north to the Julian Alps and Mont Blanc.

You can also make the ascent from the old village of **Fiumalbo**, just below the Passo Abetone that separates Emilia from Tuscany. Two other mountain lakes are just south of Fiumalbo: Lago Santo and Lago Bacio, connected by an easy footpath. Not as pretty, but more unusual, is the small Lago Pratignano, in the meadows south of **Fanano**, a little to the east of Sestola. In the spring its banks are strewn with wild flowers and carnivorous plants – bring your waders.

Giardino Esperia [map, page 144] (*Passo del Lupo;* 📞 *053 661 535;* ⊕ *mid- Jun–mid-Sep 09.30–12.30 & 14.00–18.00 Tue–Sun (Jul & Aug daily); admission donations*) This botanical garden was planted by the local branch of the CAI (Italian Alpine Club) in 1980 at the Passo del Lupo, a botanical frontier near the Monte Cimone ski area; here Alpine and Apennine flowers, trees and herbs grow side by side, along with some imports from the Himalayas.

Cimone Sci [map, page 144] (*9km south of Sestola;* 📞 *0536 62350;* **w** *cimonesci. com;* ⊕ *9.00–16.30 Mon–Fri in season, 08.30–16.30 Sat–Sun*) This ski area sprawls across the highest point of the northern Apennines, 11km south of Sestola. It's a big operation, with 27 lifts and 26 different runs of every degree of difficulty, covering some 50km, as well as an extensive and challenging park for snowboarding. Day passes go for €28 weekdays, €36 weekends (€24 and €31 for children and seniors over 65) and there's a wide range of multi-day packages and special offers available; consult the website.

EMILIA-ROMAGNA ONLINE

For additional online content, articles, photos and more on Emilia-Romagna, why not visit **w** bradtguides.com/emilia?

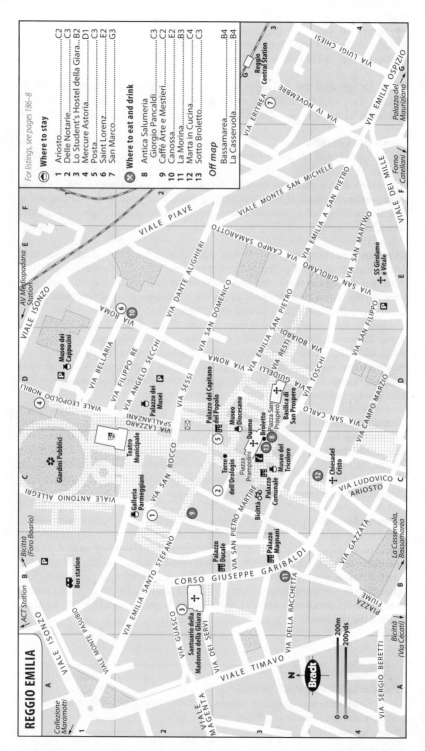

REGGIO EMILIA

6

Reggio Emilia and Surrounds

The people of Reggio all agree that they don't care if you call their town Reggio nell'Emilia, Reggio di Emilia or simply Reggio Emilia, as long as you do call them. Long the odd man out among the region's art cities, Reggio lacks the compelling attractions of Parma, Bologna or the others. Nevertheless, it is a handsome, well-organised and likeable city, and you won't regret stopping over. Reggio's hinterlands include a clutch of Baroque memories around the Po in towns such as Guastalla, Gualtieri and Correggio. To the south is one of the more attractive stretches of the Emilian Apennines, home to the famous Castle of Canossa (or what's left of it), a bit of skiing, a bit of scenery, and the outlandish Rocca di Bismantova.

HISTORY

Reggio started out as the Roman Regium Lepidi, a fortified camp town on the Via Aemilia, founded in 175BC. When Emilia was a newly founded Roman colony, this frontier area was still troubled by Celtic bandits up in the mountains, and it was good to have some legionaries around to keep the peace. As things grew more settled, Reggio developed into a flourishing commercial town, then contracted in the Dark Ages into a tiny *castrum vescovile*, a walled compound that enclosed little more than the cathedral and the bishop's palace.

The city started booming again in the early Middle Ages, becoming one of the first towns to found a *comune* in the 12th century, and then commencing one of medieval Emilia's most ambitious sets of city walls, the tidy, hexagonal circuit still traceable on the map in the ring of boulevards that replaced them in the 19th century.

Medieval Reggio was famous for violent factionalism, even by the standards of the day. On more than one occasion in the 1200s, this broke out into bloody civil war. The two contending parties were called the 'Uppers' and' Lowers'; in 1287 the Uppers expelled their rivals and demolished all their houses, and their leader, Matteo da Fogliano, used the materials to build himself a great palace. After a year of wasting the countryside and burning villages, the Lowers got back in, and served the Uppers the same way. By 1290 both exhausted parties had had enough, and they offered the city to Obizzo II d'Este as *signore*.

This sort of anarchy was followed by the rule of various *signori* in the 1300s, and in the end the city lost its independence once and for all. From 1409 to 1796 Reggio was ruled by the Este, during which time its most famous sons, Matteo Maria Boiardo (1440–91), author of *Orlando Innamorato*, and Ludovico Ariosto (1474–1533), who continued the epic in *Orlando Furioso*, were born. In the dismal 1600s Reggio managed to keep its head above water thanks to a new industry: silk manufacture. Nowadays it makes a good living from manufacturing (aircraft, among other things), and the city is noted for its numerous ballet schools, its balsamic vinegar and its Parmigiano Reggiano cheese (see box, page 243), which after all, is the real thing as much as Parma's.

GETTING THERE AND AWAY

BY AIR SACA **Aerbus** operates the shuttle from Bologna's Guglielmo Marconi Airport, via Modena to Reggio's Piazzale Europa. The price one way is €20, and tickets can be bought online (w *booking.sacaonline.it*). Coaches run about every 3 hours during the day; timetables are on the website.

BY RAIL Reggio's striking new **AV Mediopadana** station [map, page 144] (*Via del Tricolore; see also box, page 193*), in the northern suburbs bordering the A1 Autostrade del Sole, is a major stop on the Trenitalia high-speed line (Frecciarossa) from Milan, with connections southward to Bologna, Florence, Rome and Naples, and an Adriatic branch to Bologna, Ancona, Pescara, Foggia and Bari. The station is also a stop for the NTV Italo trains from Milan to Bologna and the south, and a Ferrovie Emilia-Romagna local line to Guastalla. The M5 city bus, along with the Guastalla train, provides regular connections to the city centre.

The old **central rail station** [184 G3], just east of the hexagon of boulevards on Piazza Marconi, is a port of call for all the trains on the main Rimini–Bologna–Parma–Milan line; there is another line for Mantua and the north. All the local bus lines except 5 and H will take you to the centre; buy tickets at the newsstand in the station.

BY BUS Local **ACT** lines to Novellara and Guastalla in the north, and San Polo d'Enza and Scandiano to the south, leave from the ACT station [184 B1] (✆ *0522 431667; w actre.it*) west of the centre on Viale Trento e Trieste. For Correggio, Carpi and other provincial destinations, as well as Guastalla, buses depart from the bus station [184 B1] on Viale Allegri, next to the Giardini Pubblici.

GETTING AROUND

Traffic can be fierce in Reggio, and much of the centre is closed to traffic. Most of the parking areas are located around the ring of boulevards, though you might be able to find a spot in the centre around Corso Garibaldi, Via Roma or the Giardini Pubblici.

Rent bikes from **Bicittà** (at the central station [184 G3], Via San Pietro Martire [184 C3], Via Cecati [184 B4] and the Foro Boario [184 B1]). Rates begin at €1.50/hour, or €2.00/hour for an electric bike (discounts for day rentals; deposit required).

TOURIST INFORMATION

i [184 C3] Via Toschi 1/b, cnr Piazza Prampolini; ✆ 0522 451 152; ⊕ 09.00–13.00 & 14.00–18.00 Mon–Sat, 09.30–12.30 Sun

WHERE TO STAY

UPMARKET

🏠 **Delle Notarie** [184 C3] (51 rooms) Via Palazzolo 5; ✆ 0522 453500; w albergonotarie.it. Discreet luxury & lovely rooms & apts with wooden floors in an old refurbished palace, a short walk from the cathedral; bedrooms have AC, & there's a restaurant. Closed first 3 weeks of Aug. €€€€

🏠 **Mercure Astoria** [184 D1] (108 rooms) Viale L Nobili 2; ✆ 0522 435245; w mercurehotelastoria.com. A chain & a bit drab, but comfortable & offering fine views over the municipal gardens. Garage, AC & restaurant. €€€–€€€€

MID-RANGE

🏠 **Posta** [184 C3] (38 rooms) Piazza del Monte 2; 📞0522 432944; w hotelposta.re.it. For a historic stay in the heart of Reggio, you can't beat this. Housed in the 13th-century Palazzo del Capitano del Popolo. In the 1500s the palace with its swallow-tail crenellations became an inn; the rooms are very comfortable, & the public rooms still have some frescoes. There's a bar but no restaurant; free bikes available. €€€

🏠 **San Marco** [184 G3] (50 rooms) Piazzale Marconi 1; 📞0522 452742; w hotelsanmarco-re. it. A long walk from the centre, across from the station but, if you need it, it's a very well-run, welcoming & comfortable place. €€€

BUDGET

🏠 **Ariosto** [184 C2] (22 rooms) Via San Rocco 12; 📞0522 404935. On a peaceful back street right in the centre. Family-run, very friendly & eager to help; simple, comfortable rooms. €€

🏠 **Saint Lorenz** [184 E2] (23 rooms) Via Roma 45–7; 📞0522 454049; w hotelsaintlorenz. com. Basic, but works hard to provide a pleasant stay. €€

🏠 **Lo Student's Hostel della Giara** [184 B2] Via Guasco 6; 📞0522 452323; w www. ostelloreggioemilia.it) Dbls, trpls & dorms. Baby cots available, plus laundry service & bike rental; b/fast inc. €

✖ WHERE TO EAT AND DRINK

ABOVE AVERAGE

✖ **Caffè Arte e Mestieri** [184 C2] Via Emilia 14; 📞0522 432202; w giannidamato.it. Reggio's top chef, Gianni d'Amato, offers a style with plenty of rich sauces, inventive seafood concoctions (pasta with monkfish & smoked aubergine) & fantasy desserts, in one of the loveliest garden terraces you'll see. Menus €45 & €65. €€€€

MID-RANGE

✖ **Bassamarea** [184 B4] Via Pellegrini Nobili 1; 📞0522 176373; w ristorantebassamarea.it;

🕐 lunch Sun only, dinner Wed–Sun. The place to go for seafood in Reggio, & at reasonable prices: pasta with baby clams or mussels, and mixed fries & grills. Everything's fishy but the desserts. €€€

✖ **Canossa** [184 E2] Via Roma 37; 📞0522 454196; w ristorantecanossa.com; 🕐 closed Wed & Aug. A Reggio classic where nothing ever changes (or ever should). It's all about the meat: roasts & boiled meats from the cart, steaks & chops, *scaloppini*. A grand array of pasta choices, too. €€€

REGGIO SPECIALITIES

Along with neighbouring Parma, Reggio is a major producer of **Parmesan** cheese (properly called Parmigiano Reggiano); in fact, the cheese as we know it today had its origins here, in the verdant Enza Valley between Reggio and Parma, where the pastures are so lush that cows produce the richest milk in Italy. Food historians assure us that the Etruscans made it, and to this day the finest Parmesan comes from the valley, and in particular from the town of Montecchio. The hard, grainy cheese first became popular abroad in the 17th century, in large part due to Molière, who practically lived on the stuff: it was sold by merchants from Parma, so he asked for 'Parmesan cheese', and the name stuck.

Like Modena, too, Reggio distils *aceto balsamico*, or **balsamic vinegar**, as valuable as frankincense in the Middle Ages. Other specialities of Reggio are **lasagne**, *cappelletti in brodo*, a loaf called *polpettone di tacchino*, made of minced turkey, herbs, nutmeg and cloves, and a savoury vegetable pie called *erbazzone*, sold at the local baker's and ideal for a picnic lunch; good ones are available from Forno Catellani [184 F4] (*Via Terrachini 35*).

✕ Marta in Cucina [184 C4] Vicolo Folletto 1, off Corso Garibaldi; ✆0522 435755; w martaincucina.it; ⊕ closed Sun eve & Mon. Just what you were looking for: good Emiliano tradition with a touch of real creativity (& some borrowings from southern Italy). Lots of seafood, artistic homemade breads & a formidable dessert trolley. Tasting menus €45–85. €€€

✕ La Casseruola [184 B4] Via Vezzana 1; ✆0522 453837; w lacasseruola.com; ⊕ closed Tue lunch. A local favourite recently upscaled & relocated. You can still get a good pizza or a great bargain lunch menu, or splurge on some refined dishes: *garganelli* with prawns & a touch of cocoa, or seafood kebabs. €€–€€€

CHEAP & CHEERFUL

✕ La Morina [184 B3] Corso Garibaldi 24; ✆0522 431140; w trattorialamorina.it; ⊕ closed

Tue lunch & Mon. Another old-style trattoria with all the traditional dishes, & a lot of things not often seen outside grandma's kitchen. €€

✕ Sotto Broletto [184 C3] Via Broletta 1/n; ✆0522 452276. Right under the old market arches, a practically perfect traditional trattoria. An atmosphere of austerity above crisp white tablecloths, so as not to distract from the glistening *tagliere*, homemade tortelli, & pizzas piled high with rocket. Everything good in Emilia is on the big menu somewhere. €€

✕ Antica Salumeria Giorgio Pancaldi [184 C3] Via Broletta 1/p; ✆0522 432795; w salumeriapancaldi.it. Reggio's famous *salumeria*; come here first to plan your picnic sandwiches. If you're staying in, they have a few tables to enjoy plates of their finest, along with cheeses & salads. €

WHAT TO SEE AND DO

DUOMO [184 C3] (✆*0522 433783;* ⊕ *09.00–12.30 & 16.00–19.00 daily*) On Reggio's central Piazza Prampolini, the main feature is the peculiar cathedral, topped by a single octagonal tower. Most of its original Romanesque features were remodelled away in the 16th century and replaced by an unfinished façade with fine statues by Prospero Sogari of *Adam and Eve* lounging on the cornice of the portal; in the tower niche is a gilded copper *Madonna* flanked by the cathedral donors. There are Renaissance tombs and paintings by Guercino, among others, in the gloomy interior. The best part of the Duomo was discovered only recently: some provocative crypt **mosaics** from the 4th century AD. Naked men pick olives; others present herbs and ducks to naked ladies, all of them crowned. There's a hint of some Dionysiac mysticism here, but for the present the mosaics are just leaving everyone mystified.

Back behind the Duomo in the old Archbishop's Palace is the **Museo Diocesano** [184 D3] (*Via Vittorio Veneto 6;* ✆*0522 175 7930;* ⊕ *Sep–May 09.30–12.30 Tue–Fri, 09.30–12.30 & 15.30–18.30 Sat–Sun, Jun–Jul 21.00–22.30 Wed & Fri, 09.30–12.30 & 16.00–19.00 Sat–Sun, Aug closed; admission free*), with a collection of detached frescoes, capitals and other sculptural decoration from the Duomo and other churches around the province, most of them from medieval times.

PIAZZA PRAMPOLINI [184 C3] This is the civic and ecclesiastical heart of Reggio, and the site of busy outdoor **markets** on Tuesdays and Fridays; locals like to save a few syllables by calling it simply 'Piazza Grande', as they have since the Middle Ages. But Reggio has a long and proud lefty heritage; Camillo Prampolini, born here in 1859, was one of the founders of the Italian Socialist Party.

Across the piazza is the **Palazzo del Monte di Pietà**, with its lofty **Torre dell'Orologio** [184 C3]. The 18th-century façade conceals Reggio's original town hall; after a new one was built on the other side of the square, it became the headquarters of the municipal pawn shop, a worthy institution in all old Italian cities. These developed into savings banks, the average man's only source of credit; Reggio's Monte di Pietà was here for more than 400 years.

The **Palazzo Comunale** [184 C3] (✆ *0522 456111;* ⊕ *visits by appointment*), begun in 1414 and often restored and rebuilt, occupies the southern side of the piazza. The red-white-and-green *tricolore*, later adopted as the Italian flag, first appeared here in 1797 during the second congress of Napoleon's Cispadane Republic, a very short-lived entity that covered the area between Reggio, Mantua, Ferrara and Bologna. Anyone feeling empathetically patriotic may visit the **Museo del Tricolore** [184 C3] (✆ *0522 456033;* ⊕ *09.00–noon Tue–Fri, 10.00–13.00 & 16.00–19.00 Sat–Sun; admission free*), just off Piazza Prampolini on Piazza Cassotti.

Piazza Prampolini has another surprising patriotic distinction. The Polish national anthem (*Poland Is Not Lost, As Long As We Are Living…*) was written here – also in 1797, two years after the last of the partitions wiped Poland from the map – by an exiled poet named Jozef Wybicki, who was serving in Napoleon's army and quartered in the Episcopal Palace next to the Duomo.

PIAZZA SAN PROSPERO A covered arcade called the **Broletto** [184 C3] connects Piazza Prampolini to another market square, Piazza San Prospero (*markets held Tue & Fri mornings*). The Broletto itself is usually full of produce stands, fittingly enough, since the name is an old word for a vegetable garden. Besides affording the best view of the Duomo – from behind, revealing the elegant dome and towers invisible from Piazza Prampolini – this piazza is home to the 16th-century **Basilica di San Prospero** [184 D3] (⊕ *08.30–noon & 17.00–19.00 Mon–Sat, 08.30–noon Sun*) noted for its fine choir with inlaid stalls, and the cycle of frescoes by Milanese early Baroque painter Camillo Procaccini, including the *Last Judgement*.

North of Piazza Prampolini and San Prospero, the Roman **Via Aemilia** is today Reggio's pedestrianised main shopping street, passing through Piazza Cesare Battisti, roughly the site of Roman Reggio's forum. Here is the 13th-century **Palazzo del Capitano del Popolo** [184 D3], now a hotel (Hotel Posta; page 187), after a Hollywoodish 1920s restoration that made it look more medieval than anything the Middle Ages ever dreamed of.

NORTH OF THE VIA EMILIA Medieval Reggio was never nearly large enough to fill the space inside its ambitious hexagon of walls. The old centre never extended far north of the Via Emilia; this area developed mostly over the last 200 years, and now is home to some fine *palazzi* and most of the city's cultural institutions. At its heart is the vast Piazza Martiri del VII Luglio and the renowned **Teatro Municipale** [184 C1] (✆ *0522 458811;* w *www.iteatri.re.it/Calendario.jsp; box office* ⊕ *16.00–19.00 Mon–Fri, 10.00–13.00 & 16.00–19.00 Sat*), the town's opera house built in 1852 and crowned by a surplus of musing statuary. This is one of the most lavish theatres in Italy; built to upstage the Teatro Regio in Parma, it largely succeeds. Performances (all year) of opera, concerts and plays are of a high quality, if not quite as prestigious as Parma's.

The site was originally part of the Cittadella, built by the Este to keep an eye on the Reggiani. After the fortress was demolished in 1848, the rest of the area behind the new theatre was turned into the shady **Giardini Pubblici** [184 C1], embellished with statues of Boiardo and Ariosto, but also containing a Roman tomb, the 1st-century AD **Tomb of the Concordii**, moved from its original location outside town.

Palazzo dei Musei [184 D2] (*Via Spallenzani 1;* ✆ *0522 456816;* w *musei.comune. re.it;* ⊕ *09.00–noon Tue–Fri, 10.00–13.00 & 14.00–19.00 Sat–Sun; Jul–Aug 09.00–noon & 21.00–23.00 Tue–Sat, 21.00–23.00 Sun; admission free*) A block east of the Teatro Municipale, this museum has a little bit of everything. At the entrance is

6

a room of mosaics, both Roman and some fascinating 12th-century ones from a demolished church, including fragments from a *Labours of the Months*: a two-faced Janus and Aquarius for January. Beyond that, in various collections, local pedants assembled the souvenirs of African and Amazonian explorers (a stuffed crocodile and a mounted giraffe head, neck and all), a Neolithic Venus, American Indian ceremonial costumes, a huge collection of Roman coins, mounted fish, the model of the unfinished cathedral façade, the skeleton of an ancient whale and more foetuses in formaldehyde than you have perhaps ever seen: humans, an armadillo, a snake, a piglet and several kittens.

Upstairs, the **Pinacoteca** has works by various obscure Emilian artists, notably Paolo Emilio Besenzi and Reggio's Luca Ferrari, along with a fine work by Palma Giovane, the *Compianto su Cristo Morto*. A painting friar, Fra Stefano da Carpi, adds a merry *Self-Portrait* from the 1790s, when he was 82. One room is dedicated to Renato Mazzacurati (1907–69), the 'painter of the Resistance' who did the Monument to the Partigiano in Parma. Mazzacurati was a good socialist influenced by Picasso who also had a sense of humour; besides his serious paintings commenting on the Spanish Civil War and Fascism, there are caricatures of his friends, including de Chirico, and a series of capitalists and generals made into useful wine pitchers.

Galleria Parmeggiani [184 C2] (*Corso Cairoli 2;* ☏ *052 451054;* ⏲ *same as the Palazzo dei Musei; admission free*) Across the piazza from the Teatro Municipale

THE GREAT DECEIVER

Luigi Parmeggiani, born in Reggio in 1858, started out in life as a very poor apprentice shoemaker. But this talented boy was destined for greater things. In 1881 he ducked into France to avoid military conscription. By then he was already a committed anarchist, and he joined other Italian exiles in shadowy Paris groups with names like the Straccioni di Parigi (Ragamuffins of Paris) and the Introvabili (Unfindables). In Paris, Parmeggiani found he had one special aptitude – for crime. He organised a gang of like-minded compatriots, and burgled and swindled his way to a pretty good living while hatching political plots and writing journalism, tracts and pamphlets under various assumed names. He seems to have committed a murder or two, and plotted other political crimes, though he was jailed only once, briefly.

In those days of the 'diaspora' of Italian anarchists across Europe, if you put a dozen anarchists in one room they would probably find 13 sects. Parmeggiani belonged to the tendency called 'individualism'. He cared little for organising workers or throwing bombs. Instead he believed the way to go was stealing – 'expropriation', as he called it. Let every man grab what he liked, and the revolution would come about naturally. For this prototype Abbie Hoffman, though, crime seemed always less about financing the revolution than financing Parmeggiani; he wrote that he saw no reason why revolutionaries should not 'enjoy the pleasures of life'.

While in Paris, Parmeggiani became friends with a wealthy Spanish genre painter and collector named Ignacio de León y Escosura. Along with his mother and wife, Escosura ran a gallery under the name of Louis Marcy, specialising in late medieval and Renaissance Spanish objets d'art. Many of these were very skilful fakes, produced in the Escosuras' clandestine Paris workshop. This was even better than stealing, and Parmeggiani soon took over as head of the operation. He ran the gallery after Escosura's death, enjoyed his widow as a mistress and later married his niece.

is a very peculiar building, a pastiche of Renaissance and medieval forms with monster stone hounds crawling over the fairy-tale cornice – a bit of architectural fantasy that makes a perfect home for what is probably the biggest collection of art forgeries on Earth.

This is what remains of the collections of amazing anarchist and art forger Luigi Parmeggiani (see box, below), brought here from France on the sly in the 1920s. On display are furniture, paintings, jewellery, costumes, fabrics, arms and armour, from the Middle Ages to 1900, a few real, most the work of the Marcy forgers, and some of which the real story may never be known. Looking at them, you might well wonder how they ever got away with it. So many of the works have such a strong air of William Morris Arts and Crafts about them – what the Victorians thought the Middle Ages ought to have looked like.

Not everything is in doubt. There's a large collection of the historical paintings by the faker himself, Ignacio de León y Escosura, and two rooms of works by his brother-in-law Cesare Detti, a very talented genre painter born to paint Spanish cavaliers, dwarfs with ruffs and tasty ladies in gondolas. Other paintings include an El Greco and a Ribera that may well be genuine. On the building itself, note the outlandish 15th-century portal brought over from Valencia.

Museo dei Cappuccini [184 D1] (*Via Ferraro Bonini 6;* \ *0522 580720;* w *museocappuccini.it;* ☉ *during special exhibitions only, see website for details;*

Still involved in a host of other nefarious business, by 1889 Parmeggiani was finding Paris a little hot, and he simply disappeared. What he did, in fact, was to adopt the identity of the well-known but non-existent Louis Marcy and move to London, where he and the Escosuras opened another gallery. Though he narrowly escaped prison there too, his business prospered as never before. Nobody had more money than the English – and no-one, it seemed, was easier to fool. Soon Parmeggiani had a fine house at 1 Bedford Square. He was selling his fakes to dukes and earls, and even to the Victoria & Albert Museum. He peddled a fake 'sword of Edward III' to the British Museum. For a patron, he had no less a personage than Sir John Charles Robinson, curator of the Royal Collections of Queen Victoria.

At the same time, he was still scheming anarchist intrigues and running another gang of thieves. It couldn't last forever. Parmeggiani fled London sometime before 1900. The confused years that followed saw a brief exile in South America and a stint in a French prison. He was called a police spy, and a spy for foreign powers. Once during a police raid he had to escape over the rooftops of Paris. Parmeggiani organised an unsuccessful plot to assassinate his hated fellow Reggiano, the great statesman Camillo Prampolini. For a while he edited an art journal called *Le Connaisseur*, in which he penned passionate denunciations of art forgers.

Parmeggiani closed his last gallery in 1924, and took advantage of the post-World War I political amnesties to return to Reggio with his collections. 'Marcy fakes', as they came to be known, had by then found their way into the great museums of the world, and some of them were already being condemned as frauds. The news apparently never reached Reggio, for Parmeggiani was able to finagle a deal with the city in 1932, under which he would bequeath them his supposedly priceless hoard of art in return for a life pension. The great deceiver merrily cashed their cheques until his death in 1945.

6

admission free) Rehoused in bright new quarters, but still looking for a way to stay open permanently, this monastic grab-bag has everything from Baroque paintings and ceramics to agricultural implements and crafts made by the monks. There's nothing at all antique about the special exhibitions the Capuchins put on, mostly on contemporary art and photography.

CORSO GARIBALDI Reggio's elegant boulevard, the tree-lined Corso Garibaldi, winds around the southern end of the city's ancient nucleus. It follows the original course of the Torrente Cróstolo, a stream that was rechannelled in the Middle Ages when Reggio's walls were built. Beginning at Via Emilia Santo Stefano, it passes the **Palazzo Ducale** [184 B3] of the Este, with a Neoclassical remodelling of the 1780s. It's the seat of the provincial prefecture now, and the local communists have officially renamed it Palazzo Salvador Allende. Across the street stands Reggio's most impressive church, the Santuario della Madonna della Ghiara (see below). Further down, at number 29, the **Palazzo Magnani** [184 B3] (❧ *0522 444446;* w *palazzomagnani.it*) bears a familiar Reggio landmark, a Renaissance sculpture of two-faced *Janus*, looking into the past and future from his post on a corner. The palace, home to a foundation, occasionally hosts important exhibitions of art and photography. The Corso ends in Piazza Roversi, where the view is skilfully closed by the delightful rococo façade of the little **Chiesa del Cristo** [184 C4] by Giambattista Cattani (1761).

Santuario della Madonna della Ghiara [184 D2] (🕓 *07.15–noon & 16.00–19.30 Mon–Sat*) The Santuario della Madonna della Ghiara commemorates a miracle of 1596, when a deaf-mute recovered his hearing and speech while praying to an image of the Virgin on the site. The church, begun the following year, was designed by Alessandro Balbi, with a certain influence from St Peter's in Rome. A Greek-cross plan with an extended choir, its vaulting is entirely covered by frescoes of Old Testament scenes that complement the main theme, the *Exaltation of the Virtues of Mary*. The frescoes are the work of various artists, notably the Bolognese Alessandro Tiarini and Leonello Spada. All of them take their cue from Correggio and his followers in Parma, with lush pastel colouring and sophisticated graphic sense. Also present, on one of the altarpieces, is a *Crucifixion* by Guercino.

OUTSIDE THE CENTRE
SS Girolamo e Vitale [184 E4] (*Via San Girolamo 24;* ❧ *0522 438675;* 🕓 *by appointment only, though you may be able to sneak in for a look before & after masses*) This is the most remarkable building in Reggio, though largely unknown and hidden away in a quiet corner, southeast of the centre near Piazza Tricolore. Its origins go back to the 9th century, though the current building was begun only in 1646.

The idea of the confraternity that built it was to create a model of the Holy Sepulchre in Jerusalem for symbolic pilgrimages (as at Bologna's Santo Stefano). The brothers asked the great stage designer and architect Gaspare Vigarani (see box, page 166) to give them not one but three churches, all squeezed into a very small space. Vigarani's ingenious plan works on three levels connected by stairways, one of which is a **Scala Santa**, a pilgrimage stair recalling the famous one at St John Lateran in Rome. **SS Girolamo e Vitale**, behind the entrance, is a Latin plan church with a quattrocento fresco saved from the earlier church. Underneath is a crypt, adjacent to which is **San Sepolcro**, the circular crypt modelled on the one in

Spanish starchitect Santiago Calatrava has put his brand on Reggio in a big way, winning the commission for the new station Trenitalia has built for its Frecciarossa high-speed rail line north of the city. The **AV Mediopadana** was inaugurated in 2013. At 483m in length, it certainly makes an impression. Typically for Calatrava, a basically functional building is made special with lacy exterior embellishments in gleaming white. Here, undulating waves of white girders support a louvred roof over the long track area. It's lovely in its way, but you may be excused if the thing reminds you of an exploded accordion.

Calatrava also contributed two of his signature free-form **suspension bridges**, carrying roads over the *autostrade* at the toll gates just west of the station. All these works are part of the **Città del Tricolore**, the new centre Reggio is building around the station to house university campuses, the hospital, a stadium and business and industrial parks.

Jerusalem. Above that is the best part, the beautiful, richly decorated marble vault of **SS Simone e Taddeo**, commonly called the 'Rotondo'.

According to local legend there's a great treasure hidden somewhere in the stones of the church.

Palazzo del Mauriziano [184 G4] (*Via Pasteur 11, San Maurizio, 3km east of Reggio;* \ *0522 456477;* ⊕ *soon to be reopened to the public, for now you can visit the grounds any time*) The delightful 16th-century villa called 'Il Mauriziano' was the birthplace of the most renowned of Italian Renaissance poets, Ludovico Ariosto (1474–1533). Long neglected, it has been recently restored. The entrance is through a brick triumphal arch and an avenue of poplars. Inside, the villa preserves much of its original appearance. The rooms in the east wing have everything a poet's house should have: charming frescoes of love scenes, landscapes and literati.

Collezione Maramotti [184 A1] (*Via Fratelli Cervi 66;* \ *0522 382484;* w *collezionemaramotti.org;* ⊕ *14.30–18.30 Thu–Fri, 10.30–18.30 Sat–Sun, permanent collections with guided tours by appointment only; admission free*) Achille Maramotti founded Max Mara in 1951 as one of the first prêt-à-porter fashion chains. A fair amount of the profits went into his collection of contemporary art, now on display in a sharp modernist building from the 1970s in Reggio's northern suburbs which also serves as company headquarters. The permanent collection has more than 200 works (one by Francis Bacon).

NORTH OF REGGIO

CORREGGIO Some 15km northeast of Reggio, Correggio is a pretty town of arcaded streets. It suffered in the earthquake of October 1996, though nearly all the damage seems to have been repaired. It was the birthplace of painter Antonio Allegri, better known as Correggio (d1534); his home on Borgo Vecchio was reconstructed in 1755.

Tourist information
ℹ️ Via Borgovecchio 39; \ 0522 631770; w turismocorreggio.it; ⊕ mid-Mar–mid-Oct 09.30–12.30 & 15.00–18.00 Tue–Sun, mid-Oct– mid-Mar 09.30–12.30 Tue, Thu–Fri, 09.30–12.30 & 15.00–18.00 Wed, Sat–Sun

6

Lelio Orsi (1511–87), also known as Lelio da Novellara, was a brilliant, eccentric Mannerist painter who would be better known but for some bad breaks. First, Orsi made his name in Reggio Emilia, a town with the habit of commissioning frescoes on the *outside* walls of buildings. All of these are lost today. Then, the painter got mixed up in a murder case, and was forced to take refuge in his home town of Novellara; here he spent much of the rest of his life, executing commissions and doing odd jobs for the Gonzagas. These included more outdoor frescoes, after the count decreed every house in Novellara had to have one.

Most of Orsi's works have been lost, though his innumerable drawings have always been prized by collectors. His few surviving paintings show a strong influence from Michelangelo, gained from an early trip to Rome, but his peculiar manner – bright, spiritually intense figures contrasting sharply with the gloomy, ominous backgrounds – might sometimes make you think of El Greco.

 Where to stay, eat and drink

Dei Medaglioni Corso Mazzini 8; 0522 632233; w albergodeimedaglioni.com. Housed in a converted palace, with up-to-date, comfortable & stylish rooms. There's a good restaurant, Il Correggio (€€€). Closed Aug & Christmas. **€€€**

What to see and do The brick Renaissance **Palazzo dei Principi**, begun in 1506, has a Renaissance portal and courtyard, and some bits of fresco and other decoration inside. It contains the town's **Museo 'Il Correggio'** (*Corso Cavour 7;* 0522 693296; 16.00–19.00 Sat, 10.00–12.30 & 16.00–19.00 Sun; admission free), with a *Christ* by Andrea Mantegna and some lovely cinquecento Flemish tapestries, as well as the original frescoes, fireplaces and panelled ceilings.

Correggio's main church, the Renaissance **SS Quirino e Michele** (1525) is attributed to Vignola. On Via Roma, the austere but beautiful church of **San Francesco** was recently restored after the earthquake.

NOVELLARA Northwest of Correggio, Novellara was part of the realm of the Gonzaga dukes of Mantua from the 13th century until the mid 1700s. The Gonzagas' fine 14th-century castle, the **Rocca**, now serves as both the town hall and the **Museo Gonzaga** (*Piazzale Marconi 1;* 0522 655454; 10.00–12.30 & 15.00–18.30 Sun; Aug closed; admission free), housing Roman finds, farm implements, tapestries and medieval and Renaissance frescoes, and a unique collection of faience chemists' jars, which originally contained the likes of crabs' eyes and ground stag horn. It's worth a stop on a Sunday to see the group of detached frescoes by Novellara's own Mannerist master Lelio Orsi (see box, above): odd, somewhat mystical vignettes of uncertain meaning. There is also a recently acquired Orsi church painting, an *Annunciation.*

Novellara has an important Sikh community, and the oldest Sikh gurdwara (temple) in Italy. There are more than 70,000 Sikhs in Italy; here many of them herd cows for the making of Parmigiano Reggiano cheese.

DOWN THE MUDDY OLD PO

The closer you get to the Po, the lonelier the landscapes and the more bedraggled the towns. Despite their blooming prosperity, the settlements in this area don't care much for appearances; everything is clean and tidy, though it still sometimes seems as if you're in some woebegone backwater of Calabria instead of modern northern Italy.

BRESCELLO Brescello was Roman Brixellum, an important city that was destroyed in the Greek–Gothic War of the 6th century AD; nothing of it remains. Brescello revived a little under the Este dukes, and still has a statue by Jacopo Sansovino of Ercole II d'Este in the guise of his namesake, Hercules.

Brescello is famous as the setting of Giovanni Guareschi's 'Don Camillo' books, made into a series of film comedies after World War II. Starring Fernandel and Gino Cervi as the eternally quarrelling village priest and Communist mayor, these gentle parables perfectly captured the mood of a recovering post-war Italy. They were so popular that Brescello spent much of its time in the 1950s taking care of the film crews.

 ## Where to stay, eat and drink

La Tavernetta del Lupo (12 rooms) Piazza M Pallini, Loc Sorbolo Levante; ✆ 0522 680509; w latavernettadellupo.it. Basic, pleasant accommodation, but come for the restaurant (🕐 *closed Wed;* €€€): a mix of the traditional & Italian *cucina nuova* that will surprise your taste buds, with dishes such as gnocchi made from carrots with basil & pine nuts, or salmon with raspberry vinegar & poppy seeds. There's also an unusual selection of Italian & foreign cheeses & fruity desserts, & a huge wine & spirits list. **€€–€€€**

What to see and do For fans of the films, there's the **Museo Don Camillo e Peppone** (*Via de Amicis 2;* ✆ *0522 482564;* 🕐 *09.30–12.30 & 14.30–17.30 Tue–Fri, 09.30–12.30 & 14.30–18.30 (winter 14.00–18.00) Sat–Sun; €5*) in the old Benedictine monastery, with an American tank that was used in one of the films; a wooden crucifix carved as a prop in another still does duty in the village church. In the same building Brescello has a small archaeological collection.

POVIGLIO South of Brescello, Poviglio has a small **Museo Terramara** (*Via Parma 1;* ✆ *0522 960426;* 🕐 *09.00–12.30 Wed–Thu, 09.00–12.30 & 15.00–18.15 Tue & Fri, 09.00–12.30 & 17.00–19.00 (15.00–17.30 in winter) Sat; admission free*), with finds from the recently excavated Terramara village of Santa Rosa, including utensils, jewellery, ceramics and bronze objects.

GUALTIERI Down the Po to the east, Gualtieri began as a Lombard river fortress called Castrum Walterii. Its greatest days came between 1567 and 1634, when the area belonged to the Bentivoglio family, former bosses of Bologna. One of them in particular, Cornelio Bentivoglio, proved a very useful ruler, building canals and draining swamps to make this part of the plain healthier and more profitable. In Gualtieri he created perhaps the grandest piazza in all of Emilia-Romagna, the arcaded **Piazza Bentivoglio**, with more than enough room to fit all this humble village's current 6,000 people, and their cars and tractors too.

Designed by Giovan Battista Aleotti, architect of Parma's Farnese Theatre, the piazza is a unified ensemble, seemingly a single building on three sides, crowned by a tall clocktower with the Bentivoglio arms. The fourth side, for which the façade was never completed, is the **Palazzo Bentivoglio** (🕐 *closed for restoration*). Inside it has some fine frescoes, particularly those in the Sala dei Giganti. Cornelio Bentivoglio was a friend of the poet Torquato Tasso, and the frescoes portray episodes from his *Gerusalemme Liberata* as well as mythological fancies and scenes from the Bentivoglio court.

Also in Gualtieri, you can inspect the works of a very interesting naïve painter and sculptor at the **Museo Antonio Ligabue** (*Via Giardino 27*; m *333 654 6908*; w *museoligabue.it*; ⊕ *09.30–12.30 & 15.30–18.30 daily exc Tue; €2.50*). Antonio Ligabue (d1965) specialised in colourful jungle scenes with fearsome tigers and leopards, and self-portraits of the artist looking nearly as fearsome himself. Ligabue spent some stretches in mental asylums, once for sticking a palette knife in his head, and once during the war for battering a German soldier's head in with a bottle. Beginning in the 1950s his art brought him fame and money, though neither of these seemed to please him much. RAI did a TV film about his life, *Ligabue*, in 1977.

GUASTALLA Another Po-faced town with Lombard origins, Guastalla (originally Warstal) was a strategic point for the control of the river, and attracted a lot of attention over the centuries; even in the Dark Ages, the Po was an important trade route, along which salt from the lagoon of Venice was brought up to Lombardy. At times Guastalla belonged to the Canossa, the Visconti, the Da Correggio and the Gonzaga; after 1748, it became part of the Duchy of Parma – or to give it its proper name from that point, the Duchy of Parma, Piacenza and Guastalla. Ferrante I Gonzaga gave the town its present shape in 1550, an aesthetically sophisticated Renaissance plan centred on the 'noble street', Via Gonzaga, and enclosed by up-to-date fortifications.

Tourist information
i Via Gonzaga 16; ☎0522 839763; ⊕ 09.30–12.30 & 15.30–18.30 Wed, Fri–Sun, 09.30–12.30 Thu

---

 Where to stay

🏠 **Villa Montanarini** [map, page 144] (16 rooms) Via Virgilio Mandelli 29, Villarotta di Luzzara, 10km east of Guastalla; ☎0522 820001; w villamontanarini.com. Luxurious & beautifully furnished 17th-century villa set in its own park, with a restaurant (€€€); AC, room service. €€€€

🏠 **Old River** (30 rooms) Viale Po 2; ☎0522 838401. Offers excellent AC rooms in a pleasant green setting, & parking. €€€

🏠 **Locanda Argine della Cerchia** (2 rooms) Corso Garibaldi 25; ☎0522 1840580; w locandaarginedellacerchia.it. Comfortable B&B rooms in a 16th-century building in the historic centre. €€–€€€

What to see and do Ferrante Gonzaga's statue in bronze dominates the main **Piazza Mazzini**, facing the recently restored **Palazzo Ducale**, now the home of the **Museo della Città** (⊕ *temporarily closed for restorations*), with some Roman finds, and art from medieval to modern times. Other relics of better days include the **Teatro Ruggeri** on Via Verdi (1671, rebuilt 1814), the Baroque **Chiesa dei Servi** on Corso Prampolini, and the **Biblioteca Maldotti** on Corso Garibaldi (☎ *0522 826294*; ⊕ *14.00–18.00 Mon–Fri*), which includes a small museum that often puts on exhibits of art or history.

Outside Guastalla are two Romanesque churches, the **Basilica della Pieve**, at Locazione Pieve, and the **Oratorio San Giorgio**, just over the railway from the centre.

Further down the Po, on the outskirts of **Luzzara**, the former convent of San Felice has been converted into the **Museo Arti Naives** (*Villa Superiore 32*; ☎ *0522 977612*; ⊕ *still closed after the 2012 earthquake, reopening date uncertain*), with a permanent collection of naïve art, including more works by Antonio Ligabue of Gualtieri. The museum was founded by Cesare Zavattini, a great *cinema verità* director and collaborator of Vittorio De Sica.

CANOSSA It's a spot that everyone's heard of, without knowing exactly where it is: one full of history, without much left to see. Canossa, where an emperor once humbled himself before a pope, kneeling in the snow and praying for three days begging forgiveness, lies south of Reggio off the SS513, in a place where the Apennines rise abruptly up from the plain.

History Canossa's importance began with the remarkable career of a knight named Atto Adalbert, a son of Baron Siegfried of Lucca who went to the wars in the service of the bishop of Reggio and was rewarded with the territory of Canossa. Atto built the castle here, and in AD951 he was lucky or plucky enough to manage the escape of Adelaide, rightful Queen of Italy, from her island prison on Lake Garda, where she had been put by a usurper, Berengar of Ivrea. After she took refuge with Atto, she asked Otto I of Germany to help her regain her throne. Before the year was over, Otto had sorted out Berengar and married Adelaide; 12 years later they were crowned Emperor and Empress in Rome by Pope John XII – and the Holy Roman Empire was born, or at least the post-Charlemagne, German version, with a claim to overlordship in Italy that provided the mainspring of north Italian history for the next 700 years.

As for Atto, as the Emperor's right-hand man south of the Alps, he did well. Otto made him Marquis of 'Canossiana', a territory that included Modena, Mantua, Reggio and Ferrara. He accumulated an enormous treasure, and his descendants, thereafter known as the Di Canossa, became Counts of Tuscany and remained a power in Italy for generations. The most famous member of the family was the mighty, charismatic, warlike Countess Matilda, who would occasionally don armour and lead her men into battle.

In 1077 the long pan-European battle over the control of investitures led the great reforming Pope Gregory VII to do something no pope had ever dared before – excommunicate an emperor. His timing was perfect; the German barons used the excommunication as a pretext for revolt, and Matilda, a partisan of the popes who spent most of Atto's treasure financing their cause, was instrumental in bringing Henry IV to Canossa in the snow to apologise to Gregory. Though Henry got his revenge soon after, as Gregory had to witness a sack of Rome before dying in exile, it was a turning point; for the next two centuries, popes held the moral high ground over the kings and barons of Europe.

What's left of Canossa is a rarity in Italy, a rural *comune* with no real centre that covers several villages and several castles on the hills overlooking the Torrente Enza. The territory is rugged, with sharp peaks and the strangely eroded hillsides the Italians call *calanchi*. When you finally make it up to the main castle, the Castello di Canossa, you'll see why the medieval barons found it such an attractive place. A nearly impregnable eyrie, with three circuits of walls, it dominated Emilia until the militia of Reggio captured and razed it in 1255. Later rebuilt as a mountain retreat popular with the dukes of Parma, Canossa met its definitive end when the powder house inside blew up in 1576.

Tourist information

i Terre Matildiche, Castello di Canossa 26; \0522 533315; ⊕ 09.00–12.30 & 15.00–19.00 Tue–Sun

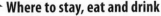 Where to stay, eat and drink

🏠 **Hotel Ristorante La Maddalena** [map, page 144] (11 rooms) Via L Pasteur 5, Loc Quattro Castella; \0522 877135; w albergolamaddalena. it. Recently renovated, simply furnished but comfortable rooms & an exceptional restaurant (🕐 *closed Wed;* €€–€€€) offering country cuisine: the best of Emilian *salumi*, stewed venison with polenta, roast guinea fowl. €€€

🏠 **Le Scuderie** [map, page 144] (6 rooms) Via Regigno 77, Loc Carpineti; m 346 423 1909; w agriturismolescuderie.it. In a restful setting, a handsome stone *agriturismo* in an 18th-century ducal hunting lodge overlooking a meadow. The friendly owners offer delicious evening meals (€€). Closed Nov. €€

✕ **La Cueva** Loc Giarretta 14, Canossa; ✆0522 876316; w ranchlacueva.it; 🕐 closed Tue eve, Mon. Just south of Canossa at Currada, an old country mill

converted into a lovely restaurant, featuring *gnocchi fritti*, great antipasti and a wide range of pasta dishes & meats, including roast boar. €€

✕ **La Torre** Piazza Carlo Sartori, San Polo d'Enza; m 328 852 3670; 🕐 closed Sun eve, Mon. Honest, old-style family trattoria with lots of *salumi* & tortelli & some interesting *secondi*, including rabbit & duck. The cook likes it hot; expect a *peperoncino* or 2 thrown in. €€

✕ **Pietranera** Via Pietranera 187, Canossa; ✆0522 870420; 🕐 closed Mon, Wed & Jan. Hearty lunches & dinners, with homemade pasta. This includes the classic *pappardelle* with boar in season, & succulent grilled lamb as a follow-up. €€

What to see and do Today the **Castello di Canossa** is a scenic and tranquil ruin with a small museum (✆ *0522 877 104;* w *www.comune.canossa.re.it;* 🕐 *09.00–12.30 & 15.00–19.00 Tue–Sun; admission free*); every now and then historical pageants are staged inside.

Matilda's capital, more than just a single strong castle, was a whole network of them, spread throughout the *comune* of Canossa and in the surrounding areas; locals call this whole region the Terre di Matilde. On a nearby peak, the picturesque 11th-century **Castello di Rossena** guarded the approaches to Canossa; now restored, it is currently up for sale.

To the north, the village of **Quattro Castella** is overshadowed by four more castles on the hills to the south (three in ruins, one turned into a villa), while another, guarding the Enza Valley road, is now the town hall of **San Polo d'Enza**.

Two more impressive castles complete Canossa's defensive array: one at **Sarzano** to the southwest, and a large one, in ruins, on the summit of Monte Antognano in the mountain resort village of **Carpineti** further south. This was a favourite residence of Matilda and went through many hands afterwards, most notoriously those of Domenico Amorotto, who received the castle in fief from Pope Julius II and so terrorised the neighbourhood that Julius's successor Leo X had him beheaded, and then ordered that his head be taken through the area to assure the populace the villain was dead. The castle was bombed by the Germans in World War II. Next to it is the Romanesque church of **Sant'Andrea**.

'Castles in the air' Maybe the best way to appreciate the castles of Canossa is by air, in a balloon. **Castelli in Aria** (✆ *0522 719518;* m *338 674 4818;* e *comunicazioneinvolo@tiscalinet.it*), in Carpineti, offers flights over the area mornings and evenings as weather permits, picnic dinner included. Book at least five days ahead in summer, two days the rest of the year.

ROCCA DI BISMANTOVA From any height in the Canossa you'll have noticed something odd on the horizon, a looming shape to the south that looks like a titanic squashed top hat. The inimitable landmark of this part of the Apennines (Dante mentions it in passing, in the *Purgatorio*), the Rocca di Bismantova from closer up resolves into a long, limestone outcrop with a flat top 1,037m high, overlooking the town of **Castelnovo ne' Monti**.

Bismantova may have been a holy place in ancient times. Castelnovo's parish church originally stood on top of it; the villagers got tired of making the long climb and moved it down to the valley stone by stone in the 1600s. Villanovan (pre-Etruscan) remains have been found on top, and both the Romans and Byzantines used it as a fortress. There is still a hermitage chapel up here, reachable in an hour or so on a path from Castelnovo, along with spectacular views over the mountains and the Po plain.

APENNINE SKIING Further south, the highest reaches of the Apennines, bordering Tuscany, are around the 2,100m **Monte Cusna**, known locally as 'Il Gigante' – the outline resembles a prone human figure. On the slopes is a small ski resort, the **Alpe di Cusna** (✆ *0522 800156;* w *infofebbio.com;* ⊕ *Thu–Sun in season, lifts run 08.30–16.30; day ski pass €20, ages 6–12 €16*) at Febbio, with three lifts and eight pistes covering all levels of difficulty, a ski school and snowboarding.

There's another ski area called **Cerreto Laghi** (✆ *0522 898164;* w *cerretolaghi.info; day ski pass: adults €30 w/ends, €18 w/days, under 14s €21/15*) to the west, laid out around two pretty mountain lakes near the border with Tuscany at the **Passo di Cerreto.** This is a bigger and more popular ski area than Alpe di Cusna, with seven lifts and 13 pistes, all but two of them easy or intermediate runs. There's a 'snow park' for snowboarders, a ski and snowboard school, plenty of trails for cross-country skiing and snowshoeing and a **skating rink** open year-round.

UPDATES WEBSITE

You can post your comments and recommendations, and read feedback and updates from other readers online at w bradtupdates.com/emilia.

SEND US YOUR SNAPS!

We'd love to follow your adventures using our *Northern Italy: Emilia-Romagna* guide – why not send us your photos and stories via Twitter (🐦 *@BradtGuides*) and Instagram (📷 *@bradtguides*) using the hashtag #emilia? Alternatively, you can upload your photos directly to the gallery on the Emilia-Romagna destination page via our website (w *bradtguides.com/emilia*).

7

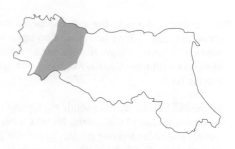

Parma and Surrounds

One of Italy's great art cities, and the second city in Emilia-Romagna after Bologna, Parma's many admirers cite her splendid churches and elegant lanes, her artworks and antiquities, the lyrical strains of grand opera that waft from her Teatro Regio – a house that honed the talents of the young Arturo Toscanini – and the glories of its famous cheese and ham at table as reasons not only to visit, but to return again and again. Even the air in Parma is lighter and less muggy in the summer than that in other cities near the Po. There are plenty of castles in the countryside, and opera lovers can trace the career of Giuseppe Verdi around his home town of Busseto.

The French daily *Le Monde* once rated Parma as the best Italian city to live in, for its prosperity and quality of life. It would, of course, since Parma is also the Italian city most influenced by French culture, thanks to a remarkable episode in the 18th century when the city filled up with Enlightenment French artists and *philosophes*, followed by a booster shot of Gallicism when it came under the rule of Napoleon's forsaken Empress, Marie-Louise. Quality of life Parma has in abundance. You'll eat well here, even by Emilia-Romagna standards, in Italy's first UNESCO Creative City of Gastronomy.

But there's more to Parma than food. It's the place to see the masterpieces of Benedetto Antelami (active 1177–1233), the great sculptor trained in Provence whose baptistry here introduced the Italians to the idea of a building as a unified work in its architecture and sculptural programme. Parma's distinctive school of art began relatively late, with the arrival of Antonio Allegri, called Correggio (1494–1534), whose highly personal and self-taught techniques of *sfumato* and sensuous subtlety deeply influenced his many followers, most notably Francesco Mazzola, better known as Parmigianino.

No town its size is more devoted to theatre and music, and none is more tolerant (or indifferent) to its perennially underachieving football team, a bottom-feeder that recently went bankrupt and has now fought its way back to Serie B. But just how French is Parma? You can mull that over while munching a crêpe, still a popular item in many Parma restaurants and street stands.

HISTORY

Parma is a fine example of how Italians have learned to adapt and even prosper in the face of continual political uncertainty. It started out as a small Roman colony on the Via Aemilia in 183BC, part of the great colonisation programme initiated after the Punic Wars; its name means 'shield'. Parma passed the Roman centuries as a fat and happy provincial town without distinguishing itself in any way.

Although it took some hard knocks from the invading Germans and Huns in the 5th century AD, it never was abandoned completely, unlike Modena. Under the short period of Byzantine rule that followed the Greek–Gothic Wars, Parma seems to have been the seat of the army treasury, and acquired the perhaps mocking nickname of Chrysopolis, the 'city of gold'. The Lombards and Franks kept it as an administrative centre, though throughout the Dark Ages the local bishops grew stronger; at some point, in the 11th century, they took control of the town's affairs.

By this time Parma, like most of its neighbours, was booming; a *comune* was established, the cathedral and the famous baptistry were begun, the walls were expanded, and the old cathedral school began developing into a university.

Parma played its role in the struggles against the Hohenstaufen; its men helped the Lombard League defeat Barbarossa at the Battle of Legnano in 1176, and in 1248 they dealt a crushing blow to Frederick II's hopes of subjugating northern Italy. The Emperor was besieging the city, and had vowed to raze it to the ground and move its people to a new town. Instead, the Parmigiani made a clever sortie while Frederick was off hunting, capturing his camp and forcing him to end the siege.

Through all this, the quarrels of pope and emperor were echoed internally by the factions of the Da Correggio and Rossi families, and the *popolo* began to assert itself. In 1250, when the Ghibelline exiles were allowed back into the city, they immediately began to plot against the *comune*. A tailor named Barisello, with 500 armed men, went to visit them all, and convinced them to behave. Barisello retained influence in the government for the next 14 years, much to the dismay of all the nobles of Emilia. Such an early outbreak of populism could not last, but under a noble *capitano del popolo* named Gilberto da Gente the commoners ran the town until 1259.

From then on, however, like its neighbours, Parma solved its addiction to factionalism by turning to boss rule. Various *signori* included Da Correggios and Rossis, and even a Della Scala from Verona. The Visconti of Milan grabbed Parma in 1346, followed in 1447 by the Sforza. Francesco Sforza's death in 1466 led to a bloody civil war, and Parma was in utter confusion for a century after; the Wars of Italy made things even worse, bringing numerous campaigns through the *contado* and almost two decades of French occupation. Yet all the troubles did not keep Parma from developing into one of the important artistic centres of the High Renaissance: San Giovanni Evangelista and the Steccata were built, and Correggio and Parmigianino were painting their most celebrated works.

THE FARNESE Parma's disarray made it an easy plum to pick for the mightiest grafter ever to sit on St Peter's throne. Alessandro Farnese, born in 1468, came from an obscure noble family north of Rome. His clerical career was made with the help of his sister Giulia (there's a nude statue of her on his tomb in St Peter's, now discreetly covered up); Alessandro set her up as mistress to the Borgia pope, Alexander VI, and soon he was collecting the revenues of no fewer than 16 absentee bishoprics, serious swag even by Renaissance standards.

When he became pope in 1534, as Paul III, he fostered learning, promoted church reform (though he also instituted the Papal Inquisition), cultivated the greatest artists of his generation, commissioning Michelangelo to paint the Sistine Chapel's *Last Judgement*, while always keeping one eye on the main business of building his family empire. The final settlement of the Wars of Italy, in which a system of Papal–Habsburg control was constructed across nearly all of the nation, gave him a chance to create a new duchy in Emilia, which in 1545 he bestowed upon his son Pier Luigi.

Pier Luigi's own ambitions, and the favour he showed towards the urban *comuni* of Parma and Piacenza, led shortly to his assassination, plotted by the Spanish King and Holy Roman Emperor Charles V and carried out by local aristocrats. His son

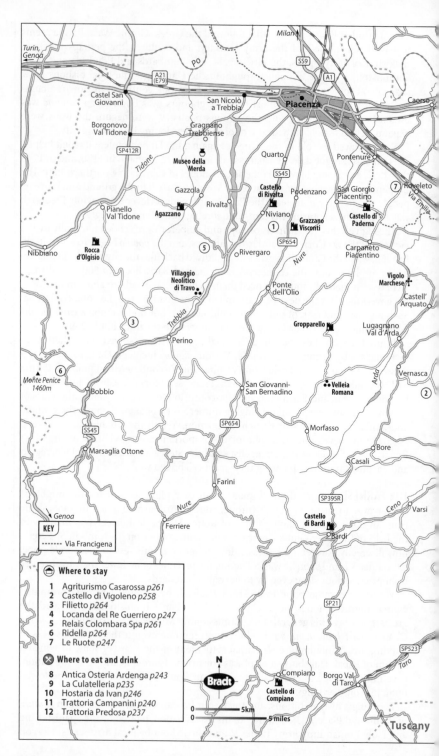

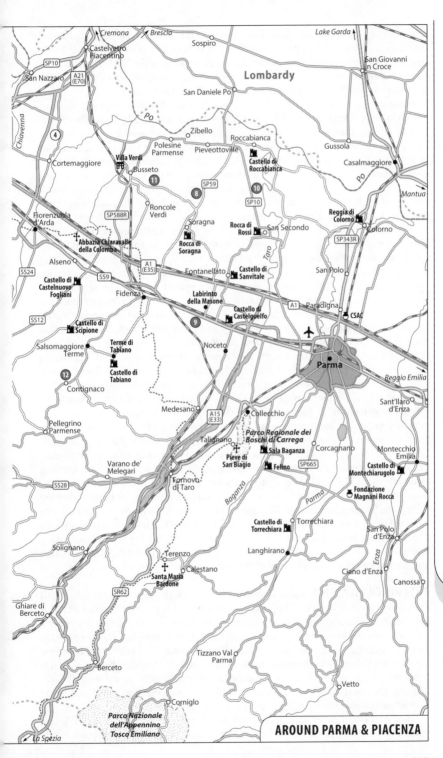

Cremona   Brescia
Castelvetro
Piacentino   Sospiro   Lake Garda
SP10   San Giovanni
in Croce
San Nazzaro   A21
(E70)   Lombardy
San Daniele Po
Po
Zibello   Roccabianca   Gussola
Polesine   Pieveottoville
Parmense   Castello di   Casalmaggiore
Cortemaggiore   Villa Verdi   Roccabianca
Busseto   11   Mantua
SP59   Reggia di
Fiorenzuola   SP588R   Roncole   8   10   Colorno   Colorno
d'Arda   Verdi   SP10   Rocca di   San Secondo   SP343R
Soragna   Rossi
Alseno   Abbazia Chiaravalle   Rocca di   San Polo
della Colomba   Soragna
SS24   A1   Fontanellato   Castello di
(E35)   Sanvitale   A1   Paradigna
Castello di   SS9   Labirinto   CSAC
Castelnuovo   Fidenza   della Masone
Fogliani   9   Castello di
SS12   Castello di   Castelguelfo
Scipione   Noceto
Salsomaggiore   Terme di   Parma
Terme   Tabiano   Reggio Emilia
12   Castello di
Contignaco   Tabiano   Sant'Ilaro
d'Enza
Medesano   Collecchio
Pellegrino   A15   Parco Regionale dei
Parmense   (E33)   Boschi di Carrega   Corcagnano   Montecchio
Talignano   Sala Baganza   Emilia
Varano de'   Pieve di   Felino   SP665   Castello di
Melegari   San Biagio   Montechiarugolo
SS28   Fornovo   Fondazione
di Taro   Baganza   Magnani Rocca
Parma
Solignano   Castello di   Torrechiara   San Polo
Torrechiara   d'Enza
Terenzo   Langhirano   Ciano d'Enza   Canossa
Santa Maria   Calestano
Bardone
Ghiare di   SR62
Bereto   Tizzano Val
Parma
Berceto   Vetto
Corniglio
Parco Nazionale
dell'Appennino   AROUND PARMA & PIACENZA
Tosca Emiliano
La Spezia

Ottavio, who ruled 1547–86, moved the capital from Piacenza to Parma and presided over a long period of prosperity and calm. The next in line, Alessandro, ruled only by correspondence, preferring to spend his time fighting in the Netherlands for the King of Spain (page 253); Parma did not seem to miss him, and the city might have been happier if it had never seen his successor, Ranuccio I, either.

Ranuccio (1592–1622) had one quality of the ideal Baroque prince, a sense of grandeur, expressed in the building of the ponderous new ducal palace, the Pilotta, and its famous theatre for elaborate court spectacles. Otherwise he was a morose, distrustful ruler, who executed more than a hundred people for a plot against him in 1612. Next came Odoardo (1622–46), who wished to emulate his grandfather, the great general Alessandro, but instead compromised the duchy's independence and nearly bankrupted it in a series of futile wars. Ranuccio II (1646–94) was a useful ruler who did his best to repair the damage, but the family that the papacy had built was now facing implacable papal enemies, out to steal their lands and titles.

The first were the Barberini, who started their own family empire when one of them became Urban VIII, and warred constantly against the Farnese in both Parma and Lazio during Odoardo's reign. Even worse was Innocent X, a pope as grasping as Paul III but without the talent and culture, who came from a rival Lazio family, the Pamphili. On a trivial pretext, he made war against the Farnese, seizing their southern Duchy of Castro in north Lazio and razing its capital to the ground.

Innocent also did his best to destroy the Duchy of Parma. Ranuccio held out, but his successor, Francesco Maria (1694–1727), found himself in such a weak position that he was eventually obliged to seek papal protection. His duchy, the second-smallest state in Italy after Lucca, had become an inconsequential Ruritanian backwater, ruled by dukes who have been described as 'tolerant more from laziness than virtue' and dominated by an equally decadent rent-collecting nobility. The city shared in the general collapse of the Italian economy after 1600, though the intensive agriculture of the countryside developed new techniques and was, like nearby Lombardy, able to remain one of the few relatively prosperous rural areas in Italy; Parmesan cheeses, exported since the Middle Ages, were still finding markets.

Like the Medici in Florence, the Farnese line sputtered to a pathetic end. Francesco Maria left no heirs, and the duchy passed to his useless glutton brother, Antonio (ruled 1727–31). After Antonio ate himself to death, Parma's fate was in the hands of the Great Powers, who were busily rearranging the map of Europe after the War of the Spanish Succession. They gave it to the talented but unemployed Charles of Bourbon, the son of Philip V of Spain and Elisabetta Farnese, niece of Francesco Maria. Charles became Carlo III of Naples, and he carted the Farnese's entire library and picture collection down south with him, along with all the furniture (though Parma and Piacenza did get many of the paintings back in the 1920s).

THE FRENCH INVASIONS Carlo III ruled Parma through a regent for 14 years until the powers reconsidered and bestowed the duchy on his younger brother Phillipe, Filippo to the Parmigiani. When Filippo got to Parma, he found that his brother had not even left him a bed to sleep on, so he sent off to Paris for a whole new kit. His wife, Babette (Louise-Elisabeth), daughter of Louis XV of France, sent home for Frenchmen to keep her company, and they came in such numbers that within a few years they made up an eighth of the population: artists, writers, architects, cooks, *philosophes*, court dandies, *gaveurs de volaille* (to make the foie gras) and, most importantly, the very useful Monsieur Guillaume du Tillot.

This gentleman, who had started out as a manservant to the King of Spain, became the duke's minister in 1759, and immediately began transforming the little

Duchy into the ideal Enlightenment state with Filippo's blessing. Du Tillot kicked out the Jesuits and appropriated their vast wealth, reduced the privileges of nobles and clergy, taxed church lands, put taxation on a more equitable basis, closed convents, reformed the university and started primary schools for the people. The French intellectuals, who enjoyed a greater freedom here than back in Paris, founded academies, museums and libraries, while the duke's favourite architect, Ennemond-Alexandre Petitot, transformed the face of the city. The new Accademia di Belle Arti, with its all-French staff, disseminated the works of Voltaire and Diderot in editions made by one of the great printers and type-designers of all time, Giovanbattista Bodoni. Parma had become one of the cultural capitals of Italy.

It was too good to last. Filippo died in 1765, leaving as successor a son, Ferdinando, who was weak, pious and entirely under the control of his wife, Maria Amalia, one of the great harridans of Italian history. Hysterically shrill, reactionary and ignorant, this daughter of Austrian Empress Maria Teresa devoted her life to small dogs, and to slandering du Tillot; in 1771 she finally succeeded in getting Ferdinando to dump him. The Jesuits came back, as did the Inquisition, and all the other reforms were undone. Most of the French went back home.

Many came back in 1796, only this time the invasion was led not by Enlightenment intellectuals, but by Napoleon's army. As long as the French were allied with Spain, the duchy remained under Spanish protection, and things continued unchanged.

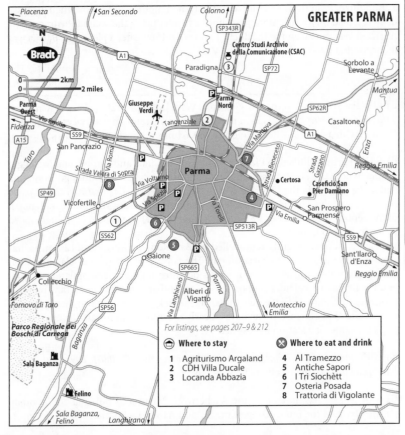

GREATER PARMA

For listings, see pages 207–9 & 212

Where to stay
1 Agriturismo Argaland
2 CDH Villa Ducale
3 Locanda Abbazia

Where to eat and drink
4 Al Tramezzo
5 Antiche Sapori
6 I Tri Siochètt
7 Osteria Posada
8 Trattoria di Vigolante

Napoleon passed through again to sort out Italian affairs in 1802, and this time the duchy was united with Tuscany in the 'Kingdom of Etruria'. While Napoleon squeezed the economy with heavy war taxes, he did give Parma a first-rate governor, Moreau de Saint-Méry. This man proved a second du Tillot, reorganising the laws and the government while promoting culture and trade. In 1814, as Napoleon fell, the allies installed another enlightened governor, this time an Italianised Irishman named Francesco Magawly-Cerati. The reforms of these two men lasted, and contributed much to the happiness of the Parmigiani in the decades to follow.

As in 1731, the Great Powers at the Congress of Vienna had determined to use the duchy to accommodate a notable in need of a throne. This time, however, the new ruler was to be no less a personage than Marie-Louise, Napoleon's second wife and late Empress of the French (see box, pages 220–1). Parma returned to its cosy Ruritanian life, and rather enjoyed being ruled by an attractive woman with a romantic past – at least until the Austrians, who pulled the strings, started forcing oppressive and unpopular policies on her. Parma became a stronghold of the secret patriotic society, the Carbonari, and Austrian troops had to put down a rebellion in 1831.

The Parmigiani let Marie-Louise live out the rest of her reign in peace. After her death in 1847, however, the duchy reverted to the Bourbons who had ruled it before the wars. The new duke, Carlo II, was a reactionary rotter, and the people of Parma forced him to flee a year later. He abdicated in favour of his son Carlo III, who was even worse; he was stabbed to death in 1854. The writing was on the wall; a child duke, Roberto I, and his well-intentioned mother and regent, the Duchesse de Berry, held on for five more years until a revolt during the second Piedmontese–Austrian War put an end to the duchy for ever. In 1860, after a plebiscite, Parma was incorporated into the Kingdom of Italy.

GETTING THERE AND AWAY

BY AIR Parma's small Aeroporto Giuseppe Verdi [map, page 205] (*Via dell'Aeroporto 44/a;* w *parma-airport.it*), is 5km northwest and currently has services to Trapani, Cagliari, Olbia and Chisinau, Moldova. Bus 6 links it hourly to the train station.

BY RAIL Parma is linked to Piacenza, Bologna, Modena and Rimini, and to Reggio Emilia, where the fast trains from Milan and Rome call. Other lines go to Brescia and to La Spezia on the Ligurian coast. The station [211 E1] (❧ *199 892 021 or 06 3000;* w *trenitalia.com*) is on Piazzale Alberto Dalla Chiesa, a 10-minute walk north of the centre (or take bus 1 or 8). Italo (w *italotreno.it*) runs buses to its high-speed trains in Reggio Emilia.

Parma's station, recently remodelled by Barcelona architect Oriol Bohigas, has already become a civic embarrassment. The good parts of the old classic station were gratuitously trashed. Now it works on three levels, for no apparent reason, and the lifts and escalators supposed to connect them seldom work. Take one that promises to bring you to the new subterranean ticket office, and you may end up in the middle of platform 4. If you have an early morning train to catch, scout out this dog's breakfast of a station in advance.

BY BUS Flixbus (w *flixbus.com*) and Baltour coaches (❧ *0861 199 1900;* w *en. baltour.it*) link Parma to other cities in Italy.

BY CAR Parma has an exit on the A1 between Milan and Bologna and another, Parma Ovest, at the intersection of the A1 and A15 to La Spezia.

GETTING AROUND

BY BUS Tep ($\searrow$ *840 222222*; **w** *tep.pr.it*) run the city and provincial buses, most departing from two separate locations on the bottom level of Bohigas's dopey train station, with no way of knowing which one to head for, and has a route-finder in English online. Tickets from the automatic machines (or *tabacchi*) are €1.20, or €2 if purchased on the bus. Prontobuses, for travel in Parma between 20.15 and 01.15, can be booked by ringing $\searrow$ 840 222223; tickets cost €2.50.

BY CAR The pedestrian zone (ZTL) stretches across both banks of the centre along Via Massimo D'Azeglio/Strada della Repubblica and north–south for two or three streets on either side of Strada Garibaldi, and is closed to traffic from 20.30 to 07.30. Parking in town can be a nightmare; there are eight free car parks (*parcheggi scambiatori*) at the main entrances to the city [map, page 205] with frequent buses into the centre (**w** *tep.pr.it*, *'Park and Ride'*). As an added bonus, the €2 bus ticket available in the car parks' machines is good for the entire day. Otherwise, your best bet is around the station or along the riverfront boulevards behind Palazzo della Pilotta, or in the underground car parks Parcheggio Toschi [210 D2] (*Viale Toschi 2*) near Piazza della Pace or Parcheggio Goito [210 D5] (*Via Goito*) to the south.

BY TAXI
🚕 **Radio Taxi** $\searrow$ 0521 252562

BY BIKE
🚲 **La Cicletteria** [210 D2] By the station; $\searrow$ 0521 281 979; **w** www.infomobility.pr.it. Hire a bike here for €1.50/hr, €12/day or €22/2 days.

Children's bikes, bike seats & helmets, & tandem & cargo bikes also available.

TOURIST INFORMATION AND TOUR OPERATORS

TOURIST OFFICE
ℹ️ **Piazza Garibaldi** [211 G7] In the Palazzo del Comune; $\searrow$ 0521 218889; **w** turismo.comune. parma.it. Offers an 'Unusual Parma' tour to otherwise inaccessible spots, with an aperitivo buffet (*€25*).

TOUR OPERATORS
Academia Barilla Barilla Center, Via Emilia Est; **w** academiabarilla.com. Offers cooking classes, & small group trips to local ham, cheese & wine producers, & tours of 'the world's biggest pasta factory'. **Food Valley** $\searrow$ 0521 798515; **w** foodvalleytravel. com. Company offering tours in & around Parma, on food, wine, art & culture, cars & outdoor activities.

🏠 WHERE TO STAY

Parma has a good range of hotels, many (not surprisingly!) with excellent restaurants. September is the busiest month, followed by July and August, and October for the Verdi festival, when booking is essential. In winter you can find real bargains.

UPMARKET
🏠 **Locanda Abbazia** [map, page 205] (10 rooms) Via Viazza di Paradigna; $\searrow$ 0521 604072; **w** locandaabbaziaparma.it. Sleep silently

in an evocative 14th-century monk's cell (they are quite spacious & come with Wi-Fi & all the mod cons), part of the CSAC (page 229). Guests can borrow bikes to make the 20min ride to Parma.

Free parking; on-site restaurant & bistro (€€€–€€€€); b/fast inc. €€€€

🏠 **Park Hotel Pacchiosi** [210 B4] (59 rooms) Strada del Quartiere 4; 📞0521 077077; w parkhotelpacchiosi.it. Built in the early 20th century, this 5-star hotel occupies a former clinic in a park on the west edge of town. Rooms have high ceilings & Carrara marble flooring & bathrooms, & sat TV with 80 films. There's also a 1st-floor piano bar, good restaurant (€€€€) with a huge wine list & underground parking. €€€€

🏠 **CDH Villa Ducale** [map, page 205] (113 rooms) Via del Popolo 35/a; 📞0521 272727; w villaducaleparma.it. 2km from the centre, an 18th-century villa that once belonged to Marie-Louise has been converted into a hotel (although only the beamed ceilings in a few bedrooms give away its age; other rooms are in the contemporary towers across the sail-topped courtyard). A quiet haven, rooms are well equipped; free parking, gym & a good restaurant (€€€€) are added bonuses. €€€–€€€€

🏠 **Sina Maria Luigia** [211 E2] (101 rooms) Viale Mentana 140; 📞0521 281032; w sinahotels. it. A large & luxurious palace in the centre, with a discreet air & choice of traditional or contemporary designer rooms – try to get 1 with a view over the *centro storico*. Its restaurant Maxim's (€€€€) is well known. €€€–€€€€

MID-RANGE

🏠 **Hotel Verdi** [210 B2] (20 rooms) Via Pasini 18 (facing the Parco Ducale); 📞0521 293539; w hotelverdi.it. Old-fashioned, refined & intimate hotel in an elegantly refurbished Liberty-style building, steeped in the well-being that the city is known for, complete with marble floors, Murano lamps & marble baths. Facilities include a garage (for small cars) & an excellent adjacent restaurant. €€€

🏠 **Mercure Parma Stendhal** [211 E3] (63 rooms) Via Bodoni 3; 📞0521 1480049; w accorhotels.com. Opposite the Piazza Pilotta, an older hotel now part of the French chain. Rooms have period furnishings, some with balconies. Garage. €€€

🏠 **NH Parma** [211 E1] (120 rooms) Viale Paolo Borsellino 31; 📞0521 792811; w nh-hotels.com. The city's newest hotel is 10mins' walk from the centre, all contemporary beige & grey, & fitted with all mod cons; fitness room; parking €10/night. Junior suites are good for families. B/fast inc. €€€

🏠 **Palazzo dalla Rosa Prati** [211 G6] (11 rooms) Strada al Duomo 7; 📞0521 386429; w palazzodallarosaprati.it. In the heart of Parma, the Palazzo offers cushy studios in a range of styles, from traditional to contemporary. B/fast inc. €€€

🏠 **Torino** [211 G6] (39 rooms) Borgo A Mazza 7; 📞0521 281046; w hotel-torino.it. Older hotel in the *centro storico* with ample, classic rooms & friendly staff. Kids under 8 stay free; garage at extra charge. B/fast in musical-themed b/fast room inc. €€€

BUDGET

🏠 **Astoria** [211 E2] (88 rooms) Via Trento 9; 📞0521 272717; w hotelastoriaparma.it. Near the station, 3-star hotel with comfortable, soundproofed rooms & a good b/fast buffet; residents can borrow bikes. €€–€€€

🏠 **Starhotels du Parc** [210 C2] (169 rooms) Viale Piacenza 12/c; 📞0521 292929; w starhotels. com. Jaunty blue hotel by the Parco Ducale. The public rooms are Liberty style & the quiet modern bedrooms have every mod con. €€–€€€

🏠 **Agriturismo Argaland** [map, page 205] (5 rooms) Strada Bergonzi, 10mins from the centre (take bus 6 to Baccanelli); m 346 012 6573; w argaland.net. Bright cheerful rooms with garden views & playground. Bike hire available; b/fast inc. €€

🏠 **Button** [211 G7] (40 rooms) Borgo Salina 7; 📞0521 208039; w hotelbutton.it. In the knot of streets behind the Duomo, & almost as cute as its name. Rooms are small but very comfortable; no restaurant but an excellent buffet b/fast. €€

🏠 **Violetta** [210 A2] (18 rooms) Viale Antonio Gramsci 37; 📞0521 983239; w hotelvioletta.it. No-frills choice west of the centre by the hospital; not all rooms are en suite, but all have Wi-Fi. €€

✖ WHERE TO EAT AND DRINK

Music and food are the Parmigiani's ruling passions; a perfect aria is greeted with the same rapt silence as a perfect dish of *anolini in brodo* or *tortelli di erbetta* (stuffed with ricotta and spinach), served with melted butter and grated Parmesan.

EXPENSIVE

✗ La Greppia [211 G5] Via Garibaldi 39; ☏0521 233686; w ristorantelagreppia.axeleroweb.it; ⊕ closed Wed. Housed in a former stable, La Greppia serves innovative cuisine, but based on local traditions. There's a delicious selection of *pasta di verdure* (made with spinach or tomatoes) & other original vegetable dishes. The *secondi* are works of art, including seafood, vegetarian & gluten-free choices. €€€€€

✗ Parizzi [211 F4] Via Repubblica 71; ☏0521 285952; w ristoranteparizzi.it; ⊕ closed all day Mon, Sun eve. A swanky place, Michelin-starred since 1980. Marco Parizzi comes from a long line of chefs & wins awards for his contemporary takes on Parma's classics. For a real blowout, get 5 friends together for a chef's table: cooking lesson, a full *menu degustazione* & 5 bottles of wine for €1,000. They also have several suites. €€€€€

ABOVE AVERAGE

✗ Al Tramezzo [map, page 205] Via del Bono 5 (just east of the centre; take bus 3 or 4 to Rocca San Lazzaro); ☏0521 487906; w altramezzo. it; ⊕ closed Sun. A wine bar that has evolved to become a top seafood restaurant, although not one for big appetites. Dishes are playfully presented, sometimes with Lego blocks. €€€€

✗ Angiol d'Or [211 G6] Vicolo Scutellari 1; ☏0521 282632; w angioldor.it; ⊕ closed Mon. Lovely place to sit out on a summer's evening while contemplating the Baptistry over a plate of *tortellini di zucca*, rigatoni with baby spinach, prosciutto & pine nuts, or lamb cutlets with a confit of courgettes with mint. Good desserts, too. €€€€

✗ Antiche Sapori [map, page 205] Strada Montanara 318, Gaione; ☏0521 648165; w trattoria-antichisapori.com; ⊕ closed Tue. The locals make a special trip south of town to this old-fashioned trattoria with a summer garden & cuisine with a difference: the chefs are Italian & Japanese. The menu changes with the seasons: look for some more unusual dishes such as caramelised aubergine with Parmesan cream & tomato sorbet, or *corzetti* (stamped pasta discs from Liguria) served with pesto. €€€€

✗ Cocchi [210 A3] Via Gramsci 16; ☏0521 981990; w ristorantecocchi.it; ⊕ closed Sat. In business since 1925, Old World elegant but not fussy, dedicated to bringing out the finest in

Parma's fine ingredients: *culatello di Zibello* with light pillowy *torta fritta*, *strolghino*, sliced beef (*tagliata*), various *bolliti*, delicately stewed *baccalà*, stuffed veal, & old-fashioned homemade vanilla ice cream. €€€€

✗ Leon d'Or [211 E2] Viale Antonio Fratti 4; ☏0521 773182; w leondoroparma.com; ⊕ closed Aug. Generations have been coming to this hotel restaurant since 1917 (now run by the great-granddaughter of the founder) to feast on generous portions of pumpkin & chestnut *torrelli* & choose dishes from the trolleys that take up half the dining room: *salumi*, vegetables, boiled & roast meats (with their sauces) & desserts. €€€€

✗ Sorelle Picchi [211 G7] Strada Farini 27/a; ☏0521 233528; w trattoriasorellepicchi.com. Welcoming place with tables outside, in the restaurant or down in the *cantina*. Besides all the classic *salumi*, it specialises in steaks, including Black Angus from the USA & Australia. Try the Rosa di Parma (fillet of beef stuffed with prosciutto & Parmigiano Reggiano). €€€€

✗ Trattoria Il Cortile [210 C4] Borgo Paglia 3; ☏0521 285779; w trattoriailcortile.com; ⊕ Closed Sun & Mon lunch. Stylish & intimate, located in a covered interior courtyard of a former post-house, Il Cortile serves a delicious mix of traditional & modern dishes – excellent homemade ravioli, sea bass baked in salt, mushrooms & truffles in season & a temptation-laden dessert trolley. It also does a special (& really good) gluten-free menu. Good wine cellar. €€€€

MODERATE

✗ Borgo 20 [211 G6] Borgo XX Marzo; ☏0521 234565; w borgo20.it; ⊕ closed Sun–Mon. A rare contemporary bistro in a city not overly fond of change, where Parma's exquisite ingredients are transformed sometimes in unexpected ways. Several vegetarian choices & gourmet pizzas, too. €€€

✗ I Tri Siochètt [map, page 205] Strada Farnese 74; ☏0521 968870; w itrisiochett.it; ⊕ closed Sun eve. Southwest of the centre (take bus 1), this osteria has a lovely summer veranda where reservations are essential for delicious food that won't break the bank. Dishes feature plenty of vegetables (relatively rare here); there are also traditional *secondi* such as *vecchia alla parmigiana* (vegetables & potatoes with minced horse-meat). €€€

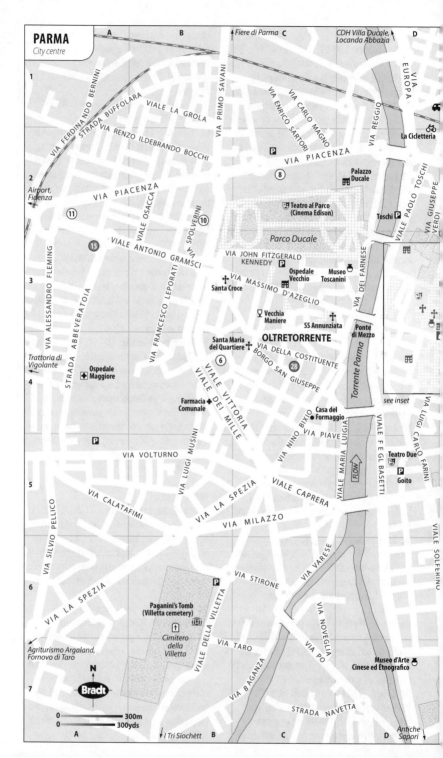

PARMA
City centre

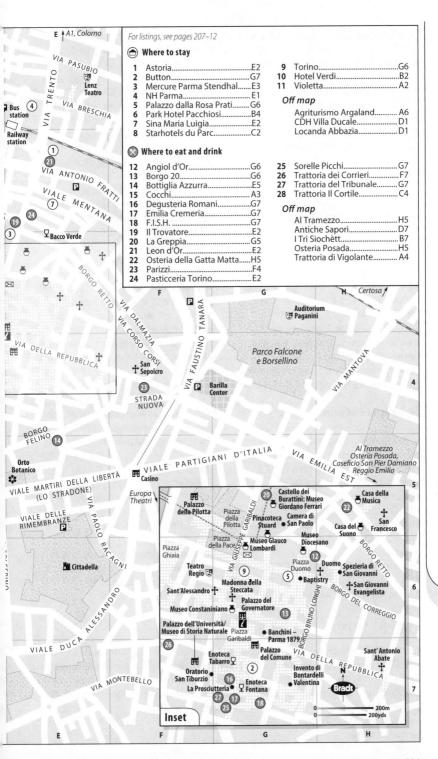

E ↑ A1, Colorno

VIA PASUBIO

VIA TRENTO

Lenz Teatro

VIA BRESCHIA

Bus station

Railway station

VIA ANTONIO FRATTI

VIALE MENTANA

Bacco Verde

BORGO RETTO

VIA DALMAZIA

VIA CORSO CORSI

VIA DELLA REPUBBLICA

San Sepolcro

VIA FAUSTINO TANARA

Barilla Center

STRADA NUOVA

Auditorium Paganini

Certosa

Parco Falcone e Borsellino

VIA MANTOVA

BORGO FELINO

Orto Botanico

VIALE MARTIRI DELLA LIBERTÀ (LO STRADONE)

VIALE DELLE RIMEMBRANZE

VIA PAOLO RACAGNI

Cittadella

VIA DUCA ALESSANDRO

VIA MONTEBELLO

VIALE PARTIGIANI D'ITALIA

VIA EMILIA EST

Al Tramezzo Osteria Posada, Caseficio San Pier Damiano Reggio Emilia

Casino

Europa Theatri

Palazzo della Pilotta

Piazza della Pilotta

VIA GIUSEPPE GARIBALDI

Castello dei Burattini: Museo Giordano Ferrari

Casa della Musica

Pinacoteca Stuard

Camera di San Paolo

Casa del Suono

San Francesco

Piazza della Pace

Museo Glauco Lombardi

Museo Diocesano

Piazza Ghiaia

Teatro Regio

Madonna della Steccata

Piazza Duomo

Duomo

Spezieria di San Giovanni

BORGO RETTO

Sant'Alessandro

Baptistry

San Giovanni Evangelista

BORGO DEL CORREGGIO

Museo Constaniniano

Palazzo del Governatore

Palazzo dell'Università/ Museo di Storia Naturale

Piazza Garibaldi

Banchini – Parma 1879

BORGO BRUNO LONGHI

Enoteca Tabarro

Palazzo del Comune

VIA DELLA REPUBBLICA

Sant'Antonio Abate

Oratorio San Tiburzio

La Prosciutteria

Enoteca Fontana

Invento di Bontardelli Valentina

Bradt

Inset

0 200m
0 200yds

For listings, see pages 207–12

Where to stay

1	Astoria	E2
2	Button	G7
3	Mercure Parma Stendhal	E3
4	NH Parma	E1
5	Palazzo dalla Rosa Prati	G6
6	Park Hotel Pacchiosi	B4
7	Sina Maria Luigia	E2
8	Starhotels du Parc	C2
9	Torino	G6
10	Hotel Verdi	B2
11	Violetta	A2

Off map

Agriturismo Argaland	A6
CDH Villa Ducale	D1
Locanda Abbazia	D1

Where to eat and drink

12	Angiol d'Or	G6
13	Borgo 20	G6
14	Bottiglia Azzurra	E5
15	Cocchi	A3
16	Degusteria Romani	G7
17	Emilia Cremeria	G7
18	F.I.S.H.	G7
19	Il Trovatore	E2
20	La Greppia	G5
21	Leon d'Or	E2
22	Osteria della Gatta Matta	H5
23	Parizzi	F4
24	Pasticceria Torino	E2
25	Sorelle Picchi	G7
26	Trattoria dei Corrieri	F7
27	Trattoria del Tribunale	G7
28	Trattoria Il Cortile	C4

Off map

Al Tramezzo	H5
Antiche Sapori	D7
I Tri Siochèt	B7
Osteria Posada	H5
Trattoria di Vigolante	A4

7

Il Trovatore [211 E2] Via Ireneo Affò 2/a; ✆0521 236905; ⊙ closed Sun. Near the station with outdoor tables, serving the classics along with options such as venison or swordfish; the complimentary glass of Prosecco on arrival gets things off to a good start. Homemade breads, biscuits & pastries. €€€

Osteria della Gatta Matta [211 H5] Borgo degli Studi 9; ✆0521 231475; w osteriagattamatta.com; ⊙ closed Mon. The food is made with lovely care at the 'Crazy Cat Inn', where the menu changes every 2 months, & often has an exotic touch – lamb chops with melted aubergines & couscous, or chocolate *millefoglia* with a namelaka of passion fruit. €€€

CHEAP & CHEERFUL

Bottiglia Azzurra [211 E5] Borgo Felino 63; ✆0521 285842; ☐; ⊙ noon–14.30 Mon, Tue & Thu, noon–14.30 & 18.00–01.00 Wed & Fri, 18.00–01.00 Sat. This popular enoteca & restaurant draws a young crowd to its long, narrow dining rooms crammed with tables. Good food on a menu that changes every week, a wide choice of Italian & French cheeses, & a big wine list. €€

Trattoria dei Corrieri [211 F7] Strada del Conservatorio 1; ✆0521 234426; w trattoriacorrieri.it. Since 1800, this place with red chequered tablecloths & traditional Parma cuisine at very reasonable prices is served in an old postal relay station near the university, where the walls are a veritable museum of old Parma photos & relics. Summer dining under a pretty grape arbour. Great *salume* with a *torta fritta* & tortelli filled with artichokes or *culatello* & tiramisu. €€

Trattoria del Tribunale [211 G7] Vicolo Politi 5/a; ✆0521 285527; w trattoriadeltribunale. it. In the heart of the historic centre, next to the

Tribunale (Court House), this family-run trattoria is a time capsule, down to its wooden chairs & starched white tablecloths. €€

Trattoria di Vigolante [map, page 205] Via Valera di Sopra 112; ✆0521 671143; ⊙ closed Mon & Tue. Old-school trattoria on the western outskirts, with a panelled interior, funky art on the walls & tables under a leafy pergola; try the *savarin di riso*. €€

F.I.S.H. [211 G7] Strada Ferdinando Maestri; ✆0521 230810; w loveitalianfish.it; ⊙ closed Sun. As in 'Fresh Italian Sea Harvest', a lifesaver for when you can't face another plate of prosciutto. It does excellent cooked & raw seafood panini as well as platters of raw fish, fry-ups & salads. €–€€

ROCK BOTTOM

Degusteria Romani [211 G7] Borgo Palmia 2; ✆0521 229816; w silvanoromaniparma.it; ⊙ closed Sun. *Salume* specialist Silvano Romani runs this informal restaurant where folks queue up for Parma 'street food' with everything from panini to platters of cheeses & ham, salads, craft beers & Prosecco. €

Osteria Posada [map, page 205] Via Mantova 72A (take bus 21); ✆0521 244302; ☐; ⊙ closed Sat–Sun lunch. Northeast of the centre, famous for excellent pizza by the metre & a menu with pasta & steaks. €

CAFÉS & *GELATERIE*

Emilia Cremeria [211 G7] Via Farini 28; ✆0521 207316; w cremeriaemilia.com. Best for creamy homemade *gelato*; other goodies too. €

Pasticceria Torino [211 E2] Strada Garibaldi 61; ✆0521 235 689; ☐ PasticceriaTorinoParma; ⊙ closed Mon. Parma's landmark pastry shop bakes all kinds of goodies & cakes; great for b/fast. €

ENTERTAINMENT AND NIGHTLIFE

Opera mobilises a more enthusiastic local audience here than just about anywhere in Italy, for regular performances in the Teatro Regio and for the glamorous Verdi Festival in Parma and Busseto (page 50), with the Arturo Toscanini International Conducting Competition following fast on its heels in late October. Parma is also home to the Emilia-Romagna Regional Orchestra and the Filarmonica Toscanini, founded in 2002; Teatri di Parma's website (w *teatridiparma.it*) lists upcoming performances.

BARS

The before- & after-dinner scene heats up along the Via Farini strip.

♀ Bacco Verde [211 E3] Via Cavallotti 33; ☎0521 230487; **f**; ⏰ 20.00–00.30. Warm & welcoming under brick vaults, the perfect place to while away an evening sipping from a long list of wines & beers & nibbling inexpensive takes on Parma classics.

♀ Enoteca Fontana [211 G7] Via Farini 24a; ☎0521 286037; ⏰ closed Sun & Mon. Popular – you can't miss it, with tables spilling out over the pavement. Although wine is the main focus, there's a good selection of grilled panini & charcuterie to make up a light meal around a bottle.

♀ Enoteca Tabarro [211 G7] Via Farina 5/b; ☎0521 200223; **w** tabarro.net. Lively wine bar with al fresco tables (or large wine barrels) along the street.

♀ T Café [211 G6] In the Palazzo dalla Rosa Prati Hotel (page 208); ⏰ closed Sun. Slick contemporary café where the cool kids hang out near the Duomo, especially for *apero* & nibbles. Try a drink Marie-Louise would have loved: a violet spritz (*crème de violette* liqueur & Prosecco).

♀ Vecchia Maniere [210 C3] Borgo Bernabei 40/a; **m** 338 312 6467; **w** birreriavecchiemaniere. it; ⏰ 18.30–01.00 Mon–Thu, 18.30–02.00 Fri– Sat. Friendly bar specialising in craft beers from around Italy, with a dozen on tap; also a vast choice of panini & other snacks.

CINEMA

🎬 Cinema Edison [210 C2] Parco Ducale, Largo VIII Marzo; ☎0521 964803; **w** solaresdellearti. it. Also run by the Solares Foundation (see *Teatro al Parco*), the Cinema Edison puts on foreign & art films.

THEATRE & OPERA

🎭 Auditorium Paganini [211 G3] Via Toscana 5/A; ☎0521 707715; **w** teatroregioparma.org. Striking glass-walled venue designed by Renzo Piano in an abandoned sugar factory.

🎭 Europa Teatri [211 F5] Via Oradour 14; ☎0521 243377; **w** europateatri.it. Experimental performances & cabaret.

🎭 Lenz Teatro [211 E1] Via Pasubio 3/E; ☎0521 270141; **w** lenzfondazione.it. A former industrial space converted into the seat of the Fondazione Lenz experimental company.

🎭 Teatro al Parco [210 C2] Parco Ducale, Largo VIII Marzo; ☎0521 992044 (theatre); **w** solaresdellearti.it. The Parco Ducale is the venue of the Teatro delle Briciole (Theatre of the Crumbs) founded in 1976, and which is a leader in children's theatre. Run by the Solares Foundation.

🎭 Teatro Due [210 D5] Viale Basetti 12/A; ☎0521 230242; **w** teatrodue.org. Contemporary theatre & dance.

🎭 Teatro Regio [211 F6] Via Garibaldi 16; ☎0521 039399; **w** teatroregioparma.org; box office ⏰ 10.00–14.00 & 17.00–19.00 Tue–Sat. Parma's temple of opera (page 218); the season runs Dec–Mar.

SHOPPING

Parma's shops are concentrated around Via Farini and Strada della Repubblica. The latter extends, a 10-minute walk from Piazza Garibaldi, to the **Barilla Center** [211 G4] (*Via Emilia Est*; ☎ *0521 247825*; **w** *barillacenter.it*; ⏰ *09.30–20.30 Mon– Sat, 10.00–20.00 Sun*), the former Barilla pasta factory, converted by Renzo Piano into a shopping mall and entertainment complex. Bargain-hunting fashionistas won't want to miss the factory outlets of **Fidenza village** (page 235).

ANTIQUES

Antiques & vintage shops line Via Nazario Sauro & surrounding lanes.

Invento di Bontardelli Valentina [211 G7] Via N Sauro 14. Cool vintage shop selling everything from 1950s robots to old petrol station signs.
Mercanteinfiera **w** mercanteinfiera.it. Reputedly the world's largest antiques fair comes

to Parma in spring & autumn. Also, see box, page 52.
Mercatino dell'Antiquariato Fontanellato. Huge market on the 3rd Sun of every month (exc Jan).
Piazza Ghiaia [211 F6] Home to a vintage fair on Tue (⏰ *09.00–19.00, Jul–Aug 18.00–23.30*).
Strada Matteo Renato Imbriani [210 C3] There's an antiques market along here every Thu (⏰ *08.00–17.00*).

FOOD & DRINK

Pick up goodies to take home, along with clothes & trinkets, at **Piazza Ghiaia/Piazza della Pace** [211 F6] (⏱ *07.00–14.00 Wed & Sat*). The Saturday **Farmers' Market** (⏱ *08.00–noon*) along Strada Matteo Renato Imbriani near the church of Santissima Annunziata is a gluttonous orgy of local products.

Banchini – Parma 1879 [211 G6] Piazza Cesare Battisti 9; **m** 349 178 6643; **w** cioccolatobanchini. it. The local masters of all things rich, luscious & chocolate; they also scoop out some superb chocolate *gelato*.

Casa del Formaggio [210 C4] Via Nino Bixio 106; ☎ 0521 230243; **w** lacasadelformaggio.it. Not only cheese, but *salumi*, fresh pasta, wines & a range of gastronomic goodies.

Caseficio San Pier Damiano [map, page 205] Strada Gazzano 35/A, Prospero; ☎ 0521 645181; **w** sanpierdamiani.com. 8km east of Parma, this dairy makes superb Parmigiano. Besides a factory shop, it offers tastings & tours; sign up online.

La Prosciutteria [211 G7] Via Farina 9/c; ☎ 0521 234 188; **w** silvanoromaniparma.it. *Prosciutti per tutti!* Also all types of *salumi*, fresh cheeses & other delights.

OTHER PRACTICALITIES

HOSPITAL
✚ **Ospedale Maggiore** [210 A4] Strada Abbeveratoia; ☎ 0521 231111

PHARMACY
✚ **Farmacia Comunale** [210 B4] Viale dei Mille 52; ☎ 0521 253 181; ⏱ 24hrs daily

POST OFFICE
✉ [211 G6] Via Pisacane Carlo 1; ⏱ 08.30–13.30 Mon–Fri, 08.30–12.30 Sat

WHAT TO SEE AND DO

PALAZZO DELLA PILOTTA [211 F5] (*Piazza della Pilotta 5;* ☎ *0521 233718;* **w** *pilotta. beniculturali.it;* ⏱ *08.30–19.00 Tue–Sat, 08.30–14.00 Sun, 13.30–19.00 1st Sun of month; adults €10, ages 18–25 €5, free 1st Sun of month*) Arriving by train or bus in Parma, one of the first buildings you notice is also, unfortunately, the most pathetic: the ungainly, never-completed and, since 1944, bomb-mutilated Palazzo della Pilotta, built for the Farnese. Begun in 1602 by the gloomy Duke Ranuccio, it was named after *pelote*, a ball game once played in its courtyard. Big as it is, it seems the Pilotta was never intended as a residence, but only to house the dukes' officials, soldiers and horses. Yet looks are deceiving – for within this patched-together shell, half of it reconstructed since the war, are Parma's greatest treasures: its archaeology museum, the Teatro Farnese, the Galleria Nazionale and the Biblioteca Palatina.

Museo Archeologico Nazionale The first-floor Museo Archeologico Nazionale was founded in 1760 during the rule of du Tillot and containing finds from the excavations at Roman Velleia and elsewhere. The single most important exhibit is the Tabula Alimentaria, a large bronze tablet that records the contributions of private citizens to a special dole. The story is an example of the Roman world at its best in the enlightened days of Emperor Trajan: the fund was established to provide relief for small farmers who were being pushed out of business by the large estates; the tablet also mentions how the government was attempting to encourage them to diversify into other crops, such as vines. When the Tabula was discovered in 1747, the local priest had it broken into pieces to sell it as scrap; an educated nobleman saved it from the forge at the last minute. Also here are Egyptian sarcophagi, Greek vases from Etruscan tombs at Vulci in Lazio, and 12 statues of the imperial family including one of Nero as a boy. Exhibits detail Emilia's prehistory, which is pretty dull except for the accomplished and mysterious Terramare culture, covered here in great detail.

Teatro Farnese To reach the Galleria Nazionale you first pass through the Teatro Farnese, built in a hurry in 1618–19 by Palladio's pupil Giambattista Aleotti to honour a planned visit of Duke Cosimo II de' Medici of Florence, who was on his way to Milan to visit the tomb of St Charles Borromeo. Aleotti even built a special booth for the duke (the original royal box, that would be much copied in subsequent theatres), but Cosimo never sat in it; he fell ill and never showed up. So the theatre had to wait another decade before its proper inauguration at the wedding, in 1628, of Margherita de' Medici and Duke Odoardo, with a performance of *Mercurio e Marte*, complete with music by Monteverdi and a *naumachia* (see box, page 216).

Unfortunately, Aleotti built the theatre of wood, for economy and acoustics, and covered it with plaster to resemble marble, and an incendiary bomb burned most of it down in 1944.

The Italians have a succinct proverbial rule to describe their feelings about their damaged monuments: *dov'era, com'era* – they like things where they were and as they were. So the Parmigiani have painstakingly reconstructed the theatre, according to the original plans and using the original methods and fragments of the original materials wherever possible. Almost all of the painted and sculptural decoration was lost, but there's an impressive proscenium flanked by statues of Alessandro and Ottavio Farnese which boasts a florid inscription honouring Ranuccio, Duke of Parma and Castro, dedicating the theatre (oddly) to 'Bellona [the goddess of war] and the Muses'. Today the theatre now hosts more performances than it ever did during ducal times, especially during the Verdi Festival (page 50).

Galleria Nazionale Although Carlo III hauled much of the Farnese collection off to Naples in 1734, his brother Filippo created the seeds of this collection in 1752 with the foundation of the Accademia Parmense di Belli Arti. This was far more than just a museum: part school, part meeting-place for intellectuals, in imitation of the Academy in Paris. Even today it plays a major role in the city's cultural life.

Among the earliest works are sculptures by Benedetto Antelami and some excellent paintings: panels showing *Male and Female Saints* by Puccio di Simone (active 1320–53) and a *Dormitio Mariae* of Niccolò di Pietro Gerini (d1415). The Early Renaissance collection features Tuscans Agnolo Gaddi, Spinello Aretino, Giovanni di Paolo, Starnina and Fra Angelico, and the Emilians Simone de' Crocifissi and Jacopo Loschi (whose charming *St Jerome* holds a toddler of a lion paternally by the paw). Loschi (d1503) was top dog in the Parma quattrocento, and you can compare his approach with that of younger painters such as Cristoforo Caselli and Filippo Mazzola who ran off to Lombardy or Venice just to escape his influence.

There are surprising works from the Cretan-Venetian painters of this era, Orthodox Greeks working in a half-Byzantine, half-Italian style, including an anonymous *Pietà* and a *Madonna* by Andrea Rico of Candia (Heraklion). Further on is the *Guarnigione del Cieco* (*Healing of the Blind Man*) from the greatest figure to come out of this exotic world, El Greco.

The star of the collection is the lovely portrait sketch of a young woman by Leonardo, *La Scapigliata* (she of the dishevelled hair). Also of note are four paintings by Cima da Conegliano, a *Madonna* by Fra Angelico, works by Bronzino and Giulio Romano, and a portrait by Sebastiano del Piombo of the handsome,

All the effort of the reconstruction of the Teatro Farnese was devoted to rebuilding a theatre that had been used exactly eight times, one that is totally impractical for either drama or music. Indeed, impracticality seems here to be refined into a divine principle; originally there was a line of statues around the rail, effectively blocking the view from the best seats. Today such a theatre, with its vast U-shaped gallery, would be fit for nothing but a political party convention, but its purpose was something we can scarcely imagine today: the Baroque court spectacle. Using themes from mythology or medieval romance, the new art of opera was combined with musical *intermezzi*, dance, equestrian shows, masques and elaborate allegorical tableaux involving sumptuous props designed by the court artists. Stage machinery created spectacular effects: monsters rose from the sea, gods descended from above, clouds rolled in to cover a change of scene.

With a modicum of Italian exaggeration, the Teatro Farnese has been called the 'first modern theatre'. Unlike his master Palladio's famous Teatro Olimpico in Vicenza, which had a fixed set of a Renaissance street scene, Giambattista Aleotti created a living theatre, with an empty stage where sets could be rearranged for each spectacle (something already being done on a much smaller scale in London's Globe Theatre, and in Spain). The huge space between the stage and the U of seats, the *platea*, was designed for the horses, for dancing and for mobile tableaux on floats. It could even be flooded by subterranean pumps for mock naval battles, *naumachia*, which became popular in the Renaissance after people read in Vitruvius how they were enjoyed by the ancient Romans.

While trying to imagine all this, consider also that the tremendous wood backdrop of columns and arches was originally covered with stucco and painted. Stage and forecourt would be illuminated by thousands of candles or oil lamps, while Jove and the Olympian gods looked down from the heavens painted on the ceiling.

Such Baroque spectacles, invented here and perfected at Louis XIV's Versailles, were the most expensive entertainments between ancient Rome and the Hollywood of D W Griffith and Cecil B de Mille. Understandably, even a duke could afford only to mount one for a very special occasion: the visit of a king or emperor, or a wedding, such as that of Elisabetta Farnese and Philip V of Spain in 1714. By 1732, when the last spectacle was presented, such colossal undertakings were already out of fashion. Afterwards, the theatre stood forlorn and forgotten.

---

foolish Medici pope *Clement VII*. Local talent of the late Renaissance is represented by Gerolamo Bedoli, Guercino, all the Carracci, Dosso Dossi, Giovanni Battista Tiuti and Bartolomeo Schedoni (d1615), the court painter to Ranuccio I, whose striking use of colour and contrast shows up in his *Last Supper* and the dreamlike *Le Marie al Sepolcro*.

Then there are Parma's own, Correggio and Parmigianino. Correggio weighs in with the *Madonna della Scodella* (1530), a seminal work for the simple humanity expressed in its portrayal of the Holy Family at rest during the return from Egypt, a *Lamentation over the Dead Christ* (1525) and the *Madonna di San Gerolamo* (1523), a *sacra conversazione* with the most unlikely grouping of the Virgin, St Jerome

above	Frescoes fill the dome of Parma's Baptistry, one of medieval Italy's marvels (SS) pages 223–4
right	The springtime enchantment of the early Renaissance lives on in Ferrara's Palazzo Schifanoia (SS) pages 285–7
below	Western Christian art was born in 5th-century Ravenna, in mosaics like these in Sant'Apollinare Nuovo (RoS/S) pages 312 & 319

left — Rimini's Arch of Augustus, the oldest triumphal arch in Italy, marked the end of the Roman Via Aemilia (AC/S) pages 370–2

below — Age-old bridges cross the Apennine rivers, like the 15th-century 'donkey-back' Ponte Alidosi in Castel del Rio (GWTW/S) page 333

bottom left — In the heart of Ferrara, the Castello Estense was the seat of the fabulous, art-loving Este dynasty (p/S) pages 278–9

bottom right — Towering over the Po marshlands, the campanile of the great medieval Abbey of Pomposa (CZ/S) pages 297–9

right	Modena's majestic 12th-century cathedral, a treasure trove of medieval sculpture (KG/S) pages 152–5
below	Parma, the city with a French flair, even boasts a mini-Versailles, the Reggia di Colorno (i/S) pages 229–30
bottom left	Parma's magnificent Romanesque Baptistry is the city's symbol (B/S) pages 223–4
bottom right	Avant-garde architecture and high-speed rail: Reggio Emilia's AV Mediopadana station, designed by Santiago Calatrava (fdm/S) page 193

above left Faenza — the town that gave the world 'faience' in the 1470s — still boasts some 60 active ceramic makers (CZ/S) pages 334–7

above right Hand-printed cloth, a 17th-century art, is still produced in Santarcangelo today (CdC) pages 383–5

below left The king of cheeses, Parmigiano Reggiano, is so valuable that regional banks accept it as collateral (ERTB) page 243

below right Parma hams aging in Langhirano, the capital of prosciutto (AP/S) page 232

above   The cinema of Fellini's childhood fantasies in Rimini has recently been restored to its Art Deco glory
(CdR) page 374

right   Italy's 'Motor Valley' around Modena and Bologna turns out some of the world's most desirable dream machines
(CF/S) pages 129, 131–2 & 170

below   Emilia-Romagna's festivals are among the most colourful in Italy; some date back to the Middle Ages
(R/S) pages 47–51 & 277

above The Parco Regionale del Corno alle Scale is a popular spot for biking, hiking and skiing in the Apennines (r/S) pages 142–3

left One of Italy's most prolific wine regions, Emilia-Romagna produces reds and whites in equal measure, along with its famous Lambrusco (ERTB) pages 44–5

below The Rocca di Bismantova, singular landmark of the central Apennines (GM/S) pages 198–9

above   One of the largest dams in Italy holds back the turquoise waters of the Lago di Ridracoli in the Casentinesi Forest National Park (N/S) page 348

right   The Apennines are high enough to provide a great day out on the slopes in winter (AZ/S) pages 54–5

above   The Porto Canale in Cesenatico, a town famous for the brightly coloured boats of its fishing fleet (AD/S) pages 379–80

left   A *trabocco*, a traditional fishing platform on the Adriatic (e/S)

below   Sunrise at Rimini (ERTB) pages 356–82

and Mary Magdalene (what could those three have been conversing about?). Parmigianino's contributions are the striking *Mystic Marriage of St Catherine* and the flirtatious *Turkish Slave*.

Among the non-Italian pictures are works by Brueghel the Younger, Van Dyck, and one of Holbein's famous portraits of the sharp-featured *Erasmus*. A Frenchman, Giovanni Sons, uses the story of *Adam and Eve* as an excuse for six wonderful Edenic landscapes with a cast of characters that includes Adam's pet cat, an ostrich, a unicorn and one of the first turkeys to appear in European art. From the Italian seicento, there are huge mythological canvases of Sebastiano Ricci, including a *Rape of Helen* that spent a couple of centuries entertaining the nurses of Parma's Foundlings' Hospital. From the next century, there's Canaletto's curious *Capriccio with Palladian Buildings* (1759), a dream vision of Venice with Palladio's losing design for the Rialto Bridge in place, framed by two of his famous buildings in Vincenza, the Basilica and Palazzo Chiericati.

Then there are gigantic black marble classical statues of *Hercules* and *Bacchus Embraced by a Faun* looted by the Farnese from the Caesars' palace on the Palatine while Paul III was pope. Besides various portraits and sculptures of the Farnese, Bourbons and Marie-Louise (including Canova's enthroned version of the empress as the Roman goddess Concordia, commissioned by Napoleon), there is the complete collection of the Academy's prize paintings. For over a century a prestigious annual competition was held here, and the winning entries offer a lesson in what passed for taste in the late Baroque; few of the winners were ever heard from again, though the 1771 prize went to a young fellow from Spain named Goya.

To show how the Baroque sensibility lingered into Napoleonic times, there is the impressive bronze and marble *Trionfo da Tavola* of 1803. Allegorical 'triumphs' made of crystal, sugar or even butter, were once the rage at dinner parties. This one, made for the Spanish ambassador to Rome, covered with allegorical knick-knacks on the Triumph of Time is one of the few anywhere to survive intact.

The last couple of centuries get a look in, too, with 19th-century paintings, views and prints of Parma by various artists, the *Three Sisters* triptych by Amedeo Bocchi of Parma (1883–1976) and a lively beach scene, *La Spiaggia* (1956) by Renato Guttuso: see if you can find Picasso among the bathers.

Biblioteca Palatina ✆ 0521 220 4419; w *bibliotecapalatina.beniculturali.it*; ⊕ 08.15–19.15 *Mon–Thu, 08.15–13.45 Fri–Sat; for Jul–Aug see website*) This library was founded in 1761 after Carlo III took the great Farnese library to Naples along with the rest of the art and furniture. It became one of Europe's first great public libraries and contains some 700,000 volumes, including incunabula, codices and manuscripts, in Neoclassical halls designed by Ennemond Petitot; like the rest of the palace, it suffered greatly from the bombings in 1944. A bust of Marie-Louise by Canova smiles benignly across the reading room.

Museo Bodoniano ✆*0521 220441;* w *museobodoni.beniculturali.it;* ⊕ *09.00–13.00 Mon–Fri by appointment only, 09.00–13.00 Sat without appointment; admission free*) A must for fans of fonts, this little museum in the Biblioteca is devoted to Giambattista Bodoni, Parma's great 18th-century printer and type designer, with examples of his work, his presses and tools, and exhibits on bookmaking and typography.

AROUND PIAZZA DELLA PILOTTA
Piazza della Pace [211 G6] Once a car park, the Palazzo della Pilotta's square was redesigned by Mario Botta into a people park, with a grassy meadow, fountain, trees

and two striking monuments: a Liberty-style **Monument to Giuseppe Verdi** (1913) by Ettore Ximenes, showing the maestro in a toga enthroned and surrounded by characters from his operas; and the vigorous cinematic **Monumento al Partigiano**, designed by the 'painter of the Resistance' Renato Mazzacurati.

Teatro Regio [211 F8] (*Entrance in Via Garibaldi;* \ *0521 039399;* w *teatroregioparma.org; guided tours* ⊕ *Sep–Jun 10.00–13.00 & 15.00–17.30 Tue–Wed, from 09.00 Thu–Sat, also 2 weeks (Mon–Fri) in Jul; €5)* Built by Marie-Louise (see box, pages 220–1) in 1829, this Neoclassical pile is one of operatic Italy's holy-of-holies, its ornate interior illuminated by a giant French chandelier. Audiences are legendarily contentious and demanding, and each year tenors and sopranos from all over the world submit either to avalanches of flowers or catcalls from the upper balconies, the *loggioni*. Toscanini began his career here playing in the orchestra, which has been renamed in his honour.

Madonna della Steccata [211 G6] (*Piazza della Steccata 9;* \ *0521 234937;* ⊕ *07.30–noon & 15.00–18.30)* Across from the Regio, the church of Madonna della Steccata stands on the site of a miracle-working image of John the Baptist painted on a wall. So many people pressed in to see it in the 1300s that a wooden fence (*steccata*) had to be built to protect it. Eventually a small oratory covered the site, to be replaced in 1521 by the present church.

It is sometimes claimed the Steccata was built according to Bramante's original design for St Peter's. Don't believe it, but its massive, Greek-cross plan does sum up one of the architectural ideas that were in the air in the High Renaissance. Various local architects worked on it over the years – the final exterior decorations were not added until 1697, and the choir in 1730 – but one great one, Antonio da Sangallo the Younger, suggested the design for the dome while passing through Parma in 1521. Having so many cooks didn't spoil this dish; despite its great bulk, and lack of a proper piazza to show it off, the church has great dignity and presence.

The chapels in its sumptuous interior are covered with 16th-century frescoes by many of the same artists who worked on the Duomo and San Giovanni: Mazzola, Bedoli and Gatti. As the city's fashionable church, the Steccata also became the shrine of its rulers. Marie-Louise's consort Count Neipperg is buried here, and the crypt is full of Farnese and Bourbons.

For all the art in this church, the most compelling attraction is the frescoed arch leading to the sanctuary. Parmigianino had painted here early in his career (some of the work on the big organ doors is his), but he was a changed man after his sojourn in Rome among the works of Michelangelo and Raphael; and these hyper-elegant Mannerist frescoes of the *Wise and Foolish Virgins*, pictured with Adam and Eve, Aaron and Moses, are his finest work in his home city. Parmigianino never finished all the painting he promised to do here, and the church canons briefly had him jailed for breach of contract – gossips said the artist's obsession with his alchemical experiments was taking up all his time.

Museo Constantiniano [211 G6] (*Piazza Steccata;* \ *0521 282854;* w *museocostantinianodellasteccata.it;* ⊕ *Sep–Jun 09.30–noon & 15.30–18.00 Mon–Fri, 15.30–18.00 Sat–Sun, Jul–Aug 09.30–noon Mon–Fri; €5, under 18s free)* The Stecccata is owned and run to this day by the Sacred Military Constantinian Order of St George, a hereditary order founded in the 1500s. After 1699 it was led by the Farnese and their heirs, the Bourbons, although they've been quarrelling over who is top dog since 1734, when Carlo III took the grand magistry with him to Naples along with all the furniture and art, which wasn't fair play according to the Parma Bourbons. It's all a bit confusing, and most of the paintings have since gone to the Galleria Nazionale, but there are some curiosities here, including the shirt Louis XVI wore at the guillotine.

Sant'Alessandro [211 G6] (*Vicolo Sant' Alessandro 1;* \ *0521 231169;* ⊕ *Jun–Oct 09.30–noon & 15.00–17.00 daily*) The Steccata completely overshadows this church of 1527 right across the street, but behind a Neoclassical façade added in the 1780s it's another colourful marble-laden treasure-house of Parma painting, performed by the city's usual late Renaissance cast of characters, including Gerolamo Bedoli Mazzola and Alessandro Mazzola. Later came Alessandro Tiarini, who frescoed the dome and pendentives (1627).

Museo Glauco Lombardi [211 G6] (*Via Garibaldi 15;* \ *0521 233727;* w *museolombardi.it;* ⊕ *09.30–16.00 Tue–Sat, 09.30–19.00 Sun (09.30–13.30 in Jul–Aug); €5, under 14s free*) The Palazzo della Riserva, just north of the Steccata, is a graceful Baroque palace that covers an entire block, with enough room for the post office, shops, and several cultural institutions including this museum.

The 'Riserva', as its name implies, was the spare palace of the duchy, used for guests. Part of this 'Casino of Nobles, Courtiers and Foreigners' was revamped by Petitot, including the severe façade of the section that holds this museum. Scholar Glauco Lombardi assembled this collection of art and objects relating to the time of the Bourbons, the Napoleonic era and the reign of Marie-Louise. Most visitors to Parma don't find the time for it, which is a pity; few museums anywhere are so successful in summoning up the spirit of a distant age.

And it was a strangely attractive age, at least seen from tranquil, refined Parma. The main room of the museum is the gorgeous Grande Sala delle Feste, designed by Petitot in pastel blue with great chandeliers. Paintings by Nattier, Fragonard and Mignard (*Portrait of Mme Sevigné*), and portraits of Marie-Louise, Napoleon and their child, the 'King of Rome', adorn the walls. There is bric-a-brac aplenty, from Marie-Louise's sewing kit and her dresses to the golden, very French Empire Corbeille de Mariage, a wedding present from Boney. Letters to the Duchess from various Bonapartes and celebrities of the day are placed in glass cases – most touchingly, in excruciatingly correct French schoolboy handwriting, from her son in Vienna, and from her nephew who would one day be Napoleon III.

Most surprising of all are the drawings of Ennemond Petitot; this seemingly dry classical architect was never given a chance to follow his fancy, but he left plans for bizarre buildings, such as a water tower shaped like an American skyscraper, and incredible designs for masquerade costumes and festival decorations that juggle the ancient Greek with the Aztec and Egyptian.

Camera di San Paolo (Camera di Correggio) [211 G5] (*Via Melloni 3/A;* \ *0521 533221;* ⊕ *08.30–14.00 (last entrance 13.30) Tue–Sat & 1st Sun of month; €2*) These two little rooms are one of the most remarkable sights in Parma. In the 1510s San Paolo's worldly abbess, Giovanna Piacenza, rebuilt the convent and hired Alessandro Araldi and Correggio to fresco its refectory and an adjoining chamber. The abbess was the centre of a learned circle of humanists; whatever they were up to may have worried the Church, for Giovanna had a long battle with the popes to avoid the cloistering of her convent. Finally, in 1524 the pope had his way and the nuns were shut in, one small, early step in the slow strangulation of Italy's

7

After a visit to the Museo Glauco Lombardi, you might suspect that Glauco Lombardi intended this museum as something of a shrine to Parma's great lady – the Parmigiani were always fond of her, even though they once chased her out of town. Maria-Luisa Leopoldina Franziska Theresia Josepha Luzia von Habsburg-Lothringen was born in 1791 at the imperial court in Vienna. A shy, introverted girl with a certain talent for art (some of her sketches and watercolours of romantic landscapes are in the museum), this emperor's daughter grew up well aware that her life would be determined according to the purposes of the dynasty.

She did not, however, imagine that she would be offered up as a sacrifice to someone her people saw as the Ogre of Europe, especially after what had happened in France to her Aunt Marie-Antoinette. In 1809, Napoleon was starting to be concerned with his succession. He did love Josephine, as much as he was capable of loving anyone, but she was never able to come up with an heir. Napoleon knew it wasn't his fault – there were already two tots crawling around the apartments of his mistresses – and he decided suddenly on a divorce. Josephine found out when she returned home one day to find that the door between their rooms had been walled up.

The logical place to look for a wife was the Habsburg court in Vienna; such a match would cement France's alliance with her most important potential rival. Count von Metternich, the Austrian foreign minister who had first suggested the idea, talked Napoleon into accepting it by pointing out it would give defeated Austria time to recover her strength, and before long the 18-year-old Marie-Louise found herself on a coach bound for France. They were married in a civil ceremony at St Cloud on April Fool's Day, 1810, and did it all over again for the priest the next day in the Tuileries.

intellectual life by the Counter-Reformation Church. No-one but the sisters saw the frescoes again until Napoleon suppressed the convent in 1810.

Refectory In 1519 Correggio had just returned from Rome, and the abbess's commission was his first chance to practise his mature style in Parma; he turned the ceiling of the refectory into a delightful arbour, with the philosophical scheme of Giovanna's devising limited to the edges. Most attempts to interpret its meaning have concluded that the theme is the 'conquest of moral virtue'. Correggio portrayed the abbess herself (some say) as the goddess Diana over the fireplace, with the enigmatic inscription *Ignem Gladio ne Fodias*, 'Do not use the sword to poke the fire'.

The rest of the scheme involves 16 putti set over lunettes of mythological emblems, painted in elegant chiaroscuro that gives them the illusion of depth. The cycle was probably meant to be read from the entrance door, beginning with the god Pan, making a great noise on a conch shell to create 'panic' (as he did at the battle of the Olympians and Titans); this is followed by allegorical figures representing perhaps Integrity and Chastity.

Next, over the fireplace wall, come the goddess Fortune, Minerva (or Bellona), the Three Graces and Adonis (or Virtue). On the next wall, the four elements, water, earth, air and fire, are represented respectively by an obscure figure called the Bonus Eventus or Genius of the City of Rome, Tellus or Africa, Juno and Vesta. Opposite the fireplace is a Philosopher, or maybe the god Saturn, then the Temple of Jupiter, the spinning Fates and Rhea Silvia (mother of Romulus and Remus),

Marie-Louise found she was pregnant three months later. Life as Empress of France proved pleasant enough, especially since her husband was hardly ever at home. Napoleon's charms were lost on her (once from a battlefield he had written a one-line letter to Josephine: 'I arrive in Paris in three weeks. Don't wash', an approach unlikely to make a favourable impression on a Habsburg princess). They last saw each other, briefly, while the allied armies were closing in on Paris in 1814. She refused to follow him to Elba, and after he threatened to have her abducted she stopped answering his letters, leaving diplomats with the delicate problem of what to do with her. The vacant Duchy of Parma proved a perfect choice; she moved in with her new lover, the Austrian General Count Neipperg, and made him prime minister. He did an excellent job, and the Parmigiani were quite content until his death in 1829.

After that, however, Metternich – who by now was making all the big decisions in Europe – decided the duchy needed a less tolerant ruler. He forced one of his minions, Josef von Werklein, on Marie-Louise as the new prime minister, and Werklein proved such a good Austrian that Parma rebelled two years later. Marie-Louise was forced to flee to the protection of the garrison at Piacenza. The troops there soon had her back on her throne, but from then on it was only as a figurehead.

The great tragedy of Marie-Louise's life was her son Napoleon-François, the 'King of Rome', now reduced to a mere Duke of Reichstadt. In 1814 she had allowed Metternich to talk her into bringing the three-year-old child to Vienna. For reasons of state, the boy had to be watched closely; the Napoleonic partisans in France were already referring to him as 'Napoleon II'. The Austrians never let him go; Metternich kept him in Vienna as a virtual prisoner. In his teens he contracted tuberculosis, and Marie-Louise was able to visit him only once, just before his death in 1832.

or else Ino and Bacchus. Returning to the beginning, the cycle is closed with the goddess Ceres, or perhaps Diana.

Much of the charm of Correggio's ceiling comes from the putti themselves, bearing attributes of Diana's hunt and pictured behind what seem to be windows into the heavens. But the putti are part of the allegorical scheme. Each is a playful comment on the figure below it: above Pan, a putto blows into another shell while a second one puts its fingers in its ears. Some are more obscure; scholars have been arguing about them, as they have about everything else here, for two centuries.

Chamber Correggio gets all the attention, but this second room frescoed in 1514 by Alessandro Araldi is quite its equal in singularity. Here too the subtle abbess dictated the scheme, believed to represent the 'conquest of spiritual virtue', with scenes on the lunettes around the cornice complemented by Biblical and mythological vignettes set in the beautiful blue decoration of the ceiling. The inscription over the fireplace may give a key: *Transimus per Ignem et Aquem ei eduxisti nos in refrigerium*, 'We passed through fire and water, and you led us to a cool place.'

Whatever sort of mysticism inspired this, it does seem that Abbess Giovanna imagined it with a decidedly feminist slant. In the main series, the first scene, *Roman Charity*, records the legend of a daughter who saved her father by nursing him. Next comes a *Burning Triumph*, from the Roman story of Paulus Emilius, whose sons all died on the same day, and then the *Lady and the Unicorn* and *Judith and Holofernes*. On the next wall, three lunettes tell the classical story of *Cleobi* and *Bitone*, sons of a priestess, who pulled the cart of Juno to the temple when the sacred oxen died, and were rewarded with eternal life. The third wall begins with a pair of feet walking on water, said to be an ancient Egyptian symbol for the impossible, followed by two scenes of women sacrificing. The triumph of virtue on the last wall is represented by the goddess Ceres, a woman killing an ape, and another dispatching a dragon.

Castello dei Burattini: Museo Giordano Ferrari [211 G5] (*Via Melloni, next to the Camera di San Paolo;* ☎ *0521 031631;* w *castellodeiburattini.it;* ⊕ *10.00–17.00 Mon, Wed–Fri, 10.30–18.30 Sat–Sun; admission free*) Part of the San Paolo convent is now home to this museum, workshop and theatre of puppetry, the biggest in Italy they say. The collection is the legacy of Giordano Ferrari and the four generations of puppet masters in his family. The puppets (*burattini*) and marionettes on display are fabulous and funny; they represent the northern, Neapolitan and Sicilian traditions, and others from around Europe and beyond. Keep an eye out for their shows: these take place on an irregular schedule, but always at 16.30.

Pinacoteca Stuard [211 G5] (*Borgo del Parmigianino 2;* ☎ *0521 508184;* ⊕ *as for the Castello dei Burattini*) This eclectic collection, the bequest of collector Giuseppe Stuard (1790–1834), offers a good selection from the Florentine and Sienese trecento, including a luminescent, recently restored *Lament over the Dead Christ* by Niccolò di Tommaso. From the Renaissance and beyond there are works by Uccello, Guercino, Jan Brueghel, Schedoni, Sebastiano Ricci, Lavinia Fontana and interesting but little-known 19th-century painters from Parma, such as Edoardo Raimondi.

PIAZZA DUOMO AND AROUND Strada Pisacane connects the Piazza della Pace to the Piazza Duomo, the strangely quiet sacred zone of an otherwise lively city. Why the odd location? In many old Italian cities (eg: Pisa, Florence, Naples) the first cathedrals in late Roman and early medieval times appeared not in the city centre, but out by the walls where the first Christian communities lived. Parma is one of these – in fact Parma's plan has changed hardly at all since the Romans built it.

Duomo [211 H6] (☎ *0521 235886;* w *piazzaduomoparma.com;* ⊕ *10.00–19.00 daily; multimedia smart guide to the cathedral, baptistry & Museo Diocesano €2*) The wide **façade** of the Duomo is all angular Romanesque, completed in 1178. Three tiers of shallow loggias create an illusion of depth around the central arched window; the pattern continues in the rich decoration of the sides, apses and dome. The **central portal**, with a pair of lions added in 1281, has reliefs of the *Labours of the Months* starting with March (in much of medieval Italy, the New Year came in with the Annunciation, at the spring equinox). The Gothic **campanile**, completed in the late 1200s, is surmounted by a copy of a gilded statue of the Archangel Raphael.

Interior Come on a sunny morning to get the full effect of one of the most ambitiously decorated cathedrals in Italy. Frescoes completely coat the tall nave, a collaborative effort painted between 1555 and 1574 by local Mannerists Lattanzio Gambara, Alessandro Mazzola, Gerolamo Bedoli Mazzola, Bernardo Gatti and Orazio Samacchini. They've fitted in most of the Bible, arranged according to the doctrine of typology; each scene from the Gospels, on the upper band, is accompanied below by the Old Testament event that somehow prefigures it.

The fresco everyone comes to see, however, is in the **dome**. Correggio's *Assumption* (1526–30) was celebrated from the moment it was revealed for its almost three-dimensional clouds, angels and saints, with masses of pink virtuous flesh getting vacuumed up into heaven. One of the first and greatest of illusionistic dome frescoes, anticipating the Baroque, it had an important influence on artists for the next two centuries – even though the Parmigiani gave it such a poor reception (one contemporary called it 'a hash of frogs' legs') that Correggio left town in disgust.

Don't let this pastel ocean of fresco keep you from noticing the cathedral's other attractions: the medieval **capitals**, some by Benedetto Antelami and his men, are excellent. Some of the best are up in the **matroneum**, the women's gallery (see page 207 for visits); an odd one portrays a *School for Wolves*. All were originally painted in bright colours. The cathedral's surviving medieval frescoes include some excellent work from a local mid-quattrocento artist named Bartolino de' Grossi and his workshop, especially the *Life of St Sebastian* in the **Cappella del Comune** and other saints' lives in the **Cappella Valeri**.

In the choir is something no Emilian cathedral can do without, an extravagant set of **intarsia choir stalls**, these made by Cristoforo da Lendinara in 1473. Nearby, under a rich Renaissance ciborium, is a **bishops' chair** sculpted by Antelami (1196) with stories of St Paul and St George. It sits under a fresco of the *Last Judgement* by Gerolamo Bedoli Mazzola, where Jesus and the cross looming out with 3D effect come uncomfortably close to the Dalí kitsch barrier. There is more Antelami in the north transept, a superb signed relief of the *Deposition from the Cross* (1178).

Baptistry [211 G6] (*Piazza Duomo;* ☎ *0521 235886;* ⊕ *Mar–Oct 10.00–18.30 daily, Nov–Feb 10.00–16.30 daily; admission inc Museo Diocesano €8; tickets are sold in the gift shop that adjoins the cathedral façade*) This octagonal Baptistry, one of the jewels of Italian Romanesque, is Parma's symbol, as much as Pisa's leaning tower. Constructed of pale rose-coloured marble from Verona, it was designed in 1196 by Benedetto Antelami, who also carved the remarkable ribbon **frieze** of animals and allegories that encircles the building. The meaning behind all the winged cats, archers, griffins and sea serpents is as elusive as that of San Paolo's ceiling (page 220); many are repeated in mirror images elsewhere in the frieze.

Antelami is also responsible for the two great doorways, the **Portale della Vergine** (north door) with reliefs of the Three Kings, the baptism of Christ, Herod's banquet (with the devil himself present, behind Salome) and the decapitation of John the Baptist; and the **Portale del Giudizio** (west door), an ambitious scene that includes the 12 Apostles, the separation of the saved and damned souls, and on the door jambs the *Six Ages of Man* and the *Parable of the Vineyard*.

The remarkable **south door**, a later work, illustrates an episode from the *Legend of Barlaam*, originally a Buddhist story from India that became popular in late

7

WHY ARE ITALIAN BAPTISTRIES NEARLY ALWAYS OCTAGONAL?

To mystics, this geometric form is said to represent the 'marriage of the earthly and the spiritual', though it may be simply a matter of tradition, following the original free-standing baptistry that Emperor Constantine built at St John Lateran in Rome. A better question would be how baptistries became an architectural genre of their own in the early Middle Ages; Parma's joins those of Florence, Pisa and Ravenna as the most glorious examples of their kind. Antelami planned it with a decorative scheme worthy of a cathedral, a *summa theologica* representing everything on heaven and earth.

Roman and medieval Europe. The scene represents a moral fable originally told by the Buddha himself; the Tree of Life appears, with two mice, one black and one white (representing night and day) gnawing at its root. The man in the tree was attracted by the honey in the beehive there (sin), but awoke the sleeping dragon (the devil), which consumes him in its fire.

Interior   Each wall of the interior is doubled to create a 16-sided space, and each is almost entirely covered with paintings in one of the most complete ensembles of Italian medieval art. The vault is divided into six distinct zones, with a starry heaven, *Christ in Glory*, flanked by the *Virgin and John the Baptist,* and in the lower two zones the *Life of St John the Evangelist* and the *Life of Abraham,* with the *Four Elements,* the *Four Seasons* and the *Four Rivers of Eden.*

Below there's a tremendous grab-bag of saints and Biblical figures painted in the 14th and 15th centuries. You might pick out two musicians: David with his harp, and St Genesius (a Roman actor who converted and was martyred) playing the violin. The fresco of the two dragon-killers, *St Michael and St George,* has been attributed by some to Buffalmacco, the Tuscan painter who may have painted the great, lost *Triumph of Death* in Pisa's Campo Santo. Also inside are Antelami's famous **reliefs** of the *Twelve Months,* with the labours and zodiacal signs, and the *Seasons,* of which only Spring and Winter survive.

Museo Diocesano [211 G6] (*Piazza Duomo, entrance on Vicolo del Vescovado;* ☉ *Mar–Oct 10.00–18.30 daily, Nov–Feb 10.00–16.30 daily*) Located in the basement of the 11th–12th century Bishop's Palace, the Museo Diocesano houses Roman mosaics discovered in 1955 in the piazza, where they formed the pavement of Parma's first Christian basilica, capitals from a cathedral that burned in the 10th century, the original statue of the Angel Raphael from the campanile, and Antelami's beautiful statues of *Michael* and *Gabriel, David* and *Habbakuk, Solomon* and the *Queen of Sheba* that once stood in the niches outside the Baptistry.

San Giovanni Evangelista [211 H6] (*Piazzale San Giovanni;* ☏ *0521 235311; church* ☉ *08.30–11.45 & 15.00–18.30 daily; monastery* ☉ *09.00–11.45 & 15.00– 17.00 Mon–Wed, Fri–Sat*) Behind its Baroque façade, San Giovanni Evangelista (1607) shelters one of the masterpieces of the High Renaissance, Correggio's *Vision of St John on Patmos* in the dome. This is one of the most carefully planned ceiling frescoes ever. Start from the door, and see how the composition gradually reveals itself as you walk down the nave.

Unfortunately, when the church was remodelled in 1587 Correggio's reputation was at a low point and all of his other decorations were lost, although a fresco of *St John Writing Down His Vision* survives over the door north of the altar. Other frescoes here are early works of Parmigianino: figures of saints on the first, second and fourth chapels on the left. And there's another remarkable intarsia choir.

The **monastery** of San Giovanni has roots going back to the 10th century, and it has three stately cloisters, two from the Renaissance. There are more frescoes by Correggio in the chapter-house and a beautiful 16th-century library with frescoes.

Spezieria di San Giovanni [211 H6] (*Borgo Pipa 1A;* ☏ *0521 233309;* ☉ *08.30– 14.00 Tue–Sat, 08.30–13.30 1st Sun of month; €2*) Herbs and medicines were always a Benedictine speciality. This pharmacy was in operation from 1298 to 1881, then sat untouched until the 1950s, when its grand Renaissance-Baroque interior was restored. It's a fascinating place, with paintings of the great doctors of antiquity,

both real and mythological: Mercury and Apollo, Galen and Hippocrates, Averroes and Avicenna. There are herbals and alembics, 16th-century carved wood cabinets and medieval pharmaceutical instruments. An altar in the back room with a 16th-century Venetian painting was for prayers to help the cures along.

San Francesco [211 H5] (*Piazzale San Francesco*) North of the cathedral complex, this is one of the finest examples of the Emilian approach to Gothic, built entirely in brick (1240–50). The church has taken some hard knocks, especially during the Napoleonic occupation, when it was used as a prison. The interior was once covered with 14th- and 15th-century frescoes; now only a few fragments remain.

Casa della Musica [211 H5] (*Piazzale San Francesco 1;* \ *0521 031170;* w *lacasadellamusica.it*) In the 15th-century Palazzo Cusani, the House of Music contains an auditorium, musical library, the archives of the Teatro Regio and the **Museo dell'Opera** (w *www.operamuseo.parma.it;* ⊕ *10.00–18.00 Wed–Sun; admission free*) dedicated to the history of opera in Parma from 1628, from the first performance in the Teatro Farnese down through the centuries, including audiovisuals on the history of music and two rooms on the city's love affair with Verdi.

Casa del Suono [211 H5] (*Piazzale Salvo D'Acquisto;* \ *0521 031103;* w *casadelsuono.it;* ⊕ *10.00–18.00 Wed–Sun; admission free*) The Casa della Musica also runs the little 'House of Sound' in the nearby church of Santa Elisabetta (1674). Along with a small collection dedicated to the history of recording and broadcasting, there are novelties: the White Room, installed with the latest in Wave Field Synthesis where you can literally feel the music; and the 224-speaker Sonic Chandelier, suspended from the dome.

PARMA'S SOUTH
Piazza Garibaldi In company with the other old gents of Parma, Garibaldi and Correggio (or at least their statues) spend their day in Piazza Garibaldi. Rare among ancient cities, Parma's main square covers almost exactly the ground of the Roman-era forum – unchanged for more than 2,000 years. Via Mazzini/Via della Repubblica, which passes through the square, is the old Via Aemilia, running as inflexibly straight a course through Parma as it did when the Romans laid it out.

Instead of temples and basilicas, the square is dominated by the yellow **Palazzo del Governatore** [211 G6], with its intricate sundials telling not only the day and the time of sunrise, but when noon comes in places from Quebec to Constantinople. The façade, along with the piazza, was redesigned by Ennemond Petitot in 1759 to update the ancient space. On the east end stands the **Palazzo del Comune** [211 G7] (\ *0521 40521;* w *comune.parma.it;* ⊕ *8.30–13.00 Mon–Fri*), a contemporary of the Palazzo della Pilotta and built in 1623 in the same blank, gloomy late Farnese manner.

Palazzo dell'Università [211 F7] (*Via dell'Università 12*) Parma's university is one of Italy's oldest, growing out of a cathedral school of the 11th century. This building, however, was a Jesuit college built in 1654, and given to the university only after the Jesuits were kicked out in 1768. An indignant plaque on the entrance records how the building was taken over as a prison and torture centre by the Fascist militias near the end of the war.

Inside is the **Museo di Storia Naturale** (\ *0521 903407;* w *musei.unipr.it;* ⊕ *16.00–18.00 Mon & Thu; admission free*) an old-fashioned natural history collection founded in 1766 by the court ornithologist. It houses mostly African plants and zoological trophies, collected in the 1880s and 90s by Vittorio Bottego of Parma (whose bronze statue stands in front of the train station) while the Italians were out empire-building in the Horn of Africa. A second section of the museum is located in the Orto Botanico (see below).

Oratorio San Tiburzio [211 F7] (*Cnr Vicolo San Tiburzio & Borgo Palmia;* ⊕ *only during special events*)
Built in 1723 over a Paleochristian church that was in turn built over a temple of Mars, this late Baroque jewel box in the Roman manner once served as the university chapel, before it was deconsecrated and abandoned for 50 years before its recent restoration.

Lo Stradone
Now the traffic-clogged Viale Martiri della Libertà, this street gives no indication that it was one of Italy's first proper boulevards. After the city's walls were demolished, Petitot laid out this stretch as the Stradone in the 1760s, lined with horse chestnut trees and marble benches, a place for the gentry to parade in their carriages following the fashion of Paris. To close the view at the end, he built the Neoclassical **Casino** [211 F5] as a café for the elite (*casino,* or 'little house', incidentally, did not imply gambling until the green tables were set up in Venice in the late 18th century).

Orto Botanico [211 E5] (*Strada Farini 90;* ✆ *0521 903433;* w *musei.unipr.it;* ⊕ *09.00–13.00 & 14.30–17.00 (summer until 18.00) Mon–Thu, 09.00–13.00 Fri; admission free*)
The university's botanical garden is a little green oasis founded in 1770 by botany professor Gianbattista Guatteri, with greenhouses added in 1793 by Petitot. It contains some 2,000 species, including succulents, carnivorous plants and the famous Parma violets (see box, opposite). It also houses the **Natural History Museum**'s collection of butterflies, local vertebrates and fossils.

Cittadella [211 E6] (*Viale delle Rimembranze;* ⊕ *Apr–Oct 07.00–21.00 daily, Nov–Mar 07.00–20.00 daily*)
South of the Stradone, the Cittadella was Alessandro Farnese's only gift to Parma. The absentee soldier-duke (see box, page 253) may never have cared to reside in his duchy, but he did spend much time and care on the planning of this fortress, a prototype of the sprawling, low forts of the Baroque era, designed to withstand artillery. This 11ha one, which had a twin in Antwerp, Belgium, was roughly the size of Parma's city centre, but Alessandro for all his planning must have missed something, for the Cittadella was never attacked without falling almost immediately. Nearly all of it, except the impressive monumental gateway (1596), has been demolished and converted into a city park.

Museo d'Arte Cinese ed Etnografico [210 D7] (*Viale San Martino 8;* ✆ *0521 257337;* w *museocineseparma.org;* ⊕ *09.00–14.00 Tue–Sat; donations*)
There are some very beautiful pieces in this collection of Chinese art collected by missionaries, along with ethnographic items from China, the Amazon and Africa.

EAST OF PIAZZA GARIBALDI
Sant'Antonio Abate [211 H7] (*Via della Repubblica 52;* ✆ *0521 233801;* ⊕ *09.00–noon & 16.00–18.00 daily*)
This eccentric church begun in 1712 is one of the most striking Baroque works in the region, designed by Ferdinando Bibiena, greatest of the famous Bolognese family of theatre architects and stage designers (his *scena per angolo* opera sets inspired Piranesi's *Carceri*). While designing operas

for Ranuccio II, he found time to give this church its unusual cross vaulting and false ceiling, set with windows to expose the heavenly scenes frescoed on the real ceiling. Nearby **San Sepolcro** [211 F4] (*Via della Repubblica 76;* ⊕ *same hrs*) was an honest Gothic church bushwhacked by the Baroque, with a bizarre slightly tilting campanile and a beautiful carved wood ceiling from the 1600s.

Certosa [map, page 205] (*Strada della Certosa 29;* ⊕ *09.00–noon & 14.00–16.00 Mon–Fri, 09.00–noon Sat; admission free*) Stendhal aficionados will be glad to know that there really is a Charterhouse of Parma although it bears no resemblance to the novelist's invention in atmosphere, architecture or history. Located 4km east of town off Via Mantova (bus 21), it was founded in 1225 but totally rebuilt in the 1600s. It now serves as a prison police school, and only the cloister is open for visits.

L'OLTRATORRENTE: PARMA'S WEST END From Piazza Ghiaia, the **Ponte di Mezzo** [210 D3] crosses the Torrente Parma to the west end. This is the most recent incarnation of the Roman bridge; if you take the underground passage near the Piazza Ghiaia market, you'll see some arches of a rebuilding job by Gothic King Theodoric. The name Torrente is an admission that the Parma is rather less than a river; for most of the year it's a trickle.

Santissima Annunziata [210 C3] (*Strada Imbriani 4;* ☎ *0521 234449;* w *annunziataparma.it;* ⊕ *07.00–noon & 15.00–19.30 daily*) Once over the bridge this church, nicknamed the Basilica del Paradiso, is a genuine surprise, a Baroque building constructed long before the Baroque was even dreamt of. Its architect, Giambattista Fornovo, collaborated with Vignola on the spectacular Villa Farnese near Rome before being summoned by Duke Ottavio in 1566 to replace the church demolished by his father for military purposes. He conceived this experimental work, an elliptical domed church with ten radiating chapels, although the new plan brought some tricky architectural problems; Fornovo's dome collapsed in 1626, but was soon rebuilt.

Museo Toscanini [210 D3] (*Borgo Rudolfo Tanzi 13;* ☎ *0521 285499;* w *museotoscanini.it;* ⊕ *09.00–13.00 Tue, 09.00–13.00 & 14.00–18.00 Wed–Sat, 10.00–18.00 Sun; admission free*) The birthplace of Arturo Toscanini (1867–1957) is a modest house, containing memorabilia and a copy of every record he ever made. Toscanini was one of the first cultural notables to become a Fascist;

> **PARMA VIOLETS**
>
> Marie-Louise was obsessed with Parma violets. Even before her arrival in Italy she wrote ahead for instructions on how to plant them, and grew them in both the Orto Botanico and at the Reggia di Colorno. She signed her letters with a violet, dressed her courtiers in violet, and wore violet capes. She commissioned the friars of Santissima Annunziata to create an essence of violets for her sole personal use. Decades after her death, around 1870, local barber Ludovico Borsari obtained the secret formula for her Violetta di Parma scent and launched his own perfume company. For the next century or so the fragrance was the rage in Paris, and Borsari was launched on a career as one of Italy's most eminent perfume makers; along with the original Violetta di Parma perfume, the firm now produces 300 different scents.

in 1919 he stood as a candidate for parliament from Milan on the same ticket as Mussolini himself. The violence of the *squadri* and the creation of the dictatorship turned him against the movement. In 1931 he was beaten up during a concert in Bologna for refusing to play the Fascist anthem *Giovinezza*, and afterwards moved to the USA.

Parco Ducale [210 C2–3] (⊕ *Nov–Mar 07.00–20.00, Apr–Oct 06.00–midnight daily*) North of Strada d'Azeglio, Parma's largest park was laid out for Ottavio Farnese in the 1560s. In its day it was one of the renowned gardens of Italy, with a spectacular sculpted fountain. By the time the Farnese trundled off to extinction, however, the park had become neglected and overgrown. In the 1760s Duke Filippo and du Tillot brought in French landscape designers and sculptors for a total makeover, under the direction of Ennemond Petitot. The result is what you see today, a reflection of the gardens of Versailles with a touch of informality. The graceful statues – satyrs and shepherdesses, naiads and classical gods – are the work of Jean-Baptiste Boudard. There is a classical ruin, built to celebrate the arrival of the horrible Maria Amalia, and a lagoon with islands and a 'Trianon Fountain'.

Palazzo Ducale [210 D2] (*Parco Ducale;* ☏ *0521 508184;* ⊕ *09.00–12.30 1st Sat of month, book via* e *prefetto.pref_parma@interno.it; admission free*) The hodgepodge Ducal Palace begun by Vignola in 1561 suffered additions and remodellings by half a dozen architects, including Ferdinando Bibiena and Petitot, over the next two centuries. The palace is now the home of the Carabinieri, but they'll let you in one morning a month to see the surviving frescoed rooms, including the Sala di Amore, the last work of Agostino Carracci. Agostino was sent here by the Farnese after the success of the fresco cycle he and his brother Annibale produced for the Palazzo Farnese in Rome, but he died before it was finished. Other rooms are frescoed with the story of Orpheus and scenes from *Orlando Furioso*. Then there's the unique Sala dei Uccelli, stuccoed by Benigno Bossi with 224 different species of bird.

Ospedale Vecchio [210 C3] (*Via Massimo d'Azeglio 45;* ☏ *0521 218019; library* ⊕ *09.00–19.00 Mon–Sat*) Behind its lengthy portico, Parma's former hospital (one of Europe's first, founded in 1201) was the most important secular building of the Oltratorrente. It was rebuilt in 1476 in the form of a Greek cross to combine all the city's little hospitals in one place. It received patients until 1926; today it houses the duchy's state archives and city's main library, the Biblioteca Civica.

Santa Croce [210 B3] (*Piazzale Santa Croce;* ☏ *0521 237610;* ⊕ *08.00–noon & 16.30–19.00 daily*) Pop into Santa Croce to see some extremely peculiar medieval capitals swimming amid a theatrical Baroque décor.

Santa Maria del Quartiere [210 C4] (*Strada del Quartiere;* ⊕ *09.00–12.15 & 16.30–19.00 Mon–Fri*) This tall, hexagonal pile (1604) was designed by Gian Battista Aleotti, architect of the Farnese Theatre. The *Paradiso* frescoed in the dome by Pier Antonio Bernabei pays tribute to Correggio.

Paganini's Tomb [210 B6] (*Villetta Cemetery, Viale della Villetta;* ☏ *0521 964042*) A native of Genoa, Niccolò Paganini, the wizard of catgut and bow (1782–1840) was so good – with his exceptionally long fingers, he could play three octaves across four strings in a hand span – that he was believed to have sold his soul to the devil, especially when he died in Nice of an internal haemorrhage before a priest could give him the last rites. His body was transported to Genoa, but the pope still refused him a Christian burial until 1876, when he was laid to rest in this little temple.

The cemetery is a 15-minute walk from the centre, or you can catch bus 1.

NORTH OF PARMA TO COLORNO

The Reggia di Colorno, 18km north, is the 'little' Versailles to Parma's Paris.

GETTING THERE AND AWAY Regional Trenord trains leave Parma hourly for Paradigna and Colorno and take 15 minutes. The fastest route by car is on the SP72.

 WHERE TO STAY, EAT AND DRINK

Locanda Abbazia See page 207 for details.

✕ Al Vèdel Via Vedole 68, Colorno; ✆0521 816169; w poderecadassa.it; ⊕ closed Mon & Tue. This superb restaurant, attached to the Podere Cadassa where *culatelli* have been cured for over 2 centuries, is the perfect place for a meal after a visit to the Reggia (see below). Now run by the 6th generation of the Bergonzi family, their *culatello* is a must, but also try the *tortél dóls di Colorno*, a dish invented for Marie-Louise: pasta pillows filled with sweet mostarda, Parmesan & plum jam, topped with melted butter & Parmesan. Also sturgeon & eels from the Po, delicious desserts & 1,500 wines. €€€

CENTRO STUDI ARCHIVIO DELLA COMUNICAZIONE (CSAC) [map, pages 202–3] (*Via Viazza di Paradigna, Paradigna;* ✆*0521 607791;* w *csacparma.it;* ⊕ *10.00–15.00 Tue–Fri, 10.00–20.00 Sat–Sun; €10*) The Abbazia di Valserena was founded in 1298, enlarged in the 17th and 18th centuries, and had some 500 monks when it was suppressed by Napoleon. Frescoes in the presbytery by Cesare Baglione survive, but most of its art has since moved to the Galleria Nazionale. The rest of the abbey now houses the University of Parma's communications archives and a contemporary art museum with sections on photography (including an unexpected collection from the US Farm Security Administration by Dorothea Lange etc), design, media, fashion, dramatic arts and more. It's a peaceful, atmospheric place, where you can stay the night (page 207).

REGGIA DI COLORNO [map, pages 202–3] (*Colorno;* ✆ *0521 312545;* w *reggiadicolorno.it; guided tours* ⊕ *10.00, 11.00, 15.00, 16.00 & 17.00 Sat–Sun year-round, also Mar & Nov 11.00 & 15.00 Tue–Fri, Apr, May, Sep & Oct 10.00, 11.30, 15.00 & 16.30 Tue–Fri, Jun–Aug 11.00 & 16.00 Tue–Fri; adults €6.50, under 7s free*) Colorno's 14th-century fortress was converted by the Sanserverino family into a residence, which the Farnese snatched up in 1612 and gradually converted into their summer home away from home. Later architects, including Ferdinando Bibiena and Ennemond Petitot, perfected its stately arcaded façade, and in 1749 Duke Philip and his wife, Louise Elisabeth, daughter of Louis XV, redid the 400 rooms to create their own 'miniature Versailles'. Later Bourbon rulers of Parma spent much of their time here, as did Marie-Louise. After Italian unification, the King of Italy confiscated its furnishings and art to embellish his own *palazzi* (poor Parma, once again fleeced of its best gear!). Today part of the Reggia contains a prestigious culinary school, ALMA, run by Gualtiero Marchesi.

The Reggia's Neoclassical interior is a bright, airy residence, more habitable than your average 18th-century palace. The 70-minute tour takes in Petitot's Sala Grande, the ducal chapel and the apartment and 'astronomic observatory' of Duke Ferdinando. The gardens had canals, an orangery – and tunnels; the later Bourbon rulers must have been nervous, for they installed escape hatches

7

leading all over the countryside, one supposedly running all the way to Parma. The French gardens, partly converted by Marie-Louise into an informal English park, suffered neglect for decades, but are now being restored according to their original Farnese design.

THE PARMA FOOTHILLS

The foothills south of Parma are the source of much happiness – almost all of the famous Parma hams are produced here, as well Parmigiano cheese, DOC Colli di Parma wines, mushrooms (*porcini* in autumn, *prugnolo* in spring) from Borgo Val di Taro, and truffles from around Calestano.

The Taro Valley was always an important route through the northern Apennines. It branches at Fornovo; one road (the SS308) follows the river before crossing the mountains into Liguria, and another (the SS62, paralleled by the A15 motorway) takes a more tortuous path over to Tuscany. Such a strategic area naturally has sprouted plenty of castles.

GETTING THERE AND AWAY Buses (✆ *840 222 222; w tep.pr.it*) go to each of the villages from Parma but rarely between them, so to do a full tour you really need a car. Fornovo di Taro and Borgo Val di Taro are stations on the Parma–La Spezia rail line. TEP bus 12 leaves Parma train station for Torrechiara, Langhirano and Traversetolo every hour excluding Sunday, although on Sundays there's a special bus at 14.30 that returns from the Fondazione Magnani Rocca at 18.00.

TOURIST INFORMATION

Fornovo Taro Via dei Collegati 19; ✆0525 2599; w iatfornovo.it; ⊕ 08.30–12.30 & 15.00–18.00 Mon–Fri, 09.00–12.30 Sun

Torrechiara Strada Castello 10; ✆0521 355009; w portaletorrechiara.net; ⊕ Nov–Feb 10.00–13.00 Tue–Sun, Mar–Oct 10.00–13.00 & 14.00–18.00 Tue–Sun

WHERE TO STAY, EAT AND DRINK

Castello di Compiano (11 rooms) Via Marco Rossi Sidoli 15, Compiano; ✆0525 825541; w castellodicompiano.com. Beautiful period rooms, including family rooms, each named after one of the local noble families. The castle's restaurant, Al Panigaccio (€€), specialises in its namesake, *panigacci*, a flatbread from northern Tuscany, served with both sweet & savoury dishes. **€€€€–€€€€€**

Taverna del Castello Via del Castello 25, Torrechiara; ✆0521 355015; w tavernadelcastello. it; ⊕ closed Mon. In a building from the same period as the castle of Torrechiara, a great place for lunch or dinner with a lovely terrace & gorgeous views; good-value menus, including seafood. **€€€€**

Villa Maria Luigia Via Galaverna 28, Collecchio; ✆0521 805489; w ristorantevillamarialuigia.it;

☺ closed Wed eve & Thu. An atmospheric place to dine in Marie-Louise's former hunting lodge on the edge of the Parco dei Boschi di Carrega. Choose between the classics (they are renowned for their stuffed quail risotto) or seafood; traditional 6-course menu €45. €€€€

✗ **Vecchio Borgo** Via Cassio 14, Borgo Val di Taro; ✆0525 99503; ☺ closed Wed. The place to go in the centre for mushroom & truffle dishes (notably the antipasti & *primi*) without fuss. Good desserts, too. €€€

WHAT TO SEE AND DO

Castello di Montechiarugolo [map, pages 202–3] (*16km southeast of Parma;* ✆ *0521 686643;* w *castellodimontechiarugolo.it;* ☺ *Mar–Nov 10.00–noon & 15.00–18.00 Sun, Mar–May also 15.00–18.00 Sat; €6*) Montechiarugolo's castle overhangs the River Enza, dwarfing the old village at its feet. Originally an 11th-century fort that took plenty of knocks during the Guelph and Ghibelline struggles, it was rebuilt by the Visconti in 1313. The main tower resembles Torrechiara, but otherwise the castle presents an austere face to the world. Inside, however, it contains antiques (including a striking wooden model of a fantasy temple by Petitot) and 15th- and 16th-century frescoes. The best are in the Camera Antica – striking allegories and scenes of human industry, attributed to Cesare Baglione. The loggia offers lovely views over the countryside.

Castello di Torrechiara [map, pages 202–3] (✆ *0521 355255;* w *castellidelducato. it;* ☺ *Jan–Mar 08.10–13.50 Mon–Sat, Apr–Oct 08.30–19.30 Tue–Fri, 10.30–19.30 Sat–Sun, Nov–Dec 09.00–16.30 Tue–Fri, 10.00–17.00 Sat–Sun, last entrance 30mins before closing; €4*) The most photogenic of all the duchy's castles, this magnificent brick fantasy is almost unchanged since it was built by Pier Maria Rossi 'Il Magnifico' (1413–82), humanist, linguist, astronomer and military captain. Visible from miles around, it's defended by a double set of walls and four mighty towers, each surrounded and linked by covered walkways. The elegant courtyard has ornate terracotta tiles; the ground floor has excellent frescoes by Cesare Baglione, who also painted the delightful cycle of acrobats performing impossible feats with hoops on the backs of lions. The castle's best frescoes, however, are by Bonifacio Bembo in the beautiful Golden Bedchamber, where Pier Maria brought his young lover Bianca Pellegrini and where he died in her arms. Bembo covered the walls with gold leaf (now gone) and a fresco cycle dedicated to their love and the Rossi's 40 other castles.

Museo del Prosciutto di Parma (*Bocchialini 7, Langhirano;* ✆ *0521 931800;* w *museidelcibo.it;* ☺ *early Mar–early Dec 10.00–18.00 Sat–Sun; €5*) Langhirano, just south of Torrechiara, is synonymous with prosciutto, and the former cattle market (1928) now holds a museum dedicated to the history and making of the famous hams. There is a tasting room (besides ham and *salumi* there's a good selection of local Colli di Parma wines) and a shop.

Fondazione Magnani Rocca [map, pages 202–3] (*Mamiano di Traversetolo;* ✆ *0521 848327;* w *magnanirocca.it;* ☺ *mid-Mar–early Dec 10.00–18.00 Tue–Sun (Jul–Aug until 19.00 Sat–Sun); adults €10, ages 6–14 €5, Parco Romantico €3*) East of Torrechiara, this eclectic, excellent collection spans some 600 years of art, housed in the beautiful villa of musicologist Luigi Magnani (1906–84). There are works by Gentile da Fabriano, Carpaccio, Lippi, Titian, Dürer, Fuseli and Goya (his magnificent *The Family of the Infante Don Luis*), Cézanne, Matisse, Renoir, Monet, de Chirico, de Pisis and Burri, with numerous drawings and engravings by Giorgio

Every region in Italy makes ham, but very few would dare to rival the subtle, glamorous, velvety, paper-thin slices of *prosciutto di Parma*, which owes its greatness to a variety of conditions that the Parmigiani swear cannot be reproduced anywhere else on the planet. The fresh hams are rounded into a fine shape, pounded with paddles until smooth, then brushed and polished. After spending a few days out in the cold, they are laid in a bed of rock salt – unlike other hams, Parma hams can get by with only a minimum of salt because of the uniquely preservative and antibacterial qualities of the air.

Air, they claim, is indeed the most important factor in the whole process. Ideally the ham should first hang in the sweet air of the hills above the Magra Valley, where it acquires the scent of pine and olives, then in the Cisa Pass, where it is subtly flavoured with the chestnut-breezes of the Apennines, before being brought down the valley of the Torrente Parma to dry from September to March at Langhirano, a town entirely devoted to curing Parma hams. The finished product is stamped with the five-pointed ducal symbol and the motto, in case you have any lingering doubt: *quello dolce è il crudo di Parma*, 'this sweet one is the raw one from Parma'.

Morandi. The villa's 12ha English-style **Parco Romantico** lives up to its name, with exotic trees, a water-lily lake, mossy statues and peacocks. It also has an excellent restaurant and bistro (€€€–€€€€).

Rocca di Sala Baganza [map, pages 202–3] (*Piazza Gramsci 1, Sala Baganza;* \ *0521 331342;* w *www.comune.sala-baganza.pr.it;* ⊕ *Apr–Oct 10.00–13.00 & 15.00–18.00 Wed–Sun, Nov–Mar 10.00–13.00 & 15.00–17.00 Thu–Sun; €4*) This sturdy fortress 10km west of Torrechiara was built by the Sanvitale lords in 1258 to defend Parma from baddies coming up the Baganza Valley, but took some hard knocks in the 2008 earthquake. Now partly owned by the *comune*, there are beautiful frescoed rooms mostly from the 15th century, including the Sala dei Busti, another dedicated to *Aeneas* and *Hercules*, and a charming small room with trompe l'œil birds seeming to fly through the ruined ceiling, frescoed by the ever-delightful Cesare Baglione. The damaged Farnese apartments are still off limits, but there's a museum of Parma wine in the former ice house.

Museo del Salame [map, pages 202–3] (*Strada al Castello 1, Felino (3km southeast of Sala Baganza);* \ *0521 931800;* w *museidelcibo.it;* ⊕ *Mar–8 Dec 10.00–13.00 & 15.00–18.00 Sat–Sun; €5*) In Emilia-Romagna Felino is synonymous not with cats, but with *salame*, and produces some 7,250 tonnes of it a year. This little museum in its 15th–18th-century castle will tell you all about it.

Museo della Pasta (*Strada Giarola 1, Collecchio;* \ *0521 931800;* w *museidelcibo. it;* ⊕ *Mar–early Dec 10.00–18.00 Sat–Sun; €5*) There had to be one. Ten different sections illustrate the past and present of homemade pasta and the commercial pasta industry, with exhibits donated by Barilla.

Parco Regionale dei Boschi di Carrega [map, pages 202–3] (*Collecchio;* w *www.parchidelducato.it*) The oldest regional park in Emilia-Romagna, this lovely lake-dotted woodland above the Taro was once the hunting reserve of Ranuccio

Farnese and a summer retreat of the dukes. Their villas, the **Casino de' Boschi**, designed by Petitot, and **Villa del Ferlaro** built for Marie-Louise, are privately owned, but the Casinetto de' Boschi, or court theatre, at Via Olma 2, is being converted into a visitor's centre (✆ *0521 836026 for hours*).

One of the walks in the park follows the Via Francigena (see box, page 235) past Talignano's **Pieve di San Biagio** (1200) (⊕ *Apr–Jul & Oct 15.00–18.00 1st & 3rd Sun of month, Aug–Sep 16.00–19.00 1st & 3rd Sun of month; at other times ring* m *366 151 0152*), which was once linked to a pilgrims' hospice. It has a vivid comedy lunette over the portal, showing St Michael and the Devil weighing souls at the Last Judgement (a subject rare in Italy to begin with), but here Satan and his grinning colleague are trying to cheat, using a hook to tip the load in their direction, although it looks like the archangel Michael is about to whack them both with his sword. Inside are a pair of medieval fonts and a few fresco fragments.

Fornovo di Taro Further up the Taro, this town has been a busy crossroads ever since it was founded as the Roman Forum Novum – for armies as much as for trade and pilgrims. Of all the battles fought around Parma, the most fateful was undoubtedly the Battle of Fornovo in July 1495. The year before, the Duke of Milan had invited the French to invade his enemy, Naples. Charles VIII obligingly took an army over the Alps and seized Naples, and then pillaged his way up the peninsula on the way home. Venice and Florence, almost alone among Italian states in seeing the danger from foreign intervention, raised an army to intercept him, and talked Milan into changing sides.

They caught up with the French here, on the banks of the Taro. The Italians had the best general, a three-to-one advantage in men, a good battle plan, and a simpleton for an opponent in Charles. Whatever his shortcomings, though, the king had a reputation for phenomenal luck, and in one of the most confusing hour-long battles in history, he managed to win. Even if his 'victory' meant only escaping Italy with his army intact, Charles had shown that Italy was a plum waiting to be picked.

Soon after, the Spaniards sent an army to restore Naples to its rightful king; in 1499 the French would be back to seize Milan, and later the Austrians and even the Swiss would be looking for bits of Italy to grab. The Wars of Italy had begun, and four decades later when it was all over Italian liberty would be dead, and the entire nation subject to the pope or foreign powers.

Santa Maria Assunta (*Piazza IV Novembre;* ✆ *0525 2218;* ⊕ *08.00–noon & 15.00–19.00 daily*) Fornovo's parish church, from the 9th century (the façade, from the 18th century, encloses the original narthex) is one of the region's best Romanesque churches, with fascinating reliefs in the manner of Antelami both inside and out for pilgrims on the Via Francigena to contemplate: a vivid scene of Hell and the Seven Deadly Sins – Avarice, with his money bags, is most prominent – also Adam and Eve, a man riding a centaur and a wrestling match. On the high altar, there's an 11th-century reliquary cross and the *Life of St Margaret of Antioch*, showing Margaret fighting both dragon and devil before her martyrdom.

Santa Maria Bardone [map, pages 202–3] (*Terenzo;* ✆ *0525 527291;* ⊕ *09.00– 11.00 & 15.00–18.00 (but best to ring ahead); €2*) Also on the Via Francigena southeast of Fornovo, this church founded in the 7th century is also famous for its reliefs by the Antelami circle. Perhaps the same sculptor as at Fornovo carved the hunting scene over the trilobed window on the façade; the scenes from the

Deposition on the dismantled pulpit are very similar to that in Parma's Duomo, only with figures of Adam and Eve on the right instead of soldiers. The *Coronation of the Virgin* has angels bizarrely popping out of vertical clouds. The holy water font, carved with a devil and a miser, is supported by a mysterious female figure.

Berceto Near the Passo della Cisa leading into Tuscany, Berceto is a picturesque village under a ruined castle. Another stop along the Via Francigena, its 12th-century **Duomo di San Moderanno** (⟍ *0525 60087;* ⊕ *07.00–13.00 & 15.00–20.00;* ⊕ *best to ring ahead*) may no longer be a cathedral, but it has a fine Romanesque portal and medieval relics inside that go back to the Lombards.

Castello di Compiano [map, pages 202–3] (*Compiano;* ⟍ *0525 825541;* w *castellodicompiano.com; guided tours* ⊕ *Mar, Oct–Dec 10.00, noon, 14.30 & 17.30 Sun, Apr–Jun & Sep 10.00, noon, 14.30 & 18.30 Sat–Sun, Jul–Aug 10.00, noon, 14.30 & 18.30 daily; €7*) Compiano, further up the Taro, was once the capital of a tiny state encompassing Bardi and Borgotaro, ruled from 1275 by the Landi family. In 1532, Emperor Charles V granted them the title of prince and the right to mint their own coins, but in 1682 they died out and their castle was forgotten until Marie-Louise made it into a prison. Now restored, it contains a hotel and restaurant (page 230), a curious museum on freemasonry, another on mountain cuisine, and sumptuous rooms of the castle's last resident, the Marchesa Lina Raimondi Gambarotta (d1987).

Castello di Bardi [map, pages 202–3] (*Bardi;* ⟍ *0525 733021;* m *380 108 8315;* w *castellodibardi.info;* ⊕ *Mar 14.00–17.00 Sat, 10.00–18.00 Sun, Apr–Jun, Sep–Oct 14.00–17.00 Mon–Fri, 10.00–19.00 Sat–Sun, Jul–Aug 10.00–19.00 daily, Nov 10.00–17.00 Sat–Sun, other months by appointment; €6*) One of the most impressive fortifications in the area, this 15th-century hilltop castle in the Val Ceno (the valley just north of the Val di Taro) was a key property of the Landi. It retains beautiful beamed ceilings, 16th-century frescoes and, they say, a ghost. It also contains an unusual Museum of Traps and Poaching; the Museo della Civiltà Valligiana with historic items from the region; and the Collezione Ferrarini-Nicoli of 60 paintings, mostly from the 20th century, all dedicated to the subject of work.

FIDENZA

More fantastic Romanesque art awaits at the Roman Fidentia Iulia, known for centuries as the Borgo San Donnino until Mussolini resurrected its old, more imperial-sounding name. For 600 years, beginning in the 9th century, the town belonged to the Pallavicino clan, and its history consists only of brief interruptions bound up with turmoil in nearby Parma; whatever faction was exiled from there often took up residence here, and on two occasions the Parmigiani sacked the town. It's a large and lively town, the province's second city, a crossroads on the Roman Via Aemilia and medieval Via Francigena, but perhaps best known these days for the factory outlets at Fidenza Village.

GETTING THERE AND AWAY Hourly trains link Parma and Piacenza with Fidenza, where you can change for Salsomaggiore or Busseto, or many of the villages in La Bassa to the north. A free shuttle bus makes the 10-minute run from the station to Fidenza Village, hourly on weekdays from 10.00 and every 40 minutes at weekends from 09.40.

TOURIST INFORMATION

 Piazza Duomo 16; ☎ 0524 83377;
w terrediverdi.it; ⏰ Nov–Mar 09.00–12.30 &
15.30–17.30 Wed–Sun (Apr–Oct also Tue)

WHERE TO STAY, EAT AND DRINK

Astoria (34 rooms) Via G B Gandolfi 5;
☎ 0524 524314; w hotelastoriafidenza.it. In the
centre, simple & fine for a night. The restaurant
(⏰ *closed Mon;* €€€) serves regional cuisine &
pizza. €€€

Osteria di Fornio Fornio, 1km west of
Fidenza; ☎ 0524 60118; w osteriafornio.it;
⏰ closed Tue & Mon eve. Lovely summer veranda
in a peaceful setting, excellent *salumi*, tasty pasta
dishes & wines. Save room for the scrumptious
tavolozz di dessert, a palette of mini goodies. €€€

Podere San Faustino Via S Faustino 33;
☎ 0524 520184; w poderesanfaustino.it; ⏰ closed

Sat lunch, Sun eve & Mon. West off the Via
Emilia, this rustic chic restaurant in a farmhouse
specialises in rich dishes, including rich pasta made
using only egg yolks and flour, & tender Angus
beef. Good wine list, too. €€€

La Culatelleria [map, pages 202–3]
Via Emilia 129, Sanguinaro; ☎ 0521 825 107;
w culatelleria.it; ⏰ 08.30–19.00 Mon–Fri,
08.30–14.30 Sat–Sun. Great place to stop between
Parma & Fidenza for platters of *salumi* & cheese,
focaccia & tortelli over bottles of Lambrusco. Book
at lunchtime or face a queue. €€

SHOPPING

Fidenza Village Via San Michele Campagna,
Fidenza; ☎ 0524 33551; w fidenzavillage.com;
⏰ 10.00–20.00 daily. Fashionistas travel from

Milan – only 1hr away – to hit this factory outlet
mall with 120 shops.

WHAT TO SEE AND DO

Duomo di San Donnino (*Piazza Duomo;* ☎ *0524 522354;* w *cattedralefidenza.it;*
⏰ *07.30–noon & 15.00–19.00*) Fidenza's cathedral is dedicated to St Domnimus,

THE VIA FRANCIGENA

Back in the 10th century, when a Bishop of Canterbury with the wonderful
name of Sigeric the Serious walked to Rome to receive his *pallium*, the route
he took had already been trodden by pilgrims for three centuries. Known as
the Via Francigena (the 'road coming from France'), the walk took 80 days
from Canterbury. It was never paved like the Via Emilia, but rather a track
between churches and abbeys where travellers could find shelter for the
night. Although the exact route occasionally varied according to political
upheavals, the standard way crossed into Italy through the Great St Bernard
Pass (where dogs with brandy casks rescued frozen pilgrims) and crossed the
Po at Piacenza, before heading to Fidenza, Fornovo di Taro, Terenzo, Berceto
and over the Cisa Pass into Tuscany.

Although the numbers walking the Via Francigena are nothing like those
heading to Compostela, Sigeric's old route has been undergoing a revival
since 2001: regions (notably Lombardy and Tuscany) have improved and
waymarked the path and a cycling route and have set up accommodation
along the way. For an official guide, map, pilgrim's passport and other
information, see the official website (w *viefrancigene.org*) or contact the
European Association of Via Francigena (*Palazzo Farnese, Piazza Cittadella 29,
Piacenza;* ☎ *0523 492792;* ⏰ *09.30–12.30 Mon–Fri*).

the chamberlain of Emperor Maximian who converted to Christianity and was martyred here in AD291 by the River Stirone. As his tomb became an important stop for Rome-bound pilgrims, a new church was begun in 1162. The lower, finished half of the façade is considered the last great work by Benedetto Antelami and his followers. The master himself probably sculpted the figures of Ezekiel and David, and perhaps the rather unusual angels welcoming families of pilgrims into the church. The rest of the façade features lively carvings of Daniel in the lion's den, Enoch in his chariot flying to heaven, the birth of Jesus and dream of Joseph, centaurs and monsters, souls in the bosom of Abraham (a delightfully surreal scene of three little faces popping out of Abe's lap), Hercules and the Nemean Lion (how did he get there?) and a frieze over the door showing the martyrdom of St Domnimus.

Don't miss the decoration on the towers. On the right there's Alexander the Great flying to heaven by holding bait on sticks over the heads of winged griffons (a favourite if bizarre medieval motif; in early Byzantine times, Alexander was mistaken for a saint). There's a lively frieze of the Seven Deadly Sins and pilgrims (including a tired dog riding a horse); on the left tower there's King Herod and the Magi.

The impressive, lofty **interior**, with its medieval matroneum and clerestory, contains a few frescoes by a trecento artist called 'Mangiaterra' ('eat-up-the-ground') for the speed of his painting; there is more Antelamian sculpture around the apse (including a scene of Winter, complete with sausages). Book ahead to visit the cathedral's matroneum

Museo del Duomo (*Via Don Minzoni 10/A;* \ *0524 514883;* ⊕ *09.30–noon & 15.00–18.00 Tue–Sun;* €3) The museum houses the cathedral treasure with a *Madonna and Child* by Antelami, and includes the crypt, with the Ark of St Domnimus.

Torre Viscontea Near the cathedral, this tower gate of 1364, all that survives of Piacenza's medieval walls, was built over a buried arch of a Roman bridge over the Stirone, where St Domnimus was martyred.

Teatro Girolamo Magnani (*Piazza Verdi;* \ *0524 517411;* ⊕ *by appointment*) Named after native son Girolamo Magnani (1815–89) who designed the scenery for 20 first performances of Verdi's operas, this little jewel box of a theatre was built by Nicola Bettoli (who also built the Reggia in Parma) in 1861, and has now been restored to its former glory.

SALSOMAGGIORE TERME

The largest and best-known of a cluster of saline water spas specialising in arthritic and rheumatic cures, Salsomaggiore was popular with Italian royalty in the early 1900s. More recently it was nationally famous for the Miss Italy bling fest which, to Salsomaggiore's chagrin, has since moved to other pastures.

GETTING THERE AND AWAY Trains run every 30 minutes from Fidenza to Salsomaggiore, 7 minutes away. Or take bus 2205 from Parma via Fidenza.

TOURIST INFORMATION
🛈 Galleria Warowland, Piazza Berzieri; \ 0524 580211; w visitsalsomaggiore.it; ⊕ Apr–Oct

09.30–12.30 & 15.30–18.30 daily, Nov–Mar 09.30–12.30 & 15.00–18.00 Mon–Fri, 09.30–12.30 Sat

WHERE TO STAY Most of Salsomaggiore's 109 hotels ask you to email in your dates before they'll tell you the price. All have restaurants.

Casa Romagnosi (39 rooms) Piazzale Berzieri; ☏0524 576543; w hotelromagnosi.it. Handsome 4-star Liberty-style hotel opposite the Terme Berzieri in the heart of town, complete with a new wellness area & infrared sauna. Free parking & bikes for guests. €€€€

Uappala Grand Hotel Salsomaggiore (167 rooms) Largo Roma 4; ☏0524 582311; w grandhotelsalsomaggioreterme.it. Classic century-old spa hotel updated with light, bright colours. It has a thermal pool with a motorised roof, herbal tea room & hammam, & jacuzzi & solarium on the roof. €€€€

Country Hotel Querce (25 rooms) Via Parma 85; ☏0524 578281; w www. countryhotelquerce.it. Homey place amid century oaks & wisteria, in a quiet setting. There's a pool, bikes to borrow, & excellent restaurant. €€€

Villa Fiorita (44 rooms) Via Milano 2; ☏0524 573805; w hotelvillafiorita.it. Handsome Liberty-style hotel in business since 1907 that recently underwent a thorough renovation. Wellness centre, free parking & sat TV. €€€

Agriturismo Antica Torre (8 rooms) Case Bussandri 197, Loc Cangelasio; ☏0524 575425; w anticatorre.it. The tower, 3km above Salsomaggiore, is from the 1400s & now the centrepiece of the Pavesi family farm. Pool & home-cooked meals made with farm-fresh ingredients. No credit cards; b/fast inc. Closed Dec–Feb. €€

Elite (28 rooms) Viale Cavour 5; ☏0524 579436; w www.hotelelitesalsomaggiore.it. A quiet choice with a garden near the centre & Terme Berzieri, with large, colourful, slightly dated rooms. Free bikes, parking & buffet b/fast inc. €€

✗ WHERE TO EAT AND DRINK

✗ Trattoria l'Oca Bianca Via Scipione Passeri 210; ☏0524 573273; w trattoriaocabianca.com; ⊕ closed Tue & Wed lunch. The 'White Goose' really does serve plenty of goose, from foie gras (melt-in-your-mouth pan fried with apples & cognac) to goose *salumi* to half-moon pasta in goose *ragù*; also duck & guinea fowl. End with lovely chocolate desserts & spirits from around the world. €€€

✗ Osteria Bellaria Via Bellaria 14; ☏0524 573600; ⊕ closed Mon. When the locals want to dine well, they head west on the Piacenza road to the Bellaria, where they put porcini mushrooms & truffles in as many dishes as possible – *sott'olio* as an antipasto, in the tortelli, in the *tortino*, on the grill, on a steak. All are simply prepared & seriously moreish – if you like mushrooms & truffles. Pretty

garden terrace, plus homemade desserts & local wines. No credit cards. €€

✗ Osteria del Castello Via al Castello 63; ☏0524 573698; ⊕ closed Wed. Rustic chic inn by the Scipione Castello [map, pages 202–3], with views from the terrace; try the unusual tortelli with green apples & sun-dried tomatoes. Exceptional desserts, too. €€

✗ Trattoria Predosa [map, pages 202–3] Loc Contignaco 83; ☏0524 578246; ⊕ closed Sun eve, Mon & Jul. Just south of Salsomaggiore at Predosa, this unpretentious trattoria serves fresh home cooking under a pergola. The menu offers a wide range of *secondi* (roast duck, *ossobuco*, fried chicken, etc), as well as the delicious pasta with truffles & mushrooms in season. €€

WHAT TO SEE AND DO
Palazzo dei Congressi (*Viale Romagnosi 7;* ☏ *0524 580222*) Built in 1898 during Salsomaggiore's golden era, this was once a grand hotel owned by the legendary Cesar Ritz, hosting Caruso, Toscanini and Queen Margherita of Italy; its beautiful Sala delle Cariatidi is still used for visiting opera performances. After the war, Ritz sold it and a new wing was added, with three stunning Liberty-style rooms designed by Ugo Giusti and decorated by Italy's greatest Art Nouveau master, Galileo Chini: the **Salone Moresco** (where Bertolucci filmed some of the *Last Emperor*), the **Taverna Rossa** and the **Loggiato Veranda**. Today the building houses municipal offices, a congress centre and, on the third floor, a **Palaeontology Museum** (*access via the*

ground-floor library; ☎ 0524 580204; ⊕ 09.00–13.00 & 14.00–17.15 Sat, 14.00–18.00 Tue & Thu, other mornings by appointment; €2.50), 'Il Mare Antico', with fossils discovered in the area from the time when it was under the sea.

Terme Berzieri (Piazza Berzieri; ☎ 0524 582723; for spa packages, see w www.salsomaggioreterme.com) Salsomaggiore's main baths are concentrated in an intriguing half-baked Liberty-style palace (1912–23) designed by Ugo Giusti and Giulio Bernardini. The lobby is still one of the grandest in Italy – a Liberty-arabesque fantasy by Galileo Chini, who produced these gorgeous murals after frescoing the throne room of the King of Siam. Inside is a little museum with some hundred ceramic and glass elements designed by Chini for the spa.

Giardino Botanico Gavinell (Loc Gaviana, Contignaco 138; ☎ 0524 578348; w gavinell.it; for guided tours ring ahead) Two kilometres east of town, this 12ha garden has more than 450 species of plants and trees, many with medicinal uses, and a medieval herb garden; also a restaurant and shop.

Castello di Scipione (Scipione Castell 60; ☎ 0524 572381; w castellodiscipione.it; guided tours on the hour ⊕ Mar & Nov 15.00–17.00 Sat, 10.30 & 11.30 Sun, Apr–Jun 15.00–18.00 Thu & Sat, 10.30, 11.30, 15.00–17.00 Sun, Jul–Oct 15.00–17.00 Thu, Fri & Sat, 10.30, 11.30, 15.00–17.00 Sun; €9) The once-powerful Pallavicino Marquesses of Busseto (pages 8–9) can trace their origins back to the 10th-century Lombards, but their castle on this wooded hill, at least according to legend, occupies a villa once owned by Scipione, the conqueror of Carthage. The Pallavicini still live here so the castle is well maintained, but the tour only takes in a few rooms, one with frescoes.

Terme di Tabiano [map, pages 202–3] (4km east of Salsomaggiore; ☎ 0524 564130; w spa.termeditabiano.it) This was Verdi's favourite spa; its stinky sulphur springs are good for the lungs, nose, throat and skin. Its T-Spatium wellness and beauty centre is housed in a curvy red building of 1999 by Marco Bardeschi, inspired by Galileo Chini and the Castello di Tabiano.

Castello di Tabiano [map, pages 202–3] (Above the Terme; m 348 895 5378; ⊕ Apr–Oct tour at 17.00 Thu–Fri, 10.00–11.30 & 15.00–16.00 Sat–Sun but ring ahead; adults €8, under 8s free) Built by the Pallavicini in the 11th century over a Roman settlement, the Castello di Tabiano helped to control the Po plain, the Via Francigena and nearby salt springs. In the 19th century it was made into a residence; the guided tour takes in the ancient vaulted wine cellar, the salons decorated with mirrors and stuccoes, the library, terraces, garden, ballroom and the 'Red Door' where Tancredi Pallavicino assassinated his brother.

LA BASSA

North of Fidenza the Via Emilia stretches the evocative fog-prone Po lowlands of the Bassa – landscapes that might look familiar if you're a fan of Parma-born director Bernardo Bertolucci, who shot several films here. For five centuries this territory made up a cohesive and remarkably long-lived feudal state; the Marquesses Pallavicino, who ruled it, were often major players in medieval Italy's factional wars (pages 8–9). Today La Bassa is the homeland of culatello and Parmigiano Reggiano, famous for its restaurants, art-filled castles, and haunting Po landscapes.

BUSSETO Busseto, the capital, is an attractive walled town that gave the world Giuseppe Verdi, and offers opera lovers a full whack of Verdian delights.

Getting there and away Fidenza has frequent buses and trains to Busseto. There are bus links to the surrounding villages, starting either in Fidenza or Busseto; for schedules see **w** tep.pr.it.

Tourist information

 Piazza Giuseppe Verdi 10; `0524 92487; **w** bussetolive.com; ⊕ Apr–Oct 09.30–13.00 & 15.00–18.30 Tue–Sun, Nov–Mar 09.30–13.00 & 14.30–17.30 Tue–Sun. Pick up the free Tourist

Card for discounts at Busseto's museums, hotels & shops. They also organise visits in the area & across the Po in Cremona, the birthplace of Stradivarius.

Where to stay, eat and drink *Map, below, unless otherwise stated*

Palazzo Calvi (6 rooms) Via di Sambosetto 26; **m** 338 135 6985; **w** palazzocalvi.com. Just outside the centre, welcoming rooms with period furnishings in the guesthouse of an 18th-century villa, in a lovely garden setting. Friendly management, & an excellent, refined restaurant (€€€€) & enoteca. Closed Jan. **€€€€**

Alle Roncole (12 rooms) Viale della Processione 179, Roncole Verdi; `0524 930015;

w alleroncole.it. By Verdi's birthplace, this locanda from the 19th century offers 5 retro rooms above the restaurant, 5 in a newer building & 2 flats for families. The good restaurant/pizzeria (⊕ *closed Thu;* €€) serves some of the more recherché dishes of Parma, including *cicciolata* (old-fashioned pig's head terrine) but also the classic tortelli & homemade desserts. **€€€**

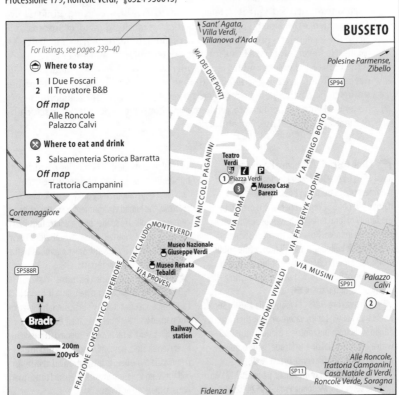

BUSSETO

↑ Sant' Agata, Villa Verdi, Villanova d'Arda

Polesine Parmense, Zibello

For listings, see pages 239–40

⊖ **Where to stay**
1 I Due Foscari
2 Il Trovatore B&B

Off map
Alle Roncole
Palazzo Calvi

✖ **Where to eat and drink**
3 Salsamenteria Storica Barratta

Off map
Trattoria Campanini

Cortemaggiore

Teatro Verdi
1 Piazza Verdi
3 ⬤ Museo Casa Barezzi

Museo Nazionale Giuseppe Verdi
Museo Renata Tebaldi

Palazzo Calvi
②

VIA DEI DUE PONTI
VIA NICCOLO PAGANINI
VIA CLAUDIO MONTEVERDI
VIA PROVESI
FRAZIONE CONSOLATICO SUPERIORE
VIA ROMA
VIA ARRIGO BOITO
VIA FRYDERYK CHOPIN
VIA MUSINI
VIA ANTONIO VIVALDI

SP94
SP588R
SP91
SP11

N
Bradt

0 ——— 200m
0 ——— 200yds

Railway station

Fidenza ↓

Alle Roncole, Trattoria Campanini, Casa Natale di Verdi, Roncole Verde, Soragna

THE 'SWAN OF BUSSETO'

To Italians Verdi is not just another great composer, but the genius who expressed the national spirit of the Risorgimento in music: Italy's equivalent of Richard Wagner (the two were both born in the same year, 1813). As a national icon in his own lifetime, Verdi could have played a role in the unification of Italy without even trying. In the 1850s, crowds at the opera screamed 'Viva Verdi!' but not just as a tribute to the composer – everybody knew it was also a not-too-subtle demand for 'Vittorio Emanuele, Re D'Italia!'

But he did try. Right from the beginning, Verdi was a sincere patriot, although he was forced to weave political themes into his operas discreetly to get them past the ever-vigilant censors. At a discouraging phase in his early career, after the death of his two small children and his wife, when he was considering giving up composing altogether, he was inspired by a lament of the captive Jews in Babylon in a libretto someone had offered him; this became the great chorus 'Va Pensiero' in *Nabucco*, his first big success, and his rendition of the lament reminded audiences, as he intended, of Italy's fight for political freedom. Through themes like these, and works based on distant periods of Italian history such as *I Lombardi* and *I Due Foscari*, Verdi was able to insert a little politics into every opera season. The censors nevertheless did their best to annoy. In an absurdity of truly operatic proportions, they forced him to transfer the setting of *Un Ballo in Maschera* from the royal court of Sweden to, of all places, Puritan Boston, since the libretto dealt with the taboo subject of regicide.

Next to music, Verdi's greatest talent seems to have been carrying grudges. The experience of losing his first chance at a job, as musical director in Busseto, when the local priests proposed their own candidate, made him an anticleric for life. He never forgave La Scala for the poor reception its audiences gave to some of his early works, and his feuds with collaborators were legendary. He never really forgave Busseto either, although after a brief spell as a member of the first Italian parliament he retired to his estate in nearby Sant'Agata, which he tended with particular care, while making himself a generous benefactor of the poor, the local hospital and school.

🏠 **I Due Foscari** (20 rooms) Piazza Carlo Rossi 15; ☎0524 930031; w iduefoscari.it. One of the finest places to stay in Busseto is, naturally, named after one of Verdi's operas, & is owned by the family of local tenor Carlo Bergonzi, who often performed in them. Rooms in the neo-Gothic, neo-Moorish building are small & cosy (the public rooms have lovely ceilings & furnishings). It also boasts one of Busseto's best restaurants, with a pretty outdoor terrace. €€€

🏠 **Il Trovatore B&B** (3 rooms) Via Musini 36; m 333 455 6893; bbiltrovatore@gmail.com. A 10min walk from the centre, a friendly little B&B with a giant sundial on the façade, large garden, parking, bikes & self-service b/fast. €€

🗙 **Trattoria Campanini** [map, pages 202–3] Via Roncole Verdi 136, Madonna Prati; ☎0524 92569;

w culatelloandwine.it; 🕒 closed Tue & Wed. Just outside Busseto, this place has been in the same family for generations. They produce their own *culatello*; the humid environment essential for its curing is supplied in spades by the winter fogs (the famously misty, moisty *culatello* capital, Zibello, is just up the road). Try it, & the other *salumi*, as well as their exquisite homemade pasta. €€

🗙 **Salsamenteria Storica Barratta** Via Roma 76; ☎0524 91066; w salsamenteriabaratta.it. Knock back Lambrusco out of white bowls in this atmospheric old inn, packed with antiques here, there & dangling from the ceiling. Verdi & his favourite soprano (& possible lover) Teresa Stolz, Respighi, Toscanini & Gabriele D'Annunzio came here to feast on *salumi*, cheese, & walnuts with various sauces. Be prepared to use your fingers: there are no forks. €

What to see and do

Teatro Verdi (*Piazza Verdi;* \ *0524 92487;* ⊕ *Nov–Mar 09.30–12.30 & 14.30–17.00 Tue–Sun, Apr–Oct 09.30–12.30 & 15.00–18.00 Tue–Sun; €4*) A statue of Verdi relaxes in an armchair in front of the castle built in 1259 by the lord Oberto Pallavicino (the subject of Verdi's first, seldom-heard, opera *Oberto Conte di San Bonifacio*). It was restored in the 19th century to look properly medieval and houses a bijou 300-seat theatre modelled after La Scala, built in the composer's honour and completed in 1868. Verdi (although he sent in a contribution and owned a box) was against its construction, complaining that the townspeople kept butting into his private life. In honour of his name ('Joe Green' in Italian) the ladies wore green and the men wore green ties at the opening night, but even then Verdi adamantly refused to ever set foot in it. The theatre hosts the International Verdian Voices Competition in June, supports its own philharmonic and chorus, and even puts on its own little winter opera season.

Museo Nazionale Giuseppe Verdi (*Viale Ziliani 1;* \ *0524 931002;* w *www. museogiuseppeverdi.it;* ⊕ *10.00–17.30 Tue–Sun (summer until 18.30); adults €9, concessions €7, under 10s free, audioguides €1*) Inaugurated in 2009, this museum has its home in the beautiful 16th-century Villa Pallavicino, just outside the town walls. Here, in 1542, the Emperor Charles V and the Farnese Pope Paul III met to make their deal: in exchange for sending the papal army to Germany to fight the Protestants, the Pope could establish the Duchy of Parma for his son. Today the rooms are devoted to the stories behind all 27 of the maestro's operas and his Requiem Mass.

Museo Renata Tebaldi (*In the former stables of the Museo Nazionale Giuseppe Verdi;* \ *0524 97870;* w *museorenatatebaldi.it;* ⊕ *Mar 10.00–12.30 & 14.30–17.00 Sat–Sun, Apr–Oct 10.00–12.30 & 15.00–17.30 Tue–Sun, other times by appointment, closed 2 weeks in Aug; €5*) Dedicated to the 'angel voice' lyrical soprano Renata Tebaldi, this museum contains memorabilia, photos, costumes, posters and more.

Museo Casa Barezzi (*Via Roma 119;* \ *0524 931117;* w *museocasabarezzi.it;* ⊕ *Mar & Nov 10.00–noon & 14.30–17.00 Tue–Sun, Apr–Oct 10.00–noon & 15.00–18.00 Tue–Sun, Dec–Feb 10.00–12.30 & 14.30–17.00 Sun, or by appointment; €4*) A memorabilia-filled Verdi shrine: this is the house of the composer's first patron, Antonio Barezzi, who hired him to teach music to his daughter Margherita (who became his first wife). Berezzi also played a major role in encouraging Verdi to persevere in music after his demoralising failure to get into the conservatory in Milan.

Casa Natale di Verdi (*Via della Procession 1, Roncole Verdi, 4km southeast;* \ *0524 97450;* w *casanataleverdi.it;* ⊕ *Feb & Dec 10.30–12.10 (last entrance) & 14.30–16.00 Sat–Sun, Mar–Sep 09.30–12.10 (last entrance) & 14.30–16.30 Tue–Sun; €5*) There are no flies on Roncole – thanks to its multimedia binaural sound, projections, videos and app, 'Verdi himself' will take you around the simple house where his parents ran a *posteria* (post office/shop/osteria) and where he was born on 10 October 1813.

Nearby, the church of **San Michele Arcangelo** is where little Giuseppe was baptised and played the 18th-century organ; a plaque recalls how in 1814, his mother, warned that Napoleon's defeated troops were rampaging in the area, took baby Giuseppe and hid with him in the belltower. Next to the church is the **tomb of Giovannino Guareschi** (page 195), who lived in the village from 1952 until his death; the local osteria, once run by his son, is packed full of memorabilia. Just outside Roncole, the **Corte Piacentine** (1820) is one of the most picturesque agricultural estates along the Po, and was used by Bertolucci for scenes in *Novecento* and *La Luna*.

Villa Verdi [map, pages 202–3] (*Sant'Agata, Villanova D'Arda, 3km north of Busseto;* \ *0523 830000;* w *villaverdi.org;* ☉ *Mar–Oct 09.30–11.45 & 14.30–18.00 Tue–Sun, Nov–Feb 09.30–11.45 & 14.00–17.00 Sat–Sun; adults €9, ages 12–18 €5)* In 1848, at the urging of his father-in-law Antonio Barezzi, Verdi bought this farm, where he installed his parents; he later added two wings and lived there with his second wife, Giuseppina Strepponi. Now owned by his descendants, there are guided tours of the house and a replica of the hotel room in Milan (with the original bed) where Verdi died in 1901. You can also visit the romantic park.

ZIBELLO AND POLESINE PARMENSE If people aren't coming to La Bassa for Verdi, they're probably after the *culatello*, the *ne plus ultra* of Emilia-Romagna's porky products. Literally 'little bum', *culatello* is made here and nowhere else. Prepared between November and February from freshly slaughtered white Zibello pigs, the finest part of the ham is deboned, salted and sometimes marinated in wine, then massaged to soften the meat and allow the salt to penetrate. After a week, the 'little bum' is tied up in a pig's bladder, then hung in the cellar to slowly mature for 12–37 months. It's exactly the same technique used in the Middle Ages, relying on the Po's unique combination of humidity, winter fogs and summer heat to create just the right mould spores (later tidied off) that produce its unique, slightly musky taste and velvet texture that melts in the mouth.

⌂ Where to stay, eat and drink

⌂ **Antica Corte Pallavicina** (8 rooms) Strada del Palazzo Due Torri 3, Polesine Parmense; \0524 936539; w anticacortepallavicinarelais.com. A reason by itself to visit La Bassa, this 14th-century farm on the Po where the Marquesses Pallavicino once cured their *culatelli* has been beautifully restored & is back in the curing business thanks to the Spigaroli family (whose ancestor worked on Verdi's farm). The ACP, as it's known, is also a chic inn with evocative period rooms & suites under beamed ceilings, with working fireplaces & views over the Po. B/fast inc. Its superb Michelin-starred restaurant (☉ *closed Mon;* €€€€€) makes exquisite use of the many ingredients produced on site, such as *faraona* (guinea fowl) slow baked with *culatello* (the ACP also uses slower-growing black pigs to make a non-DOC version that some say is even better). Tours of the estate (*from €5*) & cooking classes (*€140, creating a 4-course meal*) are available as well. €€€€€

✗ **Trattoria La Buca** Via Ghizzi 6, Zibello; \0524 99214; w trattorialabuca.com; ☉ closed Tue. A classic trattoria, now run by the 6th generation of the same family. Besides the obligatory *culatello*, look for unusual Bassa dishes such as *mariola* (fine cuts of pork, slowly aged) & *prete* (a soft cured sausage boiled for 4hrs). Also 3 rooms available (€€€€). €€€€

✗ **Ristorante al Cavallino Bianco** Via Sbrisi 3, Polesine Parmense; \0524 96136; w ristorantealcavallinobianco.it; ☉ closed Tue. The youngest Spigaroli brother Luciano runs this delightful cosy restaurant with plenty of *culatello* from the ACP (see above), but also tasty vegetarian & gluten-free dishes, made with veg plucked from his garden. Among the *secondi* is the classic Po Valley *fritto misto* (eels, frogs, catfish & *ambolina*, a local fish) & the supreme of capon, Giuseppe Verdi style. In winter, sit by the open fire. €€€

SORAGNA If you thought the Duchy of Parma was a Ruritanian historical footnote, consider Soragna, southeast of Busseto, whose Meli Lupi lords were granted in 1709 the title of Prince of the Holy Roman Empire and of Soragna, with the right to mint coins, until 1805, when Napoleon the party pooper put an end to it.

Where to stay, eat and drink

Locando del Lupo (46 rooms) Corso Garibaldi 64; ☏ 0524 597100; w locandadellupo. com. The atmospheric Locanda occupies the 18th-century coach house & outbuildings once belonging to the Meli Lupi princes, with terracotta floors, old oak beams & wrought-iron beds. €€€

✕ Antica Osteria Ardenga [map, pages 202–3] Via Maestra 6, Diolo di Soragna; ☏ 0524 599337; w osteriardenga.it; ⊕ closed Tue eve, Wed. Fetchingly atmospheric place & former possession of the Meli Lupi (Bertolucci shot several scenes of *La Luna* here.) The *salumi* hanging in the wine cellar is made *in casa*. They do delicious takes on the classics, including *anolini* in capon broth, chestnut gnocchi & roast duck or goose. €€€

What to see and do There is a castle of course, but it's one of the best: the **Rocca di Soragna** [map, pages 202–3] (*Piazza Meli Lupi;* ☏ *0524 597978; w www. roccadisoragna.it; guided tours* ⊕ *Apr–mid-Oct 09.00–11.00 & 15.00–18.00 Tue–Sun, mid-Oct–Mar 09.00–11.00 & 14.30–17.30 Tue–Sun; adults €9, under 18s €5)*

THE KING OF CHEESE

'Poets have been mysteriously silent on the subject of cheese', observed Chesterton, but Parmigiano is an exception. It appeared in Boccaccio's *Decameron*; although the description is about Basques, you can tell he really meant Emilia-Romagna:

> in a region called Cornucopia, where the vines are tied up with sausages. And in those parts there was a mountain made entirely of grated Parmesan cheese on whose slope there were people who spent their whole time making macaroni and ravioli.

Officially known as Parmigiano Reggiano, the cheese is produced in a delimited area around Parma, Modena and Reggio Emilia (see box, page 187). A true one makes the pre-grated packets stuff taste like saw dust. Each great wheel is made of 100 litres of rich milk solids, from cows grazed on the lushest meadows in Italy, and heated to 40°C while being stirred. The solid lump that forms is sieved through cloth, placed in a cylindrical container and mixed with brine. A month later a brown crust forms, and the cheese is stamped with its place of origin and date. After another seven months or so it is tapped with a hammer; a hollow sound means troublesome bacteria have formed within, and surgery is performed to preserve the cheese.

A year is the minimum ageing period, but the longer it sits in the cheese vaults, the sweeter and fuller the taste. A two-year-old cheese is called *vecchio* (aficionados claim *vecchio* is the most 'expressive'); at three years it's *stravecchio*, and at four years *stravecchione* (which makes an excellent dessert cheese, drizzled with balsamic vinegar). Winter Parmesan has a deeper, more complex flavour. You even choose where the cows graze: *pianura* (valley), *colline* (hills) or, the most prized of all, *vacche rosse di montagna* (red cows of the mountains).

The wheels are so precious that even today the Credito Emiliano banks them as collateral, and is said to have over €100 million worth in its vaults. Samuel Pepys loved his so much that he returned to his house during the Great Fire of London in 1666 to bury it before it melted (back then the average wheel of cheese was 80kg, so difficult to transport). His house in Seething Lane survived, but he never wrote if the cheese remained intact or turned into a subterranean fondue.

was begun in the 8th century and converted into a far more comfortable residential palace ten centuries later by its current owners, the Meli Lupi. One of the few castles never to have been conquered or sold, it contains furnishings going back to the 16th century and opulent frescoes, including stunning silver and gold grotesques by Cesare Baglione and the *Life of Hercules* by Niccolò dell'Abate. There's a fascinating 17th-century French tapestry of exotic animals, rooms lavishly stuccoed by the Bibiena brothers (including a spectacular 62m Poets' Gallery, with perfect acoustics), the family chapel and portraits. One depicts the local ghost, Cassandra Marinoni, wife of the Marchese Diofebo II and known as the *donna cenerina* ('the ashen lady'), who was murdered here by her brother-in-law in 1573 and never avenged: seeing her is a sign that something bad is about to happen in the family.

A monumental stair adorned with Liberty-style frescoes leads to the Great Gallery, frescoed by the Bibiena with momentous Meli Lupi events, and there's a suitably fancy throne room and nuptial chamber. An English garden, planted in the early 1800s, has fine old trees (including a massive American walnut) and 18th-century statues around the lake.

Also on the Rocca's grounds is the Castellazzi, a round building that served as the Meli Lupi's factory. It now houses the **Museo del Parmigiano Reggiano** (*Via Volta 5;* \ *0524 596129;* w *museidelcibo.it;* ⊕ *Mar–early Dec 10.00–13.00 & 15.00–18.00 Sat–Sun, other days by appointment; adults €5, under 6s free*) with historic tools, a cheese history lesson, tastings and a shop.

FONTANELLATO   Fontanellato, southeast of Soragna, resembles a little Ferrara with its moated castle in the centre, although the castle stands out from the crowd with its frescoes by Parmigianino. And there's a new attraction in town too: nothing less than a chance to get lost in the world's largest maze.

Getting there and away   Bus 2135 from Fidenza and bus 2120 from Busseto call at Fontanellato; for the Labirinto della Masone, take a train to Fidenza and a taxi (*10mins*).

Tourist information
ℹ️ Castelo Sanvitale, Piazza Matteotti 1; \0521 829055; w fontanellato.org; ⊕ Apr–Oct 09.30–12.30 & 15.00–18.00 daily, Nov–Mar 09.30–13.00 & 15.00–17.30 Tue–Sat, 9.30–12.30 & 14.30–17.00 Sun

✕ Where to eat and drink
✕ **Mezzadri**   Loc Paroletta 2; \0521 822151; w ristorantemezzadri.it. Elegant contemporary restaurant with a terrace, gorgeous *salumi* & *torta fritta* (try it with the local fizz, Fortanina Frizzante) & *tortelli con le erbette*. They also have rooms in the adjacent hotel San Vitale, same telephone number; b/fast inc (€€€). €€€.

What to see and do
Castello di Sanvitale (\ *0521 829055; guided tours* ⊕ *Apr–Oct 09.30–11.45 & 15.00–17.45 daily, Nov–Mar 09.30–11.45 & 14.30–16.45 Tue–Sat, 9.30–11.45 & 14.30–16.45 Sun; adults €8; ages 6–16 €3.50*) Fontanellato's castle was rebuilt after 1404 by a little dynasty of Sanvitale counts that got their start serving the Visconti of Milan and died out in 1951. The showstopper within is the boudoir, frescoed by a young Parmigianino in 1524, when Galeazzo Sanvitale and his wife, Paola Gonzaga, offered him refuge when he was on the run from the police after a spat with some monks in Parma. His rich, sensuous lunettes of *Diana and Actaeon* and

charming putti under a giant pergola were inspired by Correggio's Camera di San Paolo. Other frescoed rooms include the Sala delle Armi and the dining room, and there is an unusual *camera ottica* that allows you to spy on Fontanellato's piazza through a complex arrangement of mirrors.

Santuario della Beata Vergine del Rosario (*Viale IV Novembre;* \ *0521 829911;* w *santuariofontanellato.com;* ☀ *07.00–12.30 & 15.00–19.30 daily*) Most people who visit Fontanellato are here for this lavish Dominican church. Housing a much venerated, miracle-working statue of the Madonna and Child (1615), the Santuario has a perfectly elegant Baroque façade – tacked on in 1913, although nearly all the sincere if awful art inside is genuine guaranteed 17th and 18th century.

Labirinto della Masone [map, pages 202–3] (*Strada Masone 121, between A1 & SS9;* \ *0521 827081;* w *labirintodifrancomariaricci.it;* ☀ *10.30–19.00 Wed–Mon; adults €18, ages 6–12 €10*) Argentinian writer Jorge Luis Borges was always fascinated by labyrinths, and in 1977 his Italian publisher Franco Maria Ricci made him a promise: he would create the largest one in the world. Designed with Pier Carlo Bontempi and Davide Dutto at Masone, Ricci's family estate, the 8ha square labyrinth opened to the public in 2015. Consisting of 3km of paths lined with 200,000 bamboo plants, it's set within an eight-pointed star reminiscent of the planned Renaissance city of Palmanova in Friuli.

The handmade brick buildings in the centre of the maze (which you can reach without going through all the turns) were inspired by writings on Utopia over the centuries. They house a museum with Ricci's rich, eclectic art collection (the Carracci, Luca Cambiaso's *Venus Blindfolding Cupid*, Houdon, Thorwaldsen and Art Deco pieces to name just a few) and books, including a copy of everything Bodoni (page 217) ever printed. There's a bistro and café, run by the Spigaroli brothers of the Antica Corte Pallavicina (page 242), and if money is no object there are two palatial art-filled suites, available by request.

Castello di Castelguelfo [map, pages 202–3] (*Fontevivo; visible from outside only*) South of Fontanellato, in a strategic spot along Via Emilia and the Taro Valley, stands another imposing fortress with two towers that once belonged to the Ghibelline Pallavicini, but was renamed as an insult by its Guelph captors in 1407. Afterwards it changed hands countless times – but the name stuck.

NORTH OF FONTANELLATO: SAN SECONDO AND ROCCABIANCA The Rossi of San Secondo were big cheeses in these parts, and in 1523 Pier Maria Rossi III celebrated his marriage to Camilla Gonzaga by commissioning Mannerist followers of Raphael and Giulio Romano (Cesare Baglione, Orazio Samacchini, Francesco Zanguidi and Ercole Procaccini) to fresco the ceilings of the **Rocca di Rossi** (*San Secondo;* \ *0521 873214;* w *cortedeirossi.it; guided tours* ☀ *Mar–Nov on the hr 15.00–18.00 Sat, 10.00–11.00 & 15.00–18.00 Sun; €6; also* ☀ *21.30 last Sat of each month with Renaissance wedding re-enactment & tastings; book via* m *338 212 8809; €7.50*) Troilo Rossi II, an astute politician who enabled the family to coexist convivially with the Farnese, improved and restored the castle and added more frescoes. After the family died out in 1825, the Rocca was used as a prison and partly demolished – when a secret tunnel was discovered, complete with the bones of soldiers and horses. Many of the delightful frescoes, however, have survived in excellent condition, including portraits of the Caesars, giants, scenes from Ovid's *Metamorphosis*, *Aesop's Fables* and the story of the *Golden Ass of Apuleius*, culminating in the magnificent Sala delle Gesta Rossiane (1570), painted with the triumphs of the Rossi Counts to remind any visiting Farnese parvenus who's who.

Ten kilometres north, Pier Maria Rossi il Magnifico built the **Castello di Roccabianca** [map, pages 202–3] (*Piazza Garibaldi;* \ *0521 374065;* w *castellidelducato.it; guided tours* ☉ *mid-Feb–Dec 14.30 & 17.30 Sat, 10.00, 11.00, 14.30 & 17.30 Sun; €6*) in 1446 as a private residence for his lover Bianca Pellegrini (the Castello di Torrechiara, page 231, was used for their trysts). An impressive castle, once surrounded by a moat, it was purchased by the owners of the local Faled distillery. Since then, frescoes that were destroyed or carried off over the years have been copied and restored – best of all the wonderful room with scenes of Boccaccio's story of *Patient Griselda* under an astrological ceiling, said to be a map of the heavens when Pier Maria was born, although no-one is really sure. The originals are in the Castello Sforzesco in Milan.

🏠 Where to stay, eat and drink *Map, pages 202–3*

✘ **Hostaria da Ivan** Via Villa 24, Fontanelle di Roccabianca; \0521 870113; w hostariadaivan.it; ☉ closed Mon, Tue. South of Roccabianca, a rustic chic inn serving tasty traditional dishes, including *tosone fritto* (breaded & fried strips of Parmesan cheese), onion frittata & tortelli 'braided' with dandelion greens, ricotta & honey, *stracotto*, roast duck & old-fashioned *zabaione* for dessert; great wine list, too. It also has 4 dbl rooms (**€€€**). **€€€**

ALSENO Northwest of Fidenza, up the Via Emilia, Alseno is the site of the **Abbazia Chiaravalle della Colomba** [map, pages 202–3] (*Via San Bernardo 35;* \ *0523 940132;* w *chiaravalledellacolomba.it;* ☉ *08.30–noon & 14.30–18.30 daily*), the first Cistercian monastery in Emilia-Romagna and one of considerable resilience. Founded in 1136 after a visit to Piacenza by St Bernard, it was named after his abbey in Clairvaux and the dove (*colomba*) of the Annunciation. Sacked in 1248 by Frederick II, it was rebuilt in the 16th century, suppressed in 1769 and made into a hospital in 1810, when it lost its library and most of its art. The Cistercians returned only in 1937 and work in the surrounding fields.

Like all Cistercian churches, the abbey's red-brick basilica is austere, but has a chapel frescoed in the manner of Giotto; not to be missed in June during the Corpus Domini Infiorata, when the nave becomes a colourful scented carpet of rose petals and broom flowers. The 14th-century cloister is beautiful, with its remarkable 'knotted' red marble corner columns; there's a small museum of the abbey, as well as a shop selling the monk-made teas and liqueurs.

Just south of the Via Emilia, the medieval **Castello di Castelnuovo Fogliani** [map, pages 202–3] (*Castelnuovo Fogliani;* \ *0523 947 112;* ☉ *by appointment*), with a lofty swallowtail tower, was reshaped into an up-to-date palace with sumptuously decorated rooms, ornate box gardens and a park by Luigi Vanvitelli, 18th-century court architect to the King of Naples and builder of the 'Italian Versailles' at Caserta.

✘ Where to eat and drink

✘ **Da Giovanni** Via Cortina, Alseno; \0523 948304; w dagiovanniacortina.com; ☉ closed Mon & Tue. Welcoming restaurant that opened as a simple osteria in 1965 & is now famous for its superb fish, veg from the garden & its own cured *salumi*. 6-course *menu degustazione* €60. **€€€€€**

CORTEMAGGIORE In 1479 Gianludovico Pallavicino replaced Busseto with a new capital, Cortemaggiore. Although sometimes touted as one of the planned 'ideal cities' of the Renaissance, this gives too much credit to an age that, for all its talents, cared little for town design. With its neat rectangle of walls in a grid with an arcaded square and church at the centre, Cortemaggiore was only following Europe's accepted practice for laying out new towns since the 11th century; the plan is the spitting image of a medieval French *bastide*.

Cortemaggiore suffered a strange fate after the last war with the discovery of northern Italy's biggest gas deposits and the industrialisation that followed, but the old town preserves some of its Renaissance graces. At its centre, in Piazza dei Patrioti, is the **Basilica di Santa Maria delle Grazie** (1499) designed by Gilberto Manzi, who also laid out the town; it contains the tomb of Gianludovico Pallavicino and a polyptych by Filippo Mazzola, the father of Parmigianino. Other Pallavicini are buried in **Santissima Annunziata** (*Via Matteotti 27*; ✆ *0523 836536;* ◷ *by appointment, or Sun Mass at 16.30*) accompanied by paintings by Pordenone. His best – and most unusual – work is in the Cappella dell' Immacolata Concezione, showing God and St Anne at the moment of *her* virgin conception of the Virgin.

 Where to stay, eat and drink *Map, pages 202–3*

🏠 **Locanda del Re Guerriero** (4 rooms) Via Melchiorre Gioia 5, San Pietro in Cerro; ✆ 0523 839056; w locandareguerriero.it. 4km north of Cortemaggiore, a family inn with elegant eco-friendly dbls & suites in the grounds of the local castle; superb b/fast inc. **€€€€–€€€€€**

🏠 **Le Ruote** (72 rooms) Via Emilia Parmense 204, Roveleto di Cadeo; ✆ 0523 500427; w hotelleruote.com. Modern green glass hotel 10km from Cortemaggiore, with all mod cons. The excellent restaurant (**€€€**) offers vegetarian & vegan dishes, as well as the Emilian classics. **€€€**

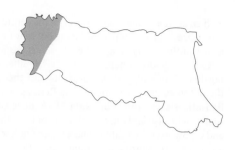

8

Piacenza and Surrounds

'Nobody comes to see us,' the Piacentini wistfully complain. It's a quiet old town, with a large medieval centre from the days when Piacenza, once the second city in the Duchy of Parma, competed with the big boys. After that good start, it fell into the shadows when first Milan and then Parma came to rule it. Nevertheless, there are several good reasons to stop.

Vying with the more famous and obvious charms of nearby Parma, Piacenza is the unassuming wallflower of Renaissance art cities, with one of northern Italy's finest cathedrals, masterpieces by Botticelli and Antonello da Messina, a memorable museum, two of the most gallant horses in Italy, and the world's most famous bronze liver. Verdant valleys stretch from Piacenza into the Apennines, where you can visit Castell'Arquato, a perfect Tuscan hill town that somehow sneaked over the Apennines, frescoed castles, the world's first shit museum and Bobbio, a candle in the Dark Ages, when it was the headquarters of Irish monasticism on the Continent.

HISTORY

Piacenza began as Placentia (Pleasant Abode), a Roman colony established at the conjunction of the Via Aemilia and the Po in 218BC, just in time to witness an important battle of the Second Punic War, when the Romans failed to stop Hannibal and his army from crossing the Apennines into Italy proper. It was a key point along the Via Francigena (see box, page 235); Holy Roman emperors such as Frederick Barbarossa would hold a parliament with their vassals in the spring of those years when they came to Italy – not in the town itself, which became a free *comune* in 1126, but on the plains of Roncaglia just east (the A24 runs through the spot now). In 1095 Pope Urban II came to Piacenza to proclaim the First Crusade.

As the site of an international trade fair, Piacenza boomed in the 12th and 13th centuries, and became an original member of the Lombard League in the fight against Barbarossa. When the *comune* began to dissolve in factionalism, it became part of the little empire of Uberto Pallavicini of Busseto (see box, pages 8–9). A local banker, Alberto Scotto (a descendant of William Douglas, who came to Italy to fight the Lombards with Charlemagne), briefly ruled it before the city was snatched by the Visconti of Milan. From then on, Piacenza's fate was never in its own hands. After the Visconti came the Sforza, and then the French, during the Wars of Italy. After the French were kicked out, Piacenza was grabbed by the papacy, and in 1545 Paul III made it part of the Duchy of Parma; it was even the capital until the locals murdered the first duke.

The city remained a backwater until the revolutions of 1848. After a plebiscite, in which the vote went 37,089 to 496, Piacenza became the first city to unite with

Piedmont in the new nation of Italy, earning itself the nickname Primogenita, or 'first-born'. In 1996, the city was awarded a gold medal for its valour and resistance in World War II.

GETTING THERE AND AWAY

BY RAIL The station [250 F2], on Piazzale Marconi, is a 10-minute walk from the centre and has frequent connections to Milan, Parma (*40mins*), Cremona, Turin and Genoa via Bobbio.

BY BUS Seta buses serve the city and the province. The bus station is at Via Colombo 3 [250 F3] (♦ *0523 390 655;* w *setaweb.it/pc*); see the website for route maps and schedules.

BY ROAD Piacenza is a major junction. The historic Via Emilia (SS9) heads to Milan and southeast to Parma, parallel to the A1 (E35). Just north of Piacenza both roads are crossed by the A21 (E70) from Turin to Cremona and Brescia. The SS45 leads southwest to the Val Trebbia, Bobbio and Genoa.

GETTING AROUND

Piacenza is easy to navigate by foot; if you need a bus, see Seta (w *setaweb.it/pc*).

BY CAR The centre's traffic limitation zone (ZTL) is in force from 08.00 to 19.00. If you're staying in the centre, ask your hotel where to park. The largest free car park is along Viale Sant'Ambrogio, by the train station.

BY TAXI
🚕 **Radio Taxi Piacenza** ♦0523 591919

TOURIST INFORMATION

ℹ️ [250 D2] Piazza Cavalli 7; ♦0523 492 001; w piacerepiacenza.it; ☺ winter 10.00–noon & 15.30–17.30 Tue–Sat, summer 09.00–13.00 & 15.00–18.00 Tue–Sat, 09.30–12.30 Sun

 WHERE TO STAY

🏠 **B&B Serena** [250 A3] (5 rooms) Via Morigi 36; m 349 802 2849; w bb-piacenza.it. In a quiet residential zone 1km west, contemporary rooms run by the owners of the adjacent Grotta Azzurra restaurant/pizzeria. B/fast inc. €€€€

🏠 **Grande Albergo Roma** [250 D2] (72 rooms) Via Cittadella 14; ♦0523 323201; w grandealbergoroma.it. Just off Piazza Cavalli, Piacenza's most prestigious hotel comes with elegant woodwork & furnishings, old-fashioned service, a garage, gym & sauna, & a restaurant/bar/lounge on the 7th floor with 360-degree views over Piacenza. €€€€

🏠 **Hotel City** [250 G4] (60 rooms) Via Emilia Parmense 54; ♦0523 579752; w hotelcitypc.it. Southeast of town on the Parma road, a modern quiet hotel with business-like rooms, bikes to rent & free parking. B/fast buffet inc. €€–€€€

🏠 **Ovest** [250 A3] (59 rooms) Via 1 Maggio 82; ♦0523 712222; w hotelovest.com. West near the Piacenza Ovest exit, convenient, contemporary hotel with well-equipped rooms in various sizes. Excellent buffet b/fast inc. €€

🏠 **Ostello Papa Giovanni XXIII** [250 C2] (10 rooms) Via Nazzaro 2A; ♦0523 490104; w ostellodipiacenza.it. Recently renovated, centrally located with en-suite sgls & dbls. €

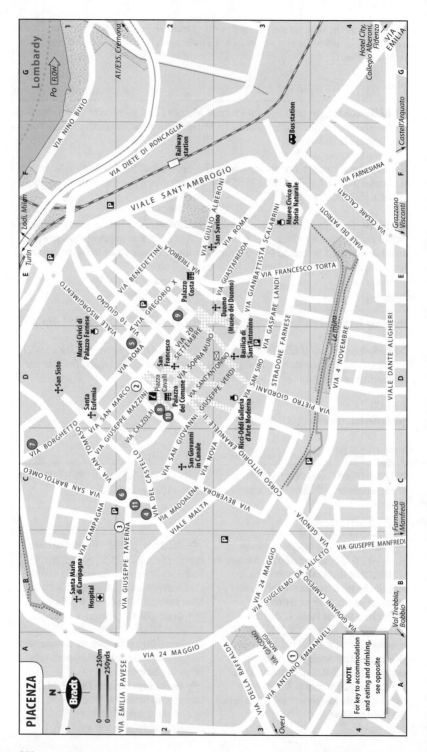

PIACENZA

N

Bradt

0 — 250m
0 — 250yds

G Lombardy

Po FLOW

A1/E35, Cremona

VIA NINO BIXIO

VIA DIETE DI RONCAGLIA

Railway station

VIALE SANT'AMBROGIO

Bus station

Turin
Lodi, Milan

Museo Civico di Storia Naturale

VIA FARNESIANA

Grazzano Visconti
Castel l'Arquato

Hotel City; Collegio Alberoni, Fidenza

VIA EMILIA

VIA CESARE CALCATI

VIALE DEI PATRIOTI

VIA GIULIO ALBERONI

San Savino

VIA ROMA

VIA TREBBIOLA

Palazzo Costa

VIALE RISORGIMENTO

VIA 10 GIUGNO

VIA GREGORIO X

VIA BENEDETTINE

9

VIA GUASTAFREDDA

Duomo (Museo del Duomo)

VIA GIANBATTISTA SCALABRINI

VIA FRANCESCO TORTA

Musei Civici di Palazzo Farnese

San Sisto

Santa Eufemia

VIA SAN MARCO

VIA ROMA

5

San Francesco

VIA 20 SETTEMBRE

VIA SOPRAMURO

Palazzo del Comune

Piazza Cavalli

VIA GIUSEPPE MAZZINI

VIA CALZOLAI

2

8

10

VIA SANT'ANTONINO

Basilica di Sant'Antonino

VIA GASPARE LANDI

Le Mura

VIA 4 NOVEMBRE

VIA SAN BARTOLOMEO

VIA SAN TOMMASO

VIA BORGHETTO

7

VIA CAMPAGNA

6

3

VIA GIUSEPPE TAVERNA

11

4

VIA DEL CASTELLO

VIA MADDALENA

VIALE MALTA

VIA NOVA

San Giovanni in Canale

VIA BEVERORA

CORSO VITTORIO EMANUELE II

VIA GIUSEPPE VERDI

Ricci-Oddi Galleria d'Arte Moderna

VIA SAN SIRO

STRADONE FARNESE

VIA PIETRO GIORDANI

VIALE DANTE ALIGHIERI

Santa Maria di Campagna

Hospital

VIA GIUSEPPE TAVERNA

VIA 24 MAGGIO

Val Trebbia, Bobbio

VIA GUGLIELMO DA SALICETO

VIA GIOVANNI CAMPESIO

VIA 24 MAGGIO

Ovest

VIA GIACOMO MORIGI

VIA ANTONIO EMMANUELI

VIA DELLA RAFFALDA

VIA EMILIA PAVESE

VIA GENOVA

VIA GIUSEPPE MANFREDI

Farmacia Manfredi

1

NOTE
For key to accommodation and eating and drinking, see opposite

250

Although they argue about small points, Piacenza follows Parma closely in the kitchen, although its classic *tortelli con la coda* are 'woven' and have 'tails'. *Pisarei e faseu*, which often appears on menus, is mini gnocchi served with beans in a tomato sauce.

✖ **Da Marco Osteria del Trentino** [250 C2] Via del Castello 71; ☎0523 324260; ⊕ closed Sun. Wood beams, white tablecloths & copper pots in the cosy dining room, but an outdoor garden terrace too. Delicious *anolini in brodo*, & along with a small selection of meats & fish there's an elaborate '*quinto quarto*' menu (a butcher's term for the 5th of the 4 main sections of an animal, aka offal). Also vegetarian choices. €€€

✖ **Trattoria San Giovanni** [250 D2] Corso Garibaldi 49a; ☎0523 321029; w trattoriasangiovanni.net; ⊕ dinner only, Sat–Sun also lunch. Black-&-white contemporary cool dining room in a 16th-century palazzo with more than 800 wines to go with its traditional Piacentine dishes, but also guinea fowl with spinach, lemon grass & red pepper corns. €€€

✖ **Enoteca da Renato** [250 D2] Via Roma 24; ☎0523 325813; ⊕ closed Mon, Sun eve. In business for more than 50 years, with 1,000-plus bottles to choose from & lovely food to match. Lively, fun atmosphere. €€

✖ **La Pireina** [250 C1] Via Borghetto 137; ☎0523 338578; ⊕ closed Mon. An old-fashioned trattoria by San Sisto, serving typical local dishes: great *salumi* & *gnocco fritto*, tortelli & meaty mains (including horse) washed down with a bottle of Gutturnio. Don't miss the *torta sbrisolona* for dessert. €€

✖ **Vecchia Piacenza** [250 C2] Calle San Bernardo 1; ☎0523 305462; ⊕ closed Mon. Just

west of the *centro*, housed in the former mint, this little place is crammed with paintings, frescoes & objets d'art. Excellent seasonal dishes (asparagus in spring) as well as refined versions of the classics; the tortelli with duck is especially recommended. €€

✖ **Food Arte da Mangiare** [250 C2] Via Taverna Giuseppe 35; m 366 980 3855; w food-artedamangiare.it; ⊕ until midnight daily. Informal, hip & often packed: no choice, but €10 lunch (salad, pasta, dessert, focaccia, glass of wine, water & coffee), or €15 with a main. In the evening choose 1, 2 or 3 veg, fish or meat courses. €

✖ **Lo Fai–Handmade Bar** [250 D2] Via Cavalletto 4; ☎0523 167 1221; 🇫; ⊕ 10.30–16.30 Mon, Tue & Thu, 10.30–16.30 & 18.00–midnight Wed, Fri & Sat. A vegan-vegetarian restaurant, with superb risotto & pasta dishes (especially with mushrooms), craft beers, organic wines & a craft shop. Daily changing menu; book ahead. €

✖ **Tosello** [250 E2] Via Francesco Daveri 10; ☎0523 324 8334; w tosellopiacenza.com; ⊕ closed Mon, Sun lunch. Informal place in a former palazzo; besides light, Roman-style pizzas, it also does a €12 all-you-can-eat vegetarian buffet. €

OTHER PRACTICALITIES

HOSPITAL
✚ [250 B1] Via Taverna Giuseppe 49; ☎0523 301111

PHARMACY
✚ **Farmacia Manfredi** [250 B4] Via Giuseppe Manfredi 72; ☎0523 457361; ⊕ 24hrs

POST OFFICE
✉ [250 D3] Via Sant'Antonino 40; ⊕ 08.30–19.00 Mon–Fri, 08.30–13.00 Sat

8

WHAT TO SEE AND DO

Although Piacenza, with just over 100,000 souls, is Emilia-Romagna's smallest provincial capital, its historic centre is larger than most. After a great start as a free city, its importance dwindled under the rule of Milan and the Farnese and, walking its long quiet streets, laid out in a business-like grid that has not changed much since the Romans, you might feel a sense of great but unfulfilled expectations. It certainly has an exceptional collection of churches – perhaps more than it ever needed.

PIAZZA CAVALLI Piacenza's excellent centrepiece takes its name from its two magnificent bronze horses, cast in the 1620s by Francesco Mochi. Riding them are Alessandro Farnese, the second Duke of Parma, and his son Ranuccio. While Ranuccio's statue is conventional, Alessandro's is the first truly dynamic equestrian statue of the Baroque era, and with a dramatic sweep of the cloak unites man and horse in an unprecedented way.

They prance in front of the **Palazzo del Comune** [250 D2] (⊕ *during temporary exhibitions*). Better known to the Piacentini as the Palazzo Gotico, it's one of Italy's most elegant city halls. Begun by Alberto Scotto in 1280, the pink and grey marble loggia contrasts with the rich red bricks and intricately ornate windows of the upper floor, all topped off with swallowtail crenellations that give away Piacenza's Ghibelline loyalties at the time it was finished.

San Francesco [250 D2] (*Via Sopramuro 46;* ☏ *0523 321988;* ⊕ *08.30–noon & 15.00–18.00 Mon–Sat, 09.00–12.30 & 16.00–19.00 Sun*) Just off Piazza Cavalli, this Gothic church begun in 1278 has a portal decorated with a relief of St Francis receiving the stigmata. Its handsome Gothic interior has survived relatively unchanged, with sculptures, tombs and remains of frescoes even though Napoleon used it as a warehouse.

SOUTH OF PIAZZA CAVALLI
Duomo [250 E3] (*Piazza del Duomo;* ☏ *0523 335154;* w *duomopiacenza.it;* ⊕ *09.00–noon & 16.00–19.00 daily*) Once Piacenza's cathedral had a proper asymmetrical medieval square, until Paul III had the area redesigned, creating a rectangular piazza more to Renaissance tastes; the Pope wanted Piacenza to look more up to date before he made a present of it to his son Pier Luigi. At least he didn't mess with the cathedral itself (1122–1233), a masterpiece of Lombard-Romanesque begun after an earthquake felled an earlier church, and only four years before the declaration of the *comune*. Viewed from the side and apse it's a picturesque confusion of columns, caryatids and galleries under an unusual octagonal cupola and the mighty **campanile** (1333), crowned by the L'Angil dal Dom, a gilded copper angel which doubles as a weather vane. There are

> ### FIVE MUSEUMS TICKET
>
> Costing €17 (*€13 children & seniors*), the 'Cinque Musei, Un Biglietto' combined entry ticket is available from any of the participating museums:
>
> Palazzo Farnese, Galleria Ricci-Oddi, Museo del Duomo, Museo di Storia Naturale, Collegio Alberoni.

The fellow on the horse may never have spent much time here but he is one of the key figures of the 1500s. Alessandro Farnese, named for his great-grandfather, who became Pope Paul III and carved out the family duchy, was born in Rome in 1545. His mother, Margaret, was Charles V's illegitimate daughter and half-sister to Philip II of Spain. Alessandro spent much of his youth in Brussels and Madrid, where he was kept as a sort of hostage by the Habsburgs to ensure Farnese good behaviour. There he got his education and became very close to his Spanish kin. As a youth he delighted in nothing more than hunting and warfare; he saw his first action at Lepanto in 1571, where he was conspicuous for his bravery – he was the first man to jump over the rail and board a Turkish galley.

The revolt of the United Provinces against the Habsburgs finally gave him a chance to lead an army. He arrived in the Netherlands in 1577, won a smashing victory at Gembloux the next year, and was named Governor General. For the next decade his armies battled furiously with William of Orange up and down the Netherlands. Twice, when diplomatic considerations made Philip II want to give up the fight, Alessandro's dogged determination kept it going. Although he never mastered the Protestant north, he met with success in the south, which he kept loyal and Catholic – just think, without him there would never have been a Belgium.

Besides his military genius, Alessandro was noted for his lack of religious fanaticism and his aversion to gratuitous violence and massacres, both characteristics sadly lacking in those times. Tyranny seldom had a more estimable servant. Alessandro almost had a chance to practise his talents on another country – he was waiting by the Channel with a big army when the Invincible Armada sank in 1588.

As for the other horseman, Ranuccio was a bad duke and a paranoid waster who reigned from his father's death in 1592 until 1622, and was best remembered for executing more than a hundred people for supposed plots against him. The best thing he ever did was to commission the statues.

sculpted capitals and columns (including a caryatid) to pick out, and an iron cage dangling from the top, placed there by Milanese boss Ludovico il Moro as a warning to malefactors.

The central portal in the pink marble and sandstone façade was rebuilt in the 1500s (retaining figures of the Zodiac and the hand of God). The right portal, sculpted with the story of Christ, is by Niccolò, who trained with Wiligelmo at Modena (see box, page 153); Wiligelmo himself may have sculpted the left portal, with the curious figure of a man riding a sheep

The transitional (from Romanesque to Gothic) **interior** features a striking striped marble floor and good 15th-century frescoes; seven piers in the nave sport reliefs by Niccolò called *formelle dei paratici* of the cloth-makers, merchants, bakers, shoemakers and other guilds who contributed to the cathedral. The remarkable **cupola** has frescoes of Old Testament prophets by Milanese painter Morazzone – his last work; he died before they were completed, in 1626, and most of the dome and the figures of the Sibyls below were done by Guercino. Other frescoes are by Ludovico Carracci and Camillo Procaccini.

Kronos: Museo del Duomo (*In the crypt;* ⊕ *09.00–noon Tue–Sat, 16.00–18.00 Wed–Sun;* €3) The crypt, with its 108 columns, is shaped like a Greek cross, and houses the relics of Piacenza's first saint, Giustina, translated here from Rome in 1001, as well as this new museum with displays on the cathedral's history, paintings, and the priceless illuminated *Codice 65* or *Libro del Maestro* (1142), a compilation of all the ecclesiastical knowledge of the day.

Palazzo Costa [250 E2] (*Via Roma 80;* ☏ *0523 306137;* m *338 745 1756;* ⊕ *by appointment for groups, but see if you can join one; admission free*) Just up Via Legnano from the Duomo, lavish Rococo Palazzo Costa was built for a wealthy Genoese family. While privately owned in part, the *piano nobile* is now a museum of the 18th-century 'ambience', with a remarkable grand stair and lavish entrance hall designed by Ferdinando Bibiena in 1693, rooms of delicate gilded stuccoes and furnishings, and among the paintings a *Philosopher* by Salvatore Rosa.

San Savino [250 E2] (*Via G Alberoni 35;* ☏ *0523 318165;* ⊕ *09.30–noon & 16.00–18.00 Mon–Fri, 09.00–10.00 & 16.00–17.00 Sat–Sun*) Also east of the Duomo, a big late Baroque façade hides a handsome Romanesque church, completed in 1107 and dedicated to the second bishop of Piacenza. In the beautiful interior, beyond some fancifully carved capitals, San Savino's main attraction is the **pavements**: a black-and-white ocean mosaic, with the occasional fish, zigzags across the nave. Two remarkable 12th-century mosaics were discovered during restoration work in 1902. One, in the presbytery, shows a classically allusive *Time*, or Fate, spinning, surrounded by the cardinal virtues: Justice, Fortitude, Temperance and Prudence – the last represented by a pair of chess players. The other, in the crypt, depicts the *Signs of the Zodiac*, the *Labours of the Months*, and a battle scene.

Basilica di Sant'Antonino [250 D3] (*Piazza Sant'Antonio;* ☏ *0523 320653;* ⊕ *08.00–noon & 16.00–18.30 Mon–Sat, 09.00–12.30 & 20.00–21.30 Sun*) Southwest of the Duomo, this basilica was the city's original cathedral. Dedicated to Piacenza's current patron saint Antoninus, a soldier in the Theban legion, it was begun shortly after his martyrdom in the 4th century AD; its 11th-century octagonal tower is believed to be the first of its kind built in Italy. In 1183, delegates of the Lombard League and Emperor Frederick Barbarossa met here to sign the preliminary agreement for the peace of Constance.

A lofty Gothic porch called the Porta del Paradiso, added in 1350, welcomed pilgrims on the Via Francigena; under this is a portal with a relief of Adam and Eve and a statue of Gregory X. Teobaldo Visconti of Piacenza was elected pope in 1271, after the longest conclave in history. He was surprised (he hadn't even taken holy orders) and at the time was on the Ninth Crusade with Edward I of England. On his return to Italy, one of his first acts was to receive a letter from Kublai Khan by way of Marco Polo's uncle and father, requesting holy oil and missionaries, initiating Marco's own travels.

Sant'Antonino's plan is unusual: the tower rises over the crossing, which is in the rear of the church, not in front of the altar. Note too how the walls of the aisles are tilted inwards towards the altar, creating a disorienting effect if you see it from the right angle. When it was done up in a Neo-Gothic style in the 19th century, it sadly obliterated some rare 11th-century frescoes.

Museo Capitolare di Sant'Antonino (*Via Chiostri Sant'Antonino 6;* ⊕ *Fri by request*) This contains the basilica's treasure and art rescued from its former chapels, including 15th-century altarpieces depicting the life of St Antoninus.

Museo Civico di Storia Naturale [250 F3] (*Via Salabrini 107;* \ *0523 334980;* w *msn.musei.piacenza.it;* ⏰ *09.30–12.30 Tue, Wed & Fri, 09.30–12.30 & 15.00–18.00 Thu, Sat–Sun; €3*) Piacenza's new museum of natural history is housed in the former abattoir, with botanical, mineralogical, zoological (mostly stuffed seabirds) and seashell collections; you can also see the big machines once used for making ice.

Ricci-Oddi Galleria d'Arte Moderna [250 D3] (*Via San Siro 13;* \ *0523 320742;* w *riccioddi.it;* ⏰ *09.30–12.30 & 15.00–18.00 Tue–Sun (Jul–Aug mornings only); €5, free 1st Sun of month*) In 1931, Piacenza gave local art enthusiast Giuseppe Ricci-Oddi (1868–1937) a derelict convent to rebuild as a handsome Neo-Renaissance gallery. His excellent collection of covers most of the Italian schools from the 19th and early 20th century, with works by Boccioni, Boldini, Carrà, Fattori, Hayez, De Nittis, Medardo Rosso, de Pisis, de Chirico, Klimt and others.

San Giovanni in Canale [250 C2] (*Via Croce 26;* \ *0523 330471;* ⏰ *07.30–noon & 15.30–19.00 Mon–Sat, from 09.00 Sun*) Dominican San Giovanni, seat of the local Inquisition, was founded in 1220 outside the walls, by a long-vanished canal to the Po. Remodelled in the 16th century, the imposing interior houses the 15th-century red Verona marble tomb of the Scotti clan, an elaborate quadratura altar and a Rosary chapel with a large *Road to Calvary* by Gaspare Landi, a Neoclassical painter from Piacenza who headed the Academy of St Luke.

NORTH OF PIAZZA CAVALLI
Musei Civici di Palazzo Farnese [250 D1] (*Piazza Cittadella 29;* \ *0523 492658;* w *www.palazzofarnese.piacenza.it;* ⏰ *09.00–13.00 Tue–Thu, 09.00–13.00 & 15.00–18.00 Fri & Sat, 09.30–13.00 & 15.00–18.00 Sun; €6, free 1st Sun of month*) The pachydermic Palazzo Farnese, once headquarters of the ducal family, was begun in 1558 by Vignola, the High Renaissance's most accomplished architect, but was never finished. But there are some lavishly decorated rooms called the **Fasti Farnese**, with precious stuccoes framing scenes of the family's favourite subject: themselves. These are impressive paintings, mostly done in the 1680s: Giovanni Draghi got the job of glorifying Alessandro Farnese, while the Venetian Sebastiano Ricci took on Paul III: *The Pope Reconciling Emperor Charles V and François I* – note the artful pose, taken from Velázquez's *Las Lanzas*, and the pope floating around in heaven on the ceiling.

In the **Pinacoteca**, a large room is dedicated to 14th-century frescoes detached from local churches, by Bartolomeo and Jacopino da Reggio, and by the 'Maestro di Santa Caterina', so called after the cycle on the *Life of St Catherine* here, all masters of the precise and virtuous line. Botticelli's lovely *Tondo* gets a room all to itself. Although painted in the 1480s, when the artist was coming under the influence of Savonarola and trading in his mythological fancies for Christian piety, his Madonna is still the familiar Venus, though a little older and wiser. The newly acquired Rizzi Vaccari collection has 14th-15th century works by Giovanni da Milano, Simone de' Crocifissi and other early masters. Later paintings are few, but big ones fit for a duke. Pride of place goes to the inimitable Ilario Spolverini, a specialist in Farnese-flattering ceremonial scenes, battle paintings and Biblical extravaganzas worthy of Cecil B de Mille: *Joshua Makes the Sun Stand Still*, and the *Hebrews Are Led through the Desert by Moses and Aaron*. Note Sala XVII, painted with trompe l'œil walls and the *Chariot of the Sun* on the ceiling by the Venetian Pietro della Vecchia.

One room holds **historic weapons**, another Vignola's enormous **wooden model** of what this palazzo would have looked like with a façade. A **Museum of**

8

the **Risorgimento** covers Piacenza's role in the great upheaval and a **Museum of Carriages** includes one that belonged to King Vittorio Emanuele and a Sicilian cart, a wonderful piece of folk art painted with scenes from Verdi's operas.

Across the courtyard from the main part of the palace is its predecessor, the 14th-century **Cittadella** built by the Visconti, housing the Archaeological Museum. The Farnese pulled most of the Cittadella down while planning its replacement; no doubt the place was an embarrassment to them, after Pier Luigi, the first duke, met his end here in 1547 when rebellious Piacentini nobles murdered him and threw his corpse out of a window into the moat. In one of the surviving rooms is the most famous Etruscan bronze of them all: a model of a sheep liver known as the **Fegato di Piacenza**, designed for apprentice *haruspices*, or augurs, diagrammed and inscribed with the names of the Etruscan deities. The Etruscans regarded the liver as a microcosm of the sky, divided into 16 houses (not 12, as in the zodiac), each ruled over by a god. The augurs looked in the liver for blemishes to see which deity had anything to communicate. The Etruscans were renowned for augury, and Roman emperors consulted their *haruspices* until the coming of Christianity; they were the last speakers of the lost Etruscan language.

San Sisto

San Sisto [250 D1] (*Via San Sisto 9;* ☏ *0523 320321;* ◷ *08.00–noon & 16.00–18.30 Mon–Fri, 08.00–11.00 & 15.00–18.00 Sat, 08.00–noon & 15.30–18.00 Sun*) San Sisto, set in an arcaded courtyard, was founded as a Benedictine convent and hospital in AD874 by Queen Angilberga, wife of Emperor Louis II. It grew incredibly wealthy, eventually becoming a daughter house of Montecassino.

The current church was the first ever built by prolific Piacentino architect Alessio Tramello (1499). Behind the imposing façade, so perfect for its time (although it was altered somewhat in the 1600s) that it could be a stage set in a late Renaissance theatre, there is an unusual interior with domes at either end, set over columned drums. Besides the chiaroscuro decoration, a feature of many of Piacenza's churches, there are good paintings: works by Procaccini, Zacchetti and Palma Giovane. Margherita d'Austria, daughter of Charles V and wife of Ottavio Farnese, is buried here in a lavish ornate tomb. The church's real prize, however, Raphael's famous *Madonna Sistina*, has been replaced by a copy; the monks sold it off long ago to a king of Poland (it's now in Dresden). Fortunately, the king did not have room in his suitcase for the excellent intarsia choir (1514), decorated with architectural scenes.

Santa Eufemia

Santa Eufemia [250 D1] (*Via Santa Eufemia 27;* ☏ *0523 320304;* ◷ *16.00–18.00 Sat, 08.00–noon Sun*) Stop by Santa Eufemia (c1100) for its elegant Romanesque façade, incorporating an arcaded portico and some good capitals, including dragons, harpies, mermaids, a monkey harpist and a fist fight.

Santa Maria di Campagna

Santa Maria di Campagna [250 B1] (*Piazzale delle Crociate 5;* ☏ *0523 490728;* w *santamariadicampagna.com;* ◷ *08.00–noon & 15.30–18.00 Mon–Sat, 07.00– noon & 15.30–19.00 Sun*) Tramelli's Madonna di Campagna (1522) replaced an ancient pilgrimage chapel outside the walls, built for a miraculous image of the Virgin. In the large field that surrounded it, Pope Urban II proclaimed the First Crusade at a Council in 1095 (in most histories the Council of Clermont in France, held later that year, is given as the site of the proclamation – only because the news made a bigger splash among the French, who were to supply most of the crusaders).

Renaissance Tuscany and Umbria developed a habit of building architectural showpiece churches just outside a town, usually in a centralised Greek-cross plan following the architectural theories of the day. Piacenza is one of the few places in northern Italy to have one, though (as at Sant'Antonino) the Piacentini eventually modified it to fit their odd penchant for backwards churches; Tramelli began the Madonna di Campagna as a Greek cross, but in the 1790s the nave was extended not to the west front, but behind the altar. The plan gives it tremendous presence; instead of looking out towards the building's focal point, you stand in it upon entering, while the arches and columns recede towards the altar under a coffered ceiling, the whole effect reminiscent of the architectural fantasy in Raphael's *School of Athens*.

Piacenza was fortunate in finding just the man to decorate this dramatic interior. Pordenone, an artist influenced equally by Titian and Michelangelo, contributed the colourful, intense frescoes (1529–31): that of *St Augustine* just to the left as you enter, and the two domed chapels on the left, the Cappella della Natività and further up, the Cappella di Santa Caterina. Bernardino Gatti assisted Pordenone on the huge dome over the crossing, where God and the prophets share space with hundreds of cavorting nude figures from classical mythology. Gatti also painted the large fresco of *St George and the Dragon* to the right of the door, and other Emilian artists (Alessandro Tiarini, Camillo Procaccini, Daniele Crespi and the Bibiena brothers, among others) also contributed, covering every square inch.

Collegio Alberoni [250 G4] (*2km southeast on Via Emilia Parmense 77;* \ *0523 322635;* w *collegioalberoni.it;* ⊕ *Sep–Jun 15.30–18.00 Sun; €4.50, free guided tours at 16.00*) This college of theology for poor boys was founded by Piacenza native Cardinal Alberoni, and contains its founder's remarkable Flemish tapestries, 16th–18th-century Flemish and Italian paintings, and an extremely rare work of

---

HOW TO BECOME RICH AND FAMOUS

A poor gardener's son, Giulio Alberoni (1664–1752) started his climb in the world as bell-ringer at Piacenza cathedral at the age of 15. An industrious, cheerful soul, he became friendly with a judge and followed him to Ravenna. In Ravenna, he met the papal vice-legate and Bishop of Piacenza, who liked the youth because he made him laugh. He employed Giulio as a chamberlain and encouraged him to take priestly orders. And when the bishop's son moved to Rome, the young priest Alberoni went along.

His big moment came during the War of the Spanish Succession, when the French commander, the Duc de Vendôme, was in Rome, and the Bishop of Parma, who had been sent as an envoy by the Duke of Parma, quit in disgust after the immensely wealthy and powerful Vendôme wiped his bottom in front of him. Father Alberoni was called in to take his place, and when the Frenchman pulled the same stunt, Alberoni is said to have kissed his buttocks and exclaimed: 'O culo del angelo!' ('Ah, the ass of an angel!') much to the duke's amusement.

Vendôme took Alberoni along to Paris, where he met Louis XIV and actively supported his grandson's claim to the Spanish throne. And when the Bourbons won the war and Philip V became king of Spain, the gardener's son from Piacenza became a wealthy grandee, cardinal, famous gourmet, and prime minister (helping the folks back home by arranging the marriage of Elisabetta Farnese to Philip V); he even received ten votes in the next papal conclave in spite of losing his position at court after his foreign intrigues proved calamitous to Spain. Alberoni spent his last days back in Piacenza in his apartments in the Collegio, enjoying all the dishes he had missed in Spain.

8

Antonello da Messina, the greatest southern painter of the 1400s, and probably the first Italian to take up oil painting: the *Ecce Homo* – an unusual composition, and the Renaissance's most sorrowful Christ.

SOUTH OF PIACENZA

The vine-covered hills and valleys south of Piacenza are some of the region's prettiest, and as usual in these parts bristle with castles. Numerous rivers flow down from the Apennines, including two main ones, the Nure and the Trebbia.

CASTELL'ARQUATO Dominating the Arda Valley, lovely Castell'Arquato is the closest to a Tuscan hill town Emilia-Romagna can offer. Starting out as a Roman military camp, the home base of the VIIIth Legion, it metamorphosed into the fortified village of a Lombard baron. Around 1200, Castell'Arquato was able to declare itself a free *comune*. It couldn't last. Alberto Scotto, boss of Piacenza, seized control in 1290; he in turn lost it after a siege to Galeazzo Visconti of Milan, before ending up languishing in the Visconti dungeons. From them it passed to the Sforza, and finally to the Farnese dukes.

Getting there and away

By rail and bus Take the train to Firenzuola d'Arda and bus E45 to Castell'Arquato. For Velleia Romana, take bus 42 from Piacenza station, but check return schedules to make sure you don't get stranded.

By car The nearest exit off either the A1 or A21 is Firenzuola d'Arda, 10km northeast of Castell'Arquato.

Tourist information

i Piazza Municipale 1; ☏ 0523 803215; w castellarquatoturismo.it; ⏱ Nov–Feb

10.00–17.00 Tue–Sun, Mar–Oct 10.00–13.00 & 14.00–18.00 Tue–Sun

Where to stay

Relais du Chateau (6 rooms) Via Sforza Calolzio 47; m 366 406 9000; w relaisduchateau. it. Located in the Liberty-style home of Luigi Illica, the librettist of Puccini & Mascagni, this boutique hotel has king-size beds, bold designer furnishings by Philippe Starck, Naoto Fukasawa, etc. There's a hot tub in the garden, & free parking; b/fast inc. €€€€€

Leon d'Oro (13 rooms) Piazza Europa 6; ☏ 0523 803222; w hotel-leondoro.com. At the entrance to the old town, a Liberty-style hotel that's been smartly redone with peaceful contemporary rooms. Free parking; excellent b/fast inc. €€€€

Castello di Vigoleno [map, pages 202–3] (8 rooms) Piazza IV Novembre 2, Vigoleno di Vernasca (10km south of Castell'Arquato); ☏ 0523 895390; w castellodivigoleno.com. Stay in a handsome suite in a fairy-tale castle, with gorgeous views all around. The most romantic ones are up in the tower; there's also a good restaurant & 'whiskeria' featuring a wide choice of bottles from across Scotland. €€€–€€€€

Villa Dircea (6 rooms) Strada Fiorenzuola 2; ☏ 0523 804150; w villadircea.it. Located at the foot of the village, peaceful pastel rooms with free parking; b/fast inc. €€€

✖ Where to eat and drink

✖ **Il Maps** Piazza Europa 3; ☏ 0523 804411; w ristorantemaps.com; ⏱ closed Mon & Tue. Contemporary arty restaurant & refined cuisine,

cheerful staff; lots of seafood, including excellent swordfish carpaccio. €€€€

✕ Stradivarius Via Sforza Calolzio 36; ☎ 0523 803381; w ristorantestradivarius.it; ⏀ closed Mon. In the castle home of the Stradivarius family of violin-making fame, a restaurant with a beautiful garden terrace. The food is an aria of delights, with specialities from Piacenza: try the pork knuckle, baked medieval style with apples. €€€

✕ Da Faccini Loc San Antonio; ☎ 0523 896340; w ristorantecastellarquato.it; ⏀ closed Wed. Classic family-run osteria that opened in 1932, offering reliable *piacentini* classics; mouthwatering pasta dishes & succulent guinea fowl slow cooked in a clay pot. €€

✕ Locanda del Verro Via Sforza Calolzio 9; ☎ 0523 803388; f. Cosy little place serving craft beers & with plates of pasta or *salumi* or a *panino*. €

What to see and do

Piazza del Municipio It's a stiff climb up to the centre of Castell'Arquato, but the reward is the elegant ensemble of the Piazza del Municipio, or Piazza Alta, little changed since the days of the *comune*. The highlight is the asymmetrical **Palazzo del Podestà**, completed after Scotto took power, with a picturesque loggia and covered stairs (Scotto was a leading Guelph, so someone else must have added the Ghibelline swallowtail crenellations). The basement now holds an Enoteca Comunale although the service can be spotty.

Collegiata di Santa Maria (*Piazza Don Cagnoni 3;* ☎ *0523 805151;* ⏀ *10.00–12.30 & 15.00–18.00 Tue–Sun*) This church turns its back to the piazza, but that's its best side, an elaborate composition of Lombard apses, gables and blind arcading. Last rebuilt in 1122 following an earthquake, it has, like Sant'Antonino in Piacenza, a Portico del Paradiso. The interior has good capitals, including a few barbaric ones recycled from the 8th-century church, along with the original font, a big one for immersion baptisms carved with a curious relief of the Trinity, represented as three equal persons. The excellent 12th-century reliefs by the altar include symbols of the Evangelists: these probably formed part of a pulpit when the church was built. There are two frescoed chapels: the Cappella di San Giuseppe is a sumptuous work of 1630 by the Piacentino Giacomo Guidotti, but it's upstaged by the second, with a lively cycle on the *Passion and the Life of Catherine of Alexandria* by an unknown artist, probably Tuscan, c1400.

Museo della Collegiata (*In the cloister;* ⏀ *Apr–Sep 09.00–12.30 & 14.30–18.30 daily, Oct–Mar 09.30–12.30 & 14.30–17.00 daily; €3.50*). Outside the church, in the tiny, timber-roofed cloister, awaits a collection of paintings starring a magnificently disturbing *Burial of a Carthusian* by the master of late Baroque macabre, Alessandro Magnasco. There is also a 15th-century altarpiece, a rare Byzantine silk pallium from the AD900s, and a mantel once worn by Paul III.

Rocca Viscontea (*Giardini Giovanni Paolo 3;* ☎ *0523 804008; guided tours* ⏀ *Nov–Feb 10.00–13.00 & 14.00–17.00 Sat–Sun, 10.30, 14.30 & 16.00 Tue–Fri; Mar–Jun & mid-Aug–Oct 10.00–13.00 & 14.00–18.00 Tue–Sun (also Mon in Apr, May & Sep); Jul–mid-Aug 10.00–13.00 & 15.00–18.00 Sat–Sun, 10.30, 11.30, 15.30, 16.30 & 17.30 Tue–Fri; €5*) This Rocca built by the Visconti in 1345 resembles an impossibly picturesque toy castle at first glance, but it did the job. It has two parts, this citadel at the top, and a connected lower one to control the slopes. Today they contain a museum on medieval life, complete with torture instruments and ghastly illustrations on how they worked. But the views from the top are lovely.

A pretty park with an avenue of trees lies beneath the lower castle, near the entrance of the town. Here too is a medieval fountain, which reveals the big

8

drawback of living in old Castell'Arquato: until the 20th century this was the town's only source of water, and people who lived at the top had to carry their supplies all the way up.

WEST OF CASTELL'ARQUATO
Vigolo Marchese [map, pages 202–3] (*6km northwest of Castell'Arquato*) A treat for Romanesque lovers: a striking church and a bijou 11th-century circular baptistry.

Velleia Romana [map, pages 202–3] (*Lugagnano Val d'Arda, on the SP14;* \ *0523 807113;* w *sbap-pr.beniculturali.it;* ⊕ *Dec–15 Mar 09.00–15.00 daily, other times 1hr before sunset; €2*) Emilia's best-preserved Roman town was never very large, but retains the foundations of a forum, temple, amphitheatre and some mysterious large carved stones that resemble bathtub plugs. Most of the finds are in Parma, including the famous Tabula Alimentaria, the largest bronze tablet ever found (page 214); others remain in the site's newly refurbished antiquarium.

Castello di Gropparello [map, pages 202–3] (*Gropparello;* \ *0523 855814;* w *castellodigropparello.it;* ⊕ *15.00 daily for guided tours, book ahead; €8; Parco delle Fiabe* ⊕ *10.00–15.00 Sun & most school holidays (see website); adults €18.50, children €16; combined ticket €19.50*) Beware the attractive castle at Gropparello, set on a spur high above the lush Val Vezzeno. Once home of honest robber barons (there are some properly baronial rooms on the guided tour), its woodlands have been turned into the Parco delle Fiabe, or 'Fairy-tale Park', Italy's 'first *parco emotivo*', where underemployed Italians dressed as gnomes, witches, druids and talking trees will do their best to amuse your offspring. In summer and school holidays they host events, and there's a medieval tavern for lunch.

GRAZZANO VISCONTI Due south of Piacenza on the N654, the village of Grazzano Visconti was rebuilt a century ago in a quaint charming neo-medieval style by Giuseppe Visconti di Modrone. Director Lucchino Visconti spent his summers here, but today it's more than a bit of a tourist trap, filled with shops and artisans, and wax and torture museums to go with the beautiful gardens.

Getting there and away Bus no 116 links Piacenza to Grazzano Visconti (*12km*). By car, take the SP654 off the Piacenza ring road. Park in the two large car parks on either side of the village.

Tourist information
𝑖 Viale del Castello 2; \ 0523 870997; w valnure. info; ⊕ 10.00–13.00 Wed–Sat, 10.00–13.00 & 14.00–17.00 Sun, Easter–May 10.00–13.00 & 14.00–17.00 daily, closed mid-Dec–Jan

✗ **Where to eat and drink** Ponte dell'Olio, 8km south of Grazzano, has long had a gold star on the Piacentini gourmet map.

✗ **Riva** Via Riva 16, Ponte dell'Olio; \ 0523 875193; w ristoranteriva.it; ⊕ closed Mon & Tue lunch. This famous place in a little *frazione* is run by one of Italy's top female chefs, Carla Aradelli. Her elegant, imaginative cuisine is based on the freshest local ingredients, so the menu changes by season. But all a bit pricey for what you get. €€€€€
✗ **Trattoria Bellaria** Loc Biana 17, Ponte dell'Olio; \ 0523 878333; w bellariatrattoria.it;

closed Thu & Sep. A mid-19th-century osteria serving traditional Piacentina cuisine, from the local *pancetta* & *coppa* to its renowned two-tailed tortelli to succulent roast duck. Lunch menu €12.50. €€

What to see and do The centrepiece, the **Castello di Grazzano Visconti** [map, pages 202–3] was built in 1395 for Beatrice Visconti, sister of the famous Gian Galeazzo. It is still privately owned by the grandson of Giuseppe Visconti, but you can book a tour of the beautiful **gardens** (*tickets at Piazza Visconti 11;* ✆ *0523 870136;* w *castellodigrazzanovisconti.it;* ⏱ *mid-Mar–late Jun & early Aug–mid-Nov afternoons Sat, morning & afternoon Sun; €7*) with fountains, a labyrinth, belvedere and children's playhouse. It's especially lovely in June when its many roses are in bloom.

There's also the **Museo delle Cere di Piacenza** (*Via Anna Visconti;* ✆ *0523 755864;* w *museodellecere.org;* ⏱ *10.30–19.30 Sat–Sun, summer also 15.00–19.00 Tue & Thu; €5.50*), your chance to see life-size models and learn all about all the movers and shakers from Piacenza's past, from Caesar's wife Calpurnia (from Piacenza) and Hannibal to Cardinal Alberoni, Marie-Louise and Verdi.

There's another castle over the River Nure, the **Castello di Paderna** [map, pages 202–3] (*Strada Paderna Montanaro 10, Pontenure;* ✆ *0523 511645;* w *castellodipaderna. it; guided tours* ⏱ *May–Jul & Sep 10.00 & 11.00 Sat–Sun; €7*). Occupied by the same family for over a thousand years, it's a rectangular walled manor of a kind once common on the Piacentino plain, a *corte*, defended by a tower and a moat. The tour includes the courtyard, a museum of historic arms, an 11th-century chapel, and the park and heirloom fruit trees (a local speciality).

SOUTHWEST OF PIACENZA: THE VAL TREBBIA

'Today I have gone through the most beautiful valley in the world,' wrote war correspondent Ernest Hemingway in 1915, after driving through the Trebbia Valley, where the wild meandering river has carved verdant hills into odd-shaped cliffs and bowls. The Trebbia's sparkling turquoise waters are among the cleanest in Italy, perfect for a swim. Castles, one of Italy's most offbeat museums and lovely places to stay dot the valley all the way up to Bobbio.

GETTING THERE AND AWAY Buses E17 and E18 from Piacenza go to Rivergaro and Travo.

 WHERE TO STAY

Relais Colombara Spa [map, pages 202–3] (19 rooms) Fraz Pigazzano, Travo; ✆0523 952146; w relaiscolombara.it. Old stone convent in the foothills, with the lights of Piacenza twinkling on the horizon at night. Beautifully furnished with period pieces, contemporary art & mod cons, plus a pool with a view & spa. B/fast inc. Superb restaurant too, with tables in a glass pavilion overlooking the view. €€€€€

Torre di San Matino (10 rooms) Rivalta di Gazzola; ✆0523 972002; w hoteltorredisanmartino.it. Romantic rooms, some with 4-poster beds & a touch of chintz under

the old wooden beams, by a 13th-century tower. Body, face & massage treatments available at the beauty/wellness centre. B/fast inc. €€€€–€€€€€

Rocca d'Olgisio (5 rooms) For details, see page 263. One of the most atmospheric places to stay; b/fast inc. €€€€

Agriturismo Casarossa [map, pages 202–3] (5 rooms) Loc Casarossa – Suzzano di Rivergaro; m 348 802 1119; w casarossapiacenza. it. Romantic, rustic chic rooms in a Liberty-style organic farm, many with sitting rooms or kitchenettes. €€€

8

🏠 **B&B Torre dei Magnani & Le Stanze del Benvegnù** (8 rooms) Loc Rallio, Travo; **m** 349 428 9924; **w** torredeimagnani.com. Two B&Bs in a 15th-century tower, with large characterful rooms, mountain bikes to rent & friendly owners. Cash only; b/fast inc. **€€–€€€**

✖ **WHERE TO EAT AND DRINK** The first 20km or so south of Piacenza has good restaurants which the Piacentini like to visit for Sunday lunch, many linked to hotels in historic buildings.

✖ **Castellaccio** Loc Marchesi di Travo, Rivergaro; \0523 957333; **w** castellaccio. it; ⏰ eves only Mon, Thu, Fri, lunch & dinner Sat–Sun. This restaurant, set in an outpost of the Renaissance Castello di Statto, has a bucolic garden and terrace overlooking the Trebbia. The cuisine matches the setting, with an elegant French touch: there are fish & vegetarian choices, perfectly aged cheeses served with warm dried fruit bread & spicy *mostarda*, & delectable desserts. **€€€€**

✖ **Antica Locanda del Falco** Strada Comunale 7, Rivalta, Gazzola; \0523 978101; **w** locandadelfalco.com; ⏰ closed Tue. Gorgeous place to dine, all wood beams, terracotta & wooden tables inside, with a century-old wisteria shading tables in the courtyard. The menu offers a delicious mix of tradition & invention: 2 can share plates of several dishes, so you don't have to choose too much. **€€€**

✖ **La Rocchetta** Strada Comunale 1, Rivalta, Gazzola; \0523 978100; **w** larocchetta.pc.it; ⏰ summer closed Mon & Thu eve, winter closed Sun eve. Lovely place in the brick vaults of the former castle stables with a pretty garden lawn. Classy cooking & a great choice of seafood or land dishes. **€€€**

✖ **Agriturismo Il Poggio Cardinale** Loc Ancarano sotto n 177, Rivergaro; \0523 958528; **w** ilpoggiocardinale.it; ⏰ closed eve Mon–Wed. Traditional to the core, serving classics such as *pisaréi e fasò* (mini gnocchi with beans in tomato sauce) with wines from Piacenza. €12 set lunch Tue–Fri. Also 7 B&B rooms (**€€**). **€€**

✖ **Caffè Grande** Piazza Paolo 9, Rivergaro; \0523 958524; **w** caffegrande.it; ⏰ closed Tue. A local institution where Piacentini cuisine is taken very seriously but updated: you'll find lovely pasta (including *anolini* in capon broth); also sous vide suckling pig with ginger & honey. **€€**

✖ **Vecchia Pergola** Piazza Roma, Gossolengo (just north of Rivergaro); \0523 778123; ⏰ closed Mon. Hearty tasty food with daily specials, *salumi* & the best *gnocco fritto* in the valley bring in the crowds; good choice of wines & outdoor seating. Be sure to book at w/ends. **€€**

ACTIVITIES The Trebbia Valley is especially popular at weekends, when people drive down from Milan. **Val Trebbia Experience** (**w** *valtrebbiaexperience.org*) lists all the campsites and all the activities in the valley. Besides pebble beaches at Rivergaro, Travo, Perino, Bobbio, Marsaglia and Ottone, there's the **River Park** (*Via Meucci 27, Rivergaro;* \ *0523 952332;* **w** *riverpark.it;* ⏰ *10.00–19.00; €10, Sat €15, Sun & holidays €18*), a laid-back family waterpark.

WHAT TO SEE AND DO

Museo della Merda [map, pages 202–3] (*Loc Castelbosco, Gragnano Trebbiense;* **w** *museodellamerda.org;* ⏰ *for guided tours only, 1 w/end a month (see website) at 11.00, 13.00, 15.00 & 17.00; adults €5, under 18s free*) Founded in 2015, the 'Shit Museum' is the brainchild of Gianantonio Locatelli, owner of a dairy farm producing Grano Padano cheese – and 100,000kg of manure every day. The tour takes in the farm's ecological biomechanical works and the nearby methane-heated castle, featuring poop-inspired exhibitions including bioluminescent installations, dung beetles (the symbol of the museum) and art and household items made from 'Merdacotta', Castelbosco's answer to terracotta, which are also on sale in the museum's Shit Shop.

Castello di Rivalta [map, pages 202–3] (*Borgo di Rivalta, Gazzola;* m *339 298 7892;* w *castellodirivalta.it; guided tours (check website for exact hours)* ⊕ *Mar–Sep 11.00 & 15.30 Wed–Fri, 11.00 & 14.00–18.00 Sat, 10.30–18.00 Sun–Tue by appointment, Oct–Feb 11.30 & 15.30 Fri, 11.00–16.40 Sat, 10.30–14.30 Sun–Thu by appointment; adults €10, ages 6–12 €8*) In a bucolic grove overlooking the Trebbia, this castle built by the Landi goes back to the 11th century, although the whole presents a stately Renaissance aspect; its round tower was built by an architect named Solari, who also designed parts of the Kremlin. Inside are period furnishings, frescoes of country life, and a room of armour with three battle flags that were carried by the Christians at Lepanto in 1571. When the castle is very busy, there's a mischievous ghost of a cook named Giuseppe who likes to turn lights off and on, close doors and move the furniture around; Princess Margaret, who spent ten summers here, met him at least once.

Rocca and Castello di Agazzano [map, pages 202–3] (*Agazzano;* \ *0523 325667;* w *castellodiagazzano.com; guided tours* ⊕ *Apr–Oct 11.00, 15.00, 16.15 & 17.30 Sun; €6*) This stronghold was begun in 1200, and mostly dates from the late 15th century. A cushier, U-shaped palace was added on the side in the 1700s, and a large French garden was planted between the two abodes. There are period furnishings and frescoed rooms to see; the cellar is full of the family's Le Torricelle wine. The grounds of Agazzano's other castle, **La Bastardina**, have been converted into a golf course.

Rocca d'Olgisio [map, pages 202–3] (*Pianello Val Tidone;* \ *0523 998045;* w *roccadolgisio.it;* ⊕ *guided tours Mar–Oct 15.00 & 16.00 Sat, 09.30, 11.30, 14.30 & 17.45 Sun; €10*) Extending over a steep ridge east of Agazzano, this picturesque fortress enclosed in six walls goes back to at least 1037. Gian Galeazzo Visconti gave it to the *condottiere* Jacopo Del Verme, and it stayed in the family until the mid 19th century, after which all its furnishings were lost. The tour takes in a 16th-century loggia, walls and gardens; trails, some challenging, go to the odd-shaped grottoes underneath.

Villaggio Neolitico di Travo (*Via al Mulino, Travo;* m *333 222 2739;* w *archeotravo.it;* ⊕ *Jul–Aug 18.00–21.00 Thu, 10.00–13.00 & 17.00–21.00 Sat–Sun, Apr–Jun & Sep–Oct 10.00–13.00 & 15.00–18.00 Sat–Sun; €2*) This Neolithic village was excavated in the 1990s. Several huts have been reconstructed, and a **museum** with finds (⊕ *same hrs*) is a 10-minute walk away in Piazza Trento.

BOBBIO

When Umberto Eco imagined the setting for the monastery in *The Name of the Rose* he had Bobbio in mind. A handsome town with many stone houses, it's practically synonymous with the abbey in its centre, founded by St Columbanus in AD612.

Columbanus was one of several scholarly Irish monks who came to the illiterate Continent as missionaries in the Dark Ages. He also founded the great abbey of Luxeuil (Vosges), although he had been forced to leave because of his outspoken views on the local Frankish barons and the Celtic observances in his church. The same thing happened in Switzerland, but Columbanus, after wandering about Europe, found a home here with the good graces of Lombard King Aistulf.

Nicknamed the 'Montecassino of the north', Bobbio was one of the first abbeys to free itself from the control of the local bishop. Its scriptorium was renowned;

by AD982, its library counted more than 700 codices, including some of the oldest Latin manuscripts and ancient Greek ones by Aristotle and Demosthenes back in a time when Greek was practically unknown elsewhere in the West. Its possessions stretched across Emilia and Liguria to Lake Garda.

Bobbio's most celebrated abbots were St Wala, a cousin of Charlemagne, and Gerbert of Aurillac. Gerbert, who had studied mathematics, science and philosophy in Toledo in Muslim Spain, was the most learned Christian of his day, so much so that he was accused of sorcery (it didn't help that he spent much of his time constructing planetary spheres and mechanical clocks). He reintroduced the abacus, Arabic numerals and armillary sphere into Europe, but ran afoul of the nobles in the Val de Trebbia when he tried to collect the abbey's rents. He went on to become the teacher of Emperor Otto III, then Archbishop of Ravenna and finally, in AD999, Pope Sylvester II.

Bobbio began to decline in the 1400s. Napoleon closed it, and its library was dispersed across Europe. Today the town is the capital of the upper Trebbia Valley, which Carla Glori's *Enigma Leonardo* (2011) suggests inspired the background to the *Mona Lisa*. It also attracts bikers; Columbanus, the wandering Irish monk, is the patron saint of motorcyclists.

GETTING THERE AND AWAY Bus E17 goes down the valley from Piacenza to Bobbio. By car, take the SS45. At weekends the narrow, winding upper valley road above Bobbio can get very busy, with few places to park.

TOURIST INFORMATION
i Piazza San Francesco 1; ℡0523 962 815;
w www.comune.bobbio.pc.it; ⊕ 09.30–12.30 &
16.00–19.00 Tue–Sat, 09.30–12.30 Sun

WHERE TO STAY
⌂ **La Torretta Bobbio** (3 rooms) Vicolo Buelli 8, Loc Piancasale; m 349 100 2120; w latorrettabobbio.it. Located 2km north of Bobbio, a charming place to stay near a pretty river beach, with a garden, & bikes to borrow. Also a suite for families & an apt. B/fast inc. €€€

⌂ **Piacentino** (18 rooms) Piazza San Francesco; ℡0523 936266; w hotelpiacentino.it. Eclectically decorated but comfortable rooms in the centre, with free parking & buffet b/fast (€7). Also a good restaurant (€€€€) with homemade pasta with mushrooms & truffles & game dishes in season, with summer tables in the pretty garden. €€–€€€

⌂ **Agriturismo Il Torrione del Trebbia** (5 rooms) Loc Morina 1; ℡0523 936204; w iltorrionedeltrebbia.com. Come here for peaceful rustic charm, stone walls & wooden beams in an old stone tower overlooking the Val Trebbia 1.5km from Bobbio. Also a good farm restaurant (*fixed menu with wine €28*). B/fast inc. €€

⌂ **Filietto** [map, pages 202–3] (10 rooms) Loc Costa Tamborlani; ℡0523 937104; w filietto.it. Beguiling little family hotel a 15min drive up in the mountains northwest of Bobbio, with lovely views, a garden, playground & a good restaurant (€€); special w/end HB rates available. €€

⌂ **Ridella** [map, pages 202–3] (12 rooms) Via Giarrone 13; Santa Maria di Bobbio; ℡0523 933130; f Albergo Ristorante Ridella. Up at Santa Maria on the slopes of Monte Penice, this peaceful family-run hotel is set in a leafy park. Also an excellent restaurant (⊕ *closed Wed;* €€) famous for its *gnocco fritto*, risotto with black truffles & grilled *involtini*. €€

⌂ **Ostello Valtrebbia** (3 rooms, 4 dorms) Via Trebbia 22, Marsaglia; m 333 247 2629; w ostellovaltrebbia.com. New, basic accommodation 10mins south of Bobbio, near the canoeing, beaches & little cataracts. B/fast €5. No credit cards. €

WHERE TO EAT AND DRINK

✗ Osteria Braceria il Barone Contrada Porta Nova 11; ☎0523 932093; w osteriailbarone.it; ⊕ closed Thu. In a palazzo, contemporary design & succulent grilled meat prepared in the open kitchen; also good pasta dishes. €€€

✗ Cacciatori Contrada di Porta Agazza 7; ☎0523 936267; w albergoristorantecacciatori. it. Near the famous bridge, serving family-style dishes such as pasta made from nettles with porcini mushrooms, *maccheroni alla Bobbiese* (made with pasta wrapped around a knitting needle) in *stracotto*. It also has 10 basic rooms (€€). €€

✗ San Nicola Contrada San Nicola 10; ☎0523 932355; w ristorantesannicola.it; ⊕ closed Mon eve & Tue. The old abbots would have been shocked to find their 17th-century convent is now a stylish restaurant with wines & spirits from around the world. Seasonal dishes accompany them, with delicious mushrooms or boar stewed with juniper; good cheeses. Wine bar in the chapel, which also does teas & chocolates (⊕ *w/ends only*). They also offer 4 comfortable B&B rooms (€€€). €€

WHAT TO SEE AND DO

Abbazia di San Colombano (*Piazza San Colombano;* ☎ *0523 962815;* w *sulleormedisancolombano.it;* ⊕ *08.00–19.00 Mon–Sat, 08.00–12.30 & 14.30– 19.00 Sun*) Largely rebuilt in the 15th–17th centuries, the abbey has few of its medieval splendours, although the basilica retains its campanile and apse from the AD800s. Note the inscription over the door: *terribilis est locus iste* ('this is a terrible place', from Genesis 28:17).

Inside are grey and gold frescoes of Columbanus's life and a fine Renaissance carved choir, but the ancient treasures are in the crypt: the Renaissance tomb of Columbanus (1480) and those of his Frankish followers SS Attala and Bertulphus. The latter are covered in carved arabesques in a style called 'langobardic' (Lombard), though they look as if Columbanus had brought them down with him from Ireland.

To the right is a marvellous, intricate wrought-iron screen from the 12th century. In 1910, parts of the mosaic pavement were discovered, with a wealth of medieval fancy in the *Labours of the Months* and zodiac. Better preserved are scenes from the Second Book of Maccabees: the wars of Judas Maccabeus (with elephants), the city of Antioch and the prophet Eleazar, along with a dragon and a 'quimera' (chimera). This one has three heads, one on its back and one on the tail, just like the famous Etruscan bronze in Florence. Where did the medieval artists get the idea?

Museo dell'Abbazia (*In the scriptorium;* ⊕ *Nov–Mar 15.00–17.00 Sat, 10.30– 12.30 & 15.00–19.00 Sun; Apr–Jun, Sep & Oct 16.30–18.30 Sat, 10.30–12.30 & 16.30–18.30 Sun; Jul–Aug 16.30–18.30 Wed–Sat, 10.30–12.30 & 16.30–18.30 Sun; €3*) This museum contains finds discovered around the abbey, including a famous 4th-century AD ivory shrine of Orpheus taming the wild beasts, an alabaster urn from the same period with reliefs, the Carolingian/Lombard tombstone of Abbot Cumian, Romanesque statuary and painting, reliquaries, and a polyptych (1522) by Leonardo's pupil, Bernardino Luini.

Museo della Città (*In the refectory;* ⊕ *same as abbey museum;* €*1.50*) Multimedia displays here cover Columbanus's life, and there's a 15th-century fresco of the *Crucifixion* with SS Columbanus and Benedict. The Delphic message over the door advises 'Nothing in excess', a reminder to the monks not to overeat.

Duomo di Santa Maria Assunta (*Piazza del Duomo;* ☎ *0523 936219*) Framed by a pair of asymmetrical towers, Bobbio's 15th-century cathedral has had a lavish

Neo-Byzantine Gothic makeover inside. Seek out the fine 15th-century fresco of the *Annunciation* discovered during the restoration in 1980.

Ponte del Gobbo Bobbio's inimitable landmark is its 280m 'hunchback bridge' over the Trebbia, a lumpy, eccentric construction where each of its 11 arches is a different size; parts of it are as old as the Romans but most of it was built by the monks in the 7th century.

Castello di Malaspina (*Strada del Torrino;* ☏ *0523 936500;* ⊕ *Jun–Sep 10.15–16.15 Tue–Sat, 10.00–13.00 & 15.00–18.00 Sun; €2*) Begun in 1304 on the site of Colombanus's first church and monastery, the castle has a square fortified tower, an ornate fireplace, a few 16th-century frescoes, and great views. Locals say there used to be a pit in the tower filled with sharp blades where enemies were tossed, if they were lucky; it beat dying in the wretched dungeon.

9

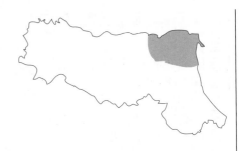

Ferrara and Surrounds

There's been a certain mystique attached to Ferrara ever since Jacob Burckhardt called it 'the first modern city in Europe' in his classic *Civilization of the Renaissance in Italy*. Whether or not Burckhardt was exaggerating can be debated endlessly; it is certain that the famous 'additions' to the medieval city in the Renaissance were far too ambitious. Ferrara, even in the most brilliant days of the court of the Este family, never had more than 30,000 citizens – not enough to fill the long, straight, rational streets laid out within the 9km circuit of its walls.

But what was a failure in the Renaissance is a happy success today. If Italian art cities can be said to go in and out of fashion, Ferrara is definitely 'in', popularised by a well-received international campaign to save its uniquely well-preserved walls, and a rebirth of interest in the city's great quattrocento painters. Thanks to the rather tyrannical Este, the charming city enclosed by those walls was one of the brightest stars of the Renaissance, with its own school of art led by the great Cosmè Tura, Ercole de' Roberti, Lorenzo Costa and Francesco del Cossa. Poets patronised by the Este produced three of the Italian Renaissance's greatest epic poems – Boiardo's *Orlando Innamorato* (1483), Ariosto's better-known continuation of the same story, *Orlando Furioso* (1532), and Tasso's *Gerusalemme Liberata* (1581).

Ferrara's career as a centre of culture – along with its economy and its civic pride – went down the drain when the popes took over in 1598. Even more than in Bologna, the nearly three centuries of papal rule meant poverty and obscurity for the city. It's been a long climb back, but today Ferrara is a contented and very prosperous city of some 135,000, with a big chemical industry leading a diversified economy. The entire city is a UNESCO World Heritage Site, and its university is rated as one of Italy's best. But don't ask about the microclimate; it's steamy and swarming with mosquitoes in summer, weirdly frosty in winter. A lot of its important buildings are still closed, under repairs from the earthquake of 2012.

Otherwise things are grand. Ferrara's good fortune is to be off the tourist track. The people who are always getting in your way in Venice and Florence have never heard of the place; seeing the sights is a stress-free delight. Do it by bike. Ferrara's proudest distinction right now is that of all European cities, it takes third place in the ratio of bicycles to people; many of the hotels are happy to lend or rent you one.

HISTORY

Ferrara is the youngest of the region's big cities. It may have been Roman Forum Alieni, a settlement whose site has never been discovered, but as far as anyone can tell the city had its beginnings in a Byzantine fortified camp, built to control trade on the Po in the 6th century. The first mention of it in the chronicles comes when the Lombards captured it in AD753. Ferrara was the first town in the region to set

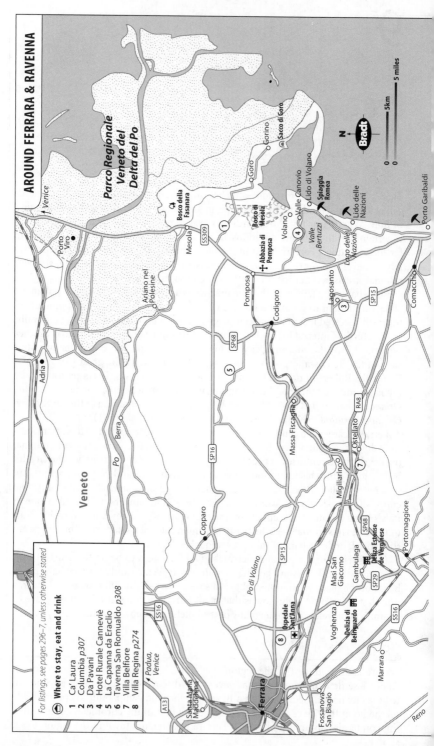

AROUND FERRARA & RAVENNA

For listings, see pages 296–7, unless otherwise stated

Where to stay, eat and drink

1 Ca' Laura
2 Columbia *p307*
3 Da Pavani
4 Hotel Rurale Canneviè
5 La Capanna da Eraclio
6 Taverna San Romualdo *p308*
7 Villa Belfiore
8 Villa Regina *p274*

Veneto

Parco Regionale Veneto del Delta del Po

Bradt

0   5km
0   5 miles

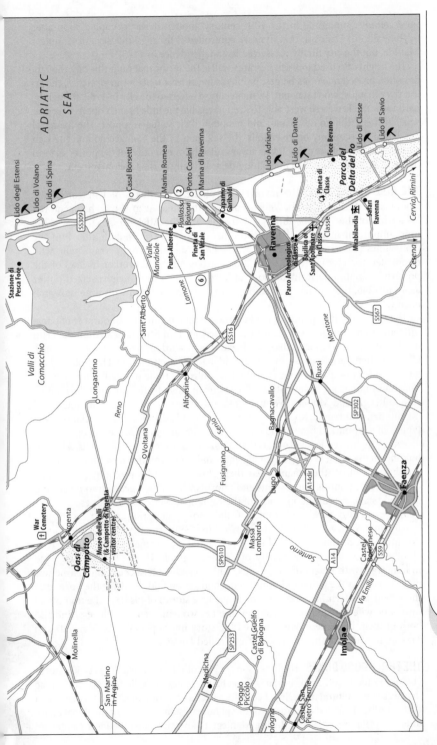

up a *comune*, sometime in the 10th century, though it was occupied soon after by Teobaldo of Canossa; that dynasty controlled it through the days of Countess Matilda, but the city finally reasserted its independence in 1115.

The mighty Po used to wash Ferrara's walls. The factor that built this city though, has often proved one of its biggest problems for, at least in its lower stretches, the Po is a river that just won't stay put. Its main course deserted the city in 1152, though by hard work the Ferrarese were able to keep navigable the little branch of the river that was left them, the Po di Volano, and maintain their status as a port. The medieval city based its economy on river tolls, the salt pans of the Comacchio and the rich agricultural land of the delta. It was always ruled by one or other of the powerful local dynasties, usually from the Ghibelline Adelardi family or the Guelph Torcelli.

THE RISE OF THE ESTE The involvement of the great dukes of Este (originally from just to the north, in the Veneto) began with Duke Azzo V, who had acquired leadership of the Guelphs through marriage with the Adelardi. Azzo VI was the most important man in Ferrara before his death in 1212, though after him the Ghibellines reasserted their power with *signori* such as Salinguerra Torelli, who dominated the city from 1222 to 1240, a strong ally (and brother-in-law) of the powerful Ezzelino da Romano, lord of Verona. When the Guelphs seized power again in 1240, they imprisoned Salinguerra and replaced him with Ezzelino's arch enemy, Azzo VII d'Este.

The rise of the Este family made Ferrara a great Guelph city, an outpost of papal influence in the north. Azzo's descendants were lords of Ferrara in an unbroken run until 1598. Azzo was succeeded by Obizzo II, a bastard in every sense of the word. Obizzo gutted the rule of law in the city and made himself a tyrant. He abolished the guilds, and threw away Ferrara's profitable control of trade on the Po in return for Venetian support for his ambitions elsewhere; in 1288–89 he extended the family's rule to Reggio and Modena. Popular gossip whispered that Obizzo had murdered his mother, and regularly committed incest with his daughters. Such claims were typical of the political propaganda of the time; they might even have been true.

Later Este proved less villainous than Obizzo, but every one was just as skilled at holding on to power. With great intelligence, and single-minded devotion to keeping the dynasty afloat, they maintained their absolute rule by promoting economic development, granting concessions and reforms when it was prudent to do so, and generally staying in the good graces of their nominal overlords, the popes.

The clan also produced some of the most interesting characters of the Renaissance, such as Niccolò II 'the Lame' (1361–88), a friend of Petrarch; his reign saw the revolt of 1385 which led the Este to build the fortified Castello. Alberto V (1388–93) founded the University of Ferrara; Niccolò III (1393–1441) engaged in long wars with neighbouring Padua, with considerable success, though he was more famous as the father of hundreds of children 'on both banks of the Po', and as the villain who terminated one of the tragic love stories of his day – he found that his young wife Parisina and his son by another woman, Ugo, were lovers, and had both of them beheaded. Byron turned the story into a poem, and Donizetti and Mascagni made that into operas, all three called *Parisina*.

THE THREE GOOD DUKES The other sons of Niccolò III – Leonello (1441–50), Borso (1450–71) and Ercole I (1471–1505) – met happier fates; each did his part to promote the city's great cultural flowering. Leonello, a friend of the architect and theorist Leon Battista Alberti, invited the most prominent humanists and artists of the Renaissance to Ferrara (Pisanello, Jacopo Bellini, Mantegna), and cultivated the local painters of the Ferrarese school, one of the most significant collections of artistic talent outside Florence. Borso continued his patronage; he also confirmed Este rule over Reggio and Modena, and was granted the title of Duke of Ferrara by the pope.

Ferrara was booming, and Ercole I had the huge addition to the city, known as the Herculean Addition, designed by his architect Biagio Rossetti. His offspring, Isabella (wife of Francesco Gonzaga of Mantua), Beatrice (married to Ludovico Sforza, il Moro, of Milan), and Cardinal Ippolito, were among the most cultured and influential people of their day. The duke was a friend and patron of poets, including Ariosto and Matteo Boiardo, whom he made a minister of state.

Ercole managed to avoid disaster in a prelude to the Wars of Italy, the 1482-3 'War of Ferrara'. The papacy, which had claimed suzerainty over the Romagna since 1278, offered Ferrara's part of the Po Delta (including the rich salt-works at Comacchio) to Venice in return for military support against Naples. The Venetians had their excuse to invade the territory, but when Florence, Milan and Spain stepped up to oppose this blatant land grab, Pope Sixtus IV and the Venetians backed down, postponing a pan-Italian conflict.

ALFONSO I When the Wars of Italy came, the Este were up to the challenge. Ercole's heir Alfonso I (1505-34) married the beautiful and unjustly maligned Lucrezia Borgia; the pair oversaw a brilliant, fashionable court, patronising Ariosto and Titian among many others and assembling one of the greatest collections of art in Europe. Alfonso also spent a lot of time casting cannons. It was a sort of hobby with him, but Alfonso was no fool. In this dangerous age, cannons were a fine thing to have, and his were the finest in Europe. With the big guns, and some carefully crafted marriages, Alfonso's skilful diplomacy helped Ferrara avoid invasion, and the Este state emerged from the wars with its independence intact, even though successive popes, Julius II, Leo X and Clement VII, all tried to destroy it.

The son of Alfonso and Lucrezia, Ercole II (1534-59), married Renée, daughter of Louis XII of France, and a Calvinist. She briefly made Ferrara Italy's last centre of Protestant thinkers, entertaining French poet Clément Marot and even sheltering John Calvin under an assumed name. Eventually relations with Rome became so touchy that she had to be imprisoned for a few days, and finally sent away.

PAPAL RULE AND RECOVERY The last Este Duke of Ferrara, Alfonso II (1559-97), patron of the unstable and unruly poet Torquato Tasso, was considered the best-educated and most courtly ruler of his day, but at the expense of his people. As the ruler of one of the few truly independent small states in Italy, Alfonso needed to lay low and avoid trouble; instead, he entertained extravagant ambitions (he once tried to get himself elected king of Poland). Such adventures, plus the expense of maintaining a glittering court, led to crushingly high taxes and neglect of the city's economy.

Worst of all, from the family's point of view, Alfonso failed to produce a legitimate heir. He tried to name a cousin, Cesare, as his successor, but Pope Clement VIII decreed that he too was illegitimate. By now the Este had few friends either at home or among the neighbouring powers, and there was no way to stop the pope from taking over Ferrara in 1598. The city was glad to see the last of the family, and it was ruled thereafter by a papal legate (though Cesare continued to rule as Duke of Modena and Reggio, where the popes had no claim; his successors kept the family state alive until the time of Napoleon).

Without the largesse of the Este, Ferrara rapidly became an artistic backwater, while the cardinals sent as legates plundered the city's treasures to enrich themselves. Under papal rule the economy rapidly foundered while the population declined considerably; visitors in the 1700s reported the city looking almost like a ghost town. After Italian unification Ferrara gradually got back on its feet; agriculture on the Po plain revived, while the city grew into a modest industrial centre. In this century, the modern 'Metaphysical School' of painting (de Chirico, Carrà, de Pisis, Morandi and others) had its origins in the city, inspired at least in part by the great frescoes in the Palazzo Schifanoia.

GETTING THERE AND AWAY

BY AIR If you're coming via Bologna's airport, the best way to get here is **Ferrara Bus&Fly** (w *ferrarabusandfly.it*). It runs eight buses a day to and from the airport, stopping at Ferrara's Centro Commerciale Il Castello [275 A7], south of the city, Ferrara Centrale railway station [275 A2], and finally the city centre on Viale Cavour, at the gardens next to the Castello Estense [275 B4]. It's a 1-hour trip; tickets cost €15 one way.

BY RAIL Ferrara is on a trunk line from Venice to Bologna, Florence and Rome. From Bologna you can change for the other main line across Emilia-Romagna and beyond, to Milan or the Adriatic coast. Trips to and from Bologna on **Trenitalia**, both on the Freccia (*20–25mins*) and regional trains (*about 50mins*) are quick and never far apart, even at night.

Regional trains to Ravenna and Rimini run about once an hour during the day; most of these stop at the major Adriatic resorts around Rimini. Check these carefully before you go. Some are direct, about a 1-hour journey, but a lot of them require a change in Bologna, and can take 3 hours or more.

An **Italo** high-speed line connects the city with Padua and Venice to the north, and Bologna, Florence, Rome and Naples to the south. Expect about six trains a day to Bologna on weekdays; with advance bookings the fare can be as low as €10.

Emilia-Romagna's regional service, **TPER**, runs lines to Codigoro, with buses from there out to the lidos on the coast (w *tper.it*; *1hr 20mins; about 14 trains/day*), and also an old narrow-gauge line to Suzzara, near Mantua in Lombardy, passing through villages that time and destiny have entirely forgotten; you can carry on from there to Guastalla in Reggio province, and even Parma and Reggio.

The **railway station** (Ferrara Centrale) [275 A2] for both services is just outside the city walls, about a kilometre from the city centre (blame the Este dukes for making Ferrara a city of great distances), but you can get in directly on city buses 1, 6, 7, 9 and 11.

BY BUS Most intercity buses leave from the **bus station** [275 A4] near the corner of the Rampari di San Paolo and the Corso Isonzo (city bus 2 connects it with the railway station). Tickets and information in the Bar PitStop2 (*Via Rampari San Paolo;* ☎ *0532 206664;* ⊕ *06.00–20.00 Mon–Sat, 08.00–13.00 Sun*). There is also an information booth in the railway station: Punto Bus (☎ *0532 599490;* ⊕ *07.15–19.15 Mon–Sat, 08.00–14.00 Sun*).

TPER's *extraurbana* buses reach most of the towns and villages of the province: frequent services to Comacchio and branches to its lidos in season, Codigoro and Pomposa, Ravenna, Bologna (Autostazione), Mesola, Cento, Modena and points in between. **LaValle** buses (w *lavalle-bus.it*) go to Ravenna and the Comacchio lidos, and to Turin, via Bologna, Piacenza, Alessandria and Asti.

Ferrara is a base for **Flixbus** (w *flixbus.it*). Its buses leave from in front of the railway station for Milan, Venice and many other northern cities, as well as for Florence, Rome and Naples.

GETTING AROUND

Ferrara's sights are concentrated in the centre, and it isn't likely you'll ever need the city's admirable bus system, run by **TPER** (**w** *tper.it*), though the numerous lines that follow the central Viale Cavour/Corso della Giovecca may come in handy to get to the railway station, or when your feet give out. Tickets are purchased in tobacco shops etc (*€1.30; €3.50 for a day ticket*); many buses have ticket machines on board though they require exact change and cost extra (*€1.50*).

The city has a relatively small Zona Traffico Limitato (ZTL), but you wouldn't much enjoy driving around the narrow streets of the medieval centre; there are several parking areas on the edges of the ZTL, signposted around the Castello Estense, and another in the Herculean Addition near the Palazzo dei Diamanti, but larger and more accessible ones can be found around Via Darsena and Piazza Travaglio at the southern walls. For complete info on parking areas, rates and current availability of spaces, see **w** ferraratua.com, a firm that operates most of them.

Almost completely flat, Ferrara has a high ratio of bicycles to humans. Bikes are available for hire at a score of places; there's a complete list, with addresses, hours and rates, on the tourist office's site (**w** *www.ferraraterraeacqua.it*), under 'Noleggio Bici'. They take *cicloturismo* seriously here. The tourist office and its website offer tonnes of info on itineraries around the province, maps, repairs and service.

TOURIST INFORMATION

i IAT [275 B4] Castello Estense; 0532 209370; **w** www.ferraraterraeacqua.it; ⏱ 09.00–18.00 Mon–Sat, 09.30–17.30 Sun. The city's MyFE Card (see box, page 278) is available to buy here.

WHERE TO STAY

UPMARKET

Alchimia [275 C3] (6 rooms, 1 apt) Via Borgo dei Leoni 122; 0532 1856 4656; **w** alchimiaferrara.it. Big, beautifully furnished contemporary rooms in a palazzo that once belonged to a Renaissance alchemist. Centrally located, private parking, terrace & garden, bike rentals available; elaborate b/fasts inc. **€€€€**

Ferrara [275 B4] (58 rooms) Largo Castello 36; 0532 205048; **w** hotelferrara. com. Designer rooms, the best with big windows overlooking the Castello Estense; hardwood floors, AC. Light b/fast inc. Free bikes; it also offers service & tours. **€€€€**

MID-RANGE

Annunziata [275 B4] (27 rooms) Piazza Repubblica 5; 0532 201111; **w** annunziata. it. Elegant hotel with big windows overlooking the Castello Estense & modern, functional rooms; excellent b/fast buffet inc, free bikes, pay parking. **€€€**

Astra [275 B3] (67 rooms) Viale Cavour 55; 0532 206088; **w** astrahotel.info. Well-furnished hotel on the main street to the station; elaborate b/fast with menus inc. **€€€**

Carlton [275 B4] (58 rooms) Piazza Sacrati; 0532 211130; **w** hotelcarlton.net. Right in the centre, a peaceful hotel with stylish rooms & contemporary design; AC. Bike rentals, service & itineraries on offer. Parking extra. Its Hotel Carlton Residence, next to the hotel, has lovely coffered-ceiling apts, sleeping 2–4 people, with all hotel services. **€€€**

Europa [275 C4] (45 rooms) Corso Giovecca 49; 0532 205456; **w** hoteleuropaferrara.com. Verdi & King Umberto stayed in this 17th-century palace near the Palazzo dei Diamanti. Bedrooms are simpler today (the place was bombed in the war), but with everything you need; some still have frescoes, & the lobby is full of 18th-century antiques; there's also a pretty garden courtyard. They have bikes for rent, & arrange tours. The Caffè Europa (page 277) is part of the

9

establishment, & its wonderful pastries figure in the hotel's b/fast (*inc*) buffets. Pay parking available. €€€

🏠 **Santo Stefano** [275 B4] (24 rooms) Via Boccacanale di Santo Stefano 21; 📞0532 242348; w hotelsantostefanofe.it. Central, bright & pleasant rooms; AC. Bikes available. Not wheelchair accessible. €€€

🏠 **Touring** [275 B4] (58 rooms) Viale Cavour 11; 📞0532 206200; w hoteltouringfe. it. Modern hotel by the Castello Estense with an underground car park & swank, AC rooms. Children are welcomed with a play area, games & other amenities. Small gym & spa; bike rentals. Ask about its shopping tours. €€€

🏠 **Villa Regina** [map, pages 268–9] (20 rooms) Via Comacchio 402, Cocomaro di Cona; 📞0532 740222; w villaregina.it. Urban escape within easy reach of the city in a beautiful converted villa set amid luxurious parkland. Free parking; there's also a restaurant (€€€) too. €€–€€€

BUDGET

🏠 **Astrolabio** [275 C2] (2 rooms) Via Borso 28; m 347 284 2068, 320 773 3663; w bbastrolabio-ferrara.it. Though 1km from the centre, this B&B more than compensates with a lovely, peaceful setting in the Herculean Addition, a garden & parking. There are 2 rooms with a common kitchen & parlour. €€–€€€

🏠 **San Paolo** [275 B5] (27 rooms) Via Baluardi 9; 📞0532 790878; w hotelsanpaolo. net. Pleasantly situated near the city walls beside Piazza Travaglio, with good rooms & service; it has less expensive 'economy rooms', special family rooms & suites. B/fast extra; bikes available. €€–€€€

🏠 **Albergo degli Artisti** [275 B5] (34 rooms) Via della Vittoria 66; 📞0532 276 1038; w albergoartisti.it. Best of the cheaper options: right in the centre of town, on a quiet side street near the Duomo. Cheaper rooms without baths. €€

🏠 **Ostello Estense** [275 B3] (20 rooms) Corso B Rossetti 24; 📞0532 201158; w ostelloferrara. it. Youth hostel in a Renaissance building next to a quiet park, close to the centre of Ferrara. Inexpensive dbls or shared accommodation, none en suite; minimal b/fast inc. There's a bar & restaurant, with FB & HB on offer. €€

✖ WHERE TO EAT AND DRINK

Ferrara's most famous dish (the favourite of Lucrezia Borgia) is spicy *salama da sugo* – a soft sausage that is cured for a year, then gently boiled for about 4 hours and eaten with mashed potatoes. The bakers of Ferrara are famous for their unique X-shaped bread, *ciupeta*, or *coppie ferrarese*. The Ferrarese like their *salumi* and cheese with that or with *pinzin*, the local version of *gnocchi fritti*. Little caps of pasta, *cappelletti*, often filled with pumpkin, are another local speciality. They do like their pumpkin; it also appears in a little tart, a *sformatino di zucca* with Parmesan cheese, as a starter. You'll find a lot of good fresh seafood here; the fishing towns of the coast aren't far away. For dessert, the unavoidable local favourite is a little chocolate bomb of a cake called *torta tenerina*.

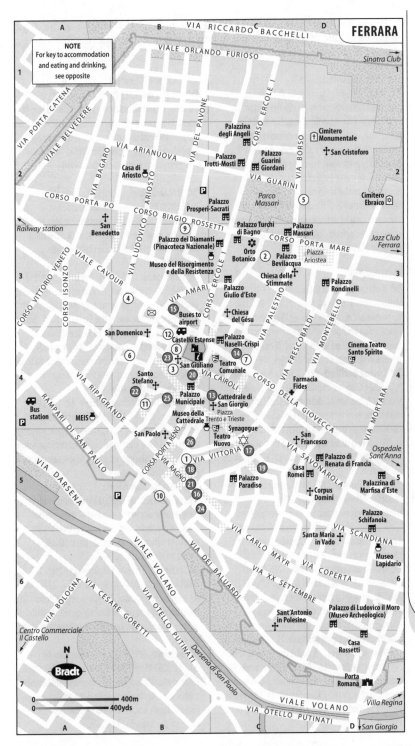

A   B   C   D

VIA RICCARDO BACCHELLI

VIALE ORLANDO FURIOSO

Sinatra Club

VIA PORTA CATENA

VIALE BELVEDERE

VIA ARIANUOVA

VIA BAGARO

CORSO ERCOLE I

VIA DEL PAVONE

Palazzina
degli Angeli

Cimitero
Monumentale

San Cristoforo

VIA BORSO

Casa di
Ariosto

Palazzo
Trotti-Mosti

Palazzo
Guarini
Giordani

VIA GUARINI

CORSO PORTA PO

VIA LUDOVICO ARIOSTO

Palazzo
Prosperi-Sacrati

Parco
Massari

Cimitero
Ebraico

Railway station

San
Benedetto

CORSO BIAGIO ROSSETTI

9

Palazzo dei Diamanti
(Pinacoteca Nazionale)

Palazzo Turchi
di Bagno

Orto
Botanico

Palazzo
Massari

CORSO PORTA MARE

Piazza
Ariostea

Jazz Club
Ferrara

VIA AMARI

CORSO ERCOLE I

Palazzo
Bevilacqua

2

Museo del Risorgimento
e della Resistenza

Chiesa delle
Stimmate

Palazzo
Rondinelli

3

CORSO VITTORIO VENETO

CORSO ISONZO

VIALE CAVOUR

Palazzo
Giulio d'Este

Chiesa
del Gésu

VIA FRESCOBALDI

VIA MONTEBELLO

4

15

Buses to
airport

San Domenico

12

Castello Estense

Palazzo
Naselli-Crispi

14

VIA PALESTRO

Cinema Teatro
Santo Spirito

6

8

23

3

San Giuliano

Teatro
Comunale

7

CORSO DELLA GIOVECCA

Santo
Stefano

20

VIA CAIROLI

Farmacia
Fides

VIA RIPAGRANDE

22

Palazzo
Municipale

13

Cattedrale di
San Giorgio

VIA SAVONAROLA

VIA MORTARA

Ospedale
Sant'Anna

Bus
station

11

25

MEIS

Museo della
Cattedrale

Piazza
Trento e Trieste

San
Francesco

San Paolo

RAMPARI DI SAN PAULO

CORSO PORTA RENO

VIA RAGNO

26

Teatro
Nuovo

Synagogue

17

Palazzo di
Renata di Francia

5

VIA DARSENA

1

VIA VITTORIA

18

19

Casa
Romei

Palazzina di
Marfisa d'Este

21

16

Palazzo
Paradiso

Corpus
Domini

Palazzo
Schifanoia

10

24

VIA SCANDIANA

Museo
Lapidario

VIA CARLO MAYR

Santa Maria
in Vado

VIA COPERTA

6

VIA BOLOGNA

VIA CESARE GORETTI

VIALE VOLANO

VIA OTELLO PUTINATI

VIA DEI BALUARDI

VIA XX SETTEMBRE

Palazzo di Ludovico il Moro
(Museo Archeologico)

Centro Commerciale
Il Castello

N

Sant'Antonio
in Polesine

Casa
Rossetti

Bradt

Darsena di San Paolo

Porta
Romana

7

0   400m
0   400yds

VIALE VOLANO

VIA OTELLO PUTINATI

Villa Regina

San Giorgio

When Renée of France came to Ferrara she brought her own vines, the origin of the local viticulture and its Vino di Bosco. Dry and aromatic, the four types of Bosco Eliceo, two red and two white, are the only DOC wines of Ferrara province.

ABOVE AVERAGE

✗ **Max** [275 B4] Piazza della Repubblica 16; ☎0532 209309; w ristorantemaxferrara. it; ◷ Mon–Fri eves only, closed Tue. Right in the centre, with tables on the terrace facing the Castello Estense. It's all luxuriously fishy & beautifully presented, from big platters of seafood antipasti, to pasta (*cappelletti* with baby clams & truffles), to the main course (grilled mixed kebabs). There's also the Bistro adjacent with the same quality at lower prices, including some remarkable seafood club sandwiches (€€€). Booking advisable. €€€€

MODERATE

✗ **Antica Trattoria Il Cucco** [275 C4] Via Voltacasotto 3; off Via C Mayr; ☎0532 760026; w trattoriailcucco.it; ◷ closed Wed. Nothing fancy, good for homemade pasta with porcini mushrooms, grilled lamb & beef. Nice outdoor terrace in summer, covered in vines. €€€

✗ **Cucina Bacilieri** [275 C5] Via Terranuova 60; ☎0532 243206; w cucinabacilieri.it; ◷ closed Sun eve & Tue. Small, intimate & sophisticated, with some very recherché dishes: guinea fowl ravioli, *baccalà* with cauliflower, almonds & truffles, foie gras with porcini & a hint of amaretto. Tasting menus €50 (*terra* or *mare*) & €75. Booking essential. €€€

✗ **L'Oca Giuliva** [275 B4] Via Boccacanale di Santo Stefano; ☎0532 207628; w ristorantelocagiuliva.it; ◷ closed Tue. Very 'slow food', with a traditional menu featuring *baccalà, salama da sugo* & *cappellacci di zucca*; the menu changes every 2 weeks. €€€

✗ **Quel Fantastico Giovedì** [275 B5] Via Castelnuovo 9, nr Piazza del Travaglio; ☎0532 760570; w quelfantasticogiovedi.it; ◷ closed Wed. Exquisite cooking, dishes prepared with an effortlessly light touch – thin slices of red tuna in a caper pesto, or squid stuffed with aubergines in a yellow pepper sauce, & game dishes in season. Save room for dessert – the chocolatey ones especially. The name, 'That Wonderful Thursday', comes from a story by John Steinbeck. Fish tasting menu €38. Coeliac menu available. Booking essential. €€€

CHEAP & CHEERFUL

✗ **Da Noemi** [275 B5] Via Ragno 31; ☎0532 769070; w trattoriadanoemi.it; ◷ closed Tue. The menu in this very popular trattoria is a textbook of traditional Ferrara cuisine, with all the *cappelletti, cappellacci* & *salumi*. Good for grilled lamb & steaks too. Everybody comes here; book well ahead. €€–€€€

✗ **Il Mandolino** [275 B5] Via Carlo Mayr 83; ☎0532 760080; w ristoranteilmandolino.it; ◷ closed Mon eve, Tue. Another neighbourhood favourite, near the Porta Paula, with a pleasant family atmosphere & all the classic dishes. €€–€€€

✗ **Al Brindisi** [275 C4] Via Adelardi 11; ☎0532 473744; w albrindisi.net; ◷ closed Mon. Hidden behind the cathedral, supposedly the oldest osteria in the world (according to the Guinness Book there's been one on this spot since 1435, mentioned in a poem by Ariosto). Now a convivial old wood-panelled enoteca with fine cheeses, *salama del sugo*, salads & its own wines; great for an inexpensive full dinner too. Outside tables. €€

✗ **Castadiva Kitchen Gallery** [275 B3] Via Amari s/n; m 338 846 1832; ◷ closed Sun eve. Off Viale Cavour near the Castello Estense, a trendy place good for a light lunch, with lots of interesting dishes on the blackboard every day: it's best at seafood salads & pasta. €€

✗ **Hostaria Savonarola** [275 B4] Piazza Savonarola 18; ☎0532 200214; ◷ until midnight daily. Practically in the shadow of the Castello Estense, a simple, non-touristy trattoria with excellent *salumi* & homemade pasta. Outside tables under the arches. €€

✗ **Zazie** [275 B5] Via San Romano 62; m 331 266 8008; ◷ 09.30–20.00 Mon–Sat, noon–22.00 Sun. A haven for vegetarians & vegans: veg couscous, lentil burgers, *riso Venere* (black rice) risotto with orange, soups; juices, herbal teas & smoothies. €–€€

✗ **Settimo** [275 B4] Via Cortevecchio 49; ☎0532 205145; ◷ closed Thu. Just behind the Palazzo Municipale. The €13 3-course dinner menu with wine & coffee included can't be beaten. Famous for its huge *cotoletta milanese* too. Get a table on the lively back terrace. €

BARS & CAFÉS

💻 **Caffè Europa** [275 C4] Corso Giovecca 51. This *pasticceria* is a local legend, part of the Hotel Europa (page 273). Delicious pastries & light lunches. €

♀ **Clandestino** [275 B5] Via Ragno 50; ✎0532 767101. Lively, popular bar with local craft beers, *piadine, salumi* & other snacks, TV sports & board games to play. €

♀ **Enotria** [275 C5] Via Saraceno 41; ✎0532 209166; w enotecaenotria.it; ⊕ closed Sun. One of the fancier *enoteche*, with a fine selection as well as *salumi* & cheeses, bruschetta & crostini. €

ENTERTAINMENT AND NIGHTLIFE

A university town, Ferrara is quite lively at night, though not for clubbing; music bars are few. Listings of forthcoming programmes in the cinema, theatre and so on can be found in the local newspaper, *La Nuova Ferrara* (w *bobobo.it/ferrara/eventi*), or on w ferrarabynight.com.

🎬 **Cinema Teatro Santo Spirito** [275 D4] Via della Resistenza 7; ✎0532 200181; w cinemasantospirito.it. Ferrara has its big multi-cinemas, but this little neighbourhood cinema is the 1 for 2nd-runs, art films, classics & children's cinema.

🎭 **Teatro Comunale** [275 C4] Corso Martiri della Libertà 5; ✎0532 205675; w teatrocomunaleferrara.it. Another of the region's spectacular 18th-century theatres, with 5 ornate tiers of boxes & scenes from the life of Caesar on the ceiling. It took decades to restore it after wartime bombings. Ferrara is a great town for dance, & most of the performances are held here, along with opera & concerts.

🎭 **Teatro Nuovo** [275 C5] Piazza Trenta e Trieste 52; ✎0532 186 2055; w teatronuovoferrara.com.

Ferrara's major venue for concerts & every other sort of show: a full season of theatre, dance, opera & operetta, & family shows.

☆ **Jazz Club Ferrara** [275 D3] Rampari di Belfiore 167; ✎0532 171 6739; w jazzclubferrara.com. A magnificent round, timbered space, in a Renaissance bastion that was part of the city's fortifications. A lot of big names have played here, though currently it's open only for special concerts.

☆ **Sinatra Club** [275 D1] Via Canalazzi 23; ✎0532 813 0123; w sinatra.it. Big compound out in the east suburbs, 5km from the city where the Ferraresi can't hear it, with a disco, concert hall & restaurant. Electro, house, hip hop & everything else (except Sinatra); check website for events.

FESTIVALS AND EVENTS

Ferrara's **Palio** may not be as famous as the one in Siena, but they claim it's the oldest horse race in the world, dating back to 1279. Held in Piazza Ariostea on the last Sunday in May, the race is the climax of a week of festivities, contested by the city's eight *contrade* (neighbourhoods). There are parades, performances by the *contrade*'s quite exceptionally skilled marching bands and flag-throwers, Renaissance markets and dinners, and races for donkeys, *putti* and *putte* (teenage boys and girls) in addition to the horses. For complete info, see the tourist office website (page 273) or w *paliodiferrara.it* (in Italian only).

For something completely different, Ferrara holds one of Europe's biggest folk festivals, the **Buskers' Festival**, or Rassegna Internazionale dei Musicisti di Strada (w *ferrarabuskers.com*; ⊕ *every evening exc Sun; free*), over ten days in late August, with more than a thousand musicians, street artists, jugglers and what have you. In mid-September, the **Ferrara Balloons Festival** (w *ferrarafestival.it*; ✎ *0532 900713*) offers hot-air balloon rides plus sports, food and cultural events.

Ferrara Musica (✎ *0532 202220*; w *ferraramusica.it*) is an international season of concerts and opera which runs from September to May. Venues include the elegant Teatro Comunale. **Ferrara Sotto le Stelle** (✎ *0532 241149*; w *ferrarasottolestelle.it*) is an alternative-rock music festival held in Piazza Castello in the first three weeks of July.

SHOPPING

The narrow streets around the Castello Estense [275 B4] are the main shopping centre, especially around Via Garibaldi, and behind the cathedral on Via Voltapaletto, Via Canonica and Via Mazzini. For trendy antique and secondhand boutiques, look around Via Ragno and Via Carlo Mayr south of the cathedral.

The big **street market** takes place on Friday mornings in Piazza Trento e Trieste [275 C4] and the other streets around the cathedral: not just food but clothes, antiques and much else. On Tuesdays there's another market in **Piazza Travaglio** [275 B5] and Via Bologna. On Friday mornings, the **Mercato Contadino** (farmers' market) sells all the best local products in Piazzetta Donatori di Sangue [275 B5], near the Porta Paola. There's another farmers' market (plus a little bit of everything) on Thursday mornings (except in winter) in Piazza XXIV Maggio [275 A3]: the **Mercato dell'Acquedotto** off Corto Isonzo around the city's ornate 1920s water tower. The **Fiera dell'Artigianato** (🕐 *until 19.30 3rd w/end of each month exc Jul–Aug*), in Piazza Savonarola in the centre [275 B4], is the place where artists and artisans display their wares.

OTHER PRACTICALITIES

HOSPITAL
✛ **Ospedale Sant'Anna** [map, pages 268–9] Via Aldo Moro 8, Cona (Cocomaro); 📞 0532 236111. The main hospital, with the only emergency room, is 10km east of the city off the RA8 motorway.

PHARMACY
✚ **Farmacia Fides** [275 C4] Corso della Giovecca 129; 📞 0532 209493; 🕐 24hrs

POST OFFICE
✉ **Main post office** [275 B3] Viale Cavour, just west of the Castello Estense

WHAT TO SEE AND DO

CASTELLO ESTENSE [275 B4] (*Piazza Castello;* 📞 *0532 299233;* w *castelloestense. it;* 🕐 *Mar–Sep 09.30–17.00 daily, Oct–Feb 09.30–17.30 Tue–Sun;* €8, *tower* €2 *extra, guided tour* €4 *extra*) At the heart of Ferrara towers the imposing Castello Estense, its elegant Renaissance towers reflected in the wide moat. It's a queer sort of building, one that doesn't seem to know whether to be a fortress or a palace; in fact it has been both. At once massive and delicate, it is also quite beautiful, the very image of suave and intelligent tyranny.

The Castello is also a part of Ferrara's precocious modernist mystique; the Metaphysical painters took it for a kind of existential symbol, and perhaps it was no accident that it inspired so many Victorian-era factory buildings.

There's no doubt about the Castello's original purpose. It was begun in 1385 after a revolt in May of that year against high taxes in which the taxman, one Tommaso da Tortona, was lynched. After clearing a huge area on the edge of what was then

SAVING MONEY IN FERRARA

The city offers a **MyFE Card** (w *myfecard.it; €12 for 2 days, €14 for 3 days, €18 for 6 days*), good for free admission to all the city's museums, plus discounts on various concerts and exhibitions, in some hotels, restaurants and shops, and on the airport shuttle, etc. It can be a very good deal if you plan to do a lot of sightseeing. Available from the tourist office and the major museums.

the town wall, Signore Niccolò II laid the first stone for his new stronghold on 29 September – the Day of St Michael, he who kicked the rebellious angels out of heaven; the symbolism was undoubtedly not lost on the Ferraresi.

The **Via Coperta**, the protected passageway running over the piazza to the old Este palace (now the Palazzo Municipale), gave the dukes a chance to reach the castle in case of further trouble; it probably inspired the famous Corridoio Vasariano that performed the same function for the Medici in Florence. In the 1400s, under Ercole I, the Este transformed the Castello into part of their residence: its crenellations were replaced by white marble balustrades, and its great halls adorned with art.

The drawbridge, with its counter-weights, still seems to be in good working order, but they'll let anybody in now. Inside the courtyard are the city tourist office, some municipal offices and the entrance to the castle residence.

A few decorated rooms survive in the ducal apartments: the best is the **Sala dell'Aurora**, Ercole II's study, with frescoes by Giovanni Settevecchi (*Day* and *Sunset*) and Bastianino (*Dawn*, *Aurora* and *Night*); they collaborated on the charming central fresco of *Time*, surrounded by putti racing chariots drawn by various beasts around a classical racecourse with obelisks. Among the other rooms are the **Camerina dei Baccanali**, and the **Salone e Saletta dei Giochi** – the games rooms, frescoed by Settevecchi with more putti wrestling and swimming, pretending to be gladiators, playing ninepins and a score of other games.

The visit includes Renée of France's unadorned Calvinist **chapel** (1590; the ceiling frescoes were added in the 19th century), and the **Torre dei Leoni**, site of the prison where Ugo and Parisina languished before their beheading (page 270). Niccolò was so angry by his betrayal that he had all the 'unfaithful women' of the city executed with them. They all still haunt this tower, according to the Ferraresi, and shrieks in the night are not unknown.

Other famous prisoners in the tower included Giulio and Ferrante, brothers of Alfonso I, who spent their lives here after attempting a conspiracy in 1506. The dukes weren't forgiving. Ferrante died after 34 years in the tower; Giulio came out with a pardon after 53 years, aged 81, walking around Ferrara in perfect health and amusing the people with his old-fashioned, threadbare clothes. The family wasn't known for its modesty either. One part of the original decoration that has disappeared are the 300 portraits of various Este princes, some by famous artists, that once covered almost all the walls.

From the ducal apartments a door leads to the lovely roof terrace, with the **Giardino degli Aranci** (1531), a grove of orange trees in huge pots; this ducal fantasy is still kept up, even though they have to bring them indoors each winter. As in many other things related to gardens, the Este were pioneers. This is probably the ancestor of all the 'orangeries' of the palaces of Europe.

PIAZZA SAVONAROLA [275 B4] Dukes can take the Via Coperta over to the Palazzo Municipale, but you'll have to go out and walk a block down Corso Martiri della Libertà, passing the **statue of Savonarola**, the fire-and-brimstone Dominican revivalist who gained control of Florence after the Medici were kicked out in 1494, and convinced the most sophisticated citizens of the Renaissance (in a Ferrarese accent, yet) to give up their treasures to the Bonfire of the Vanities; he was a native of this city. Almost underneath the Via Coperta, you can also have a look at **La Regina**, a 7-tonne *colubrina* (field culverin), one of the biggest made for Duke Ercole II. Cast in 1556, it could launch a ball over 4km, or pound down almost any castle wall. The original was melted down long ago. This one is a copy, made in the 1880s and named for Italy's beloved Regina Margherita – 'Queen Daisy', the same one they named the pizza after.

PALAZZO MUNICIPALE [275 B4] (*Piazza Municipale;* ✎ *0532 419770;* ⊕ *09.00–13.00 Mon–Fri, 09.00–13.00 & 15.00–17.00 Tue & Thu by request; admission free*) The Palazzo Municipale was begun in 1245, soon after Azzo d'Este seized control of Ferrara, and has been tinkered with ever since; its façade was redone in the 1920s in the picturesque medieval manner. The main entrance facing the cathedral is the **Volta del Cavallo**, named for the wonderful Renaissance embellishment on its right, one of the civic symbols of Ferrara. This marble arch, said to have been the work of Leon Battista Alberti, is surmounted by a bronze **statue of Niccolò III** on horseback. The companion piece on the left of the arch is an antique column with a **statue of Duke Borso**, smiling on his throne and looking for all the world like Old King Cole. It was Borso who commissioned the mystical frescoes of the Palazzo Schifanoia. Both of these statues are copies, done after Napoleon melted down the originals to make cannons.

The archway leads into a spacious courtyard, called the **Piazzetta Municipale**, now a proper city square with cafés and shops. Tourists often miss it completely, though they'll hear it in the evening, when the marching bands and flag-throwing *alfieri* practise their routines for the Palio in May. In one corner is a grand, rather Venetian-looking Renaissance monumental stair, the **Scalone d'Honore** (1481); this led directly to the dukes' apartments and was used for public ceremonies.

The parts of the Palazzo Municipale open to the public include the **Stanzino delle Duchesse**, charmingly decorated in gilt and fresco by Bastianino (Sebastiano Filippi) and his brothers, one of the last commissions of the dukes before they were forced out of the city, and the **Sala dell'Arengo**, with some very peculiar 1930s frescoes on the mythic history of Ferrara by Fascist painter Achille Funi. Once this palace was home to the Este's magnificent collection of paintings; the popes shipped it all off to Rome after 1598 and the Este had to start their collections all over again in Modena.

CATTEDRALE DI SAN GIORGIO [275 C4] (*Piazza Trento e Trieste;* ✎ *0532 207449;* ⊕ *07.30–noon & 15.30–18.30 daily exc during services, until 19.00 Sun*) It looks, if it looks like anything on this planet, a little like an old Mississippi steamboat, come paddle-wheeling up Ol' Man Po to moor itself in the piazza. A building as singular in its way as the Castello, the Cattedrale was begun in 1135. The great Wiligelmo, known for his work on Modena Cathedral, and his follower Niccolò both worked on the cathedral at the beginning, though it isn't clear who designed the building or what their original intentions were.

When it was finished, sometime before 1300, it had acquired its distinctive boxy shape, massive side gables and a façade with a Gothic false front rising above the level of the church. The upper loggia on the south side is a bit of show-offish Romanesque bravura in the Tuscan manner, with columns variously twisted, zigzagging or even tied in knots, like those on churches in Lucca. The locals say that the Devil himself twisted around all these columns the night before the consecration of the cathedral, and had to slink away with his tail between his legs in the morning when the populace joyfully applauded the ingenuity of the sculptors.

Beneath this, the **Loggia dei Merciai**, the picturesque market portico flanking the cathedral in Piazza Trento e Trieste, was erected in 1473, though there has been a market on this spot since the earliest days of the city. At the apse is a lovely candy-striped **campanile**, attributed to Alberti, begun in 1442 and never completed. The last major addition was the apse, built by Biagio Rossetti in 1498.

The cathedral's glory is its marble **portico**, guarded by porphyry lions and griffins. Niccolò executed the relief on the tympanum of *St George*, to whom the cathedral is dedicated, killing his dragon, and above it various Old Testament scenes and figures of prophets. Above the portal, a loggia shelters a *Madonna and Child* in terracotta by Cristoforo da Firenze (1427), and above the loggia is a pediment with a magnificent (though hard-to-see) 13th-century tableau of the *Last Judgement* by unknown sculptors.

The fellow in pilgrim's garb, in the niche to the right of the portal, is **Alberto V d'Este**; Alberto got in trouble with Pope Boniface IX, and in 1391 was forced to make a penitential pilgrimage to Rome. The Pope proved surprisingly lenient, and awarded Signore Alberto several advantages for his city and family, including the right to found the University of Ferrara to compete with that in Bologna.

The **interior** suffered a catastrophic remodelling under the popes in 1710, destroying most of its original works of art and leaving it with a gloomy but somewhat raffish air, helped along by the ranks of glass-bead chandeliers. On the wall over the main door, frescoes by Garofalo of *SS Peter and Paul* survived; to the right of them is a baptismal font from Byzantine times. In the last chapel on the right is a *Martyrdom of St Lawrence* by Guercino, and in the Rossetti apse Bastianino painted a fresco of the *Last Judgement*, a composition derived from the Sistine Chapel's *Last Judgement* of his master, Michelangelo.

MUSEO DELLA CATTEDRALE [275 B4] (*Via San Romano;* \ *0532 244949;* ⏱ *09.30– 13.30 & 15.00–18.00 Tue–Sun; €6*) This small but memorable museum is housed in the former church and cloister of San Romano, just across from the south side of the cathedral. Among the exhibits are the lovely marble *Madonna of the Pomegranate* (1406) by Jacopo della Quercia, some fine 16th-century Flemish tapestries, and two painted organ shutters that rank among the greatest surviving works of Cosmè Tura: an *Annunciation* full of lovely naturalistic detail (even a squirrel), and the remarkable, surreal *St George*, dispatching his dragon in a dream landscape. The 12th-century reliefs of the *Labours of the Months*, credited to followers of Parma's Benedetto Antelami, adorned the cathedral's south door before the 1710 renovations.

MEDIEVAL FERRARA The oldest streets of Ferrara around the Castello are still the shopping district and the liveliest part of town. Behind the Castello in Piazza della Repubblica is the 1405 church of **San Giuliano** [275 B4] (⏱ *currently closed for restorations after earthquake damage*), like the cathedral completely redone inside in the 1700s. One street to the west on Via degli Spadari is **San Domenico** [275 B4] (⏱ *closed for restoration*). This church, and the medieval one that preceded it, were the home of the Inquisition after the popes took over Ferrara. Inside, on a pier to the right of the entrance, you can see some claw scratches in the stone, left by the Devil himself (who is apparently never very far from Ferrara). They say Nick was eavesdropping and became outraged when one of his converts repented at the tribunal here.

SAN BERNARDINO DI SIENA

The Tuscan 'Little St Bernard' travelled across Italy on foot for 30 years in the early 1400s, raising mobs against Jews, heretics, witches and above all sodomites; when you see his logo on a church, it usually means he held a revival meeting there. In Ferrara in 1424, Bernardino railed against fancy clothes and other luxuries, a predecessor to the city's own rabble-rouser Savonarola. The people wanted to make him bishop, though he declined. Bernardino's motto 'Make it clear, make it short and keep to the point' helped him become patron saint of advertising and public relations in the 1980s.

9

From here, Via degli Spadari runs southward, following the route of a medieval canal; it changes its name to Via Boccacanale di Santo Stefano, passing several Renaissance-era houses before reaching Piazza Saint'Etienne (named for Ferrara's sister city in France) and the recently restored **Santo Stefano** [275 B4], begun in the 11th century and subjected to several later restorations. The austere but elegant façade features blind arches and four circular *rosaci*, two holding terracotta busts of St Stephen and the Virgin, and one with the Holy Name-and-sunburst logo of the great medieval preacher San Bernardino of Siena. This church is one of the few to have reopened after the 2012 earthquake, though there isn't much to see inside.

Two blocks to the east, just south of the cathedral in Piazzetta Schiatti, is **San Paolo** [275 B5] (⊕ *currently closed for earthquake restorations*), one of the last churches built under Este rule (1575) and still preserving most of its original decoration, including works by Bastianino and Girolamo da Carpi and a fresco in the apse of the *Ascension of the Prophet Elijah* by Ippolito Scarsellino, one of the last important Ferrara painters. The 10th-century campanile, called the Torre dei Leuti, is all that's left of an earlier church on this site.

Behind the church is a street that has changed its appearance little since the 1300s, the cobbled, atmospheric **Via delle Volte**, named for the vaulted passageways that connect the houses on either side. To the north, on Via delle Scienze, the **Palazzo Paradiso** [275 C5] (⊙ *0532 418200;* ⊕ *09.00–19.00 Mon–Fri, 09.00–13.00 Sat; admission free*), was begun in 1391 and named for a great fresco of heavenly scenes, now lost. The palace earned a small but confusing role in history as the setting for the Ecumenical Council of 1438, a last-ditch attempt to recover Christian unity – only 15 years before the fall of Constantinople – which was attended by both the pope and the Byzantine patriarch. This council was really only one of three, in a shambolic decade that saw two antipopes, rival councils, mutual excommunications and endless battling between Greeks and Latins over obscure points of scripture. Only a year later plague broke out around Ferrara and all the participants hightailed it off to Florence.

The palace was almost completely rebuilt in the 1590s as the home of Ferrara University. Now it is the municipal library and offices, and there is little to see outside of the university's old anatomical theatre, and the tomb of Ariosto in the Biblioteca Ariostea, which holds the original manuscript of *Orlando Furioso*.

MEIS: MUSEUM OF ITALIAN JUDAISM AND OF THE SHOAH [275 A4] (*Via Piangipane 81;* ⊙ *0532 191 2039;* w *meisweb.it;* ⊕ *10.00–13.00 & 16.00–18.00 Tue–Sun; €7*)

There seems to have been a Jewish community in Ferrara from the earliest days. As a source of taxes, they had the special protection of the Este, who did their best to protect them against preachers like San Bernardino, and the more bigoted popes such as Paul IV. By the quattrocento, the community was thriving, counting about a tenth of the total population, and it gained in numbers by taking in refugees from persecution in Portugal and Spain. Ferrara's Jews were noted as scholars and doctors.

All that changed when the popes displaced the Este in 1598. Jews were forced to wear badges on their clothing, and oppressive regulations piled up with each passing year. In 1624, the papal government forced the Jews into a ghetto with walls and gates (to be paid for by the Jews themselves) centred on what is now Via Mazzini and Via Vignatagliata. Over the next 200 years many of Ferrara's Jews left for Modena, Tuscany and other refuges of toleration. This state of affairs lasted until the Napoleonic Wars and the arrival of the French, who immediately dismantled the ghetto gates and gave the Jews equal rights.

The priest at San Francesco laughed 'It's only half *burocrazia*', and he followed that with a scholarly dissertation on why so many sights in Ferrara are still closed, so many years after the 2012 earthquake. That earthquake was a teaser. It didn't do any really dramatic damage, leaving only niggling cracks in walls and bits of falling stucco and plaster. But that damage had to be repaired, and it showed up everything that needed doing to make the city's buildings safer against the next big quake.

The Italians are the experts. With the world's greatest concentration of artistic monuments, sitting on one of its most active earthquake zones, they take the troubles in their stride. In Ferrara, their experience goes back to the quake of 1570, which destroyed much of the city. The Este dukes were fortunate to have in their employ the great architect Pirro Ligorio, who oversaw the reconstruction and wrote a book about it, the *Trattato di Diversi Terremoti*, which is still read by engineers today.

The money, as the priest told us, is always there, no problem. But the *burocrazia* parcels it out slowly, carefully. There are so many landmark buildings to fix – 620 of them in Ferrara province, not to mention far more serious jobs from the terrible recent quakes in Umbria and Abruzzo. The process involves so many offices that need to sign off on works, so many little problems discovered during reconstruction that require more investigations and head-scratching, and never enough builders and restorers with the right skills available. Have patience. It might take a few more years for everything in Ferrara to be open again, but when the job is done it will have been done right.

When the popes came back after 1815 the ghetto gates went up again, then down, then up again, according to the whims of successive popes. The end of the Papal State in the unification of Italy put a stop to the madness, and Ferrara's Jews began an era of prosperity and integration into the Italian nation, or so they thought. The sad finale, as captured in *The Garden of the Finzi-Continis* by the Ferrarese novelist Giorgio Bassani, made into the famous film by Vittorio de Sica, saw Italian authorities help the Nazis round up what remained of the community in 1943 and ship them off to the camps. Only five came back.

The museum, which opened only in 2012, has a small permanent collection and exhibits portraying the history of Italy's Jews over the centuries, with frequent special exhibitions. It is hoped to eventually be able to put on display the collections of Ferrara's old Jewish Museum in the surviving **Synagogue** [275 C5], a few streets away at Via Mazzini 95, which has been closed since the 2012 earthquake.

EAST OF THE CENTRE: CHURCHES AND PALACES From behind the cathedral, Via Voltapaletto will take you out to the east end of Ferrara and the first of the city's planned 'additions', laid out under Niccolò III in 1385 (it's a much more pleasant walk than the dull and traffic-plagued main street, Corso Giovecca). Where it crosses Via Terranuova, Voltapaletto changes its name to Via Savonarola and passes **San Francesco** [275 C5] (✆ *0532 209646;* ⊕ *08.00–noon & 15.30–18.00 daily*), one of the best of Biagio Rossetti's churches (1494); its magnificent interior, currently open in the midst of restorations, is brightened by terracotta reliefs and painted friezes in the nave, the latter by Girolamo da Carpi.

Next, at number 9, the 1475 **Palazzo di Renata di Francia** [275 D5], where Renée of France maintained her Protestant circle far from her husband's court, is now part of the university; they won't mind if you have a look at the richly decorated *piano nobile* when it's open. Behind the palace, its gardens are now a peaceful public park, the **Parco Pareschi**.

To the south on Via Pergolato, behind the church of San Girolamo, is the church and monastery of **Corpus Domini** [275 D5] (✎ *0532 209370;* ⊕ *15.30–17.30 Mon–Fri; admission free*), with a rich Baroque interior containing the austere tombs of Alfonso I, Alfonso II and Lucrezia Borgia.

CASA ROMEI [275 D5] (*Via Savonarola;* ✎ *0532 234130;* ⊕ *08.30–14.00 Sun–Wed, 14.00–19.30 Thu–Sat;* €*3*) Across from the Palazzo Renata di Francia, this fine early Renaissance palace was built for a banker who married one of the Este in 1445. Later it was the Ferrara home of the second Este cardinal, Ippolito II, son

LUCREZIA BORGIA

They told a lot of tales about Lucrezia back in her day, but then the Italians of the Renaissance had polished character assassination into an art form. In the 19th century they believed all those propaganda stories, giving us Victor Hugo's play *Lucrezia Borgia*, and the opera of the same name by Donizetti, creating the archetype of the evil femme fatale. Dante Gabriel Rossetti contributed a famous portrait of her, worriedly washing her hands after poisoning her husband.

The Borgia family were Spaniards, and they hit the jackpot in 1378 when one of their members became Pope Calixtus III. The second Borgia pope, Alexander VI, had to suffer a fair amount of politically motivated character assassination too, though outside of being a Machiavellian schemer, a libertine and possibly a closet pagan, the record says he made a thoroughly competent pope.

Alexander's daughter Lucrezia was 13 when he attained the papacy, and despite being illegitimate she immediately became the hottest marriage prospect in Italy. Lucrezia was beautiful, with a regal bearing and golden hair down to her knees, and her father had made sure she received an excellent education. Her first marriage was to Giovanni Sforza, Duke of Milan, but when the Wars of Italy began in 1494 and Sforza sided with the invading French against the pope, an annulment had to be arranged (Sforza agreed on the condition he could keep the dowry).

Lucrezia raised some scandal in the years that followed. She was suspected of having an affair with a Spanish servant, who soon after was found bobbing in the Tiber. Her second husband, Alfonso of Aragon, was murdered in 1500 for political reasons, possibly by Lucrezia's brother Cesare. Cesare was the family enforcer; some say he had tried to knock off Giovanni Sforza too.

Next, Pope Alexander sent her to Ferrara to marry Duke Alfonso I. There were intrigues here too; Lucrezia carried on a long affair with the poet Pietro Bembo, and another with her brother-in-law, the Marquess of Mantua. But Alfonso didn't seem to mind; he had affairs of his own. She was a real asset for the duke, managing his brilliant court and becoming quite the pious matron in her later years, aiding charities and providing the duke with eight children. After the birth of the last of them, in 1519, she died from complications.

of Lucrezia Borgia and one of the most influential men in Italy in the mid-16th century. This Ippolito was a great patron of the arts, and he created the greatest of all the Este gardens, the Villa d'Este at Tivoli near Rome. Here, as well as its charming frescoes in the Sala delle Sibille and Sala dei Profeti, its terracotta fireplaces and the elegant courtyards, there are some expressive detached frescoes moved here from Sant'Andrea and other disused churches, and the rooms are filled with period art and furnishings from other buildings.

PALAZZINA DI MARFISA D'ESTE [275 D5] (*Corso Giovecca 170;* ⬩ *0532 242949;* ⊕ *09.00–13.00 & noon–18.00 Tue–Sun; €4*) This palace was built for Francesco d'Este, a son of Alfonso I and father of Marfisa. It once formed part of a larger complex of buildings, now unfortunately lost, and Marfisa's retreat now seems a bit sad in the busy traffic of the Corso. Marfisa, a friend of Tasso, was beautiful and eccentric, the only member of the Este family to stay behind in Ferrara after the popes took over. She is also the subject of several ghost stories; they say Marfisa enjoyed post mortem rides through the city at midnight in a wolf-drawn carriage. The interior of her little palace, which once had a colourful majolica pavement, has been admirably restored and fitted with a fine collection of 16th- and 17th-century Tuscan and other Italian furniture, and unusual frescoed grotesques on the ceiling and cornices. Outside is a loggia with frescoes of two little girls, Marfisa and her sister. The pretty garden is now occasionally used for concerts.

At the end of Corso Giovecca, just before the walls, the big stone arch called the **Prospettiva** was built to close the view down the long straight avenue in 1703.

PALAZZO SCHIFANOIA [275 D6] (*Via Scandiana, 2 blocks south of the Palazzina Marfisa d'Este;* ⬩ *0532 244949;* ⊕ *09.30–18.00 Tue–Sun, if it's open at all – the current plan is to close the palazzo in Jan 2018 for an unknown length of time to install anti-seismic protections, but the Salone dei Mesi may be opened at times when the work permits; €3 inc Museo Lapidario, see page 287*) It's surprising there's anything left at all. The popes used this simple but exquisite palace as a tobacco factory, ruining some of the greatest frescoes of the Renaissance, and Napoleon's boys weren't too gentle with it either after they made it a barracks in 1801. *Schifanoia* translates as 'escape from boredom'. Alberto V began this *delizia*, as Este rural palaces were called, in 1385 in what was then open countryside. It was expanded and redecorated on several occasions, and took its present form in the late 15th century with architectural trim by Rossetti and a stately portal designed by painter Francesco del Cossa, displaying the Este arms.

The reason for visiting is a single bare room, the **Salone dei Mesi**, the 'collective masterpiece of the Ferrarese school', frescoed c1475 for Borso d'Este by Francesco del Cossa, Cosmè Tura and Ercole de' Roberti, and probably other hands too. Modern criticism usually credits the guiding hand behind this tremendous allegory as Tura's; busy as he was with other commissions for the Este, he left much of the actual painting to others. In their current, semi-ruined state the frescoes were at one point covered with whitewash, and only rediscovered in 1855.

The scenes of mythological and allegorical subjects represent the months of the year (*mesi*), and each is divided into three bands. On top are the **Triumphs**, each featuring the god who presides over the month in a triumphal car drawn by horses or other animals. These were inspired by Petrarch's *Trionfi*, a set of short poems with illustrations that became a popular Renaissance theme in both painting and poetry. The bottom band shows animated **scenes from the court of Borso d'Este**, each appropriate to the month.

The other inspiration comes from the occult astrology that shaped so much of Renaissance thought and life; the black central band for each month pictures the zodiacal sign and three strange, striking figures; these represent the *decans* (see box, pages 371–3) of the ancient Egyptians, who divided the zodiac into 36 zones of ten days each, three for each sign and each one ruled by its 'daemon'. The symbolism behind these *decan* figures is entirely unknown, though beyond doubt it owes a lot more to Renaissance magicians than ancient Egyptians. Some scholars identify them with constellations near the signs. They're just guessing.

Of the 12 scenes, only seven, March to September, have survived; the rest are damaged beyond restoration or even legibility:

March *Triumph of Minerva* (Aries), holding a sword and a book, in a car pulled by unicorns, with a group of scholars thought to be professors from the new University of Ferrara on the left, and ladies with a weaving loom, and the three Fates.

April *Triumph of Venus* (Taurus), with a kneeling knight in attendance, in a car drawn by swans among amorous courtiers (and lots of happy white rabbits), with the three Graces in the background. Beneath, Duke Borso gives a coin to his court jester, while on the left riders ready their mounts for Ferrara's Palio.

May *Triumph of Apollo* (Gemini), drawn by horses of four different colours, followed by the nine Muses; on the right, a fountain and a crowd of babies that have mystified critics for centuries.

June *Triumph of Mercury* (Cancer – not a crab but a lobster), drawn by black eagles, holding his caduceus and a lyre, accompanied by a white swan and a black crow, with a scene of a marketplace. Underneath is a scene from the Este *delizia* of Belriguardo showing Borsa receiving his title as lord of the city. Attributed to an unknown Maestro degli Occhi Spalancati ('Master of the Wide-open Eyes'), or possibly by Cosmè Tura.

July *Triumph of Jupiter* (Leo), holding a lightning bolt and a lotus flower, drawn by lions, accompanied by Cybele, seated facing backwards. In the background, dreaming, is Cybele's consort Attis. The bottom panel portrays the marriage of Borso's sister Bianca. In the background is the nearby monastery of Sant'Antonio in Polesine.

August *Triumph of Ceres* (Virgo), drawn by winged dragons; the background shows an image of Isis and the abduction of Proserpina; the panel is considered as an allegory of agriculture. At the bottom, Borso receives an ambassador. Possibly by Cosmè Tura or Ercole de' Roberti.

September *Triumph of Vulcan* (Libra), allegory of the mechanical arts, drawn by monkeys. In the background, Cyclopes working at a forge, a vignette of the wolf that suckled Romulus and Remus, and a scene of two lovers in bed, thought to be Venus and Mars. The court scene is unidentified, but probably the work of Ercole de' Roberti.

From the remains, **December** is thought to be Vesta, goddess of the hearth (Capricorn). On the north and south walls are fragmentary scenes of the Castello Estense, with knights on horseback

Few works so successfully capture the quattrocento delight in life and beauty, its vitality and imagination – most famously in the *Triumph of Venus* for the month of

April, with plenty of rare Renaissance kisses. Like March and possibly others, this is attributed to Francesco del Cossa. In much of this painter's work, the figures are posed with an almost superhuman grace, as in the beautiful scene of the pruning of the vines in March, or the enigmatic first *decan* of that month, a youth holding an arrow and a golden hoop.

The touch of the bizarre here comes not from Tura, little of whose work here seems to have survived, but Ercole de' Roberti, who is credited with most of September, the Triumph of Vulcan – weirdly stylised rocks, unlike anything seen in painting before or since, the god's triumphal car drawn by apes, Mars and Venus making love, and a hallucinatory vision of Vulcan's forge.

The palace has several other rooms with surviving decoration, including the 1475 **Sala dei Stucchi**, and houses an eclectic collection of medieval and Renaissance art. There's a good display of bronze medallions, including many by the originator of this Renaissance art and its all-time master, Pisanello (one is of Sigismondo Malatesta's muse Isotta degli Atti; page 369). Along with a number of fine ivories is an alabaster *Passion of Christ* by a 15th-century sculptor from Nottingham. There are also paintings, including two sombre scenes of decapitations by Scarsellino (*John the Baptist* and *Santa Margherita*).

MUSEO LAPIDARIO [275 D6] (*Via Scandiana;* \ *0532 244949;* ⊕ *09.30–18.00 Tue–Sun; joint ticket with the Palazzo Schifanoia, pages 285–7*) Across the street from the Schifanoia, on the corner of Via Camposabbionario, this is a small collection of Roman-era sarcophagi, funeral stones, sculptures and architectural fragments, along with some fine late Imperial sarcophagi.

SANTA MARIA IN VADO [275 D6] (*Via Scandiana;* \ *0532 65127;* ⊕ *08.00–noon & 15.30–19.30 daily*) Just east of the Schifanoia, on the corner of Via Borgovado, Santa Maria in Vado, designed by Rosetti and Ercole de' Roberti, was a pilgrimage church commemorating a miracle of 1171: a priest was offering Communion when blood spurted from the host and splashed up on the vaulting, where it can still be seen. The truly monumental interior has some impressive frescoes and paintings by Carlo Bononi, Camillo Filippi and others.

PALAZZO DI LUDOVICO IL MORO: MUSEO ARCHEOLOGICO NAZIONALE [275 D6] (*Via XX Settembre 124;* \ *0532 66299;* w *archeoferrara.beniculturali.it; palace & museum* ⊕ *09.30–17.00 Tue–Sun; €6*) South of the Schifanoia, the quiet old district around Via XX Settembre is the city's second planned addition, the Addizione di Borso d'Este (1451). Via XX Settembre follows the old course of the Po; the round stones used to pave the streets and in some of the houses came from the dried-up riverbed.

At number 124 is the elegant Palazzo Costabili, better known as the Palazzo di Ludovico il Moro. Designed by Biagio Rossetti, it was erroneously named after Beatrice d'Este's husband, the Duke of Milan, though it never belonged to him, but to Antonio Costabili, the Este's ambassador to Milan. It houses one of Ferrara's hidden treats, in the **Sala del Tesoro**: charming frescoes by Garofalo (c1506) of musicians and putti looking down at us from a balcony on the ceiling, an early example of trompe l'œil ceiling painting.

Upstairs is an excellent **Museo Archeologico Nazionale**, housing a collection of finds from the ancient necropolis of the Graeco-Etruscan seaport of Spina, near Comacchio, including Attic vases (one of the largest collections of red-figure vases anywhere, some by the noted painters of Athens, as well as Etruscan copies of the

Few cities made a greater contribution to the life and art of the quattrocento than Ferrara but, after touring the city and perusing the great works of the Palazzo Schifanoia and the museums, you may still leave feeling a little unsatisfied. Somehow there should be more.

For an example of why there isn't, consider Cosmè Tura. For one thing, Tura's job as court painter ironically left him little time to paint. The surviving records of the Este show that Duke Borso and Duke Ercole kept him busy designing stage sets, furniture, ceremonial costumes, tableware, cartoons for tapestries, banners, armour for mock tournaments and trappings for the horses, lavish decorations for parties and every sort of luxury trinket. Under Alfonso I and Ercole II, this same job would be taken over by Dosso Dossi, often in collaboration with poet Ariosto. He didn't get much chance to paint in Ferrara either.

Such works as Tura and his contemporaries did manage to complete are now dispersed among the museums of Europe and America, while any number of frescoes in Ferrara were doubtlessly destroyed or allowed to decay, like those in the Schifanoia, in the centuries that followed. It is just an example of the indifference that later ages would show towards the real Renaissance of art – the spontaneity, colour and brilliant imagination of the quattrocento, as opposed to the art of virtuosity and authority in the 1500s that the critics came to call the 'High Renaissance'. In the changing tides of taste and fashion, this set of blinkers didn't start to come off until the time of the pre-Raphaelites and John Ruskin, a century and a half ago.

The loss makes it that much harder to imagine the rarified world of the Este court and its artists. And not only paintings were lost. One reason the Herculean Addition is so big is that it was intended as a spacious, aristocratic district of palaces and parks. The Este were mad for gardens. Besides the orange grove on the roof of their palace (about all that survives of their projects), all the entrances to the city were beautifully landscaped – aesthetic but utilitarian as well, a kind of political propaganda designed to convey the image of a refined, orderly, well-run state. The northern wall was bordered by parks, with avenues designed to frame the towers of the Castello in the distance, and the Castello itself had a big park on its northern side. For anyone arriving by the Po, their introduction to the city would be the dukes' own hideaway, Belvedere Island, with groves and pavilions, fountains and a menagerie.

One of the pavilions was Leonello's legendary Belfiore, a masterpiece of carved wood and stone where Tura and others created a series of paintings of the Muses to inspire the ducal fancy. Nothing remains; two of Tura's magical muses survive in London's National Gallery (one mistakenly called *La Primavera*), and other works from the Belfiore (demolished 1634) have either been wrecked or are scattered round the world. The island itself, like so much else in Ferrara, has disappeared completely, lost between the ambitions of later builders and the shifting courses of the Po.

Greek work). There is also a splendid gold diadem and two canoes carved from tree trunks in the later Roman period.

If you like Biagio Rossetti's work, just down the street at number 152 you can see the modest house he built for himself, the **Casa Rossetti** [275 D7].

SANT'ANTONIO IN POLESINE [275 C6] (*Vicolo del Gambone;* ☎*0532 64068;* ⊕ *9.30–11.30 & 15.15–17.00 Mon–Fri, 9.30–11.30 & 15.15–16.30 Sat; Mass with Gregorian chant 7.30 Mon–Sat, 10.30 Sun, vespers sung 17.00 daily*) From Via XX Settembre, take Vicolo del Gambone right down to the city wall for one of the best surprises Ferrara has to offer. Few tourists ever make it to the convent of Sant'Antonio in Polesine, but just ring the bell by the door and you might get a complete guided tour from a learned nun. Built on an island in the Po before the river changed its course, Sant'Antonio was founded in 1257.

It was a cloistered convent, and so the church is divided into a *chiesa esterna* for the public, with a grand Baroque interior including a trompe l'œil ceiling by Francesco Ferrari, and a *chiesa interna* for the sisters only, which has three chapels entirely covered with some of the best early painting in Ferrara. The left one, by an unknown follower of Giotto, has the *Early Life of Jesus* on a dark background, where the *Three Kings* ride on horseback (because he couldn't draw camels); other scenes show a long-haired *Magdalene, St Dionysus* with the sun and moon, and an illustration of the old legend in which Mary hands down her girdle to St Thomas from heaven.

The centre chapel, with vaulting painted in grotesques by Bastianino, has an *Annunciation* by the Ferrarese painter Domenico Panetti, and saints from other artists of the 1400s and later. On the right, an unknown 14th-century Bolognese painter added the *Passion*, with Jesus harrowing Hell at the lower right (John the Baptist comes out first), and, in a very rare bit of medieval iconography, Jesus ascending to heaven on a ladder.

SAN GIORGIO [275 D7] (☎*0532 62231;* ⊕ *07.00–19.00 daily*) Just outside this corner of the walls (through the Porta Romana [275 D7]), and over the Po di Volano, San Giorgio was Ferrara's original cathedral from the 7th to the 12th century; the current building, mostly from the 1400s, houses the sumptuous 1475 *Tomb of Lorenzo Roverella*, Pope Julius II's physician. Also buried here is Cosmè Tura.

THE HERCULEAN ADDITION North of the Castello Estense stretches the Addizione Erculea, a testament to the prosperity and the grandiose ambitions of Ferrara in the days of Duke Ercole I. The Addition, which more than doubled the size of the city, had its practical side: the new circuit of walls that enclosed it got the Castello Estense and the rest of the city centre out of the range of Renaissance siege artillery.

Since Jacob Burckhardt, many writers have extolled the Addition as a masterpiece of rational Renaissance urban planning. That's not really true. Though Ercole's architect Biagio Rossetti was given the job of overseeing the development, the street layout is haphazard and utilitarian. It seems the duke himself had as big a hand in it as Rossetti. To Ercole, it was mostly about profit; his Addition was certainly a landmark in real estate development and promotion, a peaceful refuge of palaces and gardens for the elite. If you were a noble whose fortunes depended on your standing with the Este court, it would be an excellent idea to buy a plot from the duke to build your new mansion, and not haggle too much about the price.

Still, the Addition is uniquely beautiful, even if its aesthetic depends more on the good eye of individual architects than any tricks of planning. The combination of perfected urbanity with the absence of traffic and bustle gives it an uncanny, dreamlike air, like those old Renaissance paintings of the 'Ideal City'. Walking around it is one of the greatest delights Ferrara can offer.

Not long after the fall of the Este dynasty, travellers noted that many of the Addition's streets were already abandoned and overgrown, and even today you might detect a touch of melancholy. But the centuries of economic decadence under the popes saved much of the district from development, and kept at least something of Ercole's and Rossetti's vision intact.

Corso Ercole I and the Quadrivio degli Angeli
Originally Via degl'Angeli, the 'Street of the Angels' extending north from the Castello Estense, this was intended as the Addition's 'noble street'; you'll note how the views at its ends are closed by the matching arches of the Castello and the northern city gate, the Porta degli Angeli.

As intended, it attracted many to build palaces on and around it, including the **Palazzo Naselli-Crispi** [275 C4] by Girolamo da Carpi, better known as a painter. It has a wonderful courtyard just east of the Corso at Via Borgo dei Leoni 28. Next to it is Ferrara's Jesuit church, the 1570 **Chiesa del Gesù** [275 C3] (⊕ *08.30–11.30 Mon–Sat, 08.30–13.00 & 16.30–18.00 Sun*). Though the interior was burnt out in a 1773 fire, you can still see paintings by Bastarolo and Giuseppe Maria Crespi, and a painted terracotta group of the *Deposition* by Guido Mazzoni where the figures have the faces of Ercole I, his wife Eleonor of Aragon and members of his court.

Back on the Corso, north of Via degli Armari, is the **Palazzo Giulio d'Este** [275 C3], built for the fellow who spent his life imprisoned in the Castello (pages 278–9) and never got to enjoy it.

The centrepiece of the Addition's plan, the crossroads where the Corso meets Corso Rossetti/Corso Porta Mare, is called the **Quadrivio degli Angeli** [275 C3]. Biagio Rossetti packed this corner with three big palaces, each with a decorative carved pillar at its edge; the fourth palace was never built. Rossetti's idea of making a simple street corner, not a piazza, the centre of an urban plan inspired others across Italy, notably the Quattro Fontane of Rome and the Quattro Canti of Palermo. On the southeast corner of the Quadrivio is the 1492 **Palazzo Turchi di Bagno**, still showing the damage of World War II bombings. The 1493 **Palazzo Prosperi-Sacrati**, on the northwest corner, is notable for the lovely carved Renaissance grotesques on the portal and corner pillar. This palazzo, the biggest in Ferrara, also suffered bomb damage, and also from long service as a military barracks. It's back in shape now, and the city is still trying to find a proper use for it. The southwest corner belongs to Rossetti's greatest work, the **Palazzo dei Diamanti** (see below).

Palazzo dei Diamanti: Pinacoteca Nazionale
[275 C3] (*Corso Ercole I;* ☎ *0532 205844;* w *pinacotecaferrara.it;* ⊕ *09.00–14.00 Tue, Wed, Fri & Sat, 09.00–19.00 Thu, 09.00–13.00 Sun; €4*) Rossetti's showpiece takes its name from the 8,500 pointed, diamond-shaped stones that stud the façade – diamonds being an emblem of the Este. This spectacular building took 74 years to complete, and there's more art in its design than first appears. The little diamonds are not all the same; those on the upper levels are pointed just slightly upwards, while the lowest are pointed downwards, in order to reflect as much light as possible. They've recently all been hand-polished; the effect is striking. The building as a whole, like the other palaces at the Quadrivio, was designed to be considered not from straight on, but from the corner angle, highlighting the elegant reliefs and balcony.

The palazzo, built as a home for Duke Ercole's brother Sigismondo d'Este, has seen considerable restoration inside, and some work is still under way; whole forests must have died for the magnificent new coffered ceilings inside. The palazzo now houses the Pinacoteca Nazionale, a collection mainly of works by painters from the Ferrara school. The first rooms contain some fine medieval painting, including many works by Venetians, the greatest influence on Ferrara in the early days.

Next come rooms of Ferraresi from the quattrocento, including several little-known artists with accomplished and distinctive styles: an unknown 'Maestro

Ferrarese' and 'Maestro GZ', who contributes a *Trinità* which is reminiscent of Masaccio's famous one in Florence. There's a 'Maestro degli Occhi Spalancati' (Master of the Wide-open Eyes) and a 'Maestro degli Occhi Ammicanti' (Master of the Winking Eyes), painter of a delightful coy *Vergine con il Bambino*; Ferrara's painters were known for some of the loveliest and most naturalistic Madonnas anywhere; there is another good one from Giovanni da Modena. 'Winking Eyes' may also have done the odd *Sepoltura del Cristo* (Burial of Christ), where no-one in the picture seems overly concerned about what is taking place.

Also present are works by Mantegna, Giovanni Bellini and Gentile da Fabriano, as well as a *Madonna* and *San Petronio* by Ercole de' Roberti. Cosmè Tura weighs in with two *tondi*, the *Giudizio e Martirio di San Maurelio*. Two of the *Muses* from the lost Belfiore palace have survived, Erato and Urania, possibly from Tura's workshop.

From the Ferrarese cinquecento, the sweet Raphael-esque Garofalo (a favourite of the 18th-century critics) surprises with the fantastically complex iconography of his *Antico e Nuovo Testamente* from the church of Sant'Andrea, and some *tondi* of saints (completed with Girolamo da Carpi) from the refectory of San Giovanni degli Olivetani.

Other pieces from Ferrara's late Renaissance include works of Bastianino (Sebastiano Filippi), a series of *Fifteen Saints* by Girolamo da Carpi and Garofalo from the monastery of San Giorgio, Dosso Dossi's *Massacre of the Innocents*, and two wonderful *City Views* by Girolamo Marchesi; unlike the other Renaissance ideal cities, this one features ruins, bad dogs and washing hung on the balconies.

Later paintings include several works by Scarsellino (Ippolito Scarsella), one of the last notable artists of the Ferrara school, including a *Noli Mi Tangere* with a dramatic, dynamic composition. There are also striking religious scenes from the late Baroque Uberto and Gaetano Gandolfi. Among the many fine works by non-Ferrarese artists is Carpaccio's *Death of the Virgin*, two tremendous landscapes by Hubert Robert, and two works by the little-known Venetian Antonio Maria Marini (b1668), a *Marina in Barrasca* and *Battaglia su un Ponte*, with a dark strangeness.

Museo del Risorgimento e della Resistenza [275 C3] (*Corso Ercole I 19;*
\ 0532 244949; �” 09.00–13.00 & 15.00–18.00 Tue–Sun; €4) A building adjacent to the Palazzo houses this museum of military history from the Napoleonic Wars to World War II. Ferrara played an active role in the Risorgimento, evidenced in revolts against the popes and Austrians. Exhibits include pieces from the papal fortress that once dominated the city, torn down by the citizens in 1859, Ferrara under the Fascists and the wartime resistance.

West and north of Corso Ercole I In the western, less-developed half of the Herculean Addition, Corso Biagio Rossetti/Corso Porta Po leads to Rossetti's **San Benedetto** [275 A2], begun in 1496 to accommodate the monks of Pomposa after they had to abandon their famous monastery because of malaria (pages 297–9). It's a very unlucky church: it needed a complete restoration after being used as a barracks by Napoleon, another one after bombings in 1944, and yet another currently, after a 2007 fire wrecked much of the inside.

Just to the east at Via Ariosto 67 is the **Casa di Ariosto** [275 B2] (\ 0532 244949; �” 10.00–12.30 & 16.00–18.00 Tue–Sun; admission free), which the poet built for himself to a design by Girolamo da Carpi. 'Small,' he described it modestly, 'but suited to me' – and he paid for it with his own money, rare for poets in any age. The museum has memorabilia and rare early editions of *Orlando Furioso*, and the pretty garden out the back is used for concerts.

North of the Quadrivio degli Angeli, Corso Ercole I passes two more Rossetti palaces where it crosses Via Arianuova, the **Palazzo Trotti-Mosti** [275 C2] and **Palazzo Guarini Giordani** [275 C2]; both are now part of Ferrara University. A little further on is the last of Ferrara's palaces, the 1913 **Palazzina degli Angeli** [275 C2], home to a Ferrarese named Adamo Boari who spent his career as one of the leading architects of Mexico City, and came back home in his later years to build this charming modern house, which fits in perfectly with its Renaissance neighbours.

Orto Botanico [275 C3] (☏ *0532 293782;* w *unife.it;* ⊕ *08.30–13.30 Mon–Fri, Apr–Sep 08.30–13.30 Mon–Fri, 10.00–18.00 Sun*) To the east of the Quadrivio degli Angeli on Corso Porta Mare, behind the Palazzo Turchi-Bagni, is the university's Botanical Garden, begun in 1791. It's small, but no-one interested in things green should miss it. The beautifully kept grounds contain 16,000 specimens, with a herb garden, greenhouses, sections on exotic plants and themed gardens.

Parco Massari [275 C2] Across the street from the Orto Botanico, the Parco Massari was the gardens of the adjacent Palazzo Massari. Now it's a gracious public park full of stately trees: great cedars and oaks, and fragrant pines.

Palazzo Massari [275 C3] (*Corso Porta Mare 9;* ☏ *0532 244949;* ⊕ *currently undergoing major restorations, reopening date still uncertain*) Next to the park stands the complex of the Palazzo Massari, housing three museums which won't reopen until the works are finished. First is the **Musei Civici d'Arte Moderna e Contemporanea**, dedicated to the Metaphysical School and covering the origins of the movement in Ferrara, though most of the works are by a later painter, Ferrara's Filippo de Pisis, obsessed with still lifes and streetscapes in yellow and grey. Other notable artists present include Arnoldo Bonzaghi and painter-sculptor Roberto Melli.

Pass through the courtyard, with a sculpture by Man Ray called the *Monument au Peintre Inconnu*, to reach the **Palazzina dei Cavalieri di Malta**, seat of the Knights of Malta in 1826–34, which contains the **Museo Giovanni Boldini**, dedicated to the works of Ferrara's very own Paris salon painter, a fellow in 'imperial moustaches' who was quite fashionable in the Belle Époque; Verdi dedicated *Otello* to him. Boldini started to be influenced by French modern painting in the 1890s, but he shouldn't have bothered; he was born to paint fancy women in evening gowns. Boldini was the *Paris Match* of his age, and it was a great age for evening gowns, modelled in his portraits by countesses, an infanta of Spain, and various great ladies of France and Italy. There's a portrait of Degas (and one by Degas of Boldini), and scenes of Montmartre. Boldini's followers and contemporaries are the subject of the adjacent **Museo dell'Ottocento** – near-photographic portraits of vacant faces, and plenty of works that would have been perfect for cigar-box lids. A dissenting paintbrush is wielded by Boldini's eccentric contemporary, the symbolist Gaetano Previati.

Piazza Ariostea Across from the Palazzo Massari is the only piazza in Rossetti's plan for the Herculean Addition, the spacious and serene Piazza Ariostea, embellished with a statue of Ariosto set atop a tall column (1883). The piazza is the site of the city's biggest festival each year, the Palio di San Giorgio, during which it in fact hosts four *palii* – one for boys, one for girls, one for horses and one for donkeys – the grass terraces around the edges provide the seating for the races. Rossetti built one of his finest palaces, the arcaded **Palazzo Rondinelli** [275 D3], on the southern side of the park. On the west side, the matching **Palazzo Bevilacqua** (1499) [275 C3] was originally Palazzo Strozzi, built by a branch of the great banking family of

Florence; between the two palaces is the 1613 **Chiesa delle Stimmate** [275 C3], with a painting of *St Francis* by Guercino inside.

Cimitero Monumentale [275 D2] (🕐 *07.00–17.00 daily, summer 09.00–19.00 daily; San Cristoforo is currently closed for earthquake restorations*) Via Borso, a quiet lane lined with colourful flower shops, leads north from Piazza Ariosto to the 'Monumental Cemetery', covering a vast expanse in the northeast corner of the walls.

Monumental it certainly is. The pious Duke Borso began a Certosa (Carthusian monastery) here in 1452, and it grew into the biggest building in Ferrara – a façade over 300m wide, made of graceful arched colonnades. After Napoleon chased out the Carthusians, the city combined the Certosa and the undeveloped land around it to create the cemetery. Many famous Ferraresi are buried here, from Garofalo and other Renaissance artists to film director Michelangelo Antonioni.

The centrepiece of the complex is the matchingly huge church of **San Cristoforo** (1498), one of Biagio Rossetti's most impressive works, even if its façade was never completed. Inside, it is embellished with a huge luck-giving St Christopher, and the tombs of Borso and Marfisa d'Este. Florid 19th-century mausolea and monuments surround the church – Giovanni Boldini gets two of the biggest.

Part of the cemetery complex is the **Cimitero Ebraico** [275 D2] (📞 *0532 751337;* 🕐 *summer 09.00–18.00 Sun–Fri, winter 09.00–16.30*), along the walls by Corso Porta Mare. This was founded in the 17th century when Ferrara had a considerable Jewish population, many of them refugees from Spain; strewn with wildflowers in spring, it is one of the prettiest spots in the city.

The walls Ferrara's 9km circuit of red-brick walls, begun under the direction of Rossetti between 1493 and 1505 to enclose the Addition, was one of the prototypes for the new-model fortifications of the Renaissance, designed to withstand artillery assaults. Most of the rest was completed under Alfonso I. Both parts have a moat (which survives in part on the east side), and a low wall with a higher earth embankment behind it, planted with trees to hold it together. The best stretch is between the eastern end of the Corso Porta Mare and the former Porta degli Angeli, built by Rossetti, on the north side of the city. In many places the earth behind the walls is planted in avenues of trees; walking and cycling paths run along their length, linked with routes into the city and out to the Po.

AROUND FERRARA

VOGHENZA AND BELRIGUARDO Leaving Ferrara heading east takes you immediately into the flat and watery world of the Po Delta. To the southeast, **Voghenza** was Ferrara's predecessor, site of a Roman town that has almost completely disappeared; the bishop's seat was transferred to Ferrara's San Giorgio in the 6th century.

Just outside the village on the SP29 is the first of the *delizie*, the country palaces of the Este (there were 19 of them in all). The **Delizia di Belriguardo** [map, pages 268–9] (📞 *0532 328511;* 🕐 *9.30–noon & 15.30–19.00 Fri–Sun; €5*), begun in 1435 under Niccolò III, would have been one of the most imposing palaces in Italy in its time. The 40ha gardens, thick with lagoons, fountains and shady avenues, must have been a marvel. Unfortunately, neglect under the popes put an end to all its splendours. The gardens, enclosed by a perfect square of country roads, are now almost completely gone, ploughed over as farmland. Of the palace, all that remains are some captivating bits of fresco in the Sala delle Vigne attributed to Girolamo da Carpi and others, with ghostly caryatids and architectural trompe l'œils enclosing views over a fantasy landscape.

The Sala delle Vigne is part of the **Museo Civico di Belriguardo** (⊕ *same hrs & admission as the Delizia*), with Roman finds from the necropolis of Voghenza, Renaissance painting and ceramics from Ferrara.

DELIZIA ESTENSE DE VERGINESE [map, pages 268–9] (*Via del Verginese;* ☎ *0532 323258;* ⊕ *Nov–Mar 10.00–12.30 & 15.00–18.30 Sat–Sun, Apr–Oct 10.00–12.30 & 15.30–19.00 Sat–Sun; €3*) About 7km to the east, between the villages of Gambulaga and Maiero, you can visit another *delizia*, less grandiose than Belriguardo but thoroughly charming and in considerably better nick. Alfonso I built Verginese in c1500 for Laura Dianti, the daughter of a Ferrara hat-maker who became his mistress, and eventually his wife, after the death of Lucrezia Borgia. It's an unusual building, apparently the work of Girolamo da Carpi, with four medieval-looking corner towers. The interior is mostly 18th century, with a touch of Liberty style from later owners. It contains a collection of carved Roman grave steles and other items.

The **gardens** are being faithfully restored according to old plans and views, and some inspired guesswork. This was no mere pleasure garden, but a working garden, a *brolio*, with compartments of herbs, vegetables and flowers bounded by avenues of nut and fruit trees. It will be grand in a decade or two, but even now it provides a lesson in the beginnings of the Italian garden, and the pleasant mix of showiness and practicality in it – even the 'monumental tower' at the entrance is really a dovecote.

ARGENTA Argenta is situated on the River Reno to the southeast of Ferrara.

Tourist information
🛈 Piazza Marconi 1; ☎ 0532 330276; ⊕ May 09.30–12.30 & 15.30–18.30 daily, Jun–Aug | 09.30–12.30 Thu & Sat, Sep–Apr 09.30–12.30 & 15.30–18.30 Tue–Sat, 15.30–18.30 Sun

⌂ Where to stay
⌂ **Villa Reale** (30 rooms) 16a Viale Roiti; ☎ 0532 852334; w hotelvillarealeargenta.net. Liberty-style villa converted into a gracious hotel, | only a few minutes from the Oasi di Campotto. Rooms are comfortable, with AC; good b/fast, free parking. €€

What to see and do Argenta has an attractive quattrocento church, **San Domenico**, now housing the small Museo Civico (☎ *0532 808058;* ⊕ *Mar–Jul & Sept–Oct 15.30–18.30 Sat–Sun; €4*) with works by Garofalo, Scarsellino and others. Many towns in Italy were burned by the retreating Germans in World War II, but Argenta was the only one to be flooded by them, after the Allies had already bombed it to pieces. Argenta was on the Siegfried Line, and 625 British and Commonwealth soldiers who died at the Battle of the Argenta Gap are buried at the **Argenta War Gap Cemetery** (*Via Piangipane, 3km from Argenta;* ⊕ *daylight hours*). Just across the River Reno from the town is the tiny Romanesque **Pieve di San Giorgio**, with a carved portal showing St George and the *Labours of the Months* (1112).

All the area around the church is a detached part of the **Po Delta Regional Park** (page 4). This section, the **Oasi di Campotto** [map, pages 268–9], is one of the last completely untouched wetlands in the delta, where thousands of birds nest among the water lilies (including the rare black tern); it has been set aside as an important wildlife preserve. There are walking and cycling paths, and other parts that can be visited only by guided tour. The park visitors' centre, the **Museo delle Valli** [map, pages 268–9] (✆ *0532 808058;* w *vallidiargenta.org;* ⊕ *09.00–13.00 & 15.30–18.00 Tue–Sun, Jul–Aug afternoons closed; €3*) arranges these, and rents out electric boats and golf carts for them.

THE COAST: FROM MESOLA TO RAVENNA

The main attractions along this coast are the Po Delta and the magnificent Romanesque Abbey of Pomposa, though there are plenty of Italian family lidos in the vicinity if you're tempted to join the summer ice cream, pizza and parasol brigades.

Ferrara's portion, the southern half of the Po Delta, is only a part of the broad swathe of wetlands that closes the northern end of Italy's Adriatic coast. Other rivers, such as the Brenta, pour down from the Alps here too, creating the lagoon of Venice – that city is only 50km away.

Duke Alfonso II was the first, at least in modern times, to start draining the marshes south of the Po Delta. Much of the land was planted with rice; a large part of the rest now belongs to the **Parco del Delta del Po**, one of Italy's most important wetlands and a birdwatcher's paradise, especially in the spring and autumn migrations: prominent among the 200 species sighted here are flamingos, coots, grebes, herons, a vast assortment of ducks, black-winged stilts, and owls in the wooded sections, along with that most overdressed of sea birds, the *cavaliere d'Italia*. The white Camargue horse has also been introduced.

GETTING AROUND FER (*Ferrovie Emilia-Romagna;* w *fer.it*) narrow-gauge **trains** connect Ferrara and Bologna with Codigoro. **Buses** from Ferrara, run by TPER (*complete schedules at* w *tper.it*), radiate to the flatlands of the coast. TPER now also operates the service along the coast from Mesola and Codigoro to Ravenna (line 334).

Note that there is no convenient bus from anywhere to the lonely Abbey of Pomposa; for that you'll need a car, or else try out TPER's **Taxibus** (✆ *800 521616*) service, a kind of community transport. Line A637/A638 runs from Codigoro to Pomposa Monday to Friday, but it must be booked a day in advance. If you have a car, a new fast road (RA8) leads directly from just south of Ferrara to the beaches past Comacchio. There it meets the coast road, the SS309, between Chioggia and Ravenna. Another, slower, road also runs from Ferrara to the coast, the SS495, which passes Pomposa.

TOURIST INFORMATION Much of the coast down to Ravenna is included in the **Parco del Delta del Po** (*for information on the park:* m *346 801 5015;* w *parcodeltapo. it*). There are visitors' centres at **Campotto di Argenta** (*Via Cardenala 1;* ✆ *0532 808001*), **Comacchio** (*Corso Mazzoni 200;* ✆ *0533 81742*), **Mesola** (*Castello Estense, Piazzetta Santo Spirito;* ✆ *0533 993358*) and **Sant'Alberto** (*Via Rivaletto 25;* ✆ *0544 528710*). All of these offer helpful brochures and maps on visiting the park by horse, bike, car or boat.

ACTIVITIES The Delta Park has two main **cycling** paths: from Mesola down to the coastal villages of Goro and Gorino, and from the Abbazia di Pomposa through the coastal lagoons to Lido delle Nazioni. The park office says the best spots for **birdwatching** are along the Po di Goro near Goro and Gorino, the Bosco della Fasanara east of Mesola, the lagoon at Valle Canovio west of Volano, and along the bike path north of Lago delle Nazioni, though this always depends on the season.

Boat excursions are a popular activity here, exploring the Sacco di Goro, the mouth of the Po di Goro and the Valle di Gorino, departing from the fishing hamlets of Gorino and Goro, as well as Porto Garibaldi and Volano. There are many private operators posting their schedules and prices at the docks from March until October; for more information, contact the park offices.

MESOLA The Emilia-Romagna stretch of coast begins with Mesola, on a branch of the river called the Po di Goro, just south of the main branch. The town's landmark is its **Castello** (*Piazza Santo Spirito;* m *339 193 5943;* ⏲ *09.30–12.30 & 15.00–18.00 Tue–Sun, winter 09.30–12.30 & 14.30–17.30 Tue–Sun; €4),* the last of the *delizie* of the Este, designed for Alfonso II as a hunting and fishing lodge in 1563 by Giovanni Battista Aleotti and not completed until 20 years later. The unusual structure, a square with four towers set diagonally at the corners, is surrounded by a half-hexagon of arcaded buildings, originally quarters for the duke's guests; the space between now hosts a busy market on Saturdays. Now a centre for environmental education, the castle often hosts special exhibitions; the Castello houses a small museum devoted to the flora and fauna of the coast.

Part of the primordial coastal pine forest – preserved as the Este's old hunting grounds – survives intact in the **Bosco di Mesola** [map, pages 268–9] (⏲ *08.00–sunset Sun, Tue, Fri & Sat),* now a nature reserve and home to fallow deer, storks, spoonbills and hundreds of other birds. Not far to the west, near Italba, this varied and ever-changing coastline offers something completely different – a marooned 40ha patch of dunes, once part of the coast, called the **Moraro**.

Mesola is on the provincial border. Everything north of it is in the Veneto, and beyond the scope of this book. That entire area is in the **Parco Regionale Veneto del Delta del Po**, Italy's biggest protected wetlands, with plenty of opportunities for nature walks and bike tours, birdwatching, and other activities (*for details, see* w *parcodeltapo.org).*

Tourist information
i Piazzetta Santo Spirito; ☏ 0532 993 358;
⏲ 09.30–12.30 & 14.30–17.30 Tue–Sun

 Where to stay, eat and drink *Map, pages 268–9*

⌂ **Ca' Laura** (4 rooms, 1 apt) Via Cristina 70, Bosco Mesola; ☏ 0533 794372; w calaura. it. A lovely *agriturismo* close to the Delta del Po, ideal for people who like nature & excursions.
Swimming pool, tennis courts, golf (9 holes), picnic area & bike rental. It also has a popular restaurant, with country cooking such as rabbit & pigeon (€€). B/fast inc. €€

CODIGORO Due east of Ferrara, the last town before the coast is Codigoro, a friendly, hard-working place on the Po di Verano; there are several different 'Po's and canals as the river splits up on its way to the Adriatic. The promenade on the river has a Venetian-style **Bishops' Palace** from the 1700s. Codigoro was the centre for all the land reclamation projects carried out in this part of the Po Delta in medieval times (there's a tower built by the counts of Canossa as part of a water control scheme), and again since 1860; the town has a **Monument to the Scariolanti** (wheelbarrow-pushers) – all the local men who dug the drainage canals by hand over the decades and made this territory flourish again. A landmark on the outskirts of town is the **Garzaia** (City of the Herons), the gardens of an abandoned sugar factory that has become a favourite nesting spot for hundreds of these birds, who come back each spring; it's been made a protected area.

Where to stay, eat and drink *Map, pages 268–9*

There's nothing much in Codigoro itself; in this corner of the coast all the interesting places are hideaways out in the countryside.

🏠 **Hotel Rurale Cannevie** (16 rooms) On the Volano road, at Volano di Codigoro; 📞 0533 719014; **w** oasicannevie.com. A restored old fishing station on a small wetlands nature reserve. Comfortable rooms with AC. Bike rental available, & it can arrange horseriding tours, boat excursions & more. There's also an excellent restaurant, the **Oasi Cannevie** (📞 *0533 719142;* ⏰ *closed lunch Mon–Wed;* €€€) serving local fish specialities. B/fast inc. €€€

🏠 **Villa Belfiore** (10 rooms) Via Pioppa 27, Ostellato; 📞 0533 681164; **w** villabelfiore. com. In Ostellato, between Argenta & Codigoro, a big house furnished with old Persian carpets & antiques; it also has a big pool in the garden, & a beauty spa; b/fast inc. Cooking classes on offer. The delightful restaurant (€€€) is worth a trip in itself: solid home cooking with some distinction, & an emphasis on local produce in season; vegetarian menus available. €€€

🏠 **Da Pavani** (8 rooms) Borgo Fiocinini 13, Lagosanto, 10km south of Codigoro; 📞 0533 94182. Simple accommodation along with a restaurant (€€) that serves excellent, aromatic seafood (& meat dishes too): feast on gnocchi with crayfish, steamed seafood, or frogs & eels. Both closed Tue & Jan. €€

🍴 **La Capanna da Eraclio** Via per le Venezie 21, Loc Ponte Vicini 10km northwest of Codigoro; 📞 0533 712154; ⏰ closed Wed & Thu, & a few weeks in Aug–Sep. Welcoming & family-run. Does wonderful things to seafood, raw or cooked, or with pasta; try the chef's speciality roast eels. €€€€

🍴 **Ristorante Abbazia Pomposa** Via Pomposa Centro 16; 📞 0533 719078; **w** ristoranteabbaziapomposa.it; ⏰ closed Tue. Next to the abbey, a good choice for lunch after the visit: Emilia-style pasta dishes & lots of local seafood; outside tables. €€€

ABBAZIA DI POMPOSA [map, pages 268–9] (*Loc Pomposa on the SS 309;* 📞 *0533 719110;* ⏰ *08.30–19.00 daily;* ⏰ *museum closed Mon; €5*) South of Mesola, the SS309 continues down to the haunting and serene Abbey of Pomposa. Sometime in the troubled 6th century the early Benedictines founded their community here, lost among the trackless islets of the Po Delta. Besides being relatively safe from invaders, the fertile delta lands offered shovel-wielding Benedictines a chance to work and prosper. Hard work turned to Dark Age opulence in the 10th century, when donations from Emperors Otto I and Otto II gave Pomposa rights in the most valuable property of the region, the salt pans of Comacchio. Things got better; later rulers piled on more rights and donations, and by 1050 Pomposa's abbot was lord of 49 dependent churches and monasteries, as well as huge territories in the delta, in and around Ravenna, and as far away as Pavia in Lombardy. By this time the abbey was a noted centre of culture, with one of the biggest libraries in Italy; in this atmosphere of total tranquillity, monk Guido d'Arezzo invented the modern musical scale in the early 11th century.

Pomposa's fall was just as complete as its ascent. The rise of the medieval *comuni* cut into its power and its revenues and, when floods caused the 1152 shift in the course of the Po, they created large areas of swampland around the abbey. By 1340 it was a ghost of its former self, plagued with malaria and ruled by an absentee *commendatore*. Closing a history of a thousand years, the last monks left in 1553, finding a new home at San Benedetto in Ferrara.

Campanile The abbey is dwarfed by its great campanile, visible for miles around the delta. It was built in 1063 by an architect named Deusdedit and adorned with a unique series of mullioned windows, which progress tier by tier from a narrow slit on the bottom to a grand *quadrifore* (four arches) on top, a brilliant device that adds grace and lightness to the tower. The *patere*, painted majolica medallions that decorate the tower and other parts of the building, are all modern replacements (such things don't wear well); the originals were imported from Tebtunis, a Benedictine monastery in the oasis of al-Faiyum in Egypt that specialised in such ceramics. You'll see others like these in churches all over Italy, especially along the Adriatic coast. Oriental influence here is also shown in the striped Moorish arches of the windows, the blind arcading and the decorative patterns of brick, reminders of just how much early medieval Europe owed to the more advanced art and architecture, both Christian and Muslim, of the Middle East, North Africa and Spain.

Atrium The church, begun in the 8th century and taking its final form in the 11th, is heir to the great basilicas of Ravenna, and was probably created by architects and builders from that city, using numerous Byzantine columns, capitals and decorative stonework recycled from earlier buildings. The entrance is through a lovely **atrium**, decorated with patterned brick, reliefs and terracotta in the same manner as the courtyard of Santo Stefano in Bologna. The reliefs' stylisation is heavily influenced by the Coptic art of Egypt.

Interior Inside the church itself are some ghostly Byzantine-style saints from the original fresco decoration, probably from the 1100s. There are two baptismal fonts, one carved from an early Byzantine capital, the other a strangely primitive work of the 12th century, and a magnificent pavement, with mazelike circular designs and mosaic trim, including a strip of fantastical beasts, all done in marble intarsia by artists probably from Ravenna; most of it is 12th century, though the part nearest the altar is the oldest thing in the abbey, surviving from an earlier church of the AD500s.

Medieval frescoes For all that, the chief glory of Pomposa is its colourful 14th-century frescoes that cover nearly all its walls, the most complete and most ambitious fresco cycle of this period in Emilia-Romagna. They were the last major embellishment of the abbey, added when it was already in serious decline. Many are by Vitale da Bologna, including the faded *Last Judgement* on the west wall, with an imperial dignity and decorum the artist may have picked up from the great works of Ravenna.

Vitale is also credited with the *Maestà* (Christ in Majesty, surrounded by a mandorla) in the **apse**, surrounded by angels and saints, and the scenes below of the *Evangelists*, *Doctors of the Church* and the *Life of Sant'Eustachio*, an extremely popular medieval fairy-tale hagiography – see the saint, a Roman officer, with his famous vision of Christ between the horns of a stag while hunting; his adventures with pirates, lions and wolves; and finally the entire family's martyrdom in a bronze bull with a roaring fire underneath, while Emperor Hadrian looks on.

The frescoes on the walls of the **nave**, attributed mostly to unknown artists of Bologna, give us the entire Old Testament in the upper band, starting from the right of the altar, and the corresponding stories of the New Testament on the lower, with scenes from the Apocalypse below them, around the arches, all very much like the scheme that later artists would use in Parma Cathedral. Note the unusual scene of the story of Noah, where the ark is not a normal ship but a perfect cube (as in various esoteric traditions), floating over the ruins of the drowned world.

There are other good frescoes by some of the same artists in the monks' **chapter-house**, including a striking *Crucifixion* on a black background with gilded trim, along with the apostles and various saints, and more in the **refectory**, attributed by some to Giuliano and Pietro da Rimini: a *Last Supper* (where, as often in this region's art, the Apostles sit at a round table), balanced by a scene of the *Miracle of the Abbot Guido* where, dining with a frightened-looking archbishop, Guido calmly turns the water into wine. St Guido Strampiati was abbot here in the mid 11th century and oversaw the building of the tower and the expansion of the abbey church; the archbishop is painted as Guido's enemy Geberardo of Ravenna.

Palace and museum The abbot governed Pomposa from the beautifully austere **Palazzo della Ragione**, built in the 11th century, with the façade substantially altered in the 14th. Originally the palace was connected to the rest of the abbey by other buildings and the whole was surrounded by a high defence wall, now completely disappeared. A **museum** in the Palazzo contains items relating to the monastery, including capitals, architectural fragments and bits of frescoes.

Tourist information
Via Pomposa Centro 1, next to the Abbey; 0533 719110; Mar–Oct 09.30–13.00 & 15.00–18.30 daily, Nov–Feb 09.30–12.30 Tue–Fri, 09.00–13.00 Sat–Sun

LIDI DI COMACCHIO
Tourist information As well as those listed below, there are seasonal satellite offices in Lido delle Nazioni, Lido di Volano, Lido di Spina and Goro.

Porto Garibaldi Via Caprera 51a; 0533 329076; Jun–10 Sep 09.30–12.30 & 15.30–18.30 daily, Apr & May 09.30–12.30 & 15.30–18.30 Sat–Sun

Lido degli Estensi Viale delle Querce; 0533 327464; Jun–Aug 09.30–12.30 & 16.00–18.30 daily, Apr, May & Sep 09.30–12.30 & 16.00–18.30 Sat–Sun

 Where to stay, eat and drink If you're travelling through this part of the coast, to see Pomposa or just to enjoy the beaches and activities, you'll find that almost all of the accommodation is in this little stretch of resorts. Those that stay open off season offer some good bargain rooms.

Club Spiaggia Romea Via dell'Oasi 2; 0533 355366; w spiaggiaromea.it. Near the sea at Lido delle Nazioni. Family-oriented complex, ideal for sports lovers; hotel plus simple apts in the pines for accommodation, with nearly every conceivable sport, plus bars & disco. Extra charges for riding, bike hire, diving & 4x4 safaris. HB & FB. Open Jun–late Sep. €€€

Logonovo (45 rooms) Viale delle Querce 109, Lido degli Estense; 0533 327520; w hotellogonovo.com. One of the better choices on the Lido degli Estensi: medium-sized, modern & 5mins from the sea; with comfortable rooms & a gym, spa & pool. It caters to every kind of sport, & offers bike loans; free parking. €€€

La Pineta (52 rooms) Viale dei Lecci 2, Lido degli Estensi; 0533 327956; w hotelplazapineta. it. Typical Adriatic resort *pensione*, friendly & near the sea; all rooms have TV, AC & balconies. HB & FB; pool, spa & parking. Open Apr–Sep. €€

Milano da Perino Via Ugo Bassi 7, Porto Garibaldi; 0533 327179; w milanodapierino.it. No frills, first-rate seafood restaurant: wide variety of antipasti, raw, steamed or fried, *spaghetti vongole*, *risotto alla marinara*, grills & *fritti*. Book ahead for fish soup or lobster. €€€–€€€€

L'Angolo del Fritto Via Resistenza 74, Porto Garibaldi; m 329 335 3540. Fish, eels & prawns fried in batter; a cheap-&-cheerful local favourite take-away with a few tables outside. €

What to see and do The beach resorts along the Lidi di Comacchio begin at the Lido di Volano on the other side of the wetlands of the **Valle Bertuzzi**, where the setting sun ignites the waters in a thousand colours. The water is clean enough for all of the beaches here to have the European Blue Flag rating. Valle Bertuzzi is home to a thriving flock of flamingos, one of very few in continental Europe; you can see them nesting from April to October.

Of the resorts, the **Lido delle Nazioni** and **Porto Garibaldi** are the most interesting and best equipped. Lido delle Nazioni (in the old days it was called Pialassa, dialect for 'take it or leave it') has a long artificial lake behind it, a favourite for watersports. Beyond the lake is the beautiful **Spiaggia Romea**, home to a herd of white horses.

Porto Garibaldi's name recalls the defeated hero's refuge here after the fall of the Roman Republic in 1849 (page 13). Of all the lidos on this stretch of coast, Porto Garibaldi is the closest to being a real town. It was once the only village here and it is still a fishing port, a salty, somehow endearing place, where the beach crowd, mostly working folk from Bologna and the other cities, shares space with rusty freighters and a big wholesale fish market along the docks of the canal. Between April and September, little cruise boats depart from the Portocanale into the delta, most including a fish lunch in the ticket price. They're all independent operators; you can compare boats and prices and pick one you like.

To the south, Porto Garibaldi merges into **Lido degli Estensi**, a surprisingly attractive community full of big pine trees and decorated with stone obelisks. This lido is a little more upmarket, consisting mostly of holiday villas on shady lanes around the beach; the main street is lined with summer-only boutiques.

COMACCHIO: 'PICCOLA VENEZIA' The most important town in the delta is Comacchio. Famous for its canals and picturesque brick bridges, Comacchio is reminiscent of Venice in its history too. The town grew up in late Roman times and, while the rest of the Roman world was falling apart, Comacchio, on an island surrounded by impassable swamps and salt pans, developed into an important port, shipping its salt and fish around Italy. Between the 7th and 9th centuries it possessed one of the biggest fleets on the Adriatic, and became an important centre for trade. Venice, however, thought that one Venice in the neighbourhood was quite enough, and the larger and more energetic town occupied and destroyed Comacchio on more than one occasion. In the late 13th century Comacchio fell into the hands of the Este, who made use of its salt trade to pay the soldiers and build *delizie*.

Thanks to the Venetians, nothing is left of Comacchio's ancient glories, but it is still one of the most charming and distinctive towns in the region, and a delight to explore. In the 17th and 18th centuries, thanks to the salt and fish, Comacchio managed the singular achievement of becoming prosperous under papal rule, leaving it with a modest ensemble of Baroque churches and palaces along the canals.

Tourist information

ℹ Via Agatopisto 2; ☏ 0533 314154; ⏲ Apr–Jun, Sep, Oct 09.00–13.00 & 14.30–18.00 Mon–Fri, 09.30–18.30 Sat–Sun, Nov–Mar 09.30–18.30 & 14.30–18.00 Tue–Sat, 10.00–17.00 Sun, Jul–Aug 09.30–18.30 daily

✗ Where to eat and drink

✗ Da Vasco e Giulia Via L Muratori 2; ☏ 0533 81252; **w** vascoegiulia.it; ⏲ closed Mon & Jan. Centrally located, most popular trattoria in town: friendly, family-run, & serving good simple dishes from land or sea. €€

Activities From March to October, you can take an excursion boat (☏ 0533 81302; *leaves 11.00 daily; €12*) to the **Stazione di Pesca Foce**, where the 17th-century fishermen's huts have been converted into a museum of the old traditional fishery.

There's a seasonal restaurant there, Bettino di Foce, serving the day's catch. Other boats will take you to locations around the coast and the Valli di Comacchio.

What to see and do The centre of town, where the main Via Folegatti crosses the Canale Maggiore, has an 1824 clocktower and the 17th-century **Loggia dei Mercanti**, the old grain market. From here the very Venetian **Canale Maggiore** leads south to the **Ospedale San Camillo**; the 18th-century complex has been completely restored, and now houses the **Museo Delta Antico** (*Via Agatopisto 3;* \ *0533 311316;* w *museodeltaantico.com;* ⊕ *Nov–Feb 09.30–13.00 & 14.30–18.00 Tue–Sat, 10.00– 17.00 Sun, Mar–Jun 09.30–13.00 & 15.00–18.30 Tue–Sat, Jul–Aug 09.30–13.00 & 15.00–18.30 daily; €6*), a museum intended to give a complete overview of delta life, through exhibits on history, archaeology and the environment.

Near the Ospedale, the **Ponte degli Sbirri** ('bridge of the cops', since it led to the papal prison) crosses over to Via Pescheria, home of the **fish market** and of Comacchio's famous monumental triple bridge, the **Trepponti**, spanning two of the town's canals; a cardinal legate commissioned it from Ravenna architect Luca Danese in 1634.

From the **Cathedral** (founded AD708, current building 1868), a block east of the Loggia dei Mercanti, Corso Mazzini leads off to the **Loggiato dei Cappuccini**, one of the longest porticoes in Emilia-Romagna: 143 arches on marble columns that serve no imaginable purpose but to shade your walk to the **Santuario di Santa Maria in Aula Regia**, a wealthy monastery in Comacchio's opulent Dark Ages – though nothing there now is older than 1665.

VALLI DI COMACCHIO A *valle* isn't a valley here, but a local word for lagoon. The Valli di Comacchio, the major part of Italy's biggest wetlands area, is oddly only about a thousand years old, caused by subsidence along the coast. Gradually the freshwater lagoons turned salty and nearly all the inhabitants moved away because of floods and malaria.

The tide of battle between sea and land turned again, starting in the 15th century, with the first *bonifiche* (drainage programmes) of the Este dukes. The same 1570 earthquake that wrecked much of Ferrara also changed the course of the Po here, moving it northward to its present bed and leaving more water to soak the Valli. But the *scariolanti* (wheelbarrow men) soldiered on for centuries, drying up over 200km² of land and carving it into a tidily rectangular network of drainage canals.

There is still more than enough water about, in the sodden hinterlands just west of the town that are now mostly part of the Regional Park. Comacchio is famed for its eels, farmed in the Valli – if you're in the area between September and December, you can watch the fishermen scoop them up on their way back from the sea. Just west of Comacchio stood its ancestor, the ancient Graeco-Etruscan port of **Spina** (now miles from the sea); there's nothing to see here now, but Spina's rich necropolis produced the prize exhibits in Ferrara's archaeology museum.

10

Ravenna

Tucked away among the art towns of Emilia-Romagna there is one famous city that has nothing to do with Renaissance popes and potentates, Guelphs or Ghibellines, sports cars or socialists. Little, in fact, has been heard from Ravenna in the last thousand years. Before then, however, this little city's career was simply astounding – heir to Rome itself, and for a time the leading city of Western Europe. For anyone interested in Italy's shadowy progress through the Dark Ages, this is the place to visit.

There's a certain magic in three-digit years. History guards their secrets closely, giving us only occasional glimpses of battling barbarians, careful monks 'keeping alive the flame of knowledge' and local Byzantine dukes and counts doing their best to hold things together. In Italy, the Dark Ages were never quite so dark, never the vacuum most people think. This can be seen in Rome, but much more clearly here, in the only Italian city that not only survived but prospered through those troubled times. In Ravenna's churches, adorned with the finest mosaics ever made, such an interruption as the Dark Ages seems to disappear, and you experience the development of Italian history and art from ancient to medieval times as a continuous and logical process.

Imagining Ravenna in its golden age takes some effort. It was Venice before Venice was invented, an urban island in a lagoon with canals for streets. Imperial processions through them must have been stunning. Unlike Venice, it was connected to the mainland by causeways. It contained a mixed population of Italians and Greeks, and its greatest ruler was an illiterate German warrior – the history is somewhat complex. The advancing delta of the many small rivers that pour down from the Apennines gradually dried out all Ravenna's magic, at least on the outside, but step inside the city's ancient monuments, including eight sites on UNESCO's World Heritage list, and you'll see things you can't see anywhere else in the world.

HISTORY

Ravenna, a settlement said to have been occupied by both the Etruscans and the Gauls, first became an important Roman centre during the reign of Augustus. With its port of Classis, the city lay on an important route to the Balkans and the Danube. Set in a nearly impregnable position, surrounded by a lagoon and broad marshes, the military advantage was clear, and Classis became Rome's biggest naval base on the Adriatic.

CAPITAL OF A DOOMED EMPIRE As conditions in Italy became unsettled in the 5th century, the relative safety of Ravenna began to look very inviting to frightened emperors. Honorius moved the capital of the Western Empire here in AD402 – just in time, with the invasion of Italy by the Visigoths coming six years later, and Alaric's sack of Rome in AD409. The disaster was largely Honorius' fault. In AD408 this weak and scheming emperor had foolishly ordered the execution of his best general, the Vandal Stilicho, along with a treacherous massacre of the German soldiers in the legion that defended Italy. He also cashiered Alaric, who had been in Rome's service, and stopped paying his Visigothic army. When Alaric led his men through Italy and into Rome, he was more concerned with feeding them than seeking out plunder.

The Visigoths were soon bought off and convinced to move to Gaul, but Italy had fallen into anarchy while squabbling factions of the Imperial family continued to plot and plan behind the walls of Ravenna. After Honorius' death in AD423 such power as the Western Empire possessed had fallen to his sister Galla Placidia, ruling as regent along with army commander Aetius. Galla Placidia built San Giovanni, now the oldest church in the city; she died in AD450, and Aetius was murdered by a distrustful young Western Emperor, Valentinian III, four years later. The real power in Ravenna was now held by another German general, Ricimer, who ruled through puppet emperors. Ricimer's successor Odoacer put an end to the charade in AD476 by pensioning off the last Western Emperor, a child named Romulus Augustulus, and declaring himself King of Italy.

GOTHIC KINGDOM AND BYZANTINE RECONQUEST With the connivance of Eastern Emperor Zeno, the Ostrogoths under Theodoric invaded Italy and took Ravenna after a siege of nearly two years. Theodoric (see box, pages 322–3), who reigned AD493–526, brought peace and prosperity back to Italy, and made the fortress town of Ravenna into a proper capital, in a big building programme that included the churches of San Vitale and Sant'Apollinare. His reign saw the last flowering of Latin letters, under the influence of the Ostrogothic king's three famous councillors, Boethius, Symmachus and Cassiodorus.

Nine years after Theodoric's death, the murder of his daughter Queen Amalasuntha provided the pretext for the Eastern Empire's attempt to regain control of Italy. Justinian sent his great general Belisarius into the peninsula in AD536, touching off the terrible Greek–Gothic Wars that would consume the country for the next 25 years. Ravenna, taken by trickery in AD540, avoided the destruction Belisarius and his successor Narses spread through the rest of Italy, though few other cities were spared.

In truth, the Dark Ages for Italy begin here, brought not by barbarians but by the Byzantine heirs of the Roman Empire. But, while the rest of the country lay exhausted and devastated, pampered Ravenna perfected its embellishments. The Byzantines built more churches and more palaces, and the finest mosaic artists of Constantinople came to cement the portraits of Justinian and his consort Theodora on the walls of San Vitale.

All the effort and all the bloodshed proved meaningless when the Lombards overran a wasted Italy in AD579. After that, Byzantine rule was limited to a band of central Italy running from Ravenna to Rome, along with some port towns and enclaves in the south. These possessions were reorganised as the 'Exarchate of Ravenna' in the AD590s. The Greek exarchs, who were never popular among their new subjects, performed the occasional service in obtaining Constantinople's aid to keep the Lombards at bay throughout their period of rule. While tolerating the exarch's presence, the people of Ravenna came to rely increasingly on their own resources. When help from the east failed to appear, it was their own citizen militia, led by the politically powerful archbishops, that defended the city against invaders.

In the worst of times, the city survived as a sort of cultural time capsule, protected by its own efforts and its surrounding lagoon, still maintaining trade and cultural relations with the east, and carrying on the best traditions of classical culture single-handedly. For a Dark Age, plenty was happening. Some exarchs found the resources to embroil all Italy in war, usually battling against their arch-enemies, the popes in Rome. In the AD670s Archbishop Maurus even provoked a short-lived schism in the Church trying to win ecclesiastic independence for Ravenna.

It was a religious conflict – iconoclasm, the attempt of Byzantine Emperor Leo III to purify Christianity by destroying the sacred icons – that put an end to the Exarchate. Ravenna revolted against Byzantine rule in AD727, the same year the Venetians decided on independence and elected their first doge. While Venice's story was only beginning, Ravenna's days were numbered. With no supplies from the east to see it through a siege, the city fell to the Lombards in AD751. Six years later, however, Pepin the Short's Frankish army snatched it away from them, and the city was placed under the rule of the popes. Ravenna declined slowly and gracefully in the following centuries. Venice took over its role as leading port of the Adriatic while Classis silted up and was abandoned. The newer cities of the Romagna, such as Ferrara and Faenza, assumed a larger role in the region's economy, and even Ravenna's ancient school of Roman law was transferred to Bologna, there to become the seed of Europe's first university.

POLENTAS AND POPES Despite its declining fortunes, Ravenna managed to rouse itself in 1177, becoming a free *comune* like so many other towns in the Romagna. Originally a strong Ghibelline town, Ravenna crossed over to the Guelphs under Guido 'the Old' da Polenta in 1239. Emperor Frederick II himself came the next year to take back the city for the Ghibellines, and had Guido's father executed. Though his enemies were to hold Ravenna for decades, Guido never gave up. He finally won the city back in 1275, with the aid of the Malatesta of Rimini, inaugurating a period of family rule that was to last for a century and a half.

Already in his 80s, old Guido would have still more troubles to witness. His daughter Francesca, married to Giovanni Malatesta of Rimini, decided she liked his brother Paolo better; Giovanni killed them both when he caught them, in 1283. (The story of Paolo and Francesca would make one of the most touching and famous episodes in Dante, even though that unforgiving poet assigned them both to the Inferno.) In 1290, Guido's own sons locked him up for a time, in a plot to give the city over to the pope, but he regained control of the situation and ruled in relative peace until his death in 1310.

Guido was succeeded by his grandson Guido 'Novello', famous for offering refuge to Dante when a change in Florentine politics made the poet an exile. Dante finished the *Divine Comedy* in Ravenna, and died here in 1321. If he'd lasted a little longer, he might have found enough material for another circle in the Inferno. The first da Polenta had a reputation for honesty and sagacity that often led to their being invited to sort out the affairs of neighbouring cities (a common practice among the *comuni* when the factions could agree on an impartial referee). Guido the Old had once served as *podestà* in Florence, and in 1322 Guido Novello was spending a term as Capitano del Popolo in Bologna when his cousin Ostasio seized the city and murdered Guido's brother, Archbishop Rinaldo, who had been left in charge.

Guido Novello died in exile, and the rogue branch of the da Polenta held on to the city through the reigns of several *signori*, each worse than the last. Ostasio murdered two more close relatives before he was done; his son Bernardino starved his brothers to death after he caught them plotting against him. The next in line, another Guido, was starved to death by his own sons after they overthrew him; after that one of the sons, Obizzo, murdered all the others. It was the Venetians who finally put an end to this family fun. Venice had a commercial stranglehold over Ravenna, and its power and influence in the city steadily increased after 1400. In 1441 the Serenissima threw out the last da Polenta and ruled the city directly.

Ravenna enjoyed a brief period of renewed prosperity that lasted until the popes came back in 1509; the economic decadence brought by papal rule has been reversed only since the 1940s. Parts of the city were heavily damaged in World War II, but in the last few decades, with the construction of a ship channel and new port, the discovery of offshore gas deposits and the introduction of large chemical industries, Ravenna has become a thriving modern city – just coincidentally one with a centre full of priceless Byzantine mosaics.

GETTING THERE AND AWAY

BY RAIL Ravenna is not on the main Adriatic railway line, but there are frequent trains from Florence, Venice, Ancona and Bologna, Ferrara and Rimini. The station [306 D3] (*disabled assistance available at the station 08.00–20.00*) is in Piazzale Farini, on the eastern edge of the old town next to the ship channel, and a short walk from the centre.

BY CAR The main road to Ravenna from Bologna and central Italy, the *autostrada* A14 dir, comes to an end just west of the city where it meets the SS16 between Rimini and Ferrara, which skirts round Ravenna. Drivers approaching from the north and west normally come into the city centre along the Via di Roma, its modern main thoroughfare, which crosses the *circonvallazione* or inner ring road.

BY BUS The bus station [306 D3] is on Piazza Aldo Moro, just across the tracks from the train station (a long walk, but there's a *sottopassaggio* under the tracks for a shortcut). A number of lines run services around the Romagna, and most of Italy. You can get a bus from here to Paris, or ten different cities in Poland. These lines are mostly bucket shops, and there's no central source for information. Come down to the station and shop around. **Flixbus** (w *flixbus.it*) has stops at Via Trieste 180 [306 D4], 1km east of the railway station, and three other locations on the lidos (see its website), with bargain buses for Milan, Bergamo, Rome, Naples and many other cities around Italy.

GETTING AROUND

Be warned, it's a bit of a miasma, this storied town. Ravenna's streets just meander, with no ambition whatsoever to take you where you want to go. Whether you're walking, driving or riding a bike, it's an easy place to get good and lost.

BY BUS Sights are spread out, and city buses can come in handy here. Most of the ATM buses heading north from the train station or Piazza del Popolo (buses 1, 3, 4, 5, 8, 70, 80, 90) go past Theodoric's Mausoleum, otherwise it's a half-hour walk from the centre. Buses 1 and 70 go to Marina di Ravenna. Bus 4 from the station or Via Roma goes out to San Apollinare in Classe. Other buses from the train station or from Piazza del Popolo will take you to any of Ravenna's suburban lidos, and there's a seasonal shuttle from the station to the amusement park Mirabilandia. For information, there's the Punto Bus (⌚ *07.00–19.00*) in the train station or ring ATM (☏ *199 115 577*).

ATM also runs an ancient *traghetto* (car ferry) across the narrow inlet between Marina di Ravenna and Porto Corsini, which will amuse the children if you're on your way to the northern lidos. Buy tickets (*car €3*) from the machines on the landing.

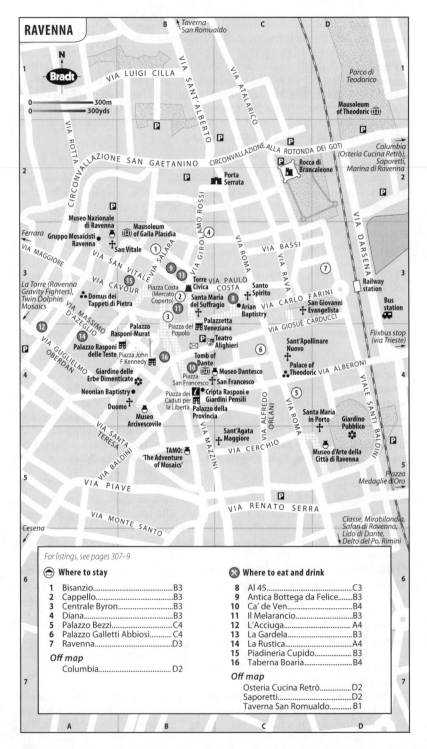

RAVENNA

Taverna
San Romualdo

VIA LUIGI CILLA

N

Bradt

0   300m
0   300yds

VIA SANT'ALBERTO

VIA ATALARICO

Parco di
Teodorico

Mausoleum
of Theodoric

CIRCONVALLAZIONE SAN GAETANINO

CIRCONVALLAZIONE ALLA ROTONDA DEI GOTI

Columbia
(Osteria Cucina Retrò),
Saporetti,
Marina di Ravenna

VIA ROTTA

Porta
Serrata

Rocca di
Brancaleone

VIA DARSENA

Ferrara

Museo Nazionale
di Ravenna

Gruppo Mosaicisti
Ravenna

San Vitale

Mausoleum
of Galla Placidia

VIA GIROLAMO ROSSI

VIA ROMA

VIA BASSI

VIA MAGGIORE

VIA SAN VITALE

VIA SALARA

4

VIA RAVA

7

Railway
station

La Torre (Ravenna
Gravity Fighters),
Twin Dolphin
Mosaics

VIA CAVOUR

15

Domus dei
Tappeti di Pietra

9

13

Piazza Costa
(Mercato
Coperto)

Torre
Civica

Santa Maria
del Suffragio

VIA PAULO
COSTA

Santo
Spirito

Arian
Baptistry

8

VIA CARLO FARINI

San Giovanni
Evangelista

Bus
station

VIA MASSIMO
D'AZEGLIO

12

Palazzo
Rasponi-Murat

2

11

3

Palazzetta
Veneziana

Piazza del
Popolo

Teatro
Alighieri

VIA GIOSUÈ CARDUCCI

Flixbus stop
(via Trieste)

14

Palazzo Raspони
delle Teste

Piazza John
F Kennedy

16

Sant'Apollinare
Nuovo

VIA GUGLIELMO
OBERDAN

Giardino delle
Erbe Dimenticate

Neonian Baptistry

Duomo

Museo
Arcivescovile

Tomb of
Dante

10

Piazza
San Francesco

Museo Dantesco

San Francesco

6

Palace of
Theodoric

VIA ALBERONI

VIALE SANTI BALDINI

Piazza dei
Caduti per
la Libertà

Cripta Rasponi e
Giardini Pensili

Palazzo della
Provincia

VIA ALFREDO
ORLANI

5

Santa Maria
in Porto

VIA ROMA

Giardino
Pubblico

VIA SANTA
TERESA

Sant'Agata
Maggiore

VIA MAZZINI

VIA CERCHIO

Museo d'Arte della
Città di Ravenna

VIA BALDINI

TAMO:
'The Adventure
of Mosaics'

Piazza
Medaglie d'Oro

VIA PIAVE

Cesena

VIA MONTE SANTO

VIA RENATO SERRA

Classe, Mirabilandia,
Safari di Ravenna,
Lido di Dante,
Delto del Po, Rimini

The **START Romagna SmartPass** (see box, page 328) is available at Bus Points and some shops and hotels.

BY BIKE Ravenna is increasingly bicycle friendly. New roads are being built, old ones closed off, and new parking areas being established on the periphery in an effort to encourage bike riding, and bring fresh air into the city centre.

TOURIST INFORMATION

There is another IAT office at the Mausoleo Teodorico (pages 320–1), and one in each of the Lidos.

 [306 B4] Piazza San Francesco 7; ☎0544 35755; w turismo.ra.it; ⏱ summer 08.30–19.00 Mon–Sat, 09.30–17.30 Sun, winter 08.30–16.00 Mon– Sat, 10.00–16.00 Sun. The Romagna Visit Card (see box, page 328) is available to buy here.

WHERE TO STAY

LUXURY
🏠 **Cappello** [306 B3] (7 rooms) Via IV Novembre 41; ☎0544 219813; w albergocappello.it. Located in a 14th-century palazzo reputed to have been the home of Francesca da Rimini. Only 7 big & lavish rooms. Charms include frescoes, wood-panelled ceilings, antique fireplaces & a romantic small restaurant (⏱ *closed Mon lunch, Sun & Aug;* €€€), as well as an enoteca (⏱ *daily;* €€) with a long wine list, *salumi*, cheeses & cakes. €€€€€

UPMARKET
🏠 **Palazzo Bezzi** [306 C4] (32 rooms) Via di Roma 45; ☎0544 36926; w palazzobezzi.com. Very central, bright, modern & elegant. Large choice of rooms from standards to suites; the Gold Room has a round dbl bed. Gym & spa, roof terrace & b/fast garden. €€€€
🏠 **Palazzo Galletti Abbiosi** [306 C4] (40 rooms) Via di Roma 140; ☎0544 31313; w hotel-ravenna-mosaico.it. Beautifully restored 18th-century palazzo in the city centre. Rooms are modern with AC, & some have frescoes on the ceilings. Impressive b/fast buffet, free bike loan; limited parking available. When it's overbooked, guests are put in a less interesting apt building down the street; ask in advance. €€€–€€€€

MID-RANGE
🏠 **Bisanzio** [306 B3] (38 rooms) Via Salara 30; ☎0544 217111; w bisanziohotel.com. Modern & serene hotel on a quiet street near San Vitale.

All AC, & a pretty inner garden. Continental b/fast inc. €€€
🏠 **Centrale Byron** [306 B3] (52 rooms) Via IV Novembre 14; ☎0544 212225. Old favourite, ageing gracefully just off the Piazza del Popolo: AC, with some very nice rooms & some much plainer ones; b/fast inc. €€€
🏠 **Diana** [306 B3] (33 rooms) Via G Rossi 47; ☎0544 39164; w hoteldiana.ra.it. Good central location, an 18th-century palace near the tomb of Galla Placidia. Comfortable hotel with a charming Baroque lobby & modern facilities in every room. 4 classes of rooms with varying prices. Baby-sitting services & bicycles for clients are a bonus. €€€
🏠 **Ravenna** [306 D3] (26 rooms) Via Maroncelli 12; ☎0544 212204; w hotelravenna. ra.it. Good choice near the station. Faded but nice. Parking & AC; b/fast inc. €€€

BUDGET
There is plenty of budget accommodation but much of it is around the port, a long walk from the centre along Via delle Industrie.

🏠 **Columbia** [map, pages 268–9] (53 rooms) Viale Italia 70; ☎0544 446038; w columbiahotel. it. Stylish modern hotel in attractive Marina Romea, to the north. 10mins' walk from the beach. Swimming pool, solarium & bike rental. Its restaurant, **Osteria Cucina Retrò** (€€), is dedicated to Romagnolo home cooking at bargain prices. Good just for a *piadina* or *crescione*, or a full dinner. Coeliac & vegetarian choices. €€

The Ravennesi are justifiably proud of all the good things that come in from the farms of the Romagna, and they feature prominently in the restaurants: top-grade olive oil from Brisighella, creamy *squacquerone* cheese.

The *squacquerone* and other cheeses come from the Romagna's white and stately Fassona cattle. Besides the cheese and milk, people here are convinced that they make the best beef in Italy, and it turns up often on local menus, especially as *tagliate* and carpaccio.

EXPENSIVE

✗ **L'Acciuga** [306 A4] Viale Francesco Baracca; ☎0544 212713; w osterialacciuga.it; ⏱ closed Sun eve, Mon. West of the centre, a place with submarinish décor where they take seafood very seriously – even the anchovies that give the place its name, which get a starring role. Creative antipasti & *primi*; try the *cappelletti* with *baccalà*. Good value. €€€–€€€€

ABOVE AVERAGE

✗ **Antica Bottega da Felice** [306 B3] Via Ponte Marino 23; ☎0544 240170; w anticabottegadifelice.com; ⏱ closed Sun. Deli/restaurant near San Vitale: *piadine, gnocchi fritti, crescioni*, stuffed courgette flowers, *tagliatelle verdi*. Book ahead; good for vegetarians. €€€

✗ **Taberna Boaria** [306 B4] Via Mentana 33; ☎0544 215258; w tabernaboaria.com; ⏱ closed Tue. Just south of Piazza del Popolo, located in a 16th-century palace, with an elegant, recently restored dining room & outside tables. They're especially talented with the pasta: with boar sauce or baby clams, or maybe with truffles. *Secondo* is all grilled meats. Try the mixed grill, but don't order it well done – they can't stand it. €€€

✗ **Taverna San Romualdo** [map, pages 268–9] Via Sant'Alberto 364; ☎0544 483 447; w tavernasanromualdo.it; ⏱ closed Tues eve. 10km north of the city on the SP1 at San Romualdo. A typically rustic Romagnolo osteria that has transformed into a sophisticated restaurant. Actually they've kept both, running out of the same kitchen. The **Osteria** side offers excellent €10–15 menus as well as *piadine* & snacks (€). In the **Ristorante** it's traditional cooking, homemade bread & pasta, wild mushrooms & game dishes in season. €€€

✗ **Al 45** [306 C3] Via Paolo Costa 45; ☎0544 212761; w al45.it. By the Arian Baptistry, with tables in a lovely medieval courtyard. The menu has a big choice of lovely things: bruschetta with porcini or oyster mushrooms (in season), *millefeuille* pastries with swordfish or Fassona steak tartare, chickpea *gnocchetti*, & a 'drunken' *zuppa inglese* for dessert. You can splurge here or settle for one of the €11–16 quick dinner menus. €€–€€€

✗ **Ca' de Ven** [306 B4] Via Corrado Ricci 24; ☎0544 30163; w cadeven.it; ⏱ closed Mon. The 'house of wine' is a Ravenna institution, a restaurant/enoteca in a beautiful building with painted ceilings. Along with the huge selection of Emilia-Romagna wines you can get just about anything, from simple *tagliere* of roast meats, cheeses or *salumi* to a full-blown *menu degustazione* (€38). Suitably calm & dark, the perfect place to while away an afternoon after a morning with the Byzantines. €€–€€€

CHEAP & CHEERFUL

✗ **La Gardela** [306 B3] Via Ponte Marino 3; m 345 401 6131; w ristorantelagardela.com; ⏱ closed Thu. A *gardela* is a grill, & they grill just about everything here, land or sea. Huge menu with lots of choices on everything. They make their own pasta daily; be sure to try *scaloppine* with *taleggio* & rocket, & sample the large collection of grappas. Centrally located & extremely good value. Outside tables. €€

✗ **La Rustica** [306 A4] Via Massimo d'Azeglio 28; ☎0544 218128; w trattoria-larustica.it; ⏱ closed Tue. Near San Vitale, charming small restaurant & very popular. Traditional Romagnolo cooking: green tortelli with hazelnut sauce, roast rabbit with rosemary, smoked goose with fennel. €€

✗ **Saporetti** [306 D2] Via N Zen 13; ☎0544 530208; w ristorantesaporetti.it; ⏱ eves only. Seriously good pizza alfresco in the garden. €€

✗ Il Melarancio [306 B3] Via IV Novembre 21; ☎ 0544 212071; w lapiadina.biz. Bespoke *piadine* & *crescioni* with a big list of interesting fillings, including their trademark caramelised figs & *squacquerone* (Romagna cream cheese). €

✗ Piadineria Cupido [306 B3] Via Cavour 43; ☎ 0544 37529; w piadacupido.net; ⊕ closed Wed. Hole-in-the-wall near San Vitale with excellent homemade *piadine, crescioni*, sandwiches & pasta dishes. €

ENTERTAINMENT AND NIGHTLIFE

There isn't much of a scene at all in Ravenna. For dancing, the action takes place in season in the informal discos and clubs along the lidos, which appear and disappear with each passing year. See w ravennatoday.it for upcoming concerts and other events.

The **Ravenna Festival** (☎ *0544 249211;* w *ravennafestival.org*) is an important music festival which runs from late May to July and reprises for a week in November. Internationally renowned musicians perform concerts, recitals and opera in the Teatro Alighieri and in some of the historic churches and palaces.

🎭 Teatro Alighieri [306 B4] Via Angel Mariani 2; ☎ 0544 215840 (box office); w www. teatroalighieri.org. The historic & delightfully ornate Teatro Alighieri (1838) stands out even in this region of grand civic theatres. Outside the Ravenna Festival it runs a regular season of opera, concerts & dance.

SHOPPING

Ravenna is a great town for **street markets**. The big ones are in Piazza Medaglie d'Oro [306 D5] (⊕ *Fri mornings*) and Piazza Costa [306 B3] (⊕ *Wed & Sat mornings*); the monumental **Mercato Coperto** in Piazza Costa has been undergoing reconstruction for years, delayed by archaeological finds, though they're still shooting for a reopening in June 2018. In summer there will be a colourful market on one of the lidos every day of the week. The main retail **shopping streets** are Via Armando Diaz, between the station and Piazza del Popolo, and Via Roma, which crosses it.

The craftsmen of Ravenna are trying to revive the art of **mosaics**, though understandably they're not always up to Byzantine levels. Items range from tacky souvenir plaques to the real thing, created on commission. Ravenna has become a major centre for modern mosaic art, in galleries and workshops around town; some offer courses in the art. The tourist office (page 307) has a complete list. A lot of them congregate around San Vitale, where the **Gruppo Mosaicisti Ravenna** [306 A3] (*Via Benedetto Fiandrini;* ☎ *0544 34799;* w *gruppomosaicisti.it;* ⊕ *08.00–17.00 Mon–Fri*) does important restorations and also keeps a gallery of reproductions and modern creations. One of the best modern designers is **Twin Dolphin Mosaics** [306 A3] (*Via Friuli 52;* ☎ *0544 403777;* w *twindolphinmosaics.com*).

WHAT TO SEE AND DO

The **Romagna Visit Card**, available to buy online or at the tourist offices, gains you free admission to some – but not all – of the major sights in Ravenna. The **Romagna SmartPass** also offers discounts on sights and entertainment (for details of both, see box, page 328).

Note also that Ravenna's sights also offer three different **joint tickets**. One of these is good for San Vitale, the Mausoleum of Galla Placidia, the Museo Arcivescovile, the Neonian Baptistry and Sant'Apollinare Nuovo (€9.50). Another gets you into

Sant'Apollinare in Classe, the Museo Nazionale and the Mausoleum of Theodoric (€10). The third combines TAMO ('The Adventure of Mosaics') museum, the Domus dei Tappeti di Pietra and the Cripta Rasponi (€7).

SAN VITALE [306 A3] (*Via San Vitale, nr Porta Adriana;* ☎ *0544 541688;* ⊕ *Mar–Oct 09.00–19.00 daily, Nov–Feb 10.00–17.00 daily exc during weddings or Mass (see calendar at* w *www.ravennamosaici.it); €9.50 joint ticket with Mausoleum of Galla Placidia, Museo Arcivescovile, Neonian Baptistry & Sant'Apollinare Nuovo*) At first this dark old church may not seem like much, but as soon as the now-automatic lights come on (a large bag of coins is no longer an essential requirement), the 1,400-year-old mosaics ignite into an explosion of colour. The mosaics of San Vitale, Ravenna's best, are one of the last great works of art of the ancient world, and one of Christianity's first. The octagonal church, begun in AD525 during the reign of Theodoric, is itself a fine example of the surprisingly sophisticated architecture from that troubled age. By the time it was finished, in AD548, the city was in the hands of Belisarius's Byzantine army; the famous mosaic portraits of Justinian and Theodora can be taken as the traditional imperial style of political propaganda.

Far from being the sorry recapitulation of old building forms and styles you might expect, San Vitale was a breathtakingly original departure in architecture. While the world was falling around their ears, late Roman architects were making revolutionary advances, using complex geometry and new vaulting techniques. In the 6th century it still wasn't entirely settled just what a church was, or what design would be proper for it. Most commonly they took the form of the Roman basilica, a secular building that housed law courts or government offices (Sant'Apollinare Nuovo and Sant'Apollinare in Classe are good examples, along with the early basilican churches of Rome). Central-plan churches were also popular, since the first big imperially sponsored building programme under Constantine, which included such novel works as the Holy Sepulchre in Jerusalem and the 'Golden Octagon' of Antioch; Ravenna's San Vitale was the next step. Their architecture derives from Roman bath complexes, mausolea and perhaps the follies and pavilions of the land-owning elite.

Take some time to admire the **exterior**, with its beautiful interplay of octagons, arches, gables and exedrae – pure proportional geometry done in plain solid brick (but for the Greek–Gothic Wars it might have been sheathed in stone). Inside, the curious double capitals on the columns are no design conceit, but an important 5th-century invention; the trapezoidal *impost capital* was specially designed to support the weight of arches. Holding up the second-floor galleries and a large octagonal cupola was an unusual design problem; these capitals and the eight stout piers around the dome were the solution. We do not know the name of San Vitale's architects, or whether they were Latins or Greeks, but the year after it was begun work commenced on the very similar church of SS Sergius and Bacchus in Constantinople, the prototype for the Hagia Sophia ten years later.

In its structure the great dome in Constantinople owed everything to the little dome of Ravenna: the innovation of the galleries, for example, in which the women were segregated during services, and the elongated apse cleverly combining the central plan favoured by eastern Christians with the basilica form needed for a court's religious ceremonies.

Nowhere in what is now Istanbul, however, or anywhere else in the east, will you find anything as brilliant as San Vitale's **mosaics**. Some of the best were undoubtedly lost during the iconoclastic troubles of the 8th century; iconoclasm, however, was fiercely resisted in Italy – it was one of the first causes of the rupture between Ravenna and Constantinople, and between the Roman and Greek churches – and most of Ravenna's art was fortunately left in peace. The colours are startling. Almost all the later Byzantine mosaics, in Sicily, Greece and Turkey, are simple figures on a bright gold ground, dazzling at first but somewhat monotonous. There is plenty of gold on the walls of San Vitale, but the best mosaics, in the choir, have deep blue skies and rich green meadows for backgrounds, highlighted by brightly coloured birds and flowers.

The two lunettes over the arches flanking the choir, each a masterpiece, show the *Hospitality of Abraham and the Sacrifice of Isaac*, and the *Offerings of Abel and Melchizedek*, set under fiery clouds with hands of benediction extended from Heaven. These sacrifices are the two events in the Old Testament that prefigure the Transfiguration of Christ. Around the two lunettes are scenes of Moses and Jeremiah; note, above the lunettes, the delicately posed pairs of angels holding golden crosses – almost identical to the fanciful figures from earlier Roman art displaying the civic crown of the Caesars, a symbol of the state from the time of Augustus. At the front of the choir the triumphal arch has excellent mosaic portraits of the Apostles supported by a pair of dolphins. Look up at the galleries and you will see more fine portraits of the four Evangelists.

The **apse** is dominated by the famous portraits of **Justinian and Theodora** – mostly, of course, of Theodora, the Constantinople dancing girl who used her many talents to become an empress, eventually coming to wear Justinian like a charm on her bracelet. Here she is wearing a rich crown, with long strings of fat diamonds and real pearls. Justinian, like Theodora, appears among his retinue offering a gift to the new church; here he has the air of a hung-over saxophone player, badly in need of a shave and a cup of coffee. His cute daisy slipper steps on the foot (a convention of Byzantine art to show who's boss) of General Belisarius, to his left. The likenesses are good – very like those in Constantinople – suggesting that the artist may have come from there, or at least have closely copied imperial portraits on display at Ravenna.

It can easily be imagined how expensive it was in the 5th century to make mosaics like these. It is said that the Hagia Sophia originally had more than four acres of them, and even the treasury of Justinian and Theodora was not bottomless; consequently most of San Vitale remained undecorated until the 17th-century bishops did the dome and the other parts in a not-too-discordant Baroque. The mosaics are such an attraction that you might miss the other features of San Vitale – including the one under your feet, a **maze** directly in front of the choir. No-one knows exactly when it was added, but such mazes were common features of late Roman and medieval churches from Britain to Algeria. No-one knows much about their significance either, though their pre-Christian symbolism may have been re-explained as a kind of substitute pilgrimage; the space at the centre was often referred to as 'Jerusalem'. You can walk this one – don't worry, you won't get lost; like all church mazes this one is a single winding path, with no wrong turns or dead ends.

Recently, part of the floor between two piers has been pulled up to reveal the original, an inlaid **marble pavement** in floral and geometric patterns that is a direct ancestor of medieval pavements in the churches of Tuscany and the south. The lower walls of the church are covered in thin sheets of precious marbles from all over the Mediterranean, much like those of the Hagia Sophia. Also worthy of note is the alabaster 6th-century **altar**, ancient reliefs of the *Throne of Neptune* and the *Sacrifice of Isaac* near the choir, and the sarcophagus of Quintus Bonus, with reliefs of the *Magi* and *Daniel in the Lions' Den*.

Either light was born here,
Or reigns here imprisoned.

Latin inscription, Sant'Andrea chapel

In Byzantine times the greatest gift an emperor could bestow on any dependent town was a few tons of gilt, glass and enamel tesserae and an artist. From Justinian's time, the art became almost a trademark of Byzantine civilisation. It was not only towns under Byzantine rule that received such favours; probably as part of diplomatic initiatives, you can see the work of Constantinople's mosaicists in Egypt, Sicily and in the mihrab of the Great Mosque of Córdoba.

Before Christianity, mosaics were a favourite Roman medium, but not always taken too seriously. They were usually reserved for the decoration of villas. Some are unquestionably great works of art (the best examples are in the Naples museum, the great villa at Piazza Armerina, Sicily, and Antakya in Turkey – ancient Antioch), but more often the productions were on the level of the famous 'Beware of the dog' mosaic in Pompeii, or prophylactic images of Priapus. It was the early Christians, with a desire to build for the ages and a body of scriptures that could best be related pictorially, who made mosaics the new medium of public art in the 6th century.

Mostly it was an affair of the Greeks, who still had the talent and the resources for it; we cannot say with absolute certainty, but it's most likely that Greek artists from the court of Constantinople created the celebrated mosaics in the churches and baptistries of Ravenna.

Western Christian art was born here, developing from the simple images – the Good Shepherd and the Cross and Stars – to the iconic Christ in Sant'Apollinare Nuovo and the beautiful scriptural scenes in San Vitale. Never, though, did the early mosaicists turn their back on the idea of art; with the ideals of the ancient world still in their minds, they naturally thought of art and religion as going hand in hand, and found no problem in serving the cause of both. Using a new vocabulary of images and the new techniques of mosaic art, they strove to duplicate, and surpass, the sense of awe and mystery still half-remembered from the interiors of the pagan temples. Try to imagine a church like San Vitale in its original state, with lamps or candles – lots of them – flickering below the gold ground and gorgeous colours. You may see that same light that enchanted the Byzantines – the light of the Gospels, the light from beyond the stars.

MAUSOLEUM OF GALLA PLACIDIA [306 B3] (*In the grounds of San Vitale;* ⏲ *see San Vitale; €9.50 joint ticket with San Vitale, Museo Arcivescovile, Neonian Baptistry & Sant'Apollinare Nuovo*) If they tried to make Galla Placidia's life into a Hollywood costumer, no-one would believe it. The daughter of Theodosius the Great, last ruler of a united and peaceful empire, she grew up between Constantinople, Rome, Milan and Ravenna amid the court intrigues that followed his death. She happened to be in Rome when the Visigoths sacked it in AD410, and at the age of 18 this princess suddenly became a very valuable bargaining chip in the hands of their leader Alaric. While negotiations were under way to return her, Alaric died, and his young successor Ataulf took his hungry people from impoverished Italy to Gaul, in

hopes of finding land and food. Galla Placidia accompanied him on this long and miserable trek, and somewhere along the way the two fell in love.

They were married in AD413 at Narbonne, and had a child, named Theodosius, in Barcelona two years later. The emperor, Galla's twisted, rotten brother Honorius, was furious, and he may well have arranged Ataulf's assassination in AD415. So failed a remarkable chance for German–Italian reconciliation, and possibly the salvation of the Empire. Galla returned to Ravenna the next year, where Honorius forced her into a second marriage, but there were more adventures to come. Galla was still Queen of the Visigoths, and worked faithfully in their interests; and perhaps as a result of this Honorius banished her in AD423 (there are also hints that he did it because Galla resisted his sexual advances).

Escaping for Constantinople, she was shipwrecked off Ephesus but miraculously saved. Honorius died the same year, heirless, and Galla sailed right back, this time as regent of the Western Empire, which she ruled for the next 13 years in the name of her son Valentinian. With such a busy life, Galla might be excused certain failures as a mother. Valentinian turned out a vicious waster, while his sister Honoria was so bad Galla had her locked up in a convent. That didn't stop her – while inside she managed single-handedly to cause the invasion of Italy by the Huns, who had previously been quiet Roman allies. Honoria smuggled out a letter to Attila the Hun, accompanied by a ring, promising to marry him if he would only come down and deliver her.

This small chapel, set in the grounds of San Vitale and originally attached to the neighbouring church of Santa Croce, never really held the tomb of Ravenna's first great patroness – she is buried somewhere near St Peter's in Rome. Nobody has peeked into the three huge stone sarcophagi, traditionally the resting places of Galla Placidia and two emperors, her second husband Constantius and her son Valentinian, and it's anyone's guess who is really inside. Galla Placidia did construct the chapel, and it was probably intended as an imperial resting place, its relative modesty a demonstration of how much the Western Empire had fallen. It is a small, gabled and cross-shaped building that is almost 2.5m shorter than when it was built: the ground level has risen that much in 1,400 years.

The simplicity of the brick exterior, as in San Vitale, makes the brilliant mosaics within that much more of a surprise. The only natural light inside comes from a few tiny slits of windows, made of thin sheets of alabaster that probably came from Egypt. The two important mosaics, on lunettes at opposite ends of the chapel, are coloured as richly as San Vitale. One represents *St Lawrence*, with his flaming gridiron; the other is a beautiful and typical early Christian portrait of Jesus as the *Good Shepherd*, a beardless, classical-looking figure in a fine cloak and sandals, stroking one of the flock. On the lunettes of the cross-axis, pairs of stags come to drink at the *Fountain of Life*; around all four lunettes floral arabesques and maze patterns in bright colours cover the arches and ceilings. Everything in the design betrays as much of the classical Roman style as the nascent Christian, and the unusual figures on the arches holding up the central vault seem hardly out of place. They are *SS Peter and Paul*, dressed in togas and standing with outstretched hands in the conventional pose of Roman senators.

The **vault** itself, a deep blue firmament glowing with hundreds of dazzling golden stars set in concentric circles, is the mausoleum's most remarkable feature. In the centre, at the top of the vault, a golden cross represents the unimaginable, transcendent God above the heavens. At the corners, symbols of the four *Evangelists* provide an insight into the origins of Christian iconography. Mark's lion, Luke's ox and Matthew's man occupy the places in this sky where you would expect the

10

constellations of Leo, Taurus and Aquarius, 90 degrees apart along the zodiac. For the fourth corner, instead of the objectionable Scorpio (or serpent, as it often appeared in ancient times) the early Christians substituted the eagle of St John.

The mausoleum was originally connected to the church of **Santa Croce** (closed to the public), also built by Galla Placidia, which you can see through the fence, along with the 9th-century **Santa Maria Maggiore**. After many rebuildings, almost nothing is left of these churches from ancient times, except the latter church's campanile (also 9th-century), one of the beautiful round towers in the Ravenna style.

MUSEO NAZIONALE DI RAVENNA [306 A3] (*In the grounds of San Vitale;* \ *0544 543724;* ☉ *08.30–14.00 Tue–Thu, 08.30–19.30 Fri & Sat, 14.00–19.30 Sun; €6, or €10 joint ticket with Sant'Apollinare in Classe & Mausoleum of Theodoric*) The medieval and Baroque cloisters attached to San Vitale now house the large collection of antiquities found in Ravenna and Classis. This is a museum well worth spending time in, for exceptional works of art such as the beautiful 6th-century Byzantine carved screens, and a unique sculpture of *Hercules Capturing the Ceryneian Hind*, also 6th-century, perhaps the last surviving piece of art made in ancient times with a classical subject, possibly a copy of an earlier Greek work. An excellent mosaic, recently moved here from a Byzantine palace excavated on Via d'Azeglio, shows *Christ as the Good Shepherd* surrounded by the *Dance of the Seasons*.

Beyond these there's a little bit of everything: Etruscan finds from the area, lead pipes and other bits of good Roman plumbing, a boy's linen shirt that has somehow survived from the 6th century, the original bronze cross from the roof of San Vitale, Byzantine forks (they invented them), swords and armour, and no end of coins and broken pots. The detailed and well-labelled **coin collection** is interesting even to the non-specialist, providing a picture history of Italy from classical times into the early Middle Ages.

Not all of the exhibits are ancient; lovely, intricately carved **ivories** (chests, portable altars and plaques from the Middle Ages and Renaissance) fill an entire room. Most are from France, with charming tableaux of medieval scenes such as tournaments and banquets. There is a good collection of **ceramics** too, not only from Faenza but from other notable Italian centres, such as Castelli, Urbino and Deruta, and a room of Byzantine **icons** from the 14th to the 17th century (it doesn't matter; over time they hardly change at all). Most of these are Italian, a reminder of the long survival of Orthodox communities here; there are works of the Cretan-Venetian school, others from the Veneto, from Russia and even Naples.

Cinquecento Italy is represented by a lavishly fancy intarsia cabinet, and by the museum building itself, which includes a domed monumental stair attributed to Bramante. To understand Ravenna and its buildings better, be sure to see the fascinating architectural models of the Neonian baptistry (page 317). The work of a modern Ravenna architect named Raffaello Trinci, its glass cross sections elaborate the proportions and geometrical theory behind the new architecture of the 6th century, a recasting of ancient sacred geometry that was to have a great influence on the cathedral builders of the Middle Ages, and a greater one on the architects of Islam.

The museum has a new attraction in a separate room, a wonderful set of **frescoes from the church of Santa Chiara**. Once part of a convent, closed by Napoleon, the church was later used as a stable and a theatre; the presbytery, with the frescoes, was walled off and forgotten, and they were discovered and detached only recently.

All the works (c1320) are by Pietro da Rimini, the Romagna's greatest painter of the trecento. They include delightful scenes from the vaulting, with the four

Evangelists paired with four great *Doctors of the Church*: Matthew with Jerome, Mark with Ambrose, John with Augustine and Luke with Pope Gregory the Great. While the Doctors sit puzzling at their desks, surrounded by books, the Evangelists come down, apparently to give them tips on the difficult points of the Scriptures. Among the other frescoes are portraits of *St Francis, St Clare* and *St Anthony of Padua*, and two of the loveliest angels of the 14th or any other century.

Look at the inside of the 16th-century cloister before you go, built over a lost *quadroporticus* that formed the entrance to San Vitale; among the architectural fragments and sculptures lying about are two huge, stately cedar trees and a sour-faced statue of Pope Clement XII.

DOMUS DEI TAPPETI DI PIETRA [306 A3] (*Via Barbiani 16;* ℡ *0544 242634;* ⏱ *Apr–Sep 10.00–18.30 daily, Oct–Mar 10.00–17.00 Mon–Fri, 10.00–18.30 Sat–Sun; €4, or €7 joint ticket with Cripta Rasponi & TAMO*) This 'House of Stone Carpets', just south of the San Vitale complex, was discovered only in 1992 during the construction of a new building. These 14 rooms of mosaic pavements, found at a level 3m underground, probably belonged to an important figure at the 5th–6th-century Gothic or Byzantine court. Don't expect another San Vitale; most of the mosaics here are simple geometric or floral designs. Some figurative scenes stand out: a charming scene of the *Four Seasons* holding hands and dancing in a circle, and Christ as the *Good Shepherd*.

PIAZZA DEL POPOLO This piazza, the centre of Ravenna, has a Venetian feel to it: the Venetians built it during their brief period of rule, and added the twin columns (like the pair in Venice's Piazzetta San Marco) bearing reliefs by Pietro Lombardo and statues of Ravenna's two patrons, San Vitale and Sant'Apollinare. The Venetians governed from the **Palazzetta Veneziana** (1444) [306 B4], embellished with Byzantine columns and heavily restored in the 19th century.

North of Piazza del Popolo on Via Ponte Marino, Ravenna has a fine example of a medieval leaning tower, the tall, 12th-century **Torre Civica** (or Torre Comunale) [306 B3], now supported by steel struts. Despite the angle of the tower, the windows near the top were built perfectly level. Byron lived for a time in a house in the nearby Via Cavour, during his affair with Countess Teresa Guiccioli. His home now houses the Carabinieri. Just around the corner on Via Ferruzzi is Ravenna's only full-blown Baroque church, **Santa Maria del Suffragio** (1734) [306 B3].

SOUTH OF PIAZZA DEL POPOLO Off the colonnaded Piazza San Francesco, a very modest Neoclassical pavilion was built in the 18th century over the **Tomb of Dante** [306 B4]. Ravenna is especially proud of having sheltered the storm-tossed poet in his last years, and the city will gently remind you of it in its street names, its tourist brochures, its Teatro Alighieri and its frequent artistic competitions based on themes from the *Divina Commedia*.

Coming here may help demonstrate just what Dante means to Italy; in all the country's more recent wars, for example, groups of soldiers have come here for little rituals to 'dedicate their sacrifice' to the poet's memory. Today there are always wreaths or bouquets from all kinds of organisations and private citizens from all over Italy. Beside the tomb is the **Museo Dantesco** [306 C4] (*Via Dante Alighieri 4;* ℡ *0544 215676;* w *centrodantesco.it;* ⏱ *Apr–Oct 10.00–18.00 Tue–Sun, Nov–Mar 10.00–16.00 Tue–Sun; €3*), set around the cloister of San Francesco and its charming fountain, with a collection of paintings, sculptures and books connected with the poet and his stay in Ravenna.

The church of **San Francesco** [306 B4] (⏲ *07.00–noon & 14.45–19.00 daily*), behind the tomb, was begun in AD460 but rebuilt in the 11th century and then thoroughly Baroqued in the 1700s. If the Greek marble columns of the nave look unusually squat, it is because a third of their height is underground. The church has been settling and sinking in the soggy ground for 1,500 years. Some of its beautiful original mosaic pavement is visible through an opening in the floor – under eight feet of water. Also in the church is the 14th-century *Tomb of Ostasio da Polenta*, first of the bad Polentas, and the unusual 1509 *Tomb of Luffo Numai*, with advice for the soul from the animal world: a bird whispers 'abstain', while a camel counsels 'endure'.

The altar was originally the fine 4th-century sarcophagus of Archbishop Liberius. In the church itself and the adjacent **Braccioforte Oratory** (behind the iron gate, next to Dante's tomb) there are some more early Christian sarcophagi. As with most of these sarcophagi scattered around the city, each one is a work of first-rate sculpture.

In front of San Francesco stands a brick palazzo that is the seat of the provincial government; behind it they have restored the walled palace gardens and a crypt with simple mosaics, called the **Cripta Rasponi e Giardini Pensili** [306 B4] (*Piazza San Francesco;* ☎ *0544 32512;* w *criptarasponi.it;* ⏲ *summer 10.00–14.00 daily, winter 10.00–14.00 Sat–Sun; €2, or €7 joint ticket with Domus dei Tappeti di Pietra & TAMO*). Just down Via Ricci from San Francesco is Ravenna's **Palazzo della Provincia** [306 B4], an ensemble of lukewarm Mussolini Deco buildings from the 1920s and 30s on a square that after the war was renamed Piazza dei Caduti per la Libertà. To the east on Via Mazzini, **Sant'Agata Maggiore** [306 C5] (⏲ *seldom open, try Sun before & after masses*) is another church founded by Theodoric, retaining another round campanile, some fine ancient capitals and an unusual ambone from the AD500s.

TAMO: 'The Adventure of Mosaics' [306 B5] (*Via Rondinelli 2;* ☎ *0544 213371;* w *tamoravenna.it;* ⏲ *Mar–4 Jun 10.00–18.30 daily, 5 Jun–Aug 10.00–14.00 Mon–Fri, Sep–7 Oct 10.00–14.00 Mon–Fri, 10.00–18.00 Sat–Sun, 8 Oct–5 Nov 10.00–17.00 Mon–Fri, 10.00–18.00 Sat–Sun, 6 Nov–30 Dec 10.00–17.00 Mon–Fri, Jan–Feb closed; €4, or €7 joint ticket with Domus dei Tappeti di Pietra & Cripta Rasponi*) As you can imagine, whenever someone digs a hole in Ravenna there's a chance they'll hit some old Byzantine's floor mosaic. A lot of them have been assembled here, filling up the deconsecrated church complex of San Niccolò. TAMO was planned as a didactic museum; you can learn a lot about the process of mosaic art here. There are modern mosaics too; the rooms around the cloister contain 21 works by different artists on themes from Dante. Finally, there's an exhibit with maps and reconstructions to show you how Ravenna looked in Roman and Byzantine times.

Despite having been used as a garage for decades, the newly restored church itself is interesting, with some colourful bits of 16th-century fresco.

PIAZZA DUOMO It's a quiet corner of the city today, but in late Roman and Byzantine times this was the busy heart of Ravenna. Like San Marco in Venice, the cathedral piazza here stood by one of the major canals, the Fossa Amnis.

Duomo [306 B4] (*Piazza Duomo;* ☎ *0554 30328;* ⏲ *08.00–noon, 15.00–18.00 Mon–Fri, 08.00–noon, 15.00–18.00 Sat–Sun*) An earthquake in 1733 wrecked Ravenna's 5th-century cathedral, west of the Piazza del Popolo, and there's little to see in the replacement except the surviving medieval pavement (now 3m below street level), the beautiful 6th-century ambone, carved with animal reliefs, and the

nicely overwrought Baroque **Cappella della Santa Vergine del Sudore**. The 'Virgin of the Sweat' was an image of Mary that was stabbed, long ago, by a drunken soldier and immediately started 'sweating' blood (Virgins don't bleed); the image later saved Ravenna from a plague and a sacking. In the chapel are two fine Byzantine sarcophagi holding the remains of San Barbagiano (a 5th-century monk) and San Rainaldo di Concorezzo (archbishop in 1303, and a defender of the Templars).

The **campanile**, another lovely, slightly tipsy round tower (10th–11th century), somehow survived. In Augustus' time, this area was the centre of the city. The forum stood just to the west, between Via d'Azeglio and Via Oberdan – now, most of it is under the walled garden of the university's law school.

Neonian Baptistry [306 B4] (*Piazza Duomo;* ✆ *0544 541688;* ☉ *Mar–Oct 09.00– 19.00 daily, Nov–Feb 10.00–17.00 daily; €9.50 joint ticket with San Vitale, Mausoleum of Galla Placidia, Museo Arcivescovile & Sant'Apollinare Nuovo*) The earthquake also spared the 'Orthodox' Baptistry, named after the 5th-century bishop Neon who commissioned its splendid mosaics. Unlike the Arian Baptistry (page 320), almost all the decoration here has survived: there is a scene of the *Baptism of Jesus* and fine portraits of the *Apostles* on the ceiling under the dome, while below the eight walls bear four altars and four empty thrones. The *Etimasia*, the 'Preparing of the Throne' for Jesus for the Last Judgement, is an odd bit of Byzantine mysticism; interestingly enough, classical Greek art often depicted an empty throne as a symbol for Zeus, only with a pair of thunderbolts instead of a cross.

Some think that the Baptistry is in part older than Neon, built over a chamber of a Roman bath complex. In the 1,500 years or so since its construction, the Baptistry has sunk more than 3m – like the Duomo and everything else on the soggy soil of Ravenna. Its floor was raised through periodic reconstructions; recent excavations have uncovered marble supporting columns down to the bottom. In the side niches are a 6th-century Byzantine altar and a huge, thoroughly pagan marble vase. The marble font, big enough for immersion baptism of adults, is from the 13th century.

Next to the Neonian Baptistry, part of the cathedral grounds has been redesigned as a herb and flower garden in the medieval-Renaissance manner, the **Giardino delle Erbe Dimenticate** [306 B4] (*Piazzetta Paolo Serra;* ☉ *09.00–12.45 & 16.00– 19.45 Mon–Sat, 10.00–12.45 Sun, closed Thu afternoons; admission free*).

Museo Arcivescovile [306 B4] (*Piazza Duomo;* ✆ *0544 541688;* ☉ *Mar–Oct 09.00–19.00 daily, Nov–Feb 10.00–17.00 daily; €9.50 joint ticket with San Vitale, Mausoleum of Galla Placidia, Neonian Baptistry & Sant'Apollinare Nuovo*) The Archiepiscopal Museum, behind the cathedral, is a small museum that receives few visitors, but this is one of the great sights of Ravenna. Its little-known treasures include the **ivory throne of Bishop Maximian**, a masterpiece of 6th-century sculpture and thought to have been a gift from Emperor Justinian, and a 6th-century reliquary, the silver *Cross of Sant'Agnello*. Among the fragments of sculpture and mosaics are works saved from the original cathedral. The large marble disc by the wall, divided into 19 sections, is an episcopal calendar, regulated to the 19-year Julian cycle to allow Ravenna's medieval bishops to calculate the date of Easter and other holy days.

The biggest surprise, however, is finding that the nondescript Archbishop's Palace, in which the museum is located, is in parts as old as anything in Ravenna. A little door at the back leads to a small chapel called the **Oratorio di Sant'Andrea**, built around AD500 during the reign of Theodoric. The mosaics on the vaults are among

Ravenna's best: in the antechamber there's a a fanciful scene of multicoloured birds and flowers, and an unusual *Warrior Christ* in full Roman armour and wielding the cross like a sword, treading a lion and snake underfoot. In the chapel itself, four angels and the four Evangelists' symbols surround Christ's monogram on the dome, and the apse bears a beautiful starry sky around a golden cross, like the one at the Galla Placidia mausoleum.

The best mosaics, however, are the excellent **portraits of saints** decorating the arches. Early Christian representations of the saints are often much stronger than the pale, conventional figures of later art. Such portraits as these betray a fascination with the personalities and the psychology of saints; such figures as St Felicitas or St Ursicinus may be forgotten now, but to the early Christians they were not mere holy myths, but near-contemporaries, the spiritual heroes and heroines responsible for the miraculous growth of Christianity, the exemplars of a new age and a new way of life.

AROUND PIAZZA DUOMO North of the cathedral complex is Piazza John F Kennedy, home to two of Ravenna's most imposing palaces: the 16th-century **Palazzo Rasponi-Murat** [306 B4] (or Spalletti) opposite 18th-century **Palazzo Rasponi delle Teste** [306 B4], now employed mostly as city offices. The Rasponi family were the big shots in Ravenna for centuries. The back of the Rasponi-Murat now houses the **Piccolo Museo di Bambole e Altri Balocchi** (*Little Museum of Dolls & Toys;* m *335 606 7703;* w *museodellebambole.it;* ⊕ *May–Sep 10.00–12.30 & 16.00– 19.00 Tue–Sun, Oct–Apr 10.00–12.30 & 15.00–18.00 Tue–Sun; €4*). This private collection became a museum in 2006; it has porcelain dolls, rag dolls, paper dolls and everything else, going back to 1860.

DOWN VIA ROMA Long, straight Via Roma, a modern thoroughfare that roughly follows one of the *decumani* of the Roman city, is always a welcome sight; it makes this eastern end of Ravenna the only part where you won't be constantly getting lost. On a map you'll notice the winding streets Via Girolamo Rossi and Via Mazzini, once roughly the course of a stream that divided Ravenna in two. The area to the east, around San Vitale, was the original city, while the part around Via Roma was an expansion of late Imperial times.

At the southern end of Via Roma, **Santa Maria in Porto** [306 D5] (*Via Roma 17;* ＼*0544 212055;* ⊕ *07.30–12.30 & 15.30–19.00 daily*) obviously isn't near the port at all; under Venetian rule this monastery was relocated from the port inside the city walls, and a new church was built in the 1500s. The gloriously ornate façade, one of the final flings of the Baroque and the favourite address of Ravenna's pigeons, was added in the 1780s. Inside are some equally fancy *pietra dura* chapel altars, an 11th-century Venetian relief of the Virgin called the *Madonna Greca*, and a prize relic, claimed as one of the urns from the wedding at Cana – it's really a 2nd-century AD porphyry vase from Alexandria.

The church's grand cloister, with the elegant early Renaissance Loggia Lombardesca facing the Giardino Pubblico behind it, houses **MAR**, the **Museo d'Arte della Città di Ravenna** [306 D5] (*Via Roma 13;* ＼ *0544 482487;* w *mar. ra.it;* ⊕ *10.00–noon Mon, Wed & Fri, 10.00–noon & 15.00–17.00 Tue & Thu; €6*), holding mostly Romagnolo artists from the Middle Ages to the 1700s. Still, the works that stand out are mostly by outsiders: paintings of the Sienese Taddeo di Bartolo and Matteo di Giovanni, a *Crucifixion* by Antonio Vivarini, and Tullio Lombardo's *funeral statue of Guidarello Guidarelli*, a 15-year-old who died at Imola fighting for Cesare Borgia. From the late Renaissance and Baroque, there are the works of local painters Luca Longhi and his daughter Barbara (*St Catherine*, really a self-portrait), Guercino's *San Romualdo*, full of operatic gesture, the Florentine Cecco Bravo's *Apollo and Daphne*, and some remarkable, almost three-dimensional compositions in chiaroscuro by a little-known late Baroque painter from Cattolica, Cesare Pronti.

The museum has been expanded considerably of late, with an important collection of modern art. It also hosts some impressive special exhibitions; check the website.

Further up Via Roma are the imposing remains of the 6th-century building traditionally called the **Palace of Theodoric** [306 C4] (📞 0544 543724; ⏰ 08.30–13.30 *Thu–Sat & 1st Sun of month; admission free*) It doesn't look anything like the *Palatium* in the mosaics of Sant'Apollinare, just next door, and the most recent judgement says it was really only the monumental narthex of a lost church; others have speculated that it was a later governmental building of some sort, or even the palace of the Byzantine exarchs. Inside there is a display of mosaic fragments discovered while excavating the area.

SANT'APOLLINARE NUOVO [306 C4] (*Via Roma 52;* 📞 0544 541688; ⏰ *Mar–Oct 09.00–19.00 daily, Nov–Feb 10.00–17.00 daily; €9.50 joint ticket with San Vitale, Mausoleum of Galla Placidia, Museo Arcivescovile & Neonian Baptistry*) After those of San Vitale, the mosaics of this 6th-century church are the finest in Ravenna. Theodoric began this as an Arian church, perhaps his own palace chapel, and after the Byzantine conquest and the suppression of Arianism it was rededicated to St Martin. The present name comes from the 9th century, when the remains of Sant'Apollinare were moved here from the 'old' Sant'Apollinare, in Classe. The tall, cylindrical **campanile**, in the style that is the trademark of Ravenna's churches, was added in the 10th century. Unlike San Vitale, Sant'Apollinare was built in the basilican form, with a long nave and side aisles. The two rows of Greek marble columns were probably recycled from an ancient temple. Above them, on walls that lean outwards rather dangerously, are the **mosaics**, begun under Theodoric and completed by the Byzantines, on panels that stretch the length of the church.

On the left, by the door, you see the *City of Classe*, with ships in the protected harbour between twin beacons, and the monuments of the city rearing up behind its walls. On the right, among the monuments of Ravenna, is the *Palatium*, Theodoric's royal palace. The curtains in the archways of the palace replace mosaics of Gothic notables and probably Theodoric himself, in the empty space at the centre, all effaced by the Byzantines – look closely and you'll still see some bit of hands and arms left on the columns.

Beyond these two urban scenes are *processions of martyrs* bearing crowns: 22 ladies on the left side, 26 men on the right; the purpose of the black Greek letters on their togas is an utter mystery. The female procession is led by colourful, remarkable portraits of the *Magi* (officially enrolled as Saints of the Church, according to the inscription above), offering their gifts to the enthroned Virgin Mary. Above these panels, more mosaics on both sides portray Old Testament prophets and doctors of the Church, as well as a series of scenes from the life of Jesus. These mosaics, smaller and not as well executed, are from Theodoric's time.

SAN GIOVANNI EVANGELISTA [306 C3] (*Via Carducci 10;* 📞 0544 212640; ⏰ 08.00–noon & 14.30–19.00 daily*) There is yet another leaning tower – almost as tipsy as the Torre Pubblico – nearby on Viale Carducci, two streets up from the railway station. This is the 12th-century campanile of San Giovanni Evangelista, a much-altered church that was begun by Galla Placidia in AD425 and is thus the oldest

church in Emilia-Romagna; she'd made a vow to the saint to build it if she was saved during her shipwreck off Ephesus, and John came through. Various reconstructions, and bombings in World War II, have seen to it that nothing is left of the original mosaics. Without them though, we can appreciate something of this architecture in its elegant, almost Scandinavian clarity and simplicity.

Even more than Ravenna's other monuments, this church has had to fight constantly against sinking into the marshy ground; the present pavement covers several earlier ones, and in the 1700s the entire church was disassembled and raised about 2m. The bombings destroyed the apse and the façade, but some recovered parts of the 13th-century **mosaic floor** – with primitive scenes of the Fourth Crusade, a unicorn, a fork-tailed mermaid (page 157) and some fantastical monsters – can be seen in the aisles.

ARIAN BAPTISTRY [306 C3] (*Vicolo degli Ariani 1;* ℡ *0544 543724;* ⊕ *May–Oct 08.30–19.30 daily, Nov–Apr 08.30–16.30 daily; €1*) Just off Via Roma, in a little square between Via Paolo Costa and Via Armando Diaz, the Arian Baptistry recalls church struggles of the 5th century. Theodoric and his Ostrogoths, like most of the Germanic peoples, adhered to the Arian 'heresy', a doctrine that mixed in elements of pagan religion and was condemned by more orthodox Christians as denying the absolute divinity of Christ. Like all heresies, this one is really the story of a political struggle, between Germans and native Italians, and between the Gothic kings and the emperor in Constantinople. Unlike Justinian, a relentless persecutor, the Goths tolerated both faiths. The Arian Baptistry preserves a fine **mosaic ceiling**, with the 12 Apostles arranged around a scene of the Baptism of Jesus. Jesus here is pictured nude, something the orthodox would never have allowed; the old man with the palm branch, across from John the Baptist, represents the River Jordan.

The baptistry belonged to the adjacent **Santo Spirito** church [306 C3] (rebuilt in the 16th century), once the Arian cathedral, while the Athenasians (orthodox) worshipped at what is now the Duomo of Ravenna. Little of the original Santo Spirito is left beyond the columns and capitals and a 6th-century ambone, and you can't get in anyhow; it currently belongs to a reclusive chapter of Eastern Orthodox monks.

MAUSOLEUM OF THEODORIC [306 D1] (*Via delle Industrie;* ℡ *0544 543724;* ⊕ *May–Oct 08.30–19.00 daily, Nov–Mar 08.30–16.00 daily; €4, or €10 joint ticket with Sant'Apollinare in Classe & Museo Nazionale*) For the real flavour of the days of the Roman twilight, nothing can beat this compellingly strange, refined yet half-barbaric building outside the old city. To reach it, head north on Via Roma, past the medieval gate called the Porta Serrata [306 C2], and turn right on the Circonvallazione alla Rotonda dei Goti. This will take you past the Venetian fortress called the **Rocca di Brancaleone** [306 C2], which was partially demolished under papal rule and is now part of a city park.

The Mausoleum of Theodoric is across the tracks in another small park on Via delle Industrie, near the port. It is totally unlike the other buildings Theodoric built in Ravenna: massive and solid, completely lacking in carved decoration and mosaics, yet quite sophisticated in its design – it is one of the few buildings in Italy designed according to the geometrically complex form of the pentagon, which is doubled to make the Mausoleum ten-sided. Some clues in the architecture have led to speculation that the architect came from Syria, but still it may have been an attempt by Theodoric, who built it before he died, to create a specifically 'Gothic' architecture.

The Mausoleum, which in the Middle Ages did service as a church, has two floors. Downstairs there is a cross-shaped chamber of unknown purpose. The second story, also decagonal though slightly smaller, contains the porphyry sarcophagus, now empty. It is a comment on the times that scholars believe this was a recycled bathtub from a Roman palace. Theodoric was hardly broke, though; he could afford to bring the stone for his tomb over from Istria – and note the roof, a single slab of stone weighing over 250 tonnes. No-one has yet explained how the Goths brought it here and raised it – or why. See also box, pages 322–3.

SOUTH OF THE CITY In the southern suburbs at Classe is the third of the great monuments of Ravenna's golden age, Sant'Apollinare in Classe. Most local trains towards Rimini stop at Classe, or take bus 4 from the train station or Via Roma.

If the children were attentive and well behaved through Ravenna's churches and museums, there are also two very special expensive treats in the area.

Basilica di Sant'Apollinare in Classe [map, pages 268–9] (*8km southeast on the SS309;* ✎ *0544 543724;* ⊕ *08.30–19.30 Mon–Sat, 13.00–19.30 Sun; €5, or €10 joint ticket with the Museo Nazionale & Mausoleum of Theodoric*) Sant'Apollinare in Classe, in fact, is literally all that remains of what was once a city in its own right, the leading port of the northern Adriatic. The little River Uniti began to silt up Classe's harbour in classical times; when the port ceased to be a Byzantine military base and the funds for yearly dredging were no longer there, the city's fate was sealed. By the 9th century Classe was abandoned. The people of Ravenna presumably carted away most of its stone, and encroaching forests and swamps erased the last traces. Today the former port is a small modern suburb, 6km from the sea.

Sant'Apollinare, a huge basilica-form church, was completed in AD549, about the same time as San Vitale. It survived its city's disappearance only because of its importance as the burial place of Ravenna's first bishop, martyr and patron saint. The exterior, in plain brick, is another finely proportioned basilica in the Ravenna manner, with another tall cylindrical campanile. Inside it's almost empty. The beautiful Greek marble columns have well-carved capitals in a unique style. Above them are 18th-century portraits of all Ravenna's archbishops, starting with Sant'Apollinare himself – important to this city where for centuries the archbishops defended local autonomy against emperors, exarchs and popes. There are a number of fine Byzantine sarcophagi around the walls, and a bit of the original pavement, recently recovered, near the altar. The altar itself is made of antique fragments, covered by a Byzantine ciborium.

The real attraction, however, is the **mosaics** in the apse (6th–7th-century), a tremendous green- and gold-ground allegorical vision of the *Transfiguration of Christ*, with Sant'Apollinare presiding and three sheep in a flower-strewn springtime landscape, representing Peter, James and John, who were with Christ on Mount Tabor. This was an important scene for early Christians, when Christ revealed his godhood to the three witnesses atop the mountain. Classical religion had been full of theophanies like this one, and it was only natural to give Christianity one too.

If this is his Transfiguration, Christ seems conspicuously absent. You'll have to look closely. From the front of the church, the mosaic seems to be a gigantic eye. The arch of the apse and the bottom of the mosaic make the almond-shaped outline, and the blue circle with the cross on a field of stars the pupil; at the centre of the cross, a tiny, faraway image of Christ is enclosed in a third circle, inducing a kind of tunnel vision into the eye towards him. The entire effect seems to have been quite intentional; once you see it, it's utterly hypnotic.

Above the Transfiguration, later mosaics (10th century) on the arch portray a *Christ in Benediction*, up in the pink pastel clouds with symbols of the Evangelists, and lines of sheep proceeding from the jewel-studded cities of Jerusalem and Bethlehem. Below the Transfiguration, as at San Vitale, there are figures (6th–7th-century) of *Four*

10

The one thing conspicuously missing from the Mausoleum of Theodoric is Theodoric himself. Later Germanic legends said his body had been carried away by Odin's white horse, Fafnir, to join the warrior heroes in Valhalla. The Italians, however, claimed it was a black horse – the Devil himself – who carried the heretic king down to Hell through the crater of Mount Etna.

Modern historians find both these reports somewhat suspicious, and suggest that Theodoric's remains were scattered after Belisarius and his Byzantines captured Ravenna in AD540. But the legends of the great king's demise nicely sum up contemporary feelings towards a ruler that the papers, had there been any, would undoubtedly have called 'controversial' in every lead paragraph.

The break-up of the Western Empire was a time of golden opportunity for a man like Theodoric. Born in AD454 on the Hungarian plains, the son of the Ostrogothic King Theudemir, Theodoric grew up in the court of Byzantium as a diplomatic hostage, kept to ensure the Ostrogoths didn't break their treaty obligations. Roman culture seems to have made little impression on him; he never even learned to read. Back home in AD472, he proved himself a proper Goth by taking his first town (Belgrade) at the age of 18; two years later he was King of the Ostrogoths.

This nation, the most talented and civilised of the Germans, had already created an empire in eastern Europe, and lost it when they were overrun by the Huns. Now, looking for a home, their king allowed the Eastern Emperor Zeno to talk him into moving to Italy, which would be theirs for the taking if they could only do away with Odoacer, a soldier who had demolished the last pretence of imperial unity by declaring himself King of Italy. Theodoric moved his people, more than 100,000 of them, over the Alps in AD488, and defeated Odoacer's army in battle. Odoacer holed up in Ravenna, and Theodoric started a siege of the impregnable city that lasted nearly two years. When Odoacer finally surrendered, Theodoric invited him to a banquet, and there he literally sliced him in half with his sword. 'What, didn't he have any bones?' the Goth laughed.

Not a very promising new ruler, the Italians must have thought. But then the barbarian surprised them by settling down and giving them three decades of the most enlightened rule they had known in centuries. Under Theodoric the

Archbishops of Ravenna, including Ursinus, who began the construction of the basilica. At the ends are later mosaics of the sacrifices of *Abel, Melchizedek* (whose sacrifice in the Old Testament prefigures the Eucharist) and *Abraham*, opposite the Byzantine Emperor *Constantine IV*, bestowing privileges on Ravenna's independent church. Archangels *Gabriel* and *Michael* appear in Byzantine court dress under a pair of palm trees, a symbol of martyrdom for early Christians, as well as an intimation of Paradise.

Parco Archeologico di Classe [map, pages 268–9] (*Via Marabina 7;* ☎ *0544 478100;* w *parcoarcheologicodiclasse.it;* ⏰ *usually 10.00–18.00 Sat–Sun but check the website before you go; €5, guided tours available*) Excavations at this site, 2km from Sant'Apollinare along the road to Ravenna, began only in 1961, and continue today. This was the port area of Classe, and they have excavated an area of commercial buildings in it. There's an itinerary that gives a good idea of its layout. Nothing spectacular to see here, but it's a real lesson in archaeology.

Elsewhere around Classe there's little to see: bits of Roman road, some foundations. Most of the city still awaits exploration. Sant'Apollinare itself is near

Kingdom of Italy became a bulwark of strength and stability. Commerce and culture, which had languished in the decadence of the late Empire, both made impressive recoveries. Roads and bridges were repaired, and cities revived.

Theodoric worked sincerely to get Germans and Romans to live together in peace, despite Gothic disdain and deep-seated Italian bigotry. An Arian Christian, like all the Goths, he practised a policy few Christians would ever have dreamed of: religious toleration and equality. To help run his government, he selected the finest men of the age from the Roman nobility, the poets Symmachus and Cassiodorus and the philosopher Boethius, who became his chief minister and most trusted adviser.

Not that Theodoric was a friend to the great landowners of the senatorial class. He treated these magnates, who owned nearly everything, and who had bled the Roman economy into penury, to something they had never before experienced – paying taxes. And the next time you hear silly prattle of how the barbarians destroyed Roman culture, think of Theodoric, promulgating a decree to protect the statues and monuments of Rome from the Romans themselves, who were grinding up the marbles for lime and melting down the bronzes for scrap.

Unfortunately for his historical reputation, and for Italy, Theodoric developed a decidedly bitter and paranoid streak in his old age. He did have his reasons. The jealous emperors in Constantinople, along with most of the senatorial class, hated him and never tired of hatching conspiracies against him. Suspecting everyone close to him, he even had Symmachus and Boethius executed in AD525, though he gave the latter enough time in prison to write *The Consolation of Philosophy*.

After Theodoric's death in AD526, court intrigues and the underlying mutual mistrust of Italians and Goths had weakened the kingdom enough to give Eastern Emperor Justinian an opportunity to try to conquer Italy. He did, though he inflicted so much damage on it, while exhausting and gravely weakening the Eastern Empire, that civilisation would need nearly five centuries to recover. The Gothic kingdom remains one of history's might-have-beens. Perhaps it was just a freak in the complex chronicle of a dying world – though there was a hint of a chance that, had it been left in peace a little longer, the Dark Ages in the West might never have happened.

the centre of a huge necropolis with some half-million burials. Some interesting things could turn up here in coming years.

Mirabilandia [map, pages 268–9] (*Savio, just beyond Classe on the SS16 10km south of the city;* w *mirabilandia.it;* ⊕ *generally Apr–Halloween 10.00–sunset; adults €35.90 (€24.90 online); children under 140cm €22.90 (online), children under 100cm free, single evening tickets (available after 17.00) €14.90*) Which destination in historic, sophisticated Emilia-Romagna attracts the most visitors each year? It's Mirabilandia, of course, and by a wide margin. This massive corporate funfair *all'Italiana* is one of the biggest in Europe. It boasts Europe's second-tallest Ferris wheel, the **Eurowheel**, and enough roller coasters to change your children's lives forever. There are musical shows, car shows, magic shows, pirate shows, and on and on. Ice cream and pizzas are never far away.

Attractions are rated 'intense', 'moderate' and 'soft'. Among the first category is 'Europe's biggest horror house', the Wild West **Legends of Dead Town** (*extra €5*). The ancient Mayans contribute **Katun**, Europe's biggest and fastest hanging roller

10

coaster; children who survive that are alternately whooshed up and dropped down smoke-belching 60m-tall **oil towers**, to see who can hold on to lunch the longest.

'Moderate' attractions are manned largely by dinosaurs and Indians. Children can ride the stone-age **Brontocars** or fly with the **Pterodactyls**. Some are sent as sacrifices to the gods of **Raratonga** and their volcano, while the bloody Apache chief Geronimo invites others into his adventure playgrounds. There's lots of water fun, including one ride with aquatic Cadillacs, though you might want to head straight to the queues for **Reset**, where you'll tour the ruins of New York with a laser pistol and score points by zapping post-apocalyptic golems and basilisks. For the less brave, the 'soft' attractions include slightly smaller dinosaurs, the inimitable Arturo the Kangaroo, and a trolley ride through the floral bowers of Bimbopoli.

Mirabilandia is owned by the Spanish Parques Reunidos, Europe's second-largest amusement park corporation, and among its virtues it may be Europe's biggest Disney-free zone. The mascot of Mirabilandia is a pale-bluish aviform named Mike the Mallard who looks like the troubled love child of Daisy Duck and Woody Woodpecker.

Mirabilandia is big business, and keeps a very complex schedule of opening dates. Consult the website before you go – it's in English – for complete details. There's a big discount for buying tickets online, and the basic ticket is good for two days.

Safari Ravenna [map, pages 268–9] (*Via dei Tre Lati in Savio, across from Mirabilandia;* ✎ *0544 690026;* w *safariravenna.it;* ⊕ *Apr–Sep 10.00–15.00 daily & selected days in Mar, Oct & Nov; age 11 & over €25, ages 4–10 €21, under 4s free*) Where one big attraction appears others are sure to follow. This one is a typical safari park with all the stars, from lions to lemurs. If you don't have a car, you can do the circuit on the *trenino* (tourist train). There's also a pedestrian trail, a reptile house and a petting farm for the kids, the Fattoria.

THE LIDOS [map, pages 268–9] It's Ravenna's strange destiny to be at once a major cultural destination, a modern industrial town and a beach resort. The string of **lidos** along its shore isn't St Tropez; they're mostly for families from the other northern cities, with a few Russians and Czechs thrown in. Whatever you plan to do, remember that Ravenna's coast has a booming population of world-class mosquitoes; guard yourself and your hotel room accordingly.

The entire coast between Casal Borsetti and the Lido di Savio is part of greater Ravenna, with a string of small resorts backed by protected pine woods and wetlands, some of them part of the Parco Regionale del Po. **Casal Borsetti** is a fishing village grown into a sleepy beach resort. Nearby are small nature reserves at Punta Alberete and Valle Mandriole, two of the last surviving freshwater swamps in the area and popular with birdwatchers. They have nature trails marked with info on local flora and fauna.

Marina Romea and **Porto Corsini** share an immense expanse of white sand, and have become built up with hotels, camping sites and holiday villages – even though bathers have to walk a 300m path through the pines to get to the beach. Porto Corsini faces the ship channel, carrying Ravenna's industry into the Adriatic, with the similar **Marina di Ravenna** on the other side, with another long, broad beach. Both of these are relaxed port suburbs where freighters rub noses with sailboats; a 2-minute ride on a weary old *traghetto* (car ferry) connects the two. Just up the canal from here are Ravenna's docks, the steelworks and the many chemical plants, but the beaches and the water are clean enough and attract big crowds.

The closest lido to Ravenna is **Lido Adriano**, built up quickly and not necessarily well, but it is popular with Russians and other foreign visitors. Just to the south of it is a relatively undeveloped hideaway with a good free beach, **Lido di Dante**.

Behind the beaches stretches a big pine forest, the **Pineta di San Vitale**, planted by the Romans to supply masts for their navy. On Via Baiona, between Porto Corsini and Ravenna, you can visit the **Capanno di Garibaldi** (m *0544 212006;* ⊕ *Mar–Oct 09.30–12.30 & 14.30–18.00 Tue–Thu, Sat–Sun; admission free*), the thatched hut where the patriot hid from the Austrians on his flight from Rome in 1849. It has been fitted out as a shrine to Garibaldi. Garibaldi had been trying to reach Venice, the only place in Italy still free after the collapse of the revolutionary movements that began in 1848. While hiding in the marshes with Austrian troops on his trail, he lost his pregnant wife, Anita, the brave Brazilian woman who fought beside him through his battles on two continents; when she died, the Austrians were so close he didn't have time to bury her. There's a monument to Anita along the SS309.

South of Ravenna the string of lidos is broken by a natural area, part of the Parco Regionale that includes, across the rail line from Sant'Apollinare in Classe, another vast and lovely pine grove, the **Pineta di Classe**, this one too originally planted by the Roman navy; just south of Classe, at Fossa Ghiaia, a slightly dodgy road leads east to a completely unspoiled expanse of dunes and wetlands on the shore, called **Foce Bevano**.

ACTIVITIES For all the industry around, the water on the lidos is in pretty good shape. All of them have earned European Blue Flag status in recent years. Swimming, however, is not allowed near the mouths of the rivers and canals. It isn't all lidos; most of the areas have a **free beach** (*spiaggia libera*); there are good ones in Casal Borsetti, on the protected areas at Lido di Classe and the dunes at Porto Corsini.

As for **watersports**, surfing and windsurfing are possible here. Beach volleyball and beach soccer are also very popular. Boats are available for deep-sea fishing, and canoes and mountain bikes for exploring the wetlands. Plenty of stables hire out **horses** for rides through the pine woods and nature reserves behind the beaches. Maria Romea may be the best-equipped lido for all of these activities, which are usually arranged by the hotels. The Maria Romea Pro Loco office (w *prolocomarinaromea.it*) has listings for these.

Lido di Dante is a popular spot for scuba-diving, thanks largely to the **Piattaforma Paguro**. This gas drilling platform blew up in 1965 and sank to the bottom at just the right depth, where it has become a proper reef, a residence of choice for all the molluscs and bivalves in the area and the whole ecosystem of sea creatures that has grown up around them; the area is now a protected reserve (*for info on diving tours* m *0544 531 140;* w *associazionepaguro.org*).

If you would rather scale a sheer concrete tower than stare at mosaics or sit on beaches, a local group called the Ravenna Gravity Fighters (m *340 146 5594;* w *ravennagravityfighters.it*) can offer Italy's tallest *arrampicata* (climbing tower), the 37m **La Torre** [306 A3].

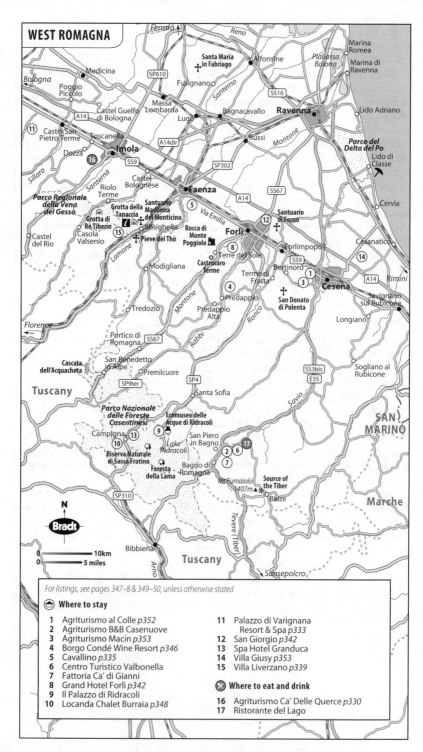

WEST ROMAGNA

Ferrara

Reno

Marina
Romea

Marina di
Ravenna

Santa Maria
in Fabriago

Alfonsine

Piallassa
Baiona

Medicina

SP610

Fusignano

Santerno

SS16

Bologna

Poggio
Piccolo

Massa
Lombarda

Lugo

Bagnacavallo

Ravenna

Lido Adriano

Castel Guelfo
di Bologna

A14

Castel San
Pietro Terme

Toscanella

Russi

Montone

Parco del
Delta del Po

Lido di
Classe

Imola

A14dir

Dozza

16

SS9

SP302

Sillaro

Castel
Bolognese

Faenza

A14

SS67

Cervia

Riolo
Terme

Santerno

Parco Regionale
della Vena
del Gesso

Grotta della
Tanaccia

Santuario
Madonna
del Monticino

SS67

5

Via Emilia

Santuario
di Forno

12

Grotta di
Re Tiberio

15

Brisighella

Forlì

Casola
Valsenio

Pieve del Thò

Rocca di
Monte
Poggiolo

Forlimpopoli

Cesenatico

Castel
del Rio

Lamone

Modigliana

Terre del Sole

8

SS9

14

Castrocaro
Terme

Bertinoro

A14

Rimini

Montone

Terme di
Fratta

1

3

Cesena

4

Predappio

San Donato
di Polenta

Savignano
sul Rubicone

Tredozio

Predappio
Alta

Ronco

Longiano

Florence

Rabbi

Portico di
Romagna

SS67

Cascata
dell'Acquacheta

San Benedetto
in Alpe

Premilcuore

SS3bis

Sogliano al
Rubicone

SP9ter

SP4

Santa Sofia

E35

SAN
MARINO

Tuscany

Savio

Parco Nazionale
delle Foreste
Casentinesi

Ecomuseo delle
Acque di Ridracoli

Campigna

9

13

Lake
Ridracoli

San Piero
in Bagno

17

10

2

6

Riserva Naturale
di Sasso Fratino

Foresta
della Lama

7

Bagno di
Romagna

N

Mt Fumaiolo
1407m

Source of
the Tiber

Bradt

Balze

Marche

SP310

Tevere (Tiber)

Bibbiena

Tuscany

0   10km
0   5 miles

Arno

Sansepolcro

For listings, see pages 347–8 & 349–50, unless otherwise stated

Where to stay

1 Agriturismo al Colle *p352*
2 Agriturismo B&B Casenuove
3 Agriturismo Macín *p353*
4 Borgo Condé Wine Resort *p346*
5 Cavallino *p335*
6 Centro Turistico Valbonella
7 Fattoria Ca' di Gianni
8 Grand Hotel Forlì *p342*
9 Il Palazzo di Ridracoli
10 Locanda Chalet Burraia *p348*

11 Palazzo di Varignana
   Resort & Spa *p333*
12 San Giorgio *p342*
13 Spa Hotel Granduca
14 Villa Giusy *p353*
15 Villa Liverzano *p339*

Where to eat and drink

16 Agriturismo Ca' Delle Querce *p330*
17 Ristorante del Lago

11

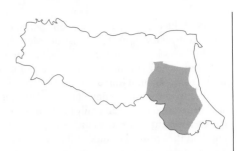

The Heart of Romagna

In a landscape apparently designed by computer, east of Bologna the big towns pop up with precise regularity along the relentlessly straight Via Emilia. They all have their attractions: fine restaurants in Imola, ceramics in Faenza, Forlì's museum and Mussolini showpieces, and Cesena's Rocca and remarkable library. But this is the place for getting off the straight and narrow – a right turn just about anywhere will take you into a part of the Apennines that is one of this region's hidden treasures, with hill towns such as Brisighella which are destinations in themselves, and little corners of Tuscany and the Marche that got away. The whole point of the Via Emilia, of course, is for all the odd bits and pieces of northern Italy to roll down to Rimini, that singular town of Fellini, ghosts and Malatesta weirdness on Italy's biggest, boisterous riviera.

IMOLA

This proud little city is best known for good food and motor racing, but when you're there Imola will take pains to remind you that it, too, is an art town.

HISTORY Imola grew up on either side of the Via Aemilia as the Roman Forum Cornelii, although it eventually became better known as Imulae ('down there') which is exactly how it appears from the surrounding hills. If the Roman name didn't stick, the street plan did, and Imola's *centro storico* is still a fairly tidy grid. This is surprising, since the town's history suffered a rude interruption: destroyed by the Lombards, it revived only gradually, around the fortified compound of its bishops. After 1300 it was in the grasp of various *signori*, often from branches of Milan's Visconti family, while engaging in the usual eternal wars against its neighbours.

Another Milanese, Caterina Sforza, author of a book on cosmetics and one of the memorable viragos of the Renaissance, married Pope Sixtus IV's nephew Girolamo Riario, and the two became rulers in Imola and Forlì after 1473, running the town at the height of its modest Renaissance glory. Riario liked to stick his nose in the

THE ROADS OF ROMAGNA

Founded in 2000, the Strada della Romagna (*headquartered at Piazza del Popolo 31, Faenza;* \0546 691298; **w** *stradadellaromagna.it;* ⊕ *08.00–13.00 Tue & Thu*) promotes independent visits, especially for motorists, offering a range of wine-and-dine packages of two or three nights, including accommodation, meals, museum, and tasting experiences along the way. Check the listing in English on its website.

affairs of the big boys, and eventually got burned for it. He took part in the failed Pazzi conspiracy against Lorenzo de' Medici, and Lorenzo was probably behind Riario's assassination in a revolt of 1488, after which Caterina was imprisoned.

Caterina had already proved her taste for politics and war four years earlier, leading an army into Rome after Sixtus's death and seizing Castel Sant'Angelo in an attempt to ensure that a pope favourable to their interests would be elected. Now she managed to escape and rally her supporters (when they pointed out that her six children were in the hands of their enemies, Caterina reportedly hoisted up her skirts and told the crowd she could still make plenty more). She eventually reconquered all her lands, and enjoyed a good bloody Renaissance vengeance on all her enemies.

However, despite putting up a fierce resistance, she was not able to save her state when Cesare Borgia attacked it in 1499. Caterina got another spell in prison, and then went to live quietly in Florence, where she married a Medici and became the mother of a worthy son, the famous mercenary captain Giovanni of the Black Bands. As for Cesare, after the death of his father, Pope Alexander VI, his little empire went up in smoke, and Imola passed under direct papal rule.

After Italian unification, Imola distinguished itself as the heart and soul of the Socialist movement. Its radical population elected Italy's first Socialist city government in 1889, seven years after sending the first Socialist deputy to parliament. This was Andrea Costa, a friend of the Russian anarchist revolutionary Bakunin; the two had gone to jail together after the failed revolt of 1874 in Bologna. Though still one of the most solidly left-wing towns in Italy, Imola is best known for its race track.

GETTING THERE AND AWAY Between Bologna and Rimini trains are fast, frequent and occasionally packed, particularly in August. Imola's station is at Piazzale Marabini 7; the bus station is on Viale Costa, a block south of the railway station (*see* w *tper.it for schedules*). For a taxi, call ☎ 0542 28122 or ☎ 0542 29746.

Driving between Bologna and the coast you have a choice between the A14 to Rimini (from which the A14 dir branches off near Imola for Ravenna) or the slow, numbingly straight and sometimes nerve-racking SS9/Via Emilia.

TOURIST INFORMATION
🛈 Via Emilia 135, Galleria del Centro Cittadino; ☎ 0542 602207; w visitareimola.it; ⏰ 08.30–13.00 Mon–Fri, 15.00–18.00 Tue, 08.30–12.30 Sat

---

SAVING MONEY IN ROMAGNA

ROMAGNA VISIT CARD (w *romagnavisitcard.it; €17*) Save up to €300 with the Romagna Visit Card, which offers free or discounted admission to more than 130 museums and other sites in the provinces of Forlì-Cesena, Ravenna and Rimini. The card includes a map, travel options, food and wine and other suggestions; purchase it online and at tourist offices.

START ROMAGNA SMARTPASS (☎ *0541 300811;* w *startromagna.it (in English); prices from €1.30, 3-day pass €11, 7-day pass €22*) START Romagna runs all the city and country buses in Ravenna, Forlì-Cesena and Rimini provinces. Its SmartPass is priced by zone and allows unlimited travel on the network, in addition to discounts on some sights and entertainment.

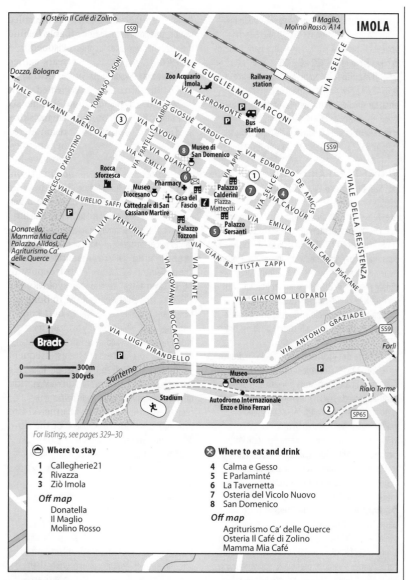

For listings, see pages 329–30

Where to stay

1 Callegherie21
2 Rivazza
3 Zió Imola

Off map
Donatella
Il Maglio
Molino Rosso

Where to eat and drink

4 Calma e Gesso
5 E Parlaminté
6 La Tavernetta
7 Osteria del Vicolo Nuovo
8 San Domenico

Off map
Agriturismo Ca' delle Querce
Osteria Il Café di Zolino
Mamma Mia Café

WHERE TO STAY *Map, above*

Callegherie21 (3 rooms) Via Callegherie 21; m 348 261 4837; w callegherie21.it. These central boutique B&B suites in an 18th-century building run by the owners of the San Domenico restaurant offer an ideal place to sleep off a perfect meal. Rooms are furnished with wooden beams, antiques & Frette linens. Private parking available; extremely good buffet b/fast inc. **€€€€**

Donatella (127 rooms) Via Gioacchino Rossini 25; 0542 680800; w imolahotel.it. Just west of the centre, hotel with all the mod cons, spa & 11th-floor rooftop pool, plus a pizzeria/ restaurant (**€€€–€€€€**) specialising in seafood. Free parking, fibre-optic Wi-Fi; b/fast inc. **€€€€**

Molino Rosso (120 rooms) Via Statale Selice 49; 0542 63111; w molinorosso.it. Outside the centre on the road to the A14, the Molino offers quiet, well-equipped rooms in various buildings. There's a good restaurant (€€€), plus beach volleyball, football pitch, 3 pools in a park, billiards & bikes for guests. €€€–€€€€

🏠 **Il Maglio** (39 rooms) Via Statale Selice 26/a; ☎ 0542 642299; w hotelilmaglio.it. In the same area, far smaller but modern & comfortable, with a good restaurant. B/fast inc. €€€

🏠 **Ziò Imola** (37 rooms) Viale Nardozzi 14; ☎ 0542 35274; w hotelzioimola.com. On a quiet

street close to the centre, a 13min walk from the station, this hotel in a handsome building from the 1920s has free bikes for guests. Buffet b/fast inc. €€€

🏠 **Rivazza** (8 rooms) Via dei Colli 39; ☎ 0542 26052; w hotelrivazza.it. Sleep in the middle of the race track in this no-frills 2-star hotel with en-suite rooms, friendly owner, Wi-Fi, free parking & good restaurant (€€) patronised by locals. €€

✕ **WHERE TO EAT AND DRINK** *Map, page 329, unless otherwise stated*

✕ **San Domenico** Via G. Sacchi 1; ☎ 0542 29000; w sandomenico.it; ⊕ closed Mon, Sun eve, Jun–Jul closed all day Sun. Gastronomes have been flocking to this temple of Italian culinary traditions since 1970. Expect deliciously fresh, seasonal dishes, prepared with the wisest & most delicate of touches, served in a slightly dated dining room or in the new summer garden, with an exquisite credit-card-shattering wine list. Tasting menus available, including an 11-course seafood menu (€170) & a 5-course business lunch (€60). €€€€€

✕ **Osteria del Vicolo Nuovo** Vicolo Coldronchi 6; ☎ 0542 32552; w vicolonuovo.it; ⊕ closed Sun, Mon. In a 17th-century palazzo, this Slow Food-approved osteria, run by Ambra (sommelier) & Rosa (chef) & their all-female staff, serves traditional dishes updated to modern tastes: wickedly good homemade pasta (gnocchi with porcini, tortellini with asparagus), rabbit roasted in Albana di Romagna wine, an assortment of vegetarian dishes, & delicious cheeses. W/day lunch (meat, fish or vegetarian) €13. €€€

✕ **Agriturismo Ca' delle Querce** [map, page 326] Via Ponticelli Pieve 30/b, Ponticelli, Malalbergo; ☎ 0542 690176; ⊕ closed Tue. 10km southwest of Imola, a jovial farm restaurant with tables under a bamboo pergola & a playground for the kids: homemade pasta with lots of grilled meats for *secondi*. €€

✕ **E Parlamintè** Via G Mameli 33; ☎ 0542 30144; w eparlaminte.com; ⊕ closed Mon, & Sun eve, May–Aug closed all day Sun. An old favourite in Imola, cheerful & family-run, where everyone comes to eat *passatelli in brodo* or *baccalà* while discussing affairs of the day – the name means 'the parliament'. €€

✕ **La Tavernetta** Via Tito Speri 6; ☎ 0542 22339; w latavernetta-ristorante.it; ⊕ closed Mon & Aug. Another very popular, very old-fashioned spot, offering plenty to choose from including seafood. Fixed-price fish menus start at €20, w/day work lunches at €13. €€

✕ **Osteria Il Cafè di Zolino** Via Luigi Tinti 1; ☎ 0542 43434; 🟦; ⊕ eves only, closed Mon. Informal place hidden away northwest of the centre, serving Romagnolo cuisine just like mamma's; don't miss the *piadine*. €€

✕ **Calma e Gesso** Via Venezia 7; ☎ 0542 850709; ⊕ closed Sun. Best bet in the centre for a quick *piadina* filled with ham, cheese & rocket, or a daily special from the chalkboard. €

☕ **Mamma Mia Café** Via Puccini 50; m 338 805 0061; w mammamiacafeimola.com; ⊕ 07.00–20.00 Sun–Wed, 06.00–noon Thu, 06.00–midnight Fri, 06.00–21.00 Sat. The hip place in Imola for b/fast, with decadent pastries (inc gluten-free), gourmet panini, wines, craft beers & nibbles. €

WHAT TO SEE AND DO In the heart of Imola's *centro storico*, the porticoed **Piazza Matteotti** probably occupies the site of the Roman forum. Its **Palazzo Sersanti** was built for Girolamo Riario during the town's heyday in 1480 by an architect named Giorgio Fiorentino. The stretch of Via Emilia west of the piazza contains some strangely clashing relics of Imola's past, from the gosh-awful Mussolinian **Casa del Fascio** (1936) to the **Farmacia dell'Ospedale** under the porticoes at number 95. This lovely pharmacy, still in business and run by the *comune*, hasn't changed much since opening in 1766, with its majolica medicine jars and a beautiful vaulted and frescoed ceiling.

Northeast of Piazza Matteotti, on Via Cavour, the **Palazzo Calderini** is the very picture of a quattrocento Florentine palace, with a rusticated ground floor, counterpoised by a graceful second storey with characteristic Florentine double windows.

COMBINED TICKET

A **combined museum ticket** (€8) is available for the Rocca Sforzesca, Palazzo Tozzoni and Museo San Domenico and can be purchased at any of those sites.

Palazzo Tozzoni (*Via Garibaldi 18;*
\ *0542 602609;* w *museiciviciimola.*
it; ⊕ *15.00–19.00 Sat, 10.00–13.00 & 15.00–19.00 Sun, Tue–Fri mornings by request; €4, or €8 joint ticket with Rocca Sforzesca & Museo San Domenico*) Palazzo Tozzoni offers a rare chance to see how a prominent family lived in the same place for 500 years. Their two older houses were combined to form a lavish rococo palace in 1738, conserving original furnishings and lots of ornate stucco and gilding, along with the family's paintings, books, coins and archaeological finds, down to the enormous mortar and pestle in the kitchen and bottles of wine from the 1860s in the cellar.

Cattedrale di San Cassiano Martire (*Piazza Duomo 10, just north of Palazzo Tozzoni;* \ *0542 22146;* ⊕ *09.00–17.00 Sun*) Imola's Romanesque cathedral was falling over in the late 18th century, when it was completely rebuilt. Inside you can pay your respects at the tomb of Imola's patron, San Cassiano, a 3rd-century schoolteacher whose martyrdom was particularly unpleasant: he was stabbed with the pens of his pagan students.

Museo Diocesano (\ *0542 25000;* ⊕ *09.00–noon & 14.00–17.00 Tue & Thu, 09.00–noon Wed, 15.30–18.30 Sat–Sun, closed Aug; admission free*) The Museo Diocesano, in the Bishops' Palace across the piazza from the cathedral, houses a small collection of paintings from Imola's churches, along with medieval illuminated books and Baroque carriages.

Museo San Domenico (*Via Sacchi 4;* \ *0542 602609;* w *museiciviciimola.it;* ⊕ *09.00–13.00 Tue–Fri, 15.00–19.00 Sat, 10.00–13.00 & 15.00–19.00 Sun; adults €4, under 20s free, or €8 joint ticket with Palazzo Tozzoni & Rocca Sforzesca*) Imola's civic museums, housed in the 14th-century convent of San Domenico, have undergone a major facelift. In the **Collezioni d'Arte della Città** are detached frescoes and a painted processional standard from Venice, all from the 1400s; a carved capital of Adam and Eve by Innocenzo da Imola, a *Madonna della Misericordia* attributed (by the Imolesi at least) to Raphael; three paintings by Lavinia Fontana, including a surprising pagan *Scena del Sacrificio*; Ludovico Carracci's busy, gory *Martyrdom of St Ursula*; and drawings by masters of the Bologna school, which are often more appealing than their glossy finished canvas. Local artists of the 19th and 20th centuries include Morandi and de Pisis.

Here too is the **Museo Archeologico Naturalistico G Scarabelli**, named after the local 19th-century scientist who donated his 'cabinet of natural history' to Imola, mostly rocks, minerals and fossils displayed in old-fashioned wood-and-glass cases plus a little archaeology, including an Egyptian mummy.

Rocca Sforzesca (*Piazzale Giovanni dalle Bande Nere;* \ *0542 602609;* w *museiciviciimola.it;* ⊕ *15.00–19.00 Sat, 10.00–13.00 & 15.00–19.00 Sun,*

The Heart of Romagna IMOLA

11

Tue–Fri mornings by request; €4, or €8 joint ticket with Museo San Domenico & Palazzo Tozzoni) Imola's landmark, the Rocca Sforzesca in the southwest corner of the old town, owes its current refined and low-slung appearance to a 15th-century rebuilding by the Duke of Milan, Galeazzo Sforza, although parts of the earlier castle were retained inside the new walls. Though the model for many similar castles throughout the Romagna and beyond, it didn't hold out for long against Cesare Borgia in 1499. Cesare had an expert on fortifications with him, a certain Leonardo da Vinci; he drew a town plan of Imola, made for improving the defences, which is now at Windsor Castle. Once the popes got their hands on the Rocca, it became a prison until 1958. Now restored, it houses a museum of arms, with a notable collection of 16th-century Lombard armour and weapons; another museum contains ceramics from the 14th–19th centuries, discovered during the castle restoration work.

Zoo Acquario Imola (*Via Aspromonte 19, nr the station;* ✆ *0542 628143;* ⓕ; ⏰ *08.30–12.30 Tue–Fri, 09.00–noon Sat–Sun; €8, but under new management; check Facebook page*) An octagonal building (a former gasometer) houses this aquarium with 50 freshwater and seawater tanks, with tropical fish, sharks, snakes and turtles.

Autodromo Internazionale Enzo e Dino Ferrari (*Via Fratelli Rosselli 2, just south of the historic centre;* ✆ *0542 655144;* w *autodromoimola.it;* ⏰ *open in late afternoons for visitors on foot or bike, if there are no events*) Inaugurated in 1953, Imola's racetrack was for many years the site of the San Marino Grand Prix, which always attracted legions of Ferrari fans. Tragically it's also famous for some of the saddest days in motor sport, when Austrian Roland Ratzenberger died on the track on 30 April 1994, followed the next day by three-time world champion Ayrton Senna, who died after hitting a concrete wall at the flat-out Tamburello corner, events that led to improved safety features on the track. Since 2006, however, it's been off the F1 calendar, although the current owners are trying to get it back on. It still hosts competitions, including world superbike championships.

Outside the track is an incredible sculpture made of a dozen red Ferrari F40s launching into the ether, by French sculptor Arman; in the nearby park is a wistful-looking bronze statue of Senna, erected in 2014; he is also remembered inside the track's **Museo Checco Costa** (⏰ *10.00–13.00 & 14.00–18.00 Mon–Fri exc Tue morning, 10.00–18.00 Sat–Sun; €7*), which houses several of his cars. Check website for special night openings.

AROUND IMOLA

CASTEL DEL RIO The small town of Castel del Rio, 25km south of Imola on the SP610, is home to **Palazzo Alidosi**. Scholars argue whether Bramante or Francesco da Sangallo designed this early 16th-century Renaissance castle for the Alidosi family, famous for its courtyard with three fountains. It now houses the municipal government and, on the second floor, the **Museo della Guerra** (m *349 155 0195*; ⏱ *14.00–18.00 Sun; admission free*), with a collection of 2,000 relics and exhibits from the wars of the 20th century. It also houses the **Museo del Castagno** (⏱ *14.00– 18.00 Sun*) dedicated to chestnuts, once a staple food in the region. The same family also commissioned the beautiful **Ponte Alidosi** over the Santerno, a 'donkey back' (*schiena d'asino*) stone bridge, a startling feat of engineering built between 1499 and 1519 in a single 42m arch, rising a steep 19m in the centre, with five rooms (used as prisons) inside it.

DOZZA Caterina Sforza was also the ruler of Dozza, a handsome spindle-shaped medieval hill town 9km west of Imola. She rebuilt the Rocca Malvezzi-Campeggi, an asymmetrical smaller version of Imola's castle with massive towers over a deep moat; the Rocca now houses the regional enoteca. Dozza itself is bright with murals, the result of the wall-painting festival, the Biennale Muro Dipinto, held in September in odd-numbered years since 1960. Sketches for the paintings, and some that have been detached from the walls, are on display in the Rocca.

Getting there and away Take bus 101 from Bologna or Imola to Toscanella, and then bus 147 to Dozza.

 Where to stay, eat and drink Dozza and its hotels are about 40 minutes away from Bologna, putting it in easy range of the capital and Imola.

🏠 **Palazzo di Varignana Resort & Spa** [map, page 326] (90 rooms) Via Ca' Masino, Varignana, 9km west of Dozza; ☎ 051 1993 8300; w palazzodivarignana.com. The setting in the hills is stunning, in a huge, immaculately maintained park reminiscent of Tuscany. The rooms & suites are contemporary, in soothing colours; pricier ones have balconies. Facilities include 5 outdoor & indoor pools, including an infinity lap pool, a panoramic gym, driving range & a remarkable state-of-the-art Varsana spa, with sensory showers, sound bath, bio sauna, you name it. The resort's elegant restaurant, Il Palazzo (⏱ *Thu–Sat eves only*), is located in the centrepiece villa of 1705, with lovely views, but there's also a less formal restaurant/lounge overlooking the pools, & the lights of Bologna. €€€€€

🏠 **Monte del Re** (38 rooms) Via Monte del Re 43; ☎ 0542 678 4000; w montedelre.it. Refined 4-star hotel in a 13th-century Franciscan convent & park in hills just above Dozza. Stylish furnishings, big beds & mod cons keep the rooms from feeling too monkish. Flowers & antiques brighten the public rooms; there's a pool (*May–Sep*) & lounge bar, an enoteca in the former ice cellar with more than 400 labels, & an elegant gourmet restaurant that offers cookery classes. €€€
✗ **Le Bistrot** Via Valsellustra 18; ☎ 0542 672122; w ristorantelebistrot.it; ⏱ closed Tues, Mon & Wed lunch. A pretty garden patio, colourful walls inside, & colourful, light versions of the regional cuisine on the plates – be sure to try the mixed desserts. €€€

What to see and do
Museo della Rocca (*Piazza Rocca Sforzesca*; ☎ *0542 678240*; w *fondazionedozza. it*; ⏱ *10.00–13.30 & 14.30–17.00 Tue–Sat, 10.00–19.30 Sun; adults €5, under 18s free*) In 1529 Pope Clement V granted Dozza's castle to the Malvezzi-Campeggi of Bologna, who converted it in part to a stately residence. When they died out in 1960, it became the property of the *comune*. There is a handsome loggia with finely carved capitals, and some of the rooms contain antiques, tapestries, family portraits, a historic kitchen and paintings by Morandi pupils Norma Mascellani and Carlo Leoni.

Enoteca Regionale Emilia-Romagna (*Piazza Rocca Sforzesca;* ☏ *0542 367700;* w *enotecaemiliaromagna.it;* ⊕ *10.00–13.00 & 15.00–19.30 Tue–Fri, wine bar* ⊕ *15.00–19.00 Sun*) More than a thousand wines from the region wait in the cellars, displayed according to the dishes they accompany best.

CASTEL GUELFO THE STYLE OUTLETS [map, page 326] (*Via del Commercio 4, Castel Guelfo di Bologna;* ☏ *0542 670762;* w *castel-guelfo.thestyleoutlets.it;* ⊕ *10.00–20.00 daily*) Some 14km north of Dozza and comprising 110 shops (including the only chance to buy Bruno Magli shoes near Bologna, where the company was born) is Castel Guelfo The Style Outlets. Free shuttle buses run from the Castel San Pietro Terme train and bus stations, and from Riccione on summer Thursdays.

FAENZA

'Faience ware' was born here in the 1470s with the invention of a new style of majolica. Terracotta would be coated with a solid white glaze using tin oxide, then rapidly, almost impressionistically, laying down coloured pigment decorated with wavy rays and peacock-feather designs in dark blues, oranges and copper greens that stood out boldly when fired. In the following century, the style achieved its peak popularity, when the potters started depicting histories, mythologies and Biblical scenes, making Faenza a household name across Europe. Besides its superb museum of ceramics and studios, the town is an open-air museum of contemporary ceramics, with some 60 pieces adorning the streets and squares.

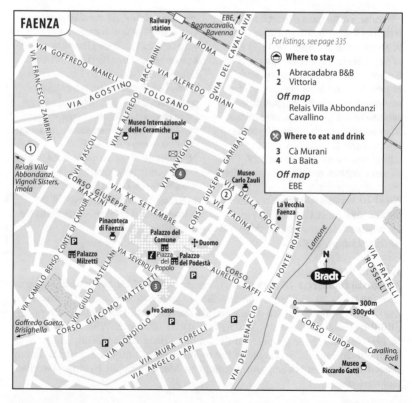

FAENZA

For listings, see page 335

🛏 **Where to stay**
1 Abracadabra B&B
2 Vittoria
Off map
    Relais Villa Abbondanzi
    Cavallino

✕ **Where to eat and drink**
3 Cà Murani
4 La Baita
Off map
    EBE

GETTING THERE AND AWAY Faenza is on the Bologna–Rimini train line, and on the scenic 'Faentina' line linking Faenza and Brisighella to Florence.

TOURIST INFORMATION

 Voltone della Molinella 2; 0546 25231; w prolocofaenza.it; May–Sep 09.30–12.30 & 15.30–18.30 Mon–Sat, 09.30–12.30 Sun, Oct–Apr

09.00–12.30 & 15.30–17.30 Tue–Sat, closed Thu afternoons

WHERE TO STAY *Map, opposite, unless otherwise stated*

Relais Villa Abbondanzi (16 rooms) Via Emilia Ponente 23; 0546 622672; w villa-abbondanzi.com. Rooms in a Neoclassical villa & former barn, just northwest of Faenza by the golf course. The pricier ones, equipped with fireplaces & antiques, are immersed in a leafy park & rose garden. There's a spa, outdoor pool & one of Faenza's best restaurants, the Cinque Cuchiai; check the website for special offers, including a package for cyclists that includes a post-ride head massage. **€€€€–€€€€€**

Vittoria (49 rooms) Corso Garibaldi 23; 0546 21508; w hotel-vittoria.com. Attractive rooms with 19th-century furnishings in a centrally located palazzo with the occasional frescoed

ceiling & an excellent restaurant with 3 designer dining rooms, including a bistro embellished with ceramics. Ceramics lessons are on offer (*from €125*) in conjunction with Matteo Zauli at the Museo Zauli (page 336). B/fast inc. **€€€–€€€€**

Cavallino [map, page 326] (80 rooms) Via Forlivese 185; 0546 634411; w cavallinohotel. it. A short drive east along the SS9: a motel-style inn with parking, garden & restaurant. B/fast inc. **€€–€€€**

Abracadabra B&B (6 rooms) Corso Mazzini 111; m 335 182 6129; w abracadabra-faenza. it. Comfy en-suite rooms with AC in the centre; no b/fast. **€€**

WHERE TO EAT AND DRINK *Map, opposite*

Cà Murani Vicolo Sant'Antonio 7; 0546 88054; closed Thu & lunch exc Sat–Sun. Handsome restaurant with a beamed ceiling, terracotta floors, wooden tables & chairs, & excellent pasta & meat dishes by chef Remo Camurani. **€€€**

La Baita Via Naviglio 25; 0546 21584; w labaitaosteria.it; closed Sun & Mon. Very comfortable old family-run deli & osteria; 1,000 different wines decorate the walls. Great choice

of cheeses & also tasting meals; the homemade *tagliatelle al ragù di Mora romagnola* is delicious. **€€**

EBE Via Mengolina 23; m 334 163 3824; EBE Faenza; 17.00–23.45 Tue–Sun. Contemporary wine & craft beer bar, with platters of *salumi* & cheeses, & little plates (try their *passatelli fritti*) & homemade desserts. Book at w/ends. **€**

WHAT TO SEE AND DO

Piazza del Popolo Faenza has a grand centrepiece in Piazza del Popolo and the adjacent Piazza della Libertà, which are at their lively best during the markets (*Tue, Thu & Sat mornings*). Public buildings with matching loggias face off on the Piazza del Popolo: the medieval **Palazzo del Comune,** originally home of the city's Manfredi rulers, with a façade added in the early 20th century, and the 13th-century **Palazzo del Podestà.** Linking the piazza to Piazzetta Nenni is a lovely double portico from the 1600s, the **Voltone della Molinella,** its ceiling frescoed with grotesques.

Duomo (*Piazza della Libertà;* 0546 664510; *Sep–Jun 07.00–noon & 16.00–18.40, Jul–Aug 07.00–noon & 17.00–18.30*) Faenza's unfinished cathedral (1474–1520) was designed by the great Florentine sculptor Benedetto da Maiano, who was 'loaned' to the Manfredi by their mates the Medici. It has some lovely Renaissance sculpture in its severe white interior, notably in the **Cappella di San Savino,** with a beautiful marble *arca* carved with reliefs by Benedetto, and some ceramic work by another Florentine, Andrea della Robbia, who also made the colourful *tondo* over the altar with the arms of the Manfredi. Also seek out the 16th-century *Pala Bonaccorsi*, by Innocenzo Francucci of Imola. There are also plenty of Baroque touches, including a bizarre flying figure of Death looming out from the pier nearest the altar. The cubic white marble altar, pulpit and bishop's chair added in 2014, however, have not exactly been met with universal approval.

Palazzo Milzetti (*Via Tonducci 15;* \ *0546 26493;* w *palazzomilzetti.jimdo.com;* ⊕ *08.30–18.30 Mon–Sat, 12.30–18.30 Sun; adults €4, under 18s free, also free 1st Sun of month*) Faenza was one of the more forward-looking towns of the Papal States in the 1700s, and it has a number of buildings in the Neoclassical style imported from Enlightenment France. The Palazzo Milzetti is the most exquisite: completed in 1802, it contains fine rooms with painted and stucco decoration influenced by the recently discovered ruins of Pompeii. The esoteric Masonic symbolism would have got the Milzettis in trouble with the Inquisition – but when they built it, Faenza was under the rule of Napoleon.

Pinacoteca di Faenza (*Via Santa Maria dell'Angelo 9;* \ *0546 680251;* w *pinacotecafaenza.racine.ra.it;* ⊕ *Oct–May 10.00–18.00 Sat–Sun, Jun–Sep 10.00–13.00 Tue–Fri, 10.00–13.00 & 15.00–19.00 Sat–Sun; adults €3, under 16s free, free 1st w/end of month*) Founded in 1798, this gallery contains an eclectic collection of finds from Roman times through Donatello (the polychrome wooden *San Gerolamo*) and Antonio Rossellino to paintings by Romagna artists, Victor Hugo and 20th-century works by Morandi, Martini, de Chircio and de Pisis.

Museo Internazionale delle Ceramiche (*Viale Baccarini 19, just north of the centre;* \ *0546 697311;* w *micfaenza.org;* ⊕ *Nov–Mar 10.00–13.30 Tue–Fri, 10.00–17.30 Sat–Sun, Apr–Oct 10.00–19.00 Tue–Sun; adults €8, under 15s free*) Founded in 1908, the MIC houses the world's largest collection of ceramics from around the world, with more than 60,000 works (don't worry – only a tenth are on permanent display). The focus is on 16th- and 17th-century Italian works; the plates from Faenza adorned with giraffe-necked Renaissance ladies were typical nuptial gifts. There are fine Liberty-style pieces by Domenico Baccarini and Francesco Nonni, and an excellent collection of later works, including ceramics by Picasso, Matisse, Chagall and Rouault.

Museo Carlo Zauli (*Via della Croce 6;* \ *0546 22123;* w *museozauli.it;* ⊕ *10.00–13.00 Tue–Sat; €6, under 12s free*) Carlo Zauli, one of Faenza's great ceramic artists, died in 2002, but his son Matteo has made his *bottega* into an art centre, with displays of works by his father and other contemporary ceramicists.

Museo Riccardo Gatti (*Via Pompignoli 4;* ✆ *0546 634 301;* w *ceramicagatti.it;* ⊕ *08.30–12.30 & 15.00–19.00 Mon–Sat; admission free*) Faenza native Riccardo Gatti was an innovative ceramicist who worked with the Futurists; the museum has a permanent collection of his pieces, starting in 1908. The Servadei family, who run the *bottega* and museum, continue to work with contemporary artists.

NORTH OF FAENZA

The plain north of Faenza is a fertile and hard-working agricultural area, and home to a number of big market towns, none of which will detain you for very long. But there are good places to eat, and don't miss Bagnacavallo's unique red wine, Bursôn, made from a vine that the Longanesi family found growing up an oak tree and which later analysis proved was unlike any other known vine. They tried making the grapes (now named *uva longanesi*) into wine, and in 1956 planted a vineyard – the rest is history.

MASSA LOMBARDA This town, 'Italy's fruit-growing capital', gets its name from the Lombard refugees who settled here in the 1250s, fleeing from the depredations of the horrible Ezzelino da Romano of Verona. Its church of **Santa Maria in Fabriago** [map, page 326], 9.5km northeast of town in the middle of nowhere on the SP58, has a 9th-century Ravenna-style round campanile.

LUGO Like the Lugo in Spain and so many other cities across Europe (Lyon, Laon, Loudon, Leiden), this Lugo gets its name from the god Lugh, the Celtic equivalent of Mercury or Hermes. Despite its ancient foundation (Neolithic finds here go back over 5,000 years), Lugo's sights are relatively recent: the 16th-century **Rocca Estense** (now the town hall) with a beautiful hanging garden, and just opposite the **Paviglione**, an arcaded square (1783) that was once the regional market for silkworms. The nearby **Teatro Rossini**, completed by Antonio Galli Bibiena in 1761, is one of the oldest in Romagna.

Near the Rocca in Piazza Baracca is a striking monument (1936) by Domenico Rambelli of Faenza honouring Lugo's most famous son and Italy's greatest World War I flying ace, Francesco Baracca (1888–1918), who shot down 34 Austrian planes before he himself was shot down. The **Museo Baracca** in his birthplace at Via Baracca 65 (✆ *0545 38105;* w *museobaracca.it;* ⊕ *10.00–noon & 16.00–18.00 Tue–Sun; €2.50*) was recently renovated in honour of the centenary of World War I. Amid memorabilia and a flight simulator recreating the wartime landscapes of Italy and Austria, there's a collection of historical postcards, a recording of Gabriele D'Annunzio's address at Baracca's funeral, and the highlight: Baracca's SPAD VII with his prancing pony emblem that recalled his days in the cavalry before becoming a pilot. After his death, his mother presented it to Enzo Ferrari, who made it the car company's symbol.

✗ Where to eat and drink

✗ **Il Trebbio Caffè Ristorante** Largo Relencini 11, Lugo; ✆0545 1891840; w iltrebbo.it; ⊕ closed Mon, & Aug. The seasonal menu changes monthly, but is always delicious & offers a change of pace with dishes such as monkfish with green spinach bread. Excellent choice of wines, & very warm, welcoming service. €€€

✗ **I Tre Fratelli** Via di Giù 56, Lugo; ✆0545 23328; ⊕ closed Mon. Pretty garden & *simpatico* owners, who prepare fresh homemade pasta & *piadine*. Excellent vegetarian choices & pizzas, as well as tasty Romagnolo dishes. €€

BAGNACAVALLO Nobody knows how Bagnacavallo (horse-bath) got its name, but this handsome old town has the distinction of having once been the property of Sir John Hawkwood, the English mercenary captain of the 1300s whose frescoed monument by Uccello is in Florence's cathedral. Its landmarks are the unique elliptical porticoed **Piazza Nuova** of 1758 and the bijou **Teatro Goldoni** (1845) in nearby Piazza della Libertà, a 'mini La Scala'. They have that *je ne sais quoi* that have made them into movie stars – nine Italian films and counting have used them as sets. Just north of the centre, up Via Pieve-Masiera (SP9) is a rare 7th-century church, the **Pieve di San Pietro in Sylvis** (⏰ *15.00–17.00 Sat–Sun, but* ☎ *0545 64363 to check*), a stop along the medieval pilgrims' Via Romea from Ravenna to Rome with apse frescoes (1320) by the Rimini school.

✕ Where to eat and drink

✕ **Osteria di Piazza Nuova** Piazza Nuova 22, Bagnacavallo; ☎ 0545 63647; w osteriadipiazzanuova.it; ⏰ closed Sun. Informal setting, creative cuisine, a good place to try *passatelli* (dumplings made with eggs, breadcrumbs & Parmesan) with baby fava (broad) beans & leeks & saffron cream, & lots of tasty seafood, too. €€

BRISIGHELLA

Brisighella, 12km south of Faenza in the Lamone Valley, is a charming colour-drenched village, a certified 'Slow City' and thermal spa with an unforgettable skyline of sharp crags crowned by the golden towers of the castle and the Torre dell'Orologio, the latter originally a respectable guard tower (1290) with a clock slapped on the front. Brisighella produced much of the clay fired in Faenza's kilns – next to the village you can see the gashes left in the hills by the old quarries. So precious was this cargo that a protected, elevated passageway, the Via degli Asini (road of donkeys), was built through the centre that could be sealed up at either end in case of attack. Be sure to visit at the weekend, when the sights are open.

GETTING THERE AND AWAY Brisighella is a station on the Faenza–Florence train line.

TOURIST INFORMATION

🛈 Piazzetta Porta Gabolo 5; ☎ 0546 81166; w brisighella.org; ⏰ mid-Apr–mid-Oct 09.00–13.00 Mon–Wed, 09.00–13.00 & 16.00–18.00 Thu–Sun, mid-Nov–mid-Apr 09.00–noon Wed & Thu, 09.00–noon & 16.00–18.00 Fri–Sun

WHERE TO STAY

Villa Liverzano [map, page 326] (8 rooms) Via Valloni 47, 5km west of Brisighella; ☏ 0546 80461; **w** liverzano.it. This enchanting hotel surrounded by wooded hills in a villa complex dates back to the 17th century & comes complete with a giant chessboard in the courtyard. The centre of an organic wine & olive estate, owner Marco Montanari has beautifully restored the property to the highest ecological standards, powered entirely with renewables. There are gorgeous views; large rooms furnished with antiques & contemporary art; an Italian garden with century trees, a pool, sauna & hammam; & a bar in the former sacristy of the church. Open Apr–Oct. B/fast inc. €€€€€

Modus Vivendi (8 rooms) Via Roma 5D; **m** 393 880 9684; **w** trattoria-lacasetta.it. A 5min walk from the train station, a hotel attached to an excellent restaurant (€€) & spa. Very helpful owner. HB, spa packages & parking available. B/fast inc. €€€

Relais Varnello (6 rooms) Via Rontana 34; **m** 338 549 8373; **w** varnello.it. West of town in a scenic hillside position near the Regional Park HQ, tranquil rooms & suites, with a garden & outdoor pool. B/fast inc. €€€

La Rocca (15 rooms) Via delle Volte 10; ☏ 0546 81180; **w** albergo-larocca.it. In the heart of Brisighella, this hotel has a panoramic terrace under the Torre dell'Orologio & coddles guests in cream-coloured rooms. The staff are wonderful & there's an excellent restaurant (€€€) under the arcades. B/fast inc. €€–€€€

Locanda La Cavallina (8 rooms) Via Masironi 8; ☏ 0546 80520; **w** locandalacavallina.it. This peaceful, colour-drenched 19th-century post-house just outside the centre has pleasant rooms, most with lovely views; there's also a garden with a panoramic pool; b/fast inc. €€

Tre Colli (8 rooms) Via Gramsci 5/7; ☏ 0546 81147; **w** albergoristorante3colli.it. Pleasant central hotel with basic rooms, among the cheapest in Brisighella. Good restaurant, too, with a €13 lunch menu. B/fast inc. €€

WHERE TO EAT AND DRINK
Brisighella is one of those places where you could go just to eat.

La Grotta Via Metelli 1; ☏ 0546 81488; **w** ristorante-lagrotta.it; ⏰ closed Wed, but in summer open Wed eve. As its name suggests, this historic restaurant is located in a cave, although there's nothing troglodyte about the kitchen: delicious sea & land food, all accompanied by homemade bread & *piadine*. Excellent-value *degustazione* menus; book ahead for the special 15 seafood antipasti (€35). €€€

Locanda La Cavallina Via Masironi 8; ☏ 0546 80520; **w** locandalacavallina.it; ⏰ closed Tue. One of the best places to eat in town; sit on the terrace overlooking the valley & enjoy delicious creative food that concentrates on locally grown produce; €11 lunch menu is a real treat. €€€

Osteria di Guercinoro Piazza Marconi 7; ☏ 0546 80464; **f**; ⏰ closed Tue & lunch exc Sun. Atmospheric from its ancient vaults down to the handwritten menu, & serving a good choice of veg dishes, as well as succulent meats. €€€

Cantina del Bonsignore Via Recuperati 4a; ☏ 0546 81889; **f**; ⏰ closed for lunch Tue, Wed, & dinner Sun. Atmospheric trattoria in the wine cellar of the monsignore's palace, with a few tables out in the lane, serving tasty ricotta & spinach tortelli, jugged boar with berries, & seafood. €€–€€€

WHAT TO SEE AND DO
Museo Civico Giuseppe Ugonia (*Piazza Porta Gabalo;* ☏ *0546 85777;* ⏰ *15 Apr–15 Oct 10.00–noon & 15.30–19.30 Fri–Sun, 16 Oct–14 Apr 15.00–18.30 Sat, 10.00–noon & 15.00–18.30 Sun; combined admission with the Rocca €3*) The small picture collection contains beautiful scenes of Brisighella by local lithographer Giuseppe Ugonia (1881–1944), as well as 18th-century ceramics and other paintings.

Brisighella has been on foodie maps for decades, thanks to its unusual thick green olive oil, the first in Italy to be designated DOP (Denominazione di Origine Protetta). It all has to do with what the French call *terroir*: it's one of the coldest places in Italy where olives grow, but it means the olives ripen more slowly and aren't plagued by the olive fruit-fly pest. The Apennines here are lower than the mountains to the west, allowing warm Tuscan breezes to dissipate the fogs and frost, while the unique chalky soil, poor in clay, maintains the summer heat. The resulting oil is very low in acidity, but richer in fat, giving it an extra-long shelf life. Three varieties grow here in the 12km zone: Nostrana of Brisighella (the bulk); Ghiaccola (the fattiest, sold as Nobil Drupa) with a grassy, peppery taste; and even rarer Orfana (bottled as Orfanella), which is mild and lighter.

In springtime, don't miss Brisighella's other one-off: *carciofo moretto*, long, pointy, reddish-purple artichokes that grow nowhere else in the world. They are tender enough to eat raw, or boiled for a few minutes and served with olive oil and salt, or in salads, or in a hundred other local recipes.

Rocca di Brisighella (*Via Rontana 64;* \ *0546 994415;* ⊕ *May–Sep 10.00–12.30 & 15.00–19.30 Sat–Sun & holidays, Oct–Apr 14.00–17.30 Sat & any day before a holiday, 10.00–noon & 15.00–17.30 Sun & holidays; combined admission with the Museo Civico €3)* The castle, built in 1310 by the Manfredi of Faenza, took its present form under the Venetian occupation of 1503–09. In the first decade of the Wars of Italy, Venice had taken advantage of the confusion to snatch territories from all its neighbours; almost every power in Italy, led by Pope Julius II, ganged up on her in the League of Cambrai of 1508. Venice was lucky to survive and keep most of its empire intact in the nine-year struggle that followed, although all the Venetian possessions in the Romagna were lost.

There are immense views from the towers over Brisighella's tile roofs and across to the **Torre dell'Orologio** (⊕ *not open to the public*) built in the 1200s by Maghinardo Pagani di Susinana, *signore* of Imola and Faenza, who earned a mention in Dante's *Inferno* (Canto XXVI) and *Paradiso* (Canto XIV). It was rebuilt many times since, lastly in 1850 when its unusual 6-hour clock was added.

Pieve del Thò [map, page 326] (*1km south of Brisighella, on the SS302;* ⊕ *mid-Apr–mid-Oct 15.00–18.00 Sun (also mid-Jun–mid-Sep 15.30–17.30 Tue–Sat), mid-Oct–mid-Apr 14.30–16.30; admission free)* Galla Placidia (pages 312–14) is believed to have founded this church on the site of a temple to Jupiter Ammone. Also known as San Giovanni in Ottavo (it's on the eighth mile of the Roman road from Faenza), it was rebuilt sometime between the 8th and 10th centuries, re-using the columns of the ancient Roman temple. Don't miss the altar, with its curious reliefs.

AROUND BRISIGHELLA

This area is a good example of the landscapes you'll see in patches along the Adriatic: not especially high hills, but curiously jagged and jumbled ones, where the back roads boom up and down like roller coasters – country favoured by Italy's masochistic weekend cyclists.

Unless you come straight from Faenza, you'll have to take roads like these (from Brisighella, it's the SP49) to get to **Modigliana**, hidden away in the valley of the

Marenzo. Modigliana has a sweet medieval centre, with lots of bridges and houses overlooking the river; it is entered by way of the **Tribuna**, a grandly picturesque bridge-gate built under Florentine rule. Above the town stands the ruined **Roccaccia** – as its name implies, even the Modiglianesi find this castle more silly than picturesque, with half its tower (divided vertically) fallen away.

In **Tredozio**, 9km south of Modigliana, the 18th-century **Palazzo Fantini** (*Via XX Settembre 91;* \ *0546 943926;* w *palazzofantini.net;* ⊕ *Apr–Sep by appointment;* €5) was once the centre of an estate that raised silkworms and hemp. There's a museum of country life in its outbuildings, as well as an immaculate Italian garden. In summer the owners host a series of concerts in its lovely courtyard.

PARCO REGIONALE DELLA VENA DEL GESSO [map, page 326] Also known as

the Parco Carnè, this park's centrepiece is an enormous vein of gypsum formed 7 million years ago which runs through Italy, but here, unusually, lies near the surface, leaving a striking landscape of outcrops, karstic hollows and dolines amid four river valleys, olive groves, caves and woodlands and ancient quarries slowly returning to nature, home to wolves, porcupines, and a range of bats and rare insects. It encompasses the 18th-century **Santuario Madonna del Monticino** on Brisighella's third hill; the chalk mine behind the church, where numerous fossils were found, is now an open-air geological museum (⊕ *always open*).

The **Centro Visite Ca' Carnè** (*Via Rontana 42;* \ *0546 80628;* w *parchiromagna.it*) has maps of hiking and cycling routes and can arrange visits into the nearby **Grotta della Tanaccia**, where finds going back to the Iron Age were discovered. The park's biggest cave, the **Grotta di Re Tiberio** [map, page 326], is to the west at Borgo Rivola in the pretty spa town of **Riolo Terme** (*book via* m *389 031 2110;* ⊕ *Sat–Sun*). The SP306 continues south of here for **Casola Valsenio**, a village known for its lavender, rare fruit orchards and massive herb garden, the **Giardino delle Erbe** (*Via del Corso 6;* \ *0546 73158;* w *ilgiardinodelleerbe.it;* ⊕ *09.00–noon & 14.00–16.00 Mon–Fri, Apr, May, Sep & Oct also 15.00–17.30 Sat, 10.00–noon & 15.00–17.30 Sun, Jun–Aug also 16.00–18.30 Sat, 10.00–noon & 16.00–18.30 Sun*), along with a shop selling seeds, jams, teas and essential oils.

FORLÌ

The Forum Livii on the Via Aemilia was elided over the centuries into Forlì, a city of more than 100,000 inhabitants which has been around for 2,000 years without calling attention to itself in any way – a rare achievement in Italy, and one that puts it on the list with the likes of Frosinone and Terni as one of the nation's most obscure provincial capitals. The city did produce one outstanding Renaissance painter, Melozzo da Forlì, but the only frescoes he left in town were blasted to bits along with much else in late 1944, when the retreating Germans dug in after the Allies breached the Gothic Line. Benito Mussolini was born in nearby Predappio, and he favoured his home area with monuments and public buildings. Being a Duce, he could get away with doing this on a massive scale, and he left Forlì a fascinating open-air museum of Mussolinian ('rationalist' is the preferred word these days) architecture.

GETTING THERE AND AWAY Forlì's airport [map, page 326], 4km southeast of the centre, has no flights at the time of writing. The train station, east of the centre in Piazza Martiri d'Ungheria, is 40m from the bus station at Via Volta 1.

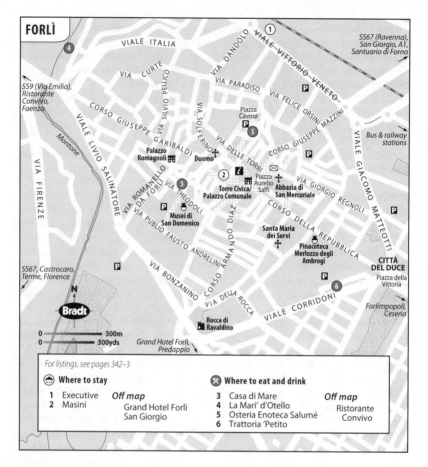

```
FORLÌ
```

VIALE ITALIA

SS67 (Ravenna),
San Giorgio, A1,
Santuario di Forno

VIA CURTE

VIA DANDOLO
VIALE VITTORIO VENETO

VIA PARADISO

CORSO GIUSEPPE GARIBALDI

VIA SILVIO PELLICO

VIA SOLFERINO

VIA DELLE TORRI

SS9 (Via Emilia),
Ristorante
Convivo,
Faenza

CORSO GIUSEPPE MAZZINI

VIALE GIACOMO MATTEOTTI

VIA FELICE ORSINI

Piazza
Cavour

Bus & railway
stations

VIA GIORGIO REGNOLI

Palazzo
Romagnoli

Duomo

Torre Civica/
Palazzo Comunale

Piazza
Aurelio
Saffi

Abbazia di
San Mercuriale

Musei di
San Domenico

CORSO DELLA REPUBBLICA

CITTÀ
DEL DUCE

Piazza della
Vittoria

Santa Maria
dei Servi

Pinacoteca
Merlozzo degli
Ambrogi

Forlimpopoli,
Cesena

SS67, Castrocaro,
Terme, Florence

VIA BONZANINO

VIA DELLA ROCCA

VIALE CORRIDONI

Bradt

```
0          300m
0          300yds
```

Grand Hotel Forlì,
Predappio

Rocca di
Ravaldino

VIA FIRENZE

VIALE LIVIO SALINATORE

Montone

VIA ROMANELLO DA FORLI

VIA THEODOLI

VIA PUBLIO FAUSTO ANDRELINI

CORSO ARMANDO DIAZ

For listings, see pages 342–3

Where to stay

1 Executive
2 Masini

Off map

Grand Hotel Forlì
San Giorgio

Where to eat and drink

3 Casa di Mare
4 La Mari' d'Otello
5 Osteria Enoteca Salumé
6 Trattoria 'Petito

Off map

Ristorante
Convivo

TOURIST INFORMATION

i Piazzetta della Misura 5; ℡ 0543 712435;
w turismoforlivese.it; ⊕ 08.30–13.00 & 15.30–
18.00, closed Wed & Sun afternoons

 WHERE TO STAY *Map, above, unless otherwise stated*

San Giorgio [map, page 326]
(57 rooms) Via Ravegnana 538; ℡ 0543 796699;
w hotelsangiorgioforli.it. Convenient for motorists,
8km east of town, just off Forlì's A14 exit;
contemporary lemony rooms & parquet floors in
the rooms, plus a techno gym & snack bar. Buffet
b/fast inc. **€€€**

Executive (84 rooms) Viale Vittorio Veneto
3; ℡ 0543 36587; w executiveforli.it. A
few minutes' walk from the *centro storico*,
comfortable business hotel, with parquet floors,
UK channels, fitness room & free parking. Buffet
b/fast inc. **€€–€€€**

Grand Hotel Forlì [map, page 326]
(52 rooms) Via del Partigiano 12/bis; ℡ 0543
479586; w grandhotelforli.com. Forlì's most
comfortable hotel, the modern 4-star Grand is just
southwest of the centre towards Castrocaro Terme
(bus 2), & comes with a rooftop terrace & pool,
wellness centre, good restaurant & free parking.
B/fast inc. **€€–€€€**

Masini (51 rooms) Corso Garibaldi 28;
w masinihotel.it. A rare central city hotel, with
good sound-proofing; try to bag a room with a
view on the top (several have balconies). B/fast
inc. **€€–€€€**

✕ WHERE TO EAT AND DRINK *Map, opposite*

✕ **Casa di Mare** Via Francesco Marcolini 29; ✆ 0543 20836; w casadimare.info; ⊕ closed Mon & Dec. Opposite the Museo San Domenico, a hip seafood restaurant that only serves the day's catch from the Adriatic, along with an exceptional choice of wines; €48 *menu degustazione*. €€€

✕ **Ristorante Convivio** Viale Bologna 346; ✆ 0543 934644; w convivioristorante.it; ⊕ closed Sun. A 5min drive west on the SS9, a cheerful place, with creative seafood & meat dishes, & a few vegetarian choices, too. Excellent foie gras & pigeon with porcini mushrooms. €€€

✕ **Trattoria 'Petito** Via Filippo Corridoni 14; ✆ 0543 35784; w trattoriapetito.it; ⊕ closed

Sun. A local favourite at the east end of town, with a cosy atmosphere, friendly staff & a kitchen using top Slow Food ingredients; anchovies from Cantabria, lovely pasta, & good choice of fish & meat *secondi*, & vegetarian choices. €€€

✕ **Osteria Enoteca Salumé** Piazza Cavour 42; ✆ 0543 36400; f; ⊕ closed Sun & Mon. Warm, welcoming place with a wide selection of local wines & seasonal small plates to choose from the chalkboard. €€

✕ **La Mari' d'Otello** Via Isonzo 51; m 389 591 6294; f; ⊕ daily, eves only. Just west of the centre, serving tasty Neapolitan-style pizza & craft beers. €

WHAT TO SEE AND DO

Piazza Aurelio Saffi From a distance Forlì seems a smaller version of Bologna: an old sprawling *centro storico* with not two tilted towers but two good straight ones sticking up on the skyline. Both are in Piazza Aurelio Saffi, Forlì's long trapezoidal main square presided over by a statue of its Risorgimento hero namesake. The shorter tower, the time-telling **Torre Civica** and the adjacent **Palazzo Comunale**, were begun in the 11th century, although the tower was dynamited by the retreating Germans in 1944 and entirely rebuilt in the 1970s. The Palazzo has some fine trompe l'œil frescoes by the Bibiena (*to see them, ring* ✆ 0543 712604).

Abbazia di San Mercuriale (*Piazza Saffi Aurelio 17;* ✆ *0543 25653;* ⊕ *07.30– 19.00*) Catercorner from Mussolini's **Palazzo della Posta** (1932), the striking 12th-century San Mercuriale is named after the city's first bishop, a great persecutor of pagans in the 4th century. Its 72m c**ampanile** (1180), Forlì's second landmark tower, has 273 steps to the top (⊕ *10.00–noon & 16.00–18.00; €2*). Note the lunette of the *Dream of the Epiphany and Adoration of the Magi* by the school of Antelami over the main portal, because the interior, buffeted by repeated renovations in the 17th– 19th centuries, has little to show besides the lovely quattrocento tomb of Barbara Manfredi, wife of Forlì boss Pino III Ordelaffi, and two works by local Renaissance painter Marco Palmezzano (*Madonna, Child and Saints* in the chapel on the right and the high altar's *Immaculate Conception*) amid an ocean of preposterous painting.

Duomo (*Piazza del Duomo;* ✆ *0543 34834;* ⊕ *06.30–noon & 16.00–19.00 daily*) West of Piazza Saffi, Forlì's big brick cathedral was completely rebuilt in 1841. Pride of place goes to the chapel dedicated to the Madonna del Fuoco (of fire) whose woodcut image on paper miraculously survived a blaze that burnt everything else to a crisp in 1428; note the painting of 15th-century firemen.

Musei di San Domenico (*Piazza Guido da Montefeltro 12;* ✆ *0543 712659;* w *www.cultura.comune.forli.fc.it;* ⊕ *09.30–19.00 Tue–Fri, 09.30–20.00 Sat–Sun; €5*) Five recently restored buildings of the 13th-century Dominican convent south of the Duomo now house the city's treasures. The **Archaeology Museum** contains finds from Neolithic times up to Etruscan helmets and a mosaic from the 6th century AD. The **Art Gallery** offers a rare chance to see (minor) paintings by Fra Angelico outside Tuscany, as well as works by his fellow Florentines Antonio Rossellino and Lorenzo di Credi, Marco Palmezzano, Il Francia and Francesco del Cossa, along with Flemish tapestries. Pride of place is held by Antonio Canova's marble *Hebe*, as rarefied a Neoclassical fantasy as you could ask for. During renovations, 14th-century frescoes on the life of St Dominic were uncovered in the convent's refectory and restored.

Palazzo Romagnoli (*Via C Albicini 12;* ☎ *0543 712627;* w *www.cultura.comune. forli.fc.it;* ⏰ *mid-Feb–mid-Jun 09.30–17.30 Tue–Fri, 10.00–18.00 Sat–Sun, mid-Jun–Sep 09.30–13.00 Tue–Sun; €5)* Another section of Forlì's civic museums is housed nearby in this 18th–20th-century palazzo. The entire ground floor is devoted to the 72 paintings of the Collezione Verzocchi: in 1949–50, local businessman Giuseppe Vezocchi offered Italy's best-known artists 100,000 lire for a painting on the subject of work, as well as a self-portrait. De Chircio, Carrà, de Pisis, Guttuso and Casorati are among those who took up the offer. The first floor has graphic works by Giorgio Morandi and sculptures by Adolfo Wildt, and 20th-century paintings from across Romagna.

Pinacoteca Melozzo degli Ambrogi (*Corso della Repubblica 72;* ☎ *0543 712659;* ⏰ *by appointment; admission free)* Located in the Palazzo del Merenda, this branch of the *musei civici* houses paintings from local churches salvaged during Napoleon's suppression, and others by Guercino, Carlo Maratta and Alessandro Magnasco (*Christ and the Adultress*), as well as Dutch and French works.

Santa Maria dei Servi (*Piazza Morgagni;* ☎ *0543 34245;* ⏰ *08.00–11.45 & 15.00– 18.30 daily)* Santa Maria is better known as San Pellegrino Laziosi, after a local 14th-century Servite saint whose 1 May feast day is celebrated with stalls selling *cedri* (citrons). It houses the finely sculpted tomb of Luffo Numai (1502) and a frescoed chapel of the 1300s.

Rocca di Ravaldino (*Via Giovanni dalle Bande Nere;* ⏰ *only during exhibitions)* At the southern corner of the city centre stands the picturesque 15th-century castle, the place where Caterina Sforza made her heroic stand against the rebels and displayed her virtue in public in 1500 (page 328) before Cesare Borgia breached the walls and captured her; the Borgia coat of arms marks the exact spot.

Città del Duce We promised you Mussolini Deco, and you'll find it at the east edge of Forlì around Piazza della Vittoria. With its towering monument to World War I, this square is the centre of an entire district laid out between 1925 and 1932 originally called the Città del Duce. Plenty of nonsense has been written about architecture under the Fascist regime. But except for the inscriptions and pasted-on fasces, Mussolini's architecture was no more 'authoritarian' than that of Paris in the 1930s, or the works of the New Deal in the USA. A little Bauhaus, a little Chicago World's Fair, wide streets and a discreet touch of travertine Roman monumentalism are the main ingredients, with recurring conceits such as the open porticoes of tall square columns. The entire ensemble is an evocative reminder of just how much Fascism, like the Baroque, depended on mass spectacles and settings appropriate to them.

It's ironic that Italy built far better under Mussolini than it ever has since 1945. But though the Fascist era produced some exceptional buildings and plans, none of them is in Forlì, although some strive to impress, such as the former Aeronautical Academy on the Piazza della Vittoria, with its huge statue of Icarus (a rather odd choice for future pilots). North of the Piazza the Duce built a grand boulevard towards the station lined with more of the same, now called Viale della Libertà.

Santuario di Forno [map, page 326] (*Via del Santuario 22, Forniolo; 8km east of Forlì;* \ *0543 61732;* ⊕ *by appointment*) Just south of the village of Carpinello stands an unusual round Renaissance temple with an octagonal dome. Built in 1500, in honour of Pietro Bianco, a pirate turned holy hermit, his Renaissance tomb and other sculptures are attributed to Agostino di Duccio or Antonio Rossellino.

INTO THE APENNINES

South of Forlì three principal routes ascend into the Apennines, each passing through pretty mountain valleys. Thank Mussolini that they are in this book at all; most dictators fill their birthplaces with big buildings, but the Duce went a step further and gave his home province something other politicians can only dream of: a little bit of Tuscany. In 1923 he redrew the frontiers, and gave what had been known since the early Middle Ages as the 'Tuscan Romagna' to the province of Forlì.

TERRA DEL SOLE Tuscany once began only 8km south of Forlì, at a planned citadel town begun in 1564 by the Archduke Cosimo de' Medici. Cosimo was consolidating his realm after conquering Siena in 1555, and Terra del Sole (Sun Land) was designed to remind the pope that Cosimo was no pushover: built as a perfect rectangle, Terra del Sole is surrounded by 13m-thick walls to repel the artillery of the day; star-shaped castles once guarded each of the two gates. In 1963 the town was divided into Florentines and Romagnolos, who compete with crossbows on the first Sunday in September in the Palio of Santa Reparata, with much swanning around in Renaissance duds.

In central Piazza dei Armi, the **Palazzo Pretorio** (\ *0543 766766;* w *terradelsole. org;* ⊕ *Jun–Sep 09.00–noon & 15.00–18.00 Mon–Sat, Oct–May by appointment; €5*) was HQ of the commissioners of the Medici's Romagna province, and now houses the tourist office and **Museo dell'Uomo e dell'Ambiente**, covering the history of Terra del Sole; there are tools, household items but also recently uncovered frescoes. The visit includes a tour of the fortifications.

Terra del Sole is part of the same commune as **Castrocaro Terme**, just to the south, complete with more Mussolini Deco in the Grand Hotel and spa, but most stylishly in the **Padiglione delle Feste** (1943), one of a few buildings in Italy completed in the middle of the war. Above all broods the **Fortezza di Castrocaro**, originally Byzantine, then papal and then Florentine, when it became the capital of their Romagna territories for 200 years. The **Museo Storico** (⊕ *Oct–May 15.00–19.00 Sat, 10.00–13.00 & 15.00–19.00 Sun, Jun–Sep 16.00–20.00 Sat, 16.00–20.00 Sun; €5*) inside has archaeological finds and special exhibitions.

For a great view down to the sea, head up 4km to the ruined **Rocca di Monte Poggiolo** [map, page 326] (*Via Ciola 3*), the Florentine fortress designed by Giuliano da Maiano (1471) only to be replaced by the Terra di Sole fortifications. Further up the SS67, other ruined castles haunt the quiet medieval towns of **Dovadola** (famous for white truffles) and **Rocca San Casciano**.

Tourist information

ℹ️ **Castrocaro Terme & Terre del Sole** Viale Marconi 20/28; \ 0543 769631; w visitcastrocaro. it; ⊕ Oct–May 09.00–13.00 daily, Jun–Sep also 16.00–19.00

ℹ️ **Municipal office** Via Fortezza 1; \ 0543 769541; w proloco-castrocaro.it; ⊕ 15.00–19.00 Sat, 10.00–13.00 & 15.00–19.00 (Jun–Sep 16.00–20.00) Sun, Mon–Fri by appt only

Where to stay, eat and drink

 Castello del Capitano delle Artiglierie
(3 rooms) Via Felice Cavallotti 2; m 338 361 6505;
w castellocapitano.com. Sleep like a Medici in the
castle that once housed the garrison defending the
Florentine side of Terra del Sole. Filled with period
furnishings, frescoes & coffered ceilings, it has a
lovely park & orchard of 'forgotten fruits' in the
former parade ground. B/fast inc. €€€€€

 **Grande Hotel & Spa Terme di Castrocaro
Terme** (117 rooms) Via Roma 2; \0543 767114;
w termedicastrocaro.it. Set in a beautiful wooded
park, with trails & a minigolf course, this stylish Art
Deco spa hotel offers beauty & health treatments,
a fitness centre, outdoor pool & rooftop terrace.
Families are very welcome; there's a kids' pool &
club to keep them happy. B/fast inc. €€€–€€€€

✖ **Trattoria Bolognesi da Melania** Piazza San
Niccolò 2; \0543 769119; w trattoriabolognesi.it;
⏲ eves only & Sun lunch. For 45 years, Castrocaro
was renowned for its fabulous restaurant, La
Frasca, & bereft when it closed. But in 2016 the
same family reopened an even more beautiful
restaurant, in an arty setting under the brick
vaults of a former convent, with a lovely terrace
overlooking the countryside. Excellent Romagnola
cuisine; try the emblematic handmade spaghetti
(*curzùl con zucchine, guanciale e pecorino di
fossa*), 1 of 6 dishes on the €32 fixed-price menu.
Excellent vegetarian choices, too. Be sure to book.
€€€

PREDAPPIO The narrow alternative route just to the east (SS9ter) passes through
lush rolling hills of vines producing Sangiovese, the red 'blood of Jove', around
Predappio, which produced Mussolini on 29 July 1883 (see box, pages 18–20). His
modest birthplace, the **Casa Natale di Benito Mussolini** (*Via Varana Costa;* \ *0543
921766;* ⏲ *mid-Jun–mid-Sep 10.00–13.00 & 14.00–18.00, other times ring in the
morning; €10*) is now used for special exhibitions. In 1957, his remains were reburied
in the local cemetery, near those of his wife, Rachele; his modest mausoleum, with
his stern bust framed in the fasces that gave his movement its name has become a
shrine for Italy's small population of retrograde blackshirts.

Mussolini left the old *comune*, **Predappio Alta**, alone with its sweeping vineyards
beneath its overgrown castle, and made his village the seat of the local government
and embellished it with public buildings, including the monumental **Casa del
Fascio**. Long in a state of decay, the building, thanks to a €5 million EU grant, is
being transformed into a museum of Fascism and its history, due to open in 2019.

Where to stay, eat and drink

 Borgo Condé Wine Resort [map, page
326] (38 rooms) Via Lucchina 47, Fiumana di
Predappio; \0543 940129; w borgoconde.it.
Midway between Forlì & Predappio, in the very
heart of the Sangiovese wine area, this luxury
hillside hotel is a world unto itself. Buggies
provide the links between the 4 buildings &
their beautiful cream-coloured suites, the lovely
pool & spa. There are 3 restaurants, including
an osteria (⏲ *year-round;* €€€) with stunning
views over the countryside, as well as the elegant
Borgo & La Cittadella del Vino Wine Bar (⏲ *both*

closed winter). Winery tours & tastings, bikes &
horseriding available. B/fast inc. €€€€€

✖ **La Vecia Cantena d'la Pre'** Piazza
Cavour 18; \0543 921095; w laveciacantena.
it; ⏲ 10.30–23.00, closed Wed eve. Informal
restaurant/enoteca above the ancient wine cellar
of the Ca' de Sanzvès estate where you can feast
on Romagnola classics, with *piadine, crescentine* or
spianate (flatbread), or perhaps just their special
PiaVina, a *piadina* made with *formaggio di fossa* &
honey. €–€€€

PORTICO DI ROMAGNA AND SAN BENEDETTO As you head into the mountains,
old Florentine associations are thick on the ground. Dante's beloved Beatrice spent
several summers in the pretty medieval town of **Portico di Romagna**, named after a
market (*porticum*) here in Roman times. It was a favourite retreat for nobility fleeing

political strife in Tuscany and Romagna, and you can still make out the three social divisions reflected in the neighbourhoods: castle and church on top, mid-level with the houses of the nobles (Beatrice stayed in her father's **Palazzo Portinari** on Via Roma), and the peasants and workers closest to the Montone River, crossed here by the humpbacked **Ponte di Maestà**. The rapid **Brusia River**, 4km south, is crossed by another humpback 18th-century bridge; the river is popular with kayakers and bathers on hot days.

Further up the Montone Valley towards the Tuscan frontier the landscape grows increasingly savage around the 9th-century **Abbazia di San Benedetto** (m *389 582 4286;* w *sanbenedettoinalpe.com*) in tiny **San Benedetto in Alpe**, which sheltered Dante after his unsuccessful bid to return to Florence from exile (*Inferno*, Canto XVI, 94–105). Its chilly stone crypt looks exactly as it did in Dante's day. There are a number of beautiful trails around San Benedetto, most spectacularly the signposted 9km walk to the **Cascata dell'Acquacheta** [map, page 326] (which also earned a mention in the *Inferno*), a bucolic, stepped waterfall (perfect for a dip, although it can dry up in high summer) with its ruined hermitage linked to the abbey.

Tourist information

 Centro Visita Parco Nazionale San Benedetto in Alpe Viale Acquacheta 6; m 349 766 7400; ⏰ mid-Apr–Oct 09.00–13.00 Sat– Sun, Aug 09.00–noon & 16.00–19.00 Tue–Sun, 09.00–13.00 Sat–Sun

Where to stay, eat and drink

🏠 **Al Vecchio Convento** (15 rooms) Via Roma 7, Portico di Romagna; 📞 0543 967053; w vecchioconvento.it. Small, charming, family-run haven in 2 buildings, 50m apart, a perfect retreat after a day in the mountains. Rooms are mostly furnished with 18th-century antiques. Also a fine restaurant (€€€) in a former barn, with a good wine list; cooking lessons & truffle hunts on offer too. €€

🏠 **Maneggio Rio Destra** (5 rooms) Via Biforco 7, San Benedetto in Alpe; m 349 159 6520; w riodestro.it. Friendly owners, simple rooms, good restaurant, & riding stable near the abbey; HB or FB terms available. €

PARCO NAZIONALE DELLE FORESTE CASENTINESI

San Benedetto borders the Casentinesi Forest National Park, along the mountainous border of Romagna and Tuscany. Established in 1993 and criss-crossed by ancient paths, its deep majestic silver firs and century-old beeches shelter eagles, wolves, roe deer, red deer, fallow deer and mouflons, introduced from Sardinia in 1870. Autumn is a great time to visit, when the air is bracing and the truffles, mushrooms and chestnuts are in season, and the forests are drenched in colour. What you won't get are many viewpoints; there are just too many trees in the way.

TOURIST INFORMATION For useful information in English, try w parks.it/parco. nazionale.for.casentinesi.

🛈 **Santa Sofia** Via Nefetti 3; 📞 0543 971375; w parcoforestecasentinesi.it; ⏰ 09.00–13.00 Mon, Wed, Fri, 09.00–13.00 & 15.00–17.00 Tue & Thu

🏠 WHERE TO STAY, EAT AND DRINK *Map, page 326*

🏠 **Il Palazzo di Ridracoli** (10 rooms) Borgo Ridracoli; 📞 0543 917570. 'Palazzo' might be an exaggeration, but this friendly family-run inn is a great place stay in the tranquil heart of the

National Park, very close to Lake Ridracoli. Also an excellent restaurant featuring porcini mushrooms & an enoteca. HB available; b/fast inc. €€€€

🏠 **Spa Hotel Granduca** (18 rooms) Via Centro 3, Campigna di Santa Sofia; 📞 0543 980051; w albergogranduca.it. Built in 1800 as a hunting lodge for the Lorraine Grand Dukes of Tuscany & converted into a hotel in 1930, the Granduca's rooms are spacious with wooden floors & ceilings, all with views over the mountains. The small spa has a Finnish sauna, Turkish bath, ice shower, mud baths & salt grotto; also an outdoor heated pool & good restaurant (€€€). B/fast inc. €€€

🏠 **Locanda Chalet Burraia** (6 rooms) Fraz Campigna di Santa Sofia 87; 📞 0543 980006; m 335 656 5764; w chaletburraia.it. Very near the Tuscan border, simple rooms in a big wooden chalet are vintage 1930s, immersed in nature, with a restaurant (€€) & bar. They can grant mushroom-hunting licences in the autumn & rent snowshoes in winter. B/fast inc. €€

WHAT TO SEE AND DO

Santa Sofia From the distance this old Tuscan town on the Bidenta resembles a mini Florence with its bridge and tall crenellated tower. There are no flies on Santa Sofia, though, with its sculpture park along the river and **Galleria di Arte Contemporanea Vero Stoppioni** (*Viale Roma 5;* 📞 *0543 975428;* 🕐 *09.30–12.30 & 15.00–18.00 Sat–Sun; €2*), housing works by Mattia Moreni (d1999) and others who won the annual Premio Campigna winter art competition.

Campigna Further up the valley, the tiny mountain hamlet of Campigna, surrounded by towering silver firs, was once owned by the Cathedral of Florence, which planted and sold the trees as masts for galleys. It's a base for the easy 3.5km Abete Bianco nature trail. In winter there's a small ski resort (1,488–1,650m) (*for info* 📞 *0543 980051*) with a lift and a black and a red run, a 'magic carpet' lift for sleds and bobsleds and some very magical cross-country and snowshoe trails through the woods, especially during a full moon.

Lago di Ridracoli [map, page 326] The turquoise lake, contained by one of the largest dams in Italy, is in the midst of another heavily forested region. Here the **Ecomuseo delle Acque di Ridracoli** (*17km from Santa Sofia on the SP4 & SP112;* 📞 *0543 917912;* w *ecomuseoridracoli.it;* 🕐 *Mar–mid-Jun & mid-Sep–mid-Nov 10.00–18.00 Sat–Sun, mid-Jun–mid-Sep 09.00–19.00 Tue–Sun (also Mon in Aug), Nov–Dec 10.00–17.00 Sat–Sun; €5*) has exhibits about the dams, and offers boat trips and canoe hire, plus e-bike hire (*€30/day, book by 14.00 the day before*) for a ride into the magical **Foresta della Lama** on the south shore of the lake. Another property of Florence Cathedral for hundreds of years, it shelters the inaccessible **Riserva Naturale Integrale di Sasso Fratino**, a rare section of primordial beech forest untouched since the last Ice Age; in 2007 it became a UNESCO World Heritage Site.

BAGNO DI ROMAGNA

The largest resort near the Casentinesi Forest National Park, lofty green Bagno di Romagna (491m) and its sister resort, San Piero in Bagno, have thermal and mud baths, and are popular summer resorts. Bagno di Romagna, like the rest of this area, was part of Tuscany in the 9th century, when Pope Adrian II granted the lands to the Bishop of Arezzo. In 1453 it came directly under the rule of the Florentines

Even the bicarbonate-alkaline and sulphurous waters which gush out at 45°C are Florentine, at least according to the locals: it is rain that fell 700 years ago, in the time of Giotto, which seeped deep into the earth to pick up heat and its special mineral qualities before gushing back to the surface. Several members of the Medici family and Benvenuto Cellini came in the Renaissance to take the waters; in winter it's fun to go for a dip in the hot pool while surrounded by snow. Bagno remains full of old Florentine touches and rusticated *palazzi*, and has another feather in its cap in its superb restaurants.

GETTING THERE AND AROUND Bagno di Romagna can be reached by START Romagna buses (see box, page 328) from the train stations of Forlì (*65km, bus 131*) or Cesena (*48km, bus 138*). Driving from the A14, take the Cesena Nord exit for the E45 to Bagno di Romagna.

From July to mid-September, **Wild Bus** runs a shuttle service one or two afternoons a week from Bagno di Romagna to the Lama Forest, Lake Ridracoli and the Ecomuseo (page 348). It can take bikes if you want to pedal there and return by bus; check schedules and book the day before at the tourist office.

TOURIST INFORMATION
i Via Fiorentina 38; ☏0543 911046; w www. bagnodiromagnaturismo.it; ⏱ Jan–Mar 09.00–12.30 Mon–Sat, also 15.30–17.30 Tue & Thu, Apr–Oct 09.00–12.30 & 15.30–18.00 daily, Nov–Dec 09.00–12.30 Mon–Sat, also 15.30–17.30 Tue, Thu, Sat–Sun

---

WHERE TO STAY
🏠 **Ròseo Euroterme Wellness Resort** (254 rooms) Via Lungosavio 2; ☏0543 911414; w euroterme.com. On the edge of town, it's the big boy at Bagno. Recently remodelled with a generous heap of beige, it offers health & beauty treatments in a lush setting, & an outdoor thermal pool. Special activities for kids; good restaurant with a cooking school. €€€€

🏠 **Grand Hotel Terme Roseo** (70 rooms) Piazza Risasoli 2; ☏0543 911016; w termeroseo. com/it. Occupies the palace of the Counts Biozzi, from the days when Bagno was part of Tuscany. Rooms have had a facelift, & come with a pillow menu; there's an indoor spa-water heated pool, gym, garden & solarium; Shiatzu massage & beauty treatments are on offer, & free bikes for guests. Continental b/fast inc. €€€

🏠 **Hotel Tosco Romagnolo** (44 rooms) Via del Popolo 2; ☏0543 911260; w hoteltoscoromagnolo.it. Peaceful place to relax with a rooftop pool, spa & famous restaurant (see below). €–€€€

🏠 **Agriturismo B&B Casenuove** [map, page 326] (5 rooms) SP43 172/D, just east of San Piero in Bagno; ☏0543 903242; w agriturismo-b-amp-b-casenuove-it.book.direct/it-it/. Peaceful, rural, friendly & free bikes for guests. B/fast inc. €€

🏠 **Al Tiglio** (16 rooms) Via Lungosavio 7; ☏0543 911522; w hotelaltiglio.com. Cheerful, charmingly old-fashioned family-run hotel with a play room & gnome-filled garden for little ones. Also a good restaurant (€€), with reasonable HB terms. B/fast inc. Closed Nov–Mar. €€

🏠 **Centro Turistico Valbonella** [map, page 326] (30 rooms) Loc Valbonella, 7km east of Bagno; ☏0543 918729; w valbonella.com. Immersed in nature, a great base for an active holiday: rustic but comfortable rooms in a 17th-century stone farm, with a restaurant, pool, tennis, stables & other activities, including a 1km track for kids through the Bosco di Gnomo Mentino, a gnome-ridden woodland. B/fast inc. €€

🏠 **Fattoria Cà di Gianni** [map, page 326] (4 rooms) Loc Cà di Gianni 159, 3km from San Piero in Bagno; ☏0543 917358; w cadigianni.it. Simple accommodation, with a riding stable, pool, family adventure park in the trees, pizzeria/restaurant & discounts at the Ròseo Euroterme spa. B/fast inc. €–€€

✗ WHERE TO EAT AND DRINK
Local specialities here include mushrooms, truffles, honey and tangy Raviggiolo cheese, a Slow Food favourite.

✗ **Paolo Teverini** In the Hotel Tosco Romagnolo (see above); ⏱ closed Mon & Tue. Paolo Teverini, one of Italy's top vegetable chefs, can make a gastronomic Mona Lisa from an onion. Beautiful seafood & meat dishes, with plenty of mushrooms in season, each dish more beautiful than the last. If you can't decide what to choose à la carte, there are fixed-price menus, & dishes offered in half portions so you can try more. Also fabulous desserts, more than 2,000 Italian & foreign wines to choose from & dessert wines by the glass. There's also a bistro, the **Prêt-à-Porter** (€€), with a vegetarian *menu di degustazione* (€28), w/day lunch (€18) & a buffet with daily specials, including homemade pasta, for a quick lunch or dinner. €€€€€

✖ **Ristorante del Lago** [map, page 326] Loc Acquapartita 147, 8km from Bagno di Romagna; \0543 903406; w albergoristorantedellago. it; ⊕ closed Mon & Tue. A family-run hotel-restaurant by the Acquapartita Lake, with a young & very talented chef. Three €47 menus to choose from (classic, contemporary or seasonal) making good use of local ingredients (ravioli filled with wild herbs in lamb sauce, quail cooked 2 ways,

slow-cooked suckling pig with courgette cream & pistachios), as well as à la carte dishes (exc Sat eve & Sun lunch). Lovely desserts & a groaning cheeseboard with France's & Italy's finest. They also have simple rooms (€€). €€€€

✖ **Da Gorini** Via Verdi 5, San Pietro in Bagno; \0543 190 8056; w dagorini.it; ⊕ closed Tue & Wed lunch. When the famous Locanda Gambero Rosso closed in 2014 after 63 years, it left a big hole in the village, but Gianluca Gorini, chef son of the owners, reopened in September 2017 with a new smart cream-coloured dining room that has been booked out since. 4-course (€40) or 7-course (€68) choose-your-own *menu degustazione*; also wines by the glass. €€€

✖ **Osteria Orso Bianco** Via Pascoli 14, San Pietro in Bagno; \0543 918297; ⊕ 18.00–02.00, closed Tue in winter. In a 17th-century vaulted cellar, a pizzeria/enoteca that also offers a good selection of craft beers. €€

WHAT TO SEE AND DO

Palazzo dei Capitani (*Via Fiorentina 38*) When the Florentines took over, they encrusted the façade of Bagno's 14th-century landmark with a big set of Medici balls (the spheres on their escutcheon; since the Medici were originally pharmacists, their Florentine opponents nicknamed the balls the 'pills') and the marble coats of arms of former captains. Besides the tourist information office, the palazzo houses a visitor centre for the Parco Nazionale Foreste Casentinesi, with exhibits on the wildlife and local geology, maps and hiking guides, etc.

Basilica di Santa Maria Assunta (*Piazza Ricosoli 13*) First mentioned in the 9th century AD, this Romanesque church houses an impressive collection of Florentine art: on the high altar, a beautiful triptych by Neri di Bicci (1468); a terracotta of *Sant'Agnese* by Andrea della Robbia; a lovely Madonna, attributed to the early 15th-century Maestro di Sant'Ivo; a *Nativity* from the same century by the Maestro del Tondo Borghese; a *Madonna and Saints* by Michele di Rodolfo del Ghirlandaio; and a *Crucifixion* by the early 18th-century Florentine Gherardini.

Source of the Tiber, Balze di Verghereto [map, page 326] (*25km southeast of Bagno di Romagna*) Old Father Tiber begins his 418km journey to Rome in a beech forest on the slopes of 1,408m **Monte Fumaiolo**. Two springs (get here from Balze on the SP43) mark the source where Mussolini erected an ancient Roman column with the inscription: 'Here is born the river / sacred to the destinies of Rome'.

BACK ON THE VIA EMILIA

FORLIMPOPOLI Although founded as Forum Popili by Roman consul Popilius Lena in 132BC, Forlimpopoli post-dates 1360, the year that papal legate Cardinal Albornoz decided to make the rebellious town an example *pour encourager les autres* and razed it to the ground. In its place he built a fat-towered Rocca on the Via

Emilia and attempted to rename the town Salvaterra. But over the next 20 years the survivors of the attack drifted back, and in 1380 the pope confirmed the position of the old ruling family, the Ordelaffi, who took over the castle. But the town is proudest of the 'great-grandfather of Italian cuisine' Pellegrino Artusi, and has adopted a new motto, the 'Città Artusiana'.

Tourist information

i Via A Costa 23; ☏0543 749250;
w forlimpopolicittartusiana.it; ⏰ 15.00–18.00
Wed & Fri, 09.30–12.30 Sat–Sun

✖ Where to eat and drink

✖ **Ristorante Casa Artusi** Via A Costa 23/27;
☏0543 743138; w casartusi.it; ⏰ closed Tue &
Wed lunch. It's never a bad idea to eat at a cookery
school; this one, with master chef Andrea Banfi at
the helm, has a large, constantly changing menu
that uses many of Pellegrino Artusi's recipes.
4-course land or sea tasting menus start at €25.
It also has boutique selling Artusi souvenirs, & an
enoteca linked to the regional one in Dozza (page
334). €€€

What to see and do

Rocca Albornoz/Museo Archeologico Civico (*Piazza Fratti 5;* ☏*0543 748071;*
w *maforlimpopoli.it;* ⏰ *09.00–13.00 Fri, 10.00–13.00 & 15.30–18.30 Sat–Sun; €4,*
under 18s free) In the 19th century the town council demolished the huge central
tower of the Rocca and made another room in the municipal theatre. This was the
scene of Forlimpopoli's second dramatic moment in history, on 25 January 1851,
when the notorious 'Ferryman' (see box, page 338), boldly interrupted a performance

THE GREAT-GRANDFATHER OF ITALIAN CUISINE

Born in Forlimpopoli in 1820, Pellegrino Artusi was the only son of a wealthy businessman, whose destiny changed when his family were among the victims of the Ferryman's gang in the theatre; one of Pellegrino's many sisters, Gertrude, was held hostage, probably raped and ended up in a mental institution. Traumatised, the Artusis moved to Florence the next year, where Pellegrino quickly made a small fortune, saw all of his many sisters married off, and in 1861 retired to devote his life to his two passions: literature and cooking.

A famed host and raconteur with white whiskers the size of kittens, Artusi firmly believed that Italian cooking was just as good as French. He travelled throughout the recently born kingdom of Italy gathering recipes, and with his faithful cooks Marietta Sabatini and Francesco Ruffilli tried them out on a scientific basis, and diligently recorded some 790 recipes for the home cook, complete with amusing anecdotes, into what became *La Scienza in Cucina e l'Arte di Mangiar Bene* (*Science in the Kitchen and The Art of Eating Well*).

Unable to find a publisher, Artusi self-published a thousand copies in 1891, dedicating the tome to his two cats. It was the first attempt at standardising a national cuisine and, before Artusi died in 1911, he saw his masterpiece sell more than 200,000 copies (in each edition he added recipes sent to him by readers, until the book had doubled in size). Reprinted countless times since, and one of the three most-read books in Italy (along with *Pinocchio* and *The Betrothed*), there are very few Italian homes today without a beloved, well-thumbed grease-spattered *Artusi*.

to demand 'a contribution of 40,000 scudi', holding hostages until they delivered the sum. The archaeological museum, in another part of the castle, has large black-and-white Roman mosaic floors (including one covered with swastikas), sculptures, inscriptions and medieval and Renaissance ceramics.

BERTINORO Medieval Bertinoro is famous for its wine and hospitality. The wine is Albana, and there's a wonderful story someone concocted that the town got its name when Galla Placidia drank some of this nectar out of a wooden mug and declared: 'O wine, you are so good I could drink you in gold!' ('*ber-ti in oro*').

The hospitality was such in old Bertinoro (now, this story is true) that the noble families constantly squabbled over who would have the privilege of hosting guests. The solution was to erect a column in the centre and hang it with a dozen rings, one belonging to each of the families; the ring to which a stranger tethered his horse decided which would be his host. The column was removed in 1570, but in 1922 its foundations were rediscovered and it was re-erected in Piazza della Libertà, complete with iron rings and views that make it the 'Balcony of Romagna'.

Getting there and away From Forlimpopoli station, a local shuttle bus goes to Bertinoro.

Tourist information

🛈 Piazza della Libertà; 📞 0543 469213;
w visitbertinoro.it; ⏱ 09.00–14.00 Mon–Fri, also
14.30–17.30 Tue & Thu

Where to stay, eat and drink

🏠 **Laresidenzanelborgo** (2 rooms)
Via Arrigo Mainardi 6; m 348 855 5841;
w laresidenzanelborgo.com. Dreamy arty B&B
in the centre with luxury linen, lovely views over
the hills & owner who will make you feel at home.
Cosy sitting room with a fireplace; fabulous b/fast
inc. €€€€

🏠 **Grand Hotel Terme di Fratta** (64 rooms)
Via Loreta 238, Fratta, 5km west of Bertinoro;
📞 0543 460911; w termedellafratta.com. Set
in a leafy park, this hotel built in the 1930s
in a spacious Greek temple style was recently
renovated; its spa/wellness centre is unique in Italy
with a choice of 7 springs, each reputedly good for
something different. The restaurant (€€€) offers
Romagnola, vegetarian & vegan menus (book for
the latter); buffet b/fast inc. €€€–€€€€

🏠 **Agriturismo al Colle** [map, page 326]
(10 rooms) Via Com le Monticino 1435, 5km
northeast Bertinoro & just south of the SS9, a few
mins from the Cesena E35 exit; 📞 0543 448868;

w agriturismoalcolle.com. Tranquil relaxing
rooms, many with canopy beds & all with private
entrances on to the garden with a pool. Superb
Romagnolo restaurant (€€€) with fresh produce
from the farm (open to non-guests); b/fast inc.
€€€

🍴 **La Divina Bistecca** Via dei Santi 3; 📞 0543
445860; 📘; ⏱ eves only, also lunch Sat–Sun.
Choose between the Paradise, Purgatory or the
Inferno rooms to feast on divine steaks, but also
much more, including gluten-free choices. Great
summer terrace, too. €€€

🍴 **Osteria Enoteca 'Cà de Bé'** Piazza della
Libertà 10; 📞 0543 444435; w cadebe.it; ⏱ closed
lunch (exc Sat–Sun), Mon & Tue in winter. Lovely
views & all the classics (including some of Artusi's
recipes). Very tender meats & excellent local wines.
€€

🍴 **La Casa della Piadina** Largo Cairoli 5/a;
m 340 791 4950; ⏱ closed Mon. Bertinoro is full of
wonderful *piadina* kiosks; this is 1 of the best. €

What to see and do

Museo Interreligioso di Arte Sacra (*Via Aldruda Frangipane 6;* 📞*0543 446600;*
w *museointerreligioso.it;* ⏱ *10.00–13.00 & 14.30–17.30 Tue–Sun; admission free*) Up

in the Rocca di Bertinoro, dating back to the 11th century (Frederick Barbarossa slept here), much has been altered over history and by many different owners; from the 16th century onwards it was the palace of the local bishops. Today it houses a museum dedicated to understanding what the three major monotheistic religions have in common.

San Donato di Polenta [map, page 326] (*Fraz Polenta, 5km south of Bertinoro; ring the tourist office for hours*) Made famous by Carduccio's poem 'La Chiesa di Polenta', Polenta was the stronghold of the famous family of that name who ruled medieval Ravenna; its Byzantine-Romanesque basilican church, often restored, still has its finely sculpted original capitals in the nave and crypt. The exterior is covered with the arms of cities from around Italy.

CESENA Cesena – now perhaps best known as the site of the European Trotting Championships in August – is almost as big as Forlì, and shares with it the honour of provincial capital. Originally a Roman fortress town, the city had more than its share of turmoil in the 14th–15th centuries. Ruled by the Ordelaffi of Forlì, it was taken over by Cardinal Albornoz in 1357. Papal rule was so oppressive that the people rose up in 1377 against the Breton troops of the papal legate Robert of Geneva, killing hundreds. In revenge, thousands of citizens were killed or forced into exile by the pope's army; Cesena was sacked and the castle burned. At the end of the year Cesena fell into the hands of the Malatesta, although it was decades before the city recovered.

The last of the family line, however, humanist and *condottiero* Domenico Malatesta, better known as Malatesta Novello (r1429–65), was also the city's great benefactor. He was married to Violante da Montefeltro, who as sister of the famous art patron, the Duke of Urbino, had received an exceptional education for a Renaissance woman. He was a friend of Cosimo de' Medici. And he left Cesena its pride and joy: a library that in 2005 was the first place in Italy inscribed on UNESCO's Memory of the World register.

Getting there and around The train and bus station is 800m from the centre, and is the base for START buses (see box, page 328) into the city and surroundings.

Tourist information

i Piazza del Popolo 9; `0547 356327; w www. comune.cesena.fc.it; ⊕ 09.30–13.00 & 15.00–18.00 Mon–Sat, 09.30–12.30 Sun

Where to stay, eat and drink

⌂ **Casali** (48 rooms) Via B Croce 81; `0547 22745; w hotelcasalicesena.com. Traditional, luxurious, the nicest hotel here, complete with a spa. Free parking &bikes for getting around. €€€€

⌂ **Villa Giusy** [map, page 326] (3 rooms) Via Cervese 6921, 10km northeast; m 338 983 8730; w villagiusybebcesena.it. Peaceful rooms in an attractive new villa with AC, a pool, nice owners, garden & shared kitchen, some with a shared bathroom. Free bikes for guests. €€€

⌂ **Agriturismo Macìn** [map, page 326] (9 rooms) Via San Mauro 5280, 7km from Cesena,

half way to Bertinoro; m 333 263 3099; w nuke. agriturismomacin.it. Stay in the quiet heart of a vineyard in a beautifully renovated farmhouse of 1890; relaxing, friendly, & delicious home-cooked b/fast inc. €€

✕ **Osteria Michiletta** Via Strinati 41; `0547 24691; w osteriamichiletta.com; closed Sun & Aug. The oldest osteria in town serves good healthy dishes, based on vegetables & freshly ground wheat & other cereals. Also meat. €€

What to see and do

Biblioteca Malatestiana (*Piazza Maurizio Bufalini 1;* \ *0547 610892;* w *www. comune.cesena.fc.it/malatestiana;* ⊕ *14.00–19.00 Mon, 09.00–19.00 Tue–Sat, 15.00– 19.00 Sun*) Inspired by the famous library of Cosimo de' Medici at San Marco in Florence, Novello hired architect Matteo Nuti, a student of Leon Battista Alberti, to build his own library in 1452 next to the beautiful cloister of San Francesco. Although the Franciscans cared for the books and copied the manuscripts, Novello gave the library to the *comune*, making it the first civic library in the world. Which prevented Napoleon from confiscating it as he did Cosimo's library at San Marco.

Astonishingly, it has survived since then in mint 15th-century condition. The portal is crowned with the Malatesta elephant sculpted by Agostino di Duccio (with the Latin motto 'Elephants aren't afraid of mosquitoes' showing just how little the Malatesta thought of their enemies). The carved wooden doors are still opened with two locks and two ornate keys: one would be held by the town council, the other by a Franciscan. Inside, under Nuti's green vaulted ceiling, 343 priceless manuscripts are still attached by chains to the 58 wooden lecterns; the light pouring through the windows allowed them to be read *in situ*.

The library also contains a priceless collection of codices going back to the 7th century and 3,200 16th-century manuscripts collected by Novello and his doctor, Giovanni di Marco da Rimini (future physician to the pope), stored in the former convent. A few are on display, including the massive illuminated choral books commissioned by Cardinal Bessarione, the Greek scholar who attempted to unite the Catholic and Orthodox churches in order to save Constantinople from the Ottoman Turks. After it fell in 1451, he donated the books to Cesena, leaving the rest of his library to St Mark's in Venice.

Rocca Malatestiana (*Via Cia degli Ordelaffi 8;* \ *0547 22409;* w *roccamalatestianadicesena.it; guided tours* ⊕ *Apr–May 10.00–19.00 Tue–Thu, 10.00–23.00 Fri–Sun, Jun–Aug 10.00–23.00 Tue–Sun, Sep–5 Nov 10.00–16.00 Tue– Thu, 10.00–22.00 Fri–Sun; €2–10.50, depending on the length of tour*) Novello also hired Matteo Nuti to repair the castle which still dominates Cesena, and to link it to the centre of town. Later improvements were carried out by Cesare Borgia, who made Cesena the capital for his ambitions in the region, which endured as long as his papa was the one with a capital P. It later served as a papal fortress and prison, complete with torture chamber, and now houses a museum of the fortress itself, with suits of armour and jousting gear, and a museum of country life and agricultural techniques. The views from the top of the walls stretch to the Adriatic.

LONGIANO Another mighty Rocca Malatestiana lords it over Longiano (12km southeast of Cesena), this one housing the **Fondazione Tito Balestra Onlus** (*Piazza Malatestiana;* \ *0547 665850;* w *fondazionetitobalestra.org;* ⊕ *Sep–Jul 10.00–noon & 15.00–19.00 Tue–Sun, Aug 16.00–20.00 Tue–Sun; €7*). Carlo Malatesta (page 358) died here in 1423. Today it hosts a foundation named after Longiano's poet, Tito Balestra (1923–76), who was a collector of modern art: there are works by de Pisis, Mafai and Rosai, and 1,800 pieces by Mino Maccari.

Longiano also sports Italy's biggest collection of cast-iron street furniture in the **Museo Italiana della Ghisa** (*Via Emilia 1671;* \ *0547 652171;* w *museoitalianoghisa. org;* ⊕ *09.00–16.00 Mon, Wed & Fri, 09.00–noon Tue & Thu; admission free*), with elegant lamps, benches, statues, door-knockers and more from as far away as Paris, Dublin and Vienna, plus an interesting collection of old postcards. Other cast-iron works are displayed in the town centre, in the 18th-century deconsecrated church of Santa Maria delle Lacrime (*Via Santa Maria 18;* ⊕ *Oct–May 14.30–18.00, Jun–Sep 15.00–18.30*).

SAVIGNANO SUL RUBICONE East of Longiano, the Via Emilia crosses a poor excuse for a stream once called the Fiumicino, that most authorities now accept as the shadowy Rubicon. Once the dividing line between Cisalpine Gaul and what was then considered Italy, which Julius Caesar crossed with his army in 49BC, thereby defying the Senate and declaring his intention to take over the Roman state, today it separates respectable Emilia-Romagna from the international beach babylon of Rimini. Cheese-lovers will want to make a detour 16km up the Rubicon to **Sogliano al Rubicone**, proud producer of DOP *formaggio di fossa* (see box, page 391), winner of the best Italian cheese prize in 2012, and a product widely available in the local cheese makers' shops.

12

Rimini and the Adriatic Riviera

Seen by the aliens from their spaceships, the Adriatic Riviera must be one of the most unusual and enticing sights of Europe. Welcome to 'Linear City' – 70km long and a few blocks deep, a mass of compacted (and mostly quite attractive) urbanity, with the SS16 and the Ravenna–Pesaro rail line on one side and a solid line of beach on the other. It's the place where Italians come because their grandparents did, where Germans come to look for Italians, the British come to fill shopping trolleys with gin, and Russians finally get a chance to wear their designer sunglasses. On any given night in August, more than 100,000 of them will be sitting down to *tagliatelle al ragù* in their hotels and thinking that life is pretty damn sweet.

There's no place like it. And right in the middle is the surprising city of Rimini, home of one of the most beguiling monuments of the Renaissance and a vortex for weirdness of all kinds, from genuine haunted castles to hallucinogenically kitschy roadside attractions and the sovereign, independent Republic of San Marino.

At first glance Italy's biggest resort may strike you as strictly cold potatoes, a full 15km of peeling skin and *gelato*, 10,000 selfie-taking teenagers with eternally whining, giggling little brothers and sisters. To many Italians, however, Rimini means pure sweaty-palmed excitement. In the 1960s, following the grand old Italian pastime of *caccia alle svedesi*, a staple of the national film industry was the Rimini holiday seduction movie, in which a bumbling protagonist with glasses was swept off his feet by some incredible Nordic goddess, who was as bouncy as she was adventurous. After many complications, embarrassing both for the audience and the actors, it could all lead to true love. For the bumbling protagonists of real life, all this may only be wishful thinking but they still come in their millions each year to 'the Beach of Europe'. As a resort Rimini has its advantages. Noisy as it is, it's a respectable, family place, relatively cheap, convenient and well organised, with the best nightlife in the north, if not all Italy. Also, tucked away behind the beachfront is a genuine old city, with a four-star Renaissance attraction.

HISTORY

Settlements around Rimini go back to the late Neolithic period, but when the site of the city itself was still a swamp, the modest metropolis of this area was the little village of Verucchio, up on the hills to the southwest. The Villanova people lived here for centuries, and maintained a trading station at the mouth of the River Marecchia. By the 5th century BC, there was enough solid ground on the coast for people to start gradually drifting down from the hills. The Villanovans were succeeded by the Umbrians, an Italic people who had expanded into parts of the Romagna Apennines, and later by the Celts, who seem to have been busy traders here.

The area was one of Rome's first conquests in Cisalpine Gaul, after their victory at the Battle of Sentinum (Sassoferrato) in 295BC. The founding of Ariminium, the first Roman colony north of the Apennines (268BC), had been a matter of some controversy in the Senate; it was a sign of Rome's resolve to conquer all of Cisalpine Gaul. The opening of the Via Aemilia in 218BC made Ariminium the natural port for all the trade of the new region, and the city grew along with it, throwing off its colonial status to become a full-fledged *municipium* in 90BC.

A rude interruption came in the Civil Wars – Ariminium sided with the populist Marius, and got thoroughly sacked by the victorious conservative general Sulla – but this setback was soon overcome. In 49BC the city picked the right horse, siding with Julius Caesar when he passed through on his way to power in Rome, and in the next century Ariminium became one of the more opulent towns of northern Italy, with an amphitheatre nearly as big as Rome's Colosseum.

Ariminium shared in the general late Imperial decay of Italy, and it must have been hit hard in the various barbarian invasions and in the Greek–Gothic Wars, when it changed hands several times. The victorious Byzantines made it the capital of a new 'Pentapolis', a province of five maritime cities (with Fano, Pesaro, Senigallia and Ancona in the Marche), ruled by a duke subject to the exarch at Ravenna, and it fell to the Lombards in AD751 along with Ravenna. By 1000 the city had shrunk to a tiny part of its Roman-era extent, a few streets around Piazza Cavour.

A *comune* was founded at some unknown date, and Rimini started to grow again with a little help from Mother Nature – the River Marecchia changed its course to flow right under the city's walls, providing a convenient new port to replace the old one that had silted up. Under the *comune*, the leading official of the city was called the Pater Civitatis. This office, and control of the city, became so identified with a single powerful family that they eventually took it as a family name – the Parcitadi. Medieval Rimini followed the usual path of the Italian cities: it built a Palazzo Comunale, made plenty of money, fought continually with its neighbours, grew dramatically and built a new set of walls (1330). It did show at least two eccentricities. It was unshakeably Ghibelline, and in the 1200s it had a large population of Cathars – the Manichaean heretics who flourished in southern France before the Albigensian Crusade. In northern Italy they were called Patarenes, but they suffered the same Church pogroms and eventual extinction.

THE HEADACHE FAMILY The Malatesta started out as Lords of Verucchio, Ghibelline backwoods barons who moved into the city in 1216. The greatest of the line, Malatesta da Verucchio (Headache from Hump), became a political power in the 1240s. In 1248, after Emperor Frederick's defeat at Parma, he saw his chance to ride a big wave. He defected to the Guelph camp, and while Guelphs were winning control all over northern Italy he managed to seize power in Rimini with the aid of the Church and neighbouring Guelph cities. The coup did not come off without resistance – 50 years of it in fact, but Malatesta was up to the challenge on every occasion, and settled the issue once and for all in 1295 by arranging a formal ceremony of reconciliation with the Parcitadi and the other Ghibellines, and then attacking them the same night while they slept. This redoubtable old warrior continued to run the city until 1312, when he was over 100, just like his neighbour and ally Guido 'the Old' da Polenta of Ravenna, whom he outlived by two years.

Malatesta left enough sons to keep control until 1334: Malatestino the Cross-eyed, Giovanni the Lame and Paolo the Fair, among others (Paolo was the lover of Francesca in Dante's famous story, Giovanni the deceived husband who did them both in). When the last of them were finally overthrown, it was another Malatesta who managed it: cousin Pandolfo, called Guastafamiglia, the 'family-wrecker', and his sons. As usual in Italy, bloody politics and great art were tripping hand in hand. While the Malatesta were having their fun, their city spawned one of the finest schools of trecento painting in Italy, including the great Pietro da Rimini.

After Guastafamiglia came Galeotto Malatesta (1364–85), succeeded by the only gentleman in the whole dynasty, Carlo, who presided over 44 years of prosperity and relative peace until his death in 1429. His time marked the height of Malatesta power and prestige; another branch of the family ruled Bergamo and Brescia, and another ruled Cesena (page 353). Carlo's nephew and successor Galeotto Roberto was more interested in piety than in ruling a city-state, and naturally all his neighbours took advantage of him, led, also naturally, by other Malatestas (yet another branch of the family, ruling at Pesaro). When a revolt broke out in Rimini, Roberto could only pray. But the Malatestas hadn't gone soft just yet. His brother Sigismondo, aged 14, raised some loyal troops and won control of the situation. Roberto packed himself off to a monastery two years later, and young Sigismondo slipped into his chair as *signore*.

Sigismondo Pandolfo Malatesta has gone into the books as one bad hombre. According to the great but sometimes credulous historian Jacob Burckhardt: 'the verdict of history ... convicts him of murder, rape, adultery, incest, sacrilege, perjury, and treason, committed not once, but often'. Burckhardt adds that his frequent attempts on the virtue of his children, both male and female, may have resulted from 'some astrological superstition'. In 1462, Pope Pius II accorded him a unique honour – a canonisation to Hell. The pope, who was behind most of the accusations, can be excused a little exaggeration. He wanted Sigismondo's land, and resorted to invoking supernatural aid and earthly propaganda when he couldn't beat him at war. For Sigismondo was one of the great *condottieri* or mercenary captains of the Renaissance; though at first the commander of the papal

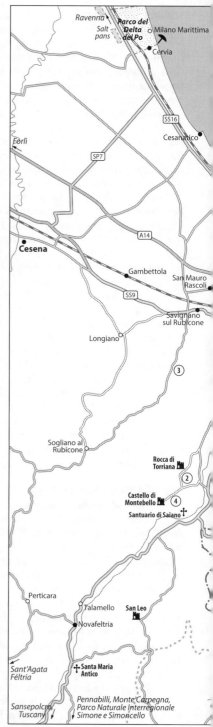

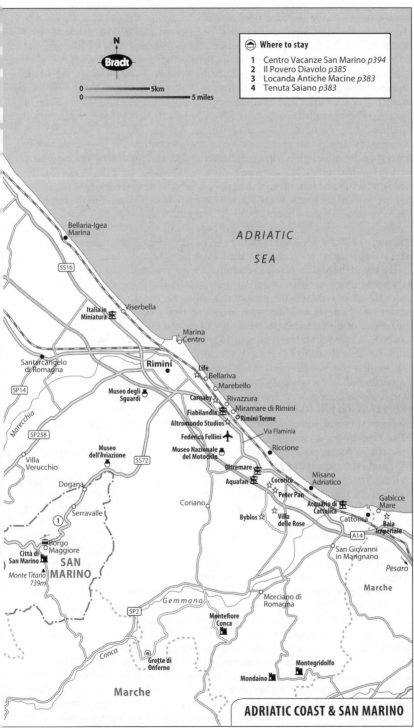

N

Bradt

| 0 | | 5km |
| 0 | | 5 miles |

⊖ **Where to stay**

1 Centro Vacanze San Marino *p394*
2 Il Povero Diavolo *p385*
3 Locanda Antiche Macine *p383*
4 Tenuta Saiano *p383*

ADRIATIC

SEA

Bellaria-Igea
Marina

SS16

Italia in
Miniatura   Viserbella

Marina
Centro

Santarcangelo
di Romagna   **Rimini**   Life
                                      Bellariva
SP14   Marebello
         Museo degli   Carnaby   Rivazzura
Marecchia   Sguardi   Miramare di Rimini
                          Fiabilandia Rimini Terme
SP258   Altromondo Studios
                     Federico Fellini   Via Flaminia
         Museo
Villa   dell'Aviazione   Museo Nazionale   Riccione
Verucchio   SS72   del Motociclo
                                    Oltremare
Dogana   Aquafan   Coconico   Misano
                                                Adriatico
         Serravalle   Coriano   Acquario di   Gabicce
                                    Peter Pan Cattolica   Mare
    ①   Byblos   Villa   Cattolica Baia
       Borgo   delle Rose   Imperiale
    Città di Maggiore   A14
    San Marino **SAN**   San Giovanni
Monte Titano ▲ **MARINO**   in Marignano
      739m   *Pesaro*
                                                    Marche
              Gemmano   Morciano di
SP2   Romagna
                        Montefiore
    Conca   Conca
              Grotte di
              Onferno   Montegridolfo
    Marche   Mondaino

ADRIATIC COAST & SAN MARINO

armies, he eventually switched sides and warred against the popes and their new champion, the 'ideal Renaissance prince' Federico da Montefeltro, the fellow who built the 'ideal Renaissance palace' at nearby Urbino (Federico, if the truth be told, was no sweetheart either, but once you start on Renaissance gossip there's no end to it).

Modern historians give Sigismondo better reviews, finding him on the whole no more pagan and perverse than the average Renaissance *signore*, and less so than many popes. Certainly, he was an able and intelligent ruler and a great patron of the arts, who brought Leon Battista Alberti, Piero della Francesca and Agostino di Duccio to work on his wonderful Temple. A long career as a successful and occasionally treacherous mercenary does not win many friends, though, and when the crisis came in his fight against the implacable Pius II, Sigismondo was on his own. By 1463 he had lost all his lands, and was allowed to keep only the city of Rimini; nearly bankrupt, he was forced to hire out his services as a mercenary again for the last five years of his life, two of which were spent fighting in Greece in the service of the Venetians. His son Roberto, called 'Il Magnifico', followed in his footsteps as a soldier, and mended fences by marrying Federico da Montefeltro's daughter. After winning a battle for Pope Sixtus IV in 1481, he was given a hero's welcome in Rome, after which he quite unaccountably died, most likely from poison.

The last of the Malatesta was a real rotter, the oppressive and violent Pandolfo IV. When the Wars of Italy began in 1494, Malatesta rule became increasingly precarious. Not only was the papacy still out to get the family, but the Riminesi, nobles and commoners alike, were becoming weary of them. Cesare Borgia, in the service of his father, Pope Alexander VI, seized the city in 1500, and though Pandolfo briefly won it back twice, in 1522 and 1527, the game was up. Papal rule proved as calamitous in Rimini as it was in that other citadel of the Renaissance, Ferrara; few places suffered as much. Famine in 1529 killed off a quarter of the population, and a French army ravaged the countryside as late as 1559.

FROM LAST RESORT TO FIRST RESORT The only notable events in Rimini's history for the next two centuries were the severe earthquakes that hit the city in 1672 and 1786. Even by the standards of the Papal State, 19th-century Rimini was a basket case, but its people played their part in the Risorgimento, joining the rebellion of 1831 and even staging one of their own in 1845.

Recovery, although perhaps no-one realised it, had already begun two years earlier from a most unexpected source – that worthless expanse of sand running along the Adriatic shore. Sea bathing had its origins as a medical cure, and a local doctor helped establish Italy's first Stabilimento Balneare in 1843. By the 1890s people were beginning to suspect that bathing might be fun, too. In the booming economy of the 1900s, the period when Italians really started to enjoy life again for the first time since the 1400s, beaches were the craze among the upper and middle classes; Rimini's famous Grand Hotel went up in 1908.

Working people got to join in, ironically, under Mussolini, who mandated paid vacations and discount holiday rail fares, and whose Dopolavoro (after work) organisation built big holiday complexes on the beaches for railroad men and factory workers and their families. After the war Rimini continued as a favourite of Italian families, and it also began to attract sun-seekers from all over Europe. Its latest metamorphosis has taken place in only the last ten years or so. Today you'll see as many signs in Russian as in English around the beaches; after the fall of the Iron Curtain, Rimini stood out as the one place that was close, friendly and relatively inexpensive. The influx of eastern Europeans only adds to the charm of the biggest, funkiest, most unpretentious and most cosmopolitan lido in Europe. Rimini is an up-and-coming place, full of confidence and more future-oriented than most Italian cities, with a busy Rimini Fiera exhibition centre, a new UFO-shaped Palacongressi for conventions, 6,000 students attending a branch of the University of Bologna and, coming in late 2018, a new museum dedicated to favourite son Federico Fellini.

GETTING THERE AND AROUND

BY AIR Regular international and domestic flights fly into Rimini's Federico Fellini airport [map, pages 358–9] (\ *0541 715711;* w *riminiairport.com*), located behind the beaches at Miramare (on the A14 coming from the south take the Riccione exit; from the north take the Rimini Sud exit). Frequent START buses (no 9) link the airport to the Rimini and Santarcangelo train stations.

BY RAIL Rimini's station [363 G1], built in 1861, is on Piazzale Cesare Battisti. It's a major junction, with direct trains from Turin, Milan, Bologna and Verona, hourly links up the coast to Ravenna, two daily direct trains to Ferrara, and 18 a day to Ancona and Rome. Cultural day-trippers who shudder at the thought of Rimini's beach madness can dip in easily – the Tempio Malatestiano (pages 369–70) is only a 10-minute walk from the station.

BY BUS Bonelli buses [363 G1] (*Piazzale Cesare Battisti 12;* *0541 662069;* w *bonellibus. net*) link the Adriatic resorts from Cesenatico to Gabicce Mare direct to L'Aquila and Rome via the *autostrada*; they also go to San Marino. Rimini's city and provincial buses are run by **START Romagna** (\ *0541 300811;* w *startromagna.it; see box, page 328*), and nearly all pass in front of the train station [363 G1]. Bus stops along the beaches are numbered; there are nine fare zones (see 'Find the Area' on START's useful English-language page). In summer, START's **Blue Line buses** and shuttles provide transport to most of the clubs and discos, departing from the station and Piazza Marvelli.

BY TAXI
🚕 **Radiotaxi** \0541 50020; w radiotaxirimini.it

BY CAR Rimini is the terminus of the Via Emilia (SS9); from the A14 Rimini Sud is the closest exit to the centre. Compared with Emilia-Romagna's other cities, parking restrictions are few, but it doesn't mean you'll find a spot by the beach in July and August. Many hotels have some kind of parking, even if it's only reserved spots along the street.

TOURIST INFORMATION

ℹ **Arimini Caput Viarum Visitor Centre** [363 E1] Corso d'Augusto 235; \0541 29833; w riminiromana.it; ⏰ Jun–Sep 10.00–12.30 & 16.30–20.00 Tue–Sat, 09.30–12.30 Sun, Oct–May 09.00–13.00 Tue & Thu, 15.00–19.00 Wed, Fri & Sat, 09.30–12.30 Sun. Information on the city & interactive exhibits on Roman Rimini with Julius Caesar as your guide.

ℹ **IAT Federico Fellini airport** [map, pages 358–9] Via Flaminia 409; \0541 378731; ⏰ summer only

ℹ **IAT Rimini FS** [363 E2] Piazzale Cesare Battisti, next to the station; \0541 51331; w riminiturismo.it; ⏰ 08.30–19.30 Mon–Sat, 08.30–12.30 Sun, closed Sun in winter

ℹ **IAT Rimini Marina Centro** [363 B2] Piazzale Fellini 3; \0541 56902; ⏰ winter 08.30–18.00 Mon–Fri, 08.30–13.00 Sat, summer 08.30–19.00 Mon–Sat, 09.00–noon Sun

ℹ **Infoline & hotel booking** \0541 53399

ℹ **Municipal Information** [363 E2] Piazza Cavour 29; \0541 704112; ⏰ 09.00–13.00 Mon–Fri, also 14.00–17.00 Tue & Thu

12

Rimini may have set up Italy's first sea-bathing establishment, but today the subject makes the city's holiday barons mildly uneasy. 'There's room for everybody,' they say, and in a way they're right. The resort has 15km of sandy beaches and 1,100 hotels – a quarter of all the hotels in Emilia-Romagna. At the usual resort ratio, that means about 85,000 beds. It could be a problem in August. If all the beds are full – plus another 25,000 or so day-trippers, campers and holiday apartment tenants – that makes 195,000 souls, or 13,000 per kilometre of beach front. With less than 10cm of shore per bum, if everyone hits the water at the same time the results could be catastrophic. Fortunately, this human tsunami will really need never happen. Many of these people at any given time will be in Rimini's 900 restaurants, 850 bars and pubs, 23 discos, 20 tennis clubs, ten riding schools, eight miniature golf courses, five theme parks, three funfairs, three bowling alleys, sailing schools and water parks.

WHERE TO STAY

A holiday in Rimini often means a modern, standard room; in August you'll probably have to take half board, which will probably be unfortunate. Most will be '*convenzionato*', ie: have arrangements with a *bagno*, offering discounts or free use of their sunbeds, umbrellas, etc.

People do not come to Rimini for scenery, charming inns or fine cuisine, but for the crowd and the endless possibilities for fun that go with it. If that sounds good, make sure to get a place in the centre where the action is. The places mentioned below are close to both the beach and *centro storico*. A third of them now stay open in the winter (there are enough conventions to make it worthwhile); by October rates plummet so low that going to Rimini can be cheaper than staying home, except on New Year's Eve, when the city is packed.

RIMINI

For listings, see pages 364–6

🛏 Where to stay

✖ Where to eat and drink

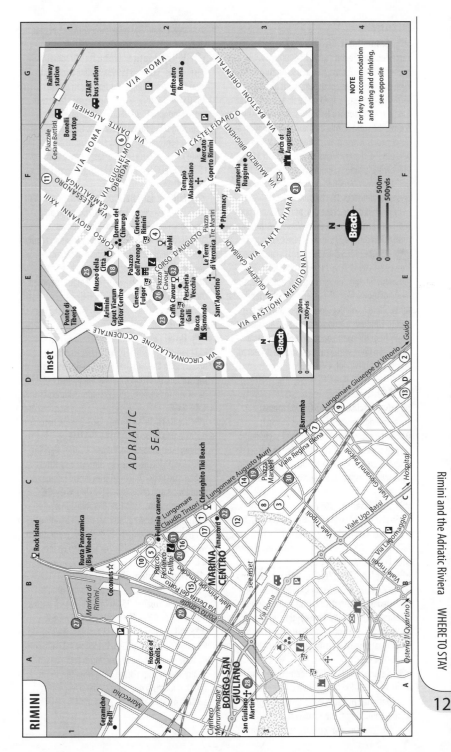

RIMINI

Inset

NOTE
For key to accommodation and eating and drinking, see opposite

LUXURY

🏠 **Grand Hotel** [363 B2] (117 rooms)
Parco Federico Fellini; 📞0541 56000; **w** www.
grandhotelrimini.com. This imposing turn-of-the-
20th-century palace of dreams with its beautiful
terrace & gardens helped make Rimini what it is
today. Young Federico Fellini was fascinated by it
& gave it a starring role in *Amarcord* (although a
hotel nearer Rome played the part), & when he
was older & richer always stayed in room 315.
Indecently luxurious, rooms glitter with well-
polished brass, Venetian antiques, & enormous
crystal chandeliers. It's the only hotel in Rimini
with its own dance orchestra, plus a heated pool
& private beach, tennis, Dolce Vita spa & fitness
centre. Rich buffet b/fast inc. €€€€€

🏠 **i-Suite** [363 D4] (54 rooms) Viale Regina
Elena 28; 📞0541 309671; **w** i-suite.it. Sleek,
luminous all-suite design hotel by the sea, with a
range of rooms from the essential to the penthouse
suite. Some have fireplaces, others have floor-to-
ceiling windows overlooking the sea. Also lovely
views from the avant-garde **i-Feel Good spa**
on the top floor, with sea-view saunas & heated
outdoor infinity pool. €€€€€

UPMARKET

🏠 **Ambasciatori** [363 C2] (62 rooms)
Viale Amerigo Vespucci 22; 📞0541 55561;
w hotelambasciatori.it. Brash, modern building
set just back from the sea, designed to attract a
youngish crowd, with an Art Deco American Bar,
pool, hydromassage & private beach. B/fast inc.
€€€€

🏠 **Ambassador** [363 D4] (53 rooms) Viale
Regina Elena 86; 📞0541 387207; **w** riminiclubhotel.
com/ambassador. Liberty-style hotel from the early
1900s overlooking the beach, with a shady garden &
pool; buffet b/fast inc. €€€€

🏠 **DuoMo** [363 E2] (43 rooms) Via Giordano
Bruno 28; 📞0541 24215; **w** duomohotel.com.
Designed by Rod Arad, colourful, shiny boutique
hotel for couples, with the reception desk in a giant
metal ring. 3 types of rooms & suites, rain showers
& open bathrooms. Parking available; b/fast inc.
€€€-€€€€

🏠 **Savoia** [363 C3] (110 rooms) Lungomare
Marri 13; 📞0541 396600; **w** savoiahotelrimini.
com. Designed by Paolo Portoghesi right on the
Marina Centro front, the Savoia offers white,
luminous contemporary rooms, spacious spa with

sea views & a private relax zone with a pool that
you can book. B/fast inc. €€€-€€€€

🏠 **Villa Adriatica** [363 B2] (84 rooms) Viale
Vespucci 3; 📞0541 54599; **w** villaadriatica.it.
Near the Parco Fellini, this hotel is in a villa of
1880 where Gabriele D'Annunzio met his great
muse Eleonora Duse. It offers lots for families,
including bikes for adults & kids. Rooms have
been recently renovated & sleep up to 4 &
there's a large terrace for b/fast, a pool, & use
of the i-Feel Good spa (see left); free parking.
€€€-€€€€

🏠 **Milton** [363 B2] (75 rooms) Via C Cappellini
1a; 📞0541 54600; **w** hotelmilton.com. In a
residential area by the beach with elegant,
soundproofed white & red rooms, including family
rooms sleeping 4. There's a good restaurant, &
garden bar, heated pool, spa (even a baby spa)
fitness centre, & b/fast with homemade breads in
the garden. B/fast inc. €€-€€€€

MID-RANGE

🏠 **Hotel Card International** [363 F2]
(53 rooms) Via Dante 50; 📞0541 26412; **w** en.
hotelcard.it. Close to the Tempio Malatestiano &
the station, this contemporary minimalist hotel
has a rooftop terrace, fitness centre & library.
€€-€€€

🏠 **Le Rose Suite Hotel** [363 D4] (50 rooms)
Viale Regina Elena 46; 📞0541 394289;
w lerosesuitehotel.com. Rooms & suites sleeping
up to 5 with kitchenettes by the sea; all with
queen-size beds. Other facilities include indoor &
outdoor heated pools, spa & parking. €€-€€€

🏠 **Napoleon** [363 F1] (60 rooms) Piazzale
C Battisti 22; 📞0541 27501; **w** napoleonrimini.
it. Pleasant hotel vintage 1973 in the *centro storico*
with big bathrooms & free parking. B/fast inc.
€€-€€€

🏠 **New Primula** [363 C3] (51 rooms) Viale
Trento 12; 📞0541 23712; **w** hotelnewprimula.
it. Also well situated, 150m from the beach with a
restaurant (€€). Buffet b/fast inc. €€-€€€

🏠 **Villa Lalla** [363 C2] (33 rooms) Viale
Vittorio Veneto 22; 📞0541 55155; **w** villalalla.com.
Midway between the *centro storico* & the beach,
family-run medium-sized hotel from the 1950s,
with big rooms & nice extras – bicycles, library
excursions, kids' activities, restaurant & parking.
€-€€€

BUDGET

🏠 **Delizia Rimini** [363 C3] (43 rooms) Viale Zanzur 11; **m** 329 081 2957; **w** deliziariminihotel. com. Basic en-suite dbls & trpls with parking, AC or fans, 5mins from the beach & a 15min walk from the centre. B/fast inc. **€–€€**

🏠 **Primavera** [363 D4] (49 rooms) Viale Lagomaggio 113; ☎ 0541 380206; **w** hotelprimavera.info. Classic friendly 2-star family hotel a 10min bus ride (no 11) from the station, a couple of streets from the beach with AC & balconies. FB in season. **€€**

SHOESTRING

🏠 **Jammin' Hostel** [363 C3] (10 dorms sleeping 4–8, 8 en-suite rooms sleeping 2–6) Viale Derna 22; ☎ 0541 390 800; **w** hosteljammin.com. 5mins from the beach, & just a bit further from the station, shared female or mixed dorms and rooms with cheap bike hire, a rooftop tiki bar & a young party atmosphere. **€**

🏠 **Sunflower City Hostel** [363 B2] Via Dardanelli 102; ☎ 0541 25180; **w** sunflowerhostel. com. Take a trip back to the 1970s in this lively hostel run by 3 ex-backpackers 10mins from the station, 200m from the beach. Dorm beds from €12/night, plus lots of activities; lockers, fans; b/fast inc. Some sgl & dbl rooms also available. **€**

✖ WHERE TO EAT AND DRINK

With *piadina* kiosks on nearly every corner you'll never starve.

EXPENSIVE

✖ **Guido** [363 D4] Lungomare Spadazzi 12; ☎ 0541 574612; **w** ristoranteguido.it; ⊕ closed lunch exc Sat–Sun. One of the top seafood restaurants in town opened its doors in 1946. Currently run by Guido's grandsons Gianpaolo & Gianluca, it still serves the freshest seafood *primi* & *secondi*, including superb oysters; 7-course *menu degustazione* €80. **€€€€€**

ABOVE AVERAGE

✖ **i-FAME** [363 D4] Lungomare Agosto Murri 65; ☎ 0541 386331; **w** i-suite.it/i-fame-rimini. php; ⊕ Jul–Aug lunch & dinner, otherwise eves only, closed Tue. The i-Suites' (see opposite) all-white, hip restaurant serves some of the most imaginative, original food in Rimini. Among the choices are a deluxe vegetarian menu (€42) & exotic seafood menu (€62). **€€€€**

✖ **Dallo Zio** [363 F3] Vicolo Santa Chiara 16; ☎ 0541 786747; **w** ristorantedallozio.it. Founded in 1965, seafood & old-fashioned charm near the Arco di Augusto popular with locals & tourists alike; try the marine lasagne & seafood-filled vol-au-vents. **€€€–€€€€**

MODERATE

✖ **Abocar Due Cucine** [363 E1] Via Carlo Farini 13; ☎ 0541 22279; **w** abocarduecucine.it; ⊕ eves only, closed Mon. In the *centro storico*, creative Italian-Argentinean restaurant with a terrace surrounding a tree dripping with fairy lights. The

menu features arty cocktails & nibbles, interesting set fish or meat menus (*from €39*) & daily specials. **€€€**

✖ **Il Pescato del Canevone** [363 E1] Via Tonini Luigi 34; **m** 366 354 1510; **w** ilpescatodelcanevone.it; ⊕ closed Mon & Sat lunch. Located in the bare brick walls of a 16th-century warehouse near the Museo della Città, the Pescato has no menu, but a blackboard offering the day's catch. Elegant atmosphere, fine wine & champagne list & service. **€€€**

✖ **L'Ingrata Grill & Cucina** [363 E2] Piazzetta San Martino 6; ☎ 0541 782490; **w** lingrata. com; ⊕ closed Mon. Just north of Piazza Cavour, contemporary restaurant with a garden, specialising in grilled meats but also in various marinated *carpacci* (raw sliced beef, goose & even pork), unusual *primi* (risotto with sautéed rabbit & preserved lemons), & fancy desserts. Good-value lunch menus. **€€€**

✖ **Molo 22** [363 B1] Via Ortigara 78/80, Darsena di Rimini; **m** 345 089 3907; **w** ristorantemolo22rimini.it; ⊕ eves only, in summer also lunch Sat–Sun. A glass-walled seafood restaurant with the best location in town: in the middle of the sea at the end of the marina boardwalk. Menus from €20; free parking. **€€€**

✖ **Osteria de' Borg** [363 A3] Via dei Forzieri 12; ☎ 0541 56074; **w** osteriadeborg.it. Head to this osteria in Borgo San Giuliano for a change from seafood, with a tantalising menu of soups, homemade pasta – try its famous *cappelletti* stuffed with carrot or *strozzapreti* with sausage & *strigoli* (bladder campion leaves) — grilled meats & other recipes from the interior of the province. Traditional 4-course menu €28. **€€€**

✕ Osteria delle Storie di Mare [363 B2] Via Fratelli Leurini 2; **℡** 0541 21101; **w** osteriadellestoriedimare.com; ⊕ closed Tue & lunch exc Sat–Sun. Succulent seafood, including the local *mazzancolle* (large prawns) & great views over the boat-filled Porto Canale; for dessert, don't miss the *sfogliatina calda di miele con la crema* (warm honey pastry with cream). **€€€**

✕ Taverna degli Artisti [363 B2] Viale Vespucci 1; **℡** 0541 28519; **w** tavernadegliartisti. com. A classic still going strong in the Marina Centro after 50 years, with photos of visiting celebrities. Come for seafood, pizzas, meats & a *degustazione* of whisky; they have almost every brand from around the world. **€€€**

CHEAP & CHEERFUL

✕ Bounty [363 C3] Via La Strada 6; **℡** 0541 391 900; **w** bountyrimini.it; ⊕ eves only. Yo ho ho! Board the ship of fun for a pirate pizza, pasta, burger & *frites*, or even a *bistecca alla fiorentina*. Corny but fun local institution at the Marina Centro, with live rock music on the terrace in summer & a DJ set every night from 23.30; in winter, country nights on Wed, disco on Sat & family night on Sun. **€€**

✕ Osteria Il Quartino [363 B4] Via Coriano 161; **℡** 0541 731215; **w** ilquartino.it. 4km from the Rimini Sud *autostrada* exit, dine in an old farmhouse or in the garden on the likes of *tagliata* & *ragù antico* or herb-filled ravioli Parma-style. Friday is Irish Angus steak night but there's also a vegetarian menu. **€€**

✕ Teatro Pane Vino e Caffè [363 E2] Piazza Cavour 6; **℡** 0541 51026; **w** teatrorimini.it; ⊕ 07.00–23.00 Fri–Wed. Front-row seats on the passing theatre that is Rimini; come for b/fast, *piadine*, pasta, hamburgers or *aperitivi*. **€–€€**

ROCK BOTTOM

✕ Casina del Bosco [363 B2] Viale Antonio Beccadelli 15; **℡** 0541 56295; **w** casinadelbosco.it; ⊕ Mar–Oct 11.30–02.00 daily. Overlooking the Parco Federico Fellini, a great place to grab a quick *piadina* lunch, with an Amarcord or a Gradisca craft beer, salad & fancy desert. **€**

✕ Piada e Cassoni da Ciana e Monda [363 C3] Viale Don Giovanni Bosco 1; **m** 348 563 2992; **w** cianaemonda.it; ⊕ 16.30–22.30 Tue–Thu, 11.30–15.30 & 16.40–22.30 Sat–Sun. Near the beach, just off Viale Regina Elena, offering a huge menu of tasty *piadine* & *cassoni* (with a pocket, similar to a pitta). **€**

GELATERIE

♈ Gelateria Biologica Santa Colomba [363 E2] Piazza Malatesta 35; **℡** 0541 149 4018; **w** gelateriasantacolomba.it. Luscious organic *gelato* (try the Brazilian coffee) & ice cream pastries, sorbet & granitas. **€**

♈ Gelateria 3 Bis [363 C3] Viale Amerigo Vespucci 73; **℡** 0541 020 966; **w** gelateria3bis. it. Best *gelato* by the beach (including a decadent Nutella flavour), as well as crêpes, frozen yoghurt, shakes & smoothies. **€**

♈ Gelateria il Castello [363 D3] Via Dario Campana; **℡** 0541 020510; **w** gelateriailcastello. com. By the Rocca Sismondo, 24 delicious flavours made fresh daily; lots of nutty & chocolate flavours, & non-dairy fruit flavours. **€**

ENTERTAINMENT AND NIGHTLIFE

BAGNI AND BEACHES When Riminesi first meet, often the first question they ask is which *bagno* they frequent. The beach is lined with 250 *stabilimenti balneari*, or *bagni* (the numbers on the roofs help helicopters locate them in case of emergencies). They vary widely: some have jacuzzis, yoga lessons, posh restaurants, sports facilities, four-poster sunbeds, etc; some have facilities for guests with disabilities, some allow dogs, some have playgrounds and activities for children. For a complete list, with their facilities, see **w** riminibeach.it/bagni-stabilimenti. There are also public beaches (Piazzale Boscovich by the port and Marebello nos 105–108 are the biggest), but by law, you can swim anywhere if you stay within 5m of the shore.

BARS On summer nights many of the *bagni* become music bars.

♀ **Chiringuito Tiki Beach** [363 C2] Lungomare Claudio Tintori 30 (Bagno 26); ☎0541 27058; w chiringuitorimini.it; ⊕ round the clock in summer. One of the liveliest beach bars, with good snacks; often with live music & theme nights (even for the over 30s).

♀ **Barrumba** [363 C3] Lungomare Murri 79; ☎0541 307541; w barrumba.it; ⊕ summer 17.00–03.00. One of Rimini's 'musts' for starting the evening with a delicious cocktail or beer; also excellent pizzas, live music & super-friendly staff. Always packed, so book.

♀ **Caffè Cavour** [363 E2] Piazza Cavour 12; ☎051 785123; f cavour.caffe; ⊕ until midnight. Classic place for an *aperitivo* with good nibbles while watching the passing crowd.

♀ **NoMi** [363 E2] Via Giordano Bruno 28; m 335 704 8607; ⊕ 07.00–02.00 daily. Sleek & stylish cocktail bar in the DuoMo hotel (page 364).

♀ **Rock Island Molo di Levante** [363 B1] Via Largo Boscovich; ☎0541 23797; w rockislandmolodilevante.it; ⊕ 18.00–03.00. A Rimini institution on stilts in the port, with a great terrace, live concerts, excellent cocktails: also the perfect place to watch the sun go down.

CLUBS AND DISCOS (See map, pages 358–9, unless otherwise stated) The Adriatic Riviera is Italy's clubland. At weekends crowds descend from within a 200km radius, and on mornings-after the road back to Bologna is often scattered with the battered cars of partygoers who didn't quite make it home. From mid-June to late August most are open every night; out of season, the indoor ones are Friday and Saturday nights only. Entrance fees are €10–€20 and usually include your first drink. In summer Blue Line all-night buses link the major venues to the main resorts; bus 11 links Rimini station to Riccione; another night bus runs from Riccione and Cattolica stations up glitzy Misano Monte (for details of buses, see page 361).

☆ **Altromondo Studios** Via Flaminia 358, Rimini; m 335 564 5740; w altromondo.com; f. Where James Brown & Ray Charles once played: a massive spaceship-style venue near the airport. Now mostly electronic music. You'll need a taxi, but they aren't too dear.

☆ **Baia Imperiale** Via Panoramica 36, Gabicce Mare; ☎0541 950 312; w baiaimperiale.net. On a scenic promontory on the Marche border, the largest club on the coast replicates an ancient Roman imperial villa, complete with colonnades, fountains, pools, statues, flaming torches, & 5 floors with all kinds of music. From Riccione, take the no 125 yellow line or the special nightclub shuttle.

☆ **Byblos** Via Pozzo Castello 24, Misano Adriatica; ☎0541 607345; w byblosclub.com. In the hills above Riccione, an old jet-setter place enjoying a renaissance: a white villa with a glassed-in gazebo, dance floor & terrace, with a mix of music, good restaurant, Italian celebrities & a chance to wear your bling. Reached by the Riccione nightclub shuttle.

☆ **Carnaby** Viale Brindisi 20, Rimini; m 335 622 2784; w carnaby.it. Young & fun-loving on the Rivazzurra: R&B & soul in the Cave, house & hits in the Dance area & a 3rd-floor party zone. Bus 11, stop 26.

☆ **Coconuts** [363 B1] Via Lungomare Tintori 5, Rimini; m 345 655 2701; w coconuts.it. Energetic Latino, reggae & hip hop by the port.

☆ **Cocoricò** Via Chieti 44, Riccione; ☎0541 605183; w cocorico.it; ⊕ 23.00–06.00 Mon–Fri, 22.00–08.00 Sat–Sun. Fatboy Slim's favourite club in Rimini is capped by a giant pyramid big enough for 2,000 party animals.

☆ **Life** Viale Regina Margherita 11, Rimini; m 347 793 3091; w liferimini.com. Rap, R&B & hip hop on 2 dance floors. Bus 11, stop 22.

☆ **Peter Pan** Via Scacciano 161, Riccione; m 393 502 7597; w peterpanclub.net. Up on Misano Monte, 1 of the biggest beasts with top DJs, with a wide range of sounds.

☆ **Villa delle Rose** Via Camilluccia 16, Misano Adriatico; m 393 502 7595; w villadellerose.net. Up on the hills, expensive glamour disco that people love or hate. Reached by the Riccione nightclub shuttle.

SPAS Rimini had the first thalassotherapy spa in Italy; its now up-to-date spa, **Rimini Terme** [map, page 363] (*Viale Principe di Piemonte 56, Miramare di Rimini*; ☎ *0541 424011*; w *riminiterme.com*; ⊕ *all year*) has seawater pools, wellness paths and much more.

THEME PARKS [map, pages 358–9] Mirabilandia (page 323) might be bigger, but this coast has its share of amusements waiting to fleece hapless parents. From late June to August, Bonelli shuttle buses (✆ *0541 662069*; w *bonellibus.it*) link the resorts to Italia in Miniatura, Oltremare, Aquafan and the Acquario di Cattolica. Discounts are available if you visit more than one; check their websites.

Acquario di Cattolica Piazzale delle Nazioni 1A, Cattolica; ✆0541 8371; w acquariodicattolica. it; ⏰ Apr–mid-Jun & 1st half Sep 09.30–16.30, mid-Jun–Aug 10.00–21.30, some w/ends at other times (see website, also for feeding times); admission €20, over 65s & under 140cm €16, under 1m free, families 50% discount on Tue. 2nd-largest aquarium in Italy, with lots of sharks, rays, penguins & otters.

Aquafan Viale Ascoli Piceno 6, Riccione; ✆0541 4271; w aquafan.it; ⏰ Jun–mid-Sep 10.00–18.30; admission (for 2 days) €30, under 140cm & over 65s €21, under 1m free. Massive water park just off the Riccione A14 exit with scary bits for teenagers, & DJs.

Fiabilandia Via Cardano 15, Rivazzurra di Rimini; ✆0541 372064; w fiabilandia.net; ⏰ see website; admission: over 130cm €23.50, under 130cm €16.50, under 3s free. 'Fairyland', an amusement park for tots.

Italia in Miniatura Via Popilia 239, Viserba di Rimini; ✆0541 736736; w italiainminiatura. com; ⏰ mid-Mar–Sep 09.30–18.30 (Aug until 19.00); Oct–Mar 09.30–16.30 Sat, Sun & holidays; admission (for 2 days) €10–€23, reduced €7–17 depending on season (see website), children under 1m free. Besides 272 mouse-sized Italian cathedrals & castles, this offers mini highlights of Europe, a ride down a flume, toy race track, science exhibits & a 7D cinema. Take bus 8 from Rimini station.

Oltremare Viale Ascoli Piceno 6, Riccione; ✆0541 4271; w oltremare.org; ⏰ Apr–mid-Sep 10.00–18.00 (Aug until 19.00), see website for other dates; admission €26. Butterfly garden, storks, farm animals, seahorses & Mississippi alligators, & bird of prey, parrot & dolphin shows.

SHOPPING

An **outdoor market** with clothes and everything else takes place in and around Piazza Tre Martiri [363 F2] (⏰ *07.00–13.00 Wed & Sat*).

Amarcord [363 C3] Viale Vespucci 67; ✆0541 56956; w amarcordromagna.it. Great place to pick up a ceramic, textile or foodie souvenir of Romagna.

Ceramiche Brolli [363 A1] Viale Cervignano del Friuli 7, Rimini Rivabella; ✆0541 780130; w ceramichebrolli.it. Ceramic workshop hidden away in a residential area.

Le Terre di Veronica [363 E2] Via Soardi 23; m 328 230 4048; w leterrediveronica.it. Funky arty & useful ceramics in the *centro storico*.

Mercato Coperto Rimini [363 F2] Via Castelfiadardo 15–21; w mercatocopertorimini.it; ⏰ 07.00–19.45 Mon–Sat. Rimini's indoor market is full of goodies, with an enormous seafood section.

Stamperia Ruggine [363 F3] Via Bertani 36; ✆0541 50811; w teleromagnole.com. Traditional Romagnola hand-stamped dishtowels, tablecloths, bags, etc.

OTHER PRACTICALITIES

HOSPITAL
⊞ [363 C4] Viale Luigi Settembrini 2; ✆0541 705 111

PHARMACY
✚ [363 E3] Piazza Tre Martiri 11

POST OFFICE
✉ [363 F3] Largo Giulio Cesare 1

You may recognise some of the street scenes of old Rimini from *Amarcord* – which wasn't filmed here, but meticulously reproduced at Cinecittà in Rome. For the fact that there is any *centro storico* at all, thank Italian determination and the *dov'era com'era* (where it was, as it was) spirit. During 1943–44, 369 bombing raids hit 82% of Rimini's buildings, possibly the highest proportion in Italy, and half of these were completely destroyed or damaged beyond repair. When the Allies took the city, they found a ghost town; nearly everyone had fled to San Marino or the hills.

TEMPIO MALATESTIANO [363 F3] (*Via IV Novembre 35;* ✆ *0541 51130;* 🕐 *08.30–noon & 15.30–18.30 Mon–Fri, 08.30–12.30 & 15.30–19.00 Sat, 09.00–12.30 & 15.30–18.30 Sun; admission free*) Some special angel (though not necessarily a Christian one) seems to have been watching over Rimini's unique Renaissance monument, the eclectic and thoroughly mysterious work that has come to be known as Tempio Malatestiano: old photos show it standing almost alone in a field of ruins. Though badly damaged, the Tempio found another unlikely angel after the war – southern US dime-store magnate Samuel Kress, whose foundation brought the nickels and dimes of Dixie to the rescue. A more thorough rehabilitation was completed more recently, and the Tempio is looking as bright and new as it did to Sigismondo and Isotta.

Whatever Sigismondo's personal habits, he was an educated man and a good judge of art. To transform this unfinished 13th-century Franciscan church into his temple he called in two Tuscan geniuses: Leon Battista Alberti to redesign the exterior and Agostino di Duccio for the reliefs inside. The project that began in the 1440s as a simple chapel soon grew into the reconstruction of the entire building, as Alberti encased the church in new exterior walls of Istrian marble. Slow in building, owing to Sigismondo's many distractions and perennial lack of funds, the temple was never completed. Work stopped completely in 1461, a disastrous time in which the *signore* was excommunicated and beset with enemies on all sides. Alberti's intentions for the completed building can be seen in a medal minted for Sigismondo at the beginning of its construction. A second-storey arch was to have been built over the portal (as in the architect's Sant'Andrea in Mantua); the gable-like pediment around it would have been rounded, and the entire work would have been dominated by a great dome, as wide as the building itself and more than doubling its height.

Scholars have been puzzling for centuries over just what sort of temple Sigismondo had in mind. Although it's been Rimini's cathedral since 1809, the temple is hardly a Christian building; lame attempts to claim it as such run up against the near-total absence of Christianity anywhere in its decoration, which celebrates astrology and the liberal arts amid an enchanted forest of allegories, putti and enigmatic symbols and mottoes. Pope Pius himself, in his long list of accusations against Sigismondo, mentioned 'the building of a pagan temple'. Some have tried to explain the work as a temple to Sigismondo's muse, Isotta degli Atti, his long-time mistress and third wife, who is buried here along with Sigismondo. But it goes deeper than that. One of the *signore*'s court scholars, Roberto Volturio, mentioned in his writings that the entire temple was full of symbols that would proclaim the doctrines of arcane philosophy to the learned, while remaining hidden to vulgar folk. That, unfortunately, includes all of us; whatever secret Neo-Platonic philosophy was current at Sigismondo's court is probably lost forever (see box, pages 371–3).

Alberti's unfinished exterior, grafting Roman arcades and pilasters on to the plain Franciscan building, grievously feels the lack of the upper storey of the façade, and the planned cupola that might have tied the composition together. The big arches on the sides were meant to hold sarcophagi of notable men; only a few were ever used, including one on the right side that holds the Greek philosopher Gemistos Plethon, whose remains Sigismondo brought back from Mistra in the Peloponnese.

Interior Inside, four pairs of chapels hold the temple's major feature, the sculptural reliefs made by Agostino di Duccio. Among the greatest works of the Renaissance, these are mostly on the pilasters on the edges of the chapels, above the recurring devices of the decorative scheme: the omnipresent monograms S and I, for Sigismondo and Isotta, together like a dollar sign, and plenty of elephants, the Malatesta heraldic symbol of strength and long memories.

In the left aisle, the first chapel contains figures of the classical sibyls and prophets, along with the Arca degli Antenati (Tomb of the Ancestors) and reliefs of Minerva and the Triumph of Scipio. The third is decorated with quite strange reliefs of children, and the fourth with allegories of the liberal arts and sciences. On the right, just inside the door is the **Tomb of Sigismondo**. The first chapel has reliefs of putti or angels, while the second has the famous fresco by Piero della Francesca (1451) of *Sigismondo and His Patron St Sigismund*, an obscure Vandal king of Burgundy. Sigismondo got the Medici in Florence to send Piero up to him, and this revolutionary artist gave him the first work of the Florentine Renaissance style north of the Apennines. Paintings of a ruler and his patron saint were common, but nothing like this calm, naturalistic one.

In the next chapel a painted *Crucifix* by Giotto is the only surviving work from the original decoration of San Francesco. Giotto had been commissioned to decorate the entire church early in the 1300s, and other works of his may well have been destroyed by Sigismondo's rebuilding. His crucifix shares the space with the **Tomb of Isotta degli Atti**, by Matteo de' Pasti. The pilasters on this side contain some of Agostino's finest work, in the allegorical panels of the planets and signs of the zodiac; note especially the enchanting Moon – Cynthia in her silver car – and a scene of 15th-century Rimini beneath the claws of the Crab, the city's and Sigismondo's natal sign.

PIAZZA TRE MARTIRI [363 F2] Named after three heroes of the Resistance who were executed here, this once dowdy piazza, now pedestrianised, unabashedly modern but harmonious, occupies the site of the Roman forum. There's a statue of Julius Caesar and stone pillar commemorating his famous *Alea jacta est* speech after crossing the Rubicon. Via IV Novembre was the *cardo maximus* (part of the original Roman paving is displayed at number 38), while the other main street running through the square, the **Corso d'Augusto**, was the *decumanus*. Here and there are fragments of ancient buildings embedded in the walls. The Torre dell'Orologio, originally from the 1500s, was rebuilt in 1759.

Piazza Tre Martiri is apparently haunted: in the 13th century the Knights Templars had an important commandery here. Witches were burned here. In the 1920s and 30s Rosicrucians, Theosophists and Mesmerisers gathered to hold seances. In the 1950s and 60s Italy's foremost mediums, Luciano and Serina Rossi, set up here, and by the 1970s Rimini had so many bizarre sects that it challenged Turin as Italy's capital of the occult.

ARCH OF AUGUSTUS [363 H3] (*South end of the Corso d'Augusto*) This monumental gateway in the city walls is actually the oldest surviving triumphal arch in Italy, built in 27BC to honour the first emperor and mark the meeting of the Via Aemilia, the

tempus loquendi, tempus tacendi
Inscription in the Malatesta Temple, Rimini

'A time to speak, and a time to be silent.' This enigmatic motto is repeated in small letters throughout the decoration of Sigismondo Malatesta's Temple in Rimini, carved on banners entwined with the trunks of Sigismondo's omnipresent stone elephants. These elephants have been faithfully keeping their secrets now for more than 500 years. But if they ever decide it is time to speak, they could tell us things about the Renaissance we never imagined.

In 1438, only 14 years before the fall of Constantinople to the Ottoman Turks, a solemn Ecumenical Council was held at Ferrara and Florence to discuss the reunion of eastern and western Christianity, with the hope of raising support in the west for military aid against the Turks. In fact, a union of the churches was proclaimed in 1439, though the haughty Byzantines, whose 'empire' by then consisted of nothing beyond part of the Peloponnese and Constantinople itself, scornfully dismissed it.

But the council was a momentous event nonetheless, if only for bringing some of Greece's most learned men to an Italy thirsting for the knowledge of classical antiquity. Among the delegation from Constantinople was Bessarion, who became a cardinal in the western Church and brought the important collection of Greek books that became the nucleus of the new library in Venice. Another was the 82-year-old George Gemistos Plethon, the last philosopher of Byzantium. Not much is known for certain about what Gemistos Plethon was really up to, courtesy of the Patriarch of Constantinople, who burned all his manuscripts after he died, but his presence must certainly have livened up the Council, for Gemistos Plethon was a thoroughgoing pagan.

His stay in Italy was one of the principal causes for a profound influx of Neo-Platonic thought, the undercurrent to so much that happened in the Renaissance. In the late Roman Empire, many Platonic ideas had got mixed up with Orphic religion, elements from Pythagoreanism, eastern mystery cults and magic, and it was in this form that Gemistos Plethon brought them back to Italy. By this time, a few surviving late Roman mystical texts were erroneously assumed to be much older. Renaissance scholars saw them as the fount of all philosophy and religion, dating back to the Egyptians and the mythical figure of Hermes Trismegistus, 'Thrice-great Hermes', founder of letters and science and the most ancient of prophets, in fact the teacher of Moses.

Marsilio Ficino, doctor, priest, philosopher and magus of Florence, was the man chiefly responsible for the dissemination of these ideas in Italy. His patron Lorenzo de' Medici had him translate some of these Hermetic books in 1471 – bidding him hold off on his translations of Plato until this more important work was finished. Ficino also translated the Enneads of Plotinus, the mystical philosopher of 3rd-century AD Alexandria, who contributed more to what came to be known as Neo-Platonism than Plato himself. While all this work was under way, Ficino led the informal 'Platonic Academy' in its discussions at the country villa of Lorenzo de' Medici. After Ficino came Pico della Mirándola, lord of that small town in the Po Valley. Pico, who wrote the

continued overleaf

12

famous manifesto of Renaissance humanism, the *Oration on the Dignity of Man*, was also a kabbalist and Hermetist. His magical 900 *Conclusiones* so shocked Rome in 1486 that Lorenzo had to intercede with the pope to get him out of jail.

Willing neither to dispose of Christianity entirely, nor to let their thought be subjected to its dogmas, these philosophers concentrated on what they saw as a 'natural religion' that lay beneath the surface of all faiths. Its origin was in ancient Egypt, with Hermes Trismegistus (or in Iran, with Zoroaster, according to Gemistos Plethon), and it reappeared in different forms through Moses, Orpheus, Pythagoras, Plato and finally Christ. Along with the natural religion went a 'natural magic'. The gods of the old religion, along with their planetary counterparts, the seven 'Governors of the sensible world', and the constellations, were considered as Platonic forms, ideas in the mind of God. To each corresponded elements in nature: stones and plants, as well as symbols, places and times. The natural magic of the Neo-Platonists consisted in manipulating these to capture the virtues of the forms in an image, constructing it of the proper materials, at the proper astrologically determined time. Such an image could be a talisman – or it could be a work of art.

We will probably never know how many Renaissance paintings and sculptures were specifically made as magical images. The famous mythological allegories of Botticelli certainly were. In the *Primavera*, for example, the three main figures represent the three 'good' planets, Jupiter, Venus and the Sun; Ficino recommended their healthy influence to counteract the gloomier side of scholarly, Saturnine natures like his own. Something similar is likely to be behind the two ambitious Neo-Platonic works of Emilia-Romagna, the Malatesta Temple and the frescoes of the Palazzo Schifanoia at Ferrara; both of these are astrologically comprehensive images of the universe as a whole. The decoration of the Malatesta Temple is particularly fascinating; it seems to draw us on, inviting us to try to solve its puzzle. Some have claimed that the Temple provides a complete exposition of Neo-Platonic doctrines, readable only to initiates, and that it was a site for secret rites of Sigismondo Malatesta and his court.

Such things could not be fully laid out in plain sight. Persecution of the humanist scholars by the Church had already appeared, in a mild form, in the 1460s under Pope Paul II, though they were encouraged under his successor Sixtus IV. There was indeed a time to speak, and a time to be silent. Less than 20 years after Pope Pius II condemned the 'pagan' Malatesta Temple, Hermeticism was at work in the Pope's own city of Siena, where artists covered the cathedral pavement with inlaid stone figures of Hermes Trismegistus himself, along with the sibyls of antiquity and philosophical allegories that cannot be interpreted today.

Via Popilia and the Via Flaminia. The small busts flanking the entrance are Jupiter and Apollo, and Minerva and Neptune.

ANFITEATRO ROMANO [363 G2] (⊕ *Always*) From the Arch of Augustus Via Bastioni Orientali runs east to a less well-preserved relic, the amphitheatre. Built in the reign of Hadrian, in AD138, this temple of Roman vileness was used for barely a century; in the unsettled 3rd century AD, when cities started to build walls, Rimini's incorporated the amphitheatre into a bastion. Most of its stones were later cannibalised, and the site was covered with houses until excavations in the 1920s.

Of all the curious baggage that came along with Neo-Platonism, none perhaps was more curious than a book called the *Picatrix*, which was probably written by the last pagans of the Middle East, the star-worshipping Sabeans of Harran, and transmitted through the Muslim world to Spain. The *Picatrix* is a book of magic that deals with the making of talismans and star images, and it is based on the 36 asterisms (star groups) called the *decans*. These originated at least 4,000 years ago in Egypt, where they often appear on coffin lids and the ceilings of tombs. Each *decan* was a daemon, a spirit something less than a god. Each one ruled a 10-day 'week' of the 360-day Egyptian calendar, and each had its moment when its stars were seen to rise just before the sun. Sirius, whose 'heliacal rising' promised the annual flooding of the Nile, was the first and most important of them.

The *decans* lost their everyday importance in Egypt after the conquest of Alexander, and the introduction of the zodiac and a new calendar. But they lived on in magic, and their great antiquity gave them special power and mystery. The *decans* were condemned by St Augustine and Origen, and as the Christians turned daemons into mere demons, the whole business began to have a whiff of the infernal about it. In the Middle Ages, though astrology was widely accepted, any old books that mentioned *decans* would have been the sort that monks kept locked away in a special place.

Ficino, in his book *De vita coelitus comparanda* (On capturing the nature of the stars), touched on the *decans*, but it was probably through some other channel that their images found their way into Renaissance art, in the magnificent frescoes planned by Cosmè Tura for Borso d'Este in the Palazzo Schifanoia at Ferrara. Under the Este that city was an important centre of the new philosophy and mysticism. In the 1470s, a chair of Platonic philosophy was established at the University of Ferrara, held by philosopher Francesco Patrizi. *Decans* were still dangerous, and in all Italy they only appear in one other place, in the frescoes by Niccolò Miretto in the Salone of the Palazzo della Ragione in Padua.

Sigismondo Malatesta died in 1468, just after his return from an expedition to the Peloponnese. What was he doing in Greece, with his city almost bankrupt and threatened by enemies on all sides? Trying to make a little money, of course, and at the same time working on his last grand gambit – that successes in Greece would restore his power and reputation, and perhaps even lead to western enthusiasm for a crusade against the Turks to reconquer Constantinople. The Turks were too strong, and Sigismondo came home empty-handed – except for the body of Gemistos Plethon, which he had dug up from Mistra and transferred to his temple at Rimini, where it is buried under a Greek inscription that proclaims him the 'Greatest of the Philosophers'.

PIAZZA CAVOUR North on Corso d'Augusto, Piazza Cavour is decorated with a lovely marble pine cone fountain of 1545 (replicated in the snowball and peacock scene in Fellini's *Amarcord*). Its glowering bronze statue of Pope Paul V was sufficiently loved in Rimini that, when Napoleon's troops came to town, they changed his name to San Gaudenzo, the city's patron saint, to keep the anti-papal troops from destroying it.

Piazza Cavour was the medieval heart of town, before Rimini grew back to fill its Roman street plan. Its **Palazzo dell'Arengo** [363 E2] has been the town hall since 1207; an arch connects it to the **Palazzo del Podestà**, built in the 1300s. The name is a bit misleading; in the 1300s there were no more imperial *podestàs* – only Malatestas. Under the arch, note the stone dated 1544 with all Rimini's standard measures and

12

Nulla si sa, tutto s'immagina (One knows nothing, one imagines everything)

Federico Fellini

The futile, frustrated Hollywood fantasies in the Cinema Fulgor are a key scene in *Amarcord*, Fellini's portrait of provincial Italy in the 1930s. On one level, the film is about Rimini: the characters, all masterfully sketched by a born caricaturist, were based on real people, and many of the vignettes really did happen, from the madman in the tree screaming 'I want a woman!' to the passing of the ocean liner *Rex*.

Romagnolo dialect poet Tonino Guerra (page 29) collaborated on the script, and the film is chock full of lyrical local colour, from the early shots of the *fogarazza*, the burning in March of the witch of winter, to the collective fantasies about romantic sheikhs in the Grand Hotel. The familiarity is increased by Fellini's jocular messing about with the traditional role of audience and director: on several occasions a pedantic lawyer tries to give a tour of Rimini while Fellini himself blows raspberries and throws snowballs at him from behind the camera. But from the beginning, everything is suspect: it's the village idiot who introduces the film, casting doubts on all that follows. For Fellini the autobiographical details were incidental; *Amarcord*, he insisted, did not mean 'I remember' (*mi ricordo*), but was rather 'like a brand of *aperitivo*' made of many things blended together.

In an interview he gave called 'The Fascism within Us', Fellini explained that one of his reasons for making the film came from his conviction that *Amarcord*'s dominant themes of adolescence and fascism are:

the permanent historical seasons of our lives; adolescence of our individual lives, fascism of our national life. That is, this remaining children for eternity, this leaving responsibilities for others, this living with the comforting sensation that there is someone who thinks for you (and at one time it's mother ... another time Il Duce, another time the Madonna ...);

brick sizes engraved on it. Both of these *palazzi* had to be substantially rebuilt after the war. The bombs totally gutted the **Teatro Galli** [363 E2], one of the last bits of Rimini still waiting to be completely redeemed. Opposite the Palazzo dell'Arengo is the entrance to a graceful old arcade of the **Pescheria Vecchia** [363 E2], or old Fish Market of 1747, evocatively lit in the evening.

CINETECA RIMINI [363 E2] (*Via Gambalunga 27;* ☎ *0541 704302;* ⓕ) Just north of the piazza, the Cineteca is part of the city library, housing films especially devoted to Rimini or made by Riminese directors. Since 2015, it has taken charge of the Fondazione Federico Fellini (w *federicofellini.it*), founded by the director's sister Maddalena in 1995. It ran into trouble when Fellini's niece, journalist Francesca Fabbri Fellini, fell out with other members and kept his Oscars and library in a feud that director Pupi Avati, head of the foundation, commented was worthy of *Amarcord* itself and would have made Fellini laugh. Nearby at Corso d'Augusto 12, the Art Deco **Cinema Fulgor** [363 E2] is a place that figured prominently in the director's personal mythology where he was introduced to the fantasy world of film. The cinema reopened in 2017 after a five-year restoration; other floors in the same building are destined to become the 'House of Cinema' as part of a Fellini Museum in 2018, with exhibits from Fellini's films, his life and *Book of Dreams* where he jotted down and drew all of his dreams.

and in the meanwhile, you have this limited, time-wasting freedom which permits you only to cultivate absurd dreams – the dream of the American cinema, or the Oriental dream concerning women; in conclusion, the same, old, monstrous out-of-date myths that even today seem to me to form the most important conditioning of the average Italian.

According to Fellini, what ultimately binds *Amarcord*'s hapless characters is confusion and ignorance; all of Rimini, in fact, is shown to be in a state of arrested development.

Unlike Bertolucci and other Italian directors, Fellini doesn't demonise the Fascists or allow his Italian audience to dismiss them as brutal perverts, as something alien to themselves; his bumbling, clownish blackshirts are as misguided as everyone else. The frequent scenes of fog and smoke not only give *Amarcord* its dreamy air, but symbolise the ignorance and alienation (at one point the fog is so thick the grandfather can't even find his own door). An enigmatic motorcyclist goes around and around; a peacock, the symbol of vanity, appears in the snow; the priest and the teachers misinform and misguide.

'The pretext of being together is always a levelling process. People stay together only to commit stupid acts,' said Fellini, and the several occasions in the film when his slightly crazy and frustrated but individually innocuous characters gather together – for the bonfire, for the Fascist holiday of 21 April, or to greet the Fascist bigwig – are when they become disquieting and truly imbecilic, caught up in the ritual, void of individual responsibility, capable of any madness.

If anyone in Rimini is on to the real intentions of their favourite son, they do not seem to hold it against him. The best caricaturists can't help making the humanity of their subjects shine through. And the director himself, for all the sardonic scolding of his interviews, was incapable of making his home town and its people seem anything but perfectly endearing.

ROCCA SISMONDO [363 D2] (*Piazza Malatesta;* ⏲ *for temporary exhibitions only*) The bulky castle of the Malatestas, which grew out of the family's complex of houses, begun when Malatesta da Verucchio moved into the city in 1216. Built by Sigismondo in 1446, and possibly designed by Brunelleschi, the great architect of quattrocento Florence, the castle was sold at a knockdown price by the last of the Malatesta, Pandolfo IV, to Cesare Borgia after he lost control of the city. Since then it has lost all its Renaissance graces to partial demolitions in the 17th and 19th centuries (the popes used it as a prison); you can see how it originally looked in Piero della Francesca's painting in the Tempio Malatestiano. The relief elephant over the gate, Sigismondo's symbol, survives, though little else does. By the end of 2018, the surrounding piazza will be pedestrianised to host another part of the Fellini Museum: the Arenas of Art, with spaces dedicated to outdoor performances etc.

SANT'AGOSTINO [363 E2] (*Via Cairoli 14, just off Piazza Cavour;* ☎ *0541 781268;* ⏲ *08.30–noon & 15.30–18.30 daily*) Not many works by the trecento school of Rimini remain in the city, but some of the best are in this church, rediscovered after an earthquake in 1916. The *Storia della Vergine* by an unknown painter (perhaps Giovanni da Rimini) show the influence of Giotto in many ways, not least of which is the use of simple architectural fantasies for backgrounds, turning such scenes as the *Presentation at the Temple* into self-contained dreamlike worlds. Dante himself appears on the left of *The Raising of Drusiana*. Other frescoes, including an enthroned *Virgin and a Christ with Mary Magdalene*, are by another anonymous painter called the 'Maestro dell'Arengo'.

MUSEO DELLA CITTÀ [363 E1] (*Via L Tonini 1*; \ *0541 793851;* w *museicomunalirimini.it;* ⊕ *mid-Jun–Aug 10.00–19.00 Tue–Sat, 10.00–13.00 & 16.00–19.00 Sun, Sep–mid-Jun 09.30–13.00 & 16.00–19.00 Tue–Sat, 10.00–19.00 Sun; €7, EU citizens under 18 free, Wed & 1st Sun of month free*) East of the Corso, in an 18th-century Jesuit monastery, the Museo della Città covers the history of Rimini from Palaeolithic times to Fellini. Roman mosaics depict exotic African scenes (a favourite subject of mosaic art in Roman homes), and a view of Ariminium's port. There are stone tickets from gladiator fights, and finds from the Surgeon's House (Domus del Chirurgo; see below): glass paste panels of fish from his waiting room and 150 medical instruments, including a rare iron tool for extracting arrow heads and a hollow ceramic foot that may have been filled with warm water and placed over a sore foot and which suggest the doctor was a military surgeon.

The Pinacoteca has a number of works by the Riminese school of the 1300s, including parts of a *Last Judgement* detached from Sant'Agostino and others by Rimini's most accomplished seicento painter, Guido Cagnacci, as well as two by Guercino and one by Guido Reni (*San Giuseppe*), the colourful *Pala di San Vicenzo Ferrer* by Ghirlandaio and his workshop, and a wonderful *Pietà* by Giovanni Bellini, with angel children commiserating instead of Mary. This work was Sigismondo's last commission, and Bellini finished it just before the *signore* died in 1468. Graphic art by Rimini-born fashion illustrator René Gruau rounds out the collection.

DOMUS DEL CHIRUGO [363 E1] Under a shelter just outside the museum, the 2nd-century AD Domus del Chirugo was discovered by chance in 1989. It once stood on the seafront, now 1km away, and burned in the mid 3rd century, its walls collapsing on to the interior and preserving its handsome mosaics (including one of Orpheus), wall frescoes and underfloor heating system.

PONTE DI TIBERIO [363 E1] (*North end of Corso d'Augusto*) This five-arched Istrian stone bridge of AD21 over the Marecchia River at the end of the Via Emilia was patched up after damage in the Greek–Gothic Wars; the Goths, under siege, had partially demolished it in an unsuccessful attempt to keep out Belisarius's army. But it has survived in good nick since.

BORGO SAN GIULIANO Just over the bridge awaits Rimini's most atmospheric neighbourhood, the compact old Borgo San Giuliano. Its cobbled lanes and colourful little houses were once the poorest part of the city because of the flooding of the Marecchia, which has since been diverted north. Colourful murals, many from Fellini's films, cover the walls; Fellini occasionally spoke of retiring here with his wife, Giulietta Masina. At its heart, the Renaissance church of **San Giuliano Martire** [363 A3] (*Piazzetta San Giuliano;* \ *0541 25761;* ⊕ *08.30–noon & 16.00–18.30 daily*) contains that saint's relics, a polyptych (1409) by Bittino da Faenza of his life and a painting of his martyrdom, the last work of Paolo Veronese.

MARINA CENTRO The buzzing heart of summertime Rimini, the Marina Centro saw the first bathing establishment in 1843. By the turn of the century, the dunes were cleared and Liberty-style villas and hotels cropped up along elegant Viale

Principe Amadeo. Fellini was born on 20 January 1920 just off of the avenue at Via Dardanelli 10, on the beach side of the rail line, near the **Piazzale Federico Fellini** and **Parco Federico Fellini** [363 B2] with its **Fountain of the Four Horses** of 1928. The famous **Grand Hotel** (page 364) of Fellinesque desires is here, and towards the beach there's the giant **Fellinia camera** [363 B2]; this was built in 1948 as a film processing kiosk, and has become an unofficial monument to the city's favourite son. Missing here is the Kursaal, with its floating dance floor built in 1872 to cement Rimini's reputation as the city of fun; young Fellini and his friends spent a lot of their youth gaping at the swells. It was demolished after the war, but you can instead ride the Marina Centro's newest attraction, the **Ruota Panoramica** big wheel [363 B1] (m *320 283 5849;* w *ruotapanoramicarimini.it;* ⊕ *10.00–midnight; €9, family rates available*).

West, over the boat-filled Porto Canale, is the **House of Shells** [363 A2] (*Via del Fante 40*), the creation of taxi driver Alfonso Rinaldi who covered his house with 12,000 mostly scallop shells, collected with the aid of local seafood restaurants. East of the Piazzale, along Lungomare Augusto Murri, are 26 side streets named after Fellini's films, in chronological order from Via Una Agenzia Matrimoniale (1953) to Via La Voce della Luna (1990) in the south.

OUTSIDE THE CENTRE
Cimitero Monumentale [363 A3] (*Piazzale Umberto Bartolani;* ⊕ *07.30–17.00 daily*) Fellini died in Rome on 31 October 1993, the day after his 50th wedding anniversary; his wife, Giulietta Masina, followed him exactly five months later. They are buried with their baby son, Pierfederico, who died of encephalitis at four weeks, near the cemetery entrance under a bronze sculpture by Arnaldo Pomodoro that resembles the prow of the *Rex* in *Amarcord*.

Museo degli Sguardi [map, pages 358–9] (*Via delle Grazie 12, Covignano di Rimini;* \ *0541 704421;* w *museicomunalirimini.it;* ⊕ *by request; admission free*) Delfino Dinz Rialto (d1979) was a diplomat and explorer who spent much of his life living among the traditional cultures of the world. He also had a good eye for art, and built up an excellent collection from the most diverse sources, with more than 3,000 pieces of ancient and modern art from Africa, Oceania and the Americas, now in the 18th-century Villa Alvarado by the hillside Santuario delle Grazie church.

Some of the standouts are the ritual equipment for a New Guinea 'spirit house', entire tree trunks carved into drums from the New Hebrides, and a Yoruba figure of Shango, the god of Santería, portrayed here in his original African form as a thunder god with a double axe.

Museo dell'Aviazione [map, pages 358–9] (*Via Santa Aquilina 58;* \ *0541 756 696;* w *museoaviazione.com;* ⊕ *09.00–18.00 (Jul–Aug until 19.00); €12*) On the border with San Marino, this collection of more than 40 mostly fighter planes (including Clark Gable's) also features uniforms, photos, model planes, and displays on the September 1944 Battle of Rimini and the Yellow Line, part of the Gothic Line.

Museo Nazionale del Motociclo [map, pages 358–9] (*Via Casalecchio 58, west of the airport;* \ *0541 731096;* w *museomotociclo.it;* ⊕ *late Apr–Oct 09.30–noon & 14.00–19.00, winter by appointment; €7, under 12s free*) At the end of a rural road, this museum houses 260 motorcycles from the late 1800s to the 1970s, with associated photos, posters, scooters, sidecars and a 10,000-volume motorcycle library.

CERVIA–MILANO MARITTIMA South of Comacchio (pages 300–1) runs a long stretch of small resorts, coastal pine woods and the Parco del Delta del Po that straggles past various lidos, full of families and convenient for a day on the beach if you're passing through. They continue to the first big centre on the coast, Cervia–Milano Marittima, with 9km of sugar-fine sand, all immaculately groomed by an endless row of *stabilimenti*. Before baking bodies on the beach became big, Cervia earned its living through 'white gold' or salt, which made it a prize from the time of the ancient Greeks, who founded the first town here – Ficocle, which was destroyed by Exarch Theodore in AD709. The Venetians influenced it or controlled it outright from the 13th century to 1509 – in 1445 they even inaugurated a 'Marriage to the Sea' on Ascension Day, modelled after their famously arrogant ceremony in Venice. After 1509 Cervia made money for the pope, who insisted that his states use his costly product and no-one else's. The vast salt warehouses, dating from 1691 and 1712, and the quadrangle of salt workers' houses in the *centro storico* are intact, and the pans still produce piles of the stuff, amid flocks of pink flamingos. Cesena's chic annex, Milano Marittima just to the north, was founded in 1912 and designed according to Ebenezer Howard's Garden City ideals.

Tourist information

Torre San Michele Via Arnaldo Evangelisti 4; ℓ0544 974400; w turismo.comunecervia.it; ⊕ mid-Sep–May 10.00–16.00 Mon–Sat, 11.00–17.00 Sun, Jun–mid-Sep 09.30–18.30 daily

Where to stay, eat and drink

Palace Hotel (135 rooms) Viale 2 Giugno 60, Milano Marittima; ℓ0544 993618; w selecthotels.it. Luxurious 5-star beach-front palace built in 2005, with all the bells & whistles, including a wellness centre, gym & pool. The hotel's excellent restaurant I Venini (⊕ *closed Nov–Jan;* €€€€€) is one of the best in town, & operates an annex on the private beach in season. Hotel open all year; b/fast inc. €€€€€

Excelsior (60 rooms) Viale Roma 104, Cervia; ℓ0544 970567; w hexcelsior.it. 100m from the beach, cheerful family-run hotel with modern orangey-pink rooms, a heated pool with retractable cover, sauna & bikes for guests. Buffet b/fast inc. €€€

Santiago (26 rooms) Viale 2 Giugno 42, Milano Marittima; ℓ0544 975477; w hotelsantiago.it. In a quiet spot 150m from the sea, with a pretty garden terrace & helpful staff. B/fast €7. €–€€

La Piazzetta Rotonda Don Minzoni 1, Milano Marittima; ℓ0544 193 5185; w lapiazzettamima. it; ⊕ closed Sat lunch & Mon in winter. A young chef runs this restaurant built around a tree. At 18.00 they serve a range of exquisite *aperitivi*; for dinner, expect creative variations on Italian classics, including dishes from Lombardy (risotto & *cotoletta Milanese*) but each a work of art. Even the kids' menu is better than most. 6-course *menu degustazione* €58. €€€€€

Osteria Il Cantinone Via XX Settembre 28; ℓ0544 977078; w ilcantinone.com; ⊕ eves only. Converted old wine shop in Cervia's *centro storico*, with big fireplace & rustic atmosphere. The homemade pasta is especially good, as are the freshly made *piadine*, *salumi* & grilled meats. €€€

Le Ghiaine Via Romea Nord 180, Cervia; ℓ0544 991696; w ristoranteleghiaine.it; ⊕ closed Mon, also lunch on Tue & Sat. The Mirella family are renowned for the best *piadine* in Romagna, but their bright, informal restaurant is also great for succulent beef dishes; just don't look for any seafood. Tasty desserts & interesting wine list, including bottles from Lebanon. €€

Casa delle Aie Via Ascone 1; ℓ0544 927631; w casadelleaie.it; ⊕ eves only & Sun lunch. Jovial, legendary establishment serving rigorously traditional Romagnolo specialities plus wine by the pitcher in an 18th-century house built for pine-nut gatherers. Vast shady terrace; on a summer's evening don't be surprised if people burst into song. You need a car (there's a big car park) or taxi. €

What to see and do

Museo del Sale di Cervia (*Via Nazario Sauro 24;* 📞 *0544 977592;* w *musa. comunecervia.it;* ⏱ *mid-Sep–May 15.00–19.00 Sat–Sun, Jun–mid-Sep 20.30–23.30 daily; €2*) Located in a warehouse along the banks of the canal that linked the salt pans to Cervia's port, this ethnographic museum is dedicated to the history of the salt pans, with tools, boats, historic salt cellars, etc, and old 'Sali e Tabacchi' signs that recall that, until 1973, salt – like cigarettes – was a state monopoly.

Casa delle Farfalle (*Via Jelenia Gora 6/d, Milano Marittima;* 📞 *0544 995671;* w *atlantide.net;* ⏱ *Jun–mid-Sep 09.30–19.00 daily, mid-Sep–May 09.30–12.30 & 14.30–17.00 Tue–Fri, 09.30–18.00 Sat–Sun; €11, under 1m tall free, family ticket (2 adults, at least 2 children) €35*) The House of the Butterflies is a huge rainforest greenhouse in the pinewood, housing some 500 butterflies from around the world. Admission includes the Casa degli Insetti (Insect House) which is home to other insects – crickets, praying mantises, beetles, bees, etc.

CESENATICO Next down the coast, Cesenatico was founded in 1302 by Cesena as its port, although it too would spend much time under the Venetians until 1509. The secret of its success is the Porto Canale, a pretty canal-like harbour that offered shelter from the storms, improved in 1502 by Leonardo da Vinci for Cesare Borgia. Cesenatico is still the base of an important fishing fleet and boasts the coast's landmark: the 115m reinforced concrete skyscraper, nicknamed the 'Ecomonster', built in 1958 and visible from all the resorts to the south towards Rimini: Valverde, Gatteo a Mare, San Mauro a Mare and Igea Mare.

Tourist information

ℹ Via Roma 112; 📞0547 673287; w cesenatico.it;
⏱ 08.30–18.30 Mon–Sat

🏠 Where to stay

🏠 **Grand Hotel Cesenatico** (78 rooms) Piazza Andrea Costa 1; 📞 0547 80012; w grandhotelcesenatico.com. Romantic family-run hotel by the sea built in 1929. Rooms have been renovated, & many have sea views; facilities include an attractive pool, garden terrace & private beach, tennis court & a restaurant (€€€€) serving Bolognese & gluten-free cuisine. Free parking; excellent b/fast buffet inc. €€€€€

🏠 **Grand Hotel da Vinci** (150 rooms) Viale Carducci 7; 📞 0547 83388; w selecthotels.it. Liberty-style 5-star luminous luxury by the sea, with princely rooms, a private beach, pools inside & out, gorgeous gardens, & Monnalisa restaurant (€€€€€), one of the best on the coast. Lots for families; b/fast inc. €€€€€

🏠 **Britannia** (40 rooms) Viale Carducci 129; 📞 0547 672500; w hbritannia.it. Refined early 1900s villa by the sea with a big flowery terrace, a pool & olive grove leading down to a private beach. Rooms have all creature comforts & there's a good restaurant, open to guests only. Good low-season deals. Open Easter–late Sep. €€–€€€€€

🏠 **Hotel Favorita** (48 rooms) Viale Venezia 22; 📞 0547 84322; w hotelfavorita.net. Modern, 3-star hotel 4mins' walk from the beach; beds & umbrellas on the beach offered if you book all-inclusive. Special offers for families, inc single-parent families. B/fast inc. €€–€€€€

✖ Where to eat and drink

✖ **Magnolia** Via Trento 31; 📞 0547 81598; w magnoliaristorante.it; ⊙ closed Wed & lunch exc Sat–Sun. This is the elegant bailiwick of chef Alberto Faccani, a master of creative seafood; there's a classic tasting menu (€70), or splash out on the Degustazione Magnolia (€95) for an unforgettable meal. Also dishes à la carte; great wine list. €€€€€

✖ **La Buca** Corso Garibaldi 41; 📞 0547 82474; w labucaristorante.it; ⊙ closed Mon. Stefano Bartolini's famous seafood restaurant in the pedestrian zone on the Porto Canale has been going strong since 1985, serving some of the best fish & shellfish right off the boat. There's also a small vegetarian menu; great wines; *menu degustazione* €68. €€€€

✖ **Osteria del Gran Fritto** Corso Garibaldi 41; 📞 0547 82474; w osteriadelgranfrittocesenatico. com. Next to La Buca, also run by Stefano Bartolini. The place for a golden *gran fritto dell'Adriatico* – a seafood fry-up. Bookings not accepted. €€–€€€

What to see and do

Museo della Marineria (*Via Armellini 18;* 📞 *0547 79205;* w *museomarineria. comune.cesenatico.fc.it;* ⊙ *Sep–May 10.00–noon & 15.00–19.00 Sat–Sun, Jun–Aug 10.00–noon & 17.00–23.00 Sat–Sun; €2*) A new building houses some of traditional (and rather beautiful) fishing and trading boats with yellow and orange sails that plied the northern Adriatic in the 19th and early 20th centuries, along with videos, and a reconstructed ship's carpentry workshop. Others float in the canal between Easter and October, with their sails raised daily depending on the weather.

Piazzetta delle Conserve In the old days some 20 enormous pits throughout the town were filled with snow and ice in winter to keep the catch fresh; an impressive one survives in the centre of this colourful little square in the *centro storico*.

MORE BEACHES: RICCIONE TO CATTOLICA Holiday madness continues through the string of resorts south of Rimini. Riccione, Misano Adriatico and Cattolica are all huge places, and in the summer they can be as crowded and intense as Rimini itself. There's really no great reason to see them for themselves, although Riccione, however, has carved out a niche beyond the beach as Italy's cycling capital. Since 1997 the national team has trained in the surrounding hills, and thousands of amateurs come to follow suit.

For the numerous theme parks in the area, see page 368.

Tourist information

ℹ Cattolica Via Mancini 24; ☎0541 966697;
w cattolicaturismo.com; ⊕ mid-May–Oct 08.30–
19.00 daily, Nov–mid-May 08.30–19.00 Mon–Fri,
09.30–12.30 & 16.00–18.00 Sat–Sun

ℹ Misano Adriatico Viale Platani 24; ☎0541
615520; **w** misano.org; ⊕ Oct–Mar 08.00–14.00
Mon–Sat, Apr 08.00–19.00 Mon–Fri, 08.00–14.00

Sat–Sun, May, Jun & Sep 08.00–19.00 daily, Jul–
Aug 08.00–14.00 & 16.00–22.00 daily
ℹ Riccione Piazzale Ceccarini 10; ☎0541
426050; **w** riccione.it; ⊕ Oct–Apr 08.00–13.30
Mon–Sat, 13.30–19.30 Sun, May–Sep 08.00–
20.00 daily

🏠 **Where to stay, eat and drink** This is a lively area on summer nights; for a list
of clubs, see page 367.

Riccione

🏠 **Grand Hotel Des Bains** (70 rooms)
Viale Gramsci 56; ☎0541 601650;
w grandhoteldesbains.com. Established in
1908 & as lavish as they come, decorated with
stuccoes & mirrors, but offering every mod con,
plus a private beach, spa, pool & fitness centre.
€€€€–€€€€€

🏠 **Dory** (56 rooms) Viale Puccini 4; ☎0541
642896; **w** hoteldory.it. The Dory was Italy's first
bike hotel, but it's also good for families, couples &
hikers, offering more than most for your money: a
choice of designer rooms, buffet b/fasts, wellness
centre, children's pool, boats & sea excursions. The
same owners run the **D-Place** (**w** d-placericcione.
it) aparthotel's contemporary rooms with
kitchenettes. **€€–€€€€**

🏠 **Adlon** (47 rooms) Viale G D'Annunzio 104;
☎0541 643550; **w** adlon.it. On the beach, another
bike hotel, hospitable & family-run, with a seaside
play park, pool, children's clubs & more. Most
rooms have balconies on the sea. **€€–€€€€**

🏠 **Augustus** (44 rooms) Viale
Guglielmo Oberdan 18; ☎0541 69322;
w riccionehotelaugustus.it. Peaceful family hotel
set back from the beach, with a heated rooftop
pool. B/fast inc. **€–€€€**

🏠 **Riccione Bike Hotels** Various locations
in Riccione; **w** riccionebikehotels.it. 'The Pirate'
and terror of the mountains, Cesena-native Marco
Pantani (1970–2004), winner of the Tour de France
and Giro d'Italia in 1998, trained here, & today so
many cyclists come to follow in his footsteps that
specialised bike hotels have sprouted up to make
them welcome, offering special packages that
provide guides, itineraries, tutors, racing bike hire,
bike storage & repairs, lockers, technical clothing

laundry, masseuses & sport doctors, energy b/fasts
& 'menus for champions' in their restaurants.
Usually in the range of €50–70/night pp.

✕ **Ristorante Green** Via Lungomare della
Libertà 15; ☎0541 178 0816; **w** hotel-atlantic.
com. Romantic terrace or candlelit dining room,
superb service & some of the tastiest seafood in
town, but also vegetarian choices. 5-course *menu
degustazione* €55. **€€€€€**

✕ **Sol y Mar** Via Lungomare D'Annunzio 190;
☎0541 648528; **w** ristorantesolymar.it. White
tables & chairs by the sand, the perfect setting for
exquisite seafood (raw or cooked) with a Japanese
touch. Good vegan dishes, too. **€€€€**

✕ **Trampolines** Lungomare della Repubblica
18; ☎0541 600702; **w** trampolines.it; ⊕ closed
Tue exc summer & Oct–Feb. Very popular spot for a
pizza by the sea, with special gluten-free choices.
Also attractive suites upstairs. **€€**

Misano Adriatico

🏠 **Locanda I Girasoli** (7 rooms) Via Ca'
Rastelli 13, Misano Monte; ☎0541 610724;
w locandagirasoli.it. One of the most delightful
places to stay or eat around here, far from the
scent of sunblock, offering country-style rooms
in a 19th-century farmhouse surrounded by
olive trees & sunflowers. There's a heated pool,
children's playground, bikes to borrow, tennis
courts, & a restaurant/pizzeria (open to non-
guests, but book) serving delicious home cooking.
B/fast inc. **€€€€**

Cattolica

🏠 **Gambrinus Mare** (20 rooms) Via Carducci
86; ☎0541 961347; **w** hotelgambrinusmare.com.
This family-oriented hotel has themed rooms &

activities for all ages, including a cheap laundry service. Good value FB & HB terms; also facilities for cyclists. B/fast inc. €€€–€€€€

🏠 **Ines** (36 rooms) Via del Prete 107; ☎0541 954775; w hotelines.it. Snazzy 3-star design hotel with 4 styles of room; kettles, bikes, an outdoor pool, sunbeds, playground & free parking. B/fast inc. €€€

✖ **Il Granaio** Via R Fabbro 18, just inland at San Giovanni in Marignano; ☎0541 957205; 🅕 Il Granaio Marignano; ⊕ closed Tue. Charming little restaurant of character, in an ancient granary, serving unusual but tasty dishes such as goose prosciutto, wholewheat pasta with broccoli & pecorino or pumpkin gnocchi with red chicory. Don't miss the *formaggio di fossa*; good wine list too. Best to book. €€

Riccione Riccione, the 'Green Pearl of the Adriatic', is perhaps the most family-oriented resort here with its long beach, gardens, and pedestrian-only Viale Ceccarini for fashionable *passeggiate*. Its **Museo del Territorio** (*Viale Lazio 6;* ☎*0541 600113;* w *www.comune.riccione.rn.it;* ⊕ *Jul–Aug 09.00–12.30 Tue–Sat & 20.30–23.00 Tue, Wed & Fri, Sep–Jun 09.00–12.30 Tue–Sat & 15.00–18.00 Tue, Wed & Fri; admission free*) goes way back in time, with its fossils of the elephants, rhinoceroses, bears and giant stags that once frolicked in the valley of the Conca south of Riccione, followed by Palaeolithic, Neolithic and Roman finds. An elegant villa houses the **Galleria d'Arte Moderna e Contemporanea Villa Franceschi** (*Via Gorizia 2;* ☎*0541 693534;* w *www.comune.riccione.rn.it;* ⊕ *Jul–Aug 08.30–12.30 Tue–Fri & 20.30–23.00 Tue–Sun, Sep–Jun 08.30–12.30 Tue–Fri & 16.00–19.00 Tue, Thu & Sat; €2*) with Italian Art Nouveau/Liberty-style works up until the late 20th century. Another villa, the **Villa Mussolini** (*Viale Milano 40*) was purchased by Mussolini's wife Rachele in 1934 for family holidays. After decades of disrepair it was restored in 2005 by the *comune* for special exhibitions.

Cattolica South of Riccione, at the mouth of the River Conca, Cattolica was founded as a station along the Via Flaminia. Its first famous tourist was Lucien Bonaparte, Napoleon's brother, and the rest is history. Some of this, along with archaeological finds and a collection of traditional fishing boats, is installed in the **Museo della Regina** (*Via Pascoli 23;* ☎ *0541 966577;* ⊕ *summer 09.30–12.30 Tue–Thu, 09.30–12.30 & 15.30–19.00 Fri & Sat, summer 09.30–12.30 Tue, 17.30–20.30 Wed–Sun; admission free*) in a 16th-century pilgrims' hostel.

San Giovanni in Marignano At San Giovanni, just inland from Cattolica, its beach and fast food, frankfurters and hamburgers have a special meaning; the villagers are known in Romagna as the Mangiatedeschi, the 'German-eaters', a tradition that San Giovanni doesn't care to commemorate. It started when two women lured in and wolfed down 17 Goths in AD539 (according to the Byzantine historian Procopius); it was the middle of the Greek–Gothic Wars, and times were hard. Perhaps they were difficult to digest, for the villagers didn't try another for 1,300 years; an Austrian soldier was apparently stewed in 1859. And such was the wartime hunger in 1944 that several retreating Germans met a similar fate. Or so they say.

13

The Marecchia Valley to San Marino

The *comuni* behind Rimini belong to the Valmarecchia, the crossroads between Romagna, the Marche and San Marino – a jumble of hills, valleys and towns, with the sea never far away. The Malatesta built castles here to protect their flanks from their many enemies, and perhaps it shouldn't come as a surprise, considering Sigismondo's special status in Hell, that most of them have ghostly legends attached to them.

Romagna used to end at Montebello, but after a referendum in 2006 seven towns further up the Marecchia in the northern Marche fief of Montefeltro voted to join Rimini province. The Montefeltro is studded with rocky crags, each crowned by yet more castles from the days when the dukes of Urbino and the Malatesta clobbered each other for control of the turf. Today it's an attractive, peaceful region, just being discovered; the late Umberto Eco had a house here.

SANTARCANGELO

Just 10km behind Rimini on the slopes of Monte Giove (Hill of Jupiter), Santarcangelo di Romagna is named after a 6th-century Byzantine church of St Michael. Famous as a birthplace of poets – and a pope, Clement XIV – Santarcangelo is the great antidote to the hedonistic coast, dedicated to the old traditions of Romagna: it has an important handicrafts tradition and a steep, labyrinthine *centro storico* of cobbled streets built over a mysterious underworld.

GETTING THERE AND AWAY From Rimini it's a short hop by train or START bus 9.

TOURIST INFORMATION
🛈 Via C Battisti 5; ☎ 0541 624270;
w iatsantarcangelo.com; ⏱ daily 09.00–13.00
& 15.30–19.30 summer, winter 09.00–13.00 &
15.00–19.00 daily

WHERE TO STAY, EAT AND DRINK

🏠 **Tenuta Saiano** [map, pages 358–9]
(4 rooms) Montebello di Poggio Torriana, 13km
southwest of Santarcangelo; ☎ 0541 675515;
m 331 677 3822; w tenutasaiano.it. Peaceful,
antique-furnished rooms in a vineyard with
windows overlooking the unspoiled Valmarecchia.
The farm supplies the veg, meats, *salumi*, etc for
the restaurant (⏱ *Thu–Sun eves;* €€€€) & for La
Sangiovesa (page 384). B/fast inc. €€€€

🏠 **Locanda Antiche Macine** [map, pages
358–9] (12 rooms) Via Provinciale Sogliano
1540, Fraz Montalbano (SP11); ☎ 0541 627161;
w antichemacine.it. Handsome rooms & suites
(2 for families) amid the olive groves on an 18th-
century estate, with a pool & beautiful garden.
Also a good Romagnolo restaurant (€€€€) under
ancient beams. B/fast inc. €€€

🏠 **Della Porta** (22 rooms) Via A Costa 85; 📞 0541 622152; **w** hoteldellaporta.com. 2 old mills converted into a charming small hotel. Rooms are furnished with country antiques & king-size beds; some ceilings have trompe l'œil frescoes. Buffet b/fast inc. **€€€–€€€€**

🍴 **Osteria & Ristorante La Sangiovesa** Piazza Balacchi 14; 📞 0541 620710; **w** sangiovesa. it; ⊕ eves only, & Sun lunch. In an 18th-century palazzo, the most picturesque place to dine in Santarcangelo, designed by poet Tonino Guerra. The *piadine* & pasta dishes are made with stoneground flour from a nearby mill. The menu changes with the season, but is firmly Romagnolo; the adjacent osteria has a fine selection of regional wines, *salumi* & cheeses. Restaurant menu €36. **€€–€€€**

WHAT TO SEE AND DO

Rocca Malatesta (*Via Rocca Malatestiana 4;* 📞 *0541 620832;* ⊕ *10.00–13.00 & 15.00–19.00 1st w/end of month;* €3) This privately owned foursquare castle is one of several that claims to have witnessed the immortal indiscretion of Francesca da Polenta and Paolo Malatesta; on moonless nights a female ghost is said to shuffle nervously about, although people think she is really the second wife of Paolo's lame brother Giovanni.

Grotte di Santarcangelo (⊕ *guided tours by appointment only, inc the medieval centre; book ahead with the tourist office (page 383);* €4.50) Besides the ghost, Santarcangelo has another mystery: some 150 artificial caves excavated in the sandstone and clay cliffs of Monte Giove, most with long access tunnels, ending in circular rooms. What were they for? Guesses range from Celtic or Mithraic places of worship to cells of Basilian monks to cellars for the local Sangiovese wine. There are legends of golden treasure, stored away and guarded by ghosts that you can hear if you stay in at night and press your ear to the ground.

Arco Trionfale di Clemente XIV (*Piazza Ganganelli*) Clement, pope from 1769 to 1774, was best known for suppressing the Jesuits and serving as one of the more honest heads of the Papal States. His home town erected this monument in 1777, although these days the locals call it the Arco dei Becchi, or 'arch of the cuckolds'.

Museo Storico Archeologico (MUSAS) (*Via della Costa 26;* 📞 *0541 625212;* **w** *museisantarcangelo.it;* ⊕ *Nov–Apr 15.30–18.30 Sat–Sun, May–Oct 16.30–19.30 Tue–Sun, also in May, Jun & Sep 10.30–13.00 Thu–Sat;* €3, free on Sun) This 17th-century palazzo houses archaeological finds and paintings, including a handsome polyptych of 1385 by Jacobello da Bonomo, and a room dedicated to Clement XIV.

Museo nel Mondo di Tonino Guerra (*Via della Costa 15;* 📞 *0541 626506;* ⊕ *10.00–12.30 & 16.30–19.00 Fri–Wed; admission free*) Santarcangelo's beloved poet and screenwriter Tonino Guerra (1920–2012) worked with all the great post-war Italian directors, including Vittorio De Sica, Antonioni and the Taviani brothers, and won an Oscar for his work in *Amarcord*. This exhibit in the former Monte di Pietà set up by his son displays his playful ceramics and other art.

Museo dei Bottoni (*Via della Costa 11;* **m** *339 348 3150;* **w** *www.bottoni-museo. it;* ⊕ *mid-Sep–May 10.00–noon & 15.00–18.00 Tue–Sun, Jun–mid-Sep 10.00–noon, 16.00–18.30 & 21.00–23.30 Tue–Sun; donations*) Giorgio Gallavotti's extraordinary button collection includes political buttons, buttons made out of dozens of different materials and show-off buttons from the 18th and 19th centuries.

Mangano del 1633 (*Via Battisti 13;* ☏ *0541 626018;* ⏱ *09.00–12.30 & 16.00–19.00; ring ahead to book guided visits on w/day mornings; €2.50*) This shop, where they make traditional hand-stamped printed fabrics with the original machinery, is the oldest business in Romagna.

Museo Etnografico (MET) (*Via Montevecchi 41;* ☏ *0541 624703;* w *museisantarcangelo.it;* ⏱ *Nov–Apr 09.00–noon Tue–Fri, 15.30–18.30 Sat–Sun, May–Oct 09.00–noon Tue–Fri, 16.30–19.30 Sat–Sun; €3, free on Sun*) A 10-minute walk from the centre, this museum has a collection of artefacts related to traditional crafts – wine, shoes, iron, cloth-printing – and musical instruments, farming, milling and popular theatre.

San Michele (*Via del Pieve, just south of the centre off SP14;* ☏ *0541 624485;* ⏱ *for services 10.00 Sun*) Dating from the 6th century, the oldest church in the diocese, handsome Ravenna-Byzantine style San Michele has lost all its decoration over the centuries, outside of fragments of mosaics and marbles found in excavations.

VERUCCHIO

Medieval Verucchio (from the Latin *verrucula*, or hump) is an attractive hill town, built on a rocky spur over the Valmarecchia, a naturally defensive spot that attracted settlers in Villanovan times. In the traumatic years of Greek and Gothic battles, it became a place of refuge; the fortress, rebuilt in the 10th century, became the cradle of the Malatesta clan with its first big shot, Malatesta il Centenario, the father of the famous Paolo and Giovanni. His descendant Sigismondo made Verucchio one of his chief citadels, and added its walls and towers. In later years its rulers included a lute player named Giovanni Maria, before it fell to the papal administrators.

GETTING THERE AND AWAY START buses 163 and 164 (see box, page 328) link Santarcangelo to Verucchio.

TOURIST INFORMATION
🛈 Piazza Malatesta 20; ☏ 0541 670222; w www.verucchioturismo.it; ⏱ Oct–Apr 09.00–13.00 Mon–Fri, 10.00–12.30 & 15.00–18.30 Sat–Sun, May–Sep 09.00–13.00 & 15.00–19.00 Mon–Fri, 09.30–12.30 & 15.00–19.00 Sat–Sun

WHERE TO STAY, EAT AND DRINK

🏠 **Oste del Castello** (29 rooms) Via dei Martiri 10; ☏ 0541 679308; w ostedelcastello.it. Handsome hotel with a range of rooms, including romantic suites with hydromassage baths. Guests have free entrance to the Grotto del Benessere, an atmospheric underground spa. It's also a bike hotel (you can rent 1 with a week's notice). Good restaurant; b/fast inc. €€–€€€€

✖ **Il Povero Diavolo** [map, pages 358–9] Via Roma 30, Torriana; ☏ 0541 675060; w ristorantepoverodiavolo.com; ⏱ eves only, closed Wed. Picturesque locale & kitchen seducing diners since 1995 with excellent *salumi*, homemade breads, delicate yet flavourful pasta dishes, wild asparagus omelettes, a wide choice of Italian & foreign cheeses, & splendid wines. You can also eat in its subterranean osteria, or just have *salumi, piadine* & cheese. €€€€

✖ **Casa Zanni** Via Casale 171, Villa Verucchio; ☏ 0541 678449; w casazanni.it. One of Romagna's best-known trattorias, founded in 1919 by Antonio Zanni, a miner who opened an eatery, serving meals to those in need. Delicious *piadine* and grilled meats are cooked while you watch; also excellent *salumi*, tagliatelle & house wine. 6-course menu €32; also vegetarian choices. €€

✗ Hostaria Ro' e Buni' Via Molino Bianco 809, Villa Verucchio; ☎ 0541 678484; **w** tenutaamalia. com; ⊕ closed Mon. Classic Romagnolo cuisine in a charming rustic 16th-century mill on the Tenuta della Garisenda wine estate once owned by Gea della Garisenda, a singer married to Senator Borsalino of the famous hats. €€

✗ Pacini Via Castello di Montebello 5, Poggio Torriana; ☎ 0541 675410; **w** ristorantepacini.com; ⊕ closed Wed. Next to the castle & going strong since 1962, Pacini serves up the hearty delights of Romagna: good homemade *salumi*, pasta & meat dishes. Its speciality is *coniglio in porchetta* (baked stuffed deboned rabbit). €€

WHAT TO SEE AND DO

Rocca Malatestiana (*Via Rocca 42;* ☎ *0541 670222;* ⊕ *Apr–Jun & Sep 10.00–12.30 & 14.30–18.30 daily, Oct–Mar 10.00–13.00 & 14.30–18.00 Sat–Sun; €4.50, or €7.50 combined with the archaeology museum*) Also known as the Rocca del Sasso for the big rock it sits on, this castle has huge views over the valley. There are costumes, weapons and coats of armour inside, and a helpful Malatesta family tree to work out who's who.

Collegiata di San Martino (*Piazza Battaglini 22;* ☎ *0541 670197;* ⊕ *08.00–19.00 daily*) Verucchio's church was rebuilt in the 19th century, but keeps older art from the town's other churches: two precious wooden crucifixes, one by the 14th-century Rimini school and the other by the 15th-century Venetian Niccolò di Pietro.

Museo Archeologico (*Via Sant'Agostino;* ☎ *0541 67022;* ⊕ *Oct–Mar 10.00–18.00 Sat–Sun, Apr–Sep 10.00–18.00 Tue–Sun; €5.50*) Between 1960 and 1975, archaeologists brought to light hundreds of tombs in a 10th–6th-century BC Villanovan necropolis (page 60). The chemical nature of Verucchio's soil is such that the grave goods are astonishingly well preserved, and suggest a society of 'shepherd kings' who occasionally made war on each other and traded amber between the Adriatic and Tuscany.

The evidence for this *civiltà verucchiese* is in this museum in a former Augustine monastery outside the Porta Sant'Agostino: burial urns, unusual ceramics, fancy gold fibulas, amber discs, weapons and helmets, parts of a wooden inlaid throne and even woollen fabrics. Recent excavations also revealed a sacred area and well at Pian del Monte.

Convento di San Francesco (*Via Convento 150, Fraz Villa Verucchio;* ☎ *0541 678417;* ⊕ *07.30–noon & 15.30–19.30 daily*) Founded in 1215, this is the oldest Franciscan foundation in Emilia-Romagna, on the site of a hut where St Francis stayed and performed several miracles, one of which was planting his staff in the ground and finding it had taken root overnight; this is said to be the tremendous, 23m 800-year-old cypress that grows in the cloister. The church has a pretty door, a trecento fresco of the *Crucifixion* by the Rimini school, and a carved choir from the 15th century. A second tree on the road to Verucchio, St Francis's oak, is a mere 400 years old.

Rocca di Torriana [map, pages 358–9] (*6km west of Verucchio*) Known as Scorticata (the Flayed) until Mussolini renamed it in the 1920s, Torriana was another key defence point in the Valmarecchia; a jagged 13th-century tower and later a Rocca Malatestiana defended the natural bulwark that rises behind the town. The story goes that Galeotto Malatesta, the same who killed his wife Francesca and brother Paolo, was himself murdered in the citadel's underground passages.

Castello di Montebello [map, pages 358–9] (*Via Casale di Montebello, 7km west of Verucchio;* ℡ *0541 675180;* w *castellodimontebello.com;* ⊕ *guided tours mid-Sep–May 14.30–18.00 Sat–Sun, also 22.30 & 23.00 Sat, Jun–mid-Sep 14.30–19.00 Tue–Sun, also 1st 2 weeks in Jun & Sep 22.30 & 23.00 Fri–Sun, mid-Jun–Aug 22.30 & 23.00 Tue–Sun; €8, ages 5–10 €4, at night €9, no children*) Another ghost, in fact one of the best-documented phantoms in Italy, haunts Torriana's second and better-preserved castle. Built on its steep cliff in the 12th century by Malatesta da Verucchio, the castle was given in 1464 by Pius II to the Counts di Bagno, and they held on to it until the 18th century; there's a guided tour that takes in antique furnishings and paintings, and wine tastings in the adjacent 11th-century church, which was converted into an armoury. The ghost is named Azzurrina. She was the little albino daughter of a captain of the guard, who vanished one stormy night in the late 14th century, and who allegedly returns on the night of the summer solstice every five years or so (lately it's during election years) to play in the castle. RAI (Italian State Radio and Television) spent one evening recording the sounds – a ball bouncing on the flagstones, skipping, a child's laughter in a thunderstorm, and the bells tolling midnight. But there are no bells anywhere near the castle. At night, they play the recording to spook visitors.

Santuario di Saiano [map, pages 358–9] (*Via Saiano 14, Torriana;* m *333 983 3848;* w *madonnadisaiano.it;* ⊕ *08.30–19.00 Sat–Thu, 16.00–21.30 Fri*) Near Montebello castle on another rocky spur high over the Marecchia, this church too was originally a castle, and keeps a round Byzantine tower from that period. The restored sanctuary has some Byzantine elements, and a miraculous 15th-century Madonna.

SAN LEO

> Only one Pope, only one God, only one Fort – San Leo!
> A Montefeltro saying

The most extraordinary of all the area's extraordinary castles hangs high over the one and only entrance into San Leo, a road that had to be cut into the living rock. Founded, according to legend, in the 4th century by St Leo of Dalmatia, a companion of Marinus (who founded San Marino), it was donated by Pepin, father of Charlemagne, to the Church. It briefly served as 'capital of Italy' in the AD960s, during the undistinguished reign of King Berengarius II, who after a siege of two years surrendered both San Leo and Italy to the German emperor Otto, who returned San Leo to the Church. Dante slept here and gave San Leo a mention in his *Purgatory*; St Francis also wandered through and preached so convincingly that one of his listeners, the Count di Chiusi, gave Francis his beloved La Verna as a retreat. And Umberto Eco called it the 'most beautiful city in Italy' (even though it's tiny, a huddle of stone houses, San Leo is officially a *città*).

GETTING THERE AND AWAY START bus 165 from Rimini station goes to San Leo. On summer Wednesdays Bonelli buses (w *bonellibus.it*) make afternoon excursions from Rimini and the coastal resorts. In summer, a shuttle goes up to the fortress from the car park.

TOURIST INFORMATION
ℹ Piazza Dante 14; ℡ 0541 916306; w san-leo.it;
⊕ 09.30–19.30 daily

WHERE TO STAY, EAT AND DRINK

Il Castello (14 rooms) Piazza Dante 11–12; \0541 916214; w hotelristorantecastellosanleo. com. Recently renovated antique-furnished rooms in a 16th-century palace in the historic centre; all the better for its excellent restaurant (€€), with tables in the piazza. €€–€€€

La Rocca (6 rooms) Via G Leopardi 16; \0541 916241; w laroccasanleo.it. This little hotel is run by the Rossi family, who offer simple rooms, terrace, garden & superb cooking (€€€):

truffles & mushrooms in season, & *secondi* such as the local speciality, *pasticciata alla Cagliostro* – marinated beef braised in wine, tomatoes & cloves. Impressive cheese & wine list. Closed Mon in Sep–Jun. €€

✗ **Il Bettolino** Via Montefeltro 4; \0541 916265; ◼ Il Bettolino San Leo; ◷ closed Wed. Dine on tasty classics, good pasta dishes with house wine in the cool vaulted stone gallery or out on the terrace. Also pizzas in the evening. €€

WHAT TO SEE AND DO

Museo d'Arte Sacra (*Piazza Dante;* \ *0541 916306;* ◷ *09.30–12.30 & 14.00–17.00 Mon–Thu, 09.30–18.15 Fri–Sun; €3*) Housed in the 16th-century **Palazzo Mediceo** along with the tourist office, this holds art from the 14th–18th centuries, including a Botticelli-like *Madonna with SS Leo and Marino* (1493) by Luca Frosino.

Pieve (*Piazza Dante;* ◷ *09.00–12.30 & 15.00–19.00 daily*) This evocative rough-walled parish church built into the side of the mountain may well date back to the time of St Leo. The ciborium over the altar has an inscription to Christ and the Madonna from the year AD882, dedicated by Duke Orso, who ruled San Leo for Pope John VIII.

Duomo (◷ *09.00–12.30 & 15.00–19.00 daily*) Opposite the Pieve, the cathedral was built by Lombard masters in 1173 to replace a 7th-century church, which in turn was built over a prehistoric shrine. After the 1400s, its bishops preferred to stay in Pennabilli, leaving the Romanesque church 'unimproved' over the centuries. The harmonious interior has ancient capitals, including a few Roman ones perhaps from the temple of Jupiter. The crypt has a bas-relief and tomb of St Leo with a 6th-century inscription.

Rocca di San Leo [map, pages 358–9] (\ *0541 926067;* ◷ *09.30–18.45 daily, winter 10.30–16.20 Mon–Fri, 09.30–18.00 Sat–Sun; €9, ages 6–14 €4, or €11 joint admission with the Museo d'Arte Sacra*) In Roman times this tremendous pinnacle was known as Mons Feretrius, referring to Jove's lightning (another castle, atop nearby Majolo, was blasted into ruins by a thunderbolt in the 1600s). There was probably a temple on top, perhaps of the same Jove Feretro to whom the Roman Consul Marcellus dedicated the corpse of the leader of the Gauls in the 3rd century BC. Mons Feretrius gave its name to Montefeltro, the old name of San Leo, and in 1158 to the ducal family who relocated to Urbino. The Malatesta seized it in the 14th century and added the square towers, but in 1441 Federico da Montefeltro, then only aged 19, tricked the defenders with a fake attack and in 1475, commissioned the great Sienese fortifications architect Francesco di Giorgio Martini to replace the old fort with the most spectacular castle in Italy, with its fat round towers hung on a sheer cliff. It overlooks the whole of the Montefeltro and the three towers of San Marino: in the autumn, the region's landmark crags and castles rise over the rolling sea of fog like an enchanted archipelago.

Martini's fortress is a perfect building of the Renaissance: balanced, finely proportioned in its lines, a structure of intelligence and style. But it proved to be

THE RISE AND FALL OF GIUSEPPE BALSAMO

Born into a poor family in Palermo in 1743, Giuseppe Balsamo began his career humbly enough by forging theatre tickets. The rest of his life reads as if it were concocted by a picaresque novelist on amphetamines.

After outlandishly tricking a gullible goldsmith in Palermo with a ghost story, Giuseppe hooked up with a famous Armenian alchemist, Altolas, who took him to Greece, Egypt and Malta, where the Grand Master of the Knights let the two seek the philosopher's stone in his laboratory. Altolas accidentally poisoned himself, but Giuseppe, thanks to a forged letter, next appears in Rome, supported by the Maltese ambassador in his business of manufacturing love potions. He found a 14-year-old Roman intriguer named Lorenza Feliciani to marry, and, after several unsuccessful machinations, Giuseppe decided there was nothing to do but recreate himself with a new name: Count Alessandro Cagliostro, the greatest magician in Europe, born in Egypt and raised by alchemists, a man who personally assassinated Pompey and gave counsel to Jesus Christ.

After years of travelling around Europe, pimping for Lorenza, staying just ahead of the law or behind bars, and exciting debate as to whether he was a scoundrel, a sage, a prophet or the Antichrist, Cagliostro rocketed to fame and fortune in London in 1776 when he gave a couple the numbers that won them £2,000 in a lottery. All at once people were pounding on his door for his numbers, his elixir of long life and his love potions. When the numbers began to lose, Cagliostro retreated to the Continent, where he made a triumphal tour – he became a counsellor to Catherine the Great, healed the blind and crippled in Strasbourg, founded his own Masonic lodge and became the protégé of the Cardinal of Rohan in Paris, one of the most powerful men and biggest dupes in France. Rohan was tricked into financing a diamond necklace for Marie Antoinette by a group of swindlers, who took the money and ran; when the queen got the bill, she had Louis XVI toss Rohan and Cagliostro into the Bastille. Ironically, it was the one time that Cagliostro was innocent, and he was soon acquitted of having anything to do with the affair.

Lorenza, however, had thought the gig was up and spilled the beans of the count's humble origins to a London journalist. Cagliostro forgave her, and the two returned to Rome and lay low, until Cagliostro caused a sensation in Rome's Masonic Lodge in September 1789 when he hypnotised a girl who accurately predicted the start of the French Revolution. This caught the attention of the Inquisition, and Lorenza, immune to her husband's love potions, confessed that the count was guilty of Freemasonry. This was enough to get him condemned to death by the Holy Office, a sentence that Pius VI commuted in 1791 to solitary confinement for life in San Leo. Cagliostro was first placed in a normal cell, but the guards were so terrified of his evil eye that he was moved to a tiny, dark, rat-infested pit where he slowly went mad and died of apoplexy four years later. According to the accounts preserved in San Leo's archives, as an unrepentant heretic, his body was buried somewhere near the fortress, in unconsecrated ground. When Napoleon showed up a few years later, freed the prisoners and asked to pay his respects to Cagliostro's grave, no-one could find it.

not quite as impregnable as it looks; in 1523, after a four-month siege, the troops of Lorenzo de' Medici the younger (who was made Duke of Urbino by his uncle, Leo X) captured it on a dark and stormy night by using ropes and ladders to scale the west face of the rock, an exploit that Vasari frescoed on to the walls of Florence's Palazzo Vecchio. The Medici were succeeded by the delle Rovere dukes, and, when they died out, by the popes, under whom it became the escape-proof Alcatraz of its day. Inside you can see Renaissance weapons, the dungeon, charts of various nasty tortures, modern art, a series of illustrations of Dante's *Inferno*, and the cell where San Leo's most famous prisoner, Cagliostro, spent the last years of his life.

SANT'AGATA FÉLTRIA

Sant'Agata Féltria huddles under the Rocca Fregoso, a fantastical castle balancing precariously on 'Wolf Rock', the Sasso del Lupo. It's liveliest in the autumn, when it holds a white truffle market on four consecutive Sundays, beginning with the second Sunday in October.

TOURIST INFORMATION

Piazza Garibaldi 3; \0541 848022; w prolocosantagatafeltria.com; 09.00–noon Tue–Sun, also 15.00–17.00 Wed, Sat–Sun.

WHERE TO STAY, EAT AND DRINK

Falcon Hotel (40 rooms) Via San Girolamo 30; \0541 929090; w falconhotel.it. Solar-powered hotel vintage 1995 just outside Sant'Agata, with a pool, views over the mountains & a restaurant (€€€) that specialises in dishes using the local cheeses, mushrooms & truffles. B/fast inc. €€–€€€€

Pian del Bosco (8 rooms) Via Guido Donegani 151, Perticara; \0541 927600; w piandelbosco.com. A charming farmhouse conversion in a panoramic setting with hammocks,

pool, tennis court & a lively pizzeria & restaurant (€€). B/fast inc. €€€

Antenna dal Morino Fraz Monte Benedetto 32; \0541 929626; closed Mon exc Jul–Aug. Rustic trattoria renowned for more than half a century as the best in the area. Come here for its homemade pasta & tasty oven-baked ham, & mushrooms & white truffles in season. If you ring ahead in the autumn, when the fireplace is crackling, you can feast on the pièce de résistance – chestnut-stuffed pheasant. €€

WHAT TO SEE AND DO

Rocca delle Fiabe (\0541 929923; w roccadellefiabe.it; Apr–Dec 10.00–noon & 15.30–18.30 Wed–Sun; €6) The Rocca Fregoso, built in the 10th century and remodelled by the indefatigable Francesco di Giorgio Martini in 1474, looks so much like a storybook illustration that the tourist office decided to change its name to 'fairy-tale castle' and use mannequins to illustrate motifs such as 'children in the woods', 'persecuted girls' and 'intrepid traveller'.

Teatro Angelo Mariani (*Piazza Garibaldi 33;* m 338 921 3702; w teatromariani. it; Oct–May 10.00–noon & 15.30–17.30 Sat–Sun, Jun–Sep 15.30–18.30 Tue–Fri, 15.30–18.30 Sat–Sun; donations) One of the oldest wooden theatres in Italy, this was built in 1605 by boss Orazio Fregoso in his Palazzone. The 19th-century curtain is painted with a scene of the town; one of the medallions depicts Angelo Mariani, 19th-century composer, friend and reputed love rival of Verdi, who once conducted here before hitting the big time.

Be sure to walk behind the theatre to the stair with a giant **snail fountain** designed by Tonino Guerra as an ode to slowness, and made of 300,000 gold and coloured tesserae by Marco Bravura of Ravenna.

Talamello is a leading producer of *formaggio di fossa*, or 'pit cheese'. Made of ewe's and/or cow's milk, the cheese is aged normally for 30 days before being placed in canvas bags and lowered into hay-lined pits dating from the Middle Ages (the custom originated from the need to hide the cheese from countless marauding armies; at some point there was a eureka moment, when someone realised the cheese actually improved while in the hole). Today the 3–10m pits are prepared in August with fires to sterilise them and eliminate excess humidity, then lined with fresh hay to maintain a constant temperature of 21°C. On 26 November, St Catherine's day, the cheeses are traditionally removed. The local version is called Ambra di Talamello (a name bestowed by Tonino Guerra). The best *fossa* has a pungent aroma, reminiscent of the forest floor and truffles; it's often used in dishes, but is also good plain or with honey.

AROUND SANT'AGATA

Perticara Just off the road to Novafeltria, lofty Perticara is tucked under another rocky crag. Sulphur has been mined here for more than 500 years, and when the Cantiere Certino, the largest in Europe, closed in 1964, it threw 1,600 men out of work. It keeps the now odour-free memory alive in the old power plant next to the landmark Vittoria shaft, in the **Museo Sulphur** (\ *0541 927576;* w *museosulphur. it;* ⊕ *mid-Mar–Jun & Sep–mid-Dec 10.00–12.30 & 15.00–18.00 Sat–Sun, Jul–Aug 16.00–19.00 Thu–Fri, 10.00–13.00 & 16.00–19.00 Sat–Sun; €6)* Inside is the reconstruction of a gallery (there are almost 100km of them underground), photos, tools and an extensive mineral collection, all translated into English.

Talamello Just east, in the chestnut forests above Novafeltria, the old hill town of Talamello still derives much of its income from its pits (see box, above). Its pride and joy, however, is a *Crucifixion* by Giovanni da Rimini, pupil of Giotto, now in the **Museo Gualtieri** (*Via Saffi 34;* \ *0541 922893;* w *gualtierimuseum. it;* ⊕ *mid-Nov–mid-May 10.30–12.30 & 15.00–18.00 Sun, mid-May–mid-Nov 10.30–12.30 & 15.30–19.00 Wed–Sun; €2)* along with 40 paintings by neo-realist Fernando Gualtieri (b1919), who spent his youth here. The **cemetery chapel** (⊕ *usually open, but check at the museum)* is covered with frescoes by Antonio da Ferrara (1473).

Santa Maria Antico [map, pages 358–9] (*just off the SP258 in Maiolo, 4km south of Novafeltria; book a visit with Mario Gianessi* m *328 568 3549)* This handsome sandstone church from the 13th century, with a marble lunette of the Madonna del Soccorso over the door, has another beloved Madonna inside, complete with Bambino, by Luca della Robbia.

PENNABILLI AND MONTE CARPEGNA

Heading into the Apennines, the upper Marecchia Valley's market town of Pennabilli basks under two crags, each capped by an 11th-century 'feather', or castle, built by the Malatesta, named Penna and Billi. Billi, with a convent clinging to its slope, now does service as a base for an iron cross, but Penna's castle is in pretty good nick, in the heart of the *centro storico*. Pennabilli runs a major antiques exhibition in July,

13

but it likes new things, too, especially contemporary art and mathematics. Above Pennabilli looms the majestic profile of Monte Carpegna (1,415m), now part of a natural park.

GETTING THERE AND AWAY Take START bus 160 from Rimini station to Novafeltria, then bus 161.

TOURIST INFORMATION
i Piazza Garibaldi 1; ✆ 0541 928659;
w pennabilliturismo.it; ⏱ 09.30–12.30 & 14.30–
17.30, winter Sat–Sun only

WHERE TO STAY, EAT AND DRINK
Hotel il Duca (42 rooms) Via Moro Aldo 12; ✆ 0541 161 3400; w hotelducamontefeltro. it. Modern, friendly hotel with a Tonino Guerra-inspired décor & airy rooms, a spa, comma-shaped outdoor pool & restaurant. Most rooms have lovely views; also parking, b/fast inc. €€–€€€

Agriturismo La Torre (3 rooms) 12km south on the Strada per Castello di Bascio 12; m 348 262 0337; **f** Agriturismo La Torre Pennabilli; ⏱ w/ends by reservation. An organic farm surrounded by nature with 3 apts & an excellent restaurant. €€

✕ Piastrino Via Parco Begni 9; ✆ 0541 928106; w piastrino.it; ⏱ closed Wed. Elegant, arty Michelin-starred cuisine that draws visitors from far & wide to this country house with a fireplace & garden, just outside the centre. White truffles are its forte; all-truffle menu €75; others start at €45. €€€€

✕ Osteria Al Bel Fico Piazza Vittoria Emanuele II 24; ✆ 0541 928810; w ristorantebelfico.it; ⏱ closed Tue. Come here for Romagna–Marche style cuisine inside or on the terrace; good choice of local wines. €€–€

WHAT TO SEE AND DO
Santuario della Madonna delle Grazie (*Piazza Sant'Agostino;* ✆ *0541 928140;* ⏱ *08.00–18.00*) The sanctuary is a handsome Renaissance church, famous for its miraculous fresco of the Madonna that wept in 1489.

Museo Diocesano del Montefeltro (✆*0541 913 750;* ⏱ *09.30–12.30 Thu, 15.00–18.30 Fri & Sun, 09.30–12.30 & 15.00–18.30 Sat; w museo-diocesano-montefeltro.it;* €5) This museum displays art gathered from the Montefeltro's churches.

Mateureka Museo del Calcolo (*Piazza Garibaldi;* ✆ *0541 928659; w mateureka. it;* ⏱ *Apr 09.30–12.30 & 14.30–17.30 Thu–Sun, May–Aug 09.30–12.30 & 15.30–18.30 (closed Mon in May), Sep–Oct 10.00–12.30 & 15.00–17.30 Sat–Sun, other times by appointment;* €5) A museum of mathematics might be the last thing you'd expect to find in Pennabilli, but there are four full storeys of exhibits, dedicated to the evolution of calculation from the ancient Sumerians to the 21st century, through all kinds of ingenious machines, magic squares (including the museum's proudest exhibit, the Vampire's Magic Square of prime numbers, the largest magic square in the world) ending with fractals, infinity, robots and virtual reality.

I Luoghi dell'Anima (Abodes of the Soul) (*Salita Valentini 1;* ✆ *0541 928578; w museoiluoghidellanima.it; installations* ⏱ *09.00–19.00 daily; admission free*) Tonino Guerra (page 29) spent his summers in Pennabilli and is buried here, and left the area seven Abodes of the Soul. Among these are the *Path of Sundials*, the *Orchard of Forgotten Fruits*, the *Street of Sundials*, the *Refuge of Abandoned Madonnas*, the *Museum of the Mustachio-ed Angel* and the *Petrified Gardens*, the latter up by the 12th-century tower, standing like an exclamation mark on the next hill, at Bascio; the website has a map.

Parco Naturale Interregionale Sasso Simone e Simoncello [map, pages 358–9] (**w** *parcosimone.it*) In 1996 this border region between Romagna and the Marche, noted for its rare wild orchids, red lilies and falcons, became a park named after two prominent mesa-like crags, 'Big and Little Simon', which would look right at home in a western. Pennabilli has a **Museo Naturalistico/Visitor Centre** (*Via dei Tigli 5;* \ *0541 928 047;* **m** *320 451 0733;* **w** *musss.it;* ⊕ *check website*) in its former abattoir, with information on the flora and fauna. Some of the most grandiose views are along the road to Mount Carpegna, a favourite challenge for cyclists.

SAN MARINO

As a perfect counterpart to the sand-strewn funfair of Rimini, just 23km inland you may visit the world's only sovereign and independent roadside attraction. Before Rimini became the Italian Miami Beach, the citizens of San Marino had to make a living from agriculture (they still make some pretty good wine) and peddling postage stamps and coins. Now, with their medieval streets crowded with 3 million day-trippers a year, the San Marinesi have been unable to resist the temptation to order some bright medieval costumes and open some souvenir stands and 'duty-free' shops. Today they have one of the highest average incomes in Europe, and Sanmarinese men have the highest life expectancy in the world. They must be doing something right.

HISTORY: THE WORLD'S SMALLEST REPUBLIC Also the world's oldest republic. According to legend, San Marino was founded as a Christian settlement on the easily defensible slopes of Monte Titano by a stone-cutter named Marinus, fleeing from the persecutions of Diocletian in the year AD310. 'Overlooked', as the San Marinesi charmingly put it, by the empire and various states that followed it, the little community had the peace and quiet to evolve its medieval democratic institutions; its constitution in its present form dates from 1243 when the first pair of 'consuls' was elected by a popular assembly. The consuls are now called Captains Regent, but little else has changed in 700 years. Twice, in 1503 and 1739, the republic was invaded by papal forces, and independence was preserved only by a little good luck and nearly always choosing the winning side.

SAN MARINO AT A GLANCE

Area 61km²
Status Constitutional republic
Population 33,203
Life expectancy Men 84.1 years, women 86.8 years
Capital City of San Marino
GDP per capita €45,365
Economy Tourism, banking, manufacturing (fabrics and electronics)
Currency Euro (€)
Telephones Although San Marino has its own area code, use the numbers in the text when calling San Marino from Italy. When calling San Marino from other countries, replace the '0549' with +378.

Napoleon, passing through in 1797, found San Marino amusing, and half-seriously offered to enlarge its boundaries, a proposal that was politely declined. It felt secure enough to shelter Garibaldi, his wife Anita and 1,500 of his followers, fleeing Rome after the fall of the republic of 1849, with an Austrian army in pursuit; when the Austrians surrounded San Marino, demanding their expulsion, Garibaldi dissolved his army in the night and made a run for the coast before dawn. Since then, the republic has been an island of peace, taking in hundreds of refugees in World War II. In 2008 the historic centre was made a World Heritage Site as 'an exceptional testimony of the establishment of a representative democracy based on civic autonomy and self-governance, with a unique, uninterrupted continuity as the capital of an independent republic since the 13th century'.

GETTING THERE AND AWAY

By bus Frequent Bonelli buses (\ *0541 662069*; w *bonellibus.it*), and Benedettini buses (\ *0549 903854*) from Rimini's train station, go to San Marino.

By car The SS72 from Rimini is the road to San Marino. There are small pay car parks up in the historic centre, but in summer it's much to easier to park in Borgo Maggiore and take the cable car [map, pages 358–9] (\ *0549 883590; €4.50 return; well signposted*) from there; in winter it shuts down. There's a discount at the car parks if you're staying at a San Marino hotel (*24hrs for €4*).

TOURIST INFORMATION There's also a useful website in English for visitors with disabilities (w *sanmarinopertutti.com*).

🛈 Contrada Omagnano 20, Città di San Marino; \0549 882914; w visitsanmarino.com; ☀ summer

08.30–19.00 (winter until 18.00) Mon–Fri, 09.30–19.00 (winter until 18.00) Sat–Sun.

 WHERE TO STAY As in Riccione, bike hotels are a speciality here, too (*see* w *sanmarinocycling.com*).

🏠 **Hotel Cesar** (18 rooms) Via Salita alla Rocca, Città di San Marino; \0549 992355; w hotelcesare.com. Eagle-eye views, especially from the corner rooms & panoramic terrace, friendly service & excellent restaurant; b/fast inc. **€€€**

🏠 **La Rocca** (12 rooms) Salita alla Rocca 37, Città di San Marino; \0549 991166; w laroccasanmarino.com. Pleasant tangerine rooms & balconies with a view in the historic centre; also family rooms. B/fast inc. **€€€**

🏠 **Centro Vacanze San Marino** [map, pages 358–9] (35 chalets) Strada San Michele 50, Cailungo; \0549 907563; w gardenvillagesanmarino.com. A good bet if you've brought the kids or just want to experience the republic's natural side, complete with farm animals, tennis, outdoor pools, bike services, mini market, restaurant & pizzeria. Large choice of chalets, tents, mobile homes (sleeping 6); local buses link it to the Città. Open all year. **€–€€€**

✖ **WHERE TO EAT AND DRINK** Besides wine, look for *fagioli con le cotiche* (bean and bacon soup) and the chocolate and hazelnut dessert *torta tre monti*.

✖ **Cantina di Bacco** Contrada Santa Croce 37, Città di San Marino; \0549 992840; w cantinadibaccosanmarino.com; ☀ closed Mon. Lots of atmosphere in this old stone-walled *cantina*

with red-checked tablecloths & old wooden seats; excellent food too, & Sanmarinese wines; good-value €16 menu. **€€€–€€€€**

✖ Piccolo Via del Serrone 17, Città di San Marino; **℡** 0549 992815; **f** ristoranteilpiccolo; ⊕ closed Mon. Another restaurant excavated out of the rock, & a good bet for seafood (try the *zuppa di pesce*) & elegant desserts. €€€

✖ Il Matterelo Via Consiglio dei Sessanta 150, Dogana; **℡** 0549 908 938; **w** ilmatterello.com. One of the most popular places in the republic, offering an enormous choice of *piadine* and filled *cassoni*. €

WHAT TO SEE AND DO Entering San Marino at the village called **Dogana** ('customs', though there are no border formalities now), you pass through a string of villages, merging together along the ferociously built-up main road and its factory outlets. San Marino, no midget like Vatican City, is 12km long at its widest extent.

At the foot of Monte Titano (739m; one of the mountains the mythological Titans piled up to reach heaven, to overthrow the gods), is **Borgo Maggiore** with most of the shops, just below the **Città di San Marino**, the citadel of the republic. This is a steep medieval hill town carefully preserved in aspic – one where you can walk past a modest house on a side street bearing a plaque that says it is the Command of the Militia, or the State Ministry of Culture and the Environment.

Not everything is as old as it looks: in the grand belvedere of Piazza della Libertà, the **Palazzo del Governo,** where the Grand Council meets and the Captains Regent have their offices, is a reconstruction of 1894 with a recent restoration by Gae Aulenti. Here in the summer, starting at 14.30, Ruritanian guardsmen in their brass buttons and epaulettes put on a changing of the guard ceremony every half-hour.

The **Museo di Stato** (*Piazzetta del Titano;* ℡ *0549 883835;* ⊕ *mid-Sep–May 09.00–17.00, Jun–Aug 08.00–20.00 daily; €3*) has archaeological finds, models of the town, works by Guercino, coins and memorabilia. The same hours and admission apply to all the museums here: the **Gallery of Modern and Contemporary Art** (*Via Eugippo;* ℡ *0549 883002*) with paintings and sculptures by Renato Guttuso, Emilio Vedova and more; the **Museo di San Francesco** (*Via Basilicus;* ℡ *0549 885132*), in a 14th-century convent, with church art and works by 20th-century figurative artist Emilio Ambron; and the (rebuilt) medieval **tower fortresses** on the three peaks that give San Marino its famous silhouette (famous to philatelists anyhow). The first, **Rocca Guaita**, was restored in 1500 and used as a prison until 1970; recently, layers of whitewash were removed to reveal some curious 19th-century prisoner graffiti. The second, the **Rocca de la Cesta**, on the highest peak of Monte Titano, contains thousands of weapons from the 12th–19th centuries; the third, **Rocca Montale,** can only be seen from outside.

Beyond these, there's a cheesy batch of private museums – Torture, Modern Weapons, Curiosities and Waxworks.

EAST OF SAN MARINO

The Conca Valley, a peaceful corner of Romagna with rolling vineyards, olive groves and fascinating caves, has yet more castles, although none was able to protect the villages in 1944–45, when the Eastern Gothic Line passed through here. START buses (page 328) head this way, but as usual to see more than one or two things in a day you'll need your own transport.

WHERE TO STAY, EAT AND DRINK

 Palazzo Viviani (53 rooms) Via Roma 38, Montegridolfo; **℡** 0541 855350; **w** palazzoviviani. com. These antique-filled suites, apts & dbls, with spectacular views over the Romagnolo–Marche frontier, are scattered through medieval buildings in the centre, with the finest ones in the palazzo itself. The complex includes 2 pools, spa & restaurant (€€€) with a panoramic terrace. B/fast inc. €€–€€€€

13

WHAT TO SEE AND DO Down on the borders of the Marche, the *comune* of **Gemmano** has the most striking natural features along the coast: the gates of hell. In 1810 a bishop of Rimini, offended to have such a thing in his diocese, changed the first letter of Inferno to an O. Now the centrepiece of a nature reserve, the **Grotte di Onferno** [map, pages 358–9] (*Via Provinciale Onferno 50;* m *389 199 1683;* f *Grotte di Onferno – Riserva Naturale; guided tours by appointment* ⊕ *15 Jun–15 Sep 09.00–noon & 15.00–18.00 daily, rest of year Sat–Sun only; €9; wear sturdy shoes & a jacket; torch & helmets are supplied*) mark the outer edge of the world's largest gypsum vein (page 341) and have peculiar breast-like formations called *mammelloni* hanging from the roof. Because of temperature inversions they emit vapours in the evening, especially in winter: these were for centuries considered a sign of hellish activity, along with the bats who adore the place – there are over 3,000, belonging to six different species. Admission includes entry into the **Museo Naturalistico and Botanical Gardens** (⊕ *same hrs*).

Overlooking the Conca Valley to the west, **Montescudo** changed hands countless times in history. The Malatesta bastions and lookout tower (1300) survived, as well as a rare Renaissance-era ice house on Via San Paolo dell'Olmo. Its two museums are just north of the centre: the hilltop Romanesque church of Trarivi, ruined in the war, is now the focal point of the **Museo della Linea Gotica Orientale** (*just off the SP41;* ✆ *0541 864 014;* w *comune.montescudo.rn.it;* ⊕ *14.00–18.00 Sat–Sun*) with photos, bomb fragments and machine guns; and the **Museo Etnografico Valliano** just east (*Via Valliano;* ✆ *0541 984 366;* ⊕ *09.00–noon Wed & Fri, 15.00–18.30 Sun; admission free*) evoking life here a century ago. The adjacent **Santuario di Valliano** has fresco fragments by the school of Ghirlandaio.

In **Montefiore Conca** to the southeast, the **Rocca Malatestiana** [map, pages 358–9] (*Piazzale Due Giugno, Monte;* ✆ *0541 980170;* w *castellomontefioreconca.it;* ⊕ *Jun–Sep 10.00–19.00 daily, also Jul–Aug until 23.00 Fri & Sat, Apr, May & Oct 10.00–18.00 Sat–Sun, Nov–Mar Sun & holidays only; €4*) stands on the highest point in the Valconca, with extraordinary views over the entire region. This castle is impressive in its sobriety, with sheer naked walls built in 1337 by Malatesta Guastafamiglia in the form of a single massive tower. It made such an impression on Giovanni Bellini that he used it in at least two of his backgrounds. Guastafamiglia made the castle cushy enough to entertain the King of Hungary in 1347, and later popes Gregory XII and Julius II and Sigismund, the Emperor of Bohemia slept here. It was reputedly impregnable, but under Sigismondo Malatesta's son Giovanni it fell to his arch-enemy Federico da Montefeltro (although only because he had managed to bribe some of the guards).

Under the popes the castle's career took a curious turn when it was given, along with the city of Fano, to pay off a debt to Constantine Comnenos, a descendant of the Byzantine emperors and Prince of Macedonia. Constantine lived in the castle until he died in 1530, but afterwards the fortress, militarily out of date, was neglected and ruined by earthquakes. Restored in 1950, the Malatesta arms are still in place over the gate; the vaulted Emperor's Room is frescoed with colourful fragments of battle scenes (1362–72) by Jacopo Avanzi.

To the southeast on the Marche border, medieval fortified **Montegridolfo**, 'one of the most beautiful villages in Italy', has been restored after years of total abandonment. It provides a convenient destination for coach tours, offering a tastefully done, measured teaspoon of the quaint and old: no ghosts, but a nice hotel (page 395). Just outside the centre, the **Museo della Linea dei Goti** (*Via Borgo;* ✆ *0541 855320;* ⊕ *15 Sep–15 Jun 15.00–18.00 Sun, 16 Jun–14 Sep 09.30–12.30 & 16.00–19.00 daily; donations*) has items saved by the locals: propaganda, postcards, weapons and films from the war.

Mondaino, just west of Montegridolfo, is a picturesque medieval burg wrapped around a pretty circular piazza that the locals call the 'frying pan'. It was famous in Etruscan times for a temple dedicated to Diana and the numerous deer (*daino*) that roamed its slopes. Its Malatesta castle is haunted by yet another pair of unhappy lovers, who were run through by a jealous husband's sword. For years they sighed, lamented, shook their chains and scared people to death, but so many paranormal addicts came to hear them that they declared, through a medium, that they were fed up and moved their ectoplasm elsewhere.

The castle now houses more solid relics in their stead: an important **Museo Paleontologico** (*Piazza Maggiore 1;* m *336 207 8570;* w *mondaino.com;* ⊕ *Sep–May 09.00–noon Mon, Wed–Sat by appointment, 10.00–13.00 & 15.00–18.00 Sun, Jun–Oct closed Sun morning; €2.50*). Some 5–10 million years ago, when the Adriatic dried up, thousands of fish perished in the mud at the bottom of the sea. They were preserved in the strata of Mondaino's sedimentary rock; fine examples are on display here (one, a lantern fish, was so well preserved that bands of fossilised DNA have been recovered), along with leaves, birds' feathers and wings, teeth belonging to the Procarcharodon megalodon, a 30m-long ancestor of the shark, and the oddball 'mummy fish'.

13

Appendix 1

LANGUAGE

PRONUNCIATION With a little practice, Italian is relatively easy to pronounce: as a cardinal rule, words are pronounced cleanly and how they are written. Unlike French or English, every letter (with the exception of silent 'h') is pronounced.

The alphabet The Italian alphabet, a variation on the Latin alphabet, is made up of 21 letters. It excludes the letters j, k, w, x, and y although, as they are considered 'foreign' letters, they are used in a variety of different circumstances for adopted words. They have, too, recently begun to creep into the likes of SMS messages and emails as a lazy substitute. For example, the hard 'ch' sound is often replaced by 'k': so *chi* (who) becomes *ki*. However, this is by no means an official alternative and many Italians frown upon its use.

a	as in **ah**
b	as in **b**ag
c	as in **c**at when preceding a, o, u and h
	as in **ch**eer when preceding e or i
d	as in **d**og, but without aspiration
e	two sounds: as the closed 'e' in p**e**t, or as an open sound as in 'air'
	For example: closed – *mela* (apple); open – *bello* (beautiful)
f	as in **f**un
g	as in **g**o when preceding a, o, u and h
	as in **g**eneral when preceding e or i
h	always silent
i	as in **i**t, or long, as in sk**i**
j	in some dialect words, sounded as a long 'i'
l	as in **l**ie
m	as in **m**an
n	as in **n**o
o	two sounds: as the closed 'o' in r**o**se or as the open 'o' in l**o**t
	For example: closed – *con* (with); open – *otto* (eight)
p	as in **p**et
q	as in **q**uick
r	the Italian 'r' is rolled or trilled, with the tongue against the forward palate and gums of the upper teeth
s	before vowels and c, f, p, q, s, t as the 's' in son, and then usually as the 's' in closed
t	a hard sound, as in **t**ell but with no aspiration
u	as in r**u**le
v	as in **v**an
z	as in the 'ds' in la**ds** or the 'ts' in lo**ts**

ch	always a hard 'c'
gh	always a hard 'g'
gli	as in the 'lli' in mi**lli**on
gn	as in the 'ny' in ca**ny**on
sc	followed by 'e' or 'i' as the 'sh' in **sh**oot

Stress and accents
A word's natural stress usually falls on the penultimate syllable:

*Ro*ma	Rome	an*da*re	to go

However, stress can also occur on the first syllable of a word:

*pub*blico	public	*man*dorla	almond

The presence of an accent at the end of a word means that the stress is placed on the last syllable:

papà	dad (whereas Papa means pope)	caffè	coffee

WORDS AND PHRASES
Basics

Yes	sì	Excuse me	Mi scusi
No	no	I don't understand	Non capisco
Thank you	grazie	Do you speak	Parla
You're welcome	prego	English?	inglese?

Meeting people

Good morning	buongiorno	My name is…	Mi chiamo…
Good evening	buonasera	What is your name?	Come ti chiami?
Hello	ciao		(informal)
Goodbye	ciao; arrivederci	I am…	Sono…
	(formal)	from England	dall'Inghilterra
Pleased to	Piacere	from Australia	dall'Australia
meet you	conoscerti	from America	dall'America
	(informal)	How are you?	Come stai?
	conoscerla		
	(formal)		

Useful questions

What does … mean?	Che significa…?	Why?	Perché?
Where is…?	Dov'è…?	How much does it	Quanto costa?
What?	Cosa?	cost?	
What is it?	Che cos'è?	Could you help me?	Mi potrebbe aiutare?

Transport/travel

bicycle	bicicletta	motorbike/moped	motocicletta/
boat	barca		motorino
bus	autobus	plane	aereo
car	macchina	train	treno
ferry	traghetto	toilets	toilette

I'd like to hire…	Vorrei noleggiare…	here	qui
a car	una macchina	there	là/li
a bicycle	una bicicletta	north	nord
Is this the road to…?	È questa la strada per…?	south	sud
		east	est
Where is the service station?	Dov'è il benzinaio?	west	ovest
		Turn right / left	Giri a destra/ sinistra
unleaded petrol	senza piombo		
diesel	diesel	straight on	sempre diritto
Please fill it up	Il pieno, per favore	Bon voyage!	Buon viaggio!

Public transport

airport	aeroporto	a return ticket	di andata e ritorno
bus stop	fermata dell'autobus	from … to …	da … a …
platform	binario	I want to go…	Voglio andare…
railway station	stazione	What time does it leave?	A che ora parte?
ticket office	biglietteria		
first class	prima classe	The train…	Il treno…
second class	seconda classe	has been delayed	è in ritardo
I'd like…	Vorrei…	has been cancelled	è stato cancellato
a one-way ticket	un biglietto di solo andata		

Hotels

Where is a good hotel?	Dov'è un buon hotel?	a room with bathroom	una camera con bagno privato
Do you have any rooms?	Avete delle camere libere?	Is breakfast included?	La colazione è compresa?
I'd like…	Vorrei…	key	chiave
a single room	una camera singola	shower	doccia
a double room	una matrimoniale	first floor	primo piano
a room with two beds	una camera con due letti	ground floor	piano terra

At the beach

water	acqua
sand	sabbia
towel	asciugamano
I would like to hire…	Vorrei affittare…
a beach umbrella/a beach palm…	un ombrellone/una palma…
with…	con…
a bed	un lettino
a deckchair	una sedia a sdraio
a chair	una sedia

Eating

Can I book a table?	*Posso prenotare una tavola?*	main course	*secondo*
		dessert	*dolce, frutta*
Do you have a table for … people?	*Ha un tavolo per … persone?*	side dish	*contorno*
		salads	*insalate*
I am a vegetarian	*Sono vegetariano*	soup	*minestra, zuppa*
a vegan	*vegano*	bread	*pane*
coeliac	*celiaco*	bread-sticks	*grissini*
Could I see the menu?	*Posso vedere il menù?*	butter	*burro*
		cheese	*formaggio*
cover charge	*pane e coperto*	egg	*uovo*
service charge	*servizio*	honey	*miele*
The bill, please	*Il conto, per favore*	ice	*ghiaccio*
Do you accept credit card?	*Accettate carte di credito?*	lemon	*limone*
		oil	*olio*
Could you please bring me…	*Mi potrebbe portare…*	omelette	*frittata*
		pepper	*pepe*
a knife	*un coltello*	salt	*sale*
a fork	*una forchetta*	sugar	*zucchero*
a spoon?	*un cucchiaio*	boiled	*bollito*
a glass	*un bicchiere*	fried	*fritta*
a cup	*una tazza*	grilled	*grigliata*
restaurant	*ristorante, trattoria*	roast	*arrosto*
lunch	*pranzo*	smoked	*affumicato*
dinner	*cena*	with meat sauce	*al ragù*
breakfast	*prima colazione*	without tomato (sauce)	*in bianco*
hors d'oeuvres	*antipasti*		
entrée/starter	*primo*		

Fish, seafood (pesce, frutti di mare)

anchovies	*acciughe, alici*	prawns	*gamberetti*
bream	*orata*	red mullet	*triglia*
baby clams	*vongole*	salmon	*salmone*
cod	*merluzzo*	salt cod	*baccalà*
crayfish	*gamberi di fiume*	sardines	*sarde*
large prawns	*gamberi*	sea bass	*branzino*
lobster	*aragosta*	small mixed fish	*pesce azzurro*
mackerel	*sgombro*	sole	*sogliola*
mixed fry	*fritto misto*	swordfish	*pesce spada*
mussels	*cozze*	trout	*trota*
oysters	*ostriche*	tuna	*tonno*

Meat (carne)

beef	*manzo*	sausage	*salsiccia*
boar	*cinghiale*	venison	*cervo*
chicken	*pollo*	boiled ham	*prosciutto cotto*
lamb	*agnello, abbacchio*	chop	*braciola*
mutton	*castrato*	cured ham	*prosciutto crudo*
pigeon	*piccione*	cutlet	*cotoletta*
pork	*maiale*	liver	*fegato*
rabbit	*coniglio*	meat on a skewer	*arrosticini, spiedini*

raw beef slices	*carpaccio*	stew	*spezzatino*
rolled, spiced pork	*porchetta*	veal escalope	*scaloppine*
steak	*bistecca*		

Vegetables (verdure)

artichokes	*carciofi*	fennel	*finocchio*
aubergine	*melanzana*	lettuce	*lattuga*
broad beans	*fave*	mushrooms	*funghi*
green beans	*fagiolini*	peas	*piselli*
white beans	*fagioli*	potato	*patata*
cabbage	*cavolo*	pumpkin	*zucca*
carrot	*carota*	salad	*insalata*
cauliflower	*cavolfiore*	spinach	*spinaci*
courgette	*zucchini*	tomato	*pomodoro*
garlic	*aglio*	chickpeas	*ceci*
onion	*cipolla*	lentils	*lenticchie*
peppers	*peperoni*	truffle	*tartufo*
asparagus	*asparagi*		

Herbs (erbe)

basil	*basilico*	sage	*salvia*
mint	*menta*	thyme	*timo*
parsley	*prezzemolo*		
rosemary	*rosmarino*		

Fruits, nuts (frutti, noci)

apple	*mela*	pineapple	*ananas*
apricot	*albicocca*	plum	*prugna/susina*
banana	*banana*	pomegranate	*melagrana*
cherries	*ciliegie*	raspberry	*lampone*
fruit salad	*macedonia*	strawberry	*fragola*
grapes	*uva*	tangerine	*mandarino*
mango	*mango*		
melon	*melone*	almonds	*mandorle*
orange	*arancia*	hazelnuts	*nocciole*
peach	*pesca*	nuts, or walnuts	*noci*
pear	*pera*		

Desserts (dolci)

cake	*torta*	tart	*crostata*
ice cream	*gelato*	trifle	*zuppa inglese*
Italian ice	*granita*		

Drinking

Could you bring me a glass of...?	*Mi porta un bicchiere di...?*	fruit juice	*succo di frutta*
still water/	*acqua liscia/*	bottle	*bottiglia*
sparkling water	*acqua gassata*	tea	*tè*
wine	*vino*	milk	*latte*
beer	*birra*	red wine/ white wine	*vino rosso/ vino bianco*

Time

What time is it?	*Che ore sono?*	year	*anno*
It is…		today	*oggi*
1 o'clock	*È l'una*	tomorrow	*domani*
2 o'clock	*Sono le due*	yesterday	*ieri*
10 o'clock	*Sono le dieci*	morning	*mattina*
day	*giorno*	afternoon	*pomeriggio*
week	*settimana*	evening	*sera*
month	*mese*	night	*notte*

Days of the week

Monday	*lunedì*	Friday	*venerdì*
Tuesday	*martedì*	Saturday	*sabato*
Wednesday	*mercoledì*	Sunday	*domenica*
Thursday	*giovedì*		

Months

January	*gennaio*	July	*luglio*
February	*febbraio*	August	*agosto*
March	*marzo*	September	*settembre*
April	*aprile*	October	*ottobre*
May	*maggio*	November	*novembre*
June	*giugno*	December	*dicembre*

Numbers

0	*zero*	17	*diciassette*
1	*uno*	18	*diciotto*
2	*due*	19	*diciannove*
3	*tre*	20	*venti*
4	*quattro*	21	*ventuno*
5	*cinque*	30	*trenta*
6	*sei*	40	*quaranta*
7	*sette*	50	*cinquanta*
8	*otto*	60	*sessanta*
9	*nove*	70	*settanta*
10	*dieci*	80	*ottanta*
11	*undici*	90	*novanta*
12	*dodici*	100	*cento*
13	*tredici*	200	*duecento*
14	*quattordici*	1,000	*mille*
15	*quindici*	2,000	*duemila*
16	*sedici*		

EMILIA-ROMAGNA ONLINE

For additional online content, articles, photos and more on Emilia-Romagna, why not visit **w** bradtguides.com/emilia?

Appendix 2

GLOSSARY

acroterion (*acroterio*)	decorative protrusion at the top of a roof gable of an Etruscan, Greek or Roman temple. Matching pieces at the corners of the roof are called antefixes (*antefissi*)
ambo, or *ambone*	pulpit, often elaborately decorated
ambulatory (*ambulatorio*)	aisle around the apse of a church
atrium (*atrio*)	entrance court of a Roman house or early church
badia	from *abbazia*, an abbey or abbey church
baldachin (*baldacchino*)	columned stone canopy above the altar of a church
basilica	rectangular building, usually divided into three aisles by rows of columns; in Rome this was the common form for law courts and public buildings, and Roman Christians adapted it for early churches; in the modern Church, a church of 'basilican' status enjoys special privileges
borgo	from the Saxon *burh* of Santo Spirito in Rome: a neighbourhood, suburb or village
bucchero ware	black, delicately thin Etruscan ceramics, usually incised or painted
campanile	belltower; *campanilismo* means local patriotism
campo santo	Christian cemetery
cardo	transverse street of a Roman castrum-shaped city (see decumanus, page 405)
cartoon (*cartone*)	preliminary sketch for a fresco or tapestry
caryatid (*cariatide*)	supporting pillar or column carved into a standing female form; male versions are called telamones
castrum	Roman military camp, always neatly rectangular, with straight streets and gates at cardinal points; later the Romans founded or refounded cities according to the same plan
cenacolo	fresco of the Last Supper, often on the wall of a monastery refectory (dining hall)
chiaroscuro	effect of contrasting light and dark areas in a painting
ciborium	tabernacle, often large and free-standing; or used in the sense of a baldachin
cinquecento	the 1500s – in the Italian manner of referring to centuries (duecento, trecento, quattrocento, etc)
comune	commune, or commonwealth, referring to the medieval free cities and their governments; today it is used equally for a city, town or village, and its local governmental body

condottiere	leader of a band of mercenaries in late medieval and Renaissance times
confraternity (*confraternità*)	religious lay-brotherhood, often serving as a neighbourhood mutual-aid and burial society, or pursuing some specific charitable work
contrapposto	dramatic but unnatural twist in a statue, especially in a Mannerist or Baroque work, derived from Hellenistic and Roman art
convento	convent *or* monastery
corte	fortified farm, usually built around a large courtyard, going back to the early Middle Ages, once common in the Po Valley; some still survive
decumanus	street of a Roman castrum-shaped city parallel to the longer axis; the central, main avenue was called the Decumanus Major
dodecapolis	federation of 12 city-states; a common form of religious or political organisation in ancient times (as with the Etruscans)
duomo	cathedral; there's no difference between a *duomo* and a *cattedrale*; the word used depends only on local preference
ex voto	offering (a terracotta figurine, painting, medallion, silver bauble, or whatever) made in thanksgiving to a god or Christian saint
forum (*foro*)	central square of a Roman town, with its most important temples and buildings; the word means 'outside' – the original Roman Forum was outside the city walls
frazione (abbreviated *Fraz*)	subdivision of a modern Italian *comune* (town, city or village), usually an outlying settlement or suburb; sometimes called a *locazione* (abbreviated *Loc*)
fresco (*affresco*)	wall painting, the most important Italian medium of art since Etruscan times (it isn't easy: first the artist draws the *sinopia* (page 407) on the wall, then this is covered with plaster, but only a little at a time, as the paint must be on the plaster before it dries – Leonardo da Vinci's endless attempts to find clever shortcuts ensured that little of his work would survive)
Ghibellines (*Ghibellini*)	one of the great medieval parties, the supporters of the Holy Roman Emperors and foes of the Guelphs
gonfalon (*gonfalone*)	banner of a medieval free city; the *gonfaloniere*, or flag-bearer, was sometimes the most important public official
graffito	originally, incised decoration on buildings, walls, etc; only lately has it come to mean casually scribbled messages in public places
Greek cross	in the floor plans of churches, a cross with equal arms; the more familiar plan, with one arm extended to form a nave, is called a Latin cross
grisaille	painting or fresco in monochrome
grotesques (*grotteschi*)	carved or painted faces used in Etruscan and later Roman decoration; Raphael and other artists rediscovered them in the 'grotto' of Nero's Golden House in Rome, and they became popular in Renaissance art

Guelphs (*Guelfi*)	one of the two great medieval factions, supporters of the pope and foes of the Ghibellines
intarsia	decorative inlaid wood or marble
Liberty style	Italian name for Art Nouveau (from London's Liberty department store)
locazione	see *frazione* (page 405)
loggia	open-sided gallery or arcade
lunette	semicircular space on a wall, above a door or under vaulting, filled by either a window or a mural painting
mandorla	in medieval art, an almond-shaped aureola surrounding figures of Christ in Majesty
matroneum	elevated women's gallery around the nave of an early church, a custom adopted from the Byzantines in the 6th and 7th centuries
narthex	enclosed porch of a church
naumachia	mock naval battle, like those staged in the Colosseum
niello	a technique of using a molten metal alloy (silver, copper, or others, plus sulphur) to emphasise lines or background in metal reliefs
palazzo	not just a palace, but any large, important building
palio	banner, and the horse race in which city neighbourhoods contend for it in their annual festivals; the most famous is Siena's
pantocrator	Christ 'ruler of all', a common subject for apse paintings and mosaics in areas influenced by Byzantine art
piano nobile	the principal floor of a palace or townhouse, where the owners reside; usually the first floor, but sometimes the ground floor
pietra dura	rich inlay work using semi-precious stones
pieve	country or village parish church
pluteo	screen, usually of marble, between two columns, often highly decorated
podestà	in medieval cities, an official with mostly judicial duties sent by the Holy Roman Emperors; their power, or lack of it, depended on the strength of the *comune*; a *comune* beset by factional strife might accept a *podestà* as impartial ruler for a limited time
popolo	in the medieval *comuni*, this meant not 'the people' in general, but the middle classes, organised in a body to protect their interests and led by a Capitano del Popolo; the poorer classes were the *popolo minuto*
predella	smaller paintings on panels below the main subject of a painted altarpiece
presepio	Nativity scene
putti	naked small children, a popular motif for decoration in antiquity, revived in the 1400s, developing into the flocks of cherubs that infested much of Italy in the Baroque era
quadratura	illusionistic style of painting, invented in Rome and perfected in mid-16th-century Bologna, that uses painted architectural elements in perspective to create imaginary space behind a wall or above a ceiling

quadrivio	crossroads
quadroporticus	enclosed rectangular portico, like a quadrangle or cloister, that leads to the main entrance of a church, a common feature in early Christian and early medieval churches
quattrocento	the 1400s – in the Italian manner of referring to centuries (duecento, trecento, quattrocento, etc)
rocca	fortress
sacra conversazione	a genre of Renaissance and later painting consisting of an enthroned Virgin Mary and baby Jesus at the centre of an informal grouping of saints
sinopia	layout of a fresco (page 405), etched by the artist on the wall before the plaster is applied; often these are works of art in their own right
stele	vertical funeral stone
stigmata	miraculous simulation of the bleeding wounds of Christ, appearing in holy men
telamon (*telamone*)	male caryatid (page 404)
tessera	square piece of glass, stone or other material used in mosaic work (plural: tesserae)
thermae	Roman baths
tondo	round relief, painting or terracotta
transenna	marble screen separating the altar area from the rest of a church
trecento	the 1300s – in the Italian manner of referring to centuries (duecento, trecento, quattrocento, etc)
triptych (*trittico*)	work of art, especially a painted altarpiece, in three sections; also diptych (*dittico*) for two sections, polyptych (*polittico*) for many, etc.
triumph (*trionfo*)	imitating the triumphal processions of Roman generals and emperors, a formal ceremony in celebration of a victory, or an artistic representation of one
trompe l'œil	art that uses perspective effects to deceive the eye – for example, to create the illusion of depth on a flat surface, or to make columns and arches painted on a wall seem real (see *quadratura*, page 406)
tympanum	semicircular space, often bearing a painting or relief, above a church portal
voussoir	one of the stones of an arch

Appendix 3

DIRECTORY OF ARTISTS

dell'Abate, Niccolò (1512–71) (*Modena: San Pietro*) Painter and sculptor of Modena, influenced by Correggio and Parmigianino; spent the years 1548–52 in Bologna, then went to the court of Henri II where he and Primaticcio founded French Mannerism, the 'Fontainebleau style'.

Aleotti, Giovan Battista (1546–1636) (*Ferrara: University and other buildings; Gualtieri: Piazza Bentivoglio*) Innovative early Baroque architect of Parma, where he designed the 'first modern theatre' for the Farnese in the Palazzo della Pilotta, and the church of Santa Maria del Quartiere.

Antelami, Benedetto (active 1150–1200) (*Parma: Baptistry and Cathedral pulpit; Fidenza: Cathedral*) Italy's first great medieval sculptor; probably studied in Provence. His trademark black niello-work borders add an elegant touch to his reliefs; his Parma Baptistry, neither ancient nor medieval, has been called 'proto-Renaissance'.

Niccolò dell'Arca (Niccolò da Bari, active 1462–94) (*Bologna: San Domenico church, Palazzo Comunale, Santa Maria della Vita*) Sculptor from Puglia who spent most of his career in Bologna, where he earned his name and his reputation from his work on the Arca di San Domenico in San Domenico church.

Baglione, Cesare (1545–1615) (*Sala Baganza, Soragna and Torrechiara*) Charming Mannerist painter from Bologna or Cremona who spent most of his career around Parma frescoing castle walls with allegories and grotesques.

Il Bastianino (Sebastiano Filippi, c1532–1602) (*Ferrara: Cathedral, San Paolo, Sant'Antonio in Polesine, Pinacoteca*) Ferrarese Mannerist with a soft touch.

Begarelli, Antonio (16th century) (*Modena: Cathedral, San Domenico*) Sculptor of fine terracotta groups in Modena.

Bianchi Ferrari, Francesco (d1510) (*Modena: Galleria Estense*) Modenese lesser-light of the quattrocento, noted for canvases full of colour and emotion.

Bibiena (or Bibbiena), Ferdinando (1657–1743) (*Colorno: Palazzo Ducale; Parma: Sant'Antonio Abate*) One of the elder members of a family of Bologna, famous for their stagings of theatre, opera and Baroque public spectacles, also talented as architects and painters. Most of the family's works are elsewhere. Another Bibiena (Antonio) built Bologna's Teatro Comunale.

Bonone, Carlo (1569–1632) (*Ferrara: Pinacoteca*) A late Ferrarese painter critics like to dismiss as a 'provincial eclectic', and not without reason; you'll see echoes of the Carracci, Correggio, Schedoni and Guercino in his work, but little else.

Cagnacci, Guido (1601–63) (*Rimini: Museo della Città*) Bolognese classicist and follower of Guido Reni, with a penchant for unusual colours; became court painter to the Habsburg emperor in Vienna.

Carracci, Agostino (1557–1602), **Annibale** (1560–1609), and their cousin **Ludovico** (1555–1619) (*Bologna: Museo Civico Medievale, Palazzo Comunale, Pinacoteca; Cento: Pinacoteca; Parma: Ducal Palace*) Of Bologna, devoted to rescuing the classicism in art from the caprices of Mannerism. Annibale went to Rome and, until the 19th century, his reputation was as high as those of Michelangelo and Raphael; his engravings of lower-class scenes, the Arti di Bologna, would influence painters in the 18th century. Agostino was more academic and less imaginative; Ludovico, a more personal, expressive artist, stayed in Bologna as head of the school.

Cavedoni, Giacomo (1557–1660) (*Bologna: Pinacoteca*) From Sassuolo, a close follower of Ludovico Carracci; developed a richly coloured palette. Never went to Rome.

Correggio (Antonio Allegri; 1494–1534) (*Parma: Cathedral, Camera di Correggio, San Giovanni Evangelista, Galleria Nazionale*) No intellectual, but a daring master of foreshortening in large works (his virtuoso frescoes in the cupola of Parma Cathedral, where the saints soar into a miasma of leggy angels), and painter of emotional nuances, charming gesture, and smoky Leonardo-esque shadowing in his more intimate scenes. His lofty reputation in the 18th century was based largely on his voluptuous mythological fancies, the inspiration for so much of this kind of art in the centuries that followed, but for these you'll have to travel to Berlin, Rome, Dresden and Paris.

del Cossa, Francesco (1436–78) Early protagonist of the Ferrarese school, original, energetic and good-humoured, influenced by miniaturists and Cosmè Tura. His best-known work is his contribution to the frescoes of the Palazzo Schifanoia in Ferrara. Miffed at being paid by the square foot, he went to Bologna, where his most important works were lost or broken up (the Griffoni altarpiece); the best survivor is the Pala dei Mercanti in Bologna's Pinacoteca Nazionale.

Costa, Lorenzo (c1460–1535) (*Ferrara: Palazzo Schifanoia; Bologna: San Petronio, San Giacomo Maggiore, Santa Maria dei Servi*) A leading artist of the Renaissance Ferrarese school, along with Cosmè Tura and Ercole de Roberti; in 1485 he went to Bologna where he became a favourite of the Bentivoglio and gradually adopted a softer, sappier style more pleasing to Bolognese tastes, bland and lifeless at its worst, graceful and tenderly melancholic at its best.

Crespi, Giuseppe Maria (called Lo Spagnuolo, 1665–1747) (*Bologna: Pinacoteca, Palazzo Pepoli Campogrande, Galleria Davia-Bargellini; Finale Emilia: Collegiata*) Late Baroque painter of Bologna, and one of its few real talents in that era, with a rare depth of feeling and sincerity.

de' Crocefissi, Simone (active 1355–99) (*Bologna: Pinacoteca*) Painter of Bologna, well within the International Gothic style, though his works become increasingly naturalistic in his later years.

Domenichino (Domenico Zampieri, 1581–1641) (*Bologna: Pinacoteca*) Pupil of Annibale and Ludovico Carracci who followed them to Rome, where by the 1620s he became the city's leading painter. A dignified classicist like Guido Reni, he held an immensely high reputation in the 18th and 19th centuries.

Dossi, Dosso (Giovanni di Lutero, c1490–1542) (*Modena: Cathedral; Ferrara: Pinacoteca*) One of the great late Renaissance Ferrara painters, influenced by the romanticism and rich colours of Venetians Giorgione and Titian. Equally at home in many genres, he excelled in landscapes and mythological subjects which renewed the spirit of magic and fantasy that characterised the earlier Ferrara school; all his best works are outside Emilia-Romagna.

Agostino di Duccio (1418–81) (*Rimini: Malatesta Temple; Modena: Cathedral*) With Donatello and Ghiberti, one of the three great Florentine sculptors of the quattrocento, known for his great elegance of line and striking originality in subject matter.

Fontana, Lavinia (1552–1614) (*Bologna: Pinacoteca; Imola: Pinacoteca*) Bolognese, daughter of painter Prospero Fontana, who herself became a rare woman painter of the Renaissance, and was elected to the Roman Academy; noted for portraits of prominent people as well as religious works.

Franceschini, Marcantonio (1648–1729) (*Modena: San Carlo; Reggio: San Prospero*) One of the more accomplished late Baroque painters of the Bolognese school; a light touch, and a gift for landscapes in conventional religious scenes.

'Il Francia' (Francesco Raibolini, 1450–1517) (*Bologna: Pinacoteca*) Bolognese, began as a goldsmith, jeweller and maker of medallions, and didn't paint until he was over 40, but soon became the most fashionable painter in the city. He was identified with the Bentivoglio family, and many of his works were destroyed after they lost power. A follower of Raphael, although the two never met.

Il Garofalo (Benvenuto Tisi, 1481–1559) (*Ferrara: Pinacoteca, Palazzo del Ludovico il Moro; Argenta: San Domenico*) Ferrarese High Renaissance, heavily influenced by Raphael; cranked out polished but imaginatively numb religious scenes by the dozen before going blind; held in high esteem by critics from Vasari to the 18th century.

Giovanni da Modena (1396–1451) (*Bologna: Pinacoteca, San Petronio*) The great quattrocento painter that nobody knows; tremendous *Last Judgement* in Bologna's San Petronio.

Girolamo da Carpi (1501–56) (*Bologna: San Salvatore, San Michele in Bosco; Ferrara: San Paolo, Pinacoteca*) Important Mannerist painter, influenced by Giulio Romano and Parmigianino, and a keen student of Roman antiquities.

Guercino (Giovanni Francesco Barbieri, 1591–1666) (*Modena: Galleria Estense; Cento: Pinacoteca, Chiesa del Rosario; Parma: Galleria Nazionale; Piacenza: Duomo; Bologna: Pinacoteca, San Luca; Reggio Emilia: Duomo, Madonna della Ghiara; Ferrara: Cathedral*) 'Squinty-eye' was born in Cento, near Bologna, but initially rebelled against the Carraccesque classicism and painted powerful, expressive atmospheric Baroque works in Rome. Ran the studio of Guido Reni after that artist's death in 1642, and succeeded him as the most popular painter in Bologna. See also box, page 133.

Lanfranco (active 1100–37) Architect of Modena Cathedral, built according to the basic principles of the northern Lombard style, with allusions to the classical basilican form. His work inspired the architects of Ferrara's cathedral.

Lanfranco, Giovanni (1582–1647) Born in Parma and trained under Agostino Carracci. Became one of the first great Baroque painters in Rome and Naples, inspired by his childhood familiarity with Correggio; nothing of his survives at home.

Lendinara (*Modena: Cathedral, Galleria Estense*) Family of quattrocento artists, especially known for their skill in creating intarsia wooden choir stalls; the most noteworthy is Cristoforo da Lendinara.

Lombardo, Pietro (1435–1515) Leading Venetian sculptor with an interest in antiquities. Pietro sculpted Dante's tomb in Ravenna; his son Antonio made Alfonso d'Este's 'marble study' but his reliefs are now in the Hermitage, St Petersburg.

Magnasco, Alessandro (known as Il Lissandrino; 1667–1749) (*Castell'Arquato: Museo della Collegiata*) Worked mostly in Milan; one of the greatest and most eccentric late Baroque painters, specialising in macabre scenes of monks and convents.

Mastelletta (Giovanni Andrea Danducci, 1575–1655) (*Modena: Galleria Estense; Bologna: Pinacoteca*) Bolognese, a master of ethereal poetic landscapes in a manner well in advance of his time, inspired by Correggio and Niccolò dell'Abate.

Morandi, Giorgio (1890–1964) (*Bologna: Museo Morandi; Traversetolo: Fondazione Magnani Rocca*) Of Bologna; generally considered the greatest Italian painter of the 20th century. An artist of geometry and tonal intimism, a few everyday objects formed his contemplative and lyrical 'personal alphabet'.

Morazzone (Pier Francesco Mazzucchelli, 1573–1626) (*Piacenza: Duomo*) Milanese fresco painter, a transitional figure between the late Renaissance and Baroque whose cool, precise line and love of contrast often harks back to the quattrocento.

Orsi, Lelio (c1511–87) (*Novellara: Museo Gonzaga; Modena: Galleria Estense*) Born in Novellara, a distinctive Mannerist painter with a touch of the bizarre and dramatic lighting effects.

Palma Giovane (Jacopo Negretti, 1544–1628) (*Reggio Emilia: Pinacoteca*) Trained by Titian, and spent early career in central Italy before returning to his native Venice to become the city's leading painter.

Parmigianino (Girolamo Francesco Mazzola, 1503–40) (*Parma: Madonna della Steccata, San Giovanni Evangelista; Fontanellato: Castello di Sanvitale*) The 'little Parmesan' started his precocious career under the influence of Correggio, with a keen interest in unusual spatial effects from the start. He went off to Rome and later returned to Bologna and Parma. According to Giorgio Vasari, he became an alchemist. The word *imparminigiare* came to mean to paint elegance at the expense of the subject. Was a major influence on Niccolò dell'Abate and many others.

de' Pasti, Matteo (active 1441–72) Painter, sculptor, medallist and architect of Verona; the collaborator of Agostino di Duccio on the interior of Rimini's Tempio Malatestiano.

Pietro da Rimini (active early 14th century) (*Ravenna: Museo Nazionale di San Vitale; Abbey of Pomposa*) Gifted member of the Rimini school, at his best capable of painting figures of delicate beauty; he is one of the few whose work remains in the region.

de Pisis, Filippo (Luigi Filippi Tibertelli, 1896–1956) (*Ferrara: Musei Civici d'Arte Moderna e Contemporanea*) Poet of Ferrara, where he met de Chirico; turned to painting in 1919. Best works are his marine still lifes, of incongruous objects on a beach, in dreamlike relationships with the surrounding seascapes.

Pordenone (Giovanni Antonio de Sacchis, 1483–1539) (*Piacenza: Madonna di Campagna*) Self-taught painter who followed Titian and Michelangelo; dramatic and slightly uncouth; died in Ferrara while designing tapestries for Ercole II.

Preti, Mattia (1613–99) (*Modena: San Biagio*) Calabrian Baroque painter, influenced by Caravaggio. Worked all over Italy including a short spell in Emilia-Romagna; most of his best work is in Malta, for the Grand Master of the Knights of St John.

Procaccini brothers Camillo (1560–1629) (*Piacenza: Duomo; Reggio Emilia: San Prospero*) and the younger and more gifted **Giulio Cesare** (1574–1625) (*Modena: Galleria Estense*) From Bologna, where they studied under the Carracci; they later moved to Milan, where they collaborated with Marazzone and Crespi, becoming key figures in the new art of the Counter-Reformation, under the influence of San Carlo Borromeo.

'Pseudo Jacopino' (active 1320–30) (*Bologna: Pinacoteca*) Unknown Riminese artist, notable for often breaking the boundaries of conventional, stylised religious works with a precocious realism.

della Quercia, Jacopo (c1374–1438) (*Bologna: San Petronio; Ferrara: Museo della Cattedrale*) Sienese, one of the greatest sculptors of the early Renaissance; died while working on the reliefs of the portal of San Petronio, Bologna.

Reni, Guido (1575–1642) (*Bologna: Pinacoteca, San Bartolomeo; Modena: Pinacoteca; Castelfranco Emilia: Santa Maria Assunta*) The 'maximum exponent of the classical ideal of the seicento', and a fastidious fellow, 'generally believed to be a virgin', his reputation peaked in the 18th and early 19th centuries, when many (such as Joshua Reynolds) considered him the greatest painter of all time, the 'divine Guido'. Those may have been the opinions of an artistically retarded age, but his reputation survives as one of the greats of his period, especially notable for his refined colouring, graceful line and curious lighting. Most of the dull works with his name on are by his studio. Most of his best ones are in Rome.

Ricci, Sebastiano (1659–1734) (*Piacenza: Musei Civici; Parma: Galleria Nazionale*) Venetian late Baroque painter who studied at Bologna and Parma and adapted the lessons to his own brilliant, virtuoso style.

de' Roberti, Ercole (c1450–96) (*Ferrara: Palazzo Schifanoia, Pinacoteca; Bologna: Pinacoteca*) One of the most powerful and inventive painters of the Ferrara school, with a very nervous line, refined colouring and metallic harshness that lends his work an unusual lyricism; followed del Cossa to Bologna, then became court artist to the Este in 1486. Some of his later works go beyond the dramatic to the ferocious; few remain in the region.

Rossetti, Biagio (1447–1516) Court architect to Ercole I of Ferrara who planned the layout of the Herculean Addition; designed the Palazzo dei Diamanti and many of the city's palaces and churches.

Scarsellino (Ippolito Scarsella, 1551–1620) (*Ferrara: Pinacoteca, Palazzo Schifanoia*) One of the last important painters in Ferrara, noted for his romantic treatment of landscapes in both religious and mythological scenes.

Schedoni, Bartolomeo (1578–1615) (*Parma: Galleria Nazionale; Modena: Palazzo Comunale*) Born in Modena, pupil of Annibale Carracci, influenced by Correggio and the Roman Baroque; known for his dramatic use of light, sculptural forms bordering on abstraction and metallic Mannerist colours. After 1607 became court painter to the Farnese in Parma.

Spada, Leonello (1576–1622) (*Bologna: San Domenico; Modena: Galleria Estense; Reggio Emilia: Madonna della Ghiara*) Born in Sassuolo near Modena; went to Malta with Caravaggio; in Bologna they called him 'Caravaggio's ape'.

Spolverini, Ilario (1657–1734) (*Piacenza: Galleria Farnese*) Court painter of the Farnese, creator of the genre of 'ceremonial painting', capturing the carefully staged processions and ceremonies of the Baroque age; also known for huge, stirring Biblical and battle scenes.

Tiarini, Alessandro (1577–1668) (*Parma: San Alessandro; Bologna: San Domenico; Reggio Emilia: Madonna della Ghiara*) Bolognese, a follower of the Carracci noted for large, dramatic compositions; later fell under the influence of Caravaggio.

Tibaldi, Pellegrino (1527–96) (*Bologna: Palazzo Poggi, San Giacomo Maggiore*) Mannerist painter, sculptor and architect inspired by Michelangelo.

Tommaso da Modena (c1325–79) (*Modena: Galleria Estense, Sant'Agostino*) One of the most celebrated painters of his day, from the Bolognese miniaturist tradition, who individualised his subjects and moved towards a more natural, objective style. Most of his work is elsewhere: commissioned by Dominicans in Treviso, and the German Emperor in Prague.

Tramello, Alessio (c1455–c1535) Architect of Piacenza, builder of many of the city's churches, including San Sisto and the Madonna della Campagna.

Tura, Cosmè (c1430–95) (*Modena: Galleria Estense; Ferrara: Museo del Cattedrale*) Son of a shoemaker, became court painter in Ferrara for more than 30 years. Equally influenced by Mantegna and Piero della Francesca, he turned the one's precise line and the other's infatuation with geometric volumes in dreamlike space into one of the most intense and eccentric styles of the quattrocento.

da Vignola, Giacomo Barozzi (1507–73) (*Parma: Palazzo Ducale; Bologna: Palazzo dei Banchi*) Innovative Mannerist architect, a favourite of the Farnese family and Pope Julius III; but you would never guess he was one of the greats of his day from his work in his native Emilia, where his most important building, Piacenza's Farnese Palace, was never finished.

Vitale, da Bologna (Vitale d'Aimò de' Cavalli, c1309–61) (*Bologna: San Francesco, Pinacoteca, Galleria Davia-Bargellini, Madonna dei Servi; Pomposa*) The most noteworthy painter of the Bolognese trecento, whose delicate, decorative art was influenced by the International Gothic art of Siena; capable of startling spatial orientation and drama, as in the St Anthony altarpiece in Bologna's Pinacoteca

Wiligelmo (active 1106–20) (*Modena: Cathedral*) Perhaps of German origin, one of the greatest and most influential of Romanesque sculptors, whose heavy stocky forms were based on medieval Ottonian manuscripts.

Appendix 4

FURTHER INFORMATION

BOOKS
Literature and poetry

Bassani, Giorgio *The Garden of the Finzi-Continis* Quartet Books, 1989. Emilia-Romagna's best-known contemporary writer spun this tale partly from his experiences growing up Jewish in wartime Bologna. Much of his other work evokes the region, including *Five Stories from Ferrara* (1956; translation Harcourt Brace 1977).

Carducci, Giosuè *Selected Verse* (translated by David Higgins) Liverpool University Press, 1994. The great poet of Italy's revolutionary era was a Tuscan, but he spent most of his life in Bologna. Includes his famous 'Hymn to Satan'.

Dante Alighieri *The Divine Comedy* (plenty of good translations). Few poems have ever had such a mythical significance for a nation. Anyone serious about understanding Italy and its world-view will need more than a passing acquaintance with Dante. If you know some Italian, try the original; Dante's 700-year-old classic is actually easier than most modern Italian poetry.

Dibdin, Michael *Back to Bologna* Vintage Crime/Black Lizard, 2003. This instalment in the author's popular Aurelio Zen detective series is an excuse for some satire on the city's academia and art worlds.

Fellini, Federico *Fellini on Fellini* Da Capo, 1996. A collection of the great director's writings and letters, and some boyhood memories of Rimini.

Gardner, Edmund Garratt *Dukes and Poets in Ferrara: A Study in the Poetry, Religion and Politics of the 15th and Early 16th Centuries* Haskell, 1982. Ferrara in its golden age, concentrating on literature.

Guareschi, Giovannino *The Complete Little World of Don Camillo* (translated by Adam Elgar) Pilot Productions, 2017. Guareschi's affectionate satires about a village priest and Communist mayor in a post-war Emilia village brought him worldwide fame, especially after they were made into a series of hugely popular films starring Fernandel (pages 22 and 195).

Newby, Eric *Love and War in the Apennines* UK General Books, 2010. Not entirely about Emilia-Romagna, but a great tale about how the famous travel writer escaped from an Italian prison camp in the war, and met the lady he would later marry.

History and art

Burckhardt, Jacob *The Civilization of the Renaissance in Italy* Harper & Row, 1975. The classic on the subject (first published in 1860), the mark against which scholars still level their poison pens of revisionism.

Deliyannis, Deborah *Ravenna in Late Antiquity* Cambridge University Press, 2010. Not only the history, but a description of the city and its marvels, its culture and its religion.

Ginsborg, Paul *A History of Contemporary Italy: Society and Politics 1943–1988* Penguin, 1990. A good modern account of national events since the fall of Mussolini.

Hale, J R, editor *A Concise Encyclopaedia of the Italian Renaissance* Thames & Hudson, 1981. An excellent reference guide, with concise, well-written essays.

Jäggl, Max *et al. Red Bologna* Littlehampton Book Services, 1977. Scholarly, very sympathetic account of how urban and social policy worked here in the post-war decades.

Levey, Michael *Early Renaissance* and *High Renaissance* Penguin 1967, 1984. Old-fashioned accounts of the period, with a breathless reverence for the 1500s – but still full of intriguing interpretations.

Murray, Linda *The High Renaissance* and *The Late Renaissance and Mannerism* Thames & Hudson, both 1977. Excellent introductions to the period; see also Peter Murray and Linda Murray *The Art of the Renaissance* Thames & Hudson, 1963.

Procacci, Giuliano *History of the Italian People* Penguin, 1971. An in-depth view from the year 1000 to the present – also an introduction to the wit and subtlety of the best Italian scholarship.

Richards, Charles *The New Italians* Penguin, 1995. Observant, amusing study of life in Italy during and since the political upheaval and financial scandals in the early 1990s.

Rosenberg, Charles *The Este Monuments and Urban Development in Renaissance Ferrara* Cambridge University Press, 1998. The story of this precocious mini-Florence in its greatest days, and how its princes mingled patronage and self-promotion.

Stokes, Adrian *Stones of Rimini* Schocken, 1988. An artist's very detailed examination of Sigismondo della Malatesta, his temple, and the artists that decorated it.

Symonds, John Addington *A Short History of the Renaissance in Italy* Smith, Elder 1893. A condensed version of the authority of a hundred years ago, but still makes fascinating reading today.

Vasari, Giorgio *Lives of the Painters, Sculptors and Architects* Everyman, 1996. Readable, anecdotal accounts of the Renaissance greats by the father of modern art history.

Music

Meier, Barbara *Verdi* (Life and Times Series) Haus Publishing, 2003. A short biography.

Pavarotti, Luciano *Pavarotti, My Own Story* and *Pavarotti: My World* Crown 1981, 1995. The great tenor details the ups and downs of his long career (they booed him once at La Scala); he's a great storyteller.

Phillips-Matz, Mary Jane *Verdi, A Biography* Oxford University Press, 1996. Very thorough and well researched on Verdi's music but especially about his complex relationship with the place where he lived, including more than a bit of scandal.

Food

Gioffre, Rosalba and Ganugi, Gabriela *Emilia Romagna* (Flavours of Italy Series) New Holland, 1999. A celebration of Italy's top food region, with lots of recipes.

Kasper, Lynne Rossetto *The Splendid Table: Recipes from Emilia-Romagna* William Morrow Cookbooks, 1992. From the National Public Radio cooking show, a good background on the region and practical recipes.

Sidoli, Richard Camillo *The Cooking of Parma* Rizzoli, 1996. Not only recipes, but a fond recollection of the village life and traditions behind the cuisine.

General

Burke, Greg *Parma: A Year in Serie A* Witherby, 1998. A quite unusual book, of interest mostly to soccer fans, but containing some insights on Parma and Italian life in general.

Novak, Stanley *Ferrari: Forty Years on the Road* Dalton Watson, 1988. A history of the early years, with lots of pictures.

Other Italy guides
For a full list of Bradt's Italy and other Europe guides, see w bradtguides.com/shop.

Abraham, Rudolf *Alpe-Adria Trail: From the Alps to the Adriatic. Hiking through Austria, Slovenia & Italy* Bradt, 2016

Di Gregorio, Luciano *Italy: Abruzzo* (3rd edition) Bradt, 2017

Whitehouse, Rosie *Liguria* (2nd edition) Bradt, 2016

CINEMA

1900, 1976. Bernardo Bertolucci's overcooked 4-hour epic about class struggle in his native region from the birth of the century up to 1945, with Robert De Niro and other top stars. Filmed in Parma, Busseto and other locations in the region.

Amarcord, 1973. Federico Fellini's bittersweet and deadly funny reminiscences of his early life in Fascist-era Rimini, in a nation kept in 'perpetual adolescence' by the state and the Church.

Beyond the Clouds, 1995. A complex allegory of love and illusion told in vignettes; the best parts are Michelangelo Antonioni's evocative scenes of his home town of Ferrara.

The Garden of the Finzi-Continis, 1970. One of Vittorio de Sica's last and best, made from Giorgio Bassani's novel on the tragic end of the Jewish community in Ferrara during World War II.

The Gold-rimmed Glasses, 1987. From another of Giorgio Bassani's Ferrara novels: gays and Jews suffer equally as morals and hope dissolve in wartime Italy.

The Little World of Don Camillo, 1952. French-Italian co-production (dir. Julien Duvivier) made from the popular novel by Giovannino Guareschi. It's village priest vs Communist mayor in a Po Valley village. A sweet parable that captures the mood of post-war Italy to perfection, so popular around Europe that it spawned a whole series of Don Camillo films. Filmed in and around Brescello.

OTHER RESOURCES

Facaros, Dana and Pauls, Michael *Bologna and Modena* (Art & Culture series), 2015. App guide to these cities and their provinces; profusely illustrated, with maps.

Facaros, Dana and Pauls, Michael *Italian Menu Decoder* (Art & Culture series), 2013. App with thousands of translations of foods and culinary terms, most with detailed explanations and food history.

Index

Page numbers in **bold** indicate major entries; those in *italics* indicate maps.

INDEX OF ADVERTISERS